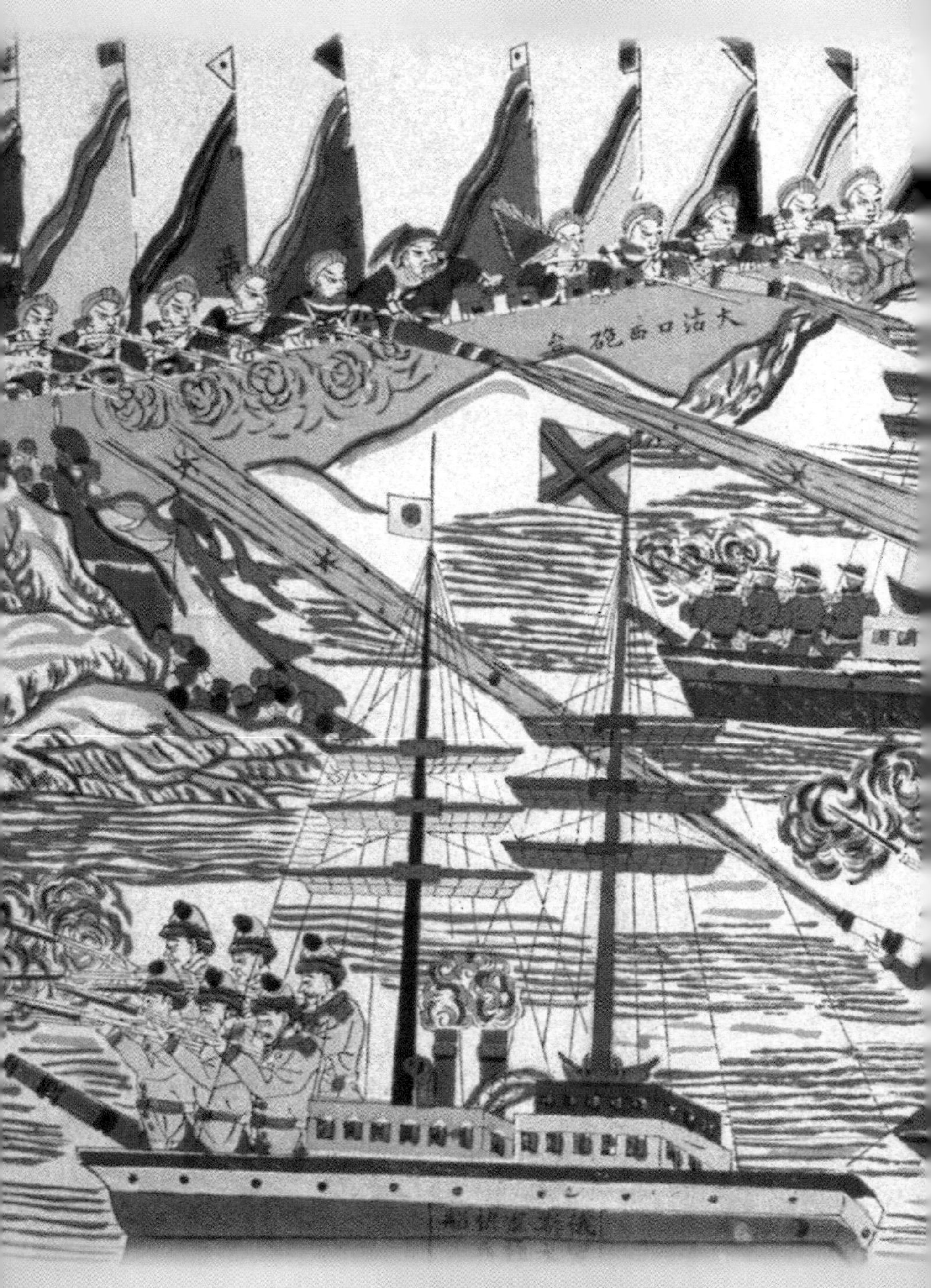

The Allied Navy Gathering at the Tagu of Tianjin. (By courtesy of the trustees of the British Library)

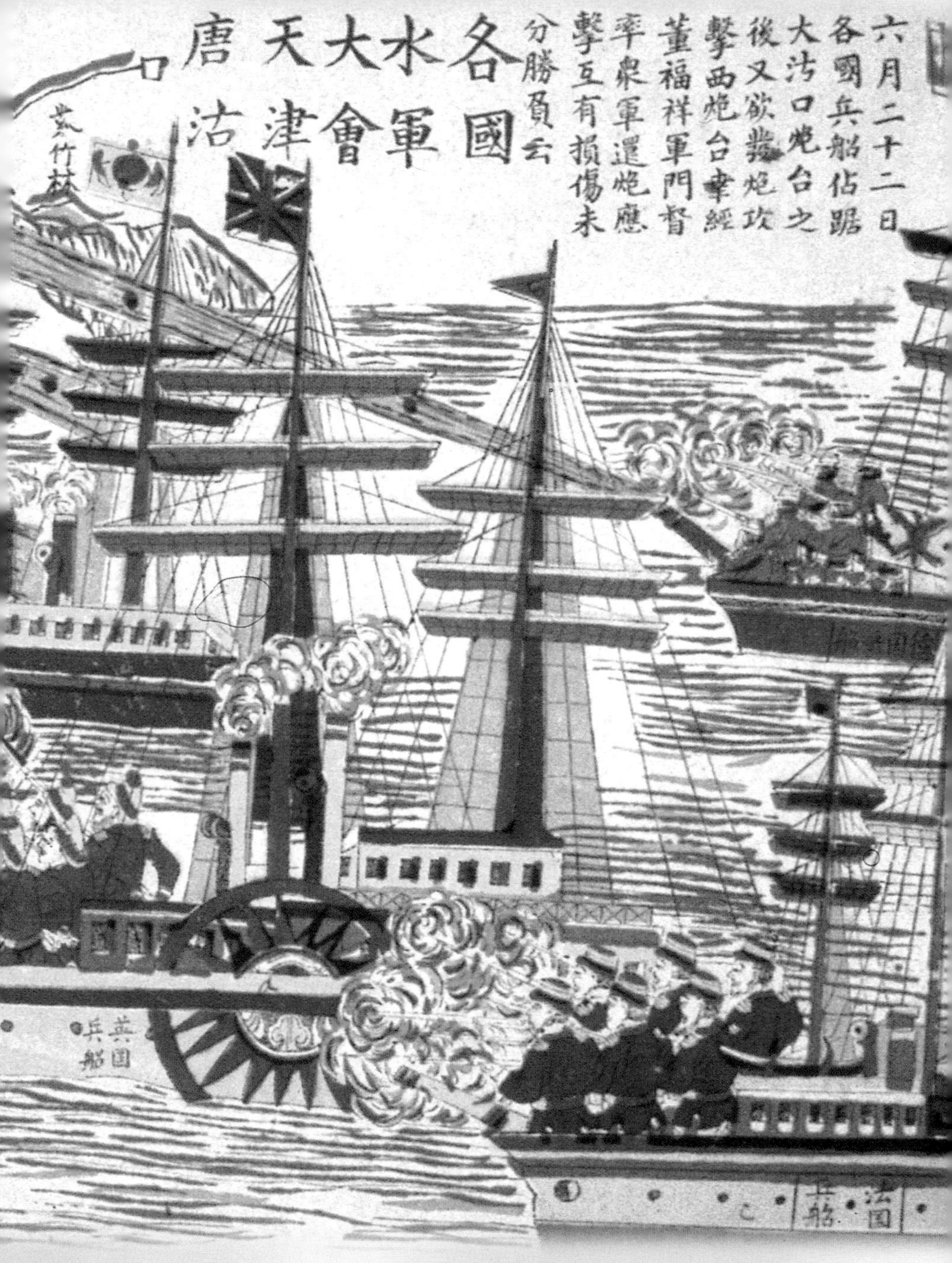

各國水軍大會天津唐沽口
六月二十二日
各國兵船佔踞
大沽口炮台之
後又欲炮攻
擊西炮台韋經
董福祥軍門督
率衆軍還炮應
擊互有損傷未
分勝負云
紫竹林
英国兵船
法国兵船

SOME DID IT FOR CIVILISATION
SOME DID IT FOR THEIR COUNTRY

Some Did It for Civilisation
Some Did It for Their Country

A Revised View of the Boxer War

Jane E. Elliott

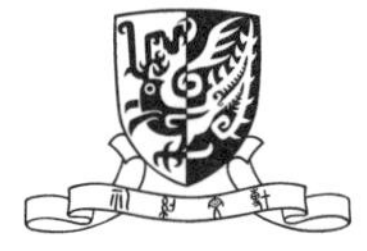

The Chinese University Press

Some Did It for Civilisation; Some Did It for Their Country: A Revised View of the Boxer War
By Jane E. Elliott

ISBN 962–201–973–0 (Hardcover)
962–996–066–4 (Paperback)

THE CHINESE UNIVERSITY PRESS
The Chinese University of Hong Kong
SHA TIN, N.T., HONG KONG
Fax: +852 2603 6692
+852 2603 7355
E-mail: cup@cuhk.edu.hk
Web-site: www.chineseupress.com

Printed in Hong Kong

To Sam Goldberg
in memorium

For Daniel Ransan
in thanks

For Chen Zhenjiang
in admiration

紀念

為祖國奮戰獻身的

偉大戰士

聶士成

In memory of General Nie Shicheng who gave his life fighting for his country against the invading Powers in 1900

Contents

Figures and Plates

Figures

Plates

Acknowledgements

To begin, I wish to acknowledge the help of Hugh Stretton, Daniel Ransan, Andrew Watson, Andrew Ramsay and David Stirling. Theirs was the best kind of help: ever-ready, unconditional and unstinting. The book could not have been begun or completed without them. Thanks to them, despite many difficulties, the research and writing remained an exciting process of continual discovery.

I also owe a great debt of thanks to the Australian Research Council for the three year Fellowship that enabled me to get this work into draft form. My thanks to the University of Adelaide for several research grants making it possible for me to acquire copies of rarely obtainable research material. I am grateful to the Australian and the Chinese Academies of Social Science for an exchange Fellowship allowing me to make contact with scholars in Beijing, Tianjin and Jinan. Discussions with Lu Yao, Su Weizhi and Li Dezheng of Shandong University, Chen Zhenjiang of Nankai University and the doyen of studies of nianhua, Wang Shucun, were of inestimable value.

My warmest thanks to Andrew Watson and all the members of the Centre for Asian Studies of the University of Adelaide for their personal friendship, their intellectual support and material support after the termination of my Fellowship. For his excellence and the delight it was to work with him, I wish to thank Chen Zhengfa of Hefei University for his help in translating the captions of the nianhua. To Xu Qinggen of Suzhou University, my deepest appreciation for arranging a stimulating but not onerous teaching programme while I completed revisions to the manuscript.

Individual scholars, librarians and archivists alerted me to valuable material throughout the time I spent working on this book. I am truly indebted to them for their erudition, their personal interest and their contribution in keeping my work at the forefront of their minds and going out of their way to supply me with references and material. In this context I would like to thank Frank Carroll (Library of Congress, retired), Gerry Groot, Mark Elvin, Margaret

Hosking (Barr Smith Library, University of Adelaide), Teruaki Kawano (Centre for Research, Defence Ministry, Tokyo, retired), Pauline Keating, Jean-Marie Linsolas (Archives de l'Armée de Terre, Château de Vincennes, Paris), Lu Yao, Mike Miller (formerly of the Marine Archives, Quantical, Virginia), Maria Rudova (State Hermitage Museum, Saint Petersberg), Gary Tiedemann, Joanna Waley-Cohen, Frances Wood (British Library) and Mitchell Yockelson (National Archives, Washington).

Most particularly, I wish to thank Bob (R. J.) O'Neill for his pertinent suggestions on an early draft of Chapter Six and for his prompt willingness to read and comment on the whole manuscript. This is the work of a historian, not a sinologist, so Bob O'Neill's comments and assistance meant a great deal to me.

Because of the inter-disciplinary nature of the work, many specialists in all kinds of fields have helped me by reading and commenting on the chapter related to their expertise. They are not too numerous to mention. My thanks to Marianne Bastid-Bruguière, Geremie Barmé, Lucy Shelton Caswell, Paul Cohen, William Coupe, Wallace Eberhard, Mark Elvin, James Flath, Gerry Groot, Robert Harrist, John Lust, Maria Rudova, Alan Trachtenberg, Dorothy Shineberg, James Starrt, Joanna Waley-Cohen, Andrew Watson and Mike Weaver. Their often trenchant comments caused me to rethink my position on many issues and their support gave me some understanding of what sort of contribution I was making to the field in question.

For help with the more technical aspects of word-processing and recalcitrant software, my thanks to Chris Gradolf and Howard Chen. The most important aspect of the book is its illustrations. I owe a great deal to Ron Blum for sharing his knowledge of early photography and for showing me his collection of rare cameras and stereographs. For their help in photographing archival material, I also wish to thank Henri de Feraudy and Alan Hoare.

Bernard Verrall taught me to write when I was a young bureaucrat. Twenty years later he gave unstintingly of his time to proofread the entire manuscript. My warmest thanks for those early lessons and for the timely support so many years later.

With dense footnotes and over 160 illustrations of all kinds, mostly published here for the first time, a book like this calls for superlative skills in steering it through the publishing process. I must record my admiration, appreciation and profundest thanks for the impeccable work done on the manuscript by Mr. Tse Wai-keung as Project Editor.

My thanks to Taylor and Francis for permission to use material that originally appeared in an article in *History of Photography*, Summer 1997 and to *American Journalism* for permission to use material that originally appeared in an article in *American Journalism*, Vol. 13, No. 3, Summer 1996.

During the six years it took to write this book I made many friends all over the world. These years were as full of delight as of personal trials, particularly with ill-health and the death of my father. For their timely and ever-ready personal and intellectual support I particularly wish to thank Chen Zhenjiang, Gerry Groot, Bob Harrist, Joanna Waley-Cohen and Frances Wood. Their understanding and support both for my work and for me as an individual gave me courage in the more difficult moments.

I have read too many acknowlegements concluding with a sentence that went something like this "Last, my thanks to Nancy for keeping Tommy, Mary and little Bill out of the way in the long years it took to write this book." I would rather record my delight in the companionship and thanks for the advice and help as research assistants offered by Oliver, Hedda and Sappho Ransan-Elliott. They made all the difference.

Illustration Credits

Every attempt has been made to contact and acknowledge the copyright holders of images and maps at the time of printing. The publisher and author would be happy to hear from copyright holders not acknowledged, so that they may be credited in future editions.

Cover, Flap and Figures 3.6, 4.4, 4.5, 6.13, 6.14. By courtesy of the Library of Congress; **Front and back endpapers, and Plates 3.14, 3.15, 3.20, 3.22.** By courtesy of the trustees of the British Library; **Plates 3.17, 3.19, 3.23, 3.24 and Figure 3.3.** By courtesy of the Bibliothèque Nationale. **Plate 3.18.** By courtesy of the Tokyo Metropolitan Central Library; **Plate 3.25.** From the private collection of Ms Kazuyo Lee; **Figure 3.2.** By courtesy of the Musée Guimet; **Figures 3.9, 3.10.** By courtesy of the Peabody Museum; **Figures 4.6, 4.7.** By courtesy of the National Archives, Washington DC; **Figures 4.8, 6.6, 6.7, 6.10, 6.11, 6.12, 6.17, 6.19, 6.20, 7.1, 7.2, 7.3, 7.4, 7.5.** By courtesy of the Musée de l'Armée de Terre, Paris; **Figures 4.9, 4.10, 4.11, 7.6.** From the private collection of Mr R. Blum; **Plate 5.1.** By courtesy of the V&A Picture Library; Figure 6.2. By kind permission of Greenhill Books, London.

Introduction

Another Millennium: The Boxer War One Hundred Years Later

"Orientalism!" bellowed Saïd. There was a hush. Then some scurried, some crept furtively but almost everybody went to a mirror and looked at themselves long and hard to see whether or not they were guilty.

* * *

There are two sets of images made about China. One set is made by foreigners. The other by Chinese. Both sets contain conflicting elements and each set is often in conflict with the other. The result of these conflicts is a series of mutual misunderstandings, some deeper and more long-lasting than others. Since the mid-eighteenth century, Chinese rulers and thinkers have been preoccupied with the problem of taking what they wanted from Western culture without disrupting the Chinese world-order as they knew it. They instinctively knew that this was impossible, and so they came up with a double-speak to deal with the situation. They took what they wanted privately while publicly declaiming for the Chinese audience that they needed nothing.[1] They operated on the assumption that if they selected only what they wanted, they could prevent undesired elements of Western culture from penetrating into Chinese thought and society. Similarly all the Western countries dealing with China saw only what they wanted to see; an El Dorado in the form of a market of teeming millions in which they could buy and sell as they pleased, governed by their own understandings of profit and loss.

To a large extent the identical motives and thus many of the same misunderstandings underpin mutual relations between China and the West today.[2] The Chinese believe that they can take Western science and technology, foreign investment and materialism without undermining their political and social world.[3] Western countries fall over each other in the race to set up joint venture companies with the Chinese. At the same time they have been continuously uneasy, thinking that they might be sitting on some giant behemoth that might erupt in their faces without warning at any time.

This study was prompted by the reaction of the Western media to the events of 4 June 1989 on Tiananmen Square. Appropriately, the study is being completed at the time of the first anniversary of the gathering of 15,000 Falun Gong members outside Zhongnanhai compound on 25 April 1999. Both the Tiananmen protesters and the Falun Gong movement arise from distinctively Chinese perceptions of Chinese needs for self-expression, political and spiritual. However, as reflected in Western media coverage, they impinge on the Western consciousness quite differently.

The Tiananmen incident provoked worldwide media outrage and a sense that the West had the "right" to "punish" China. Unarmed students, protestors and striking workers have been fired on and killed in Britain, France, Germany, Japan, South Korea and America during various peaceful demonstrations throughout the twentieth century. However, the world press of the day, while condemning these events, did not express the same degree of outrage nor the same sense of having the right to punish the country in question. After all, Britain, France and America are responsible adult members of the community of nations and can be trusted to take care of their own affairs. If unarmed protesters get shot, well, these things happen. The implication is that China is still a child to be corrected as not quite responsible for its own behaviour. Every time the writer has made this point in conversation, the response has been "Oh, but so many *more* students were shot in the Tiananmen incident." It is suggested that the number of deaths is not the issue. It is just as wrong to shoot and kill twenty unarmed demonstrators as 2,000. There is nothing very "right" about shooting unarmed demonstrators in any country while the right of lawful assembly exists.

Reporting of events concerned with the Falun Gong sect until very recently has lacked that sense of outrage, that sense of adults having the right to punish a naughty child. Members of the Falun Gong have died in police custody but there has been no talk of bringing major economic sanctions to bear on China for violation of human rights, though after the self-immolation of five members of the sect in February 2001, the Chinese government rejected US calls for freedom of religion, belief and conscience in relation to Falun Gong. In this case it would seem that the Western media has judged China to be responsible for its own affairs though developments within the Falun Gong movement may incline some foreign governments to make some statements defending the sect. It would not seem to be the number of deaths which makes the difference to Western judgments of the way China handles its affairs — nor the manner of death. Being beaten to death is probably marginally more unpleasant than being shot. Nevertheless the difference in the reporting of the two incidents is marked and has widespread repercussions.

The overtones of a moral indignation so strong as to cause various Western governments to take economic sanctions against China, naturally inflame the Western public's perception of China. At the same time these moral reverberations provoke Chinese political leaders to more extreme positions than those they might otherwise have adopted. The moral outrage and the provocation is present in international media coverage and the Chinese reaction with regard to the Tiananmen incident but not in connection with the Falun Gong movement. The difference in tone creates in this writer's mind the desire to explain the cycle of misunderstandings between China and the West which originates in the special place occupied by China in the Western mind.

There is an ambivalence with which China is regarded as a responsible political, social and economic entity capable of responding to the complexity of its own internal successes and failures. The same ambivalence is not apparent with respect to the attitude of Western governments towards Japan, towards India or any African or South American country. Thus the same response of closing or opening doors to the outside world is not part of the armoury of how these non-Western countries responded to the West in the twentieth century (with the exception of the former USSR). The Chinese all or nothing approach to the West seems extreme. The Western approach to China which apparently contains a separate special set of "rules" by which the West "allows" China to join the Western community of nations on some occasions but not on others, is also as unique as it is extreme.

A reason for the difference in Western media coverage of the Tiananmen incident and the Falun Gong movement may be thought of in terms of the twentieth century belief that democracy is sacred. "Democracy" has now put on the holy robes once worn by "Christianity." Its ties with trade are much the same as were those between Christianity and trade one hundred years ago.[4] The fourth of June 1989 showed Chinese students protesting peacefully in favour of greater democratisation. A parallel was the Taiping Rebellion, the leader of which believed himself to be a younger brother of Jesus of Nazareth. Western reporting of, involvement in, and most importantly perceived responsibility for, the Taiping Rebellion and the Tiananmen incident contains some important similarities. It also shows that in respect of Western interference alone, the Qing dynasty had roughly the same amount of power as the present Chinese government when it came to setting limits to the role the West wanted to assume. Falun Gong has not the faintest redolence of anything the West might perceive to be sacred nor can it be related in any sense to any Western country's conception of profit and loss. However, if the Chinese government persists in using violent means to put down the sect, it will inevitably earn the wide opprobrium of the international community. This will in turn irritate the Chinese government and its response will be to warn Western governments against meddling with Chinese internal affairs. The point remains that Falun Gong is very much home-grown. While many Chinese people might secretly find some of its beliefs to be credible, foreigners find it hard to identify with this latest outbreak in an ancient line of largely peasant movements in China, all with the potential to raise havoc.[5] Chinese students calling for real democratic rights are something anyone in the West, particularly the media, can identify with. Peasants talking about wheels turning in their stomachs are a bit more difficult to place in the Western cultural or media framework.

It is instructive in this context — that is, the context of democracy as being perceived as "the true way" — to compare Western attitudes to Japan or India. These two countries do not occupy the same uneasy space in the Western mind, despite Japanese explosion onto the world's stage during the 1939–1945 War. Both these countries can lay some claim to be practitioners of democracy along with all its common corruptions from cheating by every conceivable means at the polls to corruption at the level of the elected Head of State. Neither the manipulation of voters — even the forcible manipulation of voters — nor the types of corruption practised in Japan or India, somehow constitute an affront to the Western mind. May we say that a reason for this is because Indian or Japanese distortions of the "rules" have faintly familiar overtones to the Western observer.

Fundamentally the reason why China occupies a distinct and uneasy space in the Western mind is that whether during dynastic times or today, it is only too apparent that China will play along with the "rules" as and when it suits the exigencies of the Chinese leaders responsible for controlling the Chinese world-order. These rules contain an admixture of the secular and the moral unrecognisable to the Western world in the way that the same admixture prevalent in India or Japan is recognisable to the same observers. Today, just as in the time of the Qianlong Emperor (1736–1795), China takes what it wants from the West and refuses — politely in the main if it is permitted — the rest. Small countries such as Thailand may get away with this unscathed. Economically or strategically insignificant countries in Africa or South America may do likewise. However, China now constitutes a glittering gold-mine as provider of cheap labour and the mirage of an unsurpassed market for consumer goods — today more so than ever before. Its economic significance on the world stage becomes greater with every passing year.

On the principle often reiterated by tertiary students in China that it is safer and far better to turn one's critical eye to events that happened more than thirty years ago, the Boxer rising was selected for study in the light of Western media coverage of the Tiananmen incident. The events of the Boxer rising were immensely provocative, outrageous and very frightening. The newspaper-reading world was shocked by the explosive eruption onto the front page of some peasants they had never heard of before. Bands of enraged peasants killed missionaries, other foreigners, countless Chinese Christians and even Chinese people who had no association with Christianity or foreigners. They advanced first on Tianjin and then made their presence felt forcefully in the streets of Beijing. They eventually laid siege to the Legations; a siege that was not lifted for fifty-five days. During that time, barely a word reached the West concerning the health or safety of the foreigners in Beijing. The Chinese controlled the only operable telegraph lines. At the same time the Imperial Chinese Army of the North struck back at the eight invading Allied nations during an initial four weeks of ferocious and largely successful fighting.

The above is in sum the brief incident during which Western nations took upon themselves a "God-given" opportunity to impose their will on China by military force. Though China was invaded by eight foreign countries including Japan and Russia in 1900, though the armies of the eight invading Powers looted and sacked Beijing, though they succeeded in imposing heavy financial exactions on the Chinese under the terms of the Boxer Protocol, it is not apparent from the vantage point of one hundred years later, that China suffered an irreparable loss at the hands of the eight Powers. Even the word "humiliating" must be used with caution. The "humiliation" Chinese people have been taught to feel fifty to one hundred years later, does not necessarily coincide with the emotions felt by the Chinese in 1900. We do not know, in fact, what ordinary Chinese people felt as they saw the troops of the invading powers withdrawing. We have little or no idea of what kind of double-speak or, to Chinese eyes, legitimate explanations, were given for the withdrawal.[6] In stressing the danger of loading the emotions of our time onto the world-view of others one hundred years before, this writer is at variance with most scholarly writing on the way that the Boxer War was perceived at the time. The Boxer War was a particularly heady combination of potential civil war and an all-out invasion by the super powers of the day. Its relatively minor physical consequences for China are as extraordinary as the fact that China was invaded by the eight greatest Powers of the day and left intact, admittedly with an onerous indemnity to pay and an increase in foreign presence.

Indeed the use of the term "rising" as opposed to "rebellion" is the starting point for a revised interpretation of the events of summer 1900 on the North China Plain. At the beginning, the motives of some of the bands of peasants may have been questionable but for the majority the catch-cry was crystal clear: "Uphold the dynasty! Expel the foreigners!" These peasants were not, as yet, rebelling against the one who held the Mandate of Heaven. They were rising to eject foreigners. These foreigners in some places had scant authority to be on Chinese soil through the auspices of unequal treaties or treaties with no reciprocity at all, having been won by threat of force. However, in the remoter villages of Shandong, it was not at all obvious by what right and by whose permission certain foreigners took the best building sites and constructed offensive edifices. These buildings were an affront to the human eye and insulting to the heavenly eye which the peasants believed had to be consulted when any construction was considered.

If in addition to practising certain breathing techniques for the benefit of their personal health, the members of the Falun Gong sect had targeted and wrecked all buildings containing foreign-owned Internet servers and satellite and telecommunications exchanges, we would still not quite have a parallel to the Boxers. Nevertheless, by drawing this hypothetical parallel we can see what a predicament the Boxer rising brought onto the Qing Court. Itself divided into clearly distinct groups of reactionary conservatives and forward looking proponents of modernisation, the Court could sometimes lean on the Empress Dowager and at other times was obliged to follow her every whim. As far as the Court itself was concerned, the last and greatest insult had been the German annexation of Shandong in 1898. Shandong is the birth place of Confucius.

We have no definite or reliable evidence as to what went on in the Empress Dowager's mind. Suffice it to say that she belonged neither to the extreme reactionary camp, nor did she follow entirely the advice of the modernisers.[7] Whenever she could, she repelled the avaricious demands of Western powers, preventing Italy, for example, from cutting another slice of the Chinese melon in 1898. At the same time she was very alert as to the commercial advantages of some Western devices such as the railway. At heart however, she was Chinese. It is easy to see her holding her breath and staking all on one last throw of the dice. If the Boxers could sweep all the foreigners out of China, Cixi (1835–1908) was certainly not of the mould which would gainsay them. This is not speculation. We see in the torrent of conflicting decrees pouring from her dictate, beginning in 1899 and continuing after the fall of Beijing in August 1900, someone vacillating not simply because of advice being given at Court or certain events happening outside the palace walls. We see Cixi vacillating because though she certainly knew something of the might of modern Western armies, she also knew that her best armies were modern-trained and deployed to maximum strategic advantage.[8] In combination with the tens of thousands of outraged peasants it was *not* a foolish hope to pit the modern Chinese armies against the eight invading Powers. Cixi would have had more reason to reflect than most; at the age of twenty-five she had watched the British and the French burn down the Summer Palace.

This study proposes grounds for a dramatic new way of seeing the events of the siege of the Legations in the summer of 1900. Put quite simply, moderate forces either within the armed forces alone or in conjunction with the moderate to modernising factions at Court, deliberately stayed the hand of those laying siege to barricades around the Legations. This was remarked casually by one or two observers of the day. A few who wrote journals of the siege noted that the Chinese soldiers were excellent marksmen but seemed to have been ordered to fire high. Others commented frequently on the dire consequences if the Chinese chose to deploy heavy artillery against their make-shift barricades. The irrefutable evidence contained in this study makes it clear that the Imperial Chinese Army was armed with and adept at the use of the heaviest calibre, latest pattern Krupp artillery. The five wings of the newly reconstructed Wu Wei army were protecting Beijing. Both the Commander-in-Chief, Ronglu, who led the Centre Division and General Dong Fuxiang of the right wing of the Wu Wei had units of modern-trained, modern-equipped artillery under their command. Chapters Six and Seven are replete with the independent observations of many military attachés who observed demonstrations of artillery and infantry firepower put on by the various armies stationed in the North in the 1880s and 1890s. If the same artillery firepower had been directed on the Legations as had been used on the foreign settlement during the battle for Tianjin, the inadequately defended Legations would have been raised to the ground in less than forty-eight hours.

What distinguishes this work from other studies of the Boxer rising is that the emphasis is on *image makers*, not *eyewitnesses*. Some image makers were obviously also eyewitnesses. However, in distinguishing between what Chinese and foreign people of the day thought about the tumult of the Boxer War, this study uncovers three very powerful and very special groups of image makers whose thoughts and opinions have not been analysed hitherto. The first group of image makers had perhaps the most widespread power outside China and its testimony has never been invoked. None of its members ever even went to China but this does not lessen by one jot the impact of their thinking. These were the cartoonists.

The second group certainly had the most widespread influence in China, their testimony has also never been invoked and many of them never saw a foreigner. These were the Chinese woodblock artists who produced New Year Pictures (nianhua) or woodblock pictures (for newspapers). Some of them who lived close to Tianjin, Beijing or Shanghai would certainly have seen foreigners, even foreign soldiers. The majority had a tradition within which they could depict warfare, a world of colour, movement, even, it almost seems — if you concentrate on the battle scenes — sound. The unique graphics of war split out of a flat page into many dimensions, one of which, with the slightest effort of imagination on the part of the viewer becomes the sounds of the battle field. (See in particular, Plate 3.23) They took foreign soldiers, foreign weapons and foreign battle formations into their world. In so doing, they conveyed valuable and accurate likenesses of foreign soldiers to Chinese audiences already steeped in the martial conventions of Chinese woodblock arts. As image makers, they eschewed the manufacture of ghoulish baby-eating devils and drew likenesses of French, British or German officers. These likenesses bring fleeting smiles to our lips today, so extraordinary was their feel for line, for uniform, for bearing and so readily can we see in a Chinese woodcut, officers and soldiers exemplifying the huge differences between the military traditions of British, European, American, Russian or Japanese military culture.

The third group consisted of *image makers* and *eyewitnesses*. They were the foreign soldiers who fought hand to hand with the Boxers and exchanged blazing artillery duels hour after hour with the gunners of the Imperial Chinese Army. Some scholars have made sketchy reference to one or two journals but there has been no meticulous evaluation of the professional opinions of these eyewitnesses. The multitude of military documents of all kinds constitute *the* eyewitness testimony par excellence. These were professional men evaluating the performance of others in the same profession or, at least, other fighting men.

In 1900 the fairest and certainly the most explicitly accurate accounts of the Chinese as fighting men were to be found in the manuscript or printed accounts written by their enemies. If Saïd bellowed "Orientalist!" at this writer, her answer would be that the best sources are not necessarily written by those within the culture under discussion and are often those that have been most widely ignored. Furthermore, in the case of the Boxer War, it is not necessarily true that the most appropriate sources lie in the edicts sent from the hands of the Empress Dowager or letters from one Viceroy to another or oral history from a very specifically preselected group of people whose allegiance was given to the Boxers. That is, that Chinese sources originating from certain hands and destined to be read by certain Chinese audiences, need very careful handling before they can be validated insofar as certain aspects of the Boxer War are concerned. The best sources for certain types of evidence are to be found in the German, Russian, French, Italian, Austrian, British, Australian and American accounts written by a body of military men to describe the excellence of their enemies, as they saw this excellence, at the height of the struggle for Tianjin.

If you are female or illiterate or heathen or yellow or black or poor, the problem is not so much that a historian might write up your history with a hint of condescending "Orientalism." No; the problem is rather that the historian may not think to or know how to read mainstream accounts written by those with power over you, attentively enough to hear your voices. A historian who has succeeded supremely well in the writing of such history is Henry Reynolds with his book *The Other Side of the Frontier*. In this work he reconstructs Australian Aboriginal resistance to the invasion by white people into their country. Reynolds' sources show that the least likely places offer the greatest paying gold. He uses letters to and from the Secretaries of the Colonies, transcriptions of legal trials, and letters which have survived because they were written by white people for one another or to Justices of the Peace. If Reynolds had crept to look in the mirror after Saïd's loud admonition, he would have strode back to his desk and continued writing.

Turning to the greatest image makers of them all, the journalists, we are obliged to jettison many "truths" which form part of our world-view. We learn that the truth was to be found rather in the pages of the tabloid press than in the pages of *The Times*, in 1900 the pre-eminent paper in the Western world. As far as the illustrated newspapers were concerned, the Boxer rising was reported accurately to the accompaniment of pictures which were not always extremely reliable in point of correct detail. However, these pictures did less to inflame the British public against the Chinese, the lower down the social scale for which the newspaper catered. Their function as reliable information was in the main rather more significant than any overt design to instil in the minds of the British working class negative images of China and the Chinese — the Boxers in particular.

The chance does not often arise to compare Chinese illustrations of warfare destined primarily for the lower class with say, the illustrations of the same war in the *Daily Mail*. Most of the soldiers of her Majesty's forces whose mother tongue was English — as opposed to Punjabi, for example — would at least occasionally have read the *Daily Mail* or looked at the pictures. In the same way the soldiers of the Imperial Chinese Army would have seen New Year Pictures (nianhua) — an extremely well-known style of peasant woodblock prints normally produced to bring luck and good wishes for the Chinese Lunar New Year. Nianhua were reproduced in the hundreds of thousands and pasted up all over public and private spaces throughout China. This study has uncovered previously unpublished nianhua-style pictures depicting China's successful engagements not only in the first four weeks[9] of the Boxer rising but in other small wars with European powers during the nineteenth century. Thus we have a unique opportunity to evaluate the way in which men making money by purveying news both in China and in Britain, deliberately selected already extant illustrated traditions to depict soldiers of their own country in combat with enemy soldiers. This opportunity is all the more significant in terms of image making as the level of audience at which these pictures was aimed was the precise audience from which emanated the greatest preponderance of fighting soldiers, and in the case of China, fighting men. Neither Chinese nor Western owners of illustrated newspapers resorted to dis-information to portray the enemy as fiend.

This book is copiously illustrated by hitherto unpublished photographs covering the military aspects of the Boxer War. The occasion of the Boxer War in 1900 brought about one of the first uses of the photograph as reportage, as commentary rather than simply information directed to the viewers attention by a caption. It is suggested that this happened because of the particular way a brutal war fought in the "interest" of civilisation and Christianity impressed itself on the artistic sensitivity of two great American photographers, James Ricalton and Sergeant Cornealius F. O'Keefe.

It was the same contrast between motive and method that enraged the cartoonists of the day. The irony that the war was fought by inflicting unnecessary cruelty on the Chinese civilian population was openly exposed to the view of citizens in countries right around the world, as this war was supposed to be a blow for Christianity. This irony was savagely scratched before the public eye by the pens of the international corps of cartoonists. The international arena was made aware that the brutal murder, the raping and the looting of non-combatants in a war espousing the characteristics of civilisation and Christianity was a form of hypocrisy a little too close to the bone for anyone's comfort. To a man,[10] the cartoonists of the world, whether German, Spanish, Russian, British, Dutch, American, French etc., were merciless in exposing the other major forms of hypocrisy involved. The most potent was that when the Chinese bought modern Western weapons this was thought of as "civilised" but when they used them in self-defence, this was thought of as "barbaric."

The last two chapters of this study evaluate the calibre of the Imperial Chinese Army. A new strategic plan had been drawn up by the Empress Dowager and her advisors in 1898, and concentrated on defending all the approaches to the capital. Up until now, the consensus of Chinese and English-language scholarship has been that this army was yet another patchwork Qing failure. Looking at Chinese depiction of war between China and foreign countries earlier in the nineteenth century gives us the opportunity to see that all the victories claimed by the Western powers concerned, need not necessarily have been viewed as victories either by the Chinese of the day or by posterity.

With one notable exception,[11] scholars have rolled Chinese performance in the Sino-Japanese War of 1894–1895 forward into its performance in the Boxer War and labelled the lot as one big debacle. Various reasons are given for the "disastrous" performance of the Imperial Chinese Army including incompetent leadership, outdated weaponry, lack of training on the weapons they did have and a fighting force composed of a motley lot of rank and file soldiers dressed in comic opera-style uniforms. This study scrutinises these reasons one by one and finds them all wanting. In their place, a new image is created of the soldier of the modernised Imperial Chinese Army in the late Qing. It is no exaggeration to say that he emerges on the world stage and in the annals of military history as a new hero. The evidence which puts him up there where he should have been all along is the evidence of his enemies and his fellow professionals; the officers and men of the eight invading armies. Every last published or unpublished journal contains the meaningful praise given by one professional to another. In this case, as the outcome of the enemy's professionalism is often the death of some of the best-loved comrades of the journal writer, the kind of praise for the Chinese soldiers noted by the invading foreign soldiers is all the more moving. It also constitutes undeniable evidence of the actual courage and professional ability of the fighting men, mainly of the Imperial Chinese Army, but to some extent, also of the Boxers, in engagements fought directly between Boxers and foreign soldiers.

It is a pity that this testimony has not been invoked in detail before — along with supporting documents such as maps and photographs — by scholars purporting to describe the Imperial Chinese Army in the late Qing. As far as scholars of the Boxer War are concerned, it is less surprising that they failed to establish of just what mettle were the men of the Imperial Chinese Army. In so failing, however, they have deprived us of a vantage point from which we can more thoroughly survey the Boxer rising. Whether they fought for their country as Boxers or enlisted soldiers, a great many of the soldiers fighting that summer came from Shandong — some probably from the same villages, many certainly from the same counties. Lack of funds after the Sino-Japanese War had obliged China's leading statesman Li Hongzhang to demobilise many troops. Undoubtedly at least some of these were in the ranks of the Boxers.

It is important to begin a study of the Boxer rising as a peasant uprising and historiography in this context would be much the poorer without the work of Joseph W. Esherick and Paul E. Cohen.[12] As this writer sees it, however, the Boxers and their supporters were but one of three protagonists on stage that summer. Along with fighting enemy soldiers, they were also fighting against, and later with, Chinese soldiers many of whom had a similar if not identical background to themselves. Throughout Chinese history, it has been the scale of peasant risings rather than any other factor which has obliged consideration of the conflicts as insurrections, rebellions or outright civil war. In this case, however, as China was invaded by foreign countries and did declare war, we can only see the Boxer rising with any degree of accuracy, as a war, despite the invading Powers' technical evasion on this point.

Can we leave an evaluation of the Boxer War with the Boxers once more the heroes at centre-stage? The ones who were interviewed for their recollections in the vast oral history project undertaken in the early 1960s?[13] Or are we obliged to say, in the interests of a well-balanced history of what became a hotly contended war, that there were other Chinese men and their leaders who also had a concept of their country strong enough to fight and die for in the most difficult of military situations? Are we obliged to say that for those who truly want to understand the meaning of patriotism to a largely uneducated young Chinese man in 1900, we would have needed another oral history project? A project questioning former soldiers of the Imperial Chinese Army as to their motives for fighting, for resisting the invading armies so tenaciously, for following their officers to certain death, for obeying orders when being attacked by Boxers, for obeying orders when told to fight with the Boxers when they knew that the Boxers had taken their comrades, killed them in stealth and hacked their bodies to pieces?

As this writer reads the evidence, we can no longer leave the Boxers as heroes alone at centre-stage. It seems apparent that we must acknowledge fully that there were other young Chinese men prepared and willing to make the ultimate sacrifice for their country in that summer of 1900. It seems apparent that the soldiers of the Imperial Chinese Army are owed a dispassionate analysis of their equipment, training, state of preparedness and soldierliness in the sense of supporting their comrades and obeying their superiors. It likewise seems apparent that they should be subject to a dispassionate analysis of how well they performed as the modern army they were equipped and trained to be.

* * *

Some of the sources used for this study are such as would make Saïd blanch. In order to select newspapers representative in their coverage of the first six weeks of the Boxer War, some fifteen English-language newspapers were read. Some of these newspapers were directed to an exclusively working class audience; others were in parts frankly scandal sheets with headlines such as "Woman Chases Man across Three Continents for Breach of Promise." Similarly with the illustrated press, though German, French, Japanese and Russian illustrated papers were studied, the three selected for in-depth analysis were British because Britain was then at the height of its Imperial expansion and was also involved in the Boer War and the Ashanti Rebellion in 1900. Selection was based on the class background of those readers being primarily targeted. As far as Chinese newspapers are concerned, no mainland Chinese papers were found which had printed news of the events of June and July 1900, other than the *Shenbao*. It is possible that a large collection of Chinese language newspapers — or newspaper cuttings — could still be found either in libraries in California, the Marine Archives in Washington or in big collections of unsorted archival material in Germany or in Japan.

The present writer was determined to obtain some Chinese images of war, particularly the Boxer War. Exhaustive searches turned up some newspaper illustrations from a Shanghai newspaper used again by a Japanese newspaper (a very rare find) and some woodblock prints in the nianhua style. Once again, though this work contains a very comprehensive coverage by nianhua of nineteenth century wars between China and other powers, it is quite probable that there are more such nianhua in antique shops in Beijing, in museums in Germany, Taiwan or Japan, in private collections, or in the family papers of British or French men who fought in China in 1840 or 1860.[14] Given the amount of double entendre, play on words and abstruse references, the lengthy captions on the nianhua have been treated with great caution. Nevertheless, the visual evidence they provide is as extraordinary as the fact that hitherto they have not been used and evaluated as significant and invaluable historical source material regarding the clashes between various foreign powers and China during the nineteenth century.

Photographs of the Boxer War are relatively easy to uncover. They can mostly be found in Military Archives. As yet there is no extensive published collection of photographs pertaining to wars between China and foreign states or between the Imperial Chinese Army and various rebellious ethnic or peasant groups that were quelled by Chinese armies in the last half of the nineteenth century. In 1900 there were means of making immense public sales of series of photographs. The most notable for our purposes in examining the nature of image-making businesses in this pre-screen era,[15] is the stereograph. The stereograph was ubiquitous. Stereographs were also three dimensional and constituted the forerunners of machine-made home entertainment. Sets of stereographs could be bought for viewing at home or they could be borrowed from public libraries. The stereographs in this study are notable for giving viewers three dimensional access to the image of a Chinese soldier who looked remarkably similar to soldiers in America or Britain or France in point of uniform, weapons and the manifest ability to take full military advantage of the terrain.

Thanks to pioneering scholarship by William A. Coupe and Lucy S. Caswell, there has been lively debate on political cartooning and there is a superb collection of cartoons being put together by Professor Caswell at Ohio State University. The study of political cartooning, as a serious discipline owes much to the work of Professors Coupe and Caswell. Again, as with photographs, cartoons were easy to collect. It sufficed to have the conviction that the distinction between *eyewitness* and *image maker* should not automatically always fall in favour of the former as necessarily the producer of the most enlightening guidance as to how a past event was seen at the time. However, although there is some literature on the value of the political cartoon as a historical source, a great deal more work could usefully be done in this discipline. On the face of it, it would seem probable that when millions of people were breathlessly following the siege of the Legations, not knowing whether the besieged were alive or dead, cartoonists' pens would have been producing evil anti-Chinese wicked or sinister Fu Manchu imagery for public consumption in the fourteen countries producing the cartoons analysed in this book. Far from this being the case, the majority of the cartoonists produced savage anti-Western cartoons. Many of the cartoonists whose work on the Boxer rising is reproduced for discussion were internationally extremely well known at the time. They were highly sought after and internationally recognised because their acuity for the realities of the present flaming crisis was appreciated to the extent that people believed they had almost the status of political seers. They were revered in proportion to that status.

It is instructive for those accustomed to thinking of the Western press as a "free" press, to know that almost all of the great German, French, Russian and Japanese cartoonists had done long spells in prison. In Britain there was a tradition of buying up editions of newspapers containing cartoons unflattering to reigning monarchs or their families. Sometimes a cartoonist may have aggravated a political leader so scathingly that not only the cartoonist but also the editor and even the publisher were jailed as well. Yet cartooning is *the* unique source which reveals to the historian to what lengths the cartoonist in question was prepared to push his pen where it would strike the arteries of public opinion most deeply. Cartoonists also reflect the attitudes and policy of the editorial staff but the cartoonist could say things with a picture and a brief caption that an editor would never dare publish in the editorial column. As well, cartoonists held their fingers unerringly on the pulse of public feeling of the day. To do this using humour meant that a political cartoonist had to be able to assume a certain minimum knowledge of a subject in the public mind so that his graphics and caption would bring home the point. When we look at the range of cultural abbreviated "tags" the cartoonist was able to include in the knowledge that his audience would take one look at the picture and caption and laugh immediately, we are obliged to assume a fairly high level of residual knowledge of images and facts about China and the Chinese already abroad in Western Europe and America in 1900. Cartoonists cannot create symbols; excellence in their work comes from their being able to paste known symbols together, add an apt caption and have everyone understand at one glance the point they are making about the situation.

It is the source material for the two last chapters that has been plumbed to quite some depths. This material highlights the historiographical point that there are times when the historian can get the most detailed and otherwise unobtainable information from the enemy in war, the coloniser in the Empire, the captain of a slave trader, or the literate describing the illiterate. Although a very few historians have examined a couple of journals written by officers or soldiers who fought in the Boxer War, this cannot amount to a serious evaluation of the nature and development of the modern Imperial Chinese Army from 1870–1911. A deeper understanding arises from reading the letters, memoranda, observations, reports, and examining the diagrams and photographs, maps and drawings compiled by foreign military observers, some of whom spoke and wrote Chinese. Only after having looked at the entire corpus of source material written by defense attachés over the years 1870–1900, can we make a serious evaluation of the soldiers of the modernised armies in China and their performance in the Boxer War.

* * *

After Saïd's roar, the present writer did not creep back to her desk and sit there fumbling, benumbed. What she had seen in the mirror were whole bands of people whose profession obliged them to come in contact with China in 1900.[16] Their very profession — in the case of journalism, and pictorial images of China — could have tainted their evidence thoroughly with Orientalism. However, after reading a total of twenty-two newspapers and illustrated magazines, covering the months of May, June, July and August 1900, the writer discovered Orientalists to be distinctly in the minority. The correspondents for *The Times*, George Morrison and J.O.P. Bland were the worst offenders. In the case of J.O.P. Bland, for example, although he spoke fluent Chinese, this accomplishment did nothing to help him write more informed copy for his newspaper. On the contrary, it seems to have qualified him to look at Chinese people or institutions in the most "Orientalist" fashion of them all. Similarly, the illustrators, the photographers and the cartoonists — most of whom, photographers and a few illustrators excepted — had never been to China — all produced explanatory rather than defamatory or inflammatory pictures of China and the Chinese, many going so far as to criticise their own fellow countrymen, and women for their materialism and hypocrisy.

This high degree of integrity in the formation and dissemination of pictorial images led to the question "Were the Chinese similarly professional in the matter of disseminating images of foreign soldiers"? The answer must be a resounding "Yes." Although there was some anti-missionary literature printed with highly derogatory images and captions denigrating Western missionaries, this literature was neither as popular nor as ubiquitous as the xinwenzhi or the nianhua. Moreover anti-missionary literature was distributed free of charge whereas a few cash had to be expended to acquire a xinwenzhi or a nianhua.

The Boxers are very much shadowy figures in the background of this book. What this writer was looking for, she did not find. She was looking for some sense of superiority on the part of the men who wrote copy for their newspapers, who took photographs for professional distribution, who drew cartoons or who described the comportment of Chinese soldiers and their commanding officers in their journals. This book is not intended as an account of the Boxers from A–Z. It sets out to demonstrate the existence of a fairly copious residual knowledge of China and the Chinese in the public mind in Germany, France, Britain, America, Russia and Japan. It is also written not as a narrative, but so that each chapter can be read as an independent piece of thought on the subject in question. Lastly, the book also intends to show that whatever anti-Chinese core had crept into the public mind, it was emphatically not due to the work of the bodies of observers described and discussed herein, no matter how the Boxer rising may have been blown up after the event.[17] *At the time, the Boxer rising was no 4 June Tiananmen.*

Now to the final word on the study; if negative images of the Chinese were not produced by the men of the day who did not see it but drew pictures of the Boxer War, by men who saw it, wrote about it, lampooned it, took photographs and actually fought in China; who was it who did produce negative images? Did these negative images surge forth as an indignant afterthought? Did missionary literature alone, really have the power to blacken the Chinese in the public eye of the West? Or after those long fifty-five days, was there the beginnings of a deeply subterranean fear of this country once looked on benignly as a never-ending source of exotica sunk in hopeless apathy and timeless resistance to change?[18] Did the fact of facing an enemy as proficient, as well-equipped and as tenacious, cause surprise, consternation and a little doubt as to their own strength at the meetings of the highest ranking officers of the invading forces? It certainly caused alarm and uncertainty in the bars of Tianjin.

This writer believes that collective fear in international relations is a most powerful, largely non-verbalised negative force that leads to misunderstandings and eventually to the breakdown of dialogue. The mutual misunderstandings between China and Western nations are caused by cycles of breakdown of communication because both the Chinese and the Western view of developments had perceived consequences which were mutually threatening and which therefore gave rise to mutual though different fears. China may be backward, it has been said that it has lost many wars, but it remains intact and is now, in fact, increasing in power. The other reason for mutual misunderstanding lies in the perception of each country's own view of its own progress in relation to its view of the other country's progress. In the nineteenth century, when Western countries viewed China, it seemed to them that China was stagnant and that they were rushing forward along the rails of progress. China's view was that selected aspects of this progress were desirable; the others were not. The difference in these views led to attitudes of perceived superiority and perceived inferiority which were breeding grounds for fear and distrust on both sides. In the twenty-first century, it is obviously China which is moving forward at a breathtaking pace. Once again, this perception may lead to overconfidence on one side and fear and distrust on the other.[19]

At this precise juncture a new research approach presents itself which is oriented to the study of the writings of professional groups whose very profession pierces the thick camouflage of double-speak, thrown up by fear, either coming from within or without China. This book begins to fill this gap. It also calls for a more rigorous re-evaluation of the nineteenth century wars between China and Western powers, and building on Allen Fung's work, between China and Japan. To undertake such an evaluation, historians will need to speak and read English, French, Russian, German and Japanese with extreme competence. With the return of Chinese government campaigns designed to foster nationalism, studies like this one or studies of the Sino-French War using the same kind of sources will assuredly reveal some new aspects of the Chinese military that could constitute the basis of a source of legitimate pride in the minds of young Chinese. Above all, we need new biographies of the great Chinese generals and admirals written by people who take for granted the fact that they have to read accounts by Western military attachés who had many contacts in the Chinese High Command and to read how foreign officers rated particular Chinese high-ranking soldiers. It is to be hoped that after reading Chapter Six all manner of people will have a new respect for General Nie Shicheng and General Yang Mushi. It is this writer's intention to drag them out of the dusty archives and expose them to the light which reveals their extraordinary dedication and their ability to fuse what they knew of the conduct of warfare from their Chinese heritage with what they had learned from the modern Western model.

Let us leave the Boxers off stage for a moment to loot burn and kill innocent Chinese; one of their activities not emphasised in many studies of the Boxer rising. Let us bring on stage some rank and file soldiers of the Imperial Chinese Army and listen to their talk while they polish their Sam Browne belts to a lustre which would have done credit to the very best guards in Berlin or Saint Petersburg.

Unfortunately, the politics of what survives as source material has meant that we are left with no script at all from which to glean the faintest echoes of their talk. Thanks to a few remaining photographs, all we can say is that they *did* sit for hours polishing their Sam Brownes and under the ferocious eyes of successive sergeant-majors, they *did* pass inspection on parade. Sadly, we can never know anything about their attitude to their profession, to their commanders, to their comrades and to their country. Insofar as oral memories of the Boxer rising are concerned, the exigencies of the political propaganda of the day have meant that we will never hear their reminiscences. Rarely in history has a group of fighting men been more damaged by subsequent mythologies on the national and international level. American scholars "know" that the Imperial Chinese Army was corrupt and ineffective; Chinese scholars also "know" that the Imperial Chinese Army was a bunch of "losers." Dispassionate reading of this book will give rise to the idea that, in fact, the rank and file of various armies in the Imperial Chinese Army were so skilled at their profession that they managed to imbibe two separate sets of cultural constructs of how to fight wars. The Boxer War produced divisional commanders like General Yang Mushi tired, dispirited but withal proud of the resistance put up at Tianjin by himself and the soldiers under his command.

Notes

1. Joanna Waley-Cohen, "China and Western Technology in the Late Eighteenth Century," *American Historical Review*, Vol. 98, No. 5, 1993, p. 1527.
2. *South China Morning Post*, 11 May 2000: "U.S. Trade Vote Seen as Battle of Values." "Ben Gilman ... warned that the U.S. would be 'sacrificing' its most powerful annual weapon to hold the mainland to account for human rights and labour abuses. 'We cannot shrink from this battle of values,' Mr Gilman told a committee hearing on the up-coming trade vote. 'The Beijing regime has fought a vigorous public relations battle to win this philosophical argument. They have manipulated prisoner releases, effectively blackmailed dozens of countries and nearly corrupted some of our very own American corporations with their efforts'"; *South China Morning Post*, 12 May 2000: "U.S. Drafts New Anti-China Weapon." Senator Levin (Democrat), "Just increasing trade does not adequately address the complex challenges presented by China. We cannot rely on economic contact and exchange alone to lead automatically to more democracy, greater freedom and greater respect for human rights and enforcement of core worker rights." Commented the *Wall Street Journal*: "Push deeper and you will see that Mr Levin's main preoccupation seems to lie with protecting American labour unions from unfair competition and opening up World Trade Organisation proceedings to every special interest group with a bull-horn." (Both the US and China were to appear before the United Nations to answer on human rights issues); *South China Morning Post*, 13 May 2000: "Jiang Warns Brash Generals." "A military source said while most PLA officers wanted speedy action against Taiwan, Mr Jiang and his politburo colleagues favoured making a final decision after China's accession to the World Trade Organisation"; *South China Morning Post*, 14 May 2000: "Clinton's Hope for Vital Trade Vote Souring." — that is, both Presidents are being controlled by and trying to use the World Trade Organisation issue to control domestic and international issues. Interestingly, in the same article, the Danish Prime Minister, Poul Nyrup Rasmussen visited Beijing, expressed optimism (13 May) about China–EU WTO negotiations "but pointed out possible sticking points over telecommunications

and insurance." Telecommunications and insurance issues have a far more central place in negotiations over international trade agreements than do moral issues involving human rights and even — more frighteningly — considerations as to the use of armed force to settle international differences of opinion.

3. *South China Morning Post*, 14 May 2000: "Censure Aimed at Liberal Scholars." The *South China Morning Post* reported that "Departments handling ideology, culture and the media have completed preparations for countering 'Western influence' after China's accession to the World Trade Organisation." "The Publicity Department of the Communist Party Central Committee and other units have compiled new lists of avant-garde intellectuals to be criticised or gagged. While industrial and agricultural units are formulating plans to better compete with foreign goods, cultural and ideological units want to weed out 'dangerous' ideas from the West." (A Beijing source)
4. *South China Morning Post*, 11 May 2000: "U.S. Trade Vote Seen as Battle of Values." See note 2 above.
5. Falun Gong has attracted a wide cross-section of ordinary and also educated Chinese urban dwellers, even Chinese Communist Party members, as well as peasants so the movement cannot simply be characterised as a peasant movement. The Chinese government estimates the number of Falun Gong members at just over two million while the sect claims many times that number.
6. One of the conditions imposed on China as part of the Boxer Protocol was that a memorial should be erected to Baron von Ketteler, the German ambassador to China who had been killed by a Chinese soldier. In the electrically-charged atmosphere immediately preceding the siege of the Legations, von Ketteler had thrashed a young Chinese man in the street. Several journalists commented that when they asked about this memorial, they were told, "Oh, that is the memorial to the brave Chinese soldier who killed the cruel German ambassador."
7. Cixi had, however, cracked down on the brief Reform Movement of 1898 although after the Boxer War, she was at the forefront of instituting a number of reforms of all kinds.
8. Liu Beisi and Xu Qixian (eds), *Gugong zhencang renwu zhaopian huicui* (Selection of Photographs of People Kept at the Imperial Palace), Forbidden City Publishing House, Beijing, 1994. Apart from numerous photographic portraits of the Empress Dowager, this collection contains some rare photographs of palace soldiers executing military gymnastics in the modern Western style. Cixi would certainly have witnessed such exercises. My thanks to Dr Pauline Keating for obtaining a copy of this book for me.
9. Newspapers were studied for the first six weeks after the Boxers hit the news. This period includes the initial four weeks of hostilities between the eight Power invading army and the Imperial Chinese Army.
10. In 1900, there were not as yet any women political cartoonists.
11. Allen Fung, "Testing the Self-Strengthening: The Chinese Army in the Sino-

Japanese War of 1894–1895," *Modern Asian Studies*, Vol. 30, No. 4, 1996. See also Teruaki Kawano, "Allied Military Co-operation in the Boxer Rebellion and Japan's Policy," *Revue Internationale d'Histoire Militaire*, No. 70, 1988. My thanks to Mr Kawano for drawing my attention to his article.

12. Joseph W. Esherick, *The Origins of the Boxer Uprising*, University of California Press, Berkeley, 1987; Paul A. Cohen, *History in Three Keys. The Boxers as Event, Experience, and Myth*, Columbia University Press, New York, 1997.
13. In Shandong in 1960 there was a field study of Boxer activities. A second oral field investigation was undertaken in and around Tianjin in the 1980s. Those interested in such materials could begin by looking at Lu Yao et al. (eds), *Shandong yihetuan diaocha ziliao xuanbian* (Selections from Survey Materials on Fieldwork on the Shandong Boxers), Qilu shushe, Jinan, 1980. See also Lili, "Koushushi shiliao yu yihetuan yanjiu" (Oral Historical Materials and Boxer Studies). Unpublished discussion paper given at the centennial conference of Boxer Studies, Jinan, October 2000.
14. See Régine Thiriez, *Barbarian Lens: Western Photographers of the Qianlong Emperor's European Palaces*, Amsterdam, Gordon and Breach Publishers, 1998.
15. Moving pictures were in their very earliest infancy in the year 1900. However, it is notable that a large proportion of surviving short silent films took war as their theme, whether the Battle of Dagu or the Spanish-American War in the Philippines. See the collection of early motion pictures in the Library of Congress.
16. For the purposes of the present work, this writer does not consider that the group of missionaries in China in 1870–1900 constituted a "profession" having neither similar training and background nor the same goals.
17. James L. Hevia, "Leaving a Brand on China: Missionary Discourse in the Wake of the Boxer Movement," *Modern China*, Vol. 18, No. 3, July 1992.
18. It is this clichéd view of China that Joanna Waley-Cohen puts to rest in her book, *The Sextants of Beijing. Global Currents in Chinese History*, W. W. Norton and Co., New York, 1999.
19. Claude Lévi-Strauss, *Race et Histoire*, Denoël, France, 1995 (1952), pp. 41–46, has an enlightening discussion on the subject of history perceived as "stationary" and history perceived as "cumulative."

Chapter 1

Great Newspapers Report the Boxer Rising: *The Times* and the *World*

I think the greatest difference between China and the West ... is that Chinese are fond of antiquity but neglect the present. The Westerners are struggling in the present in order to supersede the past.

Yan Fu

Overnight the drama of a Chinese peasant rebellion swept the news of the Boer War and the war in the Philippines from the front page headlines in Britain and America. Groups of Chinese peasants had begun organising and drilling[1] in a movement which had taken shape as the Boxer rising by 1899. Factors which had incited the peasant insurrection included anger at European encroachment on Chinese territory,[2] resentment of the spread of Christian missionary influence, unemployment as a result of increasingly mechanised transport, mass discharging of soldiers after the Sino-Japanese War and structural changes in various Chinese armies, widespread flooding and prolonged drought.[3] The more celebrated catch-cry of the Boxers was "Uphold the dynasty! Expel the foreigners!"

The movement started in Shandong province in North China. Shandong forms the peninsular which juts out towards Japan; it was and is famous as the birthplace of Confucius and by 1900 it had been subjected to heavy missionary penetration. The Boxer movement spread rapidly and reached Beijing (Peking) in May 1900. Large numbers of Boxers in loose units roamed and drilled in the streets of Beijing, a menace equally to those Chinese who were associated with foreigners as they were to the foreigners themselves. On 16 June foreign telegraphic communication with the outside world was cut and on 20 June the Boxers laid siege to the foreign Legations in Beijing. The Boxers were joined by Muslim troops — also feared by many Chinese residents of Beijing — and other soldiers of the Imperial Chinese Army. The siege lasted for fifty-five days until it was raised by an eight-nation 20,000 strong force on 14 August.[4]

An analysis of a number of newspapers reporting the Boxer crisis in Britain, America, Hong Kong and English-language newspapers in China itself yields unexpected results. Accuracy of news coverage and emotive pejorative language in the reporting on and the portrayal of China as an independent responsible political entity were not predictable characteristics of press coverage according to which end of the socio-political spectrum the papers served. Although America's foreign policy and trade concerns in China were quite different from those of Britain, there were strong similarities between some sections of the British and American press as they reported the Boxer rising.

In this chapter the object is two-fold: to evaluate the extent to which journalists were able to report events outside racial stereotypes and to show that the Western press did not react to the Boxers in a uniform way. Insofar as the actual reporting of the Boxers themselves is concerned, accuracy and responsibility in reporting were not necessarily the exclusive hallmark of the "stately-press."[5] As a corollary, sensational reporting and coloured language were not necessarily the distinguishing characteristics of the mass-circulation newspapers reporting on a stirring event in an exotic, remote, almost inaccessible country. There is no evidence that any of the mass-circulation newspapers examined for this study used inflammatory, coloured "Fu Manchu" style language or pictures to describe the Boxers. In this chapter we will evaluate the contribution made by the reporting of the second phase of the Boxer rising to public images of China held by people from a wide social spectrum in the two major English-speaking countries of the day.

Perceptions of China varied on either side of the Atlantic for a number of reasons. Nevertheless, a detailed reading of the press coverage of the Boxer rising shows important similarities between the *Daily Mail* and the *World* as well as between the *Westminster Gazette* and the *Chicago Daily News*. These similarities reflect a high standard of responsible journalism in newspapers catering for a wide public in Britain and America. It is when we turn to the coverage of this event by *The Times*, however, that major differences appear between British and American views of China and, moreover, between British and American views of what constituted responsible journalism.

In order to evaluate the degree of responsibility displayed by British and American press coverage of the Boxer rising and the Boxers themselves, a useful approach would seem to be to concentrate on in-depth analysis of two newspapers rather than piecemeal selections from a large number of papers.[6] Turn of the century sensitivity to the standards and work of the mass-circulation press[7] led to the choice of Joseph Pulitzer's paper, the *World*, as arguably the best representative of the yellow press.[8] At the other end of the socio-political spectrum, *The Times* was chosen because of its position as the newspaper with the highest reputation of those papers comprising the "stately-press" and because of its influence on the formation of British government policy. The question of the influence of the reporting of the Boxer crisis on the formation of government policy and public opinion regarding China and Japan lies beyond the immediate scope of this study. Nevertheless, it is a question which must at least be raised in the context of a discussion of press responsibility.

Having selected *The Times* and the *World*, it was also necessary to delineate that period of the Boxer crisis most appropriate for analysis. The events divided into a first phase before the involvement of foreign troops in June 1900. Then there was a second phase of four weeks in June and July 1900 when the Chinese forces had ascendancy over the Allied invaders. Following this came the third phase of four weeks during which the Allies tried to assemble sufficient troops to march on Beijing. The fourth phase saw the taking of Beijing and the beginnings of negotiations of a punitive indemnity against the background of reckless raping, looting and indiscriminate shooting of Chinese citizens by Allied troops.[9]

There was an entrenched view in both the British and American press of China as a decaying moribund empire fit only for division by the vigorous nations of the West. Broad sections of the Chinese population were aware of this view and resented it intensely.[10] In this context, the reporting of the first four weeks of the campaign in which the Chinese were clearly defeating most Allied initiatives[11] — the second phase — constitutes the best test of the ability of the Western press to report these military successes. Previous press reporting had established an image of China that precluded the possibility of any real military preparedness or fighting ability. Moreover, the British and Americans were also involved in other major wars in 1900, notably the Boer War,[12] and the Spanish-American War in the Philippines. The magnitude of the furore over the Boxer crisis eclipsed press coverage of the Boer War and provided a highly-charged crucible in which to make a comparative evaluation of the standards of the British and American press of the day.

The Boxer rising was not just another Chinese peasant insurrection. Before it occurred, the Western press was discussing the division of China,[13] and various countries had already claimed "spheres of influence" with special rights over Chinese territory. After the rising, the talk of slicing China like a melon was heard no more.

Boxer scholarship has a long pedigree.[14] However, there has not been an analysis of English-language press coverage of the rising.[15] There has been no accurate discussion in the literature of the second phase of the rising. This was the phase which was potentially difficult for Westerners to report, namely the initial Chinese military success.[16] Nor has there been in-depth analysis of the ensuing atrocities perpetrated by Allied troops in Beijing while Western journalists and other observers looked on.[17] This writer has seen no discussion by Chinese or Western scholars of the idea that the subsequent victory for the West was a hollow one. The Empress Dowager removed her court, continued to issue Imperial edicts and Chinese diplomats dragged out the negotiations for the Boxer Protocol obtaining substantial concessions as they did so.

There may be a connection between the coverage of the first four weeks of the Allied campaign by *The Times* and the fact that no scholarly English-language work on the Boxer War has recorded the military successes of Chinese forces during this time. The establishment of such a connection does not lie within the confines of the present study. However, it is an issue which relates to the issue of press responsibility and as such, must be raised in the context of the evidence to be presented concerning the coverage of the first four weeks of the Allied campaign. As it is, many historians have a black and white attitude to outcomes: "We won; They lost." The most prominent newspaper of the day failed to report that "They" were winning at any stage. It is thus not surprising that historians who do not examine the action in detail, proceed from the outcome given by the newspaper "We won" rather than the actuality never head-lined or described by that same newspaper "We almost lost." Moreover the weight carried by *The Times* as the prominent newspaper of the day has hitherto not stimulated any scholar to show the extent of the inaccuracy of the reporting of the Boxer War by *The Times* as did Walter Lippman and Charles Merz in their celebrated analysis of the reporting of the Bolshevik Revolution by the *New York Times*.

The Times

At the turn of the century, the policy of *The Times* concerning China was that Great Britain's interest should be commercial and not territorial.[18] Both before and after the Boxer rising, *The Times* gave voice to an interest in China that stemmed from Britain's perception of her commercial interests and political relationships with Europe and Russia. Interest in and knowledge of China itself was of secondary importance. This bent dominated the thinking of its foreign editor, Valentine Chirol, who believed that in order to support her commercial and imperial interests, Britain could go as far as to propose the division of the Chinese Empire.[19] In a letter to George Morrison dated 2 March 1899, Chirol wrote:

> It seems to me that the sooner we make up our minds that the game is played out at Peking (since we are not prepared to save it by supreme measures) the better. We can then fall back upon the alternative policy of *effective* spheres of influence and make the Yang Tsze (and Canton) our own: ie. claim and maintain the same rights in those regions which we allow Russia and Germany to exercise in their spheres.[20]

In this view Chirol had the support of George Morrison, senior correspondent for *The Times*. Morrison was a radical imperialist interested in China "as a theatre of competing imperialisms."[21] The personal charisma that surrounded Morrison during his lifetime caused observers to be sharply divided as to his professional competence[22] and commitment to China itself. He was talking to Japanese representatives as early as March 1900 about a British-Japanese alliance,[23] not a clear indication of Morrison's commitment to China in the climate following the Sino-Japanese War of 1894–1895 which had heightened Chinese fear and enmity of Japan. His reporting on the events of early June 1900 showed him to be concerned with ensuring the humiliation of China and its government.[24] His account of the death of the

NEAR AN ULTIMATUM TO CHINA.

" Boxers " Openly Drilling in Peking—Foreign Powers Again Threaten to Land Troops.

SHANGHAI, May 24.—The members of the Chinese secret society known as the " Boxers " are now openly drilling at Peking, and many high Manchus, including members of the imperial clan, are joining the movement, which is becoming so threatening that the diplomatic representatives are about to take action. B. J. De Cologan, the Spanish Minister and doyen of the diplomatic corps, has made a demand upon the Tsung-li-Yamen (Chinese Foreign office), couched in the strongest terms, for the immediate suppression of the " Boxers," threatening that otherwise all the powers concerned would land troops in China.

Chicago Tribune, 25 May 1900. In line with its growing reputations as a serious reporter of foreign news, the *Chicago Tribune* is the first newspaper to define the Boxers and to indicate their connection with the ruling class.

FRENCH BOXER VICTIMS.

Massacres in the Villages and a Regiment of Troops Ambushed.

SHANGHAI, May 25.—Advices from Szuchuan, Province of Hupeh, report that "Boxers" have destroyed two villages and massacred many converts of the French missionary stations.

The General commanding at Shinanfu, it is added, sent a regiment to the scene of the disturbances. The soldiers were ambushed by the malcontents and lost twenty-six men killed.

Reinforcements have been despatched from Ichang.

WASHINGTON, May 25.—United States Minister Conger at Peking has been instructed by the State Department to inform the Chinese Government that the Government of the United States expects it to promptly and thoroughly stamp out the Boxers and to provide proper guarantees for the maintenance of peace and order and the protection of life and property of Americans in China, all now threatened by the operations of the Boxers.

The *World*, 26 May 1900. From this first report, readers would have been able to learn that Boxers were killing Chinese Christians and that Chinese soldiers sent to suppress the Boxers had suffered losses at their hands.

THE UNITED STATES AND CHINA.

(THROUGH REUTER'S AGENCY.)

WASHINGTON, MAY 25.

Mr. Conger, the United States Minister in Peking, has been instructed to inform the Chinese Government that the United States expects that it will promptly and thoroughly stamp out the " Boxers," and provide a proper guarantee for the maintenance of peace and order and the protection of the life and property of Americans in China.

The Times, 26 May 1900. Entirely dependent on information from America, this snippet gives no indication of who or what the Boxers are or why the life and property of Britons in China should not be equally endangered.

Figure 1.1 How news of the Boxers first hit the Western press.

missionaries, Mr Robertson and Mr Norman, stresses the horrific. He wrote that they "were hacked to pieces in circumstances of revolting barbarity" and linked these "murders" to Chinese government "complicity."[25]

Journalists for the English language papers in North China wrote otherwise of missionary deaths, reporting that missionaries and other foreigners had been advised by their own Consuls not to go to certain areas unless provided with Chinese guards. Furthermore they reported that in specific instances when missionaries had not complied with this advice and had been captured by antagonised sections of the Chinese populace, other Chinese citizens had attempted to rescue them.[26] Morrison was aware of these factors. He received a letter from Dr Robert Coltman, an American medical missionary in Beijing, regarding the death of the missionary Brooks.

> You will be shocked to hear of poor Brooks's murder and mutilation. Sir C. [Claude MacDonald, British Minister in Beijing] is taking it very coolly and intimating he should not have been travelling in the disturbed state of the country.[27]

George Morrison was an internationally-recognised journalist and personality. *The Times* at this time was arguably regarded as the most responsible authoritative newspaper in the world. When Morrison wrote of the behaviour of the infuriated Boxers as "revolting barbarity," his writing carried more weight for the British policy-makers reading *The Times* than did that of other journalists. Other journalists writing for other newspapers explained that, aware of the inflamed spirit of the peasantry, the Chinese government had provided guards specifically to accompany foreigners in certain areas. Morrison was neither interested in the background to peasant unrest and the build-up of the Boxer rising, nor did he give credit to the Chinese government for its determination to protect foreigners venturing into districts known to be unsafe. Chirol and Morrison's writing about China is reminiscent of the same elements Paul H. Weaver set out to criticise in the *World* in his book, *News and the Culture of Lying,* that is, to engage the feelings of the audience, to turn news into a structure of crises, to address the private, prepolitical human being not the citizen, constitutionalist and partisan.[28]

The issues concerning the permitting of correspondents to shape policy in the Far East, or even help to shape it, especially insofar as *The Times* is concerned, require a great deal more research. In choosing to analyse the second phase of the crisis, that is, the reporting of the first four weeks after the opening of hostilities by foreigners, because in this time the Chinese were achieving ascendancy over the Europeans, we must set aside the debates on Morrison's ability, contribution and influence. The months of June and July 1900 saw him besieged and incommunicado in Beijing. The personality and professionalism of the other correspondent for *The Times*, J.O.P. Bland, stationed at Shanghai, then comes into question. Although Bland spoke Chinese, unlike Morrison, he had no sympathy for or interest in Chinese culture:

> I never pass a village school house or hear these little Confucianists howling themselves into the classical condition of mental paralysis, without a feeling of gratitude for the system which has petrified the race's imagination.[29]

The year 1900 was a year of conflict which raised questions about empire and race. China was still the Middle Kingdom, although minor concessions had been made — and refused[30] — to foreign powers. The question to be addressed is to what extent could the Western press acknowledge the reasons for and report on a Chinese insurrection and Chinese military success? In order to answer this question, the following analysis of *The Times* sets out to determine whether accuracy of reporting was the greatest priority for the editors and correspondents of this prominent newspaper. Alternatively, was it the case that *The Times* fostered the writing up of news in such a way as to confirm already held perceptions of British commercial and political interests in China and existing prejudices about the Chinese held by its editor and its two foreign correspondents stationed in China?

Examination of both *The Times* editorial column and the columns written by special correspondents reveals a highly-coloured and emotive attitude to the Boxers, Chinese statesmen, Chinese military leaders and the Empress Dowager herself. There was a persistent use of adjectives such as "cruel," "ferocious," "revolting," "decayed," "reactionary," "murderous," "rigidly conservative," "malign," "ignorant," "reckless," "criminally apathetic," "corrupt," "treacherous," "arrogant," "sinister," "audacious" and "notorious."[31] Such language was not endemic in any of the other newspapers studied. Moreover, the contexts in which such adjectives were used were such as to imply a denial of the right of China as an independent sovereign nation to act in accordance with her own interests:

> That the Chinese troops who are supposed to be putting down the "rebellion" have been placed under the orders of the very general whose soldiery have been for months past a standing menace to the safety of foreigners in the province of Chi-li [Zhili] merely adds another touch of impudence to the sinister farce which is being played under the eyes of Western diplomacy in the Chinese capital.[32]

The word rebellion was placed in inverted commas to indicate *The Times'* view that the Boxer rising was solely instigated by the Empress Dowager and could be put down at her command.[33] Moreover, no attempt was made to refer to the Chinese general in question by name, let alone to indicate his probable relationship to either of the two main factions at Court, the reactionaries and the progressives. Indeed, the existence of such factions and their implications for developments in the Boxer crisis, was not a subject which came up for analysis or discussion in *The Times'* leading articles. Of the generals in command of the various wings of the Chinese army in the Beijing region, only one, General Dong Fuxiang, displayed open hostility to foreigners. His troops, as mentioned earlier, were also deeply feared by the Chinese population in and around Beijing.[34] The Commander-in-Chief of the Imperial Chinese Army, General Ronglu, was noted by contemporaries and by posterity for his professionalism and his consciousness of the need to observe the internationally-accepted codes of behaviour with regard to the rights and safety of foreign nationals.

As well as the emotive language used in *The Times'* leaders to describe the Boxers, the Imperial Chinese Army was described as "worthless … as fighting men," "mere mobs of men," "ill-armed rabble," "hordes," "swarms" and "ruffians." In terms of creating an image of China for the British public, it is suggested that such language, a direct descendant of similar language used in describing past conflicts with China,[35] initially inflated public opinion of British ability and influence. It did not reflect the nature of the Western-trained regular forces of the Chinese army nor that of some of the Boxer units which often fought with disciplined courage using state-of-the-art weapons. Other newspapers published details of China's standing army as well as noting that the Boxers were a force to be reckoned with.[36]

The language of *The Times* led to such a low estimation of the Chinese that as the China campaign wore on, the selection and elevation of rumours to facts by journalists writing for *The Times* was increasingly at variance with actual events of the Boxer War and unhelpful in explaining them. The emotive language about China which formed part of the mental baggage of journalists working for *The Times* severely affected their outlook and work. It led them to produce reporting distinguished by conflicting stories, wishful thinking, omission of events and even the discussion and analysis of events which never took place. The most notable point is that *The Times* had no journalist on the spot once Morrison had been besieged in Beijing. This emotive language, then, was an amalgam of Morrison's early reports with possible contributions by Bland about soldiers he most probably never saw and about Boxers he certainly never saw. This amalgam was finally written up by Chirol in editorials and served authoritatively to the upper-echelons of the British public and influential members of the English-speaking world.

Such journalism was not common to all British newspapers. Despite its embarrassing "scoop" in reporting the deaths of all those besieged in the Legations,[37] the *Daily Mail* produced responsible and accurate reporting of the Boxer crisis. The illustrated material in particular, brought to the British public factual information about China and the Chinese, untainted by emotive or negative images. The *Daily Mail* was the only British paper studied to give a positive analysis of the policies of the Empress Dowager. It wrote of her "marvellous success" in keeping China for the Chinese and playing off foreign ministers against each other for the last forty years. As well, it referred to the "brilliant manner" in which she had duped the foreign ministers over the last five years in the matter of foreign attempts to gain trading, mining, railway and other concessions in China.[38] Before the hostilities had broken out, the *Daily Mail* gave accurate details of the origins of the Boxer movement, did not underestimate the Boxers and noted the ineffectual nature of foreign moves as the crisis deepened.[39] By contrast, on 7 June, *The Times* voiced the opinion in a leading article that "The power of the 'Boxers' is by no means formidable in itself."

The personality and policies of the Empress Dowager could not be said in any way to have been analysed in the columns of *The Times* but were instead the continual objects of highly-emotive language.

> The impunity she has so far enjoyed … combined with her ignorance of the forces she is defying and with the malign influence of her *entourage* of eunuchs, parasites and place-hunters … has induced her to offer a direct challenge to the foreign Powers whom she has learnt to regard as incapable of acting together.[40]

As the *Daily Mail* had pointed out, the ability to take advantage of the enmity between foreign powers in order to preserve her country,[41] was one of the Empress Dowager's strengths. This point was also made extensively in the American press. On 8 June the *World* published a leading article on the Empress Dowager under the headline, "The Legend of the Strong Woman Tszu Hszi," thus becoming the first Western newspaper to refer to her by her name. This was followed with a full page article on Cixi (1835–1908) on Saturday 16 June, "The New Woman of China. The Empress Herself. First Interview with Her Ever Published." The *Chicago Daily News* analysed her reported moves based on known factors in the Chinese political situation,[42] and continued to do so as the crisis deepened.

> The intentions of the Empress Dowager are still equivocal, with a balance of the testimony on the side of a determination to expel the appropriators of a part of her country or to lose her dynasty in the attempt.[43]

Given Cixi's vacillating attitude to the Boxers, it is important to note that some journalists writing for the Western press, with the exception of *The Times*, were perceptive enough to recognise the significance of her position as the crisis intensified.

The American papers studied were all able to recognise Chinese military gains. The authority of *The Times*, however, meant that it was powerful in influencing contemporary policy-makers and was consulted as a source in later years.[44] For contemporaries and posterity, this authority dominated to such an extent that neither other organs of the British press nor any section of the American press was regarded as an equally acceptable source. For this reason it is important to note that the portrayal of facts and events in *The Times* was more persistently inaccurate than any other comparable newspaper. It also showed less understanding of any of the internal social and political pressures in China than did other newspapers.

Constant misreporting was not the case with *The Times* coverage of the Boer War. Boer tactics, strategy, motivation and victories were acknowledged from the outset of the war by *The Times*. Similarly, Boer commanders were known as "the enemy." Even towards the end of the war, it was said of them that they "did offer a very respectable resistance," and that they were capable of "delivering a somewhat mortifying check to our arms" and "daring attempts at raiding our communications."[45] When British forces lost battles, when large numbers of British soldiers were killed or captured, these events were not described in the passive tense. They were reported as actively occurring as a result of Boer military action. Throughout the campaign, concerned readers wrote letters to the editor urging that the Boers should be objects of emulation for the British army as far as training or equipment were concerned.[46] One letter criticised the War Office for sending British soldiers to fight against men with superior equipment; in this case, field glasses. No letters were written to *The Times* about Chinese superiority because they used smokeless gunpowder or because their artillery was more modern and better manned. Readers of *The Times* were made aware of Boer superiority in equipment or fighting skills but were told nothing about the fact that the Chinese had the crowning advantage in artillery duels during the siege of Tianjin. It is difficult to avoid raising the hypothesis that for *The Times*, because the Boers were white Protestants, their tactics in warfare were reported factually, in detail, and even with commendation. The Imperial Chinese Army and the Boxers themselves were "barbaric," perpetrators of "murder" or "ill-armed ruffians." The journalists writing for *The Times* clearly did not feel that there was any contradiction involved in reporting on the success of Boer guerrilla tactics and omitting to report, let alone comment on, the identical tactics used by the Boxers in conjunction with the Imperial Chinese Army.

The Times never accorded active status to Chinese military or paramilitary responses to Western aggression in the same way as it discussed Boer tactics and successes. Letters to the editor about the China crisis reflected both the tone and the factual basis of *The Times*' leading articles and reporting of the campaign. One letter proposed the kidnapping of the Empress Dowager as a solution to the Boxer crisis.[47] The point about *The Times*' view of the Chinese leadership, military and people in relation to journalism covering the Boer War and even the Ashanti Rebellion,[48] was not simply that the Chinese were viewed less favourably. *The Times* showed a consistent inability to produce responsible reporting of China's political and military institutions and its history and culture. It failed to give any background to peasant insurrections in China in general or the particular factors leading to the mass uprising in Shandong province. Above all it failed to analyse events as they were being acted on by Chinese rulers and people, preferring to take the hypothetical posture that as the Chinese were incapable of acting for themselves, Britain should intervene and settle matters as *The Times* felt they should be settled.

> We preferred to cling to our shibboleth about non-intervention in the internal affairs of foreign States — a shibboleth utterly inapplicable to the decayed politics of the East.[49]

The Chinese had already been negatively characterised by Valentine Chirol, the foreign editor, and by correspondents working in China (not all of whom spoke Chinese). The Empress Dowager had invited the wives of the foreign ministers in Beijing to afternoon tea, an initiative which had earned her praise in the *Daily Mail* of 8 June 1900. Valentine Chirol wrote to George Morrison about this incident as follows:

> I feel very strongly about exposing the representatives of refined European womanhood to the ribald jests of Palace Eunuchs and the offensive curiosity of Chinese Mandarins, who will of course represent the ceremony as a great kow-tow before the Empress and the Empress' party. However, the thing is done and there is no good kicking against accomplished facts.[50]

A reading of Sarah Conger's letters, the woman who engineered this meeting in her capacity as the wife of the American Minister (Ambassador) in Beijing, gives a completely different view of this party and of the Empress herself. Mrs Conger's view is of some consequence as she was herself "exposed to the ribald jests of Palace Eunuchs" on more than one occasion. Her writing shows that dignity, intelligence and goodwill would bridge enormous gaps of social and racial difference.[51] She also wrote in a matter-of-fact way about the courage and successes of the Imperial Chinese Army during the battle for Tianjin. It seems that her status as wife of the American Ambassador has given her testimony less weight in the eyes of posterity than that of men like Morrison, Bland or Chirol. Valentine Chirol's personal view of the Empress resurfaced in a leading article of 1900 in which we read that it was an error on the part of the British government not to have intervened on behalf of the reform movement in 1898.

> The reformers lost faith in our sincerity, and the reactionaries took heart to proceed boldly in the path on which they had entered. The attendance for the first time of the ladies of the Corps Diplomatique at a reception given by the EMPRESS while her hands were still red with the blood of the principal reformers … was regarded by both sides as a graceful submission … to accomplished facts and those who know how to make them.[52] [his emphasis]

Not only was *The Times* unable to report factual material about the elements involved in the Boxer crisis or to produce analysis of such facts as were reported by its correspondents, it also failed to ensure firsthand reporting of these events which were shaking the Western world. With the proliferation of wild and conflicting rumours, *The Times* was consistently the last newspaper of those examined to print definite and accurate news. Knowing that George Morrison, was besieged and incommunicado, its Shanghai correspondent, J.O.P. Bland made no move to approach Tianjin to be closer to the action. By contrast, in the late nineteenth century tradition of the dashing war correspondent,[53] the Irishman George Lynch of the London *Daily Chronicle*, travelled 300 miles to reach the nearest telegraph point with the first report of the capture of Tianjin by the Allied forces. He then returned to march to Beijing with the second relief expedition.[54] Similarly the *World* dispatched Frederick Palmer to cover the Boxer rising at first hand. On arrival at Tianjin, Palmer got a world scoop on the return of the British Admiral Seymour who had failed to relieve the Legations in Beijing and had been out of communication with his base for ten days. Palmer was in a quandary as to whether to accept the reliability of the telegraph service or to take his dispatch personally to Shanghai and risk missing the advance to Beijing. He finally decided to travel to Qingdao, sent a dispatch from there, went on to Shanghai, sent a duplicate dispatch and returned to catch the relief expedition which had just left Tianjin.[55]

Against this background of the opinions of Valentine Chirol, the language of the leading articles in *The Times* and the attitudes of its correspondents George Morrison and J.O.P. Bland, a detailed examination of *The Times* reporting of Admiral Seymour's abortive expedition to relieve the besieged Legations in Beijing shows *The Times* reporting conflicting and inaccurate stories day after day with little or no attempt at analysing them. By contrast, in its reporting of the Boer War, *The Times* revealed itself to be capable of criticising military leadership and organisation, perceived tactical or strategic errors and even barbaric treatment of Boer civilians by British soldiers.

In late May, Boxer groups burnt bridges and railway stations destroying nearly fifty miles of railway between Beijing and Tianjin.[56] (The distance between the two cities was approximately eighty miles). Very early on 10 June, Admiral Seymour, commanding a mixed Allied force left Tianjin intending to travel by rail to Beijing to rescue the Legations. At the time he left, he was aware of the activities of Boxer units on and around the railway line. On 11 June *The Times* published the first of many reports stating that Admiral Seymour was "believed to have reached Peking in safety." Admiral Seymour never got within thirty miles of Beijing. On 12 June the Admiral reached Langfang, a little over half-way between Tianjin and Beijing (see map showing Admiral Seymour's route Figure 7.7). In reports on 12 and 13 June, *The Times* expressed doubt as to whether the relieving force could reach Beijing before 12 June. No indication was given that either Boxer groups or Chinese regular army soldiers were responsible for the "retardation" of Admiral Seymour's force. On 13 and 14 June the foreign soldiers fought an engagement with the Boxers. On 14 June the "Defeat of the Boxers" was reported in *The Times*. On 18 June *The Times* published a report from Shanghai that the relief force was "close to Peking" and the Admiral's position was described as "serious." This report mentioned that the foreigners were confronted by troops of the Imperial Chinese Army and menaced by Boxers in the rear.

By 16 June Admiral Seymour had, in fact, decided to retreat. The reason for the long wait for definite news of Admiral Seymour was that the Chinese, in fact, controlled the only operable telegraph lines out of Beijing despite the much-vaunted Western superiority in communications. The military correspondent for the *Westminster Gazette* did finally offer his opinion that "the Chinese may, like the Boers, display a power of resistance to our arms altogether unexpected."[57] In contrast to *The Times*, the *Westminster Gazette* produced reporting in which critical analysis was applied to the various dispatches reaching the paper.[58] On 27 June the *Westminster Gazette* expressly acknowledged that the reports regarding Admiral Seymour's expedition were "exceptionally embarrassing in the nature of their information."

Admiral Seymour's dispatch printed in *The Times* on 30 June mentioned only eleven killed and forty-eight wounded. None of the reporting in *The Times* of Admiral Seymour's "anxiously" followed mission gave any indication of the dates or the nature of the engagements, which actually caused him to lose sixty-two killed and 312 wounded out of his force of 2,044.

The eventual reporting of these figures in a leading article in *The Times* on 29 June, three days after Admiral Seymour had been rescued and brought back to Tianjin, showed a marked contrast with the type of journalism practised by men such as Lynch and Palmer.

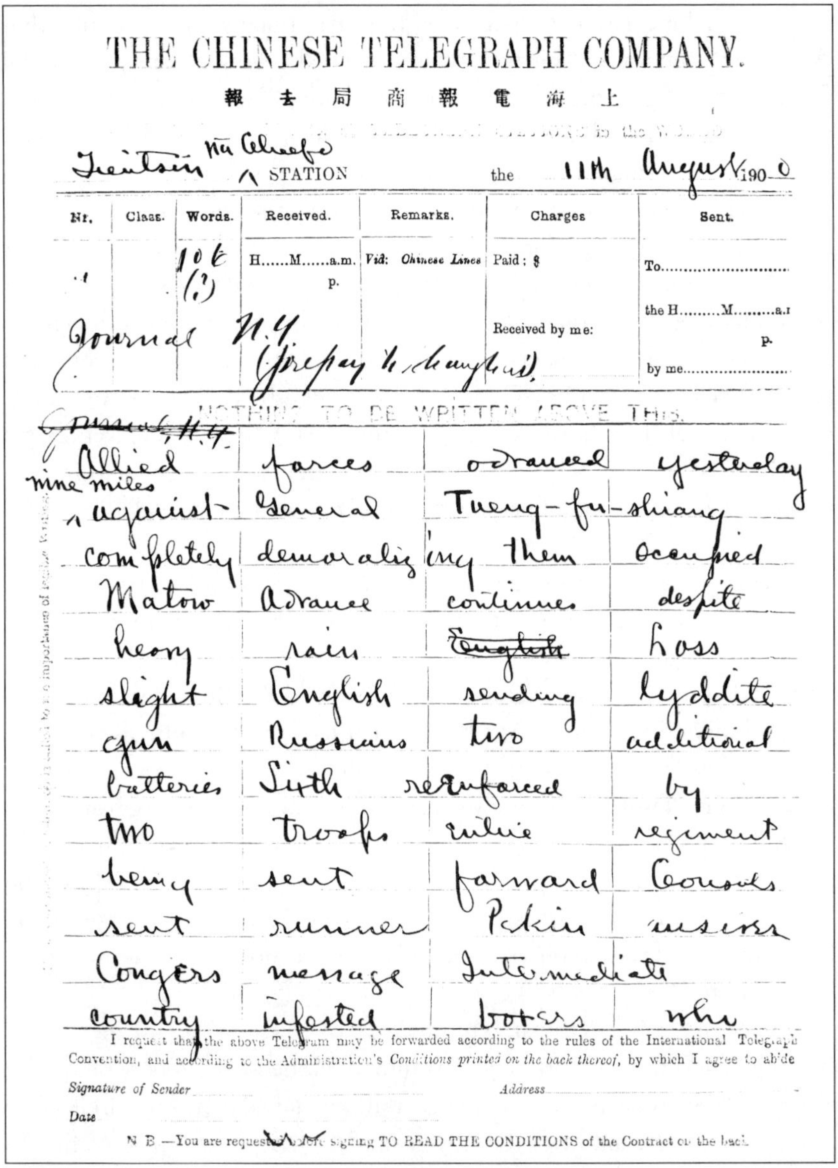

THE CHINESE TELEGRAPH COMPANY.

上海電報商局去報

Tientsin via Chefoo STATION the 11th August 1900

Nr.	Class.	Words.	Received.	Remarks.	Charges	Sent.
1		106 (?)	H......M......a.m. p.	*Vid: Chinese Lines*	Paid: $ Received by me:	To........ the H.........M.........a.m. p. by me........

Journal N.Y. (prepay to Shanghai)

NOTHING TO BE WRITTEN ABOVE THIS.

~~Journal, N.Y.~~

Allied forces advanced yesterday nine miles against General Tung-fu-shiang completely demoralizing them occupied Matow Advance continues despite heavy rain ~~English~~ Loss slight English sending lyddite gun Russians two additional batteries Sixth reinforced by two troops entire regiment being sent forward Consuls sent runner Pekin messenger Congers message Intermediate country infested boxers who

I request that the above Telegram may be forwarded according to the rules of the International Telegraph Convention, and according to the Administration's *Conditions printed on the back thereof*, by which I agree to abide

Signature of Sender .... *Address* ....

Date ....

N.B.—You are requested before signing TO READ THE CONDITIONS of the Contract on the back.

Figure 1.2(a) Telegram from Edward Wildman, an American journalist with the relieving forces marching to Beijing. From the Edwin Wildman papers, Manuscript Division, Library of Congress.

THE CHINESE TELEGRAPH COMPANY.

上海電報商局去報

STATION the 190

Nr.	Class.	Words.	Received.	Remarks.	Charges	Sent.
		~~(?)	H.....M......a.m. p.	Vià: Chinese Lines	Paid: $ Received by me:	To........ the H.........M.........a.m. p. by me........

NOTHING TO BE WRITTEN ABOVE THIS

persistently cut telegraph le hoffee
natifres Tientsin not safe
send supplies without strong
convoy Japanese war department
just received secret advices from
Pekin spies Li-Pieng Hungs
Imperial guard ten thousand
with 30 modern Krupp guns
inside city !! Tueng-Fu
~~te~~ ten thousand Forbidden city
Manchu and Honan forces
forces fifteen thousand outside
total forces forty thousand
Wildman

I request that the above Telegram may be forwarded according to the rules of the International Telegraph Convention, and according to the Administration's *Conditions printed on the back thereof*, by which I agree to abide.

Signature of Sender .... *Address* ....

Date ....

N.B.—You are requested before signing TO READ THE CONDITIONS of the Contract on the back.

Figure 1.2(b) Continued.

We are still without news from Peking and without authentic news of a positive kind from the expeditionary force under ADMIRAL SEYMOUR. We know, however, that the story brought by a Japanese ship from Ta-ku to Chifu to the effect that the ADMIRAL had returned to Tien-tsin can hardly be correct. The ship which brought it left Ta-ku early on Sunday, and the Admiralty have now received an official message from Wei-hai-wei explicitly declaring that no information of SIR EDWARD SEYMOUR's return had reached the REAR-ADMIRAL up to 2 p.m. on Sunday. A native newspaper which is said to be the organ of the well-known Mandarin SHÊNG, who has given so much trouble in his capacity as director of railway concessions, states positively that the British flag was flying on the south gate of Peking on Monday, and it is naturally presumed that this is the flag of the expeditionary force. It would be foolish to place much reliance on this story, which, however, may possibly be true. It has at least this much in its favour, that the south gate is the gate we should be tolerably sure to seize on our entry into the city. Even if this rumour were certainly well founded, our anxiety would not yet be at an end. It is, we fear, within the bounds of possibility that if the expeditionary force are at Peking they may have arrived too late to save those whom they went up to rescue. Happily there is not yet any special reason to entertain so horrible a supposition. The stories as to the murder of the German Minister and the destruction of the Legations remain unconfirmed.

From other widely distant parts of China we hear fresh news of disturbances and of attacks on Europeans. A telegram received in Berlin states that the European settlement at Tien-tsin has been bombarded; the reports of troubles in the

The Times, 20 June. Leading article. An example of the wishful thinking style of reporting which a paper of this stature did not stoop to make in other contexts.

ADMIRAL SEYMOUR'S FORCE.

(FROM OUR CORRESPONDENT.)

SHANGHAI, JUNE 20.

A despatch by Shêng's Courier Service confirms the statement that Admiral Seymour's force arrived in Peking on the 17th. No details are given of the casualties or the condition of affairs in the capital, regarding which much anxiety is felt.

The Times, 21 June.

(FROM OUR CORRESPONDENT.)

SHANGHAI, JUNE 22.

The fleet and the Consulate are still without news of Peking, but a statement has been made to-day by Shêng on the authority of a telegram from Yuan Shih-kai in Shan-tung. The latter had received news by special courier from Peking that all residents in the Legations were safe. The foreign Ministers were demanding their passports, and the Yamên appeared to be disposed to comply with their request. If the news is a fabrication the motive is not clear. If it is true it would imply the correctness of the earlier reports as to Admiral Seymour's arrival in the capital.

The Times, 25 June. Bland's analysis is not based on any logic other than the desire to believe that Admiral Seymour must have reached Peking.

(THROUGH REUTER'S AGENCY.)

WASHINGTON, JUNE 26.

Admiral Kempff has sent the following telegram from Ta-ku under yesterday's date :—

"Relief force reached Tien-tsin 23rd. Loss very small. Peking relief force, which left Tien-tsin 10th, reported be ten miles from Tien-tsin, surrounded. Force left Tien-tsin 24th render assistance."

The armoured cruiser Brooklyn will take 300 marines from Manila to Ta-ku.

The Times, 27 June.

Figure 1.3 *The Times*. Sober, dignified, false and misleading (I).

LATEST INTELLIGENCE.

THE CRISIS IN CHINA.

A telegram from the German Consul at Chifu received yesterday also alleges that ADMIRAL SEYMOUR is about 20 kilometres from Tien-tsin, hard pressed by "Boxers" and Chinese troops, and it makes the further statement that he has the foreign Ministers with him, while on Monday the German Governor of Kiao-chau telegraphed that, according to Chinese reports, the relief column had reached Peking. These assertions, as our Berlin Correspondent observes, are quite consistent with each other, and they seem to be supported by the "other tele-"grams" from ADMIRAL KEMPFF, referred to in our New York message. These telegrams, our Correspondent says, "give rise to the hope that ADMIRAL "SEYMOUR may have reached Peking, rescued "the Ministers, and been stopped when return-"ing." On the other hand, a Chifu telegram declares that there had been no news of the force since it was heard of on the 12th at Lang-fang.

The Times, 27 June. Hopeful to the last, Chinese sources could be reliable if they had "positive" news. (*The Times*, 20 June)

(FROM OUR CORRESPONDENT.)
SHANGHAI, JUNE 26.

A telegram from the British Consul at Chifu confirms the news of the relief of Tien-tsin and adds that the relieving force started on Sunday with the intention of affording assistance to Admiral Seymour, who was reported to be intrenched near Tien-tsin.

The rumour is persistent that the foreigners have left Peking escorted by native troops, but it is impossible to trace the source of or to verify such reports, which are chiefly of native origin.

The Times, 28 June. Neither Bland nor the paper for which he worked deemed of paramount importance the vulgar gathering of news at first hand.

Figure 1.4 *The Times*. Sober, dignified, false and misleading (II).

> It is circumstantially stated by our Consul at Chifu that the expedition lost 62 men killed and 312 wounded, but rumour in these regions tends to be circumstantial, and much depends upon how the news reached Chifu, without becoming known to the Rear-Admiral at Ta-ku (Dagu).

These figures were never formally acknowledged or discussed in *The Times*. Instead of acknowledging Chinese military and para-military action, the nature and extent of Boxer initiatives were simply not mentioned. In fact, the Boxers used guerrilla-type action which forced Admiral Seymour into a retreat on which he was shepherded back to Tianjin by soldiers of the Wu Wei army. The Wu Wei army consisted of five divisions and was the result of a reorganisation by Cixi of the forces in the strategically vital area around Beijing. The military circumstances of Admiral Seymour's retreat were described in detail by both soldiers and officers of the retreating Allied force and will be discussed in Chapter Seven. *The Times* was preoccupied with the unreliability of Chinese sources[59] which were quoted, however, if the news they conveyed was positive to British interests.[60] *The Times* had appointed a journalist whose concept of his profession was not such as to incline him to catch a ship from Shanghai to Tianjin and verify these and other matters. Together with the fact that Bland's services continued to be valued by *The Times* for many years after the Boxer rising, Bland's lack of initiative opens to question the degree to which *The Times* was interested in producing responsible reporting on Chinese affairs.

It is not possible to discover from Admiral Seymour's dispatch, or any other material reported in *The Times*, what role was played by the Boxers or the Imperial Chinese Army in Seymour's decision to retreat. His dispatch does not indicate which Chinese forces were responsible for forcing the Allied rescue mission back on Tianjin. Neither does the dispatch make clear why it took sixteen days for Admiral Seymour to fail to accomplish a journey of eighty miles and reach Beijing. This dispatch could not actually employ the word "retreat." The factors forcing Admiral Seymour to "withdraw on Tientsin," according to the dispatch, were shortage of provisions, being hampered with wounded and the cutting of communications with the base at Tianjin. The expedition had also run short of ammunition. There was no suggestion in the dispatch of military or paramilitary action by the Chinese as being a factor in his withdrawal. Admiral Seymour offered no explanation involving Chinese military action as to why he and his force spent five days holed up in an arsenal three miles out of Tianjin, nor why he had to ask for a relieving force to rescue his forces.

This was the age of the dashing war correspondent par excellence. American journalists arriving later in June embodied that tradition in marathon rides involving real danger to themselves in order to get their dispatches to a reliable telegraph office. George Morrison used inflammatory language to describe the behaviour of the Boxers in the earlier stages of the uprising. The other correspondent for *The Times*, J.O.P. Bland thought the events in Tianjin of so little consequence that he did not bother to come from Shanghai to see the war at first hand. (A French military attaché came especially from Tokyo to Tianjin). The editor, Valentine Chirol's general lack of interest in China and his particular blend of condescension when discussing Cixi or the Imperial Chinese Army or individual Chinese statesmen obviously influenced both Morrison and Bland. Admiral Seymour was not able to admit in his official

SIR E. SEYMOUR'S FORCE.

THE BRITISH CASUALTIES.

The War Office has received the following telegram from Colonel Dorward, dated Chifu, June 23, 11 35 a.m. :—

Seymour relieved. All British troops now in Tien-tsin.

The Foreign Office has received the following telegram from the British Consul at Tien-tsin, *via* Chifu, June 29 :—

Admiral Seymour and his force reached Tien-tsin on June 26, together with the force which had gone to his relief.

The following casualties had occurred among the British troops :—Captain Beyts killed, seven officers wounded ; 24 men killed and 91 wounded.

The returns from the foreign detachment are not yet complete.

A foreign resident at Tien-tsin has received a message through the Customs Taotai there that the Legations are still in Peking.

(FROM OUR OWN CORRESPONDENT.)

BERLIN, JUNE 29.

A telegram despatched by the German Consul at Chifu yesterday says :—

" Seymour relieved. No further details and nothing to show whether the foreign Ministers are with him. Railway communication with Ta-ku is still imperilled. The last section of the road to Tien-tsin can only be traversed by strong detachments of troops. Fifteen engineers who had taken refuge here have gone to repair the whole section to Ta-ku. The bombardment of Ta-ku (Tien-tsin ?) from the west side continues. The Chinese shells explode badly. It is alleged that three of the inhabitants are killed or wounded. Previous statements regarding destruction of property in the English settlement, where Germans chiefly live, appear to have been exaggerated."

Figure 1.5 *The Times*. Sober, dignified, false and misleading (III).

dispatch or elsewhere that he had been defeated by a combination of Boxer and Imperial Chinese Army initiatives. *The Times* was run by an editor who was not prepared to acknowledge Chinese military victories in the early stages of the war or to solicit contributions from journalists working for him which described these victories. *The Times* naturally inclined to join with Admiral Seymour in a notably successful effort to write the Boxers and regular Chinese soldiers out of their achievement in forcing the Allied Expeditionary Force to retreat to Tianjin. Of the two journalistic techniques used to describe the Boxers: the use of emotive language or ignoring their existence entirely, it was the latter which proved ultimately the most successful. Few, if any Western or Chinese scholars describe in detail the skill and courage of those Boxer units which used *modern* weapons to decimate Seymour's forces on his retreat. Anyone relying on the pages of *The Times* alone for evidence of successful Boxer military initiatives, would face a conspiracy of silence.

The details concerning Admiral Seymour's relief expedition as he officially reported it were available to readers of *The Times* on 30 June. In the interim, the anxiety regarding the fate of the relief force was intense and temporarily eclipsed concern for those in the Legations at Beijing or even those being bombarded by the Imperial Chinese Army in Tianjin. On 19 June *The Times* published a telegram from Chifu incorrectly reporting that the Admiral was back in Tianjin "having found advance impossible. The railway has been destroyed with remarkable thoroughness." The use of the passive voice should be noted here; readers of *The Times* could be forgiven for failing to discern any evidence of Boxer military initiative as a factor in Admiral Seymour's reported decision to return to Tianjin. Only five days earlier, *The Times* had reported the restoration of the broken line of communications which isolated Lord Roberts, the Commander-in-Chief of British forces in South Africa, in these terms:

> The nation cannot afford to tolerate incompetence or negligence such as must have been shown in this case; for the merest tiro knew that, when Lord Roberts depended for his supplies upon the single line of rails, running through hostile territory, a raid was only too probable and the greatest vigilance would be needed to thwart it.

Two days later, *The Times* expressly acknowledged the military ability of Boer commandos in disrupting communications:

> In spite of the number of British soldiers available under various generals to check them in all directions, the renewal of the raid on the railway and the cutting of the telegraph between Senetcal and Winburg indicate how clever and mobile they still are.[61]

Even the Ashanti Rebellion generated commentary more informed by local conditions.

> Owing to the difficulty experienced in procuring carriers, the enforcement of the labour ordinance is threatened. This, however is considered extremely inadvisable in view of the present temper of the inhabitants and the unprotected condition of the colony.[62]

Boxers, being "rabble" and members of the various Chinese armies being "worthless as fighting men," did not actively figure in *The Times* reporting of Admiral Seymour's movements. The fact that the Boxers cut the rail in front and behind the Admiral as well as cutting him off from all communications could apparently be ignored in the editorial columns. If somehow railway lines got torn up, bridges and stations burnt, water towers and rolling stock destroyed and communications cut in such a passive way, it became unclear who actively perpetrated these deeds. Readers of *The Times* were given no indication that these measures formed part of Boxer action in conjunction with Imperial Chinese Army military tactics which had a precise objective: that of forcing Admiral Seymour back on Tianjin.

Thus the course taken by *The Times* in praising the "gallant" Admiral's conduct in the face of these difficulties becomes more understandable. He was not judged irresponsible in setting out with men untrained for land warfare and insufficient food and ammunition on a railway line known to have been attacked systematically by enemy forces. He was not called to account for being cut off by that enemy for fifteen days, and finally having to be rescued though only three miles from Tianjin. *The Times* never proposed any censorial discussion of Admiral Seymour's conduct. The military principle of securing one's lines of communication applied equally in identical situations in two different campaigns occurring at the same time. As *The Times* reported the events, the principle was not substantially modified by military action in South Africa — *The Times* called for someone to take responsibility for the military lapse that allowed the Boers to cut off Lord Roberts[63] — but this same principle clearly did not apply to the action of the Boxers in China.

By 25 June, when the Admiral's retreat had brought him within three miles of Tianjin, *The Times* editorial column was still attempting an analysis of information to confirm the Admiral's arrival in the capital. Concerning this first expedition to relieve the Legations, *The Times* editorial comment showed an unwavering tendency to credit rumours reflecting positively on Allied military progress and a corresponding tendency to omit or dismiss information reporting military losses or defeats. Thus, in the absence of authentic information because of the disruption of communications, *The Times* fostered only those rumours reflecting positively on the mission.

> Another telegram published today by the organ of Shêng, Director of Railways, states that the British flag was flying yesterday over the south gate of Peking. This is presumed to indicate the arrival of Admiral Seymour's force.[64]

By contrast, a 5 June editorial comment on Lord Roberts' silence observed:

> … in our ignorance of the Boer forces between [Johannesburg] and Pretoria as well as the amount of determination they may be throwing into their defence, it is impossible to judge of his rate of progress.

Similar ignorance with regard to Admiral Seymour's whereabouts neither gave rise to an assessment of Chinese military initiatives as a factor in his having "vanished" nor to any criticism of the Admiral's lack of foresight and ability as a commander of a land force. When *The Times* was presented with evidence indicating the possibility of Chinese military successes, this was written off as some sort of "design," a strategy of disinformation deliberately used by the Chinese. There was no attempt to engage with the possibility that Admiral Seymour may have been defeated.

> The authorities at Peking are only too likely to represent the interruption of the Admiral's advance to their own menacing attitude, if not to his actual defeat by the forces at their disposal or acting under their inspiration. There are indications of such a design in some of the telegrams which reach us from Tientsin.[65]

Contrast this with the American press: *Chicago Daily News*, 14 June, "Relief Party Is Surrounded. Dispatches Received in Washington That Troops Are in Danger." The *World*, 15 June, "Chinese Oppose the Relief Column. Serious Engagement with Their Troops on the Way to Peking. Relief Party Delayed …" or with other sections of the British press. Although the editorial in the *Daily Mail* on 15 June spoke of Admiral Seymour having "to deal with an enemy of the lowest fighting power" and there being every reason to suppose that he would be able "to drive back the Boxers, and if need be, even to tackle the Chinese braves, and to seize the Empress," it also quoted on that day a dispatch from Reuters dated 13 June, "It is considered that the present force [Admiral Seymour's] will be absurdly inadequate should the Imperial troops join the Boxers." On 18 June the *Daily Mail* reported, "Rioters, however, have torn up the line both in front and behind the force, so its position is dangerous." On 19 June the editorial in the *Daily Mail* noted "Admiral Seymour … has been compelled to beat a retreat to Tientsin."

The persistence of *The Times* in wishing to give credence only to those stories that could be interpreted to demonstrate the success of the relief force, was reflected in a report on 27 June that Admiral Seymour had the Ministers of the foreign Legations with him. That is, that he had accomplished his mission. There was never any clear statement to the effect that Admiral

Seymour had failed to reach Beijing. If it could not be clearly acknowledged that Admiral Seymour had failed, then it could not be suggested that this was anything to do with Chinese military action. Lack of food and ammunition, these were the acknowledged factors "even the bravest and the most willing of troops cannot march through a hostile country without supplies and without sufficient water." But how was it that the "rabble," the "worthless ... fighting men" managed to kill sixty-two and wound 312 in a force of 2,044? This was not a question that either *The Times* nor the Admiral felt accountable to answer:

> In fairly favourable conditions a force of 2,000 Europeans might be relied upon to pull through a great deal of Chinese opposition, but in this case the physical conditions are so far from favourable as to provoke and justify the gravest apprehensions.[66]

A clearer example of writing the enemy out of a series of victorious engagements cannot be seen in any of the other newspaper accounts of the first four weeks of the Boxer campaign. In terms of image-making, the denial of military superiority to the Imperial Chinese Army and the refusal to recognise the Boxers as an effective fighting force served many purposes. It fulfilled the expectations of Chinese inferiority held by the journalists writing for *The Times*, it therefore contributed to the negative image of the Chinese held by the influential sectors of the British public, and it not only exonerated Admiral Seymour's military ineptitude, but also contributed to the nature of the whitewashing of the "gallant" and "able" Admiral. In reporting this phase of the Boxer crisis, *The Times* did not distinguish itself by its accurate reporting, its responsible analysis or by bringing authentic information about China and the Boxers to its readers.

The *World*

At the opposite end of the spectrum of journalism from *The Times* in Britain were the mass-circulation, sensationalist newspapers such as the *Daily Mail*. In order to examine the American reporting of this early part of the Boxer campaign, the *World* was selected to represent the other extreme from *The Times* on another continent. Sensationalist the *World* certainly was. Headlines such as "Professor Found Woman Under Bed," a front page headline on 25 May 1900, would not incline the reader to expect a significant degree of responsible or analytical reporting from the *World*. However, like the *Daily Mail*, the *World*'s reporting of the China crisis was more responsible than that of *The Times* in many ways. The only point of similarity was the acceptance of rumours from British or Chinese sources saying that Admiral Seymour had reached Beijing (21 June). These rumours — as was not the case with *The Times* — were superseded by a major front page headline on 24 June "Peking Unrelieved" and the story that Admiral Seymour had saved the foreign Ministers (28 June). This story was in turn superseded on 30 June by a report giving the "first authentic news of Seymour's return without the foreign envoys" under the heading: "Seymour Reports His Failure." In a highly volatile situation in which reporters were plagued by almost insurmountable difficulties in getting accurate stories, the *World*, like most other papers did publish inaccurate rumour. More exceptionally, however, it published stories retracting the earlier inaccurate headlines.

At this time the *World* was strongly anti-imperialist which led to a very clear line on American involvement and behaviour in Cuba and the Philippines and criticism of British foreign policy.[67] In domestic affairs, the *World* took a hard line on corruption among politicians and extended this to a criticism of the political patronage in overseas appointments that it saw as leading to profiteering.[68] The paper also showed a readiness to expose sharply what it alleged to be deficiencies in military leaders, an article on General Otis, commanding officer in the Philippines on 12 June containing a savage indictment of the man's personal and professional record.[69] Headlines on 4 June made the *World's* position on American involvement in the Philippines amply clear: "Taft Tells Filipinos to Yield and Be Happy.... All Sorts of Nice Presents from the Benevolent McKinley for Brown Men Who Lay Down Arms."[70] More broadly, the *World* had a larger view of "civilisation" than that espoused by *The Times*. The *World* was less ready to use the term but when it was used, this newspaper made it clear that whatever qualities were embodied in the word "civilisation," it could not be applied one for one to white Western men's behaviour; even white Western man had a tenuous grasp on civilisation.[71] Thus though the *World* undoubtedly devoted large proportions of its columns to scandal, there were elements of editorial policy favourable to a broader range of reporting style on China and the Boxer War.

In addition to the *World's* anti-imperialist line, there was frequent reporting of Chinese individuals and institutions as valid entities operating according

PEKING UNRELIEVED; MASSACRE SPREADING.

Frederick Palmer, The World's Staff War Correspondent, Arriving at Shanghai, Cables that All North China is in a War Panic.

BOXERS MOVEMENT GROWING TO SOLE POWER IN EMPIRE.

Admiral Seymour's Relief Force of 2,500 American and Foreign Troops Surrounded or Annihilated.

ONLY A FEW MILES FROM WARSHIPS, BUT NOT HEARD FROM FOR 10 DAYS.

Twenty Thousand More Troops Needed to Clear the Railway 70 Miles to Pekin—Another Regiment May Go from Manila.

(By Cable from a Member of The World Staff—the First New York Correspondent to Reach the Seat of War.)

SHANGHAI, China, June 23.—There is not a Chinese port north of Amoy to-night that is not doubtful of its security.

The Boxer movement is spreading rapidly. Chinese troops are deserting everywhere to the Boxers, who are becoming the sole authority in the Empire.

United States Consul Goodnow showed me private despatches and official advices of the gravest import. They strengthen the conviction that the situation in north China is hourly growing worse.

Few of the foreign legations are believed to have survived.

Admiral Seymour, who commands the allied foreign relief forces, is surrounded, if not annihilated, between Tientsin and Peking.

The allied forces now hold only some five miles of the Tientsin and Peking Railway [which is about seventy miles long] and are besieged at that. Not a word has been heard from the relief expedition since the 13th.

In the opinion of experts here twenty thousand troops, American, British, German, French, Italian and Japanese reinforcements, are needed under a competent commander to force a way to Peking and protect survivors of massacres.

The nearest large reinforcements are Russian reserves at Port Arthur, Japanese at Hiroshima and Americans at Manila.

Shanghai itself fears attack. Widespread terror. No one hopeful.

I expect to reach the fighting ground Monday.

FREDERICK PALMER.

Figure 1.6(a) The *World*, 24 June. Palmer's dispatch negates all possibility that the Expeditionary Force reached Beijing. It also has a compelling immediacy.

to Chinese policy dictates. While screaming headlines shouted "Save Us or Avenge Us!"[72], the actual reporting of missionary involvement and its consequences in the *World* was more detailed and offered many more points of view than that of *The Times*.[73] The Chinese ambassador to America, Wu Tingfang, was interviewed frequently by the *World* outside the period of the Boxer crisis. On 17 May 1900, under the heading "Wu Ting Fang Sarcastic," the *World* reported that he criticised the attitude of Anglo-Saxons towards women doctors and quoted his concluding advice that they should go to China to practise. Thus we see an interesting paradox in this American newspaper's reporting on China. Undeniably a paper committed to exposing political and social scandal, it was this impetus that led the paper to reveal American wrongs in domestic and international contexts. It was thus able to acknowledge the rights and/or interests of indigenous peoples and sometimes, even women. The paradox arises because the mass circulation public that the paper aimed to capture, was subjected to a range of serious articles on China which postulated China as a political entity, the institutions of which needed to be understood.[74]

The people who bought and read the 18,848,329[75] copies of the *World* sold in June 1900 were exposed to articles giving a detailed (and substantially accurate) overview of the historical origins of the Boxers;[76] they read of internal Chinese politics under such headings as "Chinese Cabinet Crisis";[77] they were given factual background on Chinese military strength and explanations of the origins, growth and power of the Chinese Ministry for Foreign Affairs;[78] they read a world scoop portrayal of the Empress Dowager, sympathetic, informative and entirely lacking in pejorative or scurrilous language.[79] Finally the US public was made aware that the nature of the Boxer troubles meant that losses and deaths at their hands were also suffered by Chinese people of all classes, Christian, non-Christian, magistrate or coolie.[80]

Another important difference between papers like the *World* and a paper like *The Times* was the value placed by the former on being first with a story; on getting a scoop. Events in China were deemed sufficiently newsworthy to send the *World*'s staff war correspondent to China. Frederick Palmer arrived at Shanghai on 24 June and his dispatch made front page headline news on 27 June as "The First Cable Message Received by Any Paper Direct from the Seat of War." Palmer's next dispatch written on board the US flagship *Newark* brought the first authentic news of the arrival at Tianjin of Admiral

WORLD GETS FIRST NEWS OF HOW M'CALLA SAVED SEYMOUR.

Frederick Palmer, The World's special war correspondent in China, yesterday sent the first authentic news of the arrival at Tientsin of Admiral Seymour's forces. Mr. Palmer's despatch was written on board of the U. S. flagship Newark, whose commander, Capt. B. M. McCalla, at the head of 150 marines, joined the allied forces which marched to the relief of the envoys at Peking.

Aside from settling definitely the fact that the Russian report of the envoys' safety was absolutely untrue, Mr. Palmer's message tells how Capt. McCalla's foresight in taking with him two weeks' supplies saved the entire allied forces of 2,700 men from annihilation

This despatch was at once telegraphed to the Secretary of State, by whom it was sent to the President. Afterward the news it contained was discussed at a Cabinet meeting. The World received the following acknowledgment from the Acting Secretary of State:

To the Editor of The World:

Your telegram relating to the situation in China is received, and I beg to thank you for it.

Washington, June 29.

DAVID J. HILL, *Acting Secretary of State.*

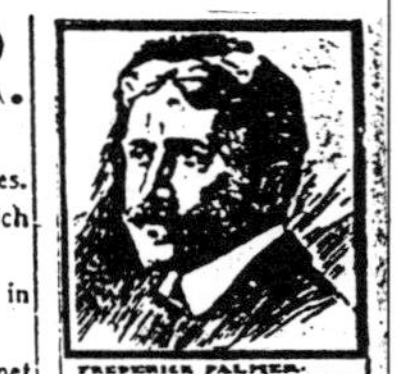

FREDERICK PALMER.

The World's famous war correspondent in China, who sent the first authentic news of Seymour's return without the foreign envoys; who sent to The World the first news of Dewey's victory at Manila, and who has achieved other notable news victories in The World's service.

BATTLE-SHIP OREGON ASHORE; SEYMOUR REPORTS HIS FAILURE

UNITED STATES BATTLE-SHIP OREGON.

Reported ashore on an island in the Gulf of Pechili, fifty miles north of Chefoo.

Peerless American Warship Was Speeding to Join the United States Squadron at Taku When She Ran Upon Hookie Island in the Miaotao Group.

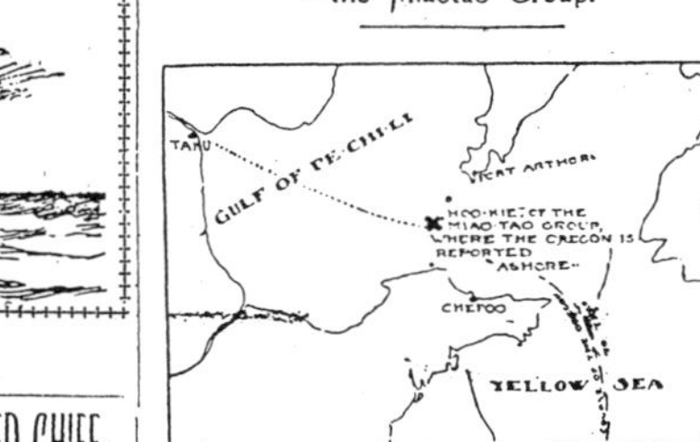

BRITISH HEAD OF PEKING EXPEDITION TELLS OF HIS DISASTROUS CAMPAIGN.

ACCUSED OF FORGERY, SAYS HE'S A NOBLEMAN

WOMEN FORM FIRE BRIGADE.

With Aid of Summer Boarders They Put Out a Blaze.

PORT JERVIS, June 29.—A fire brigade organized on emergency at Lake Kanneonga yesterday was composed largely of women. The barn of Kanneonga Inn, ...

REFUSED TO WED CHIEF-JUSTICE'S DAUGHTER.

Figure 1.6(b) The Scoop. The *World*, 30 June. No mention of McCalla's role in the retreat of the relief expedition reached *The Times*. McCalla was a fine soldier whose foresight and fighting ability played a major part in the survival of the disastrous Seymour expedition.

Seymour's forces. Palmer's reports contained details about Boxer action and Imperial Chinese Army preparations, equipment and dispositions which never appeared in *The Times*.

In addition to sending Palmer to Tianjin, the *World* reported interviews with a wide range of people, including the Chinese Ambassador in Washington, Bishop J. W. Joyce of the Methodist Church, General Scholfield, Justice Brewer, Bishop Cranston and Charles Denby, former US Minister to China.[81] These interviews spoke with moderation and dignity of a China nowhere accessible to readers of *The Times* which only published one such interview during this phase of the crisis: an interview with the German Catholic Bishop Anzer on 9 June 1900. Most of those interviewed by the *World* had considerable experience of China. The consensus of opinion was that China would not be dismembered.

In his book, *News and the Culture of Lying*, Paul H. Weaver offers an extensive negative critique of the style of journalism Pulitzer brought into being. Most particularly, Weaver wrote that:

> From day one Pulitzer's policy was to stop writing stories about events in their institutional contexts and to start writing stories that would directly engage the values and the feelings of the people among whom Pulitzer was seeking his audience.[82]
>
> It was just the kind of communication the Founding Fathers had warned about.... History showed that in the absence of institutions that shape, inform, test, check, qualify, and validate popular views, public opinion degenerated into fleeting passions engendered by passing events and manipulated by unscrupulous demagogues.... Everything the Constitution had done to make democracy safe for individual rights and prudent statecraft, Pulitzer's journalism was undoing. It took events out of their constitutional contexts.... It stressed the emotional and the immediate rather than the rational and the considered.[83]

With due respect to Paul Weaver's work, the coverage of the Boxer War by the *World* does not bear out any of the above assertions. Whether or not Wu Tingfang received more space in the columns of the *World* because he was the ambassador of an exotic country, the fact is that he received such space. Furthermore, his opinions reached a mass audience, many of whom would have had more firsthand experience of racism against the Chinese than a similar audience in Britain.[84] A newspaper which had given the amount of accurate background detail on China described above at the time of a crisis which had the potential to bring out optimum hysteria and coloured reporting, could not be said at this time in respect of this crisis to be manipulating public opinion so that it "degenerated into fleeting passions engendered by passing events" as Weaver claims in the above citation with respect to the style of journalism initiated by Pulitzer. Moreover, the journalistic innovation of the interview, a reporting style not yet adopted by *The Times*, has been shown to have been used most responsibly by the *World* both in the range of people interviewed and in the selection of their views on China which finally appeared in print.

The American public reading the yellow press had more reason to fear China and the Chinese and more experience of Chinese people in confrontational situations on American soil, than was the case in Britain. Yet the month of June saw the *World* providing a stream of factual and pictorial information from a wide variety of sources. It did not show the paper "stressing the emotional and immediate rather than the rational and the considered."

With factual information about the nature of the members of the loosely organised Boxer groups, this kind of reporting in combination with other details about Chinese political and military leaders, built up an image corresponding more to what was happening in China to Westerners as well as to Chinese people. Thus by 20 June, readers of the *World* following the Chinese crisis learned that the palace of the Viceroy of Tianjin had been burned, the Magistrate of Wingshun had been killed and many towns had been overrun by the Boxers. Thus, unlike the readers of *The Times* who were never given this kind of information, the readers of the *World* were being taught in its columns that the death of Chinese people and the destruction of their property also rated as "newsworthy." The *World* had built up an accurate image of the Boxers as a rebellious element no longer controllable by Chinese or Western authorities. This image had been built up by background articles, special interviews and headlines reporting Chinese military successes as they occurred.

An editorial on 2 July showed the *World* to be the only newspaper of those selected for this study which made the connection between the currently articulated Western notion of the dismemberment of the Chinese Empire and the "wishes or rights of the Chinese," even with the form of protest expressed by the Boxer rising. The question why the views of men like

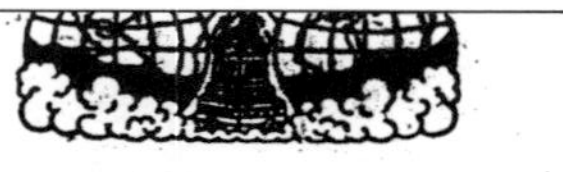

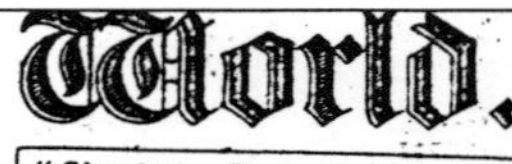

"Circulation Books Open to All."

Your for sale offers through a medium that sells. Real Estate and Business Opportunities advertised in the Sunday World find ready takers.

NEW YORK, SUNDAY, JUNE 17, 1900. Copyright, 1900, by the Press Publishing Company, New York World. 53 PAGES. PRICE FIVE CENTS.

LEGATIONS IN PEKING WRECKED,

China Cut Off from the World;

GERMANY'S ENVOY ASSASSINATED.

FIRST CRY FOR HELP OUT OF DARKEST CHINA.

Fac-Simile of Cable Despatch That Came to the World Last Sunday, Direct from Shanghai, the First Warning to the Civilized World of the Dire Events to Come.

CABLE MESSAGE.

RECEIVED at Central Cable Office, 16 Broad St., New York. June 10 1900

19 Cn Jd K K Coll Shanghai 100

World Ny

Peking ninth situation appalling railroad destroyed government refuses additional guards only four hundred all nationalities armed american missionaries all collected methodist compound furnished guard ten marines frightful reports country butcheries christians troops furnished by native government every instance amalgamated boxers without rebuke proving intent only one slender wire holds communication outside world twenty four warships taku practically defied by cabinet tsungliyamen seem mean well but powerless foreign ministers realize too late all previous promises edicts alike deceptive arouse christian world danger ourselves personally should this arrive too late avenge us committee american missionaries have endorsed above statement

635Am

Houses of Foreigners in Tientsin Burned, Together with Three English and American Churches.

10,000 CELESTIAL TROOPS JOIN BOXERS

International Force Sent to Save Ministers, Missionaries and Others Cut Off in the Interior, Supply Train Being Unable to Reach It.

HONGKONG, China, June 16.—All the legations at Peking have been destroyed.

The German Minister, Baron von Ketteler, has been killed.

The British first-class armored cruiser Undaunted has suddenly been ordered north under sealed orders. She will sail immediately.

The British first-class cruiser Terrible sailed for Taku this morning with troops.

Capt. Percy M. Scott, of the Terrible, arranged before sailing to land a twelve-pounder and other ship's guns for land service.

Trouble is brewing near West River.

Riots have broken out at Bunchow. More than a hundred refugees from there arrived at Wuchow June 12.

About 5,000 rebels have assembled at Kweilisien.

Bodies of Canton troops passed through Wuchow June 11 on their way to meet the rebels.

FOREIGN HOUSES FIRED IN THE CITY OF TIENTSIN.

SHANGHAI, June 16.—Great incendiary fires occurred last night in the eastern part of Tientsin. Three English and American churches were burned, besides the residences of many foreigners.

The train conveying the relieving party with food and

Figure 1.7 The *World*. 17 June 1900. Sensational headlines, responsible reporting. Baron von Ketteler was not, in fact, assassinated until 20 June. The reason for this discrepancy was thought by some contemporaries and by posterity to be that because of the German ambassador's personal arrogance and cruelty towards individual Chinese people, a contract had been placed on him. The assassin reached his target a few days later.

Chirol, Morrison and Bland drowned the voices brought into print by the *World*, must be asked. On the basis of this analysis, an answer pointing to the *World's* use of an inferior or irresponsible journalism which caused public opinion to "degenerate into fleeing passions engendered by passing events" would not be appropriate.

More work needs to be done on the actual nature of the popular press at the turn of the century by analysing responses to particular stories and more especially, to its pictorial content. However, it may be asserted here that there were elements of yellow journalism as practised in the coverage of the Boxer War by the *World* which favoured a more responsible portrayal of events in China than did the journalism practised by *The Times*. China was inaccessible, feared and exotic. Publishing measured analytical interviews by people who had been there, publishing pictures of places in China, publishing details about the nature of Chinese political and industrial institutions, giving the ruler of China a name and an identity qua ruler of China, publishing accurate full-page background stories on the anniversary of past conflict with China,[85] and above all sending a journalist of the calibre of Frederick Palmer to report events at first hand, all these were techniques of a journalism which, at least in respect of China, could have met the standards of the most exacting of the Founding Fathers.

By contrast, the pages of *The Times* were filled with emotive comments by a foreign editor who was less interested in and knowledgeable about China than he was about Egypt, India, Turkey and the Sudan.[86] No attempt was made to publish a wide range of the views of people interested in or knowledgeable about Chinese history and culture. Of its two foreign correspondents in China, George Morrison who was besieged in Beijing could not speak or read Chinese, and fifteen years in China as correspondent for *The Times* did not incline him to learn the language. The other correspondent, J.O.P. Bland who spoke Chinese, was stationed at Shanghai. Communications between Shanghai and the outside world were undisturbed. Neither he himself nor the editor of *The Times* thought it worthwhile for him to make the three-day risk-free boat trip to reach Tianjin, the seat of the desperate battles between the Chinese and the Allied invaders. It is difficult to avoid the conclusion that its perception of its own reputation as the paper serving the ruling class of a nation at the zenith of its imperial power overrode consideration of the actual style and content of the reporting of the Boxer War in *The Times*.

Turning to the language of the editorial columns and the headlines in the *World*, we see an image of China and the opening weeks of the Boxer campaign which is almost entirely irreconcilable with that portrayed by *The Times*. Nowhere did the Boxers "swarm" or "teem"; neither did they appear in "hordes" or "mobs." In the period under discussion they were described variously as "enemies," "insurgent," "a large force," "patriotic Chinamen" and "fanatical and ferocious" (in the context "fanatical" was descriptive of the single-mindedness of their intent rather than pejorative). Reference was made to the "fury of the Boxers."[87] In his study, *The Heathen Chinee*, McClellan claims that there was frequent use of the word "barbarian" to describe the Chinese at this time.[88] However, the word "barbarism" was used in connection with the Chinese only once in the month of June in the editorial columns of the *World*. This reference is notable in the context generated by the international hysteria consequent on the siege of the Legations. By contrast, it was used frequently in the leading articles of *The Times*, each time with additional colouring, for example, "revolting barbarity," "avalanche of Asiatic barbarism," "unyielding barbarism," "outburst of Oriental barbarism."[89] The *World*'s strongest language was employed on one occasion in condemnation of Chinese official action in connection with the perceived failure to protect the foreign envoys. This was characterised on 19 June as a "confession of outlawry and a substitution of barbarism for the peaceful intercourse of civilisation." To counterbalance this view, the leading article of 1 July pointed out that "Chinese diplomatic usages differ widely from those of Western nations."

There were many factors leading to the absence of emotive pejorative language in describing the Chinese in the editorial columns of the *World* in June 1900. Among these were a general American sympathy for the underdog,[90] American antipathy to the aggressive aspects of British imperialism and Pulitzer's own philosophy of journalism. Pulitzer had an expressed interest in advancing the welfare of mankind and held the idealistic view "that the US had a special mission in world affairs to shun the imperialistic power politics of the Old World and promote democracy among our sister states in the New."[91] More specifically, Pulitzer did not approve of the attitude in the popular press of the 1890s that news from exotic countries was a form of entertainment and a good source of fantasy and horror stories.[92] Both the leading articles on the editorial page and the feature review articles on China in June 1900 show the *World* to have reflected these concerns.

Another concern expressed in the editorial columns of the *World* was with the "facts." Judgement was withheld because of "ignorance of the actual facts" or qualified "on this statement of the facts."[93] There was a leading article on 14 June headed "The Reporter and the 'View Point'" which argued that whether in domestic politics or foreign wars,

> The duty of the correspondent is to observe and describe all that actually takes place within his range of observation, without exaggeration, distortion, omission or any form or expression of prejudice … all news reports should be photographic and phonographic, and hence free from "color" or prejudice.

The process of journalism as conceived of by those working for the *World* was one which sought to describe the facts, to publish immediately news which invalidated or superseded those facts and to offer analysis based on other facts already proven. Despite the general assumption that sensational newspapers were cavalier with facts, the headlines in the *World* throughout June gave a more accurate view of events in China than did those in *The Times*.[94] On 23 June 1900, the *World* published a report from the United States gunboat *Nashville* saying that Tianjin was being bombarded and giving the names of all the Chinese generals involved. The report noted that "the foreign residents are confined to a restricted district and as food and water are scarce they have suffered greatly." This did indeed constitute a precise statement of the facts. Moreover, this report added a detail not noted in any other newspapers examined in this study. "The Tongshan mines at Peitaiho were abandoned by soldiers and rioters flooded the mines and ruined the machinery." Thus reported, this incident became part of Western experience of an event as it might have been described had it occurred in Britain or America. The use of the word "rioters," the fact that the mines had been guarded by soldiers and the reporting of the destruction of the machinery as a possibility that the government had foreseen and attempted to prevent, gave the incident the same sort of colour as if it had occurred in Wales or Pennsylvania.

As already discussed, there were headlines conveying inaccurate news over this month, but they were corrected. There were also emotive headlines but these were rare and without exception headed factual non-emotive reporting. The one headline in this period which, succumbing to the temptations of alliteration, abandoned the usual style of the *World* and employed the language of *The Times* was "Mongol Mobs Swarm about Legations Eager to Murder."[95]

A final point about the journalism of the *World*. Like the *Daily Mail*, the *Westminster Gazette* and the *Chicago Daily News*, the *World* offered express analysis of the news itself and judgement on its accuracy according to the source of the news and other information known to be true. *The Times* while systematically denigrating Chinese sources, showed a consistent tendency to accept such sources if they contributed to a picture showing a favourable outcome for British or Allied interests. Thus there was contradictory reporting on the Chinese crisis in the pages of *The Times* which was never discussed or resolved. The absence of any attempt to reconcile contradictory reports on a story of worldwide interest in the leading British newspaper of the time is a notable feature of *The Times*' reporting of the Boxer rising. In a very fine study *Victorian News and Newspapers*, Lucy Brown commented that:

> A modern reader is struck, not so much by the biased character of the reports, some of which might be encountered today, as by the fact that they were offered in a bald, unreconciled form with no attempt to analyse or explain things to the general reader.[96]

The *World* made such attempts in a way which distinguished its reporting as unique at this time. By using such a formula as "The report [that x is happening] is taken to mean [y]," the reader got not only the *World's* interpretation but also was offered the possibility of realising that an interpretation had been made. On 16 June readers of the *World* read that:

> The report that the mixed forces will seize the Taku [Dagu] forts is taken to mean that the foreign commanders expect no aid from the Chinese Government in repressing the disorders and are determined to make Taku secure as a base from which to operate.

Some examples of the *World's* analysis are based on data perhaps not available to and certainly not reported in or taken up by *The Times*. On 22 June a comparison was made between the bombardment of Tianjin and probable events taking place in Beijing. As the *World* had already published details of the guns being used, their range and the numbers and types of Chinese forces involved, this attempt at interpretation was reasonably accurate. Attention to sources and comparatively little hysteria in reporting, meant that the *World* squashed wild rumours throughout June although, like the whole of the Western press, it succumbed in July to the story that all Westerners in Beijing had been killed. On 22 June for example, the *World* reported:

> A story was afloat here to-day that President McKinley had received a dispatch reporting a massacre of foreigners in Beijing, Minister Conger and many other Americans being among the slain. The rumour must have been our exaggerated version of Admiral Kempf's dispatch, for the *World* has ascertained with absolute certainty that the President received no other news about China to-day than what was contained in the Admiral's report.

The clearest example of responsible journalism in collecting a reliable database and using this to analyse stories as well as offering a critical interpretation of news stories, concerned the report of the massacre of foreigners at Tianjin:

> A recent census of Tientsin shows the foreign population to be about 1,000 persons.... Thus the report from Japanese sources that 1,500 foreigners at Tientsin had been massacred would seem to be grossly exaggerated. Every foreigner in Tientsin would have to be killed to bring the total up to anywhere near that number.[97]

The *World* offered its readers an outstanding coverage of the early stages of the Boxer War in terms of the quality of feature writing, reporting, editing and evaluation of news. On the same day, 23 June in a leading article "The News from China," the *World* showed the ability to offer a concise and responsible evaluation of news from a variety of sources.

Reflections

In their celebrated essay, "A Test of the News," Walter Lippman and Charles Merz surveyed the reporting of the Bolshevik Revolution by the *New York Times*.[98] They documented and condemned the erroneous reporting of this event on grounds which included the facts that "the *New York Times* index is an enormous convenience to any student of contemporary history" and "because the bound volumes are easily accessible."[99] This is also the case for *The Times*. They made a similar point about the national and international reputation of the paper. There was and is still today, a belief that great newspapers reported the truth. Furthermore, as Lippman and Merz also showed

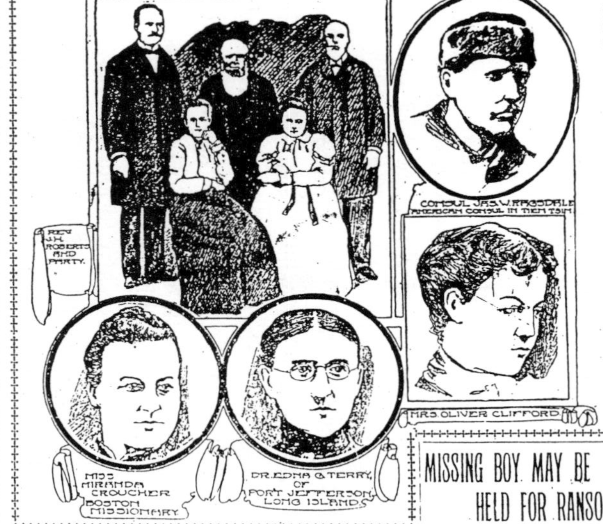

TIENTSIN IN RUINS; ANARCHY IN PEKING, 1,500 FOREIGNERS REPORTED SLAIN ALREADY.

Bombarded Five Days by Chinese Imperial Troops, Who Are Under Empress's Orders, Not by Boxers.

800 AMERICANS IN FORCE DEFENDING THE CITY.

Mobs Run Riot in Imperial Capital, Though the Foreign Ministers Are Reported to Be Safe—U. S. Soldiers to Be Rushed to Taku.

(*Copyright, 1900, by the Press Publishing Company, New York World.*)

(*Special Cable Despatch to The World.*)

Hongkong, British China, June 22.

Tientsin has been bombarded now for five days and the shelling still continues.

The attacking force consists of Chinese Imperial troops (who are under the orders of the Empress Dowager), and not of Boxers, as was at first supposed.

These imperial troops are equipped with modern weapons, including artillery, and are skilled in the arts of modern warfare, having been trained since the war with Japan by English, Russian and German officers.

The United States (converted Spanish) cruiser Don Juan de Austria has arrived at Canton, where she is awaiting orders.

800 AMERICANS IN THE BATTLE.

LONDON, June 23 (Saturday), 3 A. M.—The silence of Peking continues unbroken.

Four thousand men of the allied forces were having sharp defensive fighting at Tientsin Tuesday and Wednesday, with a prospect of being reinforced Thursday.

The Shanghai correspondent of the Daily Express cabled last (Friday) evening: "Eight hundred Americans are taking part in the fighting at Tientsin and they apparently form a part of a supplementary force, arriving with Germans and British after the conflict started. It is impossible to estimate the number of the Chinese there, but they had a surprising number of guns."

ENVOYS REPORTED SAFE.

Sheng, Director-General of Telegraphs, wires from Shanghai to the Chinese legations in Europe that the foreign legations in Peking are safe.

SOME OF THE AMERICANS AT TIENTSIN WHOSE LIVES WERE IMPERILLED BY THE BOMBARDMENT.

MISSING BOY MAY BE HELD FOR RANSOM.

Little Joe Pollio Has Disappeared, and His Relatives Believe He Has Been Kidnapped.

WAS AT PLAY IN THE STREET.

RIVAL CUT BRIDE'S THROAT AND HER OWN.

BRIDE AND GROOM ARE NOT DISCIPLINED.

Figure 1.8 The *World*, 23 June. The accuracy of this headline was discredited by the paper itself. The opening lines of this report tell a very different story about the bombardment of Tianjin. The juxtaposition of this report with the headline "Rival Cuts Bride's Throat and Her Own" is of interest in the overall context of the journalism characteristic of the *World*.

with the *New York Times*, such newspapers had enormous influence on contemporary decision makers.[100] Moreover, because of their widely-accepted position as reliable and accessible authority, their version of events was also claimed by posterity to be the correct one. Lippman and Merz believed that newspaper reporters "were performing the supreme duty in democracy: supplying the information on which public opinion feeds." They concluded roundly that "they were derelict in that duty."[101] The parallels between their analysis of the *New York Times* coverage of the Bolshevik Revolution and this briefer analysis of *The Times*' reporting of the Boxer rising are striking.

This study raises a number of questions regarding the responsibility of the press to inform its readers of which only two will be touched on in conclusion. First, that in 1900 there was a perception of a hierarchy of enemies as worthy opponents or fighting men with the Chinese being at the bottom in the British view. The second point refers to the press as provider of accurate uncoloured news coverage and analysis as the differences between the stately and the sensationalist press have been canvassed above.

On the question of perception of the enemy, it is too simplistic to say that such perception followed clear-cut lines of race and religion. Quite clearly this study has shown that Valentine Chirol's preconceived picture of the Chinese presented in emotive language influenced the ability of *The Times* to report actual Chinese military successes. Reporting in the *World* gave accurate details about the origins of the Boxers and the strength and disposition of the Imperial Chinese Army thus leading to headlines describing the war as it actually evolved in the four weeks under consideration. To explain this difference, it is necessary to look beyond racial and religious prejudice in studying the reporting of war from the last quarter of the nineteenth century up to the 1914–1918 War.

Established theatres of war such as the Balkans, the Sudan, and the far north of India were familiar territory to most experienced British war correspondents. There was nothing familiar about China. War correspondents, their editors and the newspaper reading public had been accustomed to formulating acceptable images of war. Nothing that was happening in China fitted the bill as far as *The Times* was concerned. Moreover, unlike many other British and American newspapers which sent correspondents to China, *The Times* had no man covering the events at first hand.[102] As well, the Chinese were proving decidedly worthy as fighting men. After the Imperial Chinese Army beat back the Russian Cossacks three times during the battle of Tianjin, the Russians refused to hold the railway station alone any longer. At the turn of the century, the Cossacks were universally held to be among the most redoubtable fighting men in the world. Chinese military successes were reported in the American press.[103] A partial explanation for the readiness of the American press to acknowledge Chinese military successes may lie in the different view of national interests viz à viz China. However, some credit must go to individual journalists and editors whose concept of journalism included the necessity of firsthand reporting. Aside from Palmer, another notable American journalist to cover the Boxer crisis was Wilbur Chamberlin of the *New York Sun*.[104] Chamberlin's life was cut short tragically by illness and death on his return journey from China, thus depriving newspaper reporting of one of that rare group of journalists whose attitude showed him to be unpartisan in the pursuit of his profession.

What was being purveyed was not war itself, but an image of war. This war was, moreover, being driven by bands of infuriated Chinese peasants, a concept quite usual in the Chinese context but little-known, if at all, in recent Western experience. During the First Opium War, Chinese administrative authorities had agreed to disburse massed bands of angry peasants; in 1900 Cixi vacillated and the combined Allied armies did not find it at all an easy matter to get the Boxers to lay down their arms and go home. Since this was a different kind of war from those that had been fought in other parts of other Empires, it called for the best in Western journalism. The public being an assenting partner, a study such as this one focusing on either extreme of the press and its public in two countries, allows some assertions to be made about the power of the press in making and in forming images. The conventional understanding of responsible accurate dispassionate reporting being the province of the stately press and wild, emotional and highly-coloured reporting the characteristic of the sensationalist press is untenable as far as the reporting of the first four weeks of the Allied involvement in the Boxer campaign is concerned. *The Times* systematically used emotive language to denigrate the ruler of China and Chinese political and military institutions, Chinese leaders and the Boxers themselves. It omitted any reference to Boxer or Imperial Chinese Army military success, selected news from rumour on the basis of whether such rumour could give an impression of British success and above all, failed to supply its readers with any accurate background information or firsthand reporting of the Boxer crisis. By contrast, there was nothing sensationalist or emotive about the reporting in either the British *Daily Mail* or the *World*. Insofar as the reporting of the China crisis was concerned, the readers of mass circulation newspapers in America and Britain had a wider range of more reliable material on which to base their opinions, than did the readers of *The Times*.

Notes

1. While there were superstitious elements to Boxer drill, the military history of nineteenth century China is replete with examples of well-trained gentry-led militia. These were recruited from the peasantry for training. There were even books of instructions on the organisation of local corps which were distributed to gentry and local officials. See Franz Michael, "Military Organisation and Power Structure of China During the Taiping Rebellion," *Pacific Historical Review*, Vol. 18, 1949, pp. 469–483. On the official perception of the need or otherwise to use militia, see Roger R. Thompson, "Military Dimensions of the 'Boxer Uprising' in Shanxi, 1898–1901," in Hans van de ven (ed.), *Warfare in Chinese History*, Sinica Leidensia, Brill, Leiden, 2000. My thanks to Professor Joanna Waley-Cohen for drawing my attention to this later reference.
2. In reprisal for the deaths of two missionaries, Germany occupied a part of Shandong province in November 1897. This was a particular affront to the Chinese as Shandong is the birth place of Confucius.
3. For a thought-provoking discussion of the elements of flood and drought and their effects, see Paul A. Cohen, *History in Three Keys. The Boxers as Event, Experience, and Myth*, Columbia University Press, New York, 1997.
4. Joseph W. Esherick's book, *The Origins of the Boxer Uprising*, University of California Press, Berkeley, 1987, and Cohen, op cit., are the authority on the subject. For a survey of Chinese scholarship on the Boxer rising, see David D. Buck (ed.), *Recent Studies of the Boxer Movement: Chinese Studies in History*, Vol. 20, Nos. 3–4, Spring–Summer 1987, M. E. Sharpe Inc., New York. Recent authoritative works in Chinese are Li Dezheng, Su Weizhi and Liu Tianlu, *Baguo lianjun qinhua shi* (A History of the Eight Power Allied Forces Aggression Against China), Shandong University Press, Jinan, 1990; Shi Yuceng, *Yihetuan yundong yibai zhounian jinian: Yihetuan yundong he baguo lianjun qinhua zhanzheng* (Commemoration of the Centennial of the Boxer Movement: The Boxer Movement and the Eight Allied Forces War of Aggression), Chuzhong Huiguan, Tokyo, 2000; Sun Qihai, *Tiexue bainian ji: Baguo lianjun qinhua zhanzheng jishi* (Commemoration of the Centennial of the War Against the Eight Allied Forces

Aggression), Huanghe, Jinan, 2000; Mo Anshi, *Yihetuan dikang lieqiang guafen shi* (The History of the Boxers' Struggle Against the Foreign Countries Who Wanted to Divide China), Jingji guanli, Beijing, 1997; Zhao Jianli, *Yihetuan baguo lianjun xingchou tiaoyue. Gengzi zhi bian tuzhi* (The Boxers, the Eight Invading Powers, the Boxer Protocol. Illustrated Records of the Changes That Happened in the Year 1900), Shandong huabao, Jinan, 2000.

5. J. D. Startt, *Journalists for Empire. The Imperial Debate in the Edwardian Stately Press, 1903–1913*, Greenwood Press, New York, 1991. Professor Startt uses the term "stately" press to describe such papers as *The Times*, the *Westminster Gazette*, the *Spectator* and the *Observer*.
6. The newspapers selected for the research base of this study were *The Times*, the *Westminster Gazette*, the *Spectator*, the *Daily Mail*, the *Illustrated London News*, the *Review of Reviews*, the *Chicago Daily News*, the *World*, the *Nation*, the *San Francisco Examiner*, the *North-China Herald*, the *Peking and Tientsin Times*, the *China Mail*, the *Shanghai Mercury* and the *Hong Kong Daily Press*.
7. See *Review of Reviews*, May 1900, pp. 420–433. An article on Mr Cyril Arthur Pearson, founder of the *Daily Express*. See also James D. Startt, "Good Journalism in the Era of the New Journalism: The British Press, 1902–1914," in Joel H. Wiener (ed.), *Papers for the Millions: The New Journalism in Britain, 1850's to 1914*, Greenwood Press, New York, 1988. Professor Startt's analysis of responsibility, sensationalism and accuracy shows a thoughtful appreciation of the standards of good journalism held by men of such influence as Lord Northcliffe and J. L. Garvin. Of particular interest is Startt's assertion that "there existed a quest for good journalism" among those spearheading the New Journalism (p. 281) and his assessment of Garvin's defence of the Edwardian press (pp. 292–294).
8. The latest study in the well-documented field of scholarship on Joseph Pulitzer is Paul H. Weaver, *News and the Culture of Lying*, Free Press, New York, 1994. My thanks to Professor Mark Elvin for drawing my attention to this reference.
9. Of all the foreign journalists who noted the regrettable behaviour of the invading troops, George Lynch's accounts are the most poignant. See G. Lynch, *The War of the Civilisations: Being a Record of a "Foreign Devil's" Experiences with the Allies in China*, Longmans, Green and Co., London, 1901, pp. 39, 46, 49, 142 and 182. The American photographer James Ricalton photographed corpses of Chinese civilians which accumulated overnight, clogging up the Bei river each morning. He attributed these deaths without hesitation to the invading soldiers and Imperial Chinese Army soldiers, noting their adherence to the Christian religion in this context. See C. J. Lucas (ed.), *James Ricalton's Photographs of China During the Boxer Rebellion. His Illustrated Travelogue of 1900*, Edwin Mellen Press, New York, 1990, pp. 163–164. As well as the invading soldiers and soldiers of the Imperial Chinese Army, the Boxer insurgents also killed uncountable Chinese citizens.

10. For evidence of Chinese reactions to discussions in the Western press and widely-read accounts of China such as that by Lord Charles Beresford of the division of China among the Powers, *The Break-Up of China*, Harper and Brothers, New York, 1899, see George Lanning, *Old Forces in New China*, Shanghai National Review Office, London, Probsthain, 1912, pp. 140, 148 and 150–151 and Chester C. Tan, *The Boxer Catastrophe*, Octagon Books Inc., New York, 1967, p. 14. See also Joanna Waley-Cohen, *The Sextants of Beijing. Global Currents in Chinese History*, W. W. Norton and Company, New York, 1999, p. 7.
11. The Chinese lost one important battle in the first four weeks after foreign intervention in the Boxer crisis. This resulted in the capture of the Dagu forts on 17 June after hard fighting in which Chinese gunners hit all Allied vessels taking part in the action, seriously disabling four warships. Otherwise the Chinese defeated every major Allied military initiative until the fall of Tianjin on 14 July.
12. The Ashanti Rebellion, though a small affair, also took place in mid-1900 and occasioned pro and anti-imperialist rhetoric as well as providing background for a discussion of most of the issues raised in this chapter.
13. Lord Charles Beresford's visit to China opened up newspaper debate on the relative merits of the "Open Door" policy or "slicing China like a melon." *The Times* correspondent in Beijing, George Morrison was in favour of the latter. See Lo Hui-min (ed.), *The Correspondence of G. E. Morrison*, Vol. 1, Cambridge University Press, New York, 1976; letter from Morrison to Bland, 6 December 1897, p. 52; letter from Morrison to Bland, 17 January 1898, p. 61; letter from Morrison to Bland, 14 July 1899, p. 123. The Chinese were well aware of these debates and the impetus given them by Beresford's visit.
14. At the time, the Boxer rising provoked greater publicity than did the events on Tiananmen Square of June 1989. Soon after the siege was relieved, a spate of memoirs was published by missionaries, diplomats, travellers, journalists and military men. Early silent films showing the Battle of Dagu (August 1901) and the Taking of the Walls of Beijing by the US Ninth Cavalry (January 1902) can be seen in the Library of Congress Film Archives. In China during the 1960s a massive oral history project was undertaken to interview surviving people, men as well as women, who took part in the Boxer rising. The film, "Fifty-five Days in Peking," made in 1962 starring Ava Gardner, Charlton Heston and David Niven, is still shown perennially.
15. News items from *The Times* were selected for translation by the Continental press, thus influencing a section of European public opinion. The authority on the reporting of the Boxer rising in the French press is Christine Corniot, "La Guerre des Boxeurs d'Après la Presse Française," *Etudes Chinoises*, Vol. 6, No. 2, 1987.
16. A bibliography of some of the more influential works on the Boxer rising includes Paul H. Clements, *The Boxer Rebellion: A Political and Diplomatic*

Review, AMS Press Inc., New York, 1967 (1915); Victor W. Purcell, *The Boxer Uprising. A Background Study*, Cambridge University Press, Great Britain, 1963; George Nye Steiger, *China and the Occident. The Origins and Development of the Boxer Movement*, Russell and Russell, New York, 1966; Chester C. Tan, op cit.; William J. Duiker, *Cultures in Collision: The Boxer Rebellion*, Presidio Press, California, 1978; Esherick, op cit.; Cohen, op cit. Although they all have interesting and illuminating insights, none of these works describe Chinese military successes in June/July 1900 either at all or with an acceptable degree of accuracy. Esherick even claims that the Battle of Dagu did not take place. See Esherick, op. cit., pp. 302–303. Cohen glosses over it entirely.

17. Some interesting and technically difficult work has been done by James Hevia on looting. See James L. Hevia, "Loot's Fate. The Economy of Plunder and the Moral Life of Objects," *History and Anthropology*, Vol. 6, No. 4, 1994; "Plundering Beijing, 1900–1901," unpublished paper given at the conference "1900. The Boxers, China and the World," SOAS, London, June 2001; and *English Lessons: The Pedagogy of Imperialism in Nineteenth Century China* (forthcoming).
18. *The History of the Times. The Twentieth Century Test, 1884–1912*, Kraus Reprint, London, 1971 (1947), p. 204.
19. Ibid., p. 208. Valentine Chirol's interests in the Orient centred rather on India, Egypt and Turkey than on China. See Valentine Chirol, *The Occident and the Orient, Lectures on the Harris Foundation*, 1924, University of Chicago Press, Chicago, 1924. See Lo (ed.), op cit., Letters from Chirol to Morrison of 20 October 1898, p. 101, 16 January 1899, pp. 111–112, and 2 March 1899, pp. 112–113.
20. Lo (ed.), op cit. p. 113.
21. Hugh Trevor-Roper, *Hermit of Peking. The Hidden Life of Sir Edmund Backhouse*, Alfred A. Knopf, New York, 1977, p. 28.
22. Morrison's style and attitudes earned him frequent rebukes from Chirol and suggestions regarding both the content and style of his dispatches which were of such an elementary nature as to cast some doubt on Morrison's professional ability as a journalist. See Lo (ed.), op. cit., pp. 76, 80–81, 89, 102, 105 and 106–107. Many of Chirol's letters to Morrison took the form of assuring him what a good correspondent he was and then asking him, time permitting, whether he might do something which most foreign correspondents would have been severely censured for failing to do. For example, it could have been expected of *The Times*' foreign correspondent in Beijing after a residence of over ten years there, that he might have understood the necessity of preparing an obituary of the Empress Dowager, by then a very old woman. However, he did not and earned a polite but definite rebuke from Moberly Bell for his oversight. See Sterling Seagrave, *Dragon Lady: The Life and Legend of the Last Empress of China*, Alfred A. Knopf, New York, 1992, p. 431 for Bell's letter of 24 November 1908. Although Lo Hui-Mui's edition of Morrison's letters does not contain Bell's

letter, Morrison's reply of 14 January 1909 is on p. 477.

23. *The History of the Times*, op cit., pp. 354–355.
24. See his dispatches of 1 June and 2 June 1900, for example.
25. *The Times*, 2 June 1900.
26. *The Peking and Tientsin Times*, editorial 7 April 1900. The *North China Daily Herald*, 18 June 1900, reported that the Chinese sent wires to Tianjin to get help for railway engineers being pursued by Boxers, p. 1005.
27. Lo (ed.), op cit., p. 129.
28. Weaver, op cit., p. 35 and pp. 40–41.
29. John O. P. Bland, *Houseboat Days in China*, William Heinemann, London, 1919 (1909), p. 78. This little-known book gives a clear insight into Bland's racist feelings about the Chinese. See, for example, p. 62.
30. Following the German seizure of Chinese territory, the Italians also attempted to wrest territorial concessions from the Chinese government but were prevented by the Empress Dowager. See also Waley-Cohen, op cit., p. 153 for an analysis showing that the Chinese were adept at making an apparently humiliating treaty serve Chinese purposes to the discomfort of the British.
31. This language is taken from the leading articles published in *The Times* throughout June 1900.
32. *The Times*, 6 June 1900.
33. See *The Times* leading article 6 June 1900. At this date the character of the uprising was still fluid and no responsible analyst would have felt able to comment on the precise relationship between the Court and the insurgents. Indeed, the *Westminster Gazette* saw a connection between the Boxer rising and Russia, the bête noire of British foreign affairs analysts (8 June).
34. The Hoover Institute of War, Revolution and Peace at Stanford University, holds a tape-recording of the memories of Wai H. Tan (1891–1990) concerning the Boxer rising. He recalled the looting by Dong Fuxiang's soldiers. Tan's second uncle lost all his silver and was physically maltreated by these Muslim soldiers. Dong Fuxiang's soldiers were feared alike by the Han Chinese and Western European inhabitants to such an extent that before the outbreak of hostilities with the Allied army, the Empress Dowager was obliged to order General Dong to move his soldiers to a camp-site outside the city.
35. See Private Henry Derry's account of his experiences in the First Opium War retold in the *Globe and Laurel* of November 1901 in Colonel Cyril Field, *Britain's Sea Soldiers: A History of the Royal Marines and Their Predecessors*, etc., Vol. 2, Lyceum Press, Liverpool, 1924, p. 73.
36. The *Chicago Daily News*, 2 June 1900, "The question of dealing with this large and powerful army of insurrectionists is one that will tax the powers of the foreign ministers in China and may yet lead to serious complications among the powers themselves." This early acknowledgment of the relationship between recognising the Boxers as a powerful force and giving a more accurate prediction

of future developments should be noted. Similarly, the *Daily Mail* of 8 June 1900, published a remarkably accurate article on the origins of the Boxer movement and made it clear that the Boxers should not be underestimated. The *World*, 22 May 1900, was well in advance in anticipating the significance of the crisis about to break by running an article on a hitherto unknown group of insurgent peasants. On 8 June the *World* published a special article on China's Fighting Forces. Interestingly the *Westminster Gazette* cited Morrison's reports as evidence to its readers by 5 June, "that the crisis is dangerous in the extreme" and by 9 June having synthesised reports from a wide variety of sources, the *Westminster Gazette* was asking whether the situation might not be too much for Admiral Seymour to handle. On 15 June the *Westminster Gazette* wrote, "it would be the height of folly to send a force sufficient to provoke, but wholly inadequate to cope with the conspiracy and its official supporters."

37. On 16 July the *Daily Mail* published a dispatch from a Special Correspondent in Shanghai describing the massacre of the besieged in the Legations. In London a memorial service for the victims of the massacre was arranged in St Paul's Cathedral for 23 July but cancelled on the day as doubts had begun to arise about the *Daily Mail* dispatch. As a result of the mistake, many in the European community of Beijing, including George Morrison, had the interesting experience of reading their own obituaries once the siege had been raised.
38. *Daily Mail*, 8 June 1900.
39. Ibid.
40. *The Times*, 12 June 1900.
41. "Using barbarians to control barbarians" was an age-old principle of Chinese state-craft.
42. *Chicago Daily News*, 12 June 1900.
43. Ibid., 15 June 1900.
44. Startt, op cit, p. 7.
45. *The Times*, 7 June 1900, 23 June 1900.
46. Ibid, letter to the editor by H. S. Alexander, 1 January 1900, p. 4; letter to the editor signed "Ignotus," 1 January 1900, p. 7; letter to the editor signed "British Citizen," 1 January 1900, p. 13; letter to the editor by Miles, 11 June 1900.
47. Ibid., 9 June 1900.
48. Ibid., leading article, 14 June 1900.
49. Ibid., 5 June 1900.
50. Seagrave, op cit., pp. 260–261. Chirol to Morrison, 16 December 1898.
51. Sarah P. Conger, *Letters From China*, Hodder and Stoughton, London, 1909. For more details of women's impressions of and rôle in the Boxer rising, see Susanne Hoe, *Women At The Siege, Peking, 1900*, The Women's History Press, Oxford, 2000.
52. *The Times*, 5 June 1900.

53. A book exemplifying this tradition is Frederick L. Bullard, *Famous War Correspondents*, Pitman and Sons, London, 1914.
54. R. W. Desmond, *The Information Process: World News Reporting to the Twentieth Century*, University of Iowa Press, Iowa, 1978, p. 417.
55. Frederick Palmer, *With My Own Eyes. A Personal Story of Battle Years*, Jarrolds, London, 1934, pp. 166–170. I am indebted to Professor James D. Startt for drawing my attention to this reference.
56. Seagrave, op cit, p. 314, inaccurately dates the first burning and destruction of railway lines and equipment as 5 June. This Boxer activity was, however, first reported in the *World* on 29 May. It was not reliably reported in *The Times* until 8 June. There was a report from Dalziel's Agency on 7 June; this agency was known to the world of journalism for the wild inaccuracy of its reporting at the turn of the century. In fact, soldiers of the Imperial Chinese Army were first killed by Boxers on 22 May while trying to defend the railway line. These events will be discussed in full in Chapter Six.
57. *Westminster Gazette*, 25 June, 1900.
58. Ibid, see especially p. 7, 23 June 1900, p. 7, 25 June 1900 and p. 7, 26 June 1900.
59. The unreliability of Chinese sources was referred to in leading articles in *The Times* on 15 June on 18 June and on two occasions on 20 June 1900. On 21 June 1900, it was stated that "It is impossible to place any reliance upon intelligence coming purely through native channels" and on 27 June 1900, it was reported that "An 'official's' statement that Tientsin had been relieved on Saturday by an allied force of 8,000 men was made in Shanghai yesterday, and, as our Shanghai correspondent knows Chinese officials much too well to place the smallest reliance upon their words, it was doubtless made on European authority." Tianjin was not finally taken until 14 July 1900.
60. *The Times*, 19 June 1900, reported that two of the forts at Dagu had been blown up by the Allies. "Though not officially confirmed, there is nothing improbable about this information." The forts were not blown up — a powder magazine in the south fort exploded after a chance hit by the *Algerine* — and *The Times* made no mention of the severe damage inflicted by Chinese gunners to four of the nine Allied warships which took part in this action. (See the account of the battle of Dagu in the leader on 21 June 1900 and in Chapter Seven below.) 22 June 1990, "Chinese sources say Admiral Seymour has reached Peking as M. Delcassé said and emphasised yesterday in the French Chamber, there has been nothing to show that they are incorrect." M. Delcassé had no more evidence concerning Admiral Seymour's whereabouts than anyone else in the Western world at this time and was thus not an authoritative source.
61. Ibid., 16 June 1900.
62. Ibid., 13 June 1900.
63. Ibid., 14 June 1900, "At present we are absolutely in the dark as to the officers

who are to blame. But we are quite as unable to believe that nobody was at fault as we are to admit that such mistakes should be overlooked. In the Navy there is always somebody who can be held responsible for a disaster.... Is the Army supposed to be exempt from this salutary rule?"

64. Ibid., 20 June 1900, from our own correspondent, Shanghai [that is, J.O.P. Bland].
65. Ibid., 16 June 1900.
66. Ibid., 26 June 1900.
67. The *World*, 12 June , 20 June 1900.
68. Ibid., 28 May 1900, 12 June 1900.
69. Ibid., 7 June 1900.
70. Ibid. This headline was singled out for further comment in an editorial snippet on 5 June, "'Be good and you will be happy,' says ... Taft to the Filipinos. But they seem to regard freedom as the first essential to happiness."
71. Ibid. 9 June and 16 June 1900. (See Editorial, "Where Are Missouri's Men?").
72. See Frederick Lewis Allen, "Newspapers and the Truth," first published in the *Atlantic Monthly* in January 1892 in, Tom Goldstein (ed.), *Killing the Messenger. 100 Years of Media Criticism*, Columbia University Press, New York, 1989, p. 238 for an explanation of the particular technical characteristics necessary for newspaper headline composition and, by implication, the potential for these to lead to headlines which often bear little relation to the tone of the report beneath. While there is undoubtedly substance in Weaver's point about layout (Weaver op cit., pp. 38–39), in the context of the Boxer War, the headlines used in the *World* indicate that technical reasons rather than Pulitzer's "exploitation" were responsible for some atypically emotive headlines.
73. In the month of June, *The Times*' only coverage of the issues arising from missionary presence in China was a speech made by Lord Salisbury to the London Missionary Society (20 June), the correspondence arising from this (25 June) and two short reports by Reuters on 7 June and 11 June quoting missionaries who had returned to London.
74. This study thus explains and amplifies the paradoxical nature of the *World* referred to in the *Encyclopaedia of American Journalism*, op cit., p. 351. I am indebted to Professor James D. Startt for this reference.
75. The paper claimed that it had the largest net paid circulation in America.
76. The *World*, 31 May 1900.
77. Ibid., 8 June 1900.
78. Ibid., 11 June. To put the origins of the Zongli Yamen into perspective (Masataka Banno's work remains the authority), it should be noted that the US Department of State had a total staff of thirty-eight in 1849 and in 1856 was reorganised to include fifty-seven people. Chinese affairs were placed under the charge of the second of the three clerks assigned to the diplomatic bureau, one of seven bureaux in the Department. See R. F. Wylie, "American Diplomacy in China,

1843–1857," in J. Goldstein, J. Israel and H. Conroy (eds), *America Views China: American Images of China Then and Now*, Associated University Press, New Jersey, 1991, p. 93.

79. The *World*, 17 June 1900.
80. Ibid., 20 June 1900. Seagrave's point that the actual number of European deaths in the Boxer rising was disproportionate both to the hype that surrounded them at the time and to the overwhelming number of Chinese deaths is made more succinctly by Mark Elvin in his review of Jonathan Spence's *The Search for Modern China*, see *The National Interest*, Fall, 1990, p. 88.
81. See the *World*, 3 June, 17 June, 24 June and 30 June 1900.
82. Weaver, op cit., p. 35.
83. Ibid., p. 41.
84. See Robert McClellan, *The Heathen Chinee: A Study of American Attitudes Towards China 1890–1906*, Ohio State University Press, Columbus, 1971.
85. The *World*, 24 June 1900.
86. See note 19 above. See also the following publications by Chirol reprinted from *The Times*; *The Middle Eastern Question or Some Problems of Indian Defence*, J. Murray, London, 1903; *The Indian Unrest*, MacMillan, London 1910; *India Old and New*, MacMillan, London, 1921; *India*, Scribners, London, 1926; *The Egyptian Problem*, MacMillan, London, 1920; *The Turkish Empire*, Unwin, London, 1923.
87. This language is taken from the editorial columns of the *World* throughout June 1900.
88. McClellan, op cit., p. 85.
89. *The Times*, 9 June, 18 June, 21 June, 25 June 1900.
90. S. Kobre, *Development of American Journalism*, William C. Brown, Iowa, 1969, p. 493.
91. Joyce Milton, *The Yellow Kids. Foreign Correspondents in the Heyday of Yellow Journalism*, Harper & Rowe, New York, 1989, p. 26.
92. Ibid., pp. 92–93.
93. The *World*, June 28, 1 July.
94. Ibid. **28 May**, Foreigners in Peril in the Capital of China; **29 May**, Army of Boxers Marching on Peking/Railway Station and Cars Burned and Tracks Destroyed/ Foreigners in Flight; **30 May**, Our China Legation Threatened by Boxers/Summons 100 Marines from Cruiser Newark; **31 May**, China Holds Back the Foreign Troops; **4 June**, Boxers Prepare to Attack Tientsin; **6 June**, More Americans to Fight the Boxers; **7 June**, Battle with Boxers Near Peking, Foreign Families Flee for Safety; **9 June**, Tientsin Surrounded/Foreigners in Terror; **10 June**, Boxers Burn Town and Kill Christians; **15 June**, Chinese Oppose the Relief Column; **17 June**, Legations in Peking Wrecked/China Cut Off From the World; **18 June**, We Send a Regiment From Manila to China; **19 June**, Chinese Forts Taken by the Allied Fleets/Tientsin Natives Shell the

Foreign Quarters; **23 June**, Tientsin in Ruins; Anarchy in Peking; **25 June**, Admiral Remey Ordered to China and a Full Brigade of US Troops; **3 July**, No Relief Force on the Way to Peking.

95. The *World*, 16 June 1900.
96. Lucy Brown, *Victorian News and Newspapers*, Oxford University Press, UK, 1985, p. 233.
97. The *World*, 23 June 1900.
98. See Walter Lippman and Charles Merz's influential essay, "A Test of the News," first published in *The New Republic* on 4 August 1920, in Goldstein (ed.), op cit.
99. Ibid., op cit., p. 89.
100. See Brown, op cit., pp. 262–263 for an example of politicians taking their information from the daily press. She comments on the quality of the reporting which meant that these readers "could well be excused their failure to appreciate the situation." Concerning the relationship between the authority of a newspaper and political authority at a much later date, Clifton Daniel quotes a story in which President Kennedy was told that news about the training of anti-Castro forces in Guatemala had been published in the *Nation* as well as in a Guatemalan newspaper. "But it was not news until it appeared in the *[New York] Times*," the President replied. See Clifton Daniel, "National Security and the Bay of Pigs Invasion," in Goldstein (ed.), op cit., p. 115.
101. Ibid., p. 91.
102. The word "man" is used advisedly. Aside from the well-known Nellie Bligh, there were very few women who reported on international news at the turn of the century. My research has turned up only one; Alice Tisdale Hobart who was war correspondent in Lahore in the 1890s and became editor of the *Peking and Tientsin Times*, a position she held for some time, including the period of the Boxer rising. See *China Yearbook 1903*. Apparently there was an American woman journalist who was known as a prominant writer for the social pages at Tianjin. She wrote for a publication called Town Topics. See Frederick A. Sharf and Peter Harrington, *China, 1900. The Eyewitnesses Speak, The Boxer Rebellion as Described by Participants in Letters, Diaries and Photographs*, Greenhill Books, London, p. 215.
103. *Chicago Daily News*, 23 June 1900, "Battle on in China. U.S. Marines and Other Forces Engage Chinese Troops at Tientsin. Great Loss of Life Reported. Native Soldiers Said to Have Killed Many Foreigners." Chinese troops did not, in fact, kill many foreign civilians but they did wipe out almost an entire American detachment under Colonel Liscum during the battle for Tianjin.
104. Wilbur Chamberlin's book, *Ordered to China*, Methuen, London, 1904, published posthumously, is a monument to the energy and humanity of a turn-of-the-century reporter.

Chapter 2

The Response of the British Illustrated Press: The *Daily Mail*, the *Illustrated London News* and the *Review of Reviews*

Every image of the past that is not recognized by the present as one of its concerns, threatens to disappear irretrievably.

Walter Benjamin

The stirring events of the Boxer rising produced a wealth of illustrated material during the long drawn-out summer while the world waited to hear of the fate of the foreign community and Chinese Christians made hostage in Beijing. In looking at photographs and hand-drawn pictures of this tumultuous crisis made by Westerners and Chinese, we have a unique opportunity to examine a contentious event eliciting a wide range of pictorial responses. There are not many contexts at this point in the history of pictorial reporting which allow us to analyse such diverse cultural productions purporting to describe the same events. Looking at Chinese folk art, Punch cartoons, official military photographs, Japanese woodcuts,[1] drawings of the events by artists who had never been to China, and drawings of foreign events by artists who had never left China, leads to new understanding of the assertion by William Ivins, one-time Curator of Prints at the New York Metropolitan Museum of Art that:

> at any given moment the accepted report of an event is of greater importance than the event; for what we think about and act upon is the symbolic report and not the event itself.[2]

The British illustrated press at the turn of the century was published primarily for the working class. Far from being irresponsible, hysterical or bigoted, British illustrated newspapers printed pictorial information about China and the Boxers that aimed to inform rather than inflame the British public particularly the working classes. Before turning to a detailed analysis of three illustrated British papers, a brief survey of Chinese popular pictorial imagery will be made to provide a comparison with which to evaluate the illustrated British press at the turn of the century.

The Illustrated Press in China

It would be a mistake to assume that the lack of a widespread and numerous commercial newspaper reading public in China[3] meant that there was no medium by which tens of thousands of ordinary people might see pictures of the foreigners attacking Tianjin and Beijing drawn by Chinese artists. The concept of the illustrated newspaper had been introduced as early as 1884 by Ernest Major and illustrated newspapers showing foreign news were common in Shanghai by the 1890s.[4] Although these did not have a wide circulation among ordinary people, there was also a strong Chinese pictorial tradition which did allow for the dissemination of cheap pictures on a huge scale,[5] namely the nianhua or New Year pictures. These had been made as woodcuts by specialised studios in various centres throughout China for hundreds of years. A particularly famous centre for the production of nianhua was Yangliuqing near Tianjin. It is to the justly high reputation of Yangliuqing woodcut art[6] that we owe the survival of pictures made to show the urban and rural poor in the North of China the events of the Boxer rising. Such pictures, like Western newspapers, were printed on cheap paper and were not thought of either by maker or purchasers as durable art objects. However, unlike Western newspapers, the big woodcut studios produced *coloured* woodcuts en masse which were valued by tens of thousands of people who bought them to adorn their houses both inside and out. They were bought mostly because of belief in their auspicious properties and to a lesser extent because of patriotic sentiment or a more general interest in stirring events.[7] Long before British or American working class people had cheap access to coloured pictures to decorate their homes,[8] this was an established and important tradition in China and among overseas Chinese.[9]

In times of internal or external political strife, placarding was an immediate public response in China. Placards took the form of poster-like sheets of paper with words and/or pictures pasted up in public. People gathering around the posters informed each other of their contents. Here then, there was the dimension of instant exchange of views among the onlookers, providing a forum for public political exchange in a country deemed by contemporary Western observers to be populated by people with a low to non-existent political consciousness.[10] Placards with their commentaries, particularly when enhanced with pictures, informed and inflamed public opinion in urban and rural China on internal and foreign political issues and have continued to be an important part of the Chinese political tradition until today.

The profound influence of the illustrated written word in political contexts, even in the smallest village in China, can be linked to the tradition of nianhua. The Chinese public, literate or illiterate, rural or urban, was accustomed to discussing, unravelling and comparing the complex symbolisms, homophones and double meanings contained in the words and pictures of the nianhua.[11] For one month in every year this formed the central point of most people's lives. The pictures, deliberately and personally selected from a wide range by tens of thousands of buyers — as opposed to being preselected for the public as in the Western press — were pasted in carefully chosen places inside and outside the humblest dwelling. Alexiev, the Russian sinologist and collector of nianhua wrote of:

> Chinese folk culture which is to be seen in such abundance on Chinese streets that all who walk along them during the whole month of the Chinese New Year holiday can not help but notice it — it clamours its presence, all are living by it and all are talking about it.[12]

There was even an element of audience participation in this art equivalent to the popular quiz introduced much later by the Western press.[13] Some nianhua were divided into sequences of pictures telling a story, rather like modern comic strips, and these were cut up and pasted in various parts of the home as deemed suitable by the head of the family.[14] Other nianhua in the form of calendars had blank spaces to be filled in, usually in connection with the weather, as a means of helping those working the land keep track of the days, the seasons and the phases of the moon. The oldest son in the family often filled in these sections as he was growing up.[15] The nianhua stayed up on the walls, even if faded and torn, throughout the year until more pictures were bought the following New Year. In this context, the appearance of new posters in public places and on sale as illustrated broadsheets during times of crisis, provoked immediate response from a people living in a culture with such a strong pictorial tradition.[16]

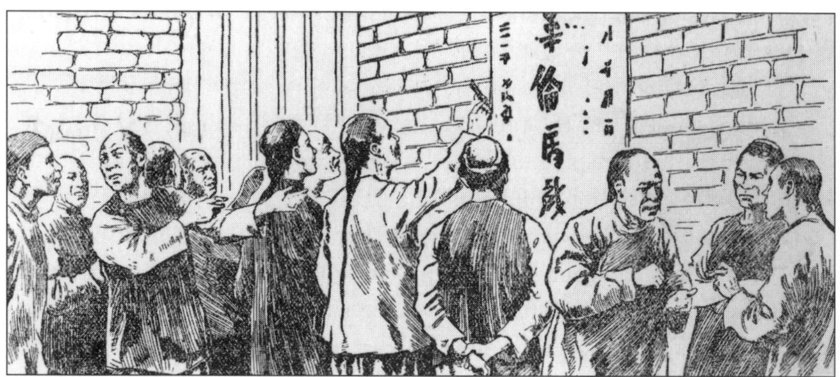

Figure 2.1 *Daily Mail*, 6 July 1900. "How the Chinese are incited to kill the 'Foreign Devil'." From the *Illustrated Missionary News* (caption from the *Illustrated Missionary News*).

A third source of illustrated news in China was the xinwenzhi, or popular newsprint, which appeared in big cities whenever there was some newsworthy event such as an earthquake, a famine, a foreign invasion, a battle or illegal acts by a mob. Episodes of the First Opium War in 1841 were pictured elsewhere in the empire by the xinwenzhi.[17] These publications did not exist as independent businesses but were another by-product for printers. Insofar as war was a popular subject, the buying and pasting up of xinwenzhi showing Chinese victories, contributed to the formation of some real sense of patriotism among the common people.[18] A fourth source of illustrations for the greater public appeared towards the end of the Qing dynasty in tracts against foreigners[19] and particularly missionaries, which again were extremely cheap, sometimes distributed free of cost, and thus had a wide circulation.

Although by the 1870s photography was socially accepted in certain milieux in China as a substitute for verity in matters of central importance to Chinese culture,[20] that is contemporaneously with America, Britain and Western Europe, for cultural reasons it was not widespread.[21] By contrast, popular desire for and exposure to illustrated material, usually associated with some form of caption and often of high artistic merit, had made even illiterate Chinese people in remote villages conversant with versions of Chinese history.[22] They were also recipients of direct deliberate cultural proselytising centuries before yellow journalism and cheap daguerreotypes or the New Journalism[23] and cheap reproductions of prints, hit America and Britain.

To begin with the issue of the respectability of popular illustrations themselves, whether in the press in the West or as huabao, xinwenzhi and nianhua in China, Jussim claims that the *New York Daily Graphic*, begun in 1873, was the first photographically illustrated paper in the world.[24] This claim may only rest if we restrict the definition of newspaper to that of a daily paper. The *China Magazine* produced in Hong Kong from 1868 to 1870 was a photographically illustrated periodical. Woodblock illustrated weekly newspapers began production a little later in China with Ernest Major's *Dianshizhai huabao*. Major's policy was to allow his Chinese editors to produce an essentially Chinese newspaper which Chinese people would want to buy and read,[25] the lasting success of the well-known *Shenbao* he founded in 1872 attesting to the integrity of his motives.[26] Chinese-owned pictorials published in increasing numbers towards the end of the Qing dynasty show the enormous influence of the pioneering *Dianshizhai huabao*.[27]

Reaction to illustrated newspapers differed widely. In China, the main objection expressed by the highly literate educated classes was to the language and style in which the news was written.[28] Exceptionally able writers such as Wang Tao, who founded the *Xunhuan ribao* in Hong Kong in 1873, had enormous influence on the development of newspapers in China because they wrote:

> with a degree of literary polish which made it respectable among the educated classes. The glory of the paper was in the daily editorial written by Wang Tao himself. His style was refined and graceful [and he] delighted the few critical scholars of that day with occasional disputations upon the classics and histories.[29]

In China, the issue was that of making newspapers themselves appear respectable in the eyes of the literate classes. As far as pictures were concerned, there was a continuing tradition from the Xia (2205 BC) of official interest in the didactic value of art.[30] Such snobbery as there was concerning painting in

Chinese society, centred rather on the issue of painting as a profession. Deliberately seeking to earn money from one's work was frowned on by Chinese scholar-philosopher artists. Interestingly, when Rowley made this point in his unsurpassed monogram on Chinese art, he used an unattributed quote saying that the eyes of "the common people" constituted the tempting lure of commercialism which would lower the artist "to earn much gold."[31] That is, that "the common people" had the disposable income and the inclination to seduce artists from the pure life of scholar-philosopher painter because they wanted art works to adorn their homes. Professor Wang Shucun writes of nianhua, the genre sought by "the common people," that although the gentry and peasantry had different tastes in art, "the execution of [New Year prints] was so skilful that the pictures also appealed to the imperial houses."[32]

The Illustrated Press in the West

In the West, attitudes towards pictorial material in newspapers were complex and contradictory, varying also from country to country, most notably between what was acceptable in America and what was regarded as de rigueur in Britain and Western Europe. Some of the same concerns prevailed on both sides of the Atlantic, particularly an interest in the didactic value of art, both its educational value as a source of new information and its role in aiding the progress of humanity on an upward moral curve.

The problematic issue of money in relation to art works also tried the thinking of British and American writers on the subject. Again, "the common people" seemed to be the stumbling block; if art were to be morally uplifting[33] it could not be seen to be cheap. No lady or gentleman would own to having other than handmade works of art hanging in their drawing rooms.[34] Yet by the turn of the century, W. T. Stead was successful in his campaign to provide an art gallery for every home.[35] His writing on the subject and the responses it elicited, seem to show that in Britain "the common people" had not as yet been exposed to the sweetening and sanctification of their daily life that Stead and many others saw as an inevitable result of having pictures in the home. There were enormous variations both geographic and temporal between Asia and the West on the issue of participation in pictorial art by the urban and rural poor and Stead's campaign suggests a rather patronising attitude. In Britain, apparently, there was a need for crusaders like Stead to fill a gap by legitimising the mass-production of cheap prints for the urban poor. In France, Germany, Vietnam, Japan and China the poor had decided for themselves generations before, that cheap woodblock prints in their homes would make a desirable addition to their lives.

The appearance of the illustrated press in the West, both the weeklies and the dailies, dramatically polarised thinking on the value of illustrations. In his pioneering work, *Photography and the American Scene* (1938), Robert Taft noted that the *Illustrated London News* had barely made its debut before Wordsworth wrote a severe indictment of the pictorial press.[36] Taft himself concluded that the selection, the layout and the false captioning of illustrated material led to the linkage of the term photograph with the idea of "sensational" journalism. While Taft's work and authority commands the greatest respect, this view is not tenable with regard to the British illustrated press under discussion. Taft himself observed that:

> the half-tone more than any other factor has been held responsible for the tremendous circulation of the modern periodical and newspaper. It has, indeed, revolutionalized the mechanics of journalism.[37]

This study of the illustrated press at the turn of the century tends to bear out the views of those who espoused the "New Journalism" in England. The *World* was an illustrated paper, par excellence. As far as the illustrated reporting of news on the China crisis was concerned, this doyen of the "Yellow Press" in America was distinguished for the transmission of factual material through its pictures. Detailed analysis in Chapter One has shown that it was not responsible for the dissemination of the "trite, trivial, superficial, tawdry, salacious, morbid, or silly" as Taft would have it.[38]

Those who espoused the "New Journalism" in England also showed a laudable desire to bring good quality journalism to the working classes. Taft experienced difficulties in his seminal work written towards the end of a career devoted to a study of facets of the very phenomenon he ultimately wrote about in such a negative vein. This shows, perhaps better than any other evidence, how deeply-rooted was the Western objection to the illustrated written word. This objection lingers to this day. It is firmly linked, not just to the illustrations themselves, but to the fact that news in this form was sought by vast masses of working men and women. Their interests were now being catered for by competing sectors of the burgeoning press and printing industry[39] intent on capturing the market they constituted. It was the distillation of pure intellect in the written form only in which the Western educated classes prided themselves. The tightly packed endlessly unrelieved columns of *The Times* constituted the ultimate expression of the views of a class and culture which equated intellect with words but certainly not pictures.

In China the poor as well as the rich had always bought pictures[40] and it was not the existence of illustrations in newspapers which proved the stumbling block for the highly educated, it was the language itself. When an indigenous illustrated press began in China, its most remarkable feature was the factual nature of the captions accompanying foreign news or contentious news concerning foreigners. Certainly there were elements of the sensational published regularly[41] but such incidents generally involved Chinese nationals only or catered to a widespread interest in the bizarre and unusual. Incidents as provocative as ones involving Westerners kicking rickshaw drivers were drawn with no fiendish exaggeration and captioned with no hysterical venom (Figures 2.2 and 2.3). This is testimony to the lack of sensationalism or use of the illustrated press to manipulate Chinese people by conveying excessively negative images of foreigners. This is not to say that other forms of Chinese illustrated material were free from the desire to depict foreigners in an exaggeratedly unfavourable way for propaganda reasons; anti-missionary literature was loaded with insulting images and captions. However, the regular illustrated Chinese press at the turn of the century did not often use pictures for this purpose.

The tradition of regularly published illustrated news in both China and the West was short. Nevertheless, in England, America and China there were many papers using captioned illustrated material with a responsibility for informing people of the facts of the incidents described which would have satisfied the most stringent turn-of-the-century morality concerning the elements of good journalism.[42] The difference between China and the West as exemplified by Britain and America was that the issue of exposing "the common people" to educational information and morally uplifting stimuli was more contentious in the West than in China. In China, the guidance and education of the common people had been the province of the throne

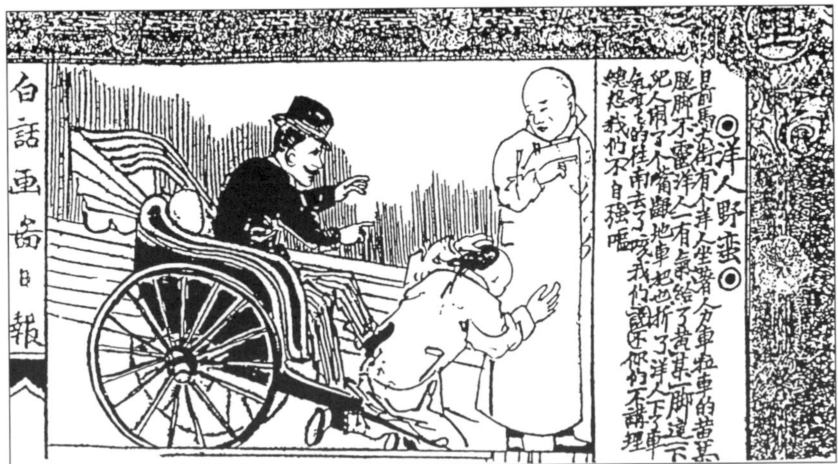

Figure 2.2 *Baihua huatu ribao*, 1908. The barbaric foreigner kicks injured rickshaw driver.

through officials for centuries. In Britain the passage of the 1870 Education Act left many influential politicians and newspaper editors uncertain as to how to cope with the newly literate public. America stood somewhere in between.

Although there were conservative publishers in America who were slow to adopt the use of illustrated material, opposing it in any form, the overwhelming popularity of the illustrated daily press meant that the public decided for the publishers the format in which it wanted to be educated and morally uplifted.

Even in the face of incontrovertible evidence from the American public that illustrated newspapers would sell by the million each month, Pulitzer himself was uncertain about using pictures. A report in the *Journalist* of 22 August 1885 stated that Pulitzer:

> left orders to gradually get rid of them, as he thought it tended to lower the dignity of his paper, and he was not satisfied that the [wood] cuts helped in its circulation.... Cockerill [editor-in-chief of the *World* until his resignation in 1891] ... found that the circulation of the newspaper went with the cuts, and like the good newspaper general that he is, he instantly changed his tactics. He put in more cuts than ever and the circulation rose like a thermometer on a hot day, until it reached over 230,000 on the day of Grant's funeral. This ought to be conclusive as to the influence of woodcuts on the circulation of a paper.[43]

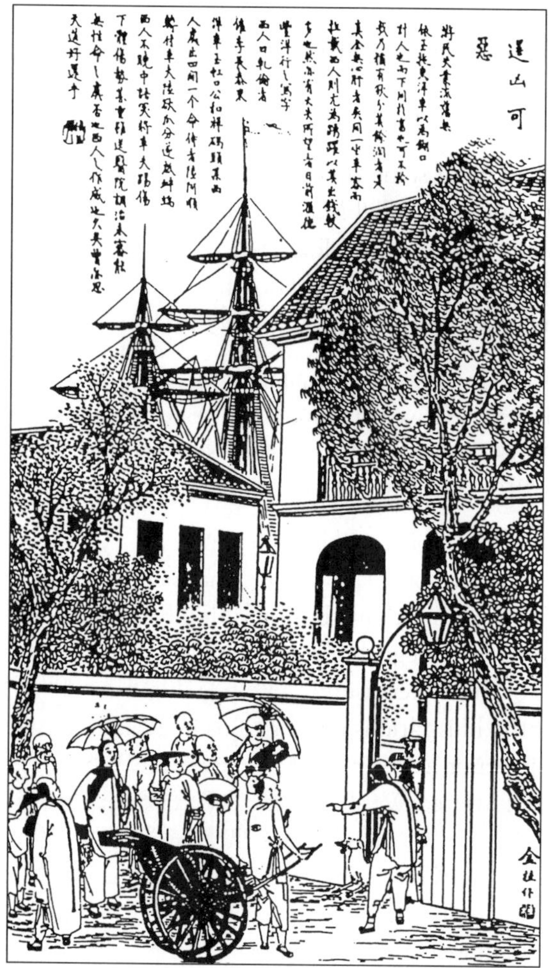

Figure 2.3 *Dianshizhai huabao*, June 1884. Problems over payment for a rickshaw ride solved by the Westerner kicking driver Li. The report notes that usually rickshaw drivers prefer Western clients as they pay better but that this time, as Li was badly hurt and had to go to hospital, the Westerner had done a long-lasting evil.

In Britain the problem of lowering the dignity and tone of a newspaper by using illustrations was compounded precisely by the widespread acceptance of them in America. In his defence of the New Journalism as espoused by the work of W. T. Stead, J. W. Robertson Scott wrote in 1889:

> The very suggestion of even an occasional illustration makes some daily newspaper conductors' hair almost stand on end — [but] why persistently and crassly fill up space with half a column of dry laboured description, when a small [illustrated] block ... would make everything as clear as possible in a moment.[44]

Because Stead had spent some time in America and knew something of its methods of journalism, his *Pall Mall Gazette* was criticised as "an Americanised sensational product."[45] In July 1892 the extreme British view of the American press appeared in a contribution to the *Welsh Review* giving voice to the mentality of those who:

> feel much thankfulness for the general sobriety and dignity of our great London ... papers. Those who have not crossed the Atlantic can have no conception of the miserable petty personalities, the shameless straining after sensation, the impertinent invasion of individual privacy of the popular press in America.[46]

Stead realised the power of the illustration and even more the caricature as an influence that crossed language barriers and roused strong feelings. What better sequence of events than those unfolding in Tianjin from June to August 1900 to test the degree of sensationalism in Western and Chinese pictorial images of the Boxer rising?

A survey of the illustrations and captions in a daily, weekly or monthly illustrated newspaper or magazine will permit an evaluation of the degree of accuracy in the illustrated Western press with regard to its coverage of the Boxer War. For the first four weeks after the Boxer crisis began, little news filtered through to the West and as we have seen, that which did was often factually incorrect, contradictory and incomplete. Although a heroic gloss was put over the failures of the Allied troops by papers such as *The Times*, there were newspapers in Britain and America which did acknowledge these failures. Hence there were some sections of the public in both countries with some kind of idea that Western civilisation was not teaching the Chinese a quick effective lesson. *The Times*, that bastion of the stately press[47] had led people to believe that this would be the inevitable outcome when superior Western-drilled troops deployed superior Western weaponry and tactics against the Chinese. By 1900 in both England and America there was a large field of illustrated newspapers. Those which have been selected in order to analyse illustrated British press coverage of China have been singled out for their popularity; the *Daily Mail*, circulation nearly one million copies a month in

1900; their reputation then and now as a leading illustrated periodical; the *Illustrated London News*, 165,000 weekly circulation in 1900; or their novelty as an illustrated monthly; the *Review of Reviews*, monthly circulation 110,000.

The *Daily Mail*

There are many outstanding aspects of the pictorial imagery of China as employed by the *Daily Mail* in June and July 1900. Foremost among these during the first four weeks of the Boxer campaign is the total absence of any pictorial reference to any aspect of military life whatever. In an age when still pictures, stereoscopes and motion pictures depicting guns, warships and soldiers drilling sold well continually, this is a notable omission, particularly for a paper Stead characterised as "now wallowing in the deepest depths of militant jingoism."[48] The second outstanding feature of these drawings is that they were the creations of British artists who had never been to China. Hence some are unrealistic in some details, but there is definitely no hint of ridicule in them or any perceptible intent to portray Chinese people as some kind of corrupt evil exotica. Lastly, the captions themselves contain nothing that could be productive of negative imagery concerning China and the Chinese.

Individuals, whether Chinese or foreign dignitaries, are all portrayed in such a way as to give the viewer some sense of their importance as public figures. Thus there is a magnificent portrait of Admiral Seymour taken from a photo and covering about one-third of the page in the issue of 28 June, while the picture labelled "A Chinese Beresford," certainly smaller and depriving the official of his name, shows an imposing figure (Figure 2.4). There is nothing about the drawing to produce an impression of inadequacy or incompetence. Feet squarely on the ground, with a heavy-jowled, clean-shaven face, this official is in every way a powerful authoritative man. Likewise, the portrait of the Empress Dowager is entirely sympathetic, there is not a sinister line in the drawing. (See *Daily Mail*, 8 June). The most unrealistic picture is that of the Emperor himself which appeared in many newspapers and magazines around this time. It was in fact captioned in the *Review of Reviews* as being of "doubtful authenticity"[49] and makes him look very much like a minor official of the Hapsburg court such as English readers would have seen in contemporary illustrations (Figure 2.5).[50]

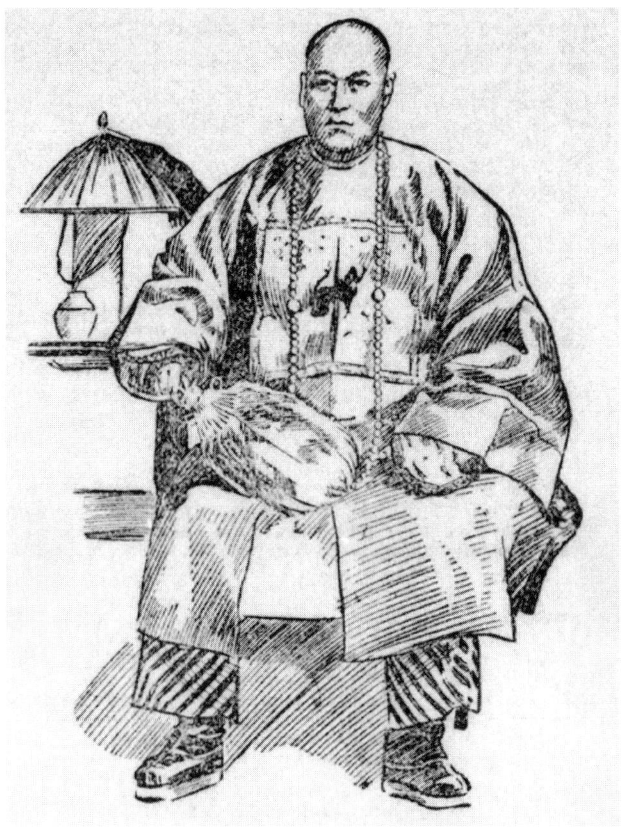

Figure 2.4 *Daily Mail*, 22 June 1900. "A Chinese Beresford."

As for the dreaded Boxers themselves, what did the *Daily Mail* make of them? Their pictorial debut came above the caption, "Captured Boxers in Charge of Chinese Policeman" (Figure 2.6). So the first message the reader got from the *Daily Mail* was that the Boxers had become an illegal group in China and that Chinese officials of the law were apprehending offenders. The men in question are cangued and chained together. Certainly, the cangue may have appeared as an exotic form of punishment to English readers, but memories of the stocks cannot entirely have died away. There is nothing exaggerated about this drawing. It is a gross oversimplification of who the Boxers were, what they were doing, and what had aroused them.

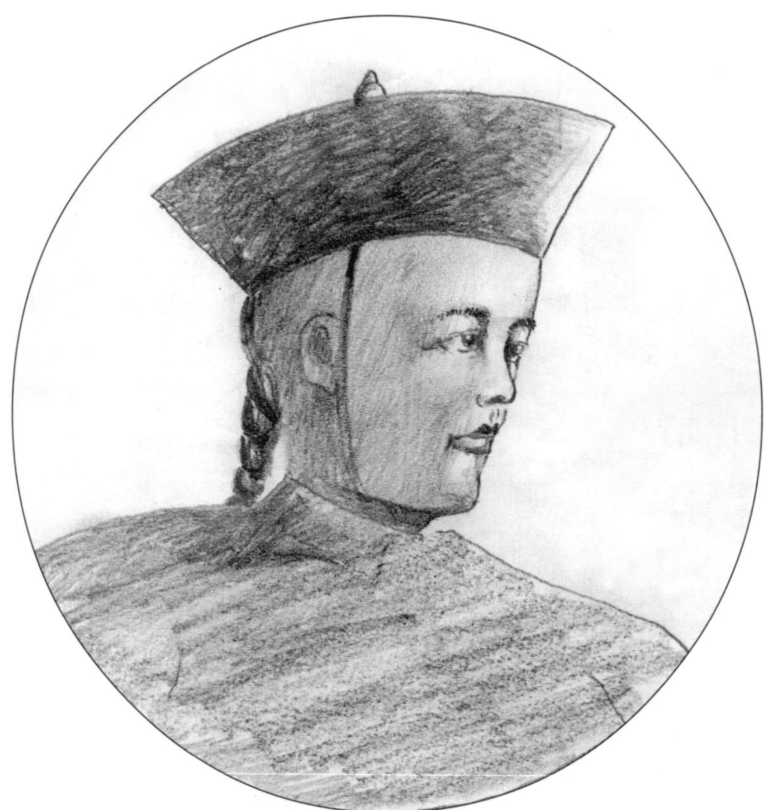

Figure 2.5 *Review of Reviews*, July 1900. Portrait of the Chinese Emperor.

Nevertheless, in the absence of any other pictorial information, this simplification is not one calculated to inspire fear and hatred of the Boxers in the minds of the thousands of English working class men and women who saw the picture at the time. In fact, this drawing exemplifies all the merits of New Journalism as its supporters defined it. There are some factually correct details in the picture. There is no exaggeration of any negative kind; for example, any suggestion that the Boxers are particularly savage, exotic or villainously barbarous has been carefully avoided. Indeed they do not look very much like Boxers at all, being dressed more like Chinese shopkeepers or merchants of the time. The drawing thus conveys some factual information, some socio-political information, and some erroneous details but cannot be said to have been deliberately intended to inspire emotive anti-Chinese feelings.

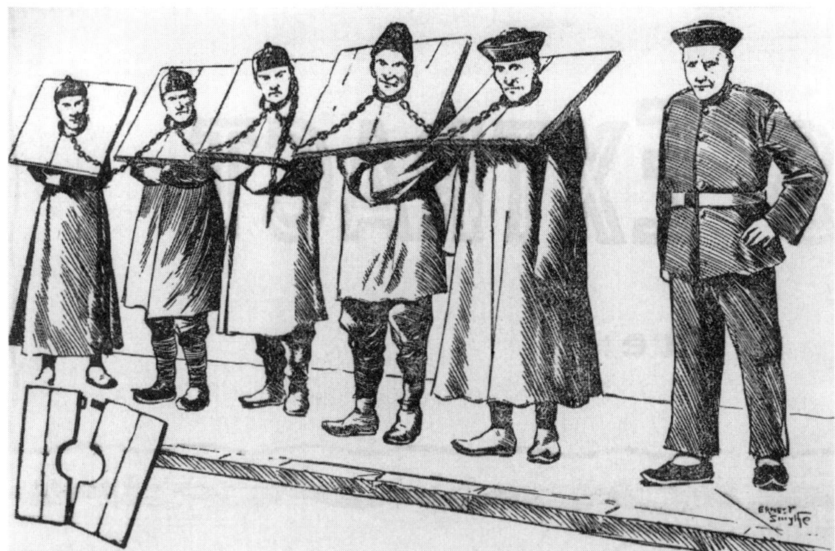

Figure 2.6 *Daily Mail*, 8 June 1900. "Captured Boxers in Charge of Chinese Policeman." Note insert showing how cangue operates.

The only other picture of the Boxers in the *Daily Mail* in this first four weeks is one captioned "The 'Old Bailey' of Pekin — 'Boxers' Being Tried" which occupies a central position on page 7 of 22 June. Many of the remarks on the first picture of Boxers stand. Aligning the Chinese system of justice with the British one by entitling the picture "The 'Old Bailey' of Pekin" would have done much to negate the popular Western image of Chinese justice as cruel, arbitrary and corrupt. Far from being like that, readers of the *Daily Mail* learnt that the Chinese authorities controlled the Boxers by similar judicial means to those used in the Old Bailey. Certainly the picture contains many erroneous details. The headwear is incorrect, the facial expressions of the yamen runners and officers of the court are unrealistic but not in any way that could inspire ridicule, fear, condescension or hatred. Genre nianhua depicting great trials and famous judges were also popular in China,[51] as were drawings of topical trials in the Chinese illustrated press (Figure 2.7).

The drama of the courtroom is one that is cross-cultural and stands the test of time. The *Daily Mail* drawing appears as a theatrical ensemble, like actors in a stage-setting which would have been familiar as well to British

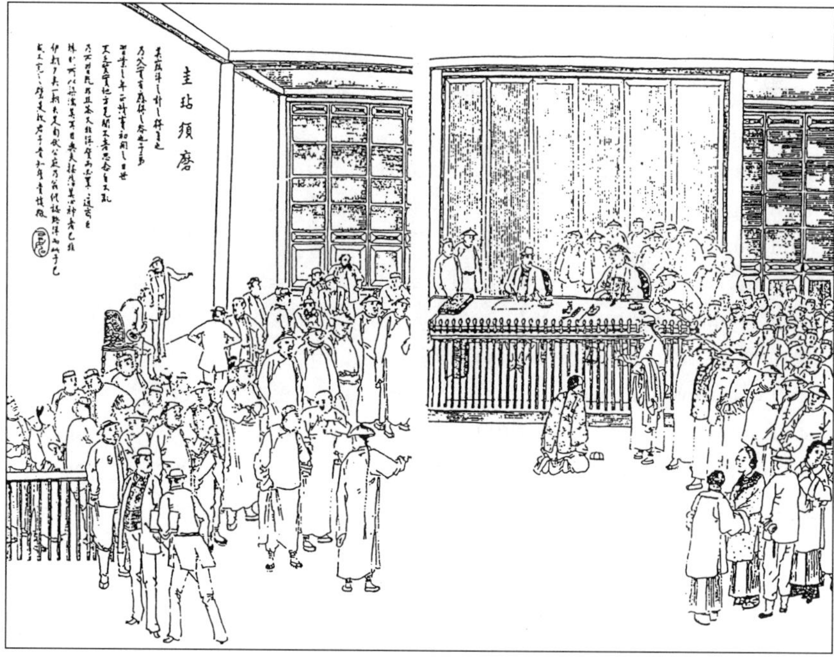

Figure 2.7 *Dianshizhai huabao*, April 1884. In this court drama, the father kneels before the bench as the one responsible for his son's theft of foreign goods.

readers, purchasers of nianhua depicting Judge Shi Shilun in the nineteenth century, Chinese readers of huabao or watchers of "Rumpole of the Bailey" today.

A final point about the *Daily Mail* pictures showing life in China. Against the background of prose in some newspapers recounting sensational rumours and horror stories, we have already noted the portrayal of the Boxers as criminals who were being brought within the reach of Chinese justice. Such images gave no ammunition to that sector of the British public who saw the Boxer rising as exemplifying the sort of "revolting" and "barbarous" behaviour to be expected from the Chinese, an attitude prevailing in the pages of *The Times* respectably uncluttered though they were by pictures. As well, researchers on the *Daily Mail* staff had unearthed old photographs of China in the absence of more up-to-date pictorial information and these were used as the basis of accurate drawings of Chinese national monuments.[52] The expectation of rapid transmission of action pictures had not yet arisen in the minds of the newspaper reading public. A drawing of French soldiers looting in Beijing in July 1900 was published in the *Graphic* on 2 March 1901, at least eight months after it happened.

Now let us examine the layout of the pictures and their function in informing the public. Far from giving the impression of crowding "the trite, trivial, superficial, tawdry, salacious, morbid or silly on the same page and of the same size as the interesting, the significant and the important,"[53] the layout of maps and pictures shows a spatially balanced judgement. The use of illustrations to convey pieces of unusual information is unmarred by sensational captions, let alone untrue verbal explanations, and results in pages so visually disposed as to draw the readers' eyes to the texts, most of which do not relate to the pictures. The illustrations thus serve a purpose in their own right; one is reminded of J. W. Robertson Scott's question, "Why persistently and crassly fill up space with half a column of dry laboured description when a small [illustrated] block ... would make everything as clear as possible in a moment?" Page seven of the *Daily Mail*, 22 June 1900 (Figure 2.8), provides a good example of these points and the use of topical Chinese material is once again presented for its interest to readers. It is definitely not verbally or artistically described so as to prejudice English readers against the Chinese. Neither the illustrations themselves, nor the attitudes towards China and the Chinese conveyed in their captions, appear in the pages of the *Daily Mail* in June and July 1900 to be in any way sensationalist, much less tawdry, salacious or hysterically anti-Chinese. From the drawings of mandarins' graves to portraits of official Chinese, to the dreaded Boxers themselves, we see pictures laid out in the best way possible to inform the public within the limits of extant knowledge.

This analysis of the *Daily Mail*'s illustrations during the first four weeks of the Chinese crisis does not support the contemporary view that the illustrated press was sensationalist and inaccurate. Such a conclusion is the more interesting when we recall that there was little pictorial information about China to hand and none at all coming from the battles which some sections of the British press, although not the *Daily Mail*, were erroneously reporting as victories for the Allied forces. In the absence of telegraphed line drawings or radioed photographs, artists working for the *Daily Mail* did not have recourse to Fu Manchu type imagery.[54] Rather, they combed through the

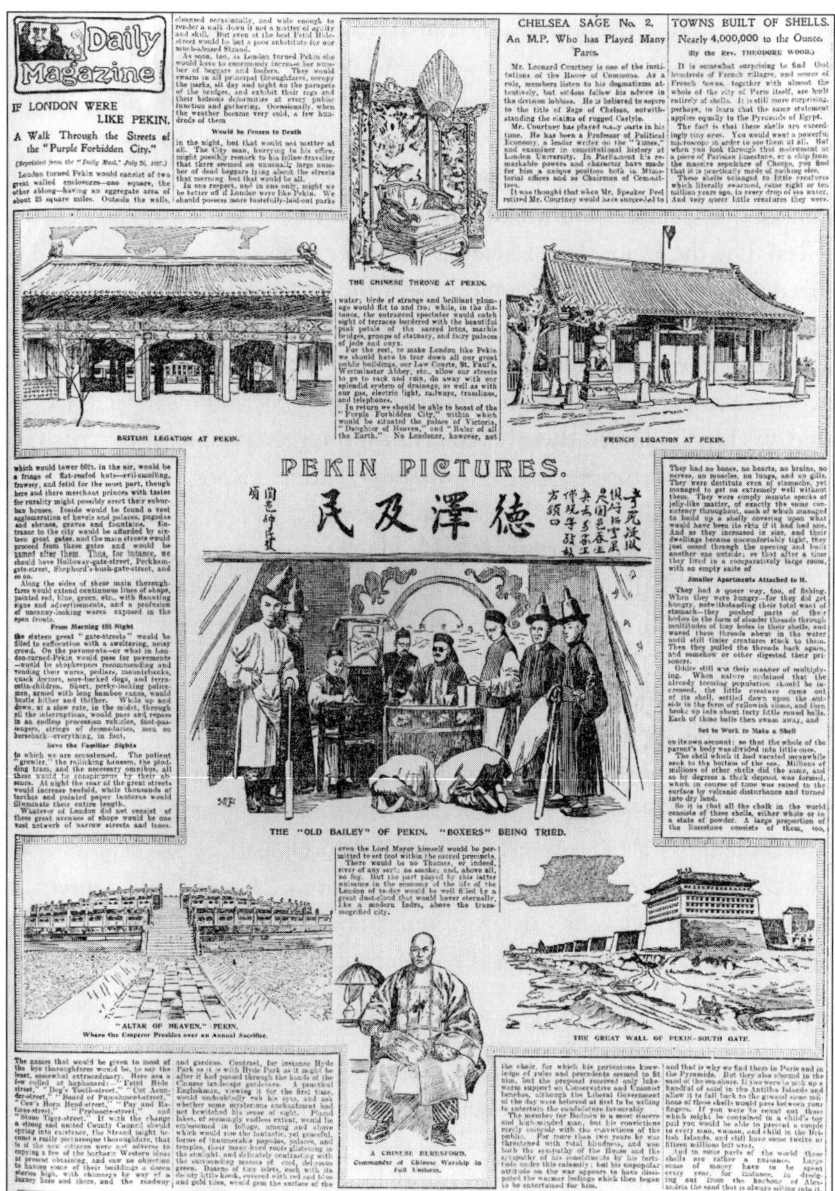

Daily Magazine

IF LONDON WERE LIKE PEKIN.

A Walk Through the Streets of the "Purple Forbidden City."

(Reprinted from the "Daily Mail," July 26, 1897.)

London turned Pekin would consist of two great walled enclosures—one square, the other oblong—having an aggregate area of about 25 square miles. Outside the walls, which would tower 60ft. in the air, would be a fringe of flat-roofed huts—evil-smelling, frowsy, and fetid for the most part, though here and there merchant princes with tastes for rurality might possibly erect their suburban houses. Inside would be found a vast agglomeration of hovels and palaces, pagodas and shrines, graves and fountains. Entrance to the city would be afforded by sixteen great gates, and the main streets would proceed from these gates and would be named after them. Thus, for instance, we should have Holloway-gate-street, Peckham-gate-street, Shepherd's-bush-gate-street, and so on.

Along the sides of these main thoroughfares would extend continuous lines of shops, painted red, blue, green, etc., with flaunting signs and advertisements, and a profusion of uncanny-looking wares exposed in the open fronts.

From Morning till Night

the sixteen great "gate-streets" would be filled to suffocation with a sweltering, noisy crowd. On the pavements—or what in London-turned-Pekin would pass for pavements—would be shopkeepers recommending and vending their wares, pedlars, mountebanks, quack doctors, sore-backed dogs, and terra-cotta-children. Short, perky-looking policemen, armed with long bamboo canes, would bustle hither and thither. While up and down, at a slow rate, in the midst, through all the interruptions, would pass and repass in an endless procession vehicles, foot-passengers, strings of dromedaries, men on horseback—everything, in fact,

Save the Familiar Sights

to which we are accustomed. The patient "growler," the rollicking hansom, the plodding tram, and the necessary omnibus, all these would be conspicuous by their absence. At night the roar of the great streets would increase tenfold, while thousands of torches and painted paper lanterns would illuminate their entire length.

Whatever of London did not consist of these great avenues of shops would be one vast network of narrow streets and lanes. The names that would be given to most of the bye thoroughfares would be, to say the least, somewhat extraordinary. Here are a few culled at haphazard:—"Fetid Hide-street," "Dog's Tooth-street," "Cut Asunder-street," "Board of Punishment-street," "Cow's Horn Bend-street," "Pay and Rations-street," "Proboscis-street," and "Stone Tiger-street." If with the change a strong and united County Council should spring into existence, the Strand might become a really picturesque thoroughfare, that is if the new citizens were not adverse to copying a few of the barbaric Western ideas at present obtaining, and saw no objection to having some of their buildings a dozen stories high, with chimneys by way of a luxury here and there, and the roadway cleansed occasionally, and wide enough to render a walk down it not a matter of agility and skill. But even at the best Fetid Hide-street would be but a poor substitute for our much-abused Strand.

As soon, too, as London turned Pekin she would have to enormously increase her number of beggars and loafers. They would swarm in all principal thoroughfares, occupy the parks, sit day and night on the parapets of the bridges, and exhibit their rags and their hideous deformities at every public function and gathering. Occasionally, when the weather became very cold, a few hundreds of them

Would be Frozen to Death

in the night, but that would not matter at all. The City man, hurrying to his office, might possibly remark to his fellow-traveller that there seemed an unusually large number of dead beggars lying about the streets that morning but that would be all.

In one respect, and in one only, might we be better off if London were like Pekin. We should possess more tastefully-laid-out parks and gardens. Contrast, for instance Hyde Park as it is with Hyde Park as it might be after it had passed through the hands of the Chinese landscape gardeners. A practical Englishman, viewing it for the first time, would undoubtedly rub his eyes, and ask whether some mysterious enchantment had not bewitched his sense of sight. Placid lakes, of seemingly endless extent, would lie embosomed in foliage, among and above which would rise the fantastic, yet graceful, forms of innumerable pagodas, palaces, and temples, their many-hued roofs glistening in the sunlight, and delicately contrasting with the surrounding masses of cool, delicious green. Dozens of tiny islets, each with its dainty little kiosk, covered with red and blue and gold tiles, would gem the surface of the water; birds of strange and brilliant plumage would flit to and fro; while, in the distance, the entranced spectator would catch sight of terraces bordered with the beautiful pink petals of the sacred lotus, marble bridges, groups of statuary, and fairy palaces of jade and onyx.

For the rest, to make London like Pekin we should have to tear down all our great public buildings, our Law Courts, St. Paul's, Westminster Abbey, etc., allow our streets to go to rack and ruin, do away with our splendid system of drainage, as well as with our gas, electric light, railways, tramlines, and telephones.

In return we should be able to boast of the "Purple Forbidden City," within which would be situated the palace of Victoria, "Daughter of Heaven," and "Ruler of all the Earth." No Londoner, however, not even the Lord Mayor himself would be permitted to set foot within the sacred precincts.

There would be no Thames, or indeed, river of any sort; no smoke; and, above all, no fog. But the part played by this latter nuisance in the economy of the life of the London of to-day would be well filled by a great dust-cloud that would hover eternally, like a modern Indra, above the transmogrified city.

THE CHINESE THRONE AT PEKIN.

BRITISH LEGATION AT PEKIN.

FRENCH LEGATION AT PEKIN.

CHELSEA SAGE No. 2.

An M.P. Who has Played Many Parts.

Mr. Leonard Courtney is one of the institutions of the House of Commons. As a rule, members listen to his dogmatisms attentively, but seldom follow his advice in the division lobbies. He is believed to aspire to the title of Sage of Chelsea, notwithstanding the claims of rugged Carlyle.

Mr. Courtney has played many parts in his time. He has been a Professor of Political Economy, a leader writer on the "Times," and examiner in constitutional history at London University. In Parliament his remarkable powers and character have made for him a unique position both in Ministerial offices and as Chairman of Committees.

It was thought that when Mr. Speaker Peel retired Mr. Courtney would have succeeded to the chair, for which his portentous knowledge of rules and precedents seemed to fit him, but the proposal received only lukewarm support on Conservative and Unionist benches, although the Liberal Government of the day were believed at first to be willing to entertain the candidature favourably.

The member for Bodmin is a most sincere and high-minded man, but his convictions rarely coincide with the convictions of the public. For more than two years he was threatened with total blindness, and won both the sympathy of the House and the sympathy of his constituents by his fortitude under this calamity; but his unpopular attitude on the war appears to have dissipated the warmer feelings which then began to be entertained for him.

TOWNS BUILT OF SHELLS.

Nearly 4,000,000 to the Ounce.

(By the Rev. THEODORE WOOD.)

It is somewhat surprising to find that hundreds of French villages, and scores of French towns, together with almost the whole of the city of Paris itself, are built entirely of shells. It is still more surprising, perhaps, to learn that the same statement applies equally to the Pyramids of Egypt.

The fact is that these shells are exceedingly tiny ones. You would want a powerful microscope in order to see them at all. But when you look through that instrument at a piece of Parisian limestone, or a chip from the massive sepulchre of Cheops, you find that it is practically made of nothing else.

These shells belonged to little creatures which literally swarmed, some eight or ten million years ago, in every drop of sea water. And very queer little creatures they were. They had no bones, no hearts, no brains, no nerves, no muscles, no lungs, and no gills. They were destitute even of stomachs, yet managed to get on extremely well without them. They were simply minute specks of jelly-like matter, of exactly the same consistency throughout, each of which managed to build up a shelly covering upon what would have been its skin if it had had one. And as they increased in size, and their dwellings became uncomfortably tight, they just oozed through the opening and built another one outside; so that after a time they lived in a comparatively large room, with an empty suite of

Smaller Apartments Attached to It.

They had a queer way, too, of fishing. When they were hungry—for they did get hungry, notwithstanding their total want of stomach—they pushed parts of their bodies in the form of slender threads through multitudes of tiny holes in their shells, and waved these threads about in the water until still tinier creatures stuck to them. Then they pulled the threads back again, and somehow or other digested their prisoners.

Odder still was their manner of multiplying. When nature ordained that the already teeming population should be increased, the little creature came out of its shell, settled down upon the outside in the form of yellowish slime, and then broke up into about forty little round balls. Each of these balls then swam away, and

Set to Work to Make a Shell

on its own account; so that the whole of the parent's body was divided into little ones.

The shell which it had vacated meanwhile sank to the bottom of the sea. Millions of millions of other shells did the same, and so by degrees a thick deposit was formed, which in course of time was raised to the surface by volcanic disturbance and turned into dry land.

So it is that all the chalk in the world consists of these shells, either whole or in a state of powder. A large proportion of the limestone consists of them, too, and that is why we find them in Paris and in the Pyramids. But they also abound in the sand of the sea-shore. If you were to pick up a handful of sand in the Antilles Islands and allow it to fall back to the ground some millions of these shells would pass between your fingers. If you were to count out those which might be contained in a child's toy pail you would be able to present a couple to every man, woman, and child in the British Islands, and still have some twelve or fifteen millions left over.

And in some parts of the world these shells are rather a nuisance. Large sums of money have to be spent every year, for instance, in dredging out from the harbour of Alexandria the sand that is always silting into it,

PEKIN PICTURES.

德澤及民

THE "OLD BAILEY" OF PEKIN. "BOXERS" BEING TRIED.

"ALTAR OF HEAVEN," PEKIN.
Where the Emperor Presides over an Annual Sacrifice.

A CHINESE BERESFORD.
Commander of Chinese Warship in Full Uniform.

THE GREAT WALL OF PEKIN—SOUTH GATE.

Figure 2.8 *Daily Mail*, Friday, 22 June 1900. Full page devoted to China.

classic illustrated authorities such as John Thomson to find background material.

Whatever characterisation of Boxers or Chinese officials, particularly the Empress Dowager — as sinister, corrupt, treacherous or barbarous — may have formed part of contemporary imagery, it did not come from the illustrations or their captions in the *Daily Mail*. The pictures drawn from photographs selected by the *Daily Mail* show no evidence of a desire to demonstrate the superiority of Western war machinery, and the corresponding feeble antiquity of Chinese military hardware and attitudes. Neither do the captions read in any derogatory or patronising way when describing Chinese cultural products as diverse as star gazing instruments, cemeteries and shoes. Cultural partisanship was not at play. Rather we see evidence of a desire to inform the public through pictures, to give tens of thousands of readers some kind of pictorial background to the world-shaking crisis in China. There is a remarkable contrast between the sobriety and reasonableness of the pictorial images of the Boxers and the Chinese leadership in the *Daily Mail*, the hysterical pejorative, repetitive language of *The Times*, and the nature of the China crisis itself with the whole of the Western world agog as to the fate of its representatives trapped in Peking.

A partial explanation for the discrepancy between the almost serene images drained entirely of violence, fear or indignation shown to the public by the *Daily Mail* would be to agree with Michael Braive in his interesting work, *The Era of the Photograph. A Social History* (1966). Braive advanced the idea that in the nineteenth century, "the consumer ... was unprepared for the appearance of spontaneity in the photograph. Technical innovations took a long time to assimilate ..."[55] and further that:

> it was not until 1900–1914, when the requirements of journalism began to exert a certain pressure on photographers to give an impression of urgency and speed, that photographers began to make feeble efforts at capturing motion.... The public without which the photograph could not survive, would have been shocked and disturbed by any such act of violence ["taking the subject — and the beholder — by force or by surprise"[56]] on the photographer's part. Habits of mind die hard.[57]

The exception he made was that the public might be more prepared to accept innovations in the photography of sport. Although it might be expected that the technical capacity to capture the violence of war inclined photographers to heed the clamourings of editors,[58] this study of photographs and drawings from photographs taken during the Boxer War, shows that they did not. A part of the explanation lies in Braive's assertion that the public was not prepared for this. A part lies in the fact that the culture of taking photographs of particular subjects — such as warfare, as opposed to death[59] — had not developed sufficiently to allow even the most innovative of photographers[60] to use the technology at their disposal to convey more striking and immediate images of war. It was not necessarily the case that the eye wished to see what the lens could see.

The *Illustrated London News*

It would be unwise to omit the *Illustrated London News* from an analysis of pictorial imagery of the Boxer War, despite Wordsworth's lament:

> Now prose and verse sink into disrepute
> Must lacquey a dumb Art that best can suit
> The taste of this once intellectual land.
> A backward movement surely have we here,
> From manhood, back to childhood …
> Avaunt this vile abuse of pictured page!
> Must eyes be all in all, and tongue and ear
> Nothing? Heaven keeps us from a lower stage![61]

Again here is an expression of the upper class British idea that the inclusion of pictures necessarily renders a text less intellectual. Perhaps it was because he was a poet that Wordsworth only mentioned the parallel with childhood and illustrated primers. He did not go so far as to associate pictures with a lower class audience; "coarse," "cheap and nasty" are descriptions that occur frequently in the literature on the subject — or to equate illustrations necessarily with sensationalism often described as "vile" or "salacious." Wordsworth's outpouring expressed purely an objection to the illustrated paper over the written page and linked its popularity with a decline in the intellectual capacity of English men and, presumably, women. It was nevertheless strongly felt. Resistance to the illustrated newspaper in the West was deeply entrenched on all sides. Yet Victorian England was to produce that tour de force in illustrated magazines, the *Illustrated London News*.

The Chinese crisis was dwarfed by the Boer War in the pages of this powerful weekly and, without going into great details about its coverage of the Boer War several points need to be made about it. The most notable were the glorification of war,[62] the animal courage of men,[63] the greatness of military leaders,[64] the explosive power of the military technology they controlled,[65] and above all the *Boys Own Annual* feats that this war allowed many chaps to perform with brilliance and daring (Figure 2.9).[66] Even the advertisers used every conceivable possible connection with the Boer War to sell anything from Bovril, tobacco, Liebig Company's Extract, to cigarettes (Figure 2.10).[67]

While a few photographs were used in almost every issue, drawings from photographs, by artists in the field or in the London office, still dominated. It is these drawings that give us an idea of the dash and brilliance that was culturally associated by the British at that time with war on the outposts of the Empire. Newspaper correspondents themselves entered into this *Boys Own Annual* world, Winston Churchill's exploits being the best-known. On 14 April 1900 the weekly carried a drawing captioned "Mr Bennett Burleigh Special Correspondent of the *Daily Telegraph*, bringing Field Marshal Lord Roberts the news that Bloemfontein had surrendered." The jaunty adventurer in Burleigh as he reins in his horse is offset by just the right degree of deference as he raises his hat to the Commander in the Field. The boys in the background stand true to their guns, the Field Marshal sits every inch a soldier under the shade of the trees. This is war in the further reaches of the Empire as public school boys may have seen it illustrated in any *Boys Annual*. Tommy Atkins — frequently mentioned as such in the columns of all newspapers, illustrated or otherwise — can be seen in the drawings of the *London Illustrated News* to be patiently slogging away at the behest of his commanding officer in all kinds of arduous situations.[68] His agonies in field hospitals are rarely depicted,[69] nor are his sorrows, such as they might have been, at the deaths of thousands of his fellows. The burial of his generals, a solemn matter, captures him staunchly playing the last post, the artist's imagination stirred by what would in the next edition, stir the British public.[70]

But China: that was something else again. Much has been written about Chinese ignorance of world geography. We may note that the veritable mania in Britain for maps so that the general public could follow the Boer War and the China crisis,[71] argues a certain ignorance on the part of most

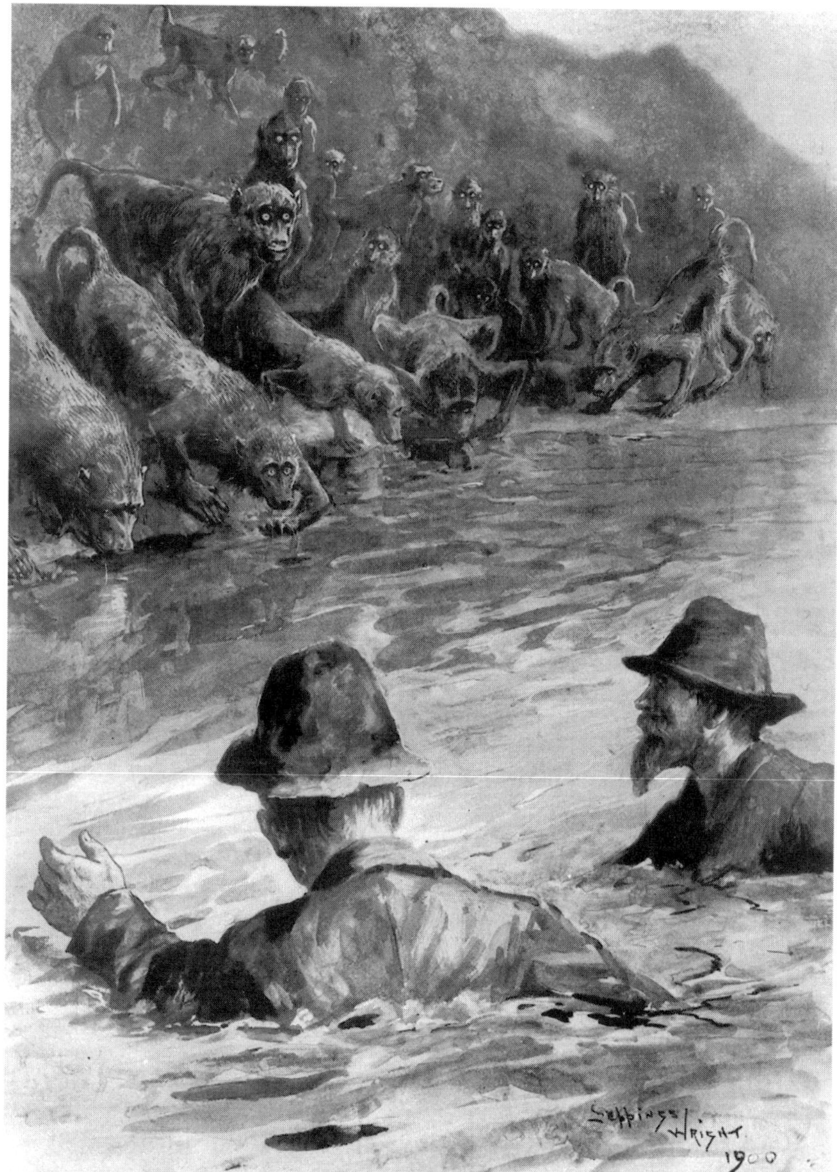

Figure 2.9 *Illustrated London News*, 30 June 1900. Boers or Baboons: An adventure on the Komati River. When they had waded halfway across the stream, the fugitives found that their progress was barred but not this time by men, although the Darwinians may contest this point. The further bank was swarming with dog-faced baboons who had come down to the water to drink. The presence of these unwelcome visitors necessitated a tedious detour of about ten miles.

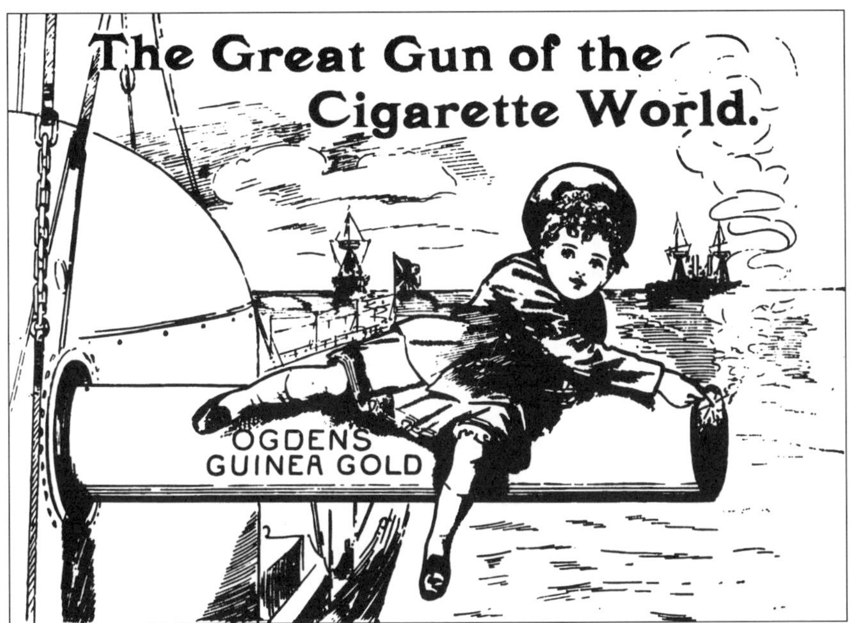

Figure 2.10 *Illustrated London News*, 30 June 1900.

English people, however well-educated, as to the exact location of Bloemfontein or, dare it be said? — Peking (Beijing). The newspapers all carried maps regularly so that people — particularly men[72] — could brush up their geography and follow the courses of the various conflicts. This was not enough, however, and special editions of maps of China were made and distributed.[73] In this way English people who in May 1900 would not have had the least idea where to look for Tientsin (Tianjin) in the vastness of China, could by June discourse knowledgeably about its situation and the geographic features surrounding it as they might bear on the China campaign (Figure 2.11).

The coverage of the Boer War and of the Boxer War in the *Illustrated London News* adds some interesting dimensions to Braive's assertion about how much the public was ready to see. The overwhelming preference for handmade illustrations of the Boer War, created week by week the sort of war with which people in England could identify as such. Certainly there were photographs but in the context of the total pictorial coverage, these lacked the vivid drama of the drawings. The picture showing the loss of the British

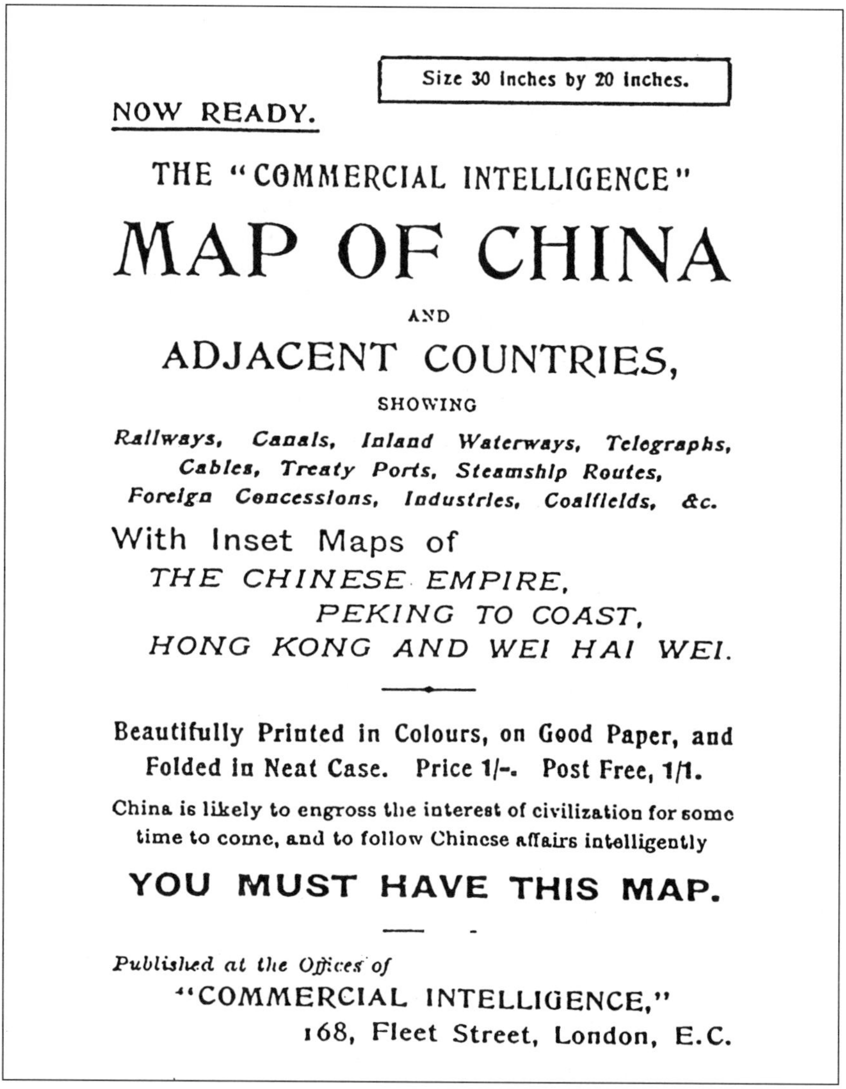

Size 30 inches by 20 inches.

NOW READY.

THE "COMMERCIAL INTELLIGENCE"

MAP OF CHINA

AND

ADJACENT COUNTRIES,

SHOWING

Railways, Canals, Inland Waterways, Telegraphs, Cables, Treaty Ports, Steamship Routes, Foreign Concessions, Industries, Coalfields, &c.

With Inset Maps of

THE CHINESE EMPIRE,

PEKING TO COAST,

HONG KONG AND WEI HAI WEI.

Beautifully Printed in Colours, on Good Paper, and Folded in Neat Case. Price 1/-. Post Free, 1/1.

China is likely to engross the interest of civilization for some time to come, and to follow Chinese affairs intelligently

YOU MUST HAVE THIS MAP.

Published at the Offices of

"COMMERCIAL INTELLIGENCE,"

168, Fleet Street, London, E.C.

Figure 2.11 *How to Read Chinese War News* (1900).

guns at Tugela river that appeared on 6 January 1900 (Figure 2.12), for example, creates a stirring image of defeated valour that no photograph of the time could emulate. The captions, too, exemplified the understated nonchalance that was a British response to the game that was war.[74] On 13 January 1900 a sketch dispatched from Ladysmith by a special correspondent before his capture bore the title "How Long Tom's Shell Disturbed the Middies' Sucking-Pig" and the description:

> A couple of days ago (November 27) a shell thrown by Long Tom, the Boer 94-pounder on Pepworth's Hill, burst just behind the Naval Battery. The middies had brought a sucking pig in a barrel and placed it behind the battery. The shell burst under the barrel, throwing it high into the air, and the pig was blown out. He came to the ground squealing terribly and was so badly injured that he had to be killed.

This report came from George Lynch, soon to go to Tientsin (Tianjin). Some of the incidents seem less amusing and open to question the depth of skin covering the British concept of fair play:

> The Boers' love of music cost some of them their lives in the trenches at Mafeking. At an advanced post one of our men played the concertina while his comrades sang. For a time the enemy took no notice, but at length curiosity prevailed; a Boer cautiously thrust his head over the breastwork, and was immediately shot down by an English sharpshooter.[75]

The *Illustrated London News* did not carry a picture of what was to become "the white flag incident" but published graphic illustrations, pointedly captioned, of Boer breaches of the white flag convention.[76] On 2 January 1900 *The Times* had also carried a report of the incident:

> A very pretty fight ... this morning. The enemy tried the white flag with Lieutenant Milford without effect, while our reply to their usual volley killed two of them, including the bearer of the flag.... The engagements yesterday and today were most creditable to our troops and distinctly a reverse for the Boers.

The nonchalance with which *The Times* wrote of the dishonouring of the internationally accepted symbol for surrender sits awkwardly with that same paper's readiness to describe the Boxers or soldiers of the Imperial Chinese Army as "treacherous." To return to the pages of the *Illustrated London News*, it was the drawings rather than photographs that produced the dominant impression of the Boer War. Drawings could depict war the way people in England and other parts of the Empire were prepared to see it and artists could select incidents which they felt exemplified what the British military effort in South Africa was all about.

Even the most cursory glance at the coverage of China shows the *Illustrated London News*, unlike the *Daily Mail*, producing both negative images and negative captions. This may have been due to lack of information — the same problem confronting the *Daily Mail* and all illustrated papers when th China crisis erupted. It may also have been due to the fact that the militar might of Western civilisation depicted frequently in the *Illustrated Londo News*, by contrast with the *Daily Mail*, was being stalemated by the "prim tive" Chinese military machine. It was often the case that the editor had great deal of power at the turn of the century. The editor of the *Illustrate London News*, the young Bruce Ingram, like Valentine Chirol of *The Times* was another one of those Englishmen who had difficulty equating the war i China with what he imagined war should be. Thus, though he could no dismiss the Boxer War — public interest in it having eclipsed that in the Boe War — his editorial directives to artists depicting the China crisis were no as informed or as precise. It may also be that Bruce Ingram shared the view of newspapermen like George Morrison and Valentine Chirol. That is, tha he had a pre-existing negative image of China. This being the case, if artist working for him produced unfavourable images of the Chinese, he might no have singled out such work as constituting unjustifiably negative information Given that all illustrated papers had the same difficulty gaining access to any pictures of China at all, it is instructive to compare the selection of pictures the creation of drawings and the captioning in a major British daily, weekly or monthly.

Not surprisingly, China first hit the pages of the *Illustrated London News* on 16 June 1900 in photographs which at that time represented the classic Western manifestations of the genre and were the least-preferred medium of the *Illustrated London News*. Of the six pictures, four were of warships and two were portraits of the leading British protagonists in the field, Admiral Seymour and Sir Claude MacDonald. The layout of this page is supremely unimaginative (Figure 2.13) and is a good example of how poorly the compositors of the *Illustrated London News* were adapting to the photograph as a medium and how much their ideas on layout were influenced by public attitudes of the day. This page with its look of a picture album on a Victorian middle-class drawing-room table, reflects more of a Western view of what constituted newsworthy images set out as in a family photograph album than do the pages of the *Daily Mail*, or indeed the events in China themselves. The Boxer War could not have been said to have been illuminated, much less represented for the public, by four photographs of British warships and two portraits of British dignitaries on the spot. As such, this Western equation of pictures of people

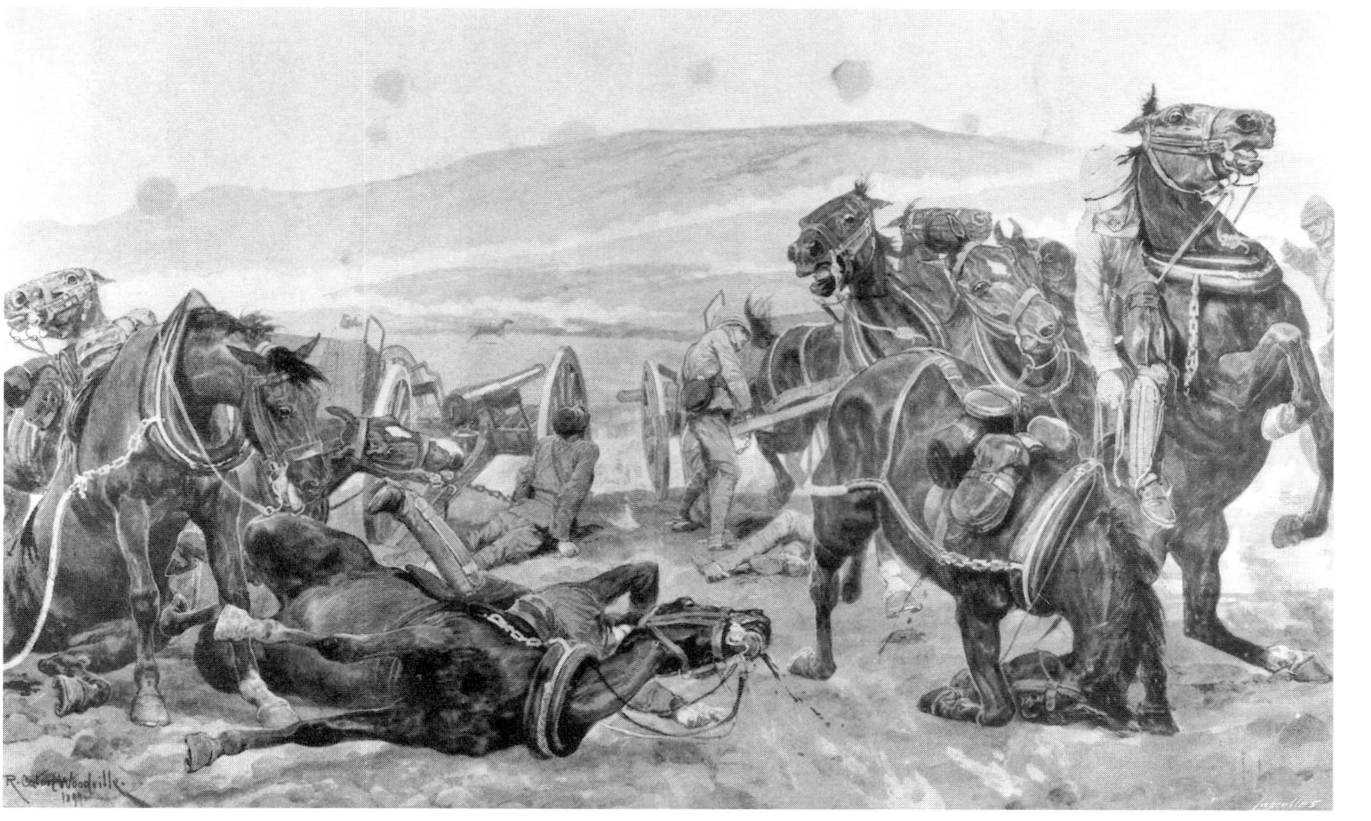

Figure 2.12 *Illustrated London News*, 6 January 1900. "The Loss of the Guns at Tugela River."

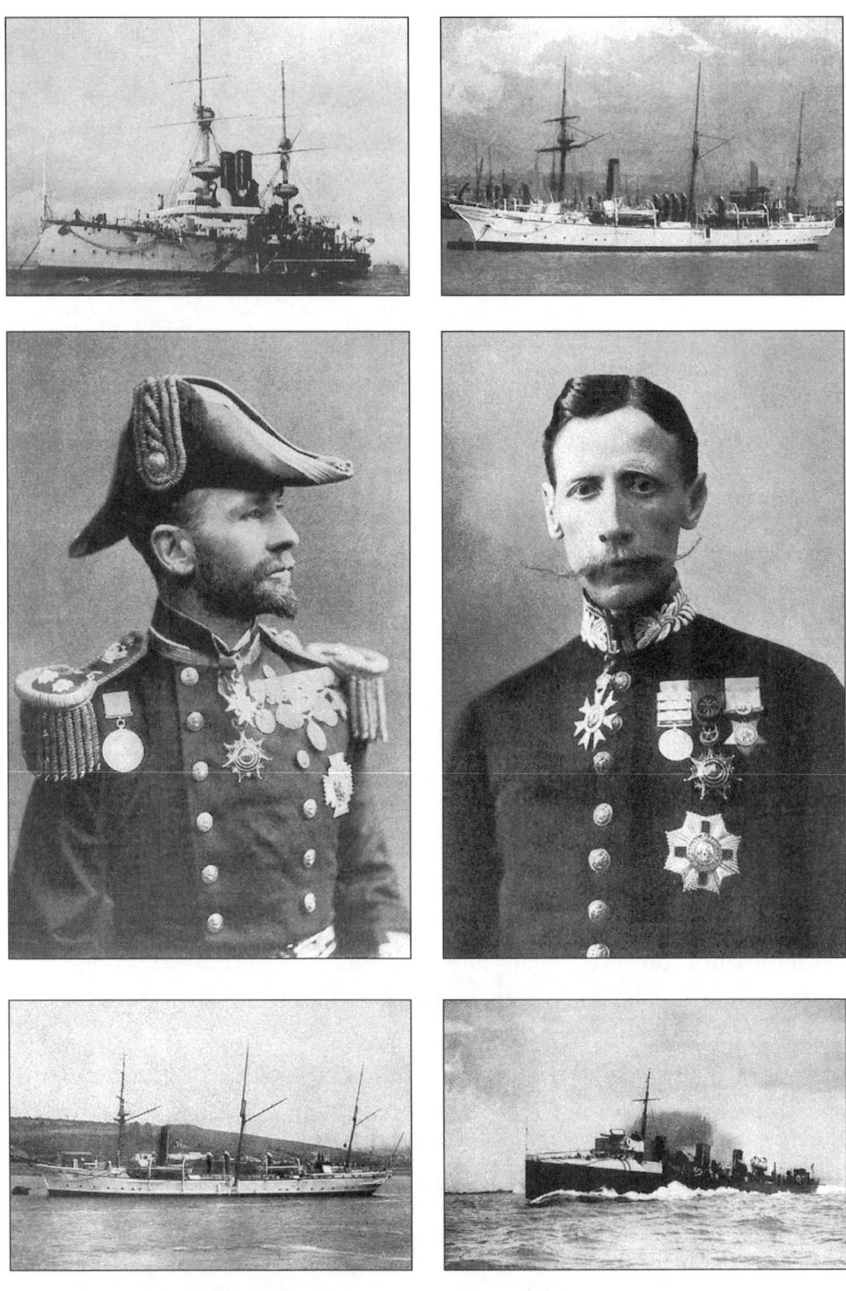

Figure 2.13 *Illustrated London News*, 16 June 1900. "Representatives of British power in China" showing full page layout.

and warships with news, popular as it was, does little to support the argument that illustrated papers were of their nature sensationalist. Rather it suggests that the pictorial eye of the public (in this case, more particularly, the middle brow eye) could only be educated very gradually.

The nineteenth century had a weakness for photographic portraiture, though far less so in China[77] than in the West. In China, significantly, portraiture was almost entirely absent from the public domain of illustrated newspapers, news sheets or New Year–style pictures.[78] In the West, there was also a plethora of cards and stereoscopes showing mechanical things — locomotives, ships, machinery, factories and so on. Contrary to contemporary received opinion, this interest was shared by all sections of the Chinese public as well, from workers and peasants, who bought Western clocks and watches as well as kerosene lighting, to leading Chinese statesmen.[79] Rudisill has commented that in the West, the increasingly technological aspect of the era was reflected in the fact that "many 'object' pictures are of machines of one sort or another — trains, steamships, a telegraph device, a 400-day clock."[80] As well, there was a demand for pictures of military hardware that increased towards the end of the century and appeared as the subject of a disconcertingly high proportion of the first motion pictures.[81]

The issues of the *Illustrated London News* for the rest of June contained photographs of buildings in China, more warships and a drawing of Chinese soldiers entering Beijing. This latter, while inaccurate is not such as deliberately to invite derision. On 30 June there were portraits of the Emperor and the Empress Dowager, marvellous, as romantic creations of what such people should look like (Figure 2.14). The portrait of the Emperor is a derivative of his representation in the Hapsburg mode and the portrait of the Empress Dowager cannot be said to look like anyone at all outside the artist's imagination. Certainly she was difficult to photograph or paint though she did appoint an official Court photographer.[82] In 1903 the American ambassador's wife, Sarah Conger, succeeded in getting her to agree to a Western woman painting her portrait,[83] but there were more authentic pictures of her available in 1900. These portraits look as if they have been created by someone who had seen a lot of Gilbert and Sullivan but certainly no official portraits of any Chinese dignitaries or heads of state. As such, they do not create a damaging impression unless it can be said that faint evocations of pantomime characters as rulers of China be damaging.

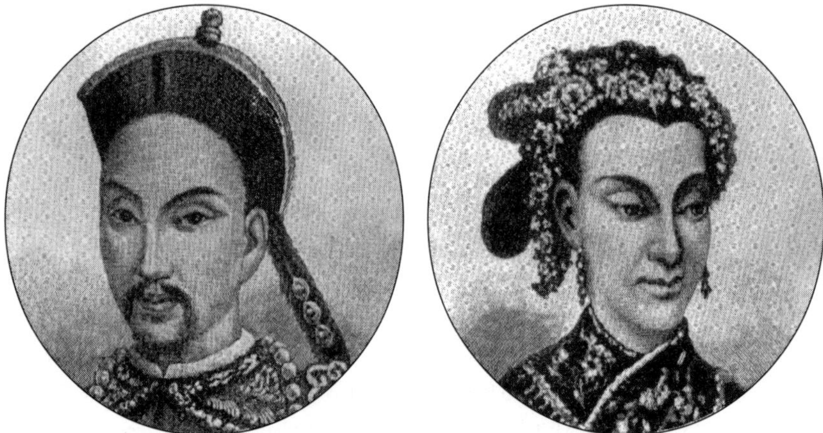

Figure 2.14 *Illustrated London News*, 30 June 1900. Portraits of the Emperor and Empress Dowager of China.

Not so the two photographs of groups of Chinese soldiers at the head of the page, captioned respectively "Possible Recruits for the Boxers: A Group of Chinese Soldiers" and "Primitive Chinese Arms: A Group of Archers." Certainly many soldiers did join the Boxers in the early weeks of the crisis, but many more stood to their modern arms as professional soldiers of the Imperial Chinese Army well used to putting down peasant risings and rebellious minorities. This particular rising gained widespread popularity because of its object in expelling the foreigners; nevertheless crack troops such as those of Generals Nie Shicheng and Ma Yukun fought both Boxers and foreigners with state-of-the-art weaponry from mid-June 1900. As to the equation of the word "primitive" with the weapons used by Chinese soldiery, two points need to be made here. First, in many cases Chinese soldiers trained with modern rifles and Krupp artillery and second, no British, French or American cavalryman of the day would have neglected his sabre drill.

The 30 June issue continues with a willow pattern-style drawing of a Chinese theatre placed opposite a photograph of the sharp angular pride of Western civilisation, "The French Flag-ship at Taku, the *d'Entrecasteaux*." The message seems clear. China is exotic but decaying. The Occident is expanding due to the sharp point of its technology. Another example of the directing of the public eye through captioning is seen on a photograph of the

Forbidden City: "The scene of the Emperor's captivity: Moat of the Forbidden City, Peking. In the Palace on the left bank the ex-Emperor is practically a prisoner." Readers of the *Illustrated London News* were expected to be conversant with the version of Chinese court politics which portrayed the Emperor as a pitiable weakling at the mercy of the Empress Dowager, a version still popular today.[84] These readers were not treated to an analysis of the motives of the reformers themselves[85] or the potential consequences for a China, besieged by hungry Western powers and expansionist Japanese ambitions, of the speedy introduction of ad hoc reform. It is possible to imagine readers looking at the photograph of the grim expanses of the moat and shuddering to think of the poor Emperor imprisoned inside. Readers of the *Illustrated London News* could certainly never have learned anything about the grim struggles at Court between Conservative forces and those advocating reform and modernisation.

The two most interesting pictures in the 30 June issue are the photographs of Tianjin captioned "The Bombardment of Tientsin: A Street in the City" (Figure 2.15) and a drawing captioned "Official China. Reading an Imperial Edict at the Yamen of a Provincial Tao-Tai or Governor" (Figure 2.16). The photograph in question is one that the *Illustrated London News* managed to obtain perhaps from a returning missionary.[86] This same photograph appeared in a French foot soldier's journal published in 1902 and was attributed to the French publishing house Larousse.[87] A reader at the end of the twentieth century has to make a special effort to look at a picture of a peaceful sunny street scene and recover the mind of the public which would accept this, suitably captioned, as a description of the bombardment of Tianjin. Ivins's observation that "at any given moment the accepted report of an event is of greater importance than the event" bears repeating in this context. Tianjin had been under heavy and accurate bombardment by Chinese military forces that successfully repulsed three Allied attempts to take the city between 18 June and 14 July. The publication of such a photograph above such a caption warrants comment.

Mr Broderick, Under Secretary for Foreign Affairs, reported to the House of Commons on 26 June that the second Allied force sent to relieve Tianjin "was frustrated by the opposition of a large body of Chinese." Mr Broderick was not alone in his reporting of events in order to minimise Chinese participation, let alone success. *The Times*, was thoroughly behind him. For

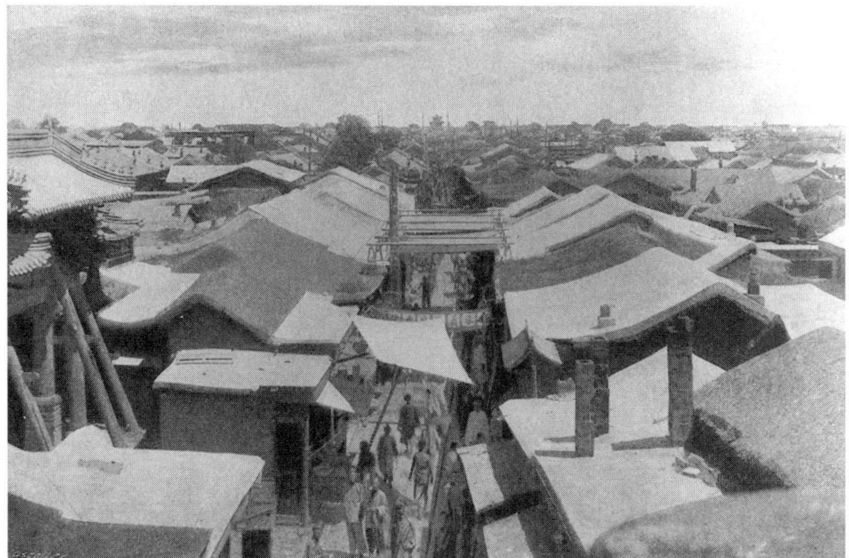

Figure 2.15 *Illustrated London News*, 30 June 1900. "The Bombardment of Tientsin: A Street in the City."

those on the frontier, Mr Broderick's performance had already been singled out as unimpressive by April 1900. In an editorial, the *Peking and Tientsin Times* noted on 7 April that Mr Broderick had not spoken on China for a long time and that "it would seem as if his long respite concerning the Far East has not deepened his perception of the situation." The *Daily Mail*, in omitting any pictorial reference to Allied Western military aggression in China or the Chinese response, also formed part of an information network on the Chinese crisis. For different reasons, the *Daily Mail* in its pictorial coverage, bled of importance both Western military action and Chinese response. However, the ultimate statement in the art of making "the accepted report of an event ... of greater importance than the event" surely is to be found in a photograph of the tranquil curves of the roofs of Tianjin sheltering passers-by from the sun as they went about their daily business, captioned "The Bombardment of Tientsin: A Street in the City." There were photographers in Tianjin taking photographs which showed the results of Allied bombardment of the city as can be seen at Figure 4.10. Nevertheless, it is notable that editors of newspapers in England, America and on the Continent did not print such photographs.

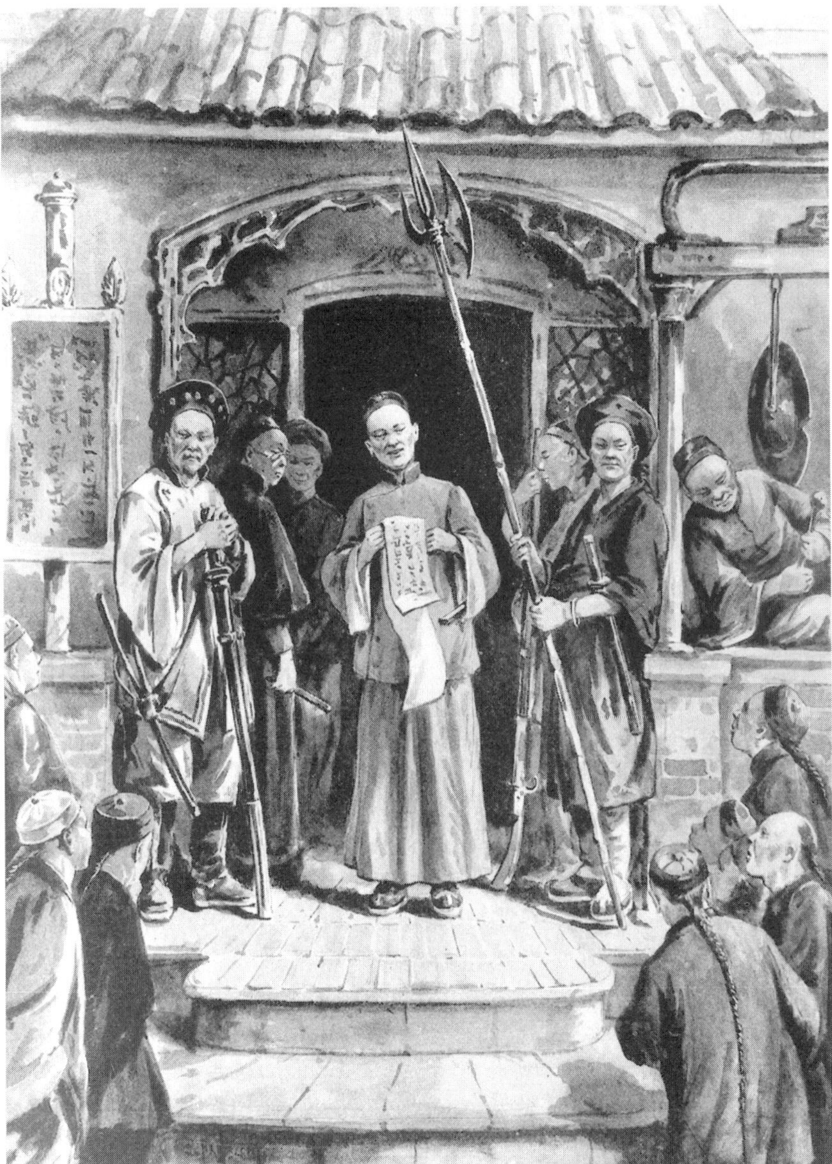

Figure 2.16 *Illustrated London News*, 30 June 1900. "Official China. Reading an Imperial Edict at the Yamen of a Provincial Tao-Tai or Governor."

Reporters and officers who went from the Boer War straight to Tianjin said that the effects of artillery fire on that city were far greater than anything they had witnessed in South Africa.[88] The *Illustrated London News* had a staff of dedicated artists not only in the field but in its London office, able to turn the slightest incident of war into a magnificent, blood-stirring picture. It was known that the Allies had been battling to take Tianjin since the fall of the Dagu forts on 17 June. How then can the publication of such a photograph on 30 June be explained? To return to Mr Broderick's report to the House. The point about this is not the report itself, but its acceptance by the House of Commons and its validation by *The Times*. No one in the House asked questions about the nature of the Chinese military forces that were repulsing Allied attacks on Tianjin; no British journalist in subsequent reporting raised questions about their position, weaponry or tactics. Mr Broderick's report went unquestioned. He described the event in such a way that it was not evident that crack Western-drilled Chinese troops using Krupp artillery more up-to-date than that possessed by the Allies had repulsed an attacking force of Russian Cossacks — at that time regarded as among the most redoubtable fighting men in the world. Mr Broderick's report of the event became the accepted version.

In the same way, the *Illustrated London News* could publish a photograph of a tranquil street scene and caption it "The Bombardment of Tientsin…." The public was not only prepared to accept this as a report of the event, we can go further and say with Braive and Jussim, the public was unprepared for more accurate visual information. By September 1900, photographs were available of some of the destruction at Tianjin and these were captioned so as to make it clear that this was the fault of the rampaging Boxers. As they had been characterised as unarmed hysterical peasants, it is difficult to see how, as such, they alone could have caused the destruction of, say, Tianjin railway station shown in a photograph in the *Illustrated London News* on 22 September.

Photographs and drawings of the destruction of Chinese temples made it clear that this was the necessary work the Allied troops had been sent to accomplish. John Schönberg's painting in the *Illustrated London News*, 1 December, "Getting at the Root of Evil: The Destruction of a Chinese Temple on the Bank of the Pei-ho" shows a British officer saluting the flaming temple. This illustration finally brought the Boxer War within the realms of British concepts of War and Empire such as they were understood, internalised and then briefed to outgoing artists by Sir Bruce Ingram. Ingram's apparent lack of empathy with what a war in China might mean, and the even-handedness of the pictorial reporting in the *Daily Mail* represent two different approaches to conveying images of China to the British public. However, the two approaches indicate the same fact about pictorial images of the day. That is, that in 1900 there was a limit beyond which editors of illustrated newspapers could not sell images of war in general, and in particular, of war in China. A version of events which concentrated on acceptable background imagery such as willow pattern pictures of theatres, or drawings of bound-foot shoes or even pictures of streets evidently untouched by the merest bullet captioned as depicting a savage bombardment, this was a version that the British public could accept. Editors could include drawings or captions more or less anti-Chinese in feeling but neither they, nor their artists, knew how to make pictures of a war in China acceptable to the British public in the same way as the *Illustrated London News* had done with the Boer War.

The last two drawings in the *Illustrated London News* selected for analysis are by the same artist. The one already mentioned, captioned "Official China. Reading an Imperial Edict at the Yamen of a Provincial Tao-tai or Governor"[89] (Figure 2.16) and the other, "Chinese Superstition. Invoking the God of War at the Gate of his Shrine."[90] There is nothing sympathetic about these drawings. What were charming sets of willow pattern chinoiserie[91] have become sharp, angular, dangerous exotica ("Chinese Superstition") or unfamiliar emblems of repressive authority ("Official China"). The artist has uniformly conveyed racial differences by infusing a leer — sinister or benevolent — into the physiognomy of every one of his official subjects and displaying incredulous-looking profiles of the members of the attending crowds.

The subtext to "Chinese Superstition" could read identically were the caption to have been "Anglican Bishop Blesses Troops" with the difference that the "deafening noise" of firecrackers would have had to be replaced with the "thunderous chords" of the organ. The subtext begins and ends as follows: "The shrine of the Chinese god of war, deserted in peace, is thronged in time of war [reference to function of firecrackers in ceremonies].... The ceremony, like other Chinese functions, is gone through gravely and without enthusiasm."

These two drawings convey a decidedly negative image of Chinese official and religious life, with the facial characteristics of the subjects being caricatures of Chinese people. The Boers do not appear similarly caricatured in pictures in the *Illustrated London News*. Nor as has been noted, do foreigners appear as caricatures in Chinese illustrated newspapers at this time. The subject of the rapid evolution of caricature in the late Qing is beyond the scope of this work. Nevertheless, preliminary research shows Qing officialdom to have born almost the full brunt of its development, both in number and type of cartoon illustrations which far outnumber the pictures of the fat foreigner in illustrated papers such as *Baihua huatu ribao* (Beijing, 1908) (Figure 2.2).

This analysis of the *Illustrated London News* shows that, unlike the *Daily Mail*, it did print captions intended to direct the readers' minds to a negative view of aspects of Chinese political and military life. As well, unlike the *Daily Mail*, prominence was given to the machinery of Western warfare which contrasted advantageously in British minds with the Chinese military world of which they had no accurate knowledge.[92] As a percentage of total information conveyed about China, that which was factual, namely drawings of buildings — from photographs as opposed to willow pattern theatre backdrops — was relatively small. Finally, pictures were drawn in such a way as to convey a prejudiced view of the Chinese and photographic material included which flagrantly deceived the public mind as to the military events being so hotly contested outside and inside the walls of Tianjin.

The Boxers were, undeniably, Chinese peasants. Like Valentine Chirol, Bruce Ingram had no experience of what a peasant uprising in China might mean. As he could not bring the Boxers themselves within his vision of what war was all about, he resorted to attempting to make the war in China conform to his image of other wars which had been fought in the British Empire. This did not mean that he would have gone so far as specifically to ask artists working for *The Illustrated London News* to portray the Boxers as sinister or evil or treacherous. It simply meant that pictures of the Boxers themselves or soldiers of the Imperial Chinese Army were not part of the way Ingram thought it best to represent the China crisis. Moreover, he made no effort to get photographs of the Imperial Chinese Army or to find someone who had recently returned from China to brief his artists about the appearance of the Boxers.

It was not until February 1901 that the London-based artist Amedee Forestier drew a picture for the *Illustrated London News* that came from exactly the same mould as "Boers and Baboons" of 30 June 1900 (Figure 2.9). The original sketch done by John Schönberg is entitled "The Return From Paotingfu: Tumbling in the Quicksand." The sketch shows three prominent British cavalrymen trying to ford a stream. In the mid-foreground is a Chinese coolie carrying a load in a manner totally atypical of the way any coolie would have carried such a load. As well, his facial features are obscured and his overly stocky figure does not constitute a representative image of a Chinese coolie of that time. There are three other coolies sketched very dimly in the background but there is little about this picture to suggest that the action was happening in China. By 1901 John Schönberg had captured the ambience of crossing rivers as those dramas had appeared in South Africa. He was still having difficulties, however, drawing Chinese people in a Chinese landscape.[93]

There is, however, nothing about the coverage of China by the *Illustrated London News* that could be said to be sensationalist, tawdry or salacious. Quite the opposite, for these pages were not intended to reach the urban poor as their primary target. Thus it would seem that it was not the fact of being illustrated but rather the class base of its readership which influenced the reaction to and selection of pictures of the war in China. The educated middle classes were being further educated with different inflections from those conveyed to the educated working classes. For the former, photographs of military leaders and military might arranged as in a family photograph album, drawings of willow pattern chinoiserie, just a few drawings depicting Chinese people in a slightly negative vein and, with the illustration of the destruction of the Chinese temple, a suggestion of a return to what war was all about for the middle class British public of this era: subduing rebellious natives on the fringes of Empire.

The *Review of Reviews*

The *Review of Reviews* was edited by W. T. Stead who had marked religious views and a personal interest in mysticism.[94] The *Review of Reviews* contains a unique pictorial version of China showing in itself, and by contrast with other British and American papers, the positive limits one culture could reach when choosing and describing images of another. The *Review of Reviews* was comfortable with the medium of photography; indeed some issues, such as that of April 1900, contained only photographs in the section "The

Progress of the World" and all devoted to the Boer War. Moreover, Stead published photographs showing Boer successes. "The ten guns captured by the Boers at Colenso arriving at Pretoria"; photographs showing British failure: "British officers being moved from the model schools, Pretoria to the Watervale Prison," and even photographs showing British military action which contravened the consensus of what constituted just warfare as recently decided at the Hague Peace Conference in 1899.[95] Magnificent artists' impressions of British military heroes were printed as the frontispiece to monthly issues. In April, a drawing of General Kitchener and his staff at the Battle of Omdurman which, while not immediately topical, was nevertheless stirring stuff, and a drawing of Baden-Powell at the head of the month of June. The drawing of Baden-Powell is the drama of war personified as opposed to his depiction in *Boys Own Annual* mode in the *Illustrated London News*. The keen-eyed, do-or-dare, immaculately accoutred horseman of the *Review of Reviews* bears little resemblance to the casual stance of the man and his wee dog captioned by the *Illustrated London News*: "His wish realized: Colonel Baden-Powell in 'a warm corner'." Stead's Baden-Powell looks as though he is riding for God first and after that the Empire; perhaps that is why the shadowy figures behind him show various degrees of discomfort or are downright unrealistic models on the wrong screen. Although the *Review of Reviews* was not averse to providing its reading public with images of heroic British military leaders, it also published variously as frontispieces, "After the Descent from the Cross: at Oberammergau" in July and Sir Joshua Reynolds' painting "The Cherub Choir" in September, softening touches to the warlike images. This painting published as a frontispiece in the year 1900 constituted testimony to the strength of the personal views of the editor rather than a craven fanning of the public's feverish interest in wars.[96]

When it came to the crisis in China, it could be expected that Stead's views on the issue would be extremely influential in the selection of pictures and cartoons that appeared in his *Review*. Characteristically, Stead saw the Boxers' point of view, describing them as a:

> secret society, hostile to foreigners, conservative of national traditions and resentful of the extent to which the foreign Governments with their engineers and railways, have forced their way into China. If we can imagine what Primrose Leaguers would feel if Russia were to establish herself at Portsmouth, while Germany seized Harwich, and France Dover, and Russian, French and German

> engineers were carefully arranging to exploit the resources of the country, we may realize what the ordinary Chinaman feels at the ever-growing aggression of Europeans ... he adopts the time-honoured practice of forming a secret society and getting up a riot [and proceeds] triumphantly to pillage and slay *after the fashion of insurgents everywhere.*[97] [emphasis added]

The *Review of Reviews* was the only one of the three illustrated papers to publish a number of photographs of Chinese dignitaries including "The Emperor as a Child" showing "Prince Chang," "Kwang-su" and the "Emperor's Brother"; "Kwang-su, 16 years old with his father" and a photograph of Li Hongzhang.[98] This last must have been taken on the occasion of Li's London visit in 1896 also extensively reported and illustrated by the *Review of Reviews.* All of these photographs bear identifying captions with no subtext. This raises the Chinese dignitaries in question to the status of people about whom one should know something — there is no need to explain any more about them in either a negative or positive tone than there would be if the subject were Count Bismarck or Count Mouraviev. It is the *Review of Reviews* which publishes the best example of the portrait of the Chinese Emperor already referred to as "in the Hapsburg mode" and beneath the caption is written "(Of doubtful authenticity)" (Figure 2.5).

As to the most contentious figure of all, the Empress Dowager, she appears twice, in both cases reputedly from drawings by Chinese artists.[99] These pictures give different impressions of Cixi (1835–1908). The article accompanying these pictures gives a balanced and sane overview of Cixi's life and political influence. In a later edition, the *Review of Reviews* quoted an article by R. S. Gundy interpreting the events of 1898 as a struggle between the capital represented by the Empress and reactionary statesmen and the provinces represented by the Emperor and the younger literati, mandarins and merchants. Gundy's analysis was that "The Empress is not, however, hopelessly opposed to reform. Her object is to strengthen the dynasty."[100] The pictures chosen by Stead to depict the Empress Dowager are well attuned to this more complex analysis of her motives in national and international politics.[101] Both are in the traditional mode (traditionally portraiture was a branch of painting looked down on by the Chinese as not constituting a high artform).

One shows her as a younger woman posing very gracefully if somewhat informally with one knee up on a porcelain stool. Her facial features conveyed the standard idea of Chinese womanly beauty at the time and there was a lap dog at her feet with which any European royal personage or aristocrat might sympathise. The other shows her sitting with her hands in her sleeves, wearing full ceremonial robes and head-dress, gazing unswervingly at all who might look upon her.[102] These portraits had been unearthed by careful research; the first certainly has something of the exotic about it, but the exotica has been provided by a Chinese artist and to a British eye conveyed more of the flowing grace of an ancient civilisation than sinister taloned murderess. The second shows a determined regal woman conscious of her position of Head of State, but then the British public was accustomed to the phenomenon; their own Queen had just been reported as picnicking that very summer in her own forest in the Highlands. We know her Muselman was with her but her dogs were not mentioned in the *Daily Mail* report.[103]

In his leader in July headed, "The Revolt of the Yellow Man," Stead broke away completely from the ideas of Valentine Chirol or the founder of the *Illustrated London News*, Herbert Ingram. He was of the opinion that "we are maintaining a vast army of missionaries to undermine the whole religious faith of the nation" and that those "engaged in propagating Christianity in the Far East have not always fulfilled their duties with the necessary tact and consideration." He observed that "it is not surprising that the fury of the Boxers should be directed principally against mission houses and churches."[104] In view of this, the photograph selected and captioned simply "A View of Tientsin" is worth comment (Figure 2.17). On first sight, this photograph creates an almost physical shock caused by the blunt uncompromising architecture of the cathedral. There were people who could look out of the framework of their own culture and see its manifestations anew, through the eyes of people of another culture. John Thomson, the great photographer who was in Tianjin in 1872, after its people had burned the cathedral for the first time in 1870, had this to say:

> We [saw] the ruins of the Roman Catholic Cathedral, by far the most striking object in Tientsin, and I could not help thinking at the time that, from what I know of the Chinese character, this noble structure must have been a dreadful eyesore to the natives, towering as it did high above any of their most sacred buildings, and drawing down evil influences from the sky.[105]

Stead would not have had a great variety of views of Tianjin from which to select. It is therefore interesting that he should have chosen one depicting

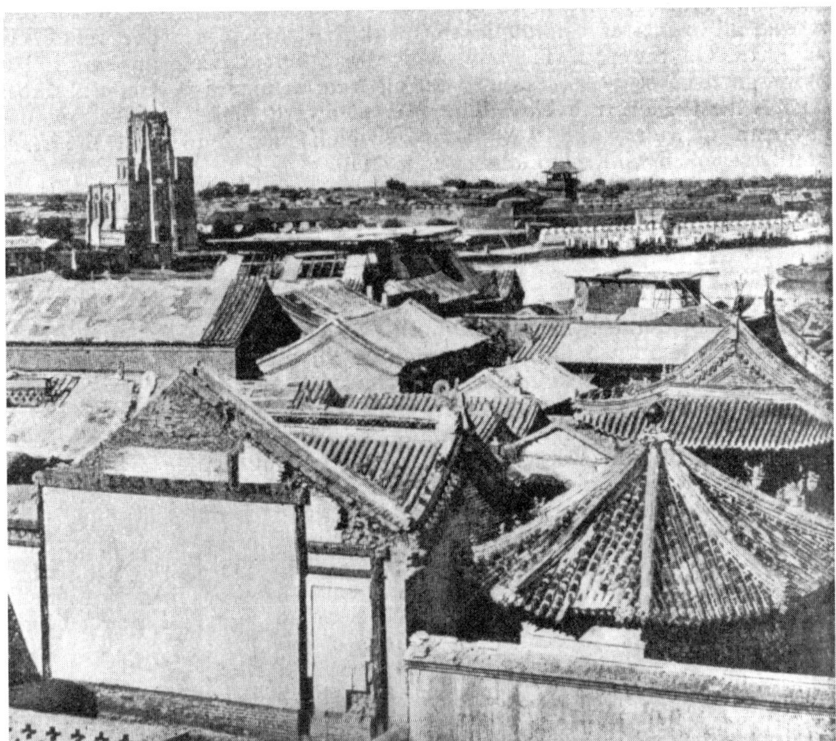

Figure 2.17 *Review of Reviews*, July 1900. "A View of Tientsin."

a Christian cathedral when his remarks in his leading articles and in reviews of others' works on the benefits of Christianity in China[106] were so trenchantly against interference with Chinese religious practices. This photograph was not published in any other periodicals examined for this study. Further striking photographic evidence to indicate that the Western eye could see the Chinese viewpoint that the cathedral was disturbing in 1900 will be discussed in Chapter Four. Photographs in the *Illustrated London News* make it clear to readers of the day that the missionaries did consider the problem of the offensiveness to the Chinese of the style of Western architecture. The London Missionary Society's hospital in Tianjin was built entirely using Chinese architectural conventions and the cathedral in Beijing was an interesting hybrid, a Gothic body flanked by Chinese wings.[107] This architectural concession did not save the building in 1900.

It is in the leader of August 1900, headed "The Revolt Against the

Paleface" that we see the publication of images vindicating the New Journalism. These pictures entirely refute the charges of mindlessness or sensationalism. As well, they show that in the twilight of Victorian England, editors could give coverage to and sections of the British public would buy pictures showing evidence of the viewpoint of the culture with which England was in conflict. These were Chinese anti-missionary posters captioned as such with no specific subtext explaining them in any way. Visually their overall meaning is quite obvious. Many specifics may not have been apparent to the readers of the *Review of Reviews* unused to the homophones and double-meanings which even illiterate Chinese villagers of the day would grasp and discuss when the captions on such a poster had been read out aloud. The captions of the two posters read as follows: "Attacking Foreigners, Burning Books" and "The Boxers Are Forcing the Foreigners to Eat Shit" (Figures 2.18a and 2.18b).

Both posters have subtexts aligning the missionaries in the most insulting way for Chinese peasant readers with pigs and dogs, their writing with farting and bullshit and their desecration of Chinese religious traditions as criminal.[108] This is the crude and violent language devised to express and channel the feelings of an already inflamed peasantry.[109] Stead's informed interest in China, his continued support of the Chinese viewpoint in his editorials, and the tenor of his reviews of others' work[110] suggest that whether or not he sought specialist help in translating the posters, he would have published them as they stood.

The important points about these posters are first that they are not appearing in a minor, small-circulation missionary newspaper[111] where they reached a select and gratifyingly horrified audience. As they appear in the *Review of Reviews*, this propaganda value as exemplars of the primitive ignorance of Chinese anti-foreignism is stripped from the posters. In the context of Stead's leaders, they appear as background information to explain Chinese feelings about and reactions to foreign aggression. Second, the fact that the posters are not translated gives them a dignity and authenticates the depth of the anger they contain. Those readers of the *Review of Reviews* who could read the Chinese characters, could have been expected to have some understanding of the Chinese viewpoint. If such readers did not like Stead's position on the China crisis, they would not have been buying the *Review of Reviews* by August 1900. For those who could not read Chinese, the posters

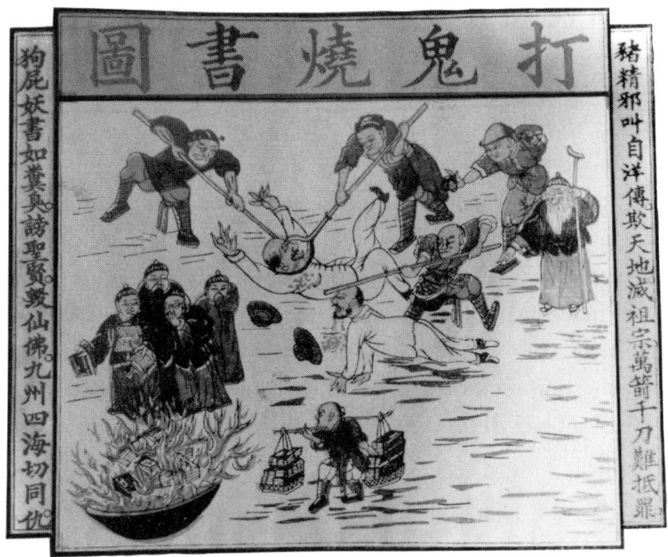

Figure 2.18(a) *Review of Reviews*, August 1900. "Attacking Foreigners, Burning Books."

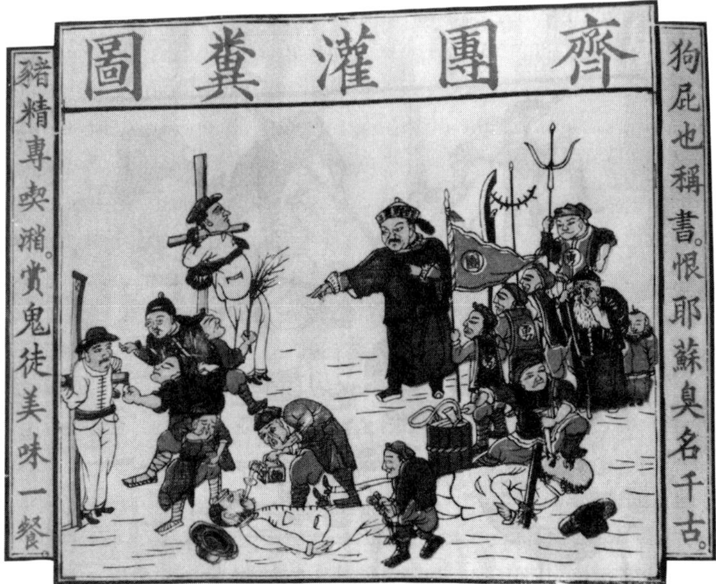

Figure 2.18(b) *Review of Reviews*, August 1900. "The Boxers Are Forcing the Foreigners to Eat Shit."

serve as factual indications of the events in China as drawn by Chinese artists and described by Chinese calligraphy. Thus the Chinese version of events is dignified by appearing pictorially and verbally as information before the British public in a major periodical. This information is not demeaned, inflated or justified in any way by caption, subtext or text. In the most difficult of contexts, war, China has been allowed to represent itself to a group of English readers by an editor who felt that such representation could and should stand alone as self-explanatory material complementing the whole of the visual material he had selected to cover the Boxer War. Whether or not most readers gave these posters no more than a cursory slightly surprised glance, it was a triumph for the New Journalism and for journalism itself, that they appeared as they did in the *Review of Reviews* in August 1900.

Reflections

In the persons of Harmsworth, Stead and Ingram (young even in an age of bright young reporters, being only twenty-two when he took over provisional editorship of the *Illustrated London News* which he retained until 1963) we have three quite different philosophies of journalism, and three men actively involved in the production of their papers. Overall, China did not fare too badly in their hands. Explosive events could so easily have led to exaggerated negative portrayals of China and the Chinese during the celebrated fifty-five days when the Middle Kingdom had the whole of the Western world over a barrel. The fact was that these editors published illustrated papers as their content has been described, tending overall more to inform readers than otherwise. Certainly there were pictures which showed the exotic, the theatrical — after all China was exotic. Buckingham Palace and the Forbidden City could not then, as now, have been said to occupy the same kind of place in the mind's eye of Westerners. Significantly, we have seen that there were also pictures which equated the processes of Chinese legal and political life with those of the Western world. The only periodical to stand out in this respect and to see in the exotic and the different, something sinister or inferior, was the *Illustrated London News*.

With the inevitable time lag, despite Western "superiority" in communications, it was not until late August and mid-September that the *Illustrated London News* carried action drawings from artists' impressions of the war in

China. The most notable of these appeared on 15 September and depicted the "Charge of the Japanese Cavalry among the Bamboos outside Tientsin." The features of the Japanese cavalrymen in question are notably lacking in any Oriental accent — they are cavalrymen first and foremost, depicted in the genre made so thrilling by the artists of this great weekly. The Chinese were deprived of some of their military capacities while being given the Oriental qualities London-based artists thought suitable, while the Japanese were deprived of their racial features in order to give them the military capacities it had been acknowledged that they had displayed.

John Schönberg, special artist for the *Illustrated London News*, had great difficulties drawing either the Japanese or the Chinese. His first drawing from China appeared in the 6 October issue and in general, he solved this difficulty by choosing subject matter that did not dwell too much on the ability to capture the likeness of an Asian person. His drawing published on 27 October of Boxers awaiting sentence, could as well have represented the inmates of just about any poor house in the United Kingdom. Even the distinctive hairstyle, so readily caricatured by artists who had never been to China, almost eluded Schönberg's pen. His tranquil river scenes, however, with just a hint of the influence of Chinese landscape painting, would have gratified all those Westerners who ascribed to the understanding of a timeless Empire decaying softly and gracefully under its own weight. As these constituted the majority of Schönberg's output — only one sketch of the Boxers was published — the surge of fear and indignation incited in the British public could be smoothed away as images depicting their old-established prejudices began to dominate once more.

The *Illustrated London News* had a long tradition having been founded in 1842 by Sir Bruce Ingram's grandfather, Herbert Ingram, as a more profitable alternative to the marketing of a patent pill. While his grandfather's dabbling in the seamy side of quack medicine could not have affected the young Bruce Ingram, he would certainly have grown up with family traditions regarding the imperative to publish a respectable illustrated weekly. The path he took in designing an illustrated magazine using expensive paper and exclusive technical processes in order to compete with papers like the *Daily Mail*, the *Daily Telegraph* and the *Graphic* showed him to have decided that his market lay in a respectable middle and upper-middle class readership. Many of the commemorative editions he brought out are now collectors' items, magnificent tributes to the illustrated medium and to his insight as to what it could achieve. Both his presentation of the Boer War (subsequently given greater depth by his own service in the 1914–1918 War) and China form two sides of the same coin designed to fit the purses of a British middle-class readership.

Not so either Harmsworth or Stead. In an interview with Pearson, founder of the *Daily Express*, Stead wrote:

> As one half of the world does not know how the other half lives, it is probable that many of those who belong to the cultured classes in this country have never seen *Tit-Bits*, *Answers*, or *Pearson's Weekly*. This does not deter many of them from commenting in more or less disparaging tones upon the efforts which Sir George Newnes, Mr Harmsworth and Mr Pearson have made to supply the great mass of readers turned out by our elementary schools with interesting reading matter.[112]

Stead quoted Pearson to have similar views to his own on what was newsworthy and what the public could be expected to take an interest in. Both men conceived their readership to consist of people who were averse to being bludgeoned with one view or its opposite over a particular issue. As well, they clearly saw their readers as people who could be expected to show some interest in well-reported stories about places they had never heard of or even thought to take an interest in. Stead had also interviewed George Newnes (founder of *Tit-Bits*, a penny weekly in 1881) on 20 May 1886 in the *Pall-Mall Gazette* and was whole-heartedly behind this paper with its appeal to "the apolitical readers of limited literacy who had been spawned in part by the Education Act of 1870." Alfred Harmsworth contributed to *Tit-Bits* at the age of seventeen and later used it as a model.[113] Harmsworth was the greatest exponent of New Journalism of them all. In Stead, we see a man who was aware of successful journalistic innovations designed to appeal to working-class readers, a man who was ever ready to point to the worth and the content of these papers which readers of his own publications would never buy or read.

As far as China was concerned, the British working-class reader was quite safe in the hands of Alfred, Lord Harmsworth. Not a single picture appeared in the *Daily Mail* during the China crisis which could have given rise to a popular conception of China and the Chinese as superstitious, treacherous, cruel, primitive, opium-sodden barbarians. As for Stead, not only were his leading articles sympathetic, not only did he amass written evidence of the Chinese viewpoint and stories of the inappropriate behaviour of foreigners in China,[114] he took the ultimate step of permitting the Chinese viewpoint to appear in his pages uncensored. The printing of the Chinese anti-foreign posters in the *Review of Reviews* in August 1900 remains a high point in the history of the attempts by one culture to understand the viewpoint of another.

Notes

1. There are some rare unsigned Japanese woodblock prints depicting the capture of Beijing. These were probably cheap single sheet issues. An example of such a print may be seen at Plate 3.25.
2. E. Jussim, *Visual Communication and the Graphic Arts: Photographic Technologies in the Nineteenth Century*, R. R. Bowker Co., New York, 1974, p. 3. A classic study amplifying Ivins's assertion is Herschel Chipp's *Picasso's Guernica. History Transformations, Meanings*, London, Thames and Hudson, 1989.
3. R. S. Britton, *The Chinese Periodical Press 1800–1912*, Kelly and Walsh, Shanghai, 1933, describes the various types of gazettes which circulated widely in Imperial China. Of the most celebrated, the *Peking Gazette*, he quotes Samuel Wells Williams in his well-known book *The Middle Kingdom*,

   > [the *Peking Gazette*] is very generally read and talked about by the gentry and educated people in the cities, and tends to keep them more acquainted with the character and proceedings of their rulers, than the Romans were of their sovereigns and senate. In the provinces, thousands find employment by copying and abridging the Gazettes for readers who cannot afford to purchase the complete edition.

   See Britton, op cit., p. 10. In this context the opening sentences of Lin Yutang's *A History of the Press and Public Opinion in China*, Institute of Pacific Relations, Shanghai, 1936, p. 2, is worth quoting. "China, like many other ancient countries was blessed with the absence of newspapers. The ancient people of China just did not have to read newspapers." The rest of his work documents the exercise of power by the people in criticising the governments of the day on topics of current importance.
4. Some examples of illustrated newspapers, a genre that blossomed copiously at the end of the Qing, include *Shenbao tuhua* (Shanghai, 1909); *Mingquan huabao* (Shanghai, 1911); *Zhongwai renwu shanshui huabao* (Shanghai, 1908); *Zhongwai renwu huabao* (Shanghai, 1908); *Zhongwai ribao* and *Baihua huatu ribao* (Beijing, 1908). These illustrated papers cover a wide range of subjects from flowers and birds to abnormal pregnancies, to scenes of robberies in homes, scandals in brothels, and stories about foreigners.
5. *Arts Asiatiques*, Vol. 35, Paris, 1978; Danielle Eliasberg, "Imagerie Populaire

Chinoise du Nouvel An," p. 11, estimated that at its height the Yangliuqing studio was able to produce 20 million prints annually. She quoted G. Pommerantz-Liedtke, *Chinesische Neujahrsbilder*, Dresden, 1961, p. 33, as saying that between 1850 and 1880, 30,000 people in thirty different villages, both adults and children, were employed in this production.

6. There is disagreement in the literature on the artistic merit of the folk art prints. Kuo Li-ch'eng, who wrote the endnotes to *The Graphic Art of Chinese Folklore*, National Museum of History, Republic of China, 1977, for example, being of the school that those producing the prints were "mere artisans conversant with the conventions of the times. Few were artists. A spirit of plodding craftsmanship was unavoidable." Wang Shucun leads the group of scholars, including foreign sinologists, who have the highest regard for the artistic worth of the woodcuts. In his book, *Ancient Woodblock New Year Prints*, Foreign Language Press, Beijing 1985, p. 2, Professor Wang Shucun links the folk art tradition to classical Chinese painting. His plausible explanation is that with the rise of landscape, flower and bird painting and the decline of figure painting, after the Yuan dynasty (1271–1368), it was the artisans producing traditional woodblock prints, who inherited the ancient elegant tradition of Daoist and Buddhist figure painting. Professor Maria Rudova also observed to the writer that she holds this view. It would appear that there is an international difficulty with acknowledging the artistic merit of folk art. In her article, "Finding the Tradition in Folk-Art: An Art Educator's Perspective," *Journal of Aesthetic Education*, Vol. 20, No. 3, 1986, pp. 94–106, Kirsten G. Congden provides some interesting background as to why this might be. The two critical issues are first that the works have widespread popularity and therefore do not come within the rarefied realms of art galleries, art critics and the top echelons of the art world. Second, the objects thus produced are anonymous, cheap and sold in great quantities. Thus it is unlikely that they will come to be seen by the community as objects of high intrinsic monetary worth. In the West this latter factor is all too often a dominant one in considerations of the artistic merit of most art forms. Sally Price's work, *Primitive Art in Civilized Places*, University of Chicago Press, 1989, is illuminating on this point. In this context, the difference should be noted between anonymous Chinese woodblock prints and signed woodblock prints by Japanese artists, worth a great deal of money.
7. Maria Rudova, *Chinese Popular Prints*, Aurora Art Publisher, Leningrad, 1988, has drawn on the scholarship of Vasili Alexiev, the Russian sinologist who began collecting nianhua seriously in 1906. She uses his interpretations of the woodcuts throughout her book and there are many examples explaining why particular prints were thought to be auspicious in particular contexts.
8. Stead's campaign in the *Review of Reviews*, beginning in May 1900, for an Art Gallery in every home, shows that coloured pictures were not part of the quality of working-class British life at that time, p. 436, "Sometimes in grimy

manufacturing towns I have almost been in despair at the thought of the sooty squalor which met the eye everywhere. The more soot and squalor there may be around us in the streets ... the more need there is to make bright and glad the walls of the lairs we live in."

9. J. Thomson, *The Straits of Malacca, Indo-China and China or Ten Years' Travels, Adventures and Residence Abroad*, Samson Low, Marston, London 1875, p. 171, describes Chinese New Year decorations he saw in a Chinese merchant's house in Cholon, Indo-China.
10. This myth was repudiated by contemporary observers such as Thomson, op cit., p. 45; R. S. Gundy in his article "The Coup d'Etat in China" reprinted from the *Fortnightly Review* in the May edition of the *Review of Reviews*, pp. 554ff, spoke of "the intervention of public opinion, generally believed not to exist in China" as being a factor in preventing the deposition of the Emperor after the failure of the 1898 Reforms; and Lin Yutang, op cit., p. 4, sets out to write about the "movements of fearless criticism of national affairs [which] form glorious chapters in the history of Confucian scholars, and should amply destroy the theory that the Chinese are by nature born indifferent to public affairs." That is, this Western theory was still current by the 1930s. Revisionist scholarship is beginning to put these myths to rest. See Joanna Waley-Cohen, *The Sextants of Beijing. Global Currents in Chinese History*, W. W. Norton and Company, New York, 1999.
11. See Rudova, op cit., Alexiev's interpretations contain endless examples of homophones and double meanings; for example, those for pictures 18, 37–38, 48, 52, 58, 103. Eliasberg, op cit., p. 12 also mentions the importance of symbolism and plays on words which were such an integral part of the nianhua, the Chinese language being so rich in homophones.
12. Quoted in Rudova, op cit., p. 11.
13. See W. T. Stead's interview with Pearson, founder of the *Daily Express*, *Review of Reviews*, May 1900, pp. 420–433.
14. I am indebted to Professor Wang Shucun for this information.
15. Rudova, op cit., text accompanying picture 52.
16. *Illustrated London News*, 25 August 1900, p. 272, gives an artist's impression of a picture of one of the "semi-religious and political drawings which the Boxers scatter broadcast over the country." The picture is standing up beside a street puppet theatre showing an anti-foreign play, a missionary being depicted as a puppet in the form of a pig.
17. Britton, op. cit., pp. 5–6.
18. See Chapter Three for a detailed discussion of the relationship between actual events, the depiction of those events and a rise of the sense of nationalism and a knowledge of the outside world on the part of the Chinese peasantry.
19. See Joseph Esherick, *Reform and Revolution in China: The 1911 Revolution in Hunan and Hubei*, University of California Press, Berkeley, 1976, pp. 25, 47–48,

133. In his work, *China in Convulsion*, Oliphant, Anderson and Ferrier, London 1901, p. 70, the American missionary Arthur H. Smith said that after the Tianjin massacre of 21 June 1870, "For a long time the sale of 'massacre fans' was carried on, the people evidently enjoying the pictures of the ruin of property and the slaughter of foreigners."

20. C. Worswick and J. Spence (eds), *Imperial China. Photographs 1850–1912*, ANU Press, Canberra 1980, p. 9. Professor Spence tells the story of Wu Kedu, the censor of Gansu province, who before committing suicide over the succession issue, asked in a letter to his son to be buried close to the tomb of the Emperor Tongzhi, writing,

    > No doubt you will desire to take home my remains, but do not do so. What you may do is take the small photograph I had made when I left Peking and have a full portrait made from it in our home and bring that together with my robes to the family ceremony.

    Professor Spence commented that "The photograph was not yet of high enough status for burial as proxy for the living body, but its accuracy … was unquestioned." For attitudes towards photography of the dead in the West, see Michel F. Braive, *The Era of the Photograph. A Social History*, Thames and Hudson, London, 1966, pp. 31 and 79.

21. It is common knowledge that Chinese country people objected to having their photo taken until well into this century (the writer has seen scowls and turned heads when tourists attempted to take photographs of old ladies in the remote areas of the New Territories in 1991). It is less well known that the introduction of the camera produced similar superstitious reactions in Britain and Europe. Thomson, op cit., p. 463, mentioned early British reaction. R. A. Sobieszek, "Photography and the Theory of Realism in the Second Empire: A Reexamination of a Relationship," in van deren Coke (ed.), *One Hundred Years of Photographic History — Essays in Honor of Beaumont Newhall*, University of New Mexico Press, Albuquerque 1975, p. 149, quotes the reaction of the German newspaper, *Leipziger Anzeiger*, immediately after the public announcement of the invention of photography in 1839:

    > To want to fix fugitive reflections is not only an impossibility, as very serious experiments have shown here in Germany, but the desire borders on sacrilege. God created men in His image and no human machine is able to fix the image of God; it would be necessary for Him to suddenly betray His own eternal principles in order to permit a Frenchman, in Paris, to launch into the world an invention so diabolical.

22. Thomson, op cit., pp 437–438.

23. Raymond L. Schults, *Crusaders in Babylon. W.T. Stead and the Pall Mall Gazette*, University of Nebraska Press 1972, has a helpful and complete definition of what constituted the New Journalism in Britain. See pp. 29ff, especially pp. 30–33.

24. Jussim, op cit., p. 277. See also Robert Taft, *Photography and the American Scene. A Social History, 1839-1889*, Dover Publications, New York, 1938, p. 58. Frank Leslie's *Illustrated Newspaper* (1856) contained reproductions of Brady's portraits, although these would have appeared as engravings from the daguerreotype.
25. Britton, op cit., p. 63.
26. Ibid., p. 68. Major retired in 1889 and returned to England. Huang Xizhuan was editor from 1896 to 1906.
27. See note 4 above.
28. Britton, op cit, p. 50.
29. Ibid., pp. 43–49.
30. George Rowley, *Principles of Chinese Painting*, Princeton University Press, Princeton, 1970 (1947), p. 12. See also Chiang Yee, *The Chinese Eye. An Interpretation of Chinese Painting*, Methuen, London 1960 (1935), pp. 10, 21, 64 and Robert E. Harrist "A Letter from Wang Hsi-chih and the Culture of Chinese Calligraphy," in Robert E. Harrist and Wen C. Fong (eds), *The Embodied Image. Chinese Calligraphy from the John B. Elliott Collection*, the Art Museum, Princeton University, 1999.
31. Rowley, op cit., p. 13.
32. Wang, op cit., p. 6.
33. R. Rudisill, *Mirror Image. The Lure of the Daguerreotype on American Society*, University of Mexico Press, Albuquerque, 1971, p. 190, quotes Marcus Root who wrote extensively on the daguerreotype as having the view that,

    > improvement of public taste and patriotism would come from the didactic uses of photography as a symbolic medium. Photography, conceived of as an agent for improvement of the public and as a source of increased public happiness, would seem to embody the ideal of art ...
34. Jussim, op cit., p. 277.
35. *Review of Reviews*, London, June, July, August, September 1900.
36. Taft, op cit., p. 447.
37. Ibid., p. 445.
38. Ibid., p. 448.
39. Jussim, op cit., p. 101.
40. The earliest reference to gluing paintings on to a part of the house is to the gluing of door gods on either side of the door posts in the Sui and Tang dynasties.
41. From many examples, two are selected from the *Dianshizhai huabao* in 1884. The first one of May 1884 recounting the circumstances of the suicide of a prostitute working in a clandestine brothel owned by the Cao family and the second one of August 1884, reporting the appearance on the Tinwan river of a pair of beautiful female legs cut off at the hip and subsequent police failure to take action on the matter.
42. Editors like Stead and Pulitzer regularly published leading articles or short

articles on the editorial page giving their views on what constituted good journalism. As representatives of a new wave of newspapers catering for a working-class readership, they had an additional crusading zeal which found expression in frequent definition of — and thus defence of — their ideals on journalism.

43. Taft, op cit., p. 421.
44. Schults, op cit., p. 30.
45. Ibid., footnote 8, p. 33.
46. Ibid.
47. A term coined by Professor James Startt in his book *Journalists for Empire. The Imperial Debate in the Edwardian Stately Press, 1903–1913*, Greenwood Press, New York, 1991, to describe such papers as *The Times*, the *Westminster Gazette*, the *Spectator* and the *Observer*.
48. *Review of Reviews*, May 1900, p. 431.
49. Ibid, July 1900, p. 31.
50. Zhao Jianli, *Yihetuan baguo lianjun xinchou tiaoyue. Gengzi zhi bian tuzhi* (The Boxers, the Eight Invading Powers, the Boxer Protocol. Illustrated Records of the Changes That Happened in the Year 1900), Shandong huabao, Jinan, 2000, p. 35 has a photographic portrait of the Guangxu Emperor in the Chinese tradition of photographic portraiture. This tradition clearly shows an entirely different cultural attitude in terms of the Chinese expectation of what a photographic portrait should look like. See J. Elliott, "Why Western Cultural Inhibitions Prevented the Exploitation of a Technology for Over Half a Century. An Analysis of Chinese and American Photographs of the Boxer Rising," unpublished paper, Centre for Asian Studies, University of Adelaide, 1995, p. 6. My thanks to Yao Koubao and Fan Qinhua of Huabao Craft Store, Suzhou for their assistance in redrawing almost illegible microfilm prints.
51. Rudova, op. cit. Under the heading "Literary and Theatrical Pictures" discusses the pictorial rendering of plays about judicial cases and picture 164 shows Judge Shi Shilun.
52. The classical photography of John Thomson, Felix Beato and the American photographer William Henry Jackson was used extensively as background illustrative material during the Boxer crisis. Given that Beato's photographs were taken in 1859–1860 and Thomson's in 1868–1874, the life of a photograph as a newsworthy item can be seen to have been considerably longer at this time in the history of the illustrated press. This was the case from the very beginnings of the history of the illustrated press in England, see Mason Jackson, *The Pictorial Press. Its Origin and Progress*, New York, 1969 (1885), p. 69, where Jackson notes that during the British Civil War woodcuts "were frequently repeated, sometimes used where they had no relation to the subject treated," p. 109, that during the same period a woodcut of an officer was used "evidently not executed for this special occasion, the officer being in the costume of the

preceding reign," and p. 121, that "sometimes the same woodcut is used to represent more than one person." See also Frederick A. Sharf and Peter Harrington, *The Boxer Rebellion. China, 1900. The Artists' Perspective*, Greenhill Books, London, 2000, pp. 43, 58 and 59.

53. Taft, op cit., p. 448.
54. J. Goldstein, J. Israel and H. Conroy (eds), *America Views China, American Images of China Then and Now*, Associated University Press, New Jersey, 1991. See the essays by J. G. Utley and Sandra M. Hanley. See also J. L. Hevia, "Loot's Fate. The Economy of Plunder and the Moral Life of Objects," *History and Anthropology*, Vol. 6, No. 4, 1994.
55. Braive, op cit., p. 183.
56. Tom Goldstein has edited some seminal writings on journalism in the US including Lippman and Merz's celebrated essay, "A Test of the News," which first appeared in the *New Republic* on 4 August 1920. For a nineteenth century view of the shock and violence of "taking the subject ... by force or by surprise," see L. Brandeis and S. Warren, "The Right to Privacy," first published in the *Harvard Law Review*, 15 December 1890, in Tom Goldstein (ed.), *Killing the Messenger. The First 100 Years of Media Criticism*, Columbia University Press, 1989.
57. Braive, op cit., p. 269.
58. See Hearst's persistent telegrams to Edward Wildman asking him to get action pictures of the Boxer rising. Wildman papers, Manuscript Division, Library of Congress.
59. There is a great deal in the literature on Western attitudes to the photography of the dead, the most revealing and pathetic story being told in Rudisill, op cit., p. 219. See also Braive, op cit., p. 175, Taft, op. cit., p. 30 and Alan Trachtenberg, *Reading American Photographs. Images as History. Mathew Brady to Walker Evans*, Hill and Wang, USA, 1989, p. 32.
60. See especially the career of the American photographer James Ricalton. Ricalton was in China during the Boxer War and was the first photographer to succeed — at great personal risk, to which he was apparently impervious — in taking a photograph of a shell leaving the muzzle of a gun during the Russo-Japanese War. He was sixty years old at the time. The newspaper rights for this eventually successful photograph sold for $5,000, an enormous amount of money in 1905. See C. J. Lucas (ed.), *James Ricalton's Photographs of China During the Boxer Rebellion. His Illustrated Travelogue of 1900*, Edwin Mellen Press, New York, 1990, pp. 47–50.
61. Taft, op cit., p. 447.
62. *Illustrated London News*, 10 March 1900, p. 331.
63. Ibid., 10 February 1900, p. 191.
64. Ibid., see photographic portraits of British generals and heroes such as Baden-Powell throughout, with an emphasis also on their aristocratic connections

where possible. Lord Roberts and Colonel Baden-Powell were the subjects of frequent and varied portraits both painted and photographic. See Lucien Bodard, *La Vallée des Roses*, Grasset, Paris, 1977, pp. 334, 336, and 371–372, on the heritage of the British aristocracy in leading men in war.

65. *Illustrated London News*, 13 January and 28 April 1900, p. 17.
66. Ibid., Supplement, 30 June 1900, pp. vi–vii.
67. Ibid., 13 January 1900, p. 64; 27 January 1900, p. 133; 3 February 1900, p. 165; 30 June, p. 887.
68. Ibid., 13 January 1900, pp. 52–53; 17 February 1900, p. 215; 24 February 1900, pp. 262–263.
69. The *Illustrated London News* contained relatively few drawings and photographs of the wounded, concentrating on depicting such scenes as little Queen Victoria herself, or other members of the royal family, bringing flowers to the bedside of a wounded man. See Matthew Paul Lalumia, *Realism and Politics in Victorian Art of the Crimean War*, UMI Research Press, Michigan, 1984, p. 62. By contrast, the American *Harper's Monthly Magazine* contained both photographs and artists' impressions of Boer field hospitals, and in his book *Meine Kriegs-Erlebnisse in China. Die Expedition Seymour*, Wilhelm Köhler, Westfalen, 1902, Captain Paul Schlieper included many drawings pertaining to all aspects of the problem of wounded soldiery during the ignominious retreat of the first Allied attempt to relieve the foreign Legations in Beijing.
70. *Illustrated London News*, 20 January, p. 87.
71. An article on "mapomania" appeared in the *Illustrated London News* on 29 June 1900, p. 87. A semi-humorous portrait of "A Strange Epidemic Rife in Up-to-date Suburbia" whereby every man wanted to follow the latest developments on maps provided by a wide range of printers eager to cash in on this craze which was proving destructive of domestic harmony. In the endpapers of books on China being published at this time, maps were being offered for sale. As a further piece of evidence for "mapomania," the *Illustrated London News* carried a picture on 9 June 1900, p. 780, of a father showing his little daughter where to pin the British flag on the map.
72. The *Daily Mail* "mapomania" emphasised this interest as a masculine one that finally drove the ladies out of their homes, so absorbing was the mania.
73. See, for example, *How to Read Chinese War News. A Vade-Mecum of Notes and Hints to Readers of Despatches and Intelligence from the Seat of War, with a Coloured War Map and a Glossary of Military Technical Terms, Local Titles, Places, Phrases, etc*, T. Fisher Unwin, London, 1900.
74. Lucien Bodard, op. cit., writing of the 1860 British and French expedition to China describes the nonchalant, almost bored attitude of British aristocratic senior officers towards the sport which is war. See especially, pp. 336–337 and 357.
75. *Illustrated London News*, 19 May 1900, Supplement, p. 2.

76. Ibid., 26 May and 29 September 1900 reported white flag incidents when the Boers had breached the white flag convention but not the incident in early January 1900 when the British had breached this convention.
77. Worswick and Spence, op cit., contains a number of superb portraits taken by Miller and Thomson of Chinese people from a wide range of socio-economic backgrounds. Li Hongzhang was always eager to have his photograph taken and gave Thomson an introduction to Zeng Guofan who unfortunately died before Thomson had the opportunity to photograph him. See Thomson, *Malacca*, op cit., pp. 462–463.
78. See discussion of the xinwenzhi of the great Chinese General Liu Yongfu in Chapter Three.
79. Li Hongzhang, who fully understood the benefits of well-orchestrated publicity, had himself photographed while travelling by train and at the arsenal he created. The Library of Congress also holds an original moving picture of Ackerman presenting Li Hongzhang with a Mutoscope from the American Mutoscope and Biograph Company in Beijing on 14 January 1901. The film was released in 1902.
80. Rudisill, op cit., p. 235.
81. Of the earliest surviving moving pictures in the Library of Congress film archives, made between 1896 and 1904, a noticeably large percentage is devoted to re-creations of war, films of guns, even tear-jerkers such as "The American Soldier in Love and War" filmed in July 1903 with reference to the war in the Philippines.
82. Liu Beisi and Xu Qixian (eds), *Gugong zhencang renwu zhaopian huicui* (Selection of Photographs of People Kept at the Imperial Palace), Forbidden City Publishing House, Beijing, 1994. My thanks to Dr Pauline Keating for obtaining a copy of this book for me.
83. Katharine A. Carl, *With the Empress Dowager of China*, Evelyn Nash, London, 1906.
84. In his introduction to the photographs he selected with Jonathan Spence, see *Imperial China*, op cit., p. 144, Clark Worswick perpetuates a simplistic negative account of the Empress Dowager. Worswick relies solely on Marina Warner whose work is not notable for its balance or its attention to a wide variety of Chinese and foreign language sources.
85. Wen Ching, *The Chinese Crisis from Within*, Grant Richards, London, 1901, shows himself well aware of and able to cater to Western, particularly British, taste for tales of salacious doings in the Manchu court. The enthusiasm and colour of his writing on these subjects quite outshines his ability to give the reader a clear idea of the 1898 reform movement and its intentions.
86. Sharf and Harrington, op. cit., p. 42 give an example of some photographs of buildings of the London Missionary Society submitted by Reverend George Owen and redrawn for the *Daily Graphic*.

87. See Soldat Silbermannn, *Journal de Marche d'un Soldat Colonial en Chine*, Henri-Charles Laveuzelle, *Extrait de la Revue Coloniale*, Paris, 1902, p. 127.
88. George Lynch, *The War of the Civilisations. Being a Record of a "Foreign Devil's" Experiences with the Allies in China*, Longmans Green and Co., London 1901, p. 22. A. H. Savage-Landor, *China and the Allies*, Vol. 1, William Heinemann, London, 1901, p. 178.
89. *Illustrated London News*, 30 June 1900, p. 879.
90. Ibid., 7 July 1900, p. 16.
91. Ibid., 30 June 1900, p. 881.
92. Zhang Junbao and Yao Yunzhu, "Differences Between Traditional Chinese and Western Military Thinking and Their Philosophical Roots," *Journal of Contemporary China*, Vol. 5, No. 2, July 1996, p. 213, "generally speaking Chinese military thinking allots a weightier part to the human factor while the Westerners give a higher priority to the weapons factor." See also p. 217.
93. Sharf and Harrington, op cit., p. 57.
94. Edith K. Harper, *Stead the Man: Personal Reminiscences*, W. Rider, London, 1918.
95. *Review of Reviews*, June 1900, pp. 542–543. On the Hague Peace Conference and its implications for China, see Roger R. Thompson, "Military Dimensions of the 'Boxer Uprising' in Shanxi, 1898–1901," in Hans van de Ven (ed.), *Warfare in Chinese History*, Vol. 47, Sinica Leidensia, Brill, Leiden, 2000.
96. In an article in *Harper's Monthly Magazine*, September 1900, p. 611, "The Teuton Tug of War," the celebrated American journalist Julian Ralph, remarked on the misconception of the English public as phlegmatic. As far as war was concerned, he noted that English people were positively "mercurial," their spirits alternately soaring and being dashed down with the latest news from the front. Accounts of the street scenes in London after the relief of Mafeking would tend to support this observation.
97. *Review of Reviews*, June 1900, p. 513. See also topic of the month, July 1900, "The Revolt of the Yellow Man," pp. 35–41.
98. Ibid, July 1900, pp. 28, 30 and 136.
99. Ibid, July 1900, pp. 22 and 26. This latter picture also appeared in the *Daily Mail* which had sympathetic coverage of the Empress Dowager.
100. Ibid, June 1900, p. 554.
101. See also the analysis of Cixi in "Character Sketches," *Review of Reviews*, July 1900, pp. 21–32.
102. When Miss Carl, the first foreigner to have such intimate access to Cixi, finished her portraits of the Empress and one was to be shipped to America, it had to be boxed and carried upright through the streets and those people in its path had to prostrate themselves. See Carl, op. cit., pp. 297–298. In his thought-provoking study on American photography, Alan Trachtenberg, op. cit. makes some interesting points about the power or otherwise of a full frontal portrait.

See especially his discussion of photographs of Negro slaves, p. 56, as opposed to those of middle-class Americans, p. 28. John Tagg also identifies the portrait photograph as empowering or robbing the subject of dignity. In this latter case, his examples include the advent of the compulsory photography of criminals and lunatics. See John Tagg, *The Burden of Representation. Essays on Photographies and Histories*, MacMillan Education, Minneapolis, USA, 1988, pp. 35, 63–64, 160.

103. *Daily Mail*, 8 June 1900, p. 4.
104. *Review of Reviews*, July 1900, pp. 35–38.
105. J. Thomson, *Illustrations of China and Its People. A Series of Two Hundred Photographs with Letterpress Descriptive of the Places and People Represented*, Vol. 4, Samson Low, Marston, London 1874. The pages are not numbered, but Thomson's remark is to be found in the caption to illustration 8. He was obviously impressed by the provocation the cathedral offered to the Chinese as he mentioned it also in his book *Malacca*, op cit., p. 483, "standing as it did so much above what the Chinese themselves hold most sacred in their yamens and shrines, must in itself have stirred up a bitter feeling against foreigners."
106. *Review of Reviews*, August 1900, p. 146. Stead is scathing in his review of an article by Mr D. Z. Sheffield, formerly president of the North China College, entitled "Chinese Civilisation: the Ideal and the Actual." This article was published in the July 1900 issue of *Forum*.
107. *Illustrated London News*, 23 June 1900, p. 837 and 30 June 1900, p. 872. There is a fascinating undated photograph of a Christian church that has been constructed almost entirely with Chinese architectural conventions in mind. It is not tall and it has two layers of roofs each of which is tiled and turned up at the lower corners in the Chinese style. The photograph itself is very small and in poor condition. It may be seen as a loose item in the Archives Militaires de l'Armée de Terre, Series 7N1665.
108. My thanks to Mr H. C. Li and Mr C. C. Hsü for their assistance with translating these posters and other material.
109. Some contemporary observers and many scholars today have a tendency to think of the Boxer rising as a sudden excrescence, an extraordinary flare up. A serious study of visual material associated with anti-foreign protests in the late Qing, reveals just how widespread and deeply-felt was the resentment against foreigners among the rural poor. Studies using county gazettes, letters and memorials by officials and imperial decrees, uncover the groundswell of anti-foreign hatred revealed by a study of clay statues, "massacre fans," anti-foreign posters and anti-foreign nianhua on sale in the market place in Tianjin in 1870 and again in 1900. See also Mark Elvin, *Another History. Essays on China From a European Perspective*, Wild Peony Pty Ltd., Australia, 1996. Mark Elvin's essay "Mandarins and Millenarians: Reflections on the Boxer Uprising of 1899–1900" contains the best appraisal this writer has seen of the extent to which Christianity

could be said to be a contributing background factor to the Boxer rising. See also Judith Wyman, "The Ambiguities of Anti-foreignism: Chongqing, 1870–1900," *Late Imperial China*, Vol. 18, No. 2, December 1997. My thanks to Dr Gerry Groot for drawing my attention to this latter reference.

110. *Review of Reviews*, July 1900, p. 93. Stead summed up the missionary A. H. Smith's celebrated bestseller, *Village Life in China*, as "a somewhat disappointing book on a subject of supreme interest at the present moment."
111. In a stimulating paper, "Catholic Images of the Boxers," *The American Asian Review*, Vol. 9, No. 3, Fall 1991, pp. 41–66, Jean-Paul Wiest points out the range of European Catholics reached by the bi-monthly *Les Annales de la Propagation de la Foi* and gives a fine analysis of the impact of Catholic missionary accounts of the Boxer troubles (pp. 56–60). However, the total numbers reached by such missionary publications were minor in comparison with the vast circulation of the great British and American secular dailies. As Wiest describes the long-term cultural impact of the deaths of Jesuit priests and their converts in China in 1900, there would appear to be a difference between the Catholic and Protestant mentality regarding the incidents of the Boxer rising; yet another interesting point of investigation stimulated by a paper proposed by Wiest himself as a starting point for a number of new aspects of research on the Boxer crisis.
112. *Review of Reviews*, July 1900, p. 420.
113. Schults, op cit., p. 194.
114. *Review of Reviews*, July 1900, pp. 35–36.

Chapter 3

Pictures of War in Nineteenth Century China[1]

He could have been nothing on earth but an English officer and the observant might have placed him in the cavalry perhaps from his heron-like legs and his walk. Whether they could have specified the regiment, I am not sure.

Elspeth Huxley

The most widespread genre of Chinese imagery of war, namely the nianhua or popular New Year picture is worthy of serious attention as an irreplaceable source of information about developments in the Chinese armies during the nineteenth century. Made by anonymous folk artisans,[2] these woodblock prints are revelatory of the Chinese image of soldiers of various foreign armies fighting on Chinese soil. They also convey a great amount of accurate detail about foreign soldiers: their uniforms, their weapons, their flags and their way of fighting. As a cultural object, the social significance of the nianhua was enormous and multifaceted. For those wishing to develop an understanding of the nianhua as a cultural text, James Flath's excellent study is worthy of serious attention.[3] The nianhua were extensively and readily available sources of pictorial images with lengthy commentaries covering the wars between China and the outside world from at least 1840 onwards. Nianhua constituted an enormous influence on the urban and rural poor from whose ranks came not only the Boxers of Shandong, but any peasants, soldiers or bandits who took part in the vast range of peasant rebellions against the Qing State.

Popular pictures in the form of nianhua describing real events form the smallest percentage of subject matter typical of the genre.[4] Nianhua depicting real military engagements in well-known museums and published collections form the basis of this study. The objective was to find what sort of aspects of war and with what kinds of detail the nianhua artisans chose to illustrate the conflicts between China and foreigners over the period 1840 to 1900. No attention is focused on the artists themselves and no research has been done to establish how they learned the facts about foreign soldiery that are depicted in the nianhua reproduced in this chapter. This constitutes a further field of study.

Large numbers of nianhua survive in collections in China, Taiwan, Russia, Britain, America and France and the interesting question is, why was such a small proportion of these pictures devoted to real events in daily life and why was the proportion devoted to actual military events even smaller? Because these nianhua were designed by workshops essentially as commercial ventures for the mass public of their day, it is argued that this very public exerted consumer influence on the owners and artisans of the great woodcut centres of China. This being the case, the woodblock studios followed public interest and produced woodcuts primarily of subjects related to prosperity and good wishes and secondarily, prints of scenes from popular operas and well-known romantic historical stories. However, as Flath remarks, "there can be no simple approach to connecting market with culture."[5] Flath reminds us of the entire context in which nianhua were sold. It seems clear that production of nianhua depicting real events constituted a break from traditional nianhua and therefore from traditional modes of selling and viewing and even display.

Nianhua depicting real events or military clashes were of relatively little interest to the peasantry until the late nineteenth century when foreign encroachment began to reach out widely to smaller villages and upset beliefs regarding magic and the spiritual world as well as the sense of justice shared by peasants in the hinterland. Nevertheless, print runs of nianhua showing wars between China and foreign countries sold so well as to necessitate a second, even a third edition.[6] It should be said that nianhua depicting real events in war helped in the formation of a sense of national identity. Those peasants who bought or saw such woodblock prints from 1840 up to the 1930s must have begun to have some understanding of and interest in the victory or defeat of China by foreign forces. Certainly, these pictures often depicted

Chinese victories when the reality was that China had been defeated. However, they constituted an important force in arousing national sentiment in the minds of the rural and urban poor.[7]

This is not the place for a debate about the meaning of "patriotism" and "nationalism" for the Chinese peasantry and urban poor over the years 1840 to 1900.[8] Suffice it to say that over these years, thanks to a number of sources within folk culture as much as to foreign influence of any kind, the common people were exposed to a good deal of information about clashes between China and foreign Powers. Such knowledge began to inform a sense of patriotism, a necessary basis for the development of a sense of nationalism. No simple connection between nianhua of real battles and the development of a sense of nationalism is proposed. Nevertheless, it can be said that for those who saw and, more importantly, for those who discussed such nianhua pasted up in public places, they had a vital function in teaching people to distinguish some kinds of Chinese soldiers from other kinds of Chinese soldiers and in distinguishing some kinds of foreign soldiers from other kinds of foreign soldiers.

As a genre forming visual perception of warfare, the nianhua woodblock prints are of historical interest and importance for a number of reasons. Analysis of woodblock prints depicting the Chinese armies at war with various foreign states constitutes a hitherto unused source of evidence about the weaponry and training of Chinese armies of the day. It also constitutes fascinating visual material revealing penetrating Chinese artistic impressions of European and Japanese soldiery. Statements about the aesthetic worth and technical expertise of traditional folk art are difficult to substantiate with a degree of acceptable objectivity.[9] The nianhua genre existed within a multitude of traditions of printed imagery in China; the wealth and range of woodblock illustrations in books, cheap tracts and single-sheet publications was immense.[10] As well, it is instructive to draw parallels with contemporary traditional European folk woodblock prints depicting war.[11]

It is impossible to approach the genre of the popular woodblock print in China without considering the religious implications of New Year prints.[12] Among these, there were crucial religious and magical elements related to martial arts and depicted constantly in popular nianhua. These religious and magical elements as well as a strong sense of good and evil and their consequences pervade the nianhua. They were practised by earthly heroes in well-known historical romances and by immortals and semi-immortals in fiction and opera. There has not yet been a scholarly evaluation of the religious impact on the peasantry and urban poor of nianhua depicting martial arts traditions comparable to the connections between martial arts and opera drawn by Bruce Doar and also Joseph Esherick[13] or by Robert Hegel and Barbara Ward's studies of audiences of vernacular drama and regional opera.[14]

There has been a call for the need for "studies not catalogues" of nianhua.[15] Our interest here is in what nianhua tell us of Chinese concepts of victory and defeat and what they reveal of contemporary Chinese and foreign military technology. It is not simple to pronounce on whether the nianhua tell us more about popular perceptions of the military and less about the real elements of the Chinese and foreign military they depict. They do both although overall it is their function in depicting real information about the military in which we are most interested.

The nianhua embodied important religious elements. Of interest here are the nianhua linking martial arts with the struggles between popular heroes and/or between immortals and semi-immortals. As well, it is instructive to draw a brief comparison with contemporary European folk woodblock prints depicting war. There is another aspect of nianhua, one of cardinal significance in the way Chinese artists depicted war and Chinese audiences perceived it. This is the romantic historical genre of nianhua. Both religious and historical elements united in nianhua depicting famous historical romances, popular themes of which were displays by martial arts heroes or the widely known military engagements of the great Chinese epic romances such as *The Three Kingdoms* and *Watermargin*.[16]

There is a large body of scholarship that discusses the influence of nianhua in general.[17] Of concern here is the specific influence of nianhua depicting fictional battles or images of real wars. The artists producing nianhua of images of war utilised many conventions already known and accepted as depicting war in the romantic historical and operatic battles so beloved by the Chinese and so accessible to the illiterate men and women[18] in both rural and urban China.[19] An interesting aspect of these popular pictures of war was the varying nature of the response by foreigners resident in China to the nianhua.[20]

Peculiar to Chinese folk woodblock prints as opposed to their equivalents in Europe, Japan or Vietnam, are the extensive descriptions written on the pictures and the labelling of different parts, persona and places in the pictures. These pictures were selected and bought by illiterate Chinese, even in the remotest parts of the countryside, from itinerant peddlers who could sing the stories and point out the labelling or in cities at Chinese New Year or at any other time from vendors who, likewise, could recite all the written material on every picture they had for sale.[21] Purchasers of woodblock prints describing wars between Chinese and foreign armies were thus buying more than a picture. They were buying an extensive written commentary on the action, a commentary not paralleled in any way in the traditional folk woodblock art of European countries as can be seen by a comparison of Plate 3.12 and Figure 3.1 with any of the Chinese woodcuts.[22]

These commentaries, as opposed to a title and one or two sentences in other folk woodblock art traditions, bring us to the final aspect to be addressed. Specific titles and lengthy commentaries on military action lead us to the question of the extent to which the nianhua constituted an accurate account of the battles they depicted. Did these pictures, together with the commentaries on them, represent the battles in question more or less accurately than the equivalent woodblock prints made in European countries and Japan? Did they, in fact, explain anything distinctively Chinese about popular conceptions of warfare? An in-depth analysis of nianhua depicting war will lead us to the idea, already present in the literature on warfare between Western and non-white Western peoples, that there are differing cultural responses to defeat and victory in warfare and that concepts of victory and defeat are not necessarily accepted in the same sense in respect of the same battle, by the contending forces involved.

In recent times we have seen the example of Saddam Hussein's refusal to concede defeat "by recourse to a familiar Islamic rhetoric that denied that he had been defeated in spirit, whatever material loss he had suffered." Comments Keegan, this "robbed the coalition's Clausewitzian victory of much of its point."[23] Even more recently, a French journalist commenting on NATO intervention in Yugoslavia wrote "NATO has had to adapt its strategy and redefine its understanding of its goals in the war."[24] The Chinese tradition is expressed by Zhang Junbao and Yao Yunzhu,

> China's huge human resources, its unbeatable national spirit and its history of

> always denying final victory to any foreign invader, are taken as counter threats to the use of even nuclear weapons.[25]

Through a discussion of particular nianhua, this will be shown to have been the case in China in the First Opium War, the Sino-French War and the Boxer War. In asking these questions concerning culture-specific concepts of victory and defeat, this chapter will continue the work of historians who wish to initiate an approach to the study of warfare between Europeans and non-Europeans in the nineteenth century embodying a more sophisticated knowledge of cultural attitudes to warfare and being less black-and-white and outcome-oriented.

> China is not, like Turkey, a sick man, it is a corpse ready to be dismembered, a corpse which offers itself up to the knife.

Paul Claudel, Vice-Consul for France in Shanghai was far from alone in this opinion that he expressed in 1898.[26] Given the international view of China as the weakest of nations, how was it then, that after so many "humiliations," China fought her way against the armies of eight Western nations in 1900? How was it that China remained not only intact but with sufficient cultural, economic, political and military life to continue to exist as a nation despite the dire predictions and burdensome reparations inflicted by the "civilised" West?

Nianhua, the Historical Traditions and Martial Arts, Architectural and Landscape Traditions and the Symbolic Presence of Heroes, Heroines or Immortals

At the time of Chinese New Year, the major consumer interest in nianhua was in those whose subject matter depicted door gods and other gods, symbols of wealth, abundance, healthy boy children and success in the examinations which would lead these boys to lucrative posts as officials. Works exuding benevolent wishes and displaying for the peasants, images of beautiful women with their male offspring and the sumptuous interiors of wealthy homes were the most popular and sought after during Chinese New Year.

However, the main centres of production of woodblock prints produced hundreds of thousands of pictures all year round.[27] Substantial proportions of these pictures were of historical or theatrical subjects. Evelyn Rawski noted

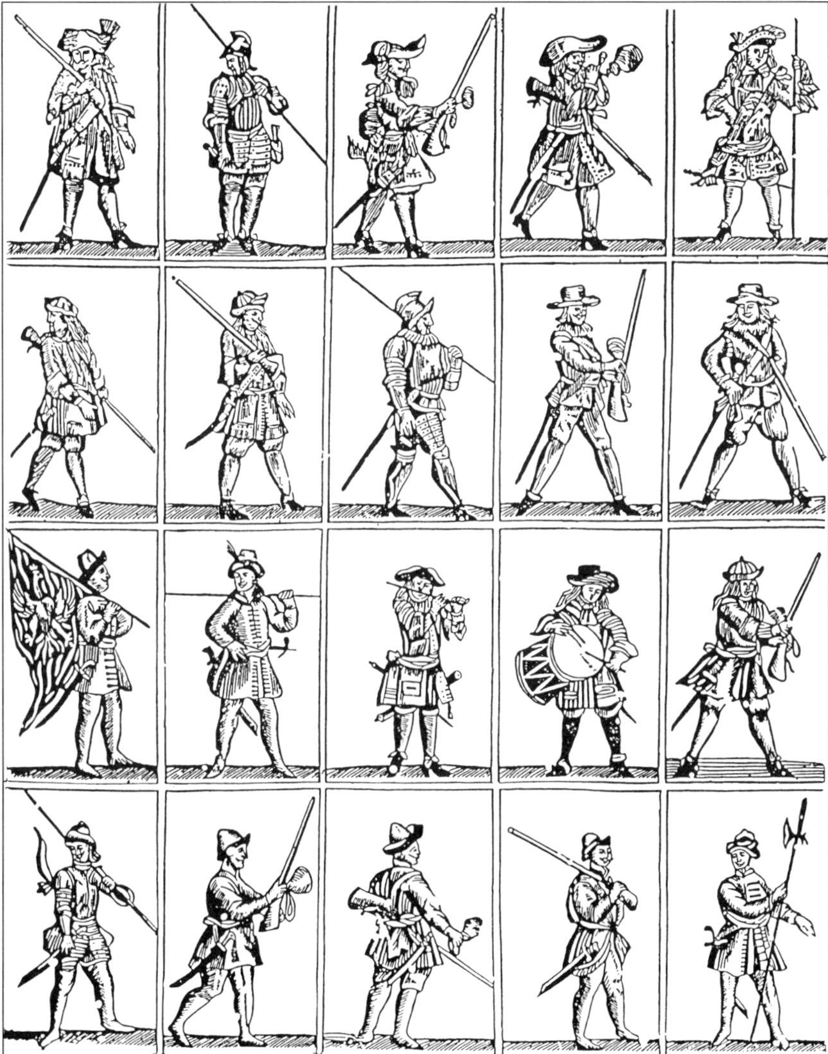

Figure 3.1 A print of various soldiers uniforms — Imagerie des Pays Bas.

that "by late Qing times, even illiterates lived in what was basically a literate culture."[28] More than any other folk art form and markedly different from European folk art woodcut traditions, the nianhua were responsible for creating a constant literary milieu in the daily life of the Chinese peasantry.

The great Russian sinologist Alexiev was overwhelmed by the impact of the highly-coloured nianhua in every street in China at Chinese New Year.[29] We may add four observations to this. First the same dazzling exterior display was evident on other important feast days and was thus a continuous part of the visual world of the peasantry and urban poor. Second, nianhua pasted up inside the homes of the illiterate poor remained on the walls until pasted over by a new woodblock print of the owners' choice. Third, a majority of the nianhua carried extensive captions that their owners would have known by heart. In pre-literate China, writing was revered and the memories of the illiterate tuned to perfect recall of stories and other written material of interest.[30] Fourth, in addition to teaching the audience ways of seeing,[31] nianhua provided informal impetus for public discussion wherever they were pasted up in public places

Another folk art form complimenting that of the world of the nianhua was that of the drama or the opera. Paul Cohen has made some pertinent connections between Boxer spirit possession and theatrical performance. There were also connection between attendance at temples and spirit possession.[32] Dramatic operas and plays were performed in large market towns and smaller villages often to mark some religious or festive occasion. These were, however, the objects of surveillance and censorship by the gentry elite. With some justification, they were sometimes judged to be potentially licentious or rebellious.[33] Sometimes sects sponsored theatrical performances to attract new members.[34] Censorship of nianhua is not mentioned in the literature as being a regular consideration for the owners and artisans in woodblock print studios.[35] Indeed, censorship of popular pictures in China did not occur on anything like the scale on which it was practised in eighteenth and nineteenth century France, Germany, Britain, Russia or Japan.[36] Writing in 1918, Chen Duxiu claimed that:

> Chinese opera ... was the first cause of the Boxers.... The gods invoked by the Boxers were mostly opera heroes with their "theatrical makeup" and "martial posturing" ["theatrical makeup" and "martial posturing" were integral to nianhua depicting opera scenes as seen in Plates 3.3, 3.4, 3.5 and 3.7] : Guan Yu, Zhang Fei, Zhao Yun, Sun Wukong ... and the like. Opera is particularly popular in Tianjin, Beijing and Fengtian, so it was exceptionally easy for the Boxers to spread. When the Boxer gods presented themselves, their speech was modelled on the spoken parts in the operas and their gestures were modelled on the prescribed movements of the opera actors. These were things that people from Tianjin and Beijing saw with their own eyes; it's not something I'm making up.[37]

Huge numbers of nianhua depicting popular dramas, episodes from the great historical romances and other episodes from actual history were chosen and displayed in the homes of the rural and urban poor throughout China. After nianhua devoted to benevolent good wishes and prosperity, the most popular subject matter of nianhua was that depicting stories from the dramatic and operatic traditions and from real or romanticised historical episodes and their heroes and heroines. Thus a vast illiterate group of people were choosing to spend money from their tiny cash surplus on articles of consumption that would not only brighten their homes but that were also vividly illustrated stories they knew by heart already. These pictures illustrated stories about heroes and heroines whose prowess, moral values and martial skills were highly regarded and intimately known by the peasants whether or not they themselves had ever had the chance to see any of the plays or operas illustrated by the popular pictures they had bought.[38]

It was through the nianhua that Chinese peasants even in the poorest and most remote areas of the country had a detailed and extensive understanding of the history of their country, of its heroes and heroines and of the great triumphs and tragedies of past dynasties. Such detailed knowledge, despite the fact that some of it was fictional — even the fiction was deeply imbued with Chinese moral and cultural values regarding heroism, virtue, evil, victory and defeat — is the kind of knowledge which locates illiterate people in their geographical space and in time. Put simply, this was precisely the kind of knowledge that inspired in the illiterate poor a love for their country, the patriotism which countless European observers found lacking in the Chinese.[39] As such, the nianhua constituted an important influence in the lives of the peasants who participated in the Boxer rising; an influence of at least as great a significance as the influences of opera and storytellers.

Joanna Waley-Cohen shows that the results of the Qianlong Emperor's desire to propagandise or broadcast his military successes were to draw different groups of minority peoples together "under the single roof of nationalism." She argues that twentieth century nationalism and its close association with militarism is deeper-rooted than has been suggested by historians who focus on the nineteenth-century "Western impact." Her work draws convincing links between the Emperor's attempt to militarise Chinese culture and the development of nationalism.[40] The style and subject matter of Chinese nianhua, though not part of the "high art" discussed by Waley-Cohen, supports her contention that the vast range, number, and genre-range of artworks devoted to military subjects led to a sense of Chinese national identity through the artistic glorification of military conquest. What the Qianlong Emperor was doing from the top downwards was echoed by what the artisan folk woodblock artists were doing from the bottom upwards.[41]

An important aspect of the nianhua is that they show a highly particularised, commonly shared perception of military values, knowledge and culture — and one that dates from earliest childhood memories. Paul Cohen gives examples of boys who believed that a particular hero from *The Three Kingdoms* had entered into their bodies.[42] Styles differ slightly from major woodblock printing studios in one region to those of other regions. Nevertheless, stylistic treatment of the same subject is remarkably similar as can be seen by the two pictures illustrating the episode of the ruse of the empty city from *The Three Kingdoms* (Plates 3.1 and 3.2).[43] In any region, every boy — and most girls — would have known the story of the ruse of the empty city. Then there was the influence of the opera and in particular, operas telling of great military events. Lin Yutang has this to say about the drama and the opera:

> Apart from teaching the people an intense love of music the theatre has taught the people.... A knowledge of history quite amazing, crystallizing ... the folklore and entire literary tradition and historical tradition in plays of characters that have captured the heart and mind of common men and women. Thus any amah has a livelier concept than I have of many historical heroes from her intimate knowledge of Chinese plays, as I was prevented from attending the theatres in my childhood ... and had to learn it all piecemeal from the cold pages of a history book.[44]

We may add to Lin Yutang's observation that not only the amahs of his childhood, but generations of peasants and urban poor as well, lived in a physical world in which the smallest hovels displayed pictures of these traditions on their inside and outside walls. A selection of typical nianhua of opera scenes and episodes from famous historical romances may be seen in Plates 3.1, 3.2, 3.3, 3.4, 3.5, 3.6 and 3.7.[45]

Writers who have connected some aspects of popular culture with rebellion have not mentioned the vital role of nianhua.[46] Many hundreds of thousands of people in remote villages rarely saw an opera or witnessed a play.[47] However, they may have had fairly regular opportunities to listen to itinerant storytellers, a large proportion of whose repertoires were the heroic deeds of men and women in the great historical romances. The important points to note are that first, nianhua were chosen by the consumer. Outside the period of Chinese New Year and other major festivals, the stock of a peddler bringing nianhua to tiny far-off villages, contained great numbers of pictures of much-loved heroes of the romantic and actual epic events of the Chinese past.[48] While the prints were priced at rock bottom, so was disposable consumer power. Thus the selection of one, possibly two or three prints by the head of the household was a much-deliberated affair. Second, once chosen and paid for, these highly coloured, often exquisitely drawn action images, were pasted up carefully in particularly selected places on the walls of the peasants' homes.[49] Famous battles drawn with dramatic élan in fast moving, blood-stirring scenes were on display continually in the home. The storytellers came and went, even the smallest theatre troupes might never reach the remotest villages and visits to the bigger market towns were rare and of short duration, seldom involving the whole family. The place where people from the remotest areas could have seen theatre as a whole family was at the temple fairs which were almost ubiquitous.[50]

For these reasons, the vivid, brightly coloured scenes of historical battles based on operas or romantic historical fiction came to have an enormous visual and emotional impact on the imaginations of all those who saw them. The nianhua tradition with its pictures and its texts was vital in the process of shaping the concepts held by peasants and the urban poor of justification of war, conduct of war, victory in war and valour in action. The impact of nianhua was far greater than we can conceive of today in a world saturated as it is with images of all kinds. Their impact was also greater as they were cultural texts viewed, recited and discussed in very particular cultural contexts. Whether or not the artisan who produced them was anonymous, he (sic) lived in the social, cultural and physical world of his art. The forces that shaped him meant that what he produced as folk art reflected moral, religious and social values in a way that a photograph made into a lithographic print could not.

Chinese mass culture manifested an intense interest in the martial arts.[51] Feats of individual strength, and skill in boxing and swordsmanship found expression in particular schools of martial arts. These schools were often actual breeding grounds for dissidents engaged in anti-dynastic activities.

The intermingling of the magical, the spiritual, the romantic historical and the martial arts traditions occasionally found expression in widespread seditious action. As well, there was a uniquely Chinese element of understanding of just or righteous principles more central to the beliefs of the common people than to those of the elite.[52] When justice or righteousness was violated, a practitioner of martial arts or a group of such practitioners held it to be their duty to right the wrong of the injured person or persons. From time immemorial in China, such fusion of magic and martial arts had led to minor and large-scale peasant insurrections. Imperial authority had large numbers of precedents to justify its injunctions that anyone who claimed a special relationship with spiritual authority was breaking the law.

In the 1760s, during campaigns in the Jinchuan area, vital to establishing Qing control of Tibet, the Qianlong Emperor expressly inveighed against his commanders allowing Qing troops to fall prey to belief in magic perpetrated by Buddhist lamas. While he himself did not believe in supernatural forces or religion, he came to understand that these factors constituted a drastic and deleterious effect on troop morale. "There was a presumption that members of such [religious] sects [were] almost by definition susceptible to disaffection against the state [and] might gain access to black magic that could be turned to treacherous purposes."[53] "Qianlong liked to attribute his own victories to divine assistance and could not allow others to do the same."[54]

By the 1870s, this fusion of the magical, the spiritual, the martial arts and popular anger started to be directed against the increasing and unwanted foreign presence in China. The woodblock studios judged the new orientation of peasant resentment and a small percentage of prints began to be produced showing pictures of real wars as opposed to the well-loved romantic historical battle scenes. Many of these nianhua bore captions with a decidedly Chinese moral view of the conflict at hand. In this way, popular art reflected, and in turn began to teach illiterate Chinese men, women and children a new and growing perception of injustice to their country because of foreign intrusion — as opposed to internal social injustice.

The most popular historical romances contained a popular religious and magical element, *The Journey to the West* and *The Story of the White Snake* being two of the more well-known examples.[55] Thus peasants were exposed to a visual tradition depicting extreme individual valour and this often in battle against immortals, sorcerers, heavenly generals, monsters and demons.

They also relished battles involving many different Chinese equivalents of Robin Hood and countless stories of heroes who were chivalrous and gallant, suppressing the evil and pacifying the good, championing the poor and assisting those in peril.[56] The element of justice and of the hero emerging triumphant because of the moral righteousness of his cause is arguably a distinctive part of Chinese popular understanding of military philosophy and as such, is not paralleled by any European traditions regarding the veneration of a particular military hero.[57] The nianhua kept alive in the minds of peasants the idea that a particular hero triumphed because his cause was just rather than because his weapons were superior or his army large.[58] In such stories, elements of superstition were entwined with tales of gallantry and highly positive moral qualities. Earthly heroes in these stories were locked in combat with immortals or semi-immortals; in their turn, the immortals could and did intervene in earthly battles. This admixture of the religious and the lay had no similarly widespread equivalent in European woodblock folk imagery.[59] Neither was the mastery of colour and line in Europe in any way comparable to the work of the great centres of woodblock folk art in nineteenth century China.

Every Chinese village in which these pictures of mortal and immortal courage was displayed, had a tradition of being called to form militias, either against local robbers — particularly in times of famine — or during small or large scale rebellions.[60] A picture such as "The Capture of Bai Juhua"[61] (Plate 3.7, see also detail, Plate 3.5) emphasises the weapons and combat stance of the individual heroes trying to capture the evil Bai Juhua. It is reasonable to postúlate a connection between the symbols understood in pictures like this and the various martial stances of their protagonists with a still out of any of the popular historical kung fu films which have been produced over the last twenty years. This leads to the proposition that there is an unbroken visual tradition describing valour and skill in the martial arts linking the peasants who took part in the Boxer rising with Chinese cinema audiences of today.[62]

Our understanding of the religious, magical and superstitious elements of the Boxer rising — the drilling, the invulnerability beliefs, the elements of hypnotic trance-like behaviour — can be amplified by a careful survey of the nianhua depicting battle scenes or scenes of individual combat. These were created by folk woodblock artists from their visual realisation of the Chinese historical traditions known so intimately by the peasantry. The connections between boxing skills and religion were multifarious and formed a very real part of the lives of many illiterate men, as shown in the nianhua print "The Xuanmiao Temple of Suzhou" (Plate 3.8).[63] In the middle foreground we see a group of tea-drinkers, by their clothing and physical bearing, members of the educated classes,[64] while virile men stripped to the waist perform boxing exercises in the foreground. Paul Cohen points out that:

> the locations of altars and boxing grounds at which possession rituals were commonly enacted were, as often as not, the very same places — the open spaces in front of temples — at which village theatrical performances were staged, in conjunction (usually) with religious festivals and fairs.[65]

The temple being an important centre of boxing activity as well as the base for martial arts sects and rural defence leagues, it is little surprising that major battles took place in temples.[66] The stance of these boxers in the Xuanmiao temple is identical with the stance of the heroes in the picture of "The Capture of Bai Juhua" (Plate 3.7, see also detail, Plate 3.5), a picture produced by another unknown artist in a completely different studio at a different time. Both pictures were drawn by artists with the same visual conception of Chinese boxing traditions. Here real life practice, actions in drama and depiction in nianhua are all fused into a particular tradition of the stance taken by a valiant hero when fighting. These traditions continued well into the twentieth century. Haideng (1902–1989) was a monk devoted to the teaching of martial arts and was asked to teach a special force of the People's Liberation Army (PLA) in Jinan. He taught them martial arts and was also fêted by PLA officers and photographed with Defence Minister Chi Haotian and Vice-President Wu Lanfu. Famous PLA officers were trained in Shaolin temple, Henan province. Xu Shiyou who performed heroically in the battle of Nanjing had had extensive training in martial arts.

Connections between boxing, triad societies, banditry and outlaws were problematic for officials and gentry alike over many generations. At the same time, the peasantry was enrolled in local militia units and drilled by village heads under gentry auspices.[67] Much of the drill they practised could as well be used to serve authority as to undermine it.[68] This selection of nianhua out of hundreds of possible and equally suitable contenders, demonstrates that as in everyday life, so in the stories, individual martial prowess and drilled ranked battle order served both good and evil, mortals and immortals in the historical romances. This concept of martial prowess, military gallantry and the triumph of the hero with the just cause was inextricably intermingled in the concept of war held by the common people. There was a fusion between nianhua of fictitious battles and nianhua of real battles; nianhua depicting mythological heroes drilling and pages out of traditional military drilling manuals of the late Qing.[69] Ultimately, there were the nianhua of real battle order and photographs of military drill showing similar battle order (see Plates 3.9, 3.10, 3.14 and Figure 3.2).[70]

The picture "Mountain of Flowers and Fruit"[71] (see Plate 3.11) shows Monkey, the hero and one of the three disciples of Monk Xuanzhang in the classic mythological novel *Journey to the West*. Monkey is commanding the military drill of the small monkeys on the mountain of flowers and fruit. In the picture, Monkey is sitting fully armoured in the upper centre while young monkeys are drilling under him. Some are charging each other in formation; others watch the fight under strict discipline.[72] A comparison between this nianhua and a page out of a drill manual for training traditional armies in the late Qing, shows that while some of the weapons being used are different, (naturally, this nianhua does not depict guns), the stances and formations of the drilling soldiers are similar. They combine the Chinese tradition of martial arts with the influence of the drill of the Manchu bannermen (see Plate 3.16 and compare this with Plate 3.9). One wonders to what extent the postures of Chinese martial arts had influenced the Manchu drill.

It is clear that the mutual influence of fiction and reality had evolved a culturally distinctive military tradition and that this tradition, illustrated by highly colourful, symbolic and stylised nianhua was accessible all over China to the poor from whose ranks came the soldiers, the rebels and the bandits. In this tradition, heroism and valour were reinforced by the stories of the great epics, glorious deeds of courage on the battlefield and the artistic depiction of both fiction and reality that was permanently on display to the rural and urban poor. The heroism, valour and glorious deeds of courage in question externalised Chinese values with respect to these qualities. As well, there was an important difference between China and the West with respect to the subject of war art; that is, the class-base of those in the pictures who could be seen to be acting with heroism and valour. In Chinese nianhua, vast numbers of ordinary soldiers were clearly the main subject of the action. In Chinese nianhua of real or fictional battles, the hero could be a much-idolised

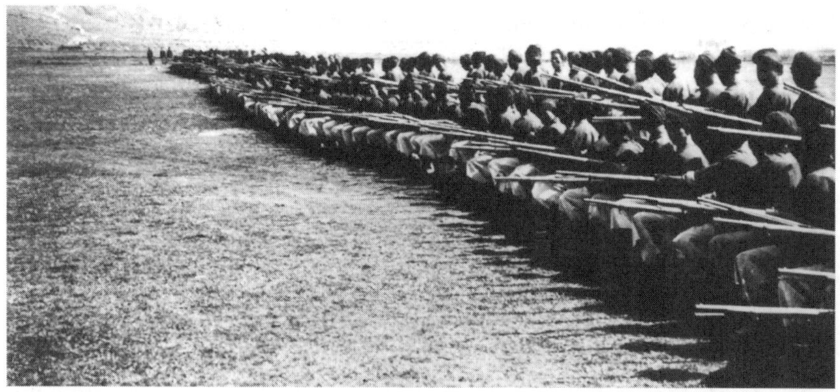

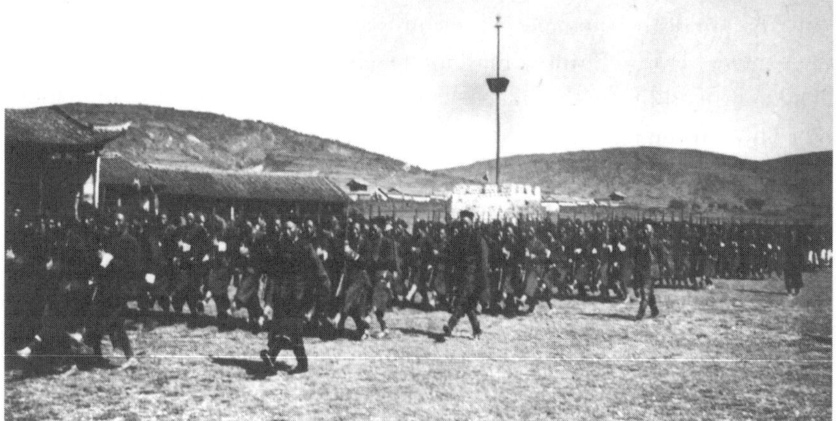

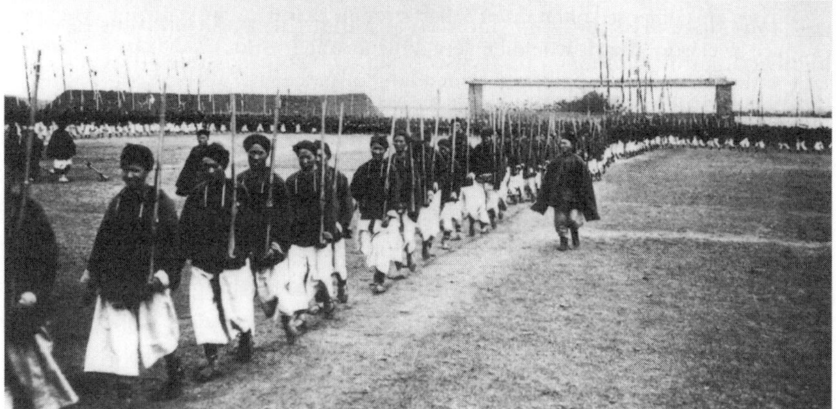

Figure 3.2 Imperial Chinese Army soldiers drilling in Yunnan, 1896–1904. (By courtesy of the Musée Guimet)

commoner who had reached official military status because of his mastery of martial arts. Such commoners who could not sit for the examinations for civilian positions were able to take the equivalent examinations for military positions and had a real chance of passing. Once in the ranks of officialdom, their martial arts training and background better equipped them for the wider variety of military engagements common in dynastic China.[73] It was only gradually in the second half of the nineteenth century, particularly in Britain, that battle painting became a socially accepted form of "high" art in the West.[74] Even then, it was decades before the common man, in the form of the ordinary soldier "dying under a bush"[75] was incorporated into either "high" art or the cheap woodcuts or prints for peasants and industrial workers or the petit bourgeoisie in images which until then were strikingly lifeless in comparison to the Chinese nianhua tradition (see Plate 3.12 and Figure 3.1).[76]

The xinwenzhi[77] depicting a real engagement with the French "Our Triumphant Military Report from Liang Shan" (Lang Son) (see Plate 3.3)[78] also shows those Chinese soldiers with traditional swords and shields adopting a similar battle stance to the drill formation of the small monkeys or to the drill books of the Manchu bannermen. As there has been so much written about the antiquated nature of the military in the late Qing,[79] it is interesting to note W. D. Bernard's observation about these shields during the First Opium War:

> They are composed of ratans or canes, strongly twisted or woven in together, and are so elastic, that it would be very difficult to cut through them with a sword; and even a musket-ball fired from a long distance and hitting them at all in a slanting direction, would be turned off.[80]

Bernard sailed with the *Nemesis* from 1840 to 1843. His account leaves us with the evidence that the shields used by the Chinese armies during action against the British in the First Opium War were not useless antiquated exotica; in fact they were more than adequate when facing British soldiers of the day. The shields had not been made to face an enemy with "superior weapons;" nonetheless they proved their worth. When held at the appropriate angle, they were effective against musket fire. Many of the nianhua depicting the battles of the Sino-French War show only a small proportion of the troops bearing shields; most are armed with rifles (see Plate 3.13).[81] This research has uncovered no photographic evidence or military intelligence reports describing the Imperial Chinese Army indicating that troops bore shields by the time of the Boxer rising.

Qing armies joined the troops of Liu Yongfu in fighting the French and the overall evidence of the nianhua points to the fact that Chinese troops of these various armies were no longer equipped with shields. There is very little pictorial evidence indicating the retention of troops bearing swords and shields by the 1880s; a notable exception is the xinwenzhi describing the battle of Liang Shan that took place on 29 March 1885 (Figure 3.3). It is possible that the character of an irregular army under such a charismatic leader as Liu Yongfu would actually, or in popular imagination, have been retained by continuing such traditional military signifiers as banners and shields.[82] The next ten to twenty years saw armies even in remote Yunnan province, as well as in Shanghai, Shandong and Tianjin adopting the modern uniforms which can be seen in the photographs in Figure 3.2 and in Chapter Six. However, at the same time, some armies under distinctive traditional leaders such as Dong Fuxiang continued to wear traditional uniforms and headgear and to contain some shield-bearing units. By the time of the Boxer rising, only two nianhua were uncovered by this research showing Chinese soldiers bearing shields. These nianhua depict a portion of the Chinese army led by Dong Fuxiang (see Plates 3.10 and 3.14). During the Boxer rising, the Muslim soldiers of General Dong's army wore traditional uniform and carried state-of-the-art weapons.[83]

In addition to what they reveal about culturally accepted visual depictions of military action, nianhua describing famous episodes from the epic historical romances and those describing real events, exhibit the same artistic traditions with respect to landscape and military architecture. Fortresses may be seen drawn in exactly the same manner whether in nianhua describing famous historical epics, such as the ruse of the empty city from *The Three Kingdoms*, or in operas, such as the nianhua describing Pan Li Hua's great defeat of Yang Fan,[84] or in nianhua depicting real events, such as "The Siege of the Beicang Cathedral During the Boxer Rising"[85] (Plate 3.16), "Land Mines in Tianjin, Victory Against the Aggressor by General Dong"[86] and "The Defeat of the French at Bac Ninh by Liu Yongfu"[87] (Plate 3.17). The fortresses in the nianhua depicting real events were not, in fact, similar in construction or appearance but the woodblock artists drew on a popular tradition which

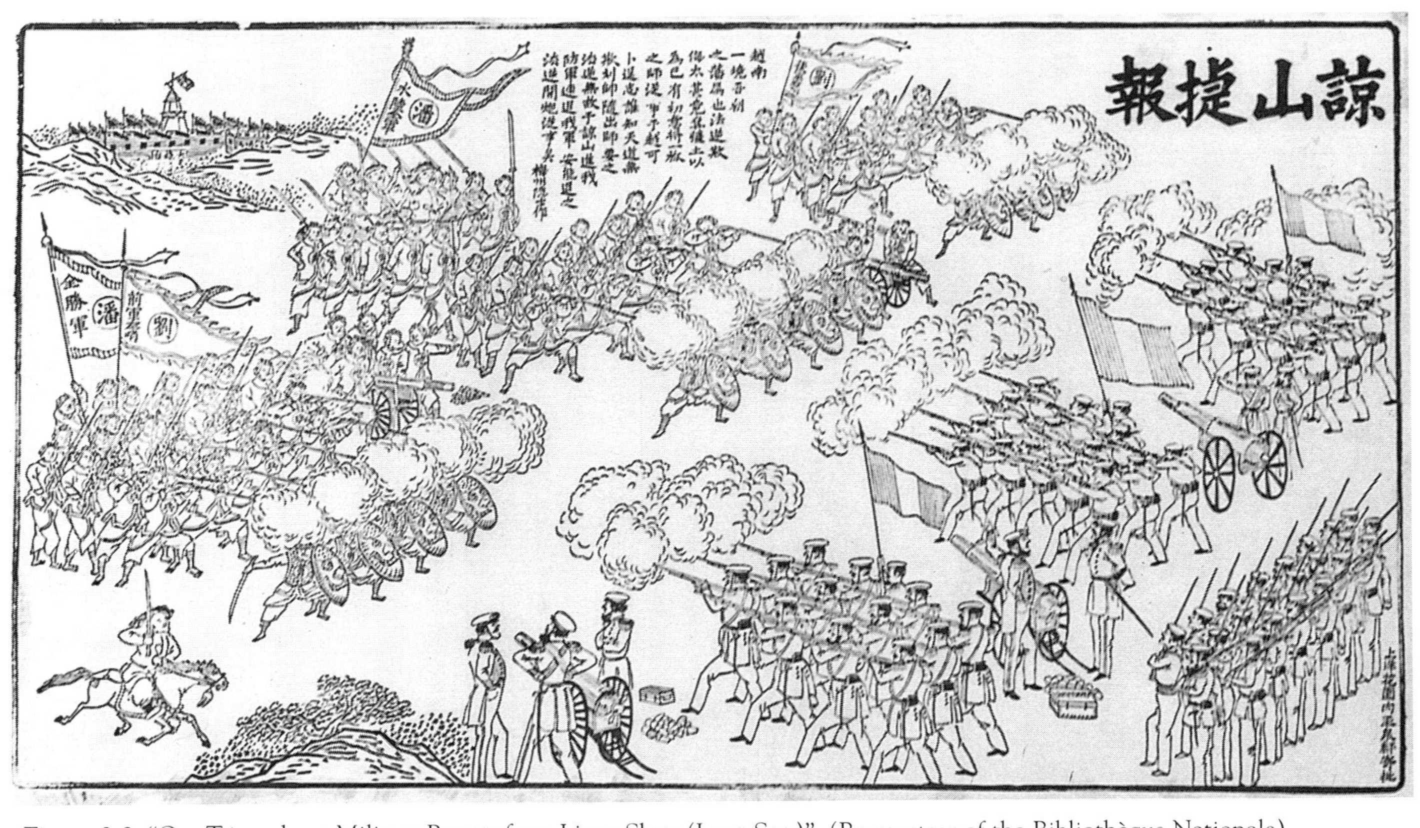

Figure 3.3 "Our Triumphant Military Report from Liang Shan (Lang Son)". (By courtesy of the Bibliothèque Nationale)

showed a military fortress drawn in a stylised way to indicate its status as such. As with the case of weapons or uniforms, an interesting point is the preservation of continuity for the audience with traditional architectural forms being generally used in nianhua while only a few actually depict new constructions to house artillery.[88]

By the 1880s in the Sino-French War and the 1900s in the Boxer rising, all the fortresses in question were equipped with modern Krupp artillery. The documentary evidence of American consuls as well as European and British military attachés describes a constant rebuilding or rearming of fortifications from 1840 to 1900. Thus while in respect of certain types of weapons and military hardware, many nianhua broke with tradition and drew the weapons and ships, for example, fairly accurately, the artists often situated the action in a traditional context using conventions well familiar to the viewer. This supports Flath's observations about nianhua as containing stereotyped visual representations.[89]

The nianhua showing Liu's defeat of the French at Bac Ninh (Bei Ning) is a good example of a stylised landscape with rocks, trees and mountains drawn in a traditional manner comparable to the nianhua of "The Battle at Chang Ban Po,"[90] a story also from *The Three Kingdoms* and also a popular opera. (See also Plate 3.6). The connections between popular and classical Chinese art are complex and range outside the purposes of this discussion, though several of the nianhua of the battles of the Sino-French War show the influence of classical Chinese art in the drawing of rocks and mountains.[91] These particular nianhua are signed with pen-names and may well be the work of artists who made a living outside the world of the traditional woodblock print studios.[92] Similarly, the nianhua depicting sea battles while, significantly relatively few in number, also show direct links with classical Chinese art.[93]

A final category in which there is a strong link between the world of romantic historical nianhua and the nianhua of real events, is that of the heroic and/or supernatural. There was a particular convention used by traditional woodblock artists to denote intervention in military (or any other) action by the immortals. This convention bears a slight resemblance to the modern convention used in cartoons to indicate speech as emanating from a particular person in a cartoon frame. Such nianhua can be commonly seen in all major published collections, some particularly good examples being in the collections edited by Maria Rudova and those by the great

Chinese scholar of the nianhua, Wang Shucun. For want of a better term, we will refer to this convention as that of a "balloon" (See, for example, Plate 3.4). Such a "balloon" may contain symbols[94] or heroes and immortals. While this convention is not common in nianhua depicting real battles, it may be seen in the nianhua of the battle of Yangcun (Plate 3.18)[95] and the nianhua of the battle for the Beicang Cathedral (Plate 3.16). Thus commonly understood folk art symbolism was harnessed by woodblock artists to indicate layers of action in real battles.

In the fictional nianhua, the "balloon" convention added symbolic meanings to military (or other) action. These meanings were well understood by the illiterate peasant audience. In fact, during real battles, there is a complex simultaneity of action that is difficult if not impossible to illustrate. Contemporary nineteenth century Western art, whether popular or "high" art, made little or no attempt to illustrate this simultaneity. Instead a single subject was most commonly chosen, often the death of a great general (a subject which present research has failed to discover — and would not expect to discover[96] — in the nianhua tradition) or, for example, a naval battle. Such a battle would typically have been depicted in "high" art as a long distance view of ships firing their cannons across a large expanse of sea with no evidence of the sailors at the guns or otherwise locked in action engagements with an enemy.[97] Commonly, European folk woodblock art showed a warship being the entire subject of the picture,[98] thus giving no indication to the audience buying the print, of any element of action, struggle, conflict and death.

Art historians of the European tradition have described the lengthy evolution of war paintings that finally came to show war as the most destructive and disruptive of the social activities of humankind.[99] The Chinese woodblock prints, though highly stylised, all make a surprisingly modern statement about the impersonal power and chaotic destruction of the force of war. This may be to do with the fact that, in contrast to European war paintings or woodblock prints, the common soldier — whether Chinese or foreign — is present everywhere, often with his leaders in his ranks. There is a powerful artistic effect in the nianhua of guns exploding, bodies flying, buildings breaking open, soldiers being executed on the field of battle, ships sinking, men floundering in the water. All these elements give the nineteenth century Chinese woodcuts a "modern" look. They display the impersonal random destructive force of war in a way that was not apparent in European art, whether "high" art or woodblock art for the masses, until the twentieth century.

Action, struggle, conflict and death were the very substance of the folk art tradition in China. Lust writes of popular art's devices for suggesting movement:

> The free flight of the Immortal is there as well as the armoury of the old Daoist magic (control of rain, thunder, etc.) and the spirit arsenals of medieval origins, the magic troops and weaponry. Combat, the simulation of flights of projectiles, spirit or secular, on the flat surface, give rise to an excitement that a designer might find irresistible, to the point of interrupting the flow of the plot[100]

The symbolism and conventions of the dramatic and romantic historical traditions of the nianhua were ideally suited to conveying the variety and intensity of battle as well as the distance from their own humanity, actually required by men who had to fight in battle. Chinese pictorial traditions emphasised the heroic stances of valorous fighting men.

The more complex realms of art criticism lie completely beyond the province of this study. The interest here is in what nianhua tell us about the wars in question and about Chinese folk woodblock traditions regarding the evocation of warfare as well as in the new factual material introduced, material that had never been part of any Chinese tradition. The nianhua reproduced here were ideally suited to convey a pictorial sense of the clamour, the confusion, the collective and individual heroism and the heroic stirring of men's minds and hearts in battle.

The nianhua of real battles differ from the nianhua of fictional battles. In the latter, highly formulaic stock scenes were presented while the former, from the nianhua of the First Opium War to those of the Boxer War, all contain some kinds of detail which stamp them as having departed, even if only slightly, from the conventions of the traditional nianhua. It must be emphasised that the heroism we see displayed in the nianhua, the hearts and minds that are stirred, are almost always those of the ordinary soldier/peasant. His general or commanding officer may be seen in the picture, usually distinguished because he is mounted, but aside from that distinction, he is one more heroic man fighting. The nianhua make him no greater or less than his men. These elements were present in an entirely different heroic mode in Western "high" art which effectively obliterated the blood and guts of soldiers killing and being killed, concentrating instead on the bloodless deaths of the heroic commanding officers.[101]

The symbolic representation of supernatural elements common in the historical nianhua, added a further artistic technique potentially able to indicate simultaneous action on the battlefield. It also showed an element of quasi religious intervention. Such intervention might commonly have been interpreted — in the case of the two nianhua of action in the Boxer rising mentioned above (Plates 3.16 and 3.18) — as the importance of mighty forces for good fighting on the side of the Boxers in their struggle to combat evil in the form of the pervasive foreign invasion of China. This intrusion was brought to a violent head by an inflamed peasantry holding strong views about good and evil and the necessity of fighting to preserve the former and to crush the latter.

In summary, it is clear that there was a Chinese folk art tradition adept at describing the drama of war, the confusion and consequences of close combat and a multitude of separate simultaneous engagements on the same battlefield. Plate 3.12, "The Defence of Paris" is a woodblock print produced for mass sale, to which, incidentally, many of Paret's comments on the nature and composition of "high" art are relevant. It is typical of European woodblock prints depicting warfare. A comparison between this print and the nianhua of battles, shows that the parallel Chinese tradition had a liveliness and a force, and above all, a profusion of common men fighting, nowhere apparent in its Western counterparts.[102] This profusion of common men fighting is more particularly noted in the nianhua of real battles than in those of fictional battles. In the latter, there are conventions to indicate the chaos of war while in the former, we see the woodblock artists struggling as individuals[103] to reproduce the chaos of war. (See Plate 3.23) The nianhua drew on the illustrations of the great Chinese historical religious and romantic historical epic novels, dramas and plays. As these literary works were imbued with ethical values and commentaries on heroism, valour, chivalry, good and evil, the folk artists developed artistic symbols and conventions to illustrate these values in woodblock pictures of fictitious battles. The pictures of real battles could be expected to contain and to convey many of these same symbols and values.

As the nianhua began to show modern weapons and modern uniforms, so there was also the beginning of the depiction of military formations and postures outside traditional conventional understanding derived from opera and romantic historical novels. The protagonists were drawn in action which showed not only the nature of their modern weapons[104] but also the posture[105] and formations adopted to fight with these weapons, either in hand-to-hand conflict or in larger scale infantry clashes or cavalry duels. The nianhua formed a bridge between the Chinese military culture associated with traditional uniforms, weapons, fortifications and foreign military culture associated with the concepts of soldiering and the modern ways being adopted by the modernised Chinese armies. They had a vital function as purveyors of information about new elements in soldiering and warfare to the masses of illiterate people all over China.[106] Both Western and Chinese sources alluded to the fact that the issue of modern, i.e. foreign-style uniform, for example, was a paramount consideration with Chinese military leaders insofar as the effect uniform would have on the peasantry.[107]

Nianhua showed men fighting using postures and in formations which derived from fictional historic-religious martial arts traditions and elements of Manchu drilling, a combination actually practised by peasants in preparation for small-scale militia action. All these fictional and actual military characteristics were incorporated by woodblock artists into pictures showing real military events. James Flath's observes that:

> The challenge of writing cultural history through predominantly graphic texts begins by defining which structures were most relevant to the society in question and how the structures were understood and configured through the graphic text[108]

Making specific Flath's general observation, it can be seen that the nianhua showed in what ways warfare was relevant to and understood by the common people and how it entered their very lives. These characteristics of the nianhua can be seen to have been influential in determining the ethos, the practice and the whole environment in which the peasantry of Shandong began drilling in 1899 and conceived of their military intervention against the unwelcome foreign presence in 1900. These characteristics illustrated the entirety of the world out of which most of the peasants on the North China Plain conceived the morality and the nature of their military moves.[109] There had been successful peasant military action against foreign intervention before, notably in Guangzhou during the First Opium War and in Fuzhou during the Sino-French War. The fury of the Boxer movement swept the missionaries out of North China and brought foreign trade to a standstill. The Boxer rising is steeped in the visual imagery drawn by folk artists for the peasants (as opposed to illustrated anti-foreign literature produced under gentry auspices).[110] This imagery gave life, colour, and a strong indication of the morality behind Chinese mass cultural traditions regarding military action and its righteousness. The nianhua tradition was thus enormously important in shaping peasant concepts of justification of war, conduct of war, victory in war and valour in action.

The Nianhua as Evidence of a Distinctively Chinese Way of Looking at the Results of Clashes Between Chinese and Foreigners

There are two important collections of nianhua of actual military action between Chinese and various European powers in the nineteenth century. One of these consists of thirty-two nianhua of the Sino-French War held in the Bibliothèque Nationale in Paris. Another of thirty to forty nianhua, many of which describe the Boxer rising and other battles with foreigners, is housed in the British Library.[111] Apart from these collections, research has uncovered nianhua depicting war in published collections of nianhua and scattered in various museums and libraries around the world.[112] There are also nianhua to be found in published works used as illustrations by authors writing at the time about the particular war in question.[113]

Before going on to analyse some nianhua showing real wars, it is of interest to note that these nianhua have received no attention in English or Chinese language scholarship. The literature concentrates on nianhua devoted to prosperity, good wishes, boy children, historical romances and opera.[114] Official censorship occasionally suppressed other popular art forms, particularly drama and opera. The woodblock artisans were free to produce prints of subject matter of their own choosing, a significantly different situation from that prevailing in European countries, particularly France and Germany at this time.[115] Given this freedom and given that woodblock folk art studios were business propositions, we must conclude that when any new run of prints was mooted, the tastes and interests of the rural and urban poor were a dominant consideration. John Lust describes the process whereby:

> the master supplied an uncoloured draft which was expected to be impeccable [and] was hung up for discussion by the [studio] team on its quality, its likely impact and reception by the public.[116]

It is no coincidence that the majority of the nianhua depicting real wars date from the Sino-French conflict. The demonstrations of fury on the part of the common people after the French destruction of Fuzhou, can be singled out as one of the several most ferocious manifestations of anti-foreign feeling in the nineteenth century.[117] In producing large numbers and many print runs of these nianhua, the woodblock studios mirrored the intense interest in the war as well as a perception of a striking change in the traditional concepts of warfare.

The increasing tempo and geographical spread of foreign encroachment into many parts of the Chinese hinterland was judged with acute prescience by woodblock studios and some individual woodblock artists[118] to be a new issue arousing violent popular resentment. This unwanted foreign presence added a new dimension to the peasant world view and found expression in bitterness about economic, religious and social changes seen to be provoked or instigated by foreigners. Such changes began to be witnessed almost daily by more and more peasants. The peasantry attributed the undesired changes to foreign intervention in all aspects of their daily lives.[119] The nianhua depicting battles with foreigners indicate, among other things, a popular perception that issues of justice, valour, good and evil had ceased to be entirely generated by and satisfactorily interpreted through traditional Chinese folk art forms. The nianhua depicting real wars, though relatively and absolutely few in number, gave immediate expression to changes forced by foreigners on the Chinese peasantry and the illiterate urban poor; changes to which they had already begun to respond with savage outbursts.

The Roman Catholic cathedral in Tianjin was burned down and many nuns and priests were killed in 1870, ten years before the Sino-French War. No nianhua depicting this event have been uncovered by this research but it is unlikely that there were none made and sold.[120] Thanks to the nianhua, changes at the village level caused by small numbers of foreigners could now also be discussed[121] by peasants in the context of war between China and hitherto unknown specific foreign countries. The element of discussion involving a number of people viewing a nianhua together as they stood in a common public space was extremely important in Chinese popular culture.

The importance of the nianhua lies not merely in what people saw, how they saw it — that is in what cultural context and tradition of looking — but also in what they provoked people to *say* to each other about it. The nianhua and their captions provided new information and new subjects of discussion to the illiterate rural and urban poor while being presented in the continuum of traditional forms they understood. It is for this reason that the nianhua showing wars between China and foreign countries constitute vital evidence of rapid and radical changes in mass perceptions of patriotism.

The most concrete evidence concerning the geographic spread of these nianhua and re-issues of them in new crisis situations comes from foreigners who saw them and complained about them. Nianhua showing real wars were seen by foreign business men, missionaries and diplomatic representatives in all major coastal cities as well as Tianjin, Beijing and smaller towns throughout Zhili, Shandong, Guandong and Yunnan. Comments on the re-issue of these prints date from the 1880s and some of the prints carry evidence of being re-issued.

The Opium War and the Development of Chinese Military Technology

The first nianhua devoted to a real battle uncovered by this research describes an incident in the Opium War, the battle of Foshan. It was originally printed in colour and is reproduced in black and white in Cyril Field's work (Figure 3.3).[122] In view of the widely accepted cliché — still current in accounts of fighting during the Boxer rising — that Chinese soldiers feared hand-to-hand combat, Bernard's eye-witness testimony should be emphasised:

> As far as personal bravery could aid them, they were by no means an enemy to be despised. The spear and the bayonet frequently crossed each other; *perhaps more frequently than the bayonets of Europeans do,* [emphasis added] — and in not a few instances, the *long* [Bernard's emphasis] spear was *more than a match for the shorter bayonet* [emphasis added] ... indeed, many of our men learnt to their cost, that they had held the Chinese far too cheap.[123]

The concept of honour in close fighting is a cultural one, and therefore unsusceptible to any single definition. It forms part of the various histories and traditions of soldiers from many different nations. There have been scathing comments on the courage of the Chinese soldiery made by late

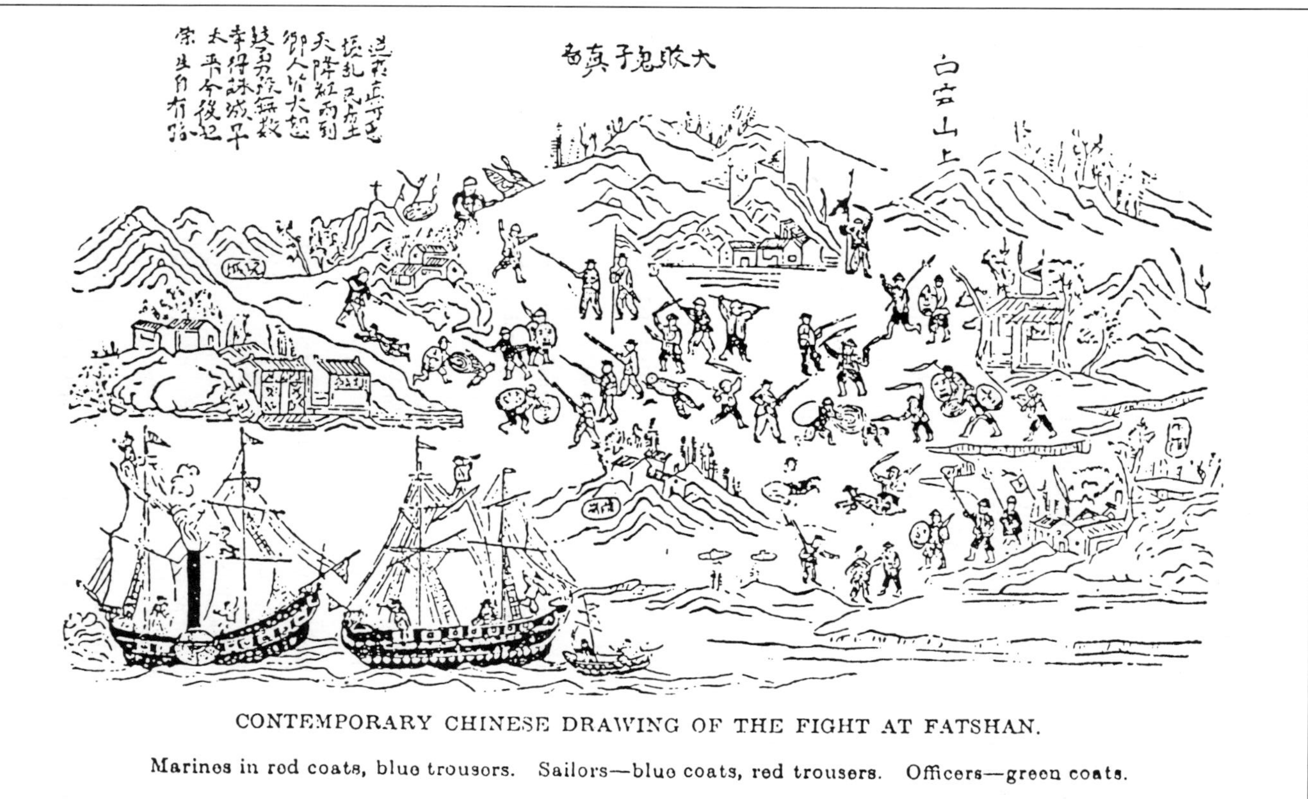

CONTEMPORARY CHINESE DRAWING OF THE FIGHT AT FATSHAN.

Marines in red coats, blue trousers. Sailors—blue coats, red trousers. Officers—green coats.

Figure 3.4 "The Battle of Fatshan."

nineteenth and twentieth century writers who have no contemporary eye witness evidence on which to base these comments. Thus we need to stress that the Chinese did, in fact, measure up to contemporary European military cultural values in this and other respects, such as their willingness and ability to fight at night which Westerners believed them incapable of until the action in the Boxer rising.[124] However, in other cultures there were warriors who saw no dishonour in fighting at a distance as the Crusaders found when they fought the Muslims.[125]

This nianhua is contemporary with that referred to by Wang Shucun "Firing the Cannon at Captain Charles Elliot" (1839).[126] A number of interesting observations can be made about the way the combatants are depicted. The long-tailed coats and trousers of the British military uniform at this time are realistically portrayed in the centre background. The stance and posture of the two British officers on board ship looking through telescopes is accurately re-created and it is obvious that the British are being attacked by peasant groups with no common specifically military attire and no overall leadership. While the British soldiers are armed with muskets and attached bayonets, the Chinese peasants do not appear to have any standardised weaponry. They all carry shields, those same shields that the Englishman Bernard pronounced at the time to be very effective. For the rest, they appear to be armed with a selection of metal-tipped pikes and short swords singled out by the same observer to be formidable weapons:

> [the English] were frequently compelled to charge with the bayonet for the Chinese, who hovered about them, seeing that they could not use their firelocks [they were fighting in a thunderstorm] came boldly up to attack them with their long spears, which are formidable from their length.[127]

From this quote, we see the much-vaunted European "superiority in firepower" to have been a very limited one indeed. A great deal of the action during the First Opium War took place in the rain or in humid conditions prohibitive to successful use of muskets which still had to be hand-filled with gunpowder.[128] One writer, drawing on Bernard wrote that:

> The British troops had to resort to the bayonet, which proved sometimes not a very successful weapon when matched against the long spears of the Chinese, and put the British momentarily at a disadvantage.[129]

Keegan's generalisation is an excellent example of one of the myths which have formed in the Western mind about Chinese military preparedness and capacity, based as it is on no particular eyewitness account of any specific military action:

> There is no more pathetic episode in military history than that of the Manchu bannermen of the nineteenth century pitting their outmatched composite bows against the rifles and cannon of the European invaders.[130]

Zhang Junbo and Yao Yunzhu write at length of the difference between Western military philosophy which places the highest regard on the power and modernity of weaponry in contrast with the Chinese military philosophy which stresses the human factor in war.[131] This Western tradition may be seen in the French and American performance in Indo-China. For both the French and the Americans "Technology became a necessary force multiplier, sustaining the initiative by substituting shock and firepower for numbers."[132]

The nianhua of the First Opium War depicts a mêlée in which neither the British soldiers nor the Chinese peasants clearly have the upperhand. In the centre middle ground there are three British marines advancing in what may be a regular formation, while in the right foreground Chinese peasants may be seen in an orderly advance proceeding from the village to kill and capture British marines. There is nothing at all in this woodblock print to indicate any kind of caricature of the foreign invaders. The drawings of the British soldiers, while primitive, convey a realistic depiction of their appearance, stance and weaponry in the sense that a European, looking at this woodcut would recognise with ease the style of the British uniforms of the day and the bodily postures of the British soldiers. Moreover, in one coloured copy of the print under disucssion, the marines were depicted in red coats and blue trousers, the sailors in blue coats and red trousers and the officers in green coats. While colours of clothing may have been changed in reprints of some kinds of nianhua, the nianhua discussed in this chapter show a remarkable fidelity to accuracy of colour and particularly to accuracy of line in reprints showing foreign soldiers' uniforms and foreign national flags. This can be seen in the discussion below of the print "The Chinese Take the City of Bac Ninh by Assault" that was re-issued as a print showing the fighting in the Boxer War.

A large quantity of accurate information had been communicated to the artisans responsible for the Opium War print. The artisans, in their turn, have produced a depiction of an enemy, not some stylised grotesque monsters. If the folk artist in question had not actually seen British soldiers, this would argue strongly that folk artists actively sought information which would enable them to reproduce the hated foreign intruders as accurately as possible rather than to caricature them. Caricature was an element in other genres of folk art depicting invading foreign soldiers (see Figure 3.5) but it is not to be seen in the nianhua. If the artists had seen foreign soldiers, the ability to reproduce their military bearing is notable. Information about colours of uniforms and flags could easily be conveyed to the artist; less tangible was the factor of the military bearing of the foreign soldiers. This is so aptly conveyed in the nianhua discussed in this chapter that it is difficult not to assume that some of the artists had been to some big coastal city where they could have seen foreign soldiers. Thereafter, other artists, formed in a tradition that allowed for stereotyping, would have been able to re-create foreign military bearing from prints they had seen that showed foreign soldiers.

The caption on the Opium War print "A Real Picture of Defeating Foreign Ghosts" contains no unnecessarily inflammatory language about the British. They are described as "really abominable" because they molested villagers and plundered their houses. This was however, quite typical of the contemporary behaviour of any large group of bandits, pirates or rebels in South China. Naturally, this is undesirable aggression but, as such, there is nothing about it making it particularly horrendous or offensive in the cultural context as understood by both sides. The caption goes on to say that fortunately this enemy was destroyed early so that peace will certainly be assured. It is this kind of wording that made foreigners so indignant about nianhua, a common reaction being that these woodblock prints gave a completely false picture of the military engagements in question.

However, as the British did withdraw on this — and many future occasions — the caption seemed a reasonable summary from the point of view of the artisans producing a print of the engagement for Chinese peasants. They knew that vast numbers of peasants, from 7,000 to 8,000 men, had turned out on several occasions, notably in late May 1841 on the heights around Guangzhou. They also knew that the British had not been able to disperse them and that the numbers of Chinese peasants threatening the British increased daily. Finally, on the authority of a Chinese official, the peasants understood that they were to disperse and all the British warships left

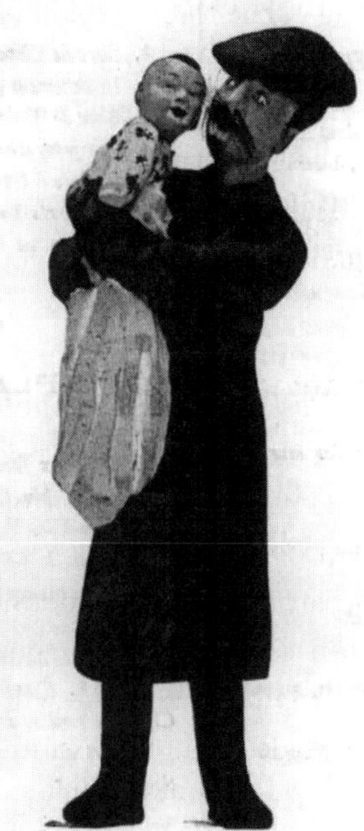

Figure 3.5 Clay statue of French soldier made and sold in Tianjin, 1900.

Guangzhou by the first week of June. Looked at from the eyes of the Chinese who had seen or heard about this conflict, purchased this print and had the text read to them, it would have appeared to be an accurate summary of the action.

To contemporary Westerners, to Westerners discussing the fate of China at the turn of the last century, and for subsequent Western scholarship, it seemed clear that the Chinese had lost the Opium War under particularly humiliating circumstances due to technological inferiority.[133] This constitutes a difference of view point regarding victory and defeat that contains cultural factors more complex than those embodied in the old adage "they won the battle but they lost the war." On the literary level, the level at which the Chinese court and civilian and military leaders operated, military philosophy was embodied in the ideas of Sun Zi, not Clausewitz. To be sure, Clausewitz had not as yet written down his ideas but the European cultural conception of warfare that led to his writings was already in evidence by the 1840s.

For the Chinese, on the contrary, war was certainly not always regarded as an extension of state politics to be fought to the absolute end using absolutely every resource. Moreover, despite Chinese traditional military culture stressing the human factor rather than the weapons factor, it would be a gross misrepresentation to portray Chinese military and civilian leadership of the day as uninterested in progress in weapons technology. Anyone wanting to make a serious evaluation of China's technological progress in response to wars with foreigners from 1839 onwards,[134] should note that during the actual course of the Opium War itself, the Chinese constructed war vessels with important modifications based on the observations they had made of enemy ships.[135] Knowledge of these technological modifications spread almost instantaneously to all areas of China in which improved defence technology was deemed urgently needed.[136] That is, that in point of speed in adaptation to contemporary foreign naval technology, the Chinese performed remarkably well by international standards. Chinese performance in the development of military technology between 1870 and 1900 will be discussed in detail in Chapter Six in the context of the general view in the literature that performance in this area was lamentable. It is therefore of interest to note that active interest in technological progress related to military affairs was an on-going factor, at least from the time of the Qianlong Emperor.

In less than the space of two years during the First Opium War, the

Chinese invented, manufactured and deployed artillery pieces and even gun carriages with important and effective modifications copied from the enemy. They also manufactured and deployed war vessels with, relatively speaking, massive technological advances, while throwing up new and vastly improved fortifications.[137] Of weighty significance in forming a judgement on Chinese ability to adapt swiftly to new technology even during the actual course of a war, is the fact that during the First Opium War a work called *Essentials of Gunnery* published in 1643 was reprinted in 1841. This work was written by the Jesuit Adam Schall in conjunction with a Chinese colleague.[138] The optimum use of artillery can thus be seen to have been a clear priority for the Chinese military. There already was some Chinese language literature on the subject and they reprinted this literature at the first sign of a requirement for maximum information when they perceived the nature and strength of British aggression.

There have been too many disparaging generalisations made about war junks. Chapter Six contains a photograph of some particularly effectively armed war junks, possibly used in action against the pirate-infested waters of South China. (See Figures 6.5, 6.6a and 6.6b). In the most recent literature on the First Opium War there is still a tendency to write confidently of British naval superiority based on British use of shallow drafted vessels.[139] The fact was that the British, two of their ships being hors de combat or insufficiently powerful, "ordered shell-guns to be fitted in three of the captured war-junks, to assist in the attack upon the French Folly."[140] These junks were later fully described by Bernard in terms of "their extreme ingenuity"[141] Thus it was the Chinese war junks, noted by Bernard as being immaculately kept, mounted with heavy guns, neatly stored fire-buckets and coiled ropes, that were able to support the British heavy artillery. Ironically then, the subsequent successful British naval action was only made possible by the use of Chinese war junks, British vessels being inadequate for the conditions. The argument that British naval superiority was responsible for all outcomes during the First Opium War is clearly unsustainable. Revisionist scholarship has already begun to give credit to the Chinese in respect of their speedy capacity to adopt desired Western technology.[142]

The nianhua were accurate reflections of the way the incidents of the First Opium War appeared to the peasants. Thus for many peasants who did not come into direct contact with the foreigners, folk art had begun to produce a broad view of foreign intervention in China, and its consequences. This view contained traditional elements but also conveyed new information that can be recognised today as accurate when compared with other visual representations of conflict between Chinese and foreigners at this time. In the main, the texts written on the nianhua also constitute verifiably accurate descriptions of the military action in question. On the peasant level, the level of those who fought in the First Opium War and suffered its consequences in their own villages, it was clear that the foreigners had appeared, bombed military and civilian installations and departed. It was also quite evident that they had left after mass peasant mobilisation that had been dispersed by the Chinese authorities. The peasants were not to know that the British, unable or unwilling to disburse the peasants through military action, had ordered Chinese officials to send the peasants back to their villages.[143] Thus in the cultural understanding of both ruling class and peasantry, the overall effect of the British having destroyed some war junks, some guns and a few gun emplacements as well as some civilian property was insignificant, physically, culturally and politically, in comparison with the fact that they had left. Here again, there is a clear example of contemporary Chinese understanding of victory being very different from the foreign — in this case, the British — understanding of victory:

> ... among the large-scale mortifications were a number of less spectacular but significant triumphs: at the government level, for instance, the diplomatic successes and at the level of ordinary Chinese people, successful acts of resistance to foreign powers.[144]

We must be very careful indeed when attributing the word "humiliation" to the feelings of Chinese peasants and officials after the events of 1839–1840. From this discussion, it would seem clear that the nianhua reflected the perception of Chinese peasants — and would certainly have been a part of official thinking — and that they were not humiliated at all. It is this very phenomenon connected with the nianhua, namely the inability or refusal of the Chinese to perceive defeat, that angered foreigners up to and including the Sino-Japanese War of 1894–1895.

Lucien Bodard is another writer who makes the points that the European victory was a hollow one even in the eyes of the victors, let alone the eyes of the Chinese and also that what appeared indicative of triumph and victory in Europe seemed meaningless in Beijing not only to the Chinese but to the

Europeans concerned. Writing of the British and French triumphal entry into Beijing in 1860, Bodard makes it clear that all aspects of Chinese response to the British and French "victory" robbed that "victory" of meaning to the extent that the foreign commanders began to feel that they had "lost face."[145] It would take an accumulation of such instances, the development of mass media and the actual ability of the foreigners to enforce the treaties they signed with China on the basis of these minor military forays, before Chinese people of all classes could culturally recognise and accept that they had, in fact, suffered a major defeat and, consequently, to feel humiliation. In commenting on the impact of the First Opium War at the time, we cannot definitely ascribe to Chinese officials and Chinese peasants ideas that came to take root in the Chinese psyche only after many more military engagements with foreigners.[146]

Chinese Folk Artists' Impressions of Foreign Soldiery

Isolated nianhua have survived depicting various Chinese engagements with the French, the Japanese, the Russians and other representatives of the eight Powers involved in the suppression of the Boxer rising. The form of the nianhua continued to be used into the 1920s (Figure 3.6).[147] Rather than analyse a narrowly selected group of nianhua, a better way of demonstrating Chinese folk artists' ability to recreate the unknown within the bounds of the traditional, is to survey the nianhua of actual battles as widely as possible.

The First and Second Opium Wars were very rapid affairs sprung quickly on the Chinese. The Sino-French War lasted long enough for artists in the huabao tradition to be sent by their employers to the battle lines. Insofar as the depiction of war is concerned, it is improbable that very many of the Chinese woodblock artisans ever went to the battle lines in any of the conflicts before 1880. That they produced such stirring prints is testimony to the vast treasury of pictorial emphasis on war in Chinese popular culture and in Imperially-sponsored commemoration of war.[148] Whether the woodblocks were of real or imaginary wars, popular art expressed the Chinese cultural view of everything implied by war: heroism, valour, death, destruction, triumph and disaster.

The prints discussed in this chapter show small but significant differences in detail more than in style or content, depending whether they depict actual

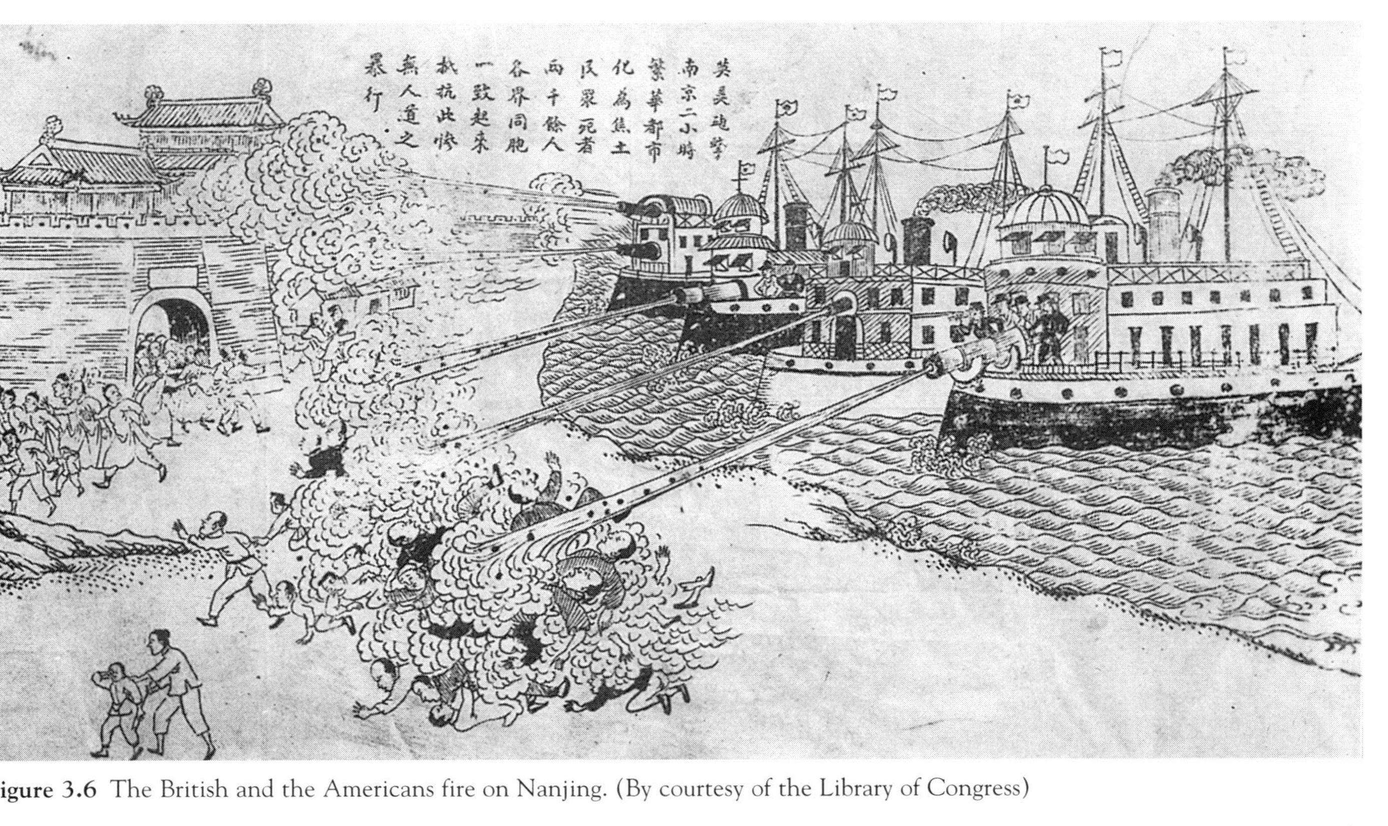

Figure 3.6 The British and the Americans fire on Nanjing. (By courtesy of the Library of Congress)

wars or well-known fictional battles. Colours of uniform, the correct rendition of the flags of various foreign countries, types of weaponry, foreign military formations as well as intangible details such as the bearing of foreign soldiers — by no means homogenous — a detachment of Sikh cavalry sat on horseback quite differently to a detachment of Cossacks — all these pieces of information constituted a new set of data about foreigners that was being brought into the world of the rural and urban poor by artists using the folk woodblock tradition. This factual, media-type element was not the case with nor part of the intended multiplicity of the traditional functions of the fictional nianhua. Elsewhere we have noted that it was a regrettable but discernable phenomenon that artists drawing for newspapers in Western countries learnt more about China during times of military clashes. It would seem from this discussion that this was possibly also a factor for Chinese woodblock artists in studios outside Shanghai and Tianjin. On any trip into the city, these artists would have had countless opportunities to see foreign soldiery on all sorts of ordinary and ceremonial occasions. They may also have got information from the great Chinese illustrated weekly, the *Dianshizhai huabao*. However, this huabao and others were not printed in colour. As few mistakes in details of colouring have been found in any of the nianhua of real battles, we may conclude that woodblock artists had seen these kinds of details or were concerned about this kind of accuracy, and deliberately sought for and applied this knowledge with precision within the nianhua tradition when they produced prints of real wars from the Opium War onwards.

The Chinese were also aware of the importance of eyewitness reporting of war. The work of woodblock artists and professional illustrators shows that whenever there was an opportunity, Chinese artists were sent to report on war or preparations for war.[149] The big nianhua studios outside Tianjin and the centres for distribution of nianhua and xinwenzhi at Shanghai and Guangzhou were all places where folk artists and woodblock artisans would have been able to go and see foreign soldiers engaged in peacetime activities such as firing salutes for ceremonial purposes, standing on guard duty in the foreign concessions and forming guards of honour for visiting Chinese and foreign dignitaries.[150] They would have had the opportunity to see their uniforms, their distinctive military way of standing, marching and deploying their weapons.

In the discussion of the print of the First Opium War, we noted that the artist had captured the exact way a European sailor or officer would stand when looking through a telescope. Similarly, the print showing Liu Yongfu's defeat of the French at Bac Ninh gives an excellent rendition of a senior French officer on horseback urging on his men to scale a city wall (Plate 3.17).[151] It is not merely the uniform that captures a culture-specific type of authority constituting the stance and bearing of Western military leaders, it is also the way the officer is drawn seated on horseback. Even the drawing of the horse itself shows an awareness on the part of the artist that Western cavalry and its officers were trained to ride their mounts quite differently from their Chinese counterparts (See details at Platess 3.18a and 3.18b). A comparison with two mounted Chinese officers in the right hand foreground shows that uniforms, weapons, drill, concept of appropriate comportment under battle conditions, even the horse itself[152] were completely different and accurately drawn by the artist to show this difference. Though there were Western-drilled Chinese troops involved in these battles, the woodblock artists continued to draw Chinese soldiers the way their public wanted to see them: in traditional uniform dress and mostly in traditional battle formation. The first nianhua showing Western influence in uniform and battle formation uncovered in this research were printed to illustrate the Boxer rising.

Another print depicting a surprise encounter between Admiral Sun Junmen and Admiral Courbet at night (Plate 3.19)[153] also shows a remarkable internalisation by the Chinese artist of the differences in bearing (and therefore the different cultural attitudes towards military training and to command) between senior Chinese and French officers. The differences between rank and file Chinese and French soldiers is also accurately conveyed. An essential point grasped by the Chinese woodblock artist is that a foreign general is larger in stature than one of his own soldiers. One would hesitate to characterise the drawing of the French officer depicted in this print as outright parody. He is as much characteristic of French officers of the era as the drawing of Admiral Sun Junmen is characteristic of a hero in a romantic historical story depicted by a nianhua. Admiral Sun is instantly familiar as showing the influence of the theatrical make-up and posture of a hero of *The Three Kingdoms* in a nianhua of the time or in a romantic historical film made in the 1990s. A comparison between the depiction of Admiral Sun Junmen and a number of the characters in Plate 3.3, particularly Zhu Hu and Zhu Lung makes this point clear. The stylised military door gods may also have been in the back of the artist's mind when he was drawing the facial features of Admiral Sun Junmen.[154]

While any Chinese peasant would see the connection between Admiral Sun Junmen and one of the heroes of *The Three Kingdoms*, French viewers would also recognise by his stance alone, that Admiral Courbet is a high-ranking French officer. By stance and facial features alone, irrespective of uniform, he could not, for example, be a British or a German senior officer. The fact that Courbet is on foot and has been taken by surprise is sufficient to account for his discomfort. There is no deliberate intent to parody. French viewers of the day had been exposed to countless paintings and prints particularly of Napoleon, horsed, dignified, all a great soldier and leader should be. They were accustomed to paintings of other great admirals and generals dying nobly and bloodlessly while anonymous soldiers out of view in the very distant background were winning the battles. Thus it would have required quite a mental effort to see a French admiral at a disadvantage, let alone at the mercy of a Chinese admiral. Nevertheless a French viewer would have recognised — and still does recognise in this woodcut — an accurate representation of a senior French officer.

This discussion has centred on the officers. It should also be noted that the stance and bearing of the Chinese soldiers illustrate much of what has been said earlier about the influence of martial arts and some of the weapons used in martial arts. The stance of foreign rank and file soldiers is depicted quite differently. The dominant impression conveyed by the representation of the two French soldiers is one of complete confusion, although again, there is nothing about the facial features of the soldier facing Admiral Courbet, or of Courbet himself for that matter, to indicate a deliberate caricature.

Nianhua showing foreign soldiery, particularly senior officers, almost without exception create a faithful likeness of the uniform, stance and bearing of foreign soldiers of the day, no matter how small the officer might be in the overall context of the picture. In the centre of the foreign lines in the nianhua, "English and French Forces Engaged in Battle with the Boxers" (Plate 3.10), we see three officers on horseback. The two closest to the viewer are drawn in such a manner as to capture exactly the body language of mounted foreign officers in action. A comparison with the mounted Chinese officer occupying a similar position in the opposing battle line shows the accuracy with which the woodblock artist has portrayed two completely

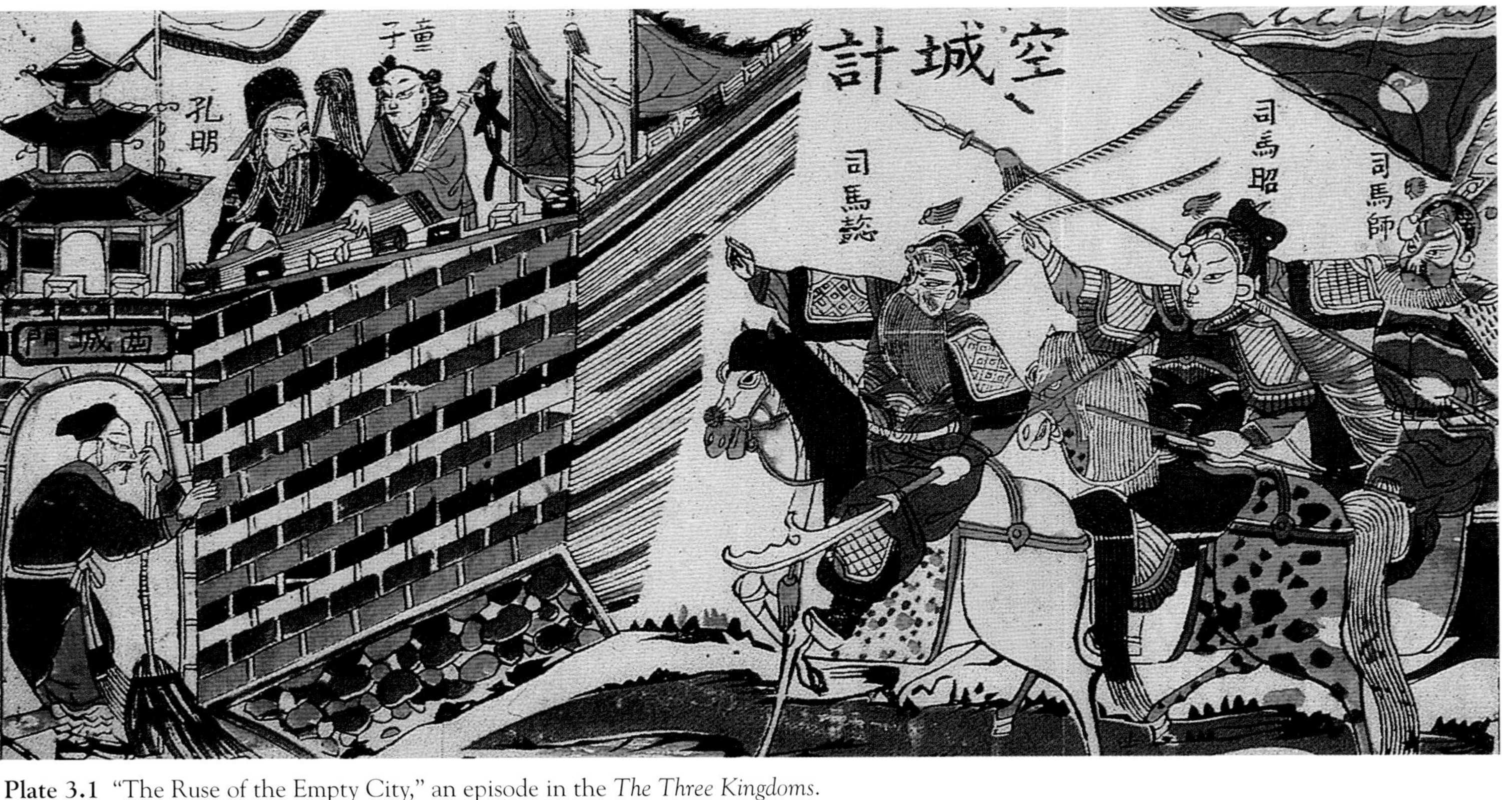

Plate 3.1 "The Ruse of the Empty City," an episode in the *The Three Kingdoms*.

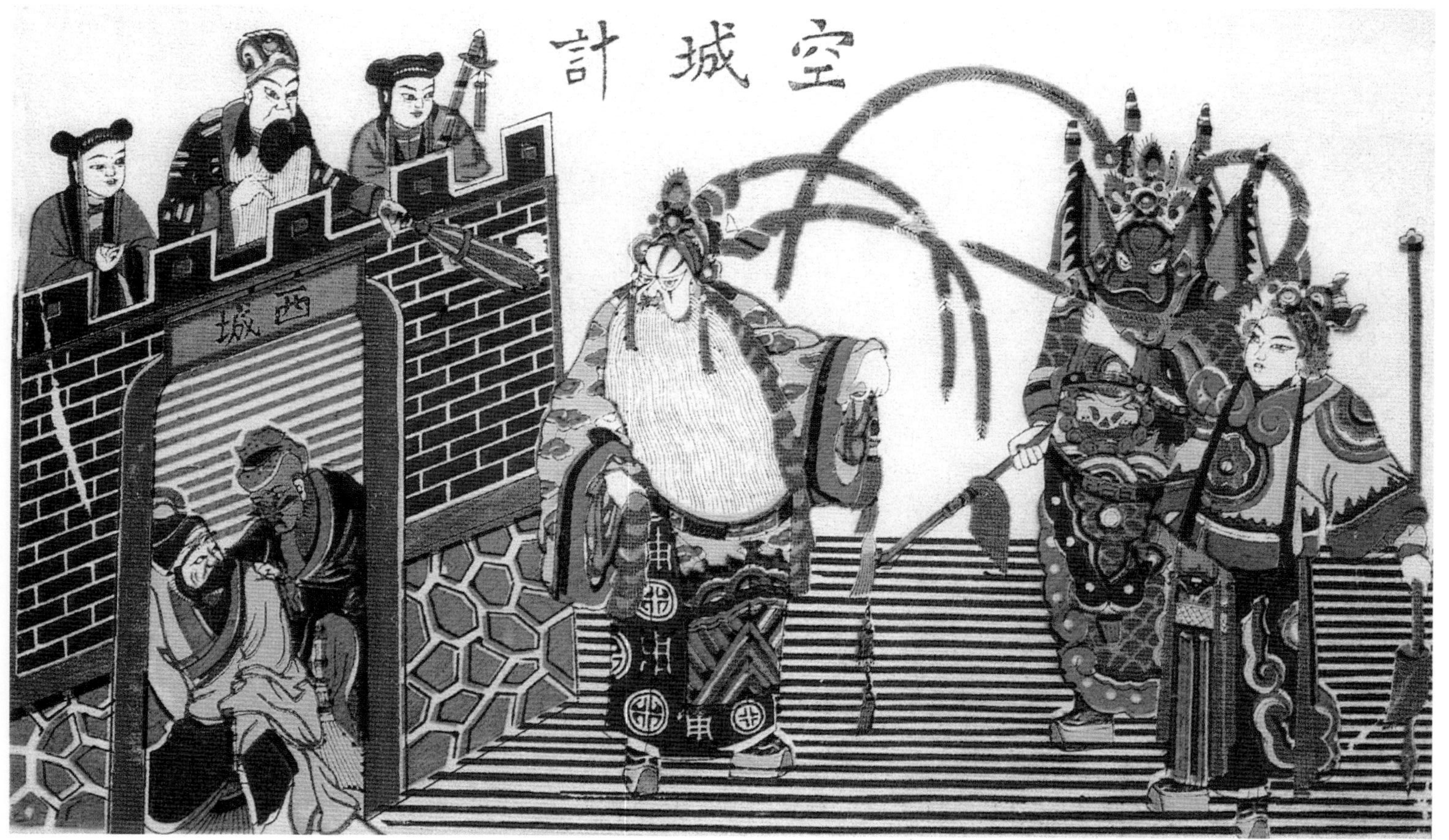

Plate 3.2 "The Ruse of the Empty City," an episode in *The Three Kingdoms*.

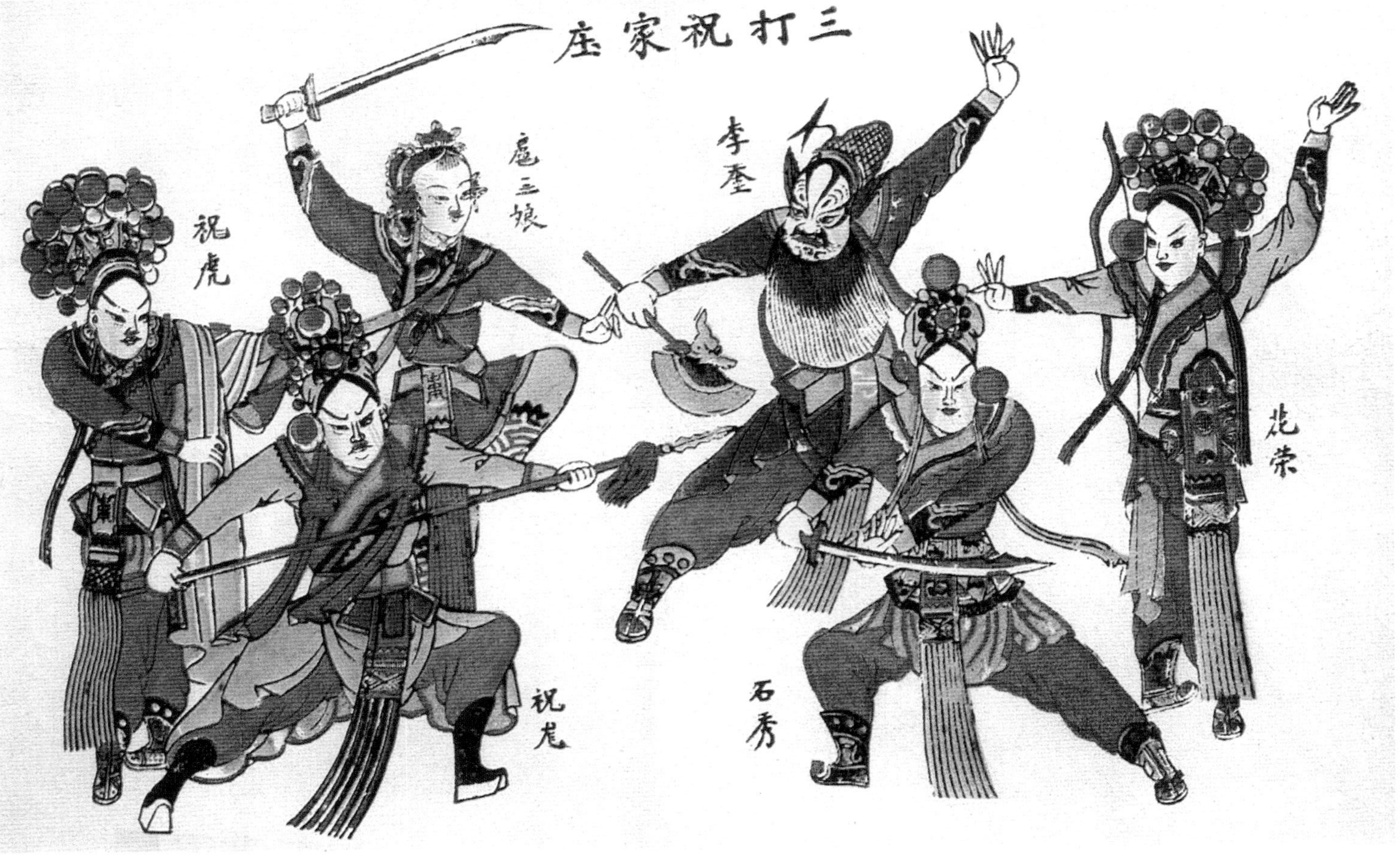

Plate 3.3 "Three Attacks on the Zhu Family Village," an episode from *Watermargin*.

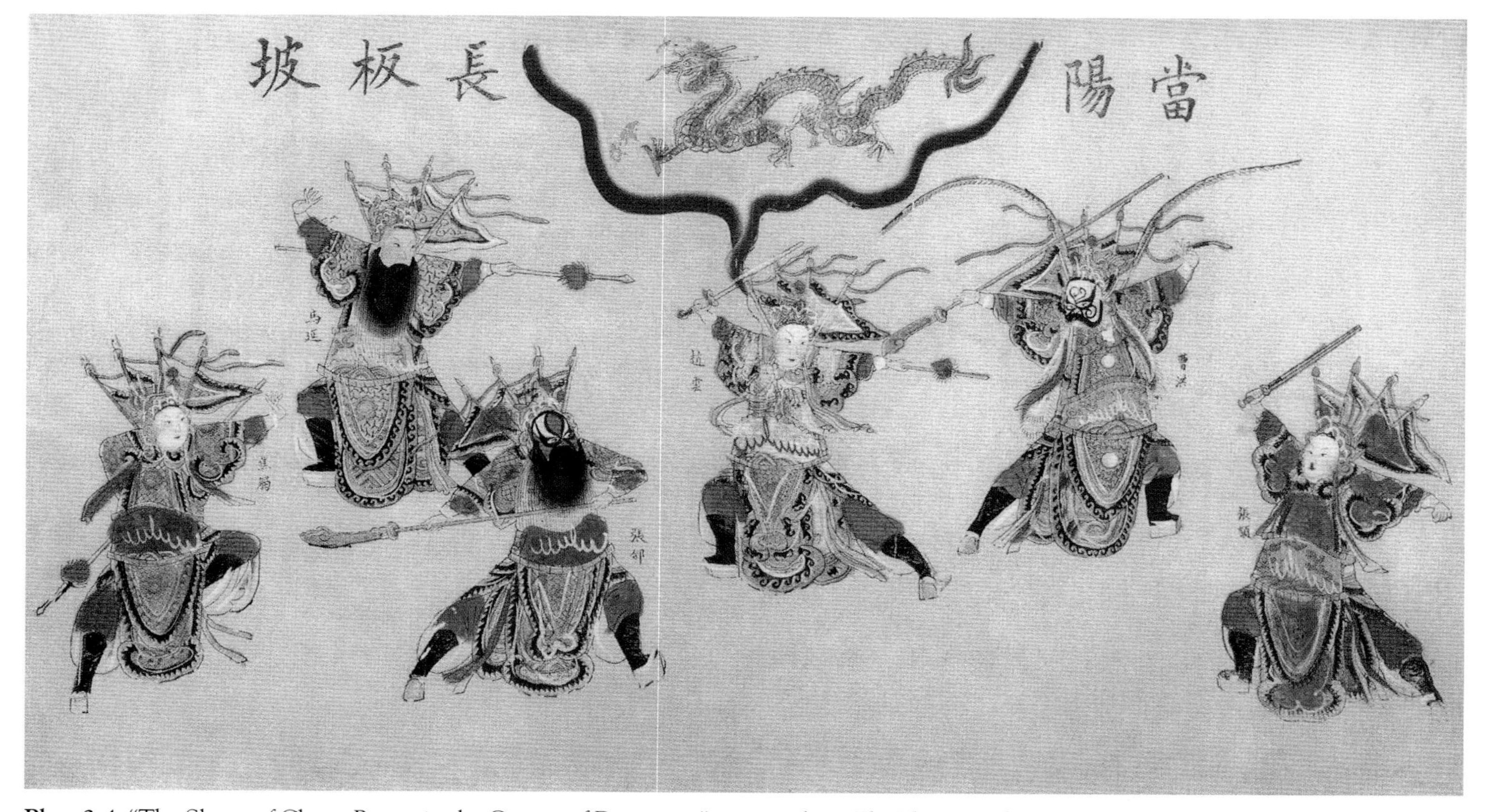

Plate 3.4 "The Slopes of Chang Banpo in the County of Dangyang," an episode in *The Three Kingdoms*.

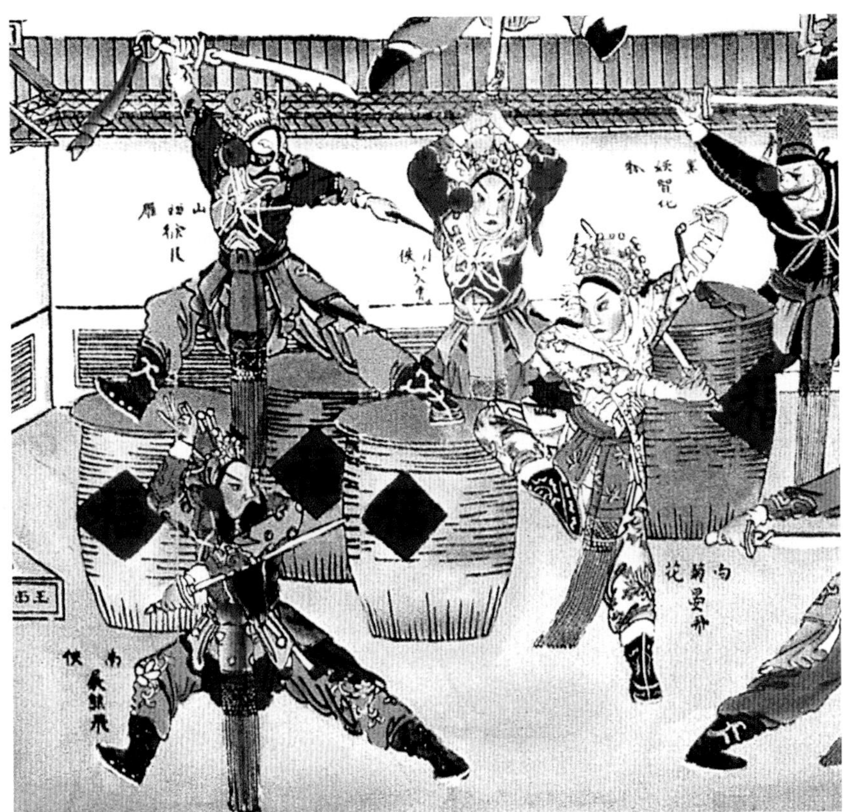

Plate 3.5 “The Capture of Bai Juhua” (detail).

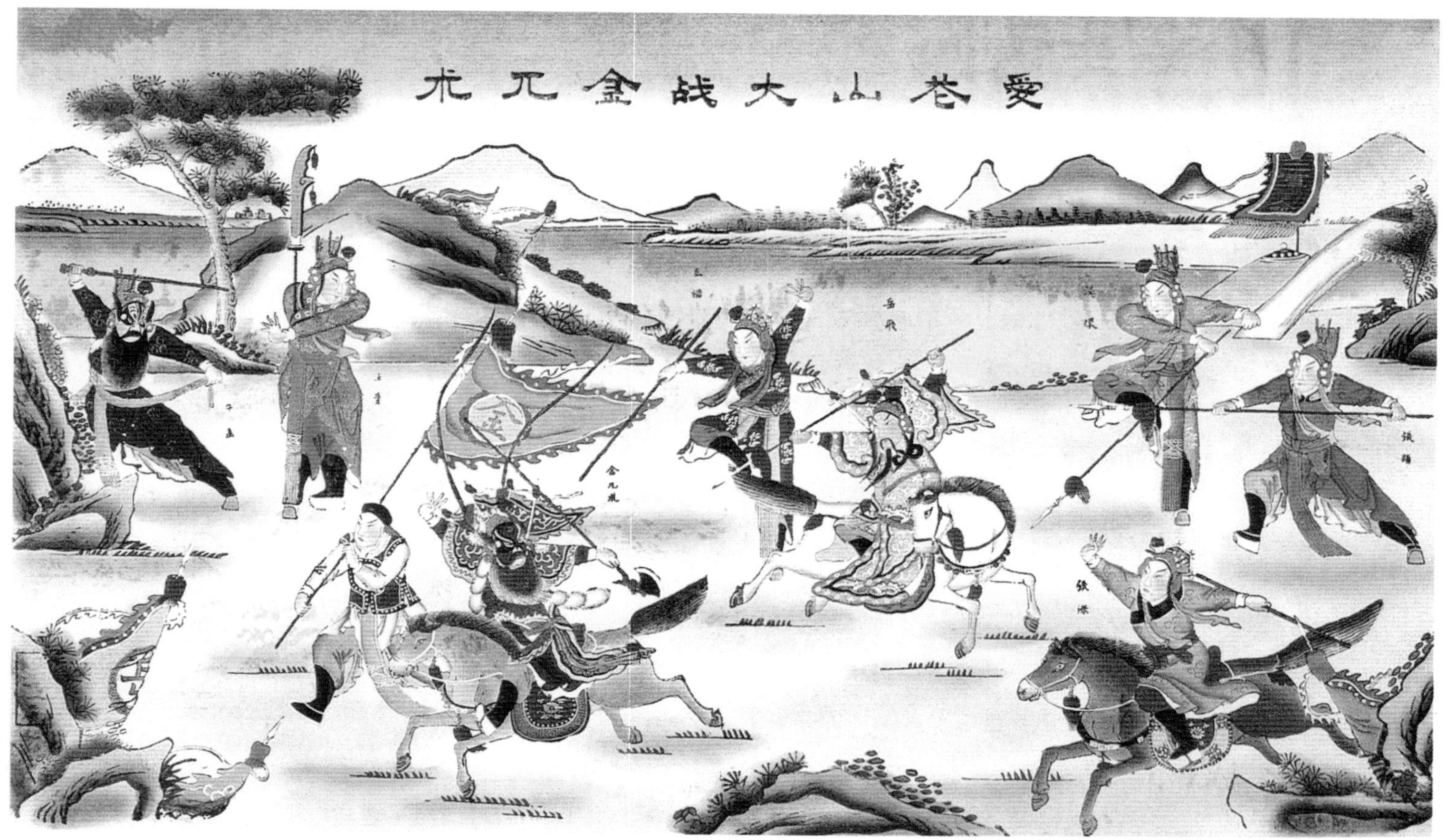

Plate 3.6 "The Battle with Wuzhu at Aihua Mountain."

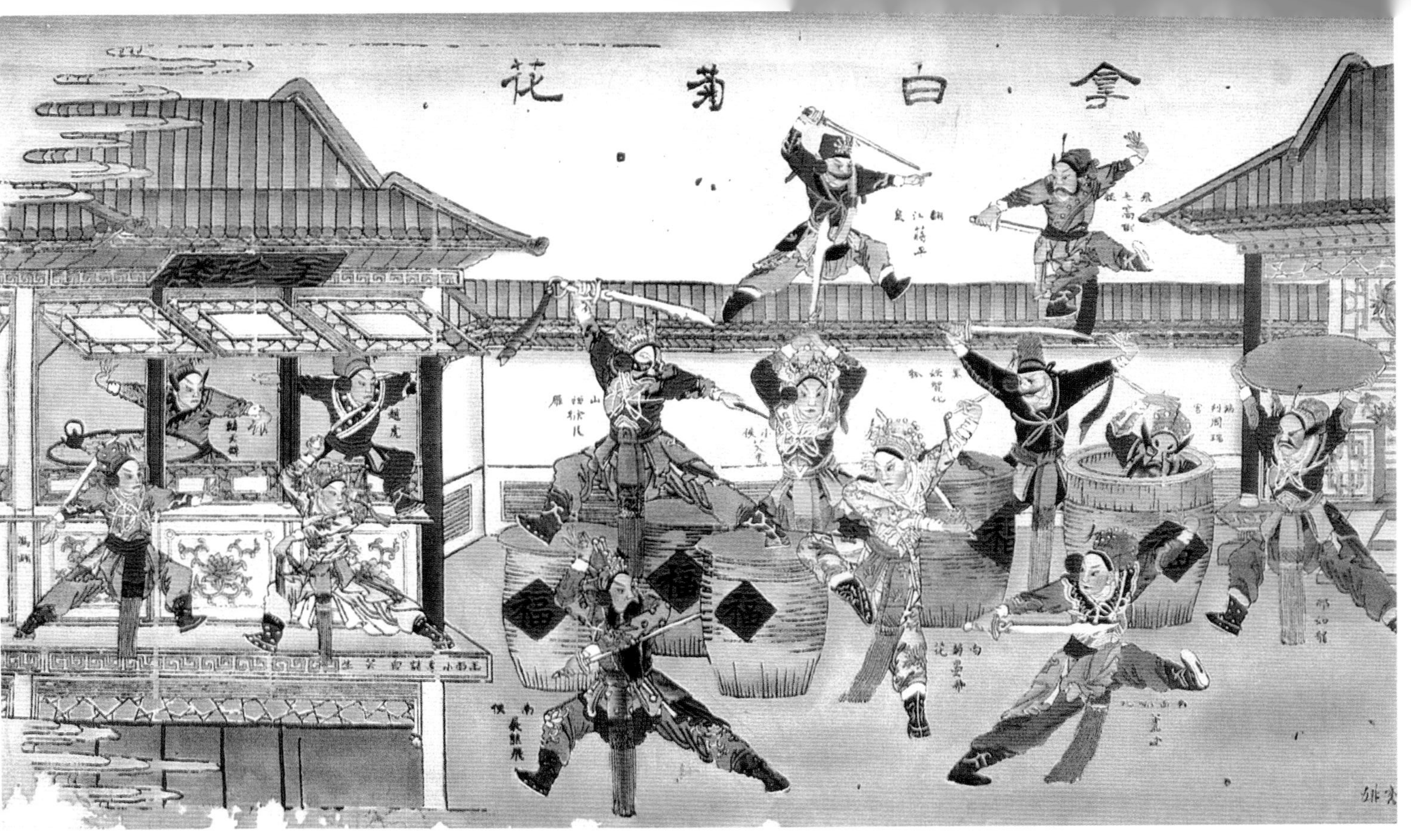

Plate 3.7 "The Capture of Bai Juhua."

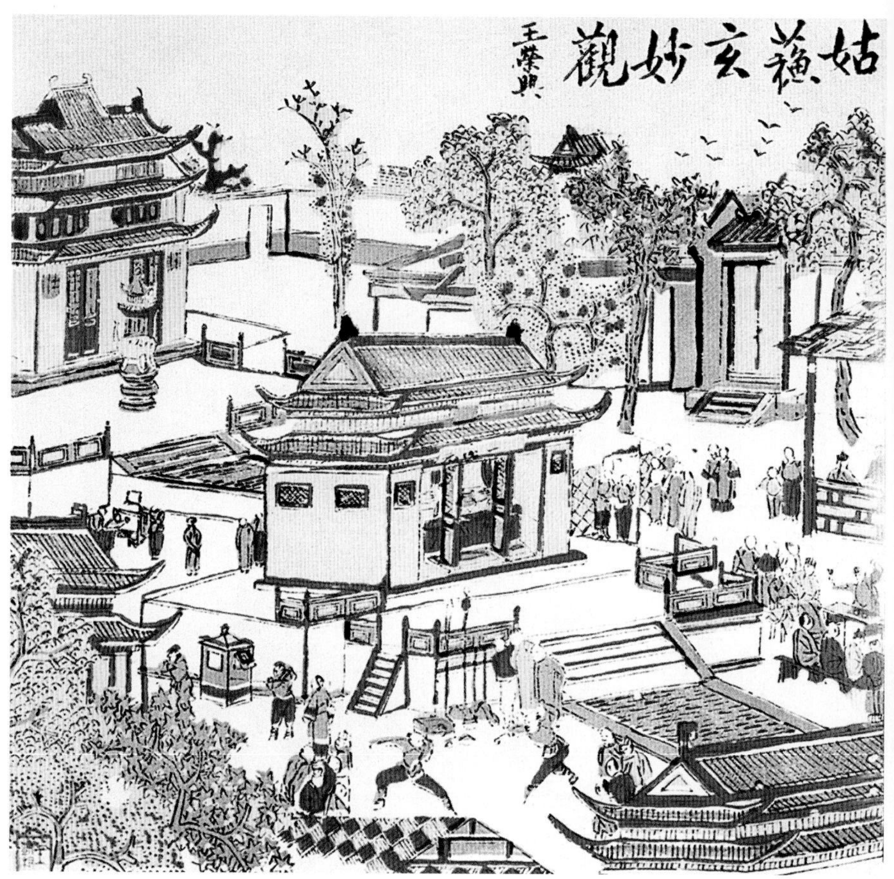

Plate 3.8 "The Xuanmiao Temple of Suzhou."

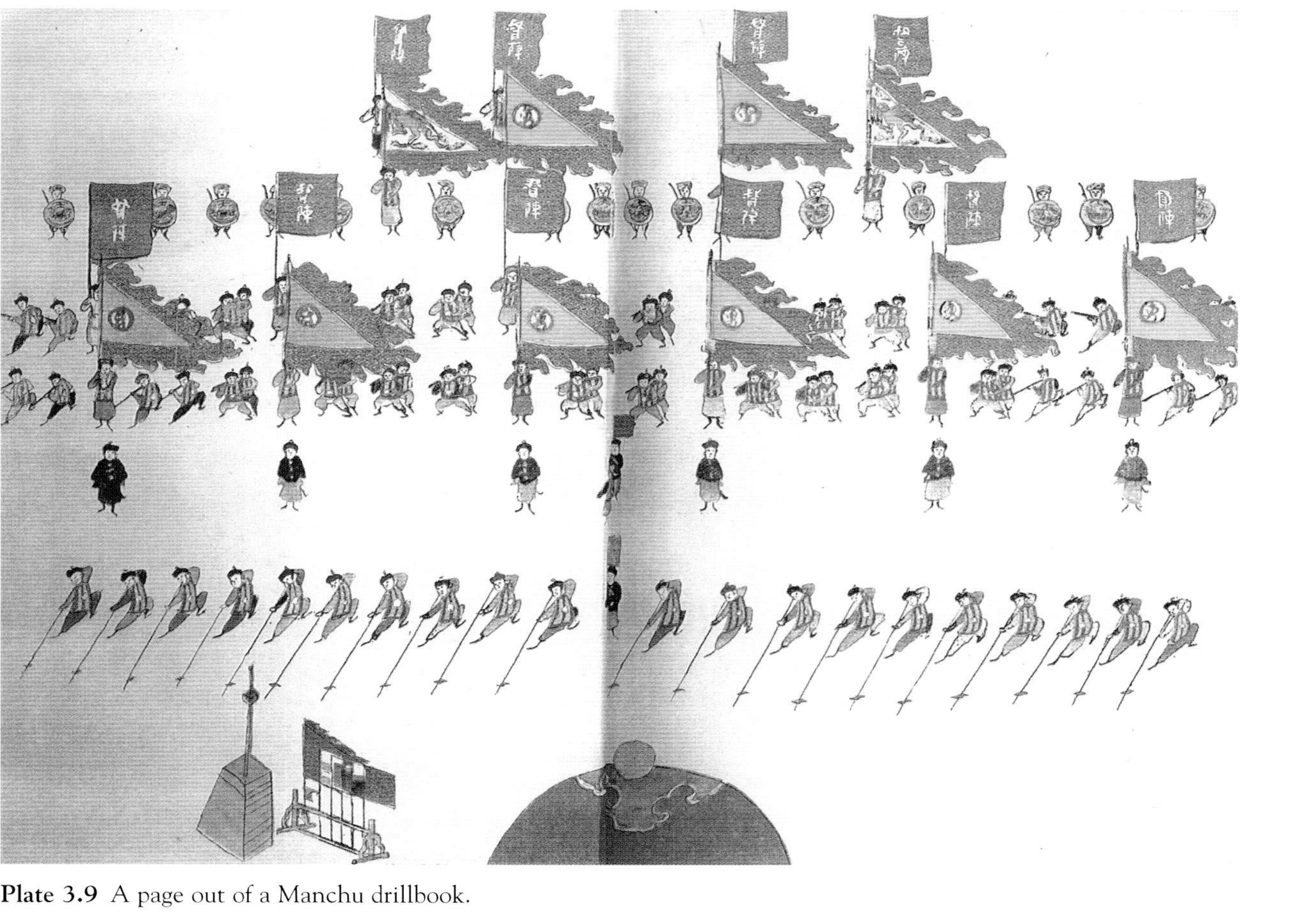

Plate 3.9 A page out of a Manchu drillbook.

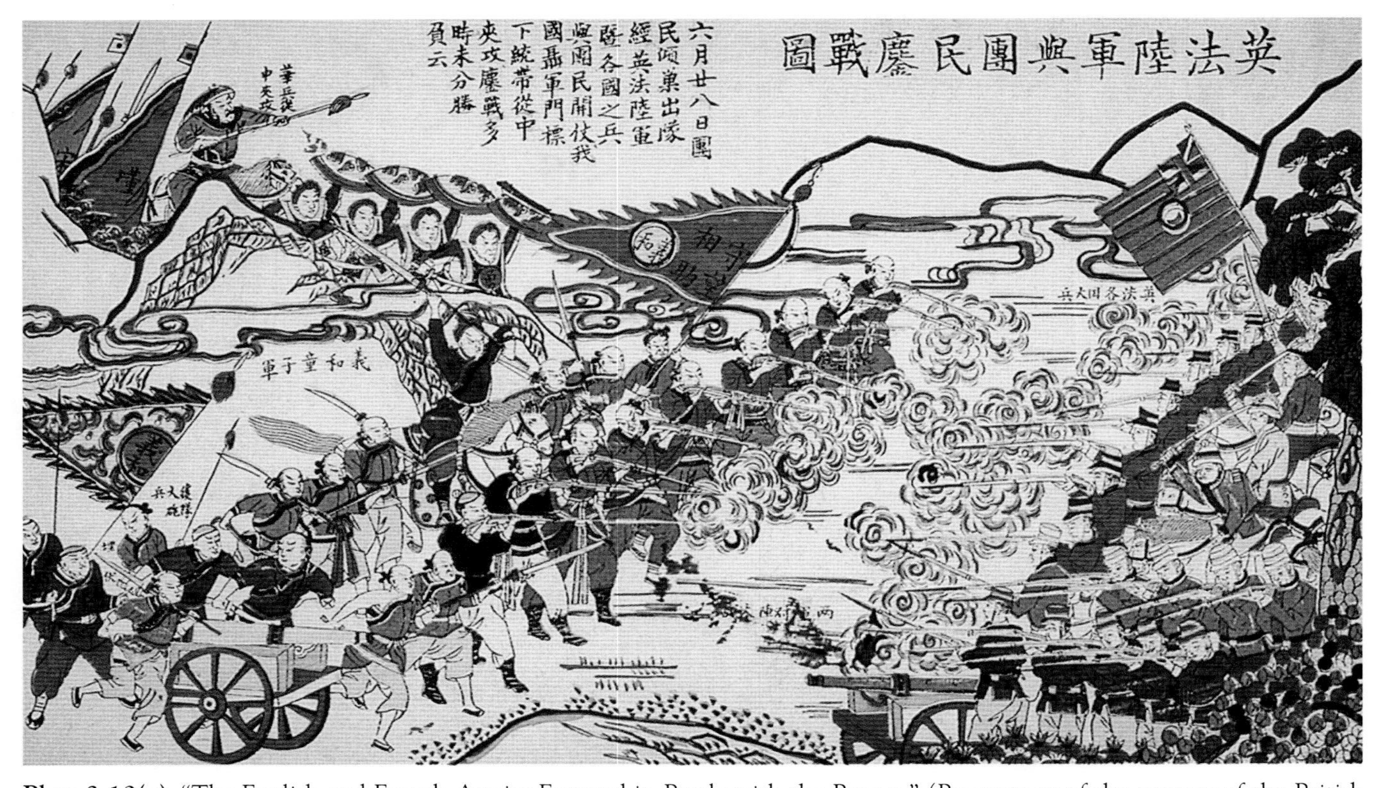

Plate 3.10(a) “The English and French Armies Engaged in Battle with the Boxers.” (By courtesy of the trustees of the British Library)

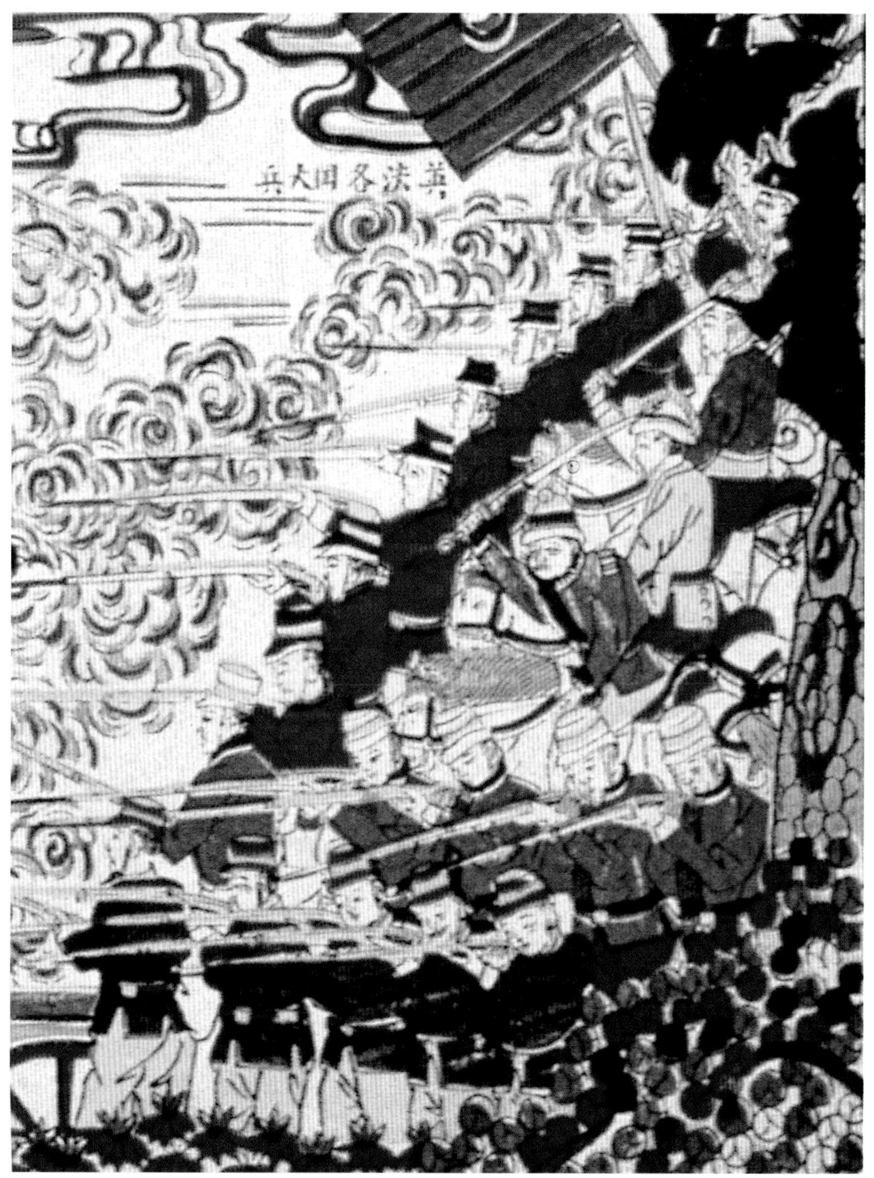

Plate 3.10(b) "The English and French Armies Engaged in Battle with the Boxers." (detail)

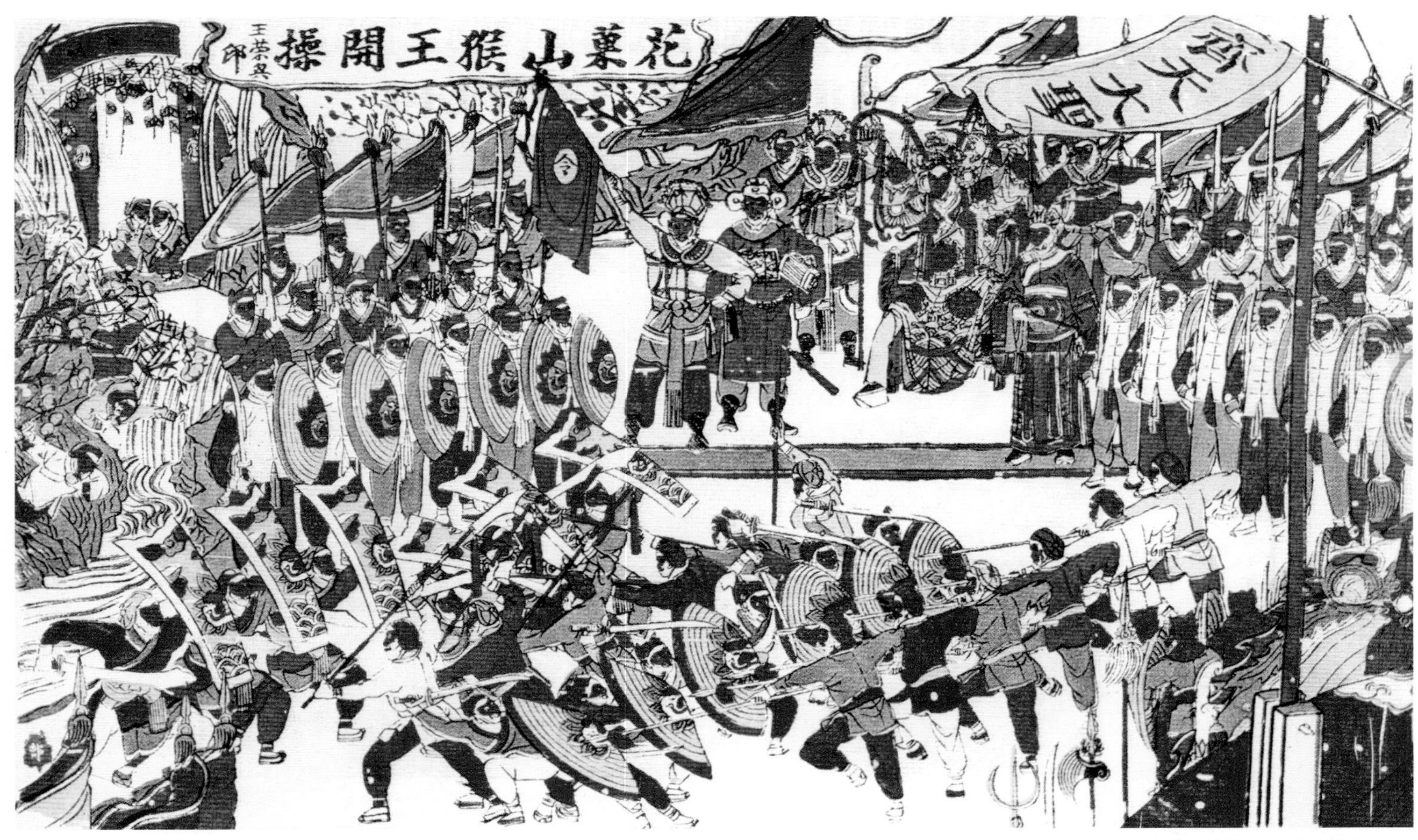

Plate 3.11 "Mountain of Flowers and Fruit," an episode from *The Journey to the West*

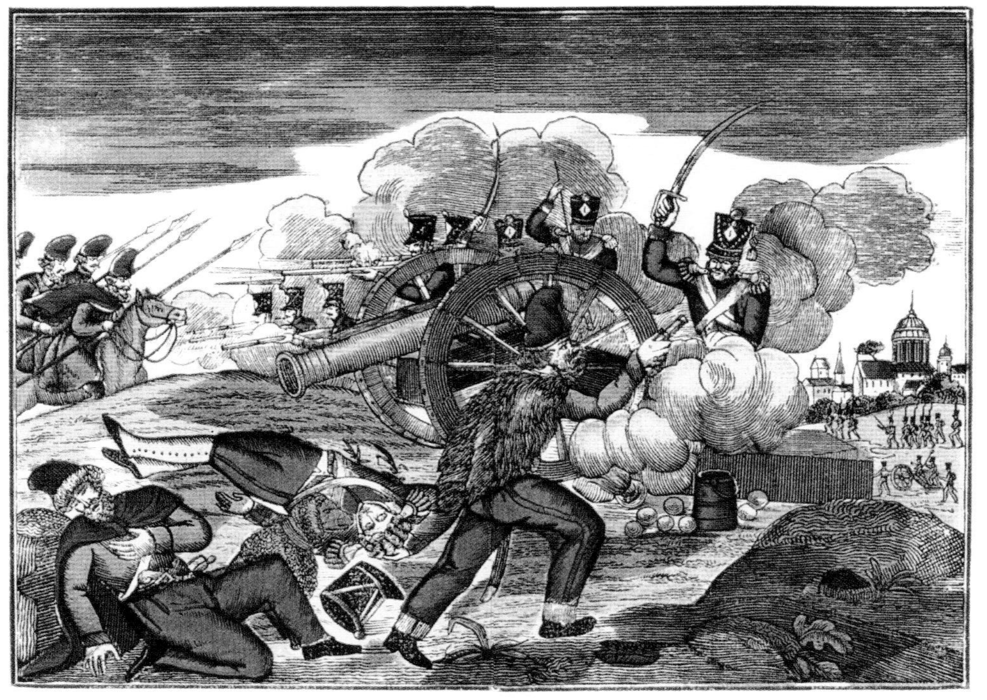

Plate 3.12 "The Defence of Paris," an Epinal print.

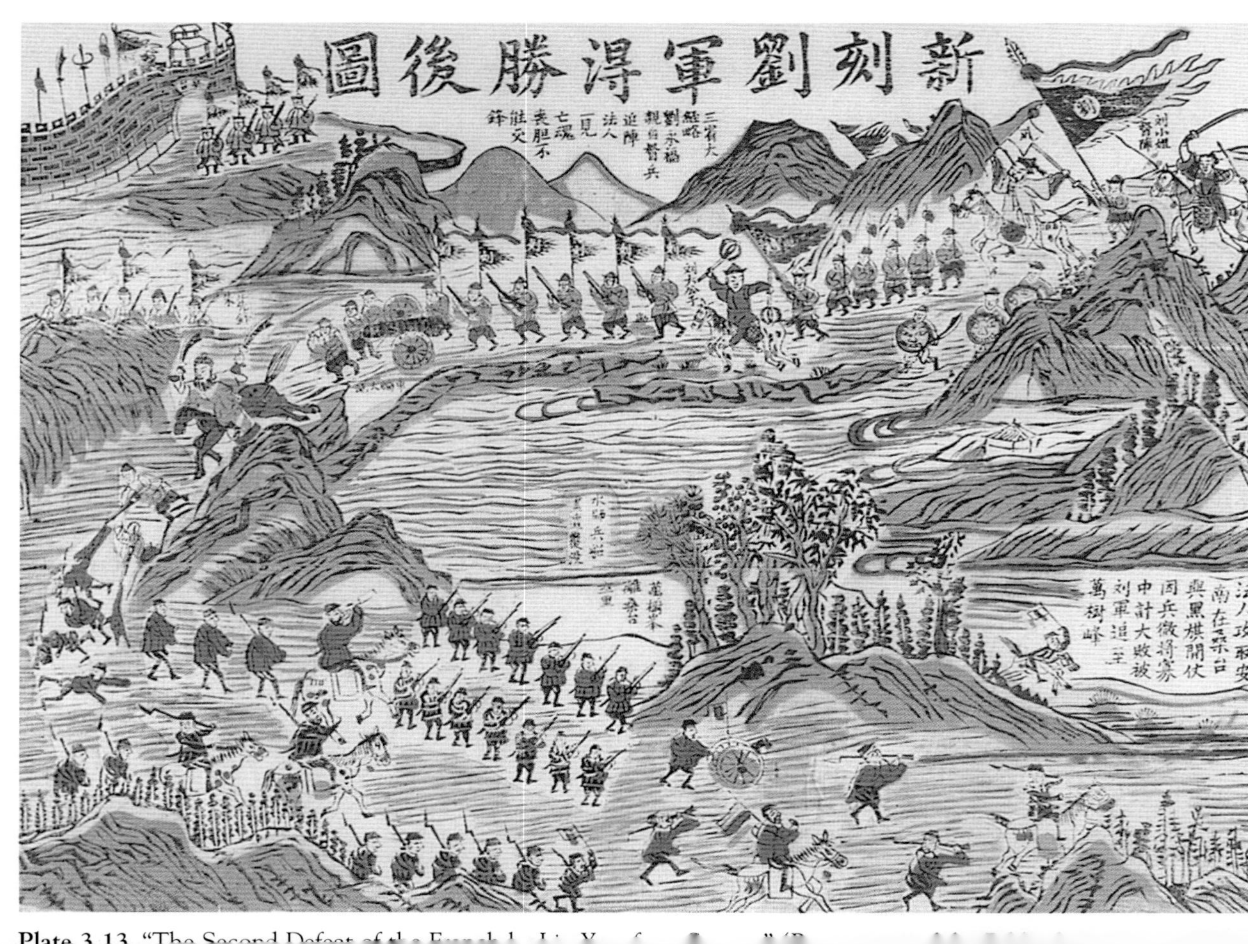

Plate 3.13 “The Second Defeat of the French

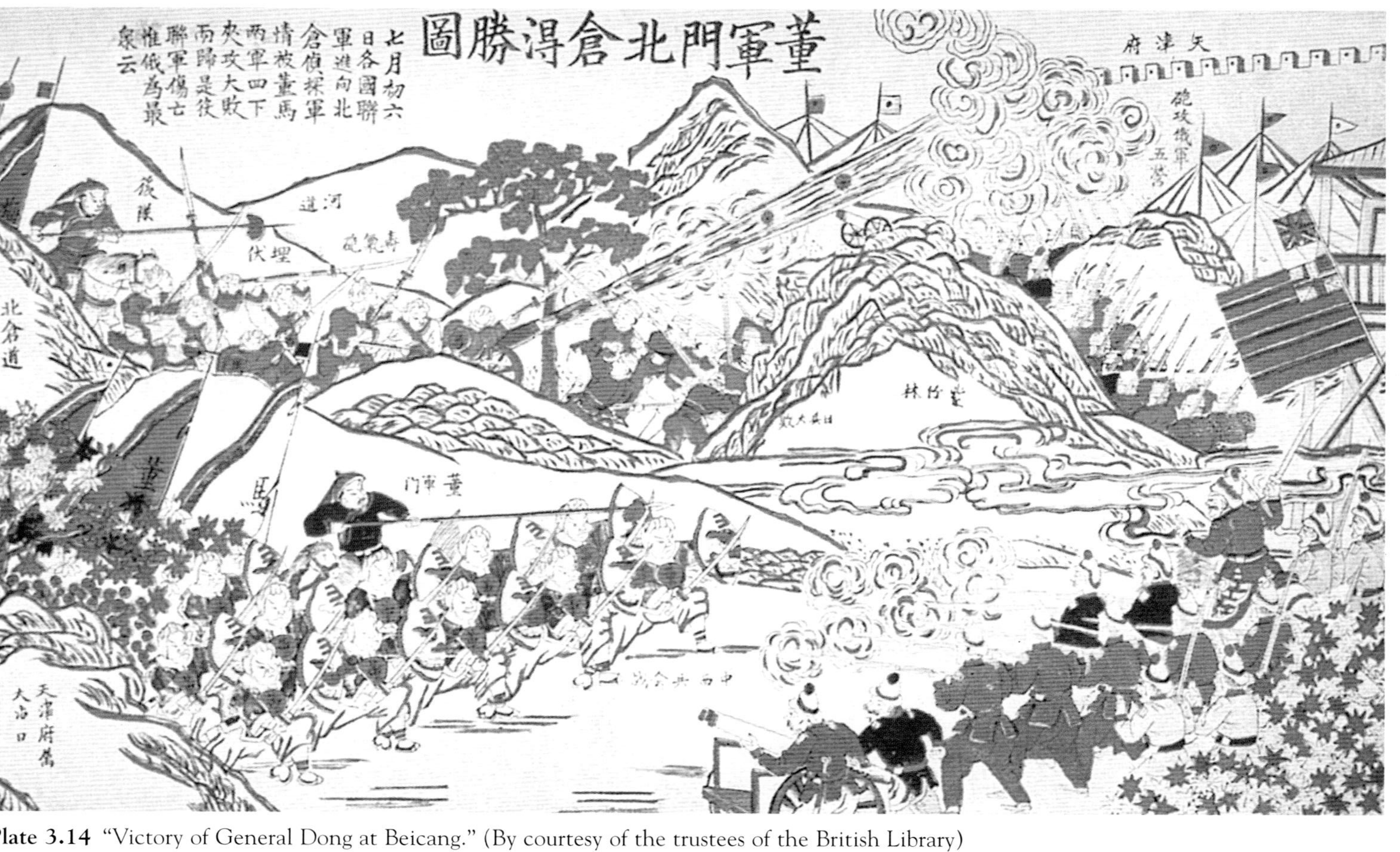

Plate 3.14 "Victory of General Dong at Beicang." (By courtesy of the trustees of the British Library)

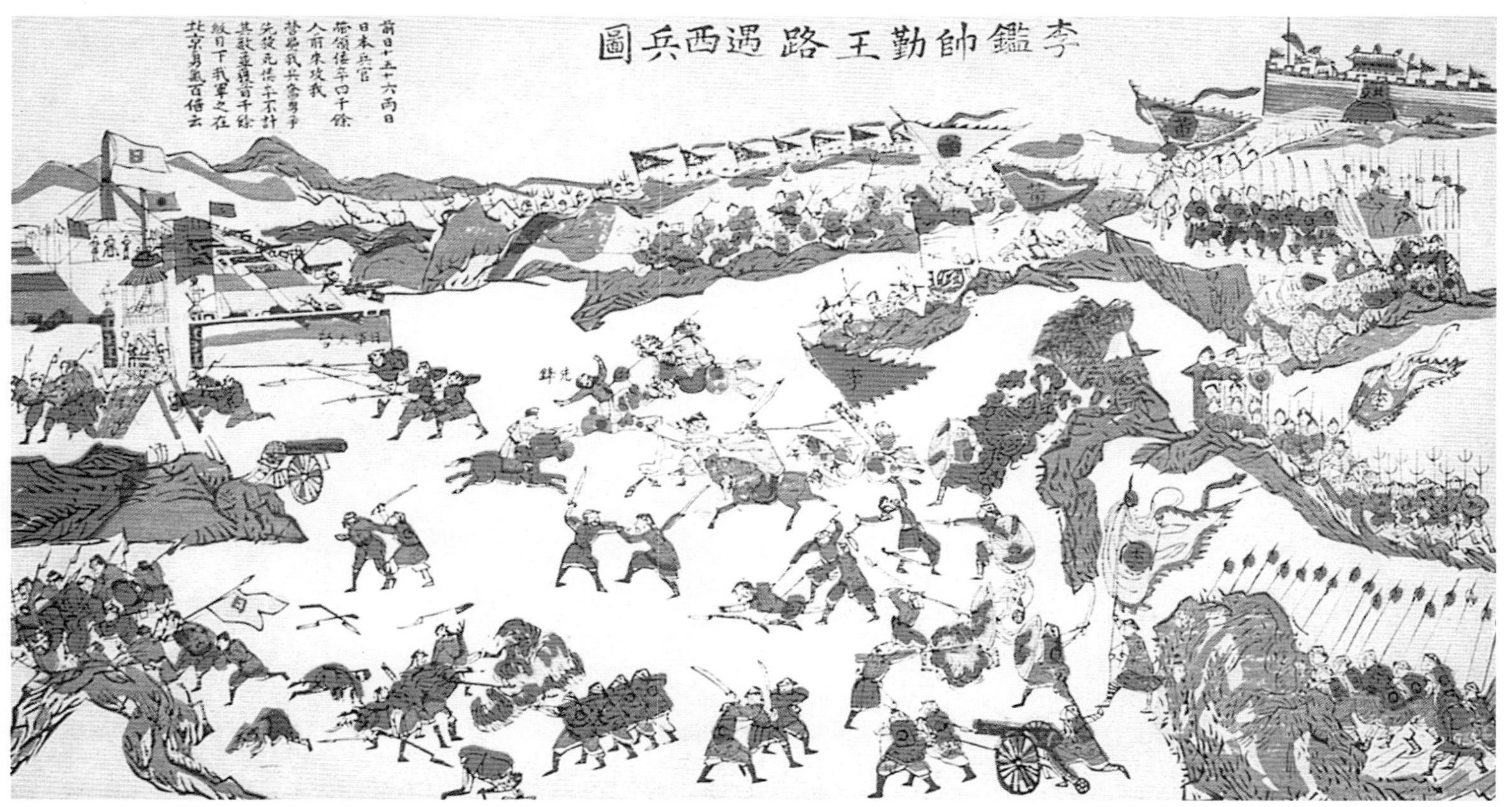

Plate 3.15 "The Chinese Repulse Four Thousand Japanese." (By courtesy of the trustees of the British Library)

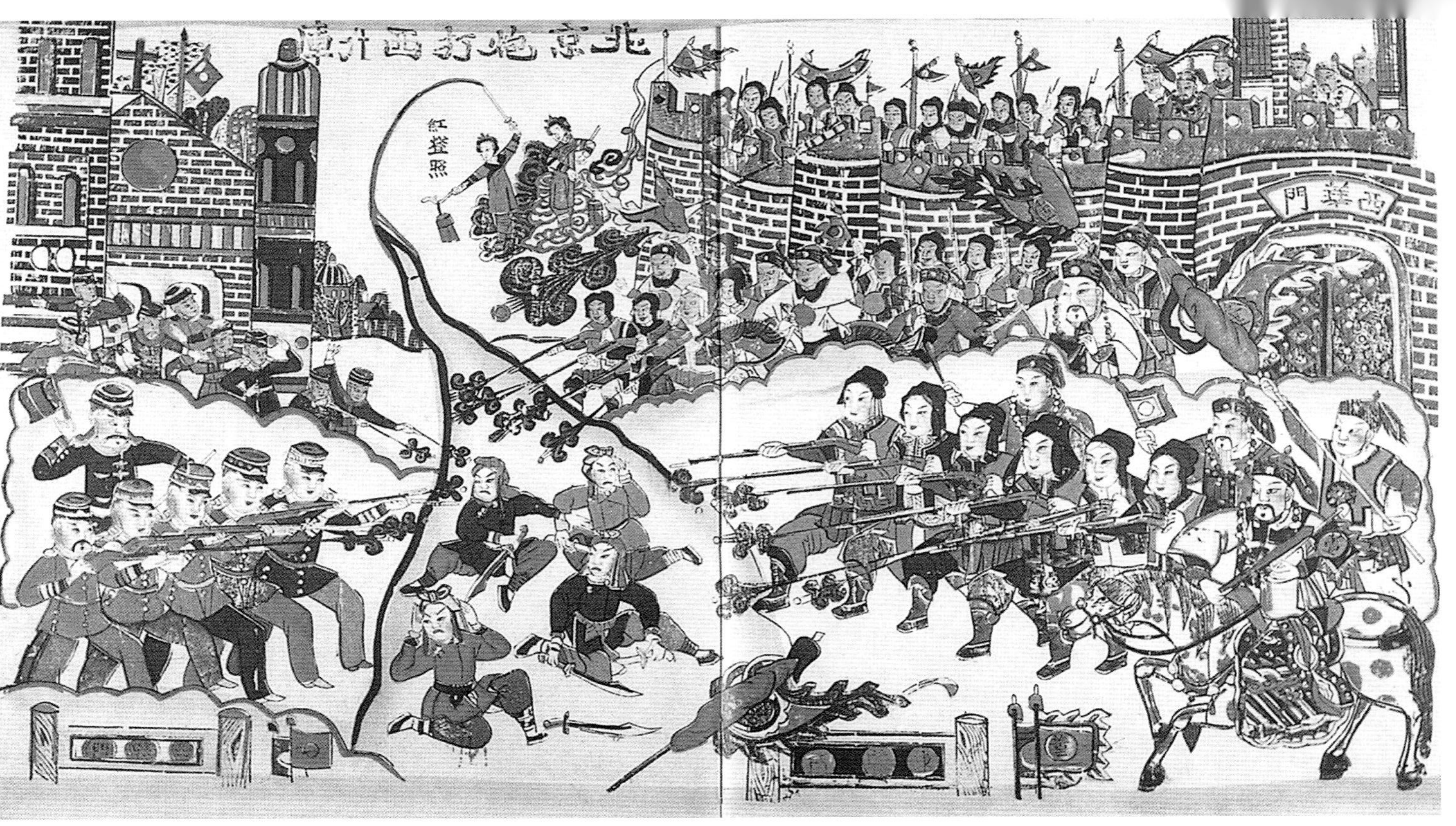

Plate 3.16 "The Siege of Beicang Cathedral."

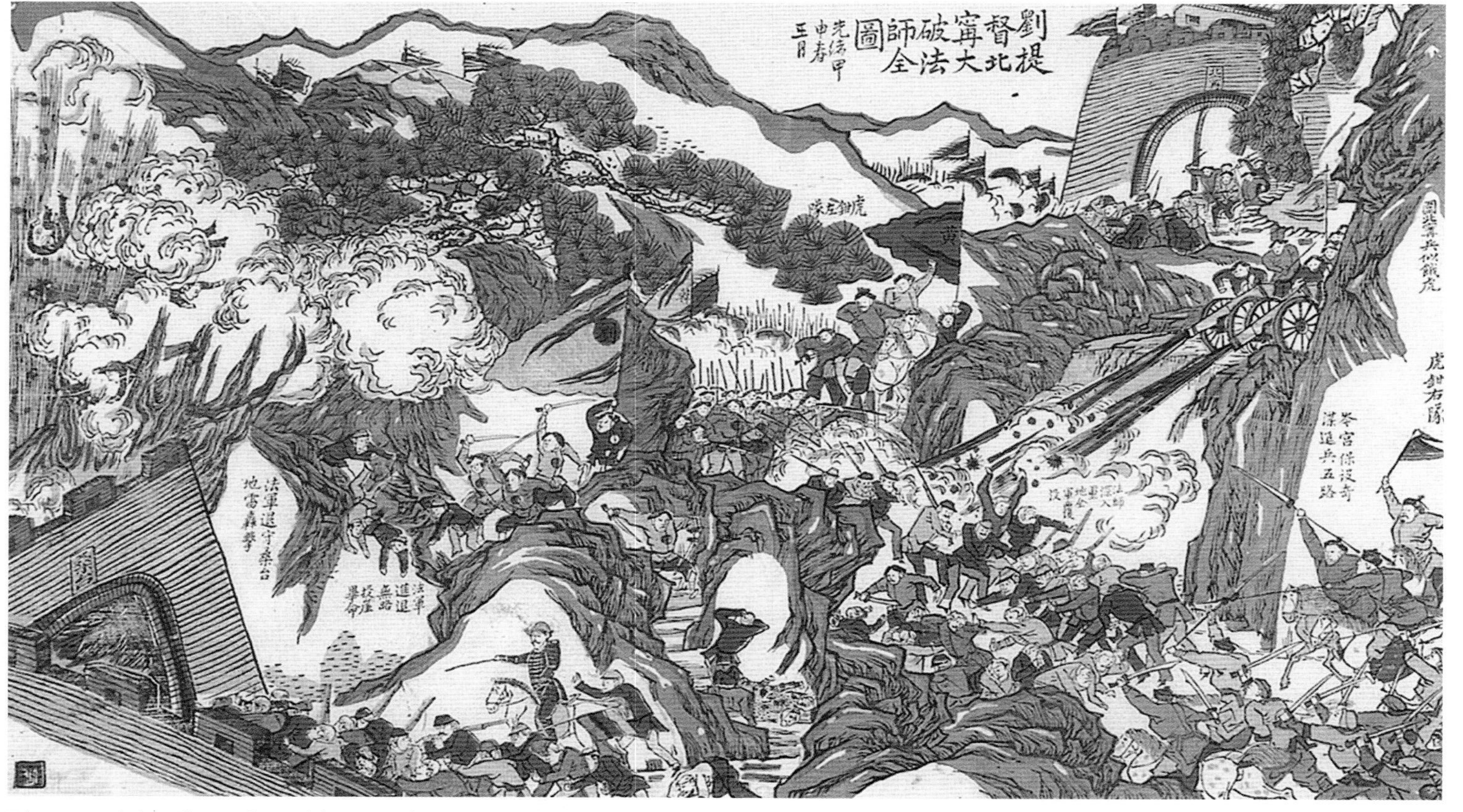

Plate 3.17(a) "The Defeat of the French at Bac Ninh by Liu Yongfu." (By courtesy of the Bibliothèque Nationale)

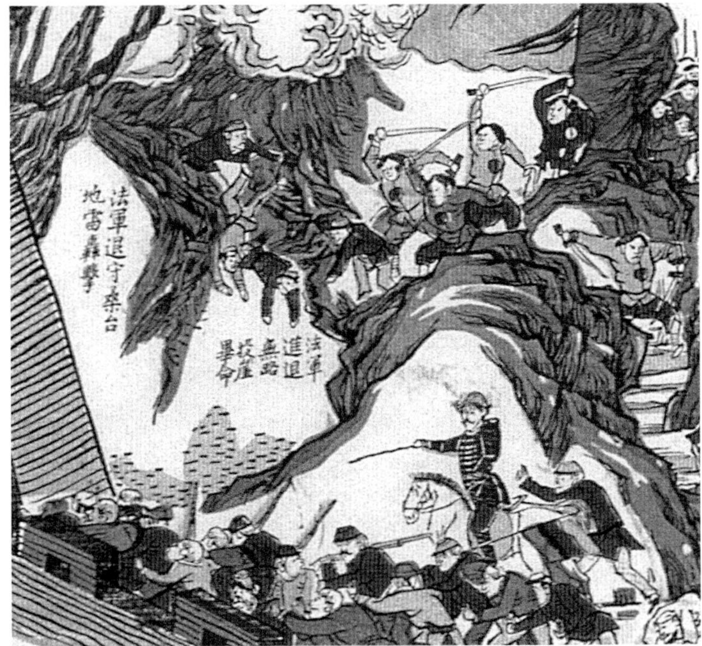

Plate 3.17(b) "The Defeat of the French at Bac Ninh by Liu Yongfu" (detail showing mounted French officer).

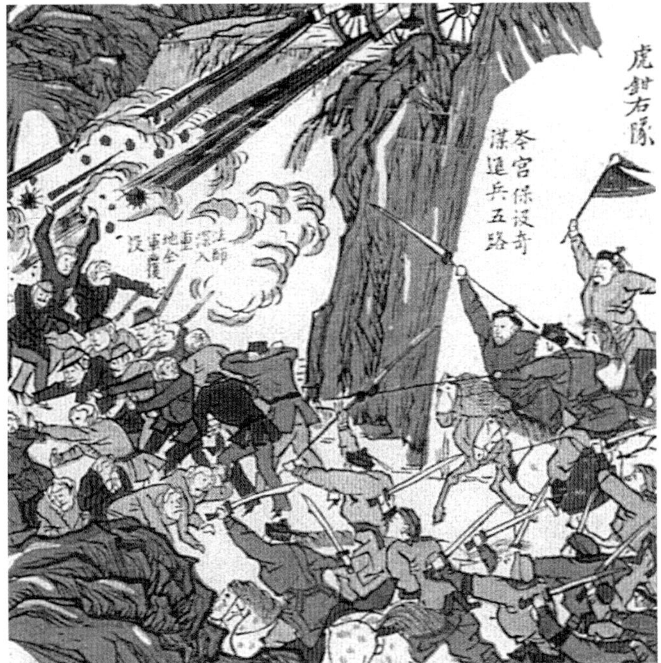

Plate 3.17(c) "The Defeat of the French at Bac Ninh by Liu Yongfu" (detail showing mounted Chinese officers).

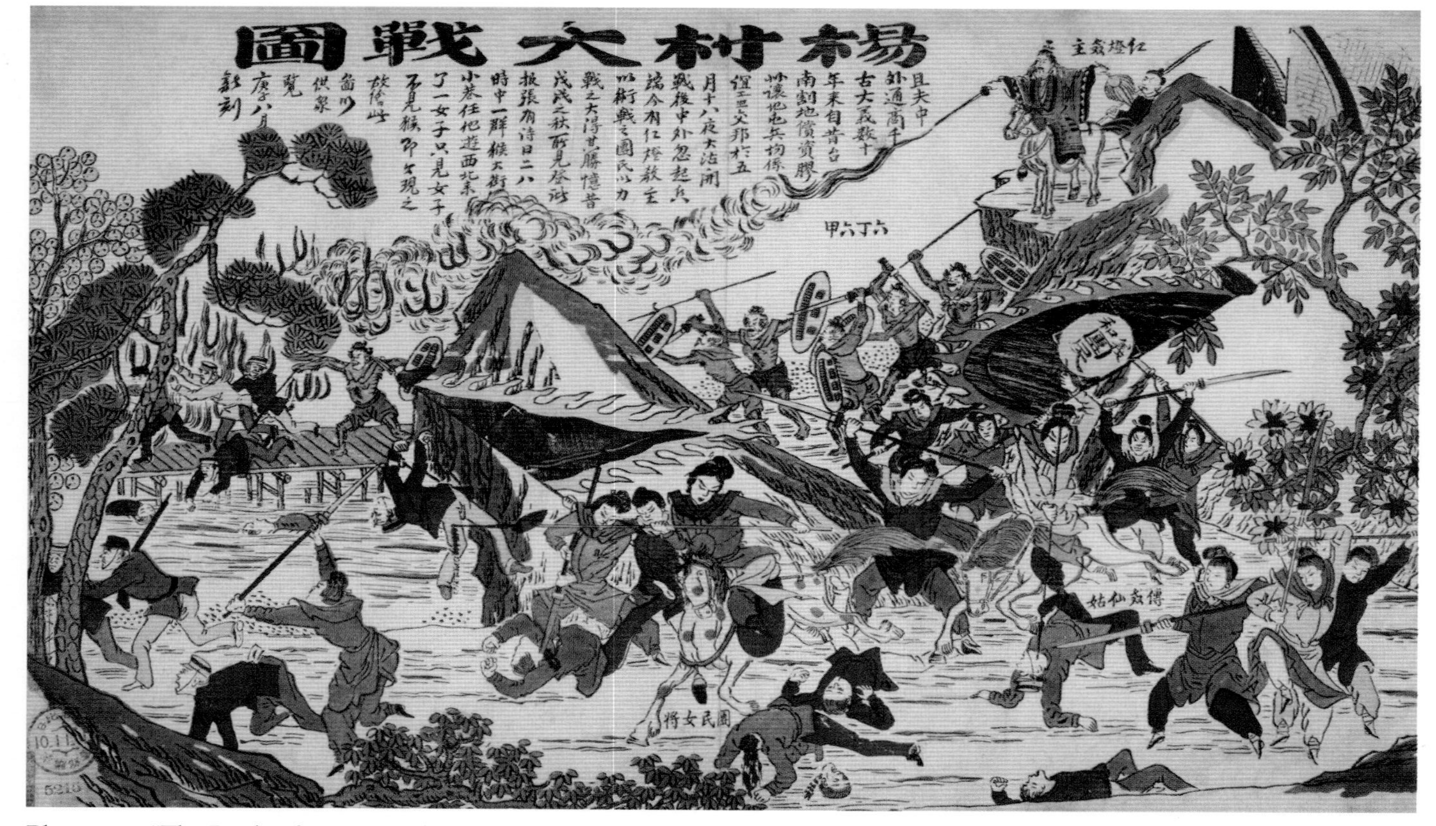

Plate 3.18 "The Battle of Yangcun." (By courtesy of the Tokyo Metropolitan Central Library)

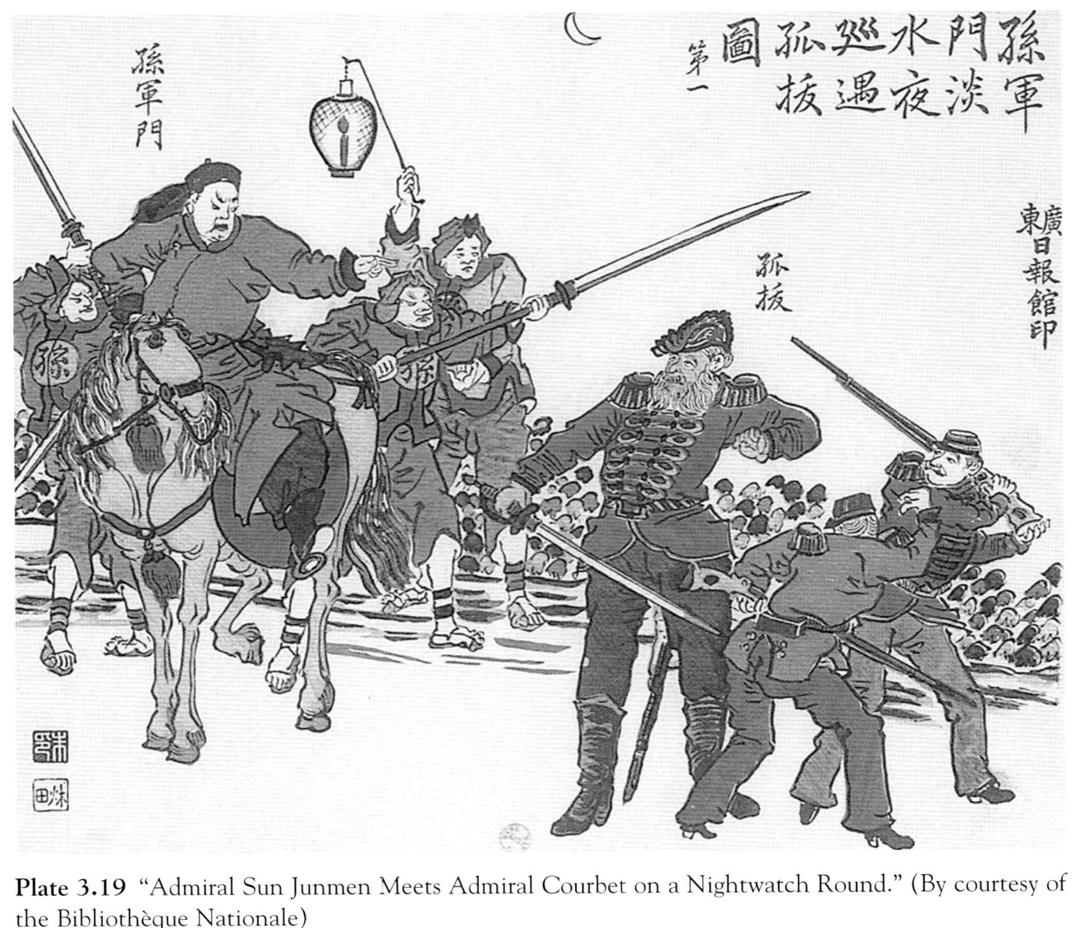

Plate 3.19 "Admiral Sun Junmen Meets Admiral Courbet on a Nightwatch Round." (By courtesy of the Bibliothèque Nationale)

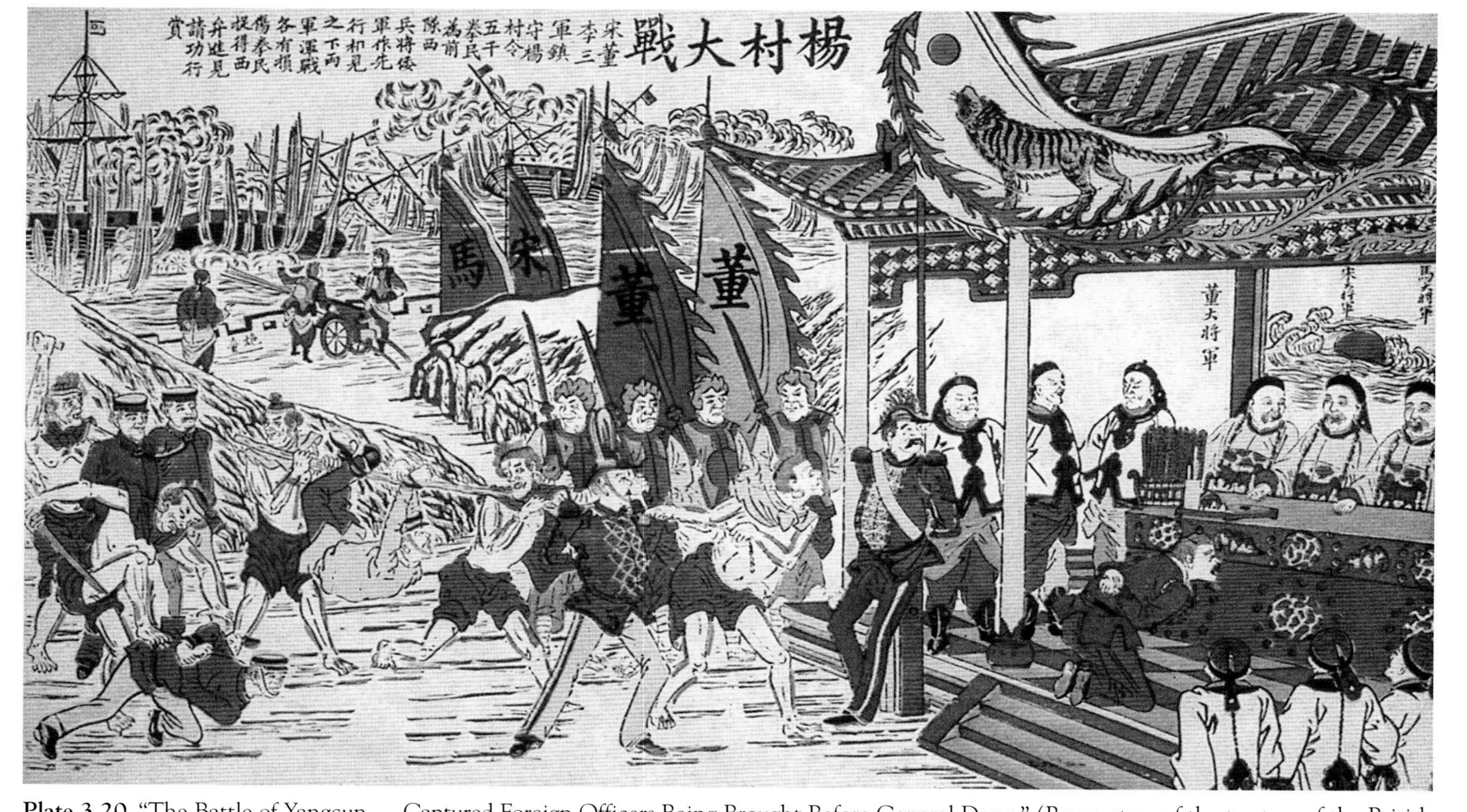

Plate 3.20 "The Battle of Yangcun — Captured Foreign Officers Being Brought Before General Dong." (By courtesy of the trustees of the British Library)

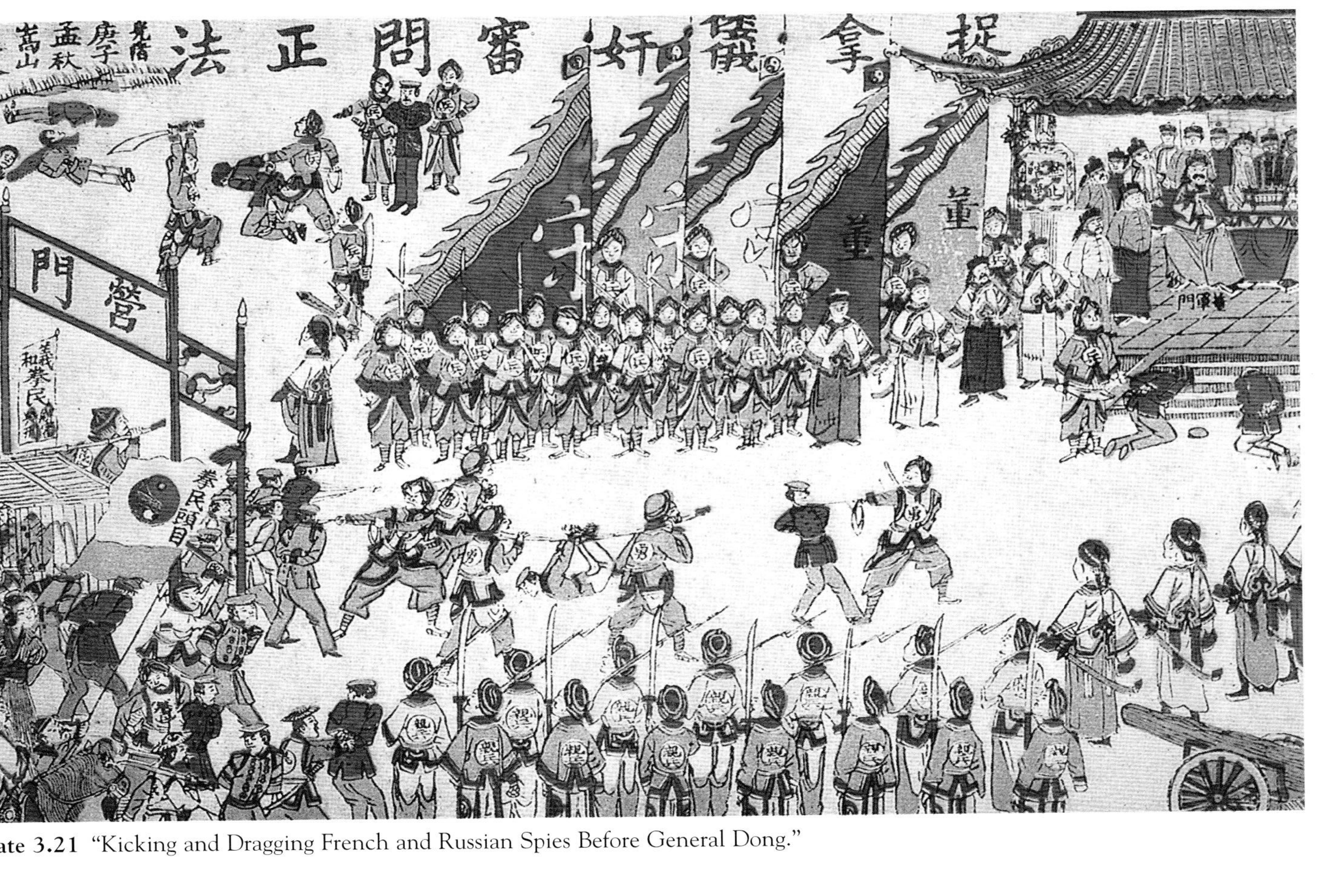

Plate 3.21 “Kicking and Dragging French and Russian Spies Before General Dong.”

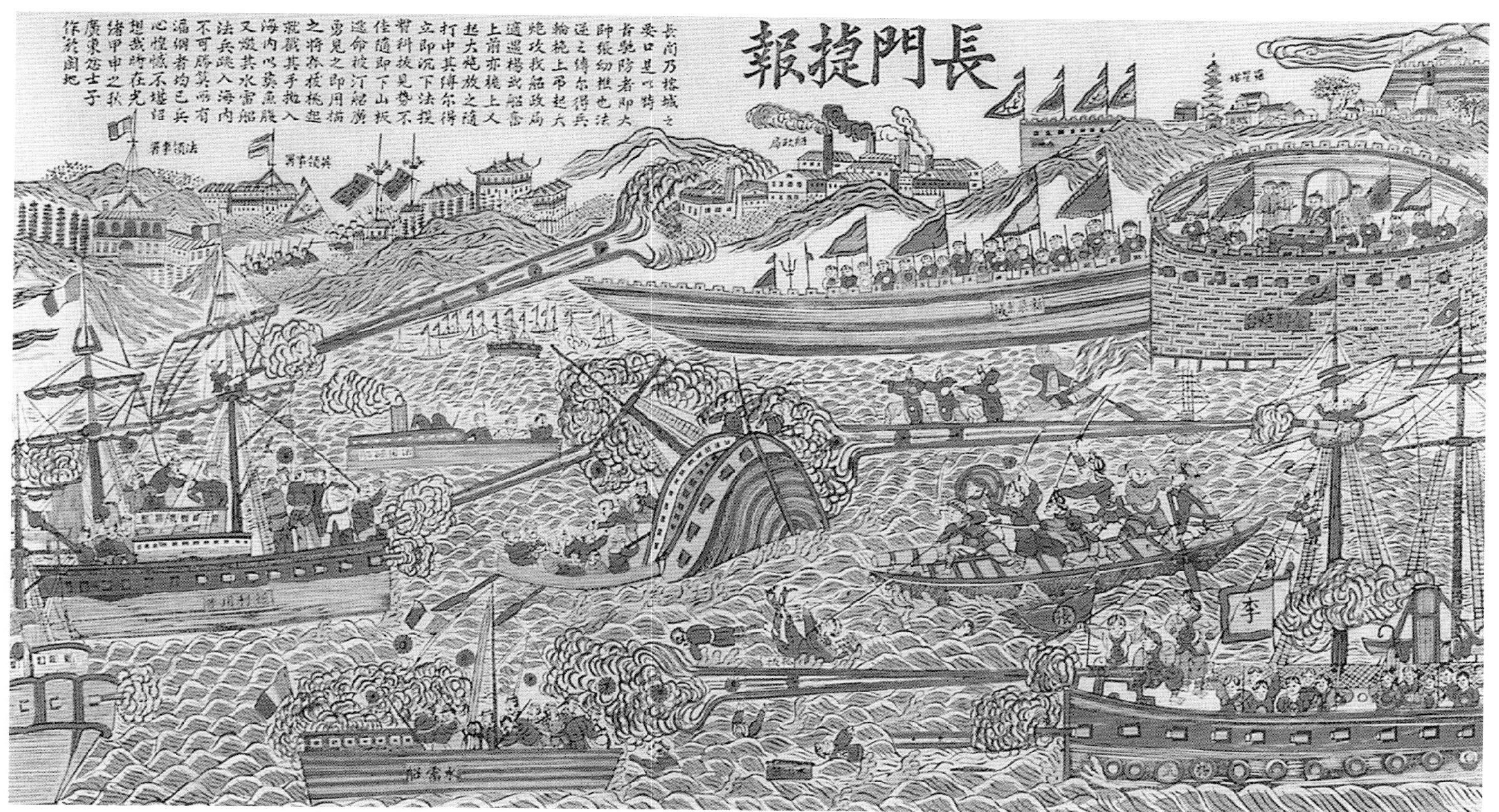

Plate 3.22 “The Battle of Fuzhou.” (By courtesy of the trustees of the British Library)

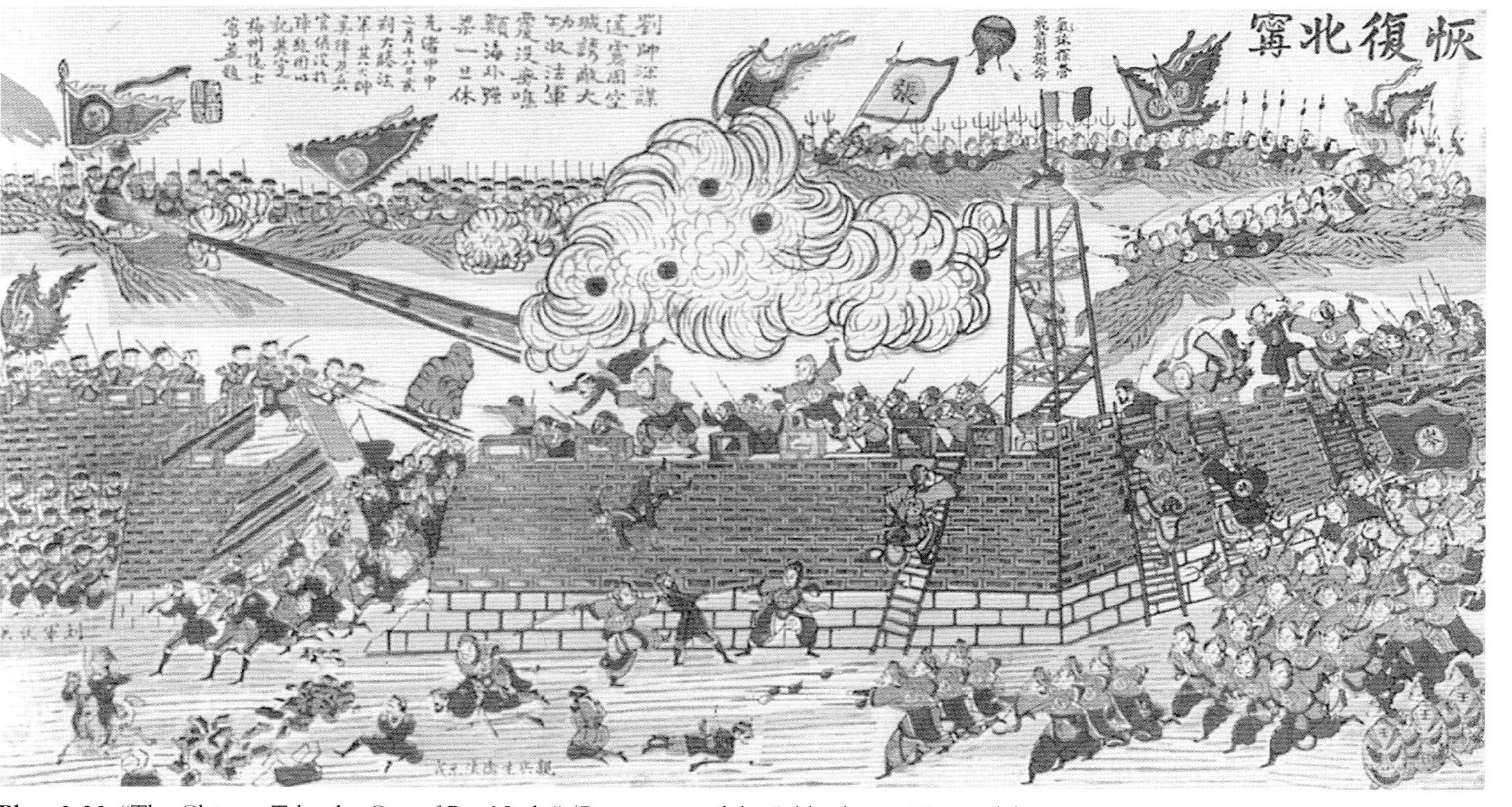

Plate 3.23 "The Chinese Take the City of Bac Ninh." (By courtesy of the Bibliothèque Nationale)

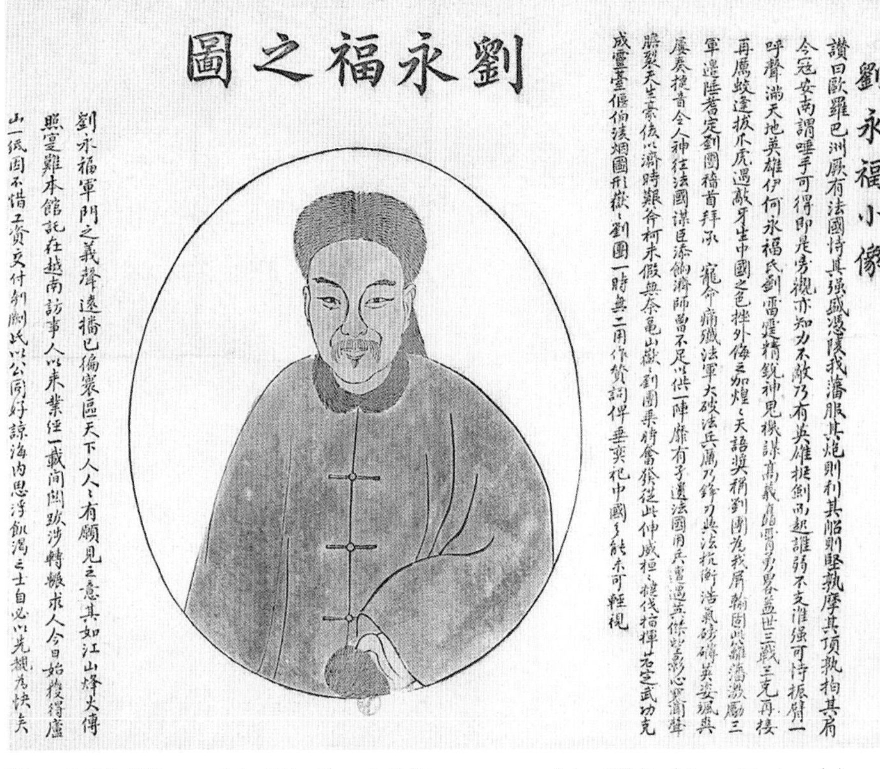

Plate 3.24 "Xinwenzhi of Liu Yongfu." (By courtesy of the Bibliothèque Nationale)

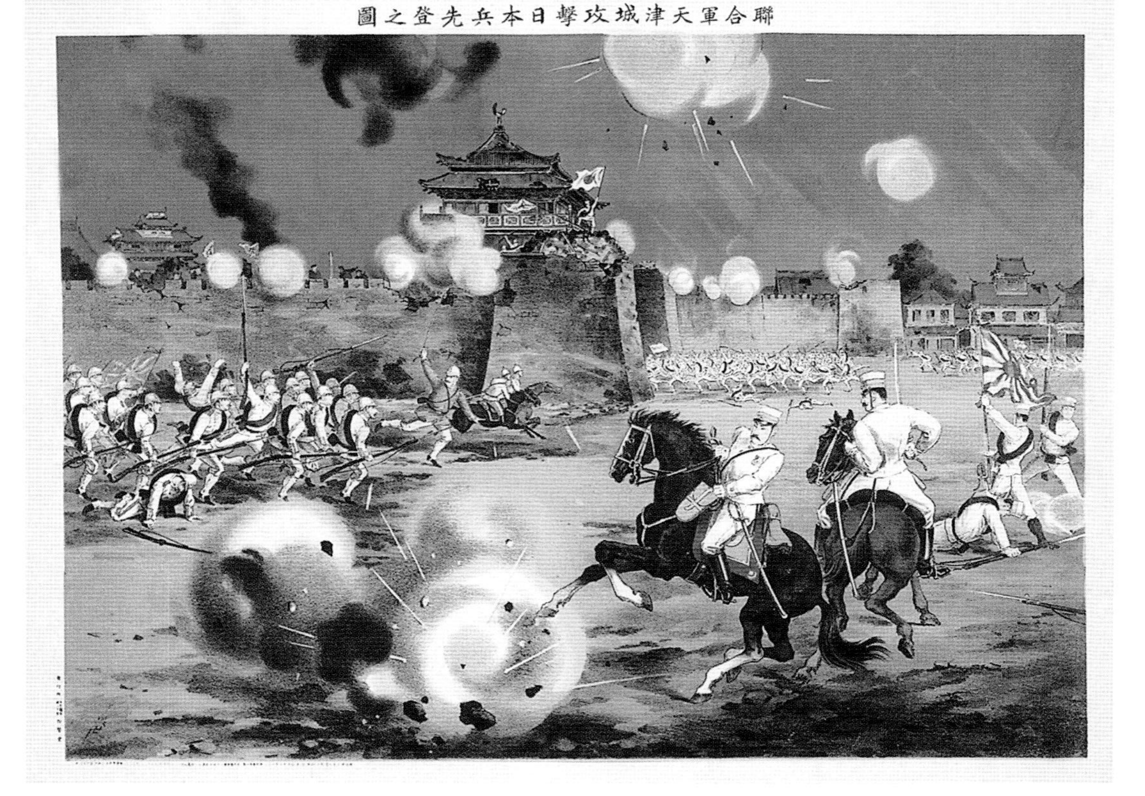

Plate 3.25 Japanese soldiers assault Tianjin. (From the private collection of Ms Kazuyo Lee)

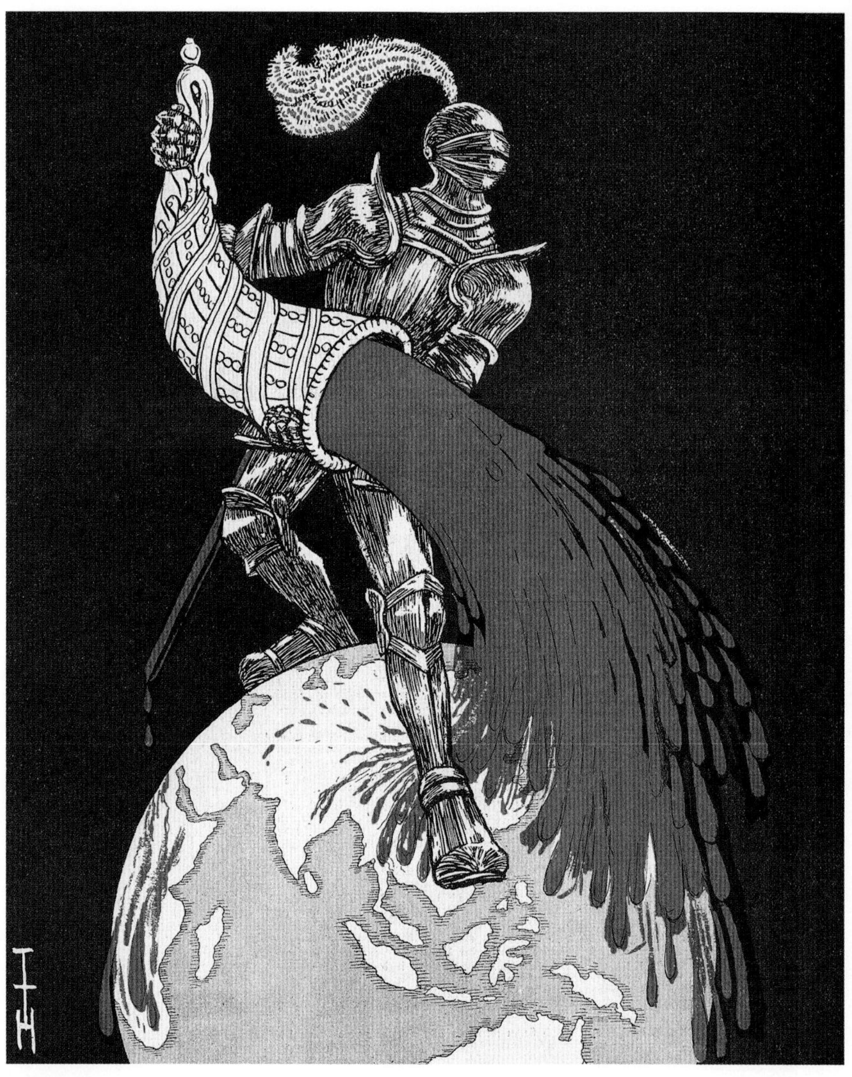

Plate 5.1 The Europeans pour the blessings of their culture over the world. (By courtesy of the V&A Picture Library)

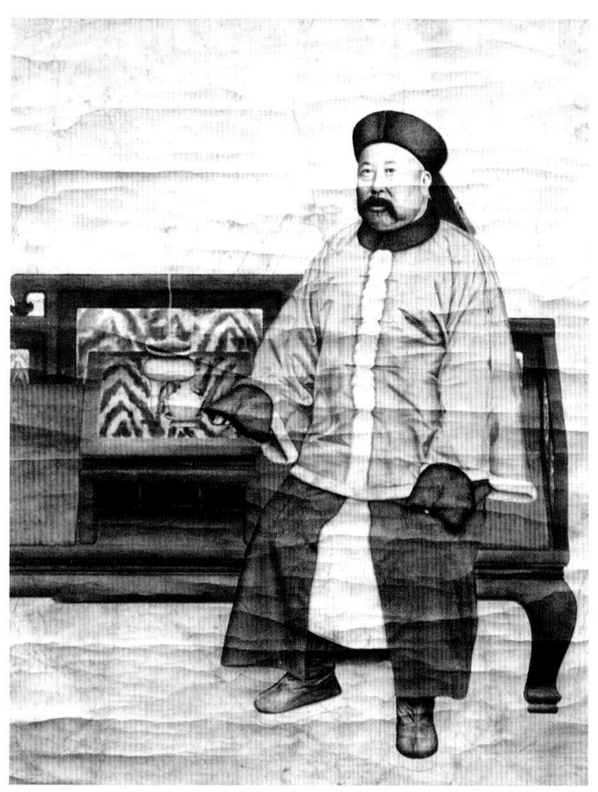

Plate 7.1 Portrait of General Nie Shicheng. (From the Tianjian Yihetuan Museum)

different military traditions (See also Plate 3.17).[155] It would appear from the nianhua that both forces are similarly armed and similarly deployed; that is, that the Chinese army is one of the modern armies. Indeed, the text informs us that one of General Nie Shicheng's commanding officers came to join the battle and that it was as shown in the picture, an engagement between evenly matched forces. General Nie's men wore blue tunics that, while not cut exactly in the Western manner, approached Western uniform style. General Nie's men also wore Western-style headgear (Figures 3.7 and 3.8).[156] General Dong Fuxiang also joined the Chinese forces and in the top left hand corner we see a Chinese officer, who, if not Dong himself, is certainly a traditionally-trained senior Chinese officer commanding soldiers bearing traditional Chinese shields. Dong Fuxiang's troops were in fact armed with modern weapons which did not permit the possibility of carrying a shield but they wore traditional uniforms.

Traditional Chinese military uniforms have been characterised by at least one scholar as "absurd."[157] This characterisation conveys a personal cultural perception of what constitutes appropriate military dress that has no place in

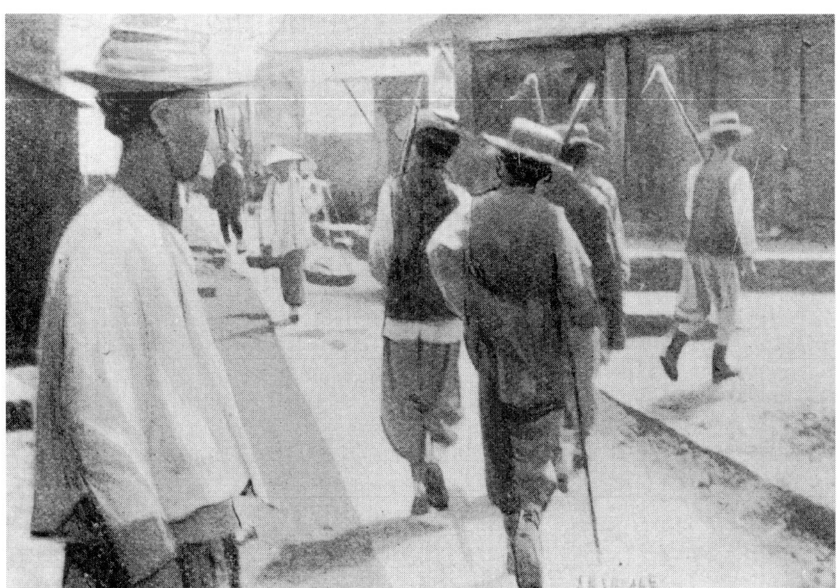

Figure 3.7 Chinese soldiers. Hand-tinted photograph by Arnold Savage-Landor c. 1900.

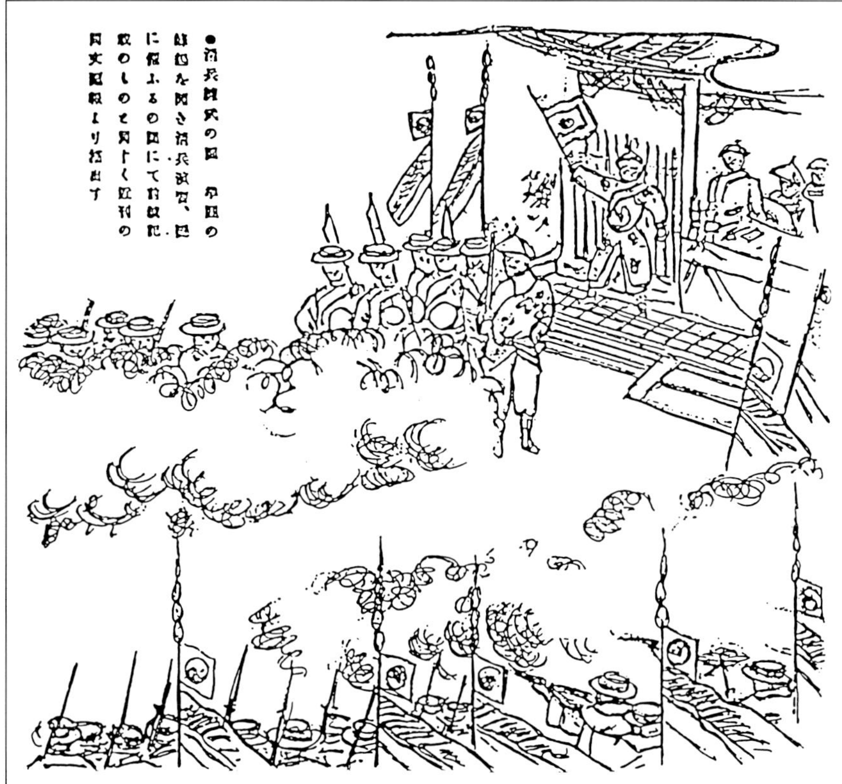

Figure 3.8 Chinese newspaper illustration showing Chinese soldiers training, *Manchoho*, 30 June 1900.

scholarly debate about the military in any of its manifestations. Cultural connotations about what constitutes appropriate "soldierly" uniform are deeply rooted to this day. Deeply rooted not only in the minds of the soldiers who wear the uniforms in question but also in the minds of the civilian populations from which the soldiers are drawn. For civilian nationals, the uniform worn by the military of their country represents to them the epitome of a fighting man. Historians of the cultural roots of war need to be aware of their own cultural prejudices in this matter as well as to be completely versed in the culture, traditions and the history of the uniforms worn by soldiers in their own culture.

Another nianhua which shows the same remarkable ability to capture the distinctive bearing of foreign soldiers and officers is "The Battle of Yangcun — captured Foreign Officers brought before General Dong" (Plate 3.20).[158] British artists did not see any Chinese soldiers or officials until after the fall of Beijing in August 1900. However, British artists, while not always able to draw a convincing representation of a Chinese officer or soldier, did not produce ridiculous caricatures (see Figure 7.1). This nianhua and another, "Kicking and Dragging French and Russian Spies Before General Dong" (Plate 3.21),[159] show foreign soldiers at a complete disadvantage; that is, after they have been captured and are being brought before senior Chinese commanders for trial. This latter image shows men whose bodyline is quite different from that of Chinese soldiers. This bodyline resulted from years of drilling in the Western manner of the era. It also came from the fact that the soldiers in question wore their uniforms with particular pride in the fit and cut of the uniform itself.[160] This pride embodied distinctive cultural ideas as to what constituted "an officer and a gentleman" or "a soldier of Her Majesty's X or Y regiment."[161]

The most outstanding distinction between Chinese and foreign soldiers stemmed from a culture specific sartorial notion of what a man — and more precisely — a fighting man, should look like. Chinese soldiers wore leggings under long baggy trousers; Western soldiers all wore tight-fitting trousers. In the eyes of Chinese observers, it was the wearing of trousers by foreign men that led them to walk so fast and in so undignified a fashion like labourers and that caused them to be known as "straight long-legs."[162] British and Continental European officers, particularly cavalry officers, were fanatical about the cut of their jackets and breeches. This fanaticism continued until the 1939–1945 War. The writer has known many officers who fought in this war and who persisted in keeping as a close secret the name and address of their personal military tailor. At its most ridiculous, this extremist and highly personal attitude towards uniform (the very contrary to the initial reason for uniform which is to impose an outward conformity on the group wearing that uniform),[163] resulted in jackets being so close-fitting after the Napoleonic wars, that officers were unable to raise their sword arms.[164] However, the Western notion of what constituted appropriate uniform for soldiers and high official dignitaries so closely permeated the view of contemporaries, that when they saw Chinese high-ranking officers, soldiers or officials in traditional Chinese garb, they could only see the "theatrical," the "unmanly."[165]

This difference in the physical cut of the uniform gave rise to two quite different perceptions of individual military strength and soldierly prowess. The salient point is that the nianhua never represent the foreign soldiers as ridiculous or as some detestable "Other," as does the anti-missionary propaganda of the early 1890s reproduced in W. T. Stead's *Review of Reviews* and discussed in Chapter Two.[166] Thanks to the contrast offered by the illustrated and blatantly anti-foreign, anti-missionary propaganda, we are able to see that the standard of accuracy of the artisans drawing foreign soldiers was at least as high as the standard of accuracy with which British, American and European [167] artists depicted Chinese soldiers.

The Chinese artisans responsible for these two woodblock prints (Plates 3.20 and 3.21) have captured some of this Western military uniform cult. While the soldier being led along by his Chinese captor at the centre of Plate 3.21 is only a member of the rank and file, he nevertheless has been drawn walking as a Western soldier wearing military dress would be obliged by his training and his uniform to walk. A glance at the stance of all the Chinese soldiers in all the nianhua shows none with their legs in a similar posture to that of the Western soldier. The fact that Western soldiers wore leather boots as opposed to the cloth boots and shoes worn by the Chinese also affected their stance and their bearing. Even into the twentieth century, Western military officers of this epoch could be recognised by their bearing when wearing civilian clothing long after retirement.

The uniform itself was, though immensely important, obviously only partly responsible for this phenomenon. Uniforms were worn by officers in contexts such as ceremonial drilling with their companies, dining at the mess and on glittering gala occasions.[168] All these situations produced Western officers whose physical posture and facial expressions were as well, if not better, characterised by Chinese folk artists than they were by contemporary full-face Western photographic portraits (see Figure 2.12). Chinese artists knew little or nothing about the general and specific military cultures that produced these officers, but the product was so distinctive that the artists had no trouble re-creating it. Chinese commanding officers were, however, fully aware of the effect an armed body of military men in unfamiliar uniform would have on Chinese soldiers or civilians. During the First Opium War, in March 1840, Commissioner Lin organised a mock battle "dressing some of the assailants in red clothes, in order to habituate the defenders to the sight of the colour of the enemy's costume."[169] During the Boxer rising, the uniforms of General Nie's Western-trained troops were also seen by Chinese civilian authorities to be potentially problematic in that the villagers may have reacted with fear and/or hostility towards these strange uniforms.[170]

To return to Plate 3.20, in the middle ground on the left-hand side we see three Chinese artillerymen. Chinese artillerymen had been photographed in Western uniform since the 1870s (see Figure 6.14). These particular artillery troops are dressed in traditional Chinese uniform. The stance of the man to the left of the artillery piece is modified by the fact that he is engaged in some kind of discussion. The stance of the other two Chinese artillerymen is upright and soldierly in a Western sense, despite the fact that they are wearing traditional Chinese uniforms. The weapons used by the Chinese artillery were imported from the West and were always the most up-to-date in point of arms technology. All soldiers trained to use them had been drilled in ways similar to contemporary Western artillery drill since the 1870s. These three artillerymen, despite their Chinese uniform, have nothing of the traditional Chinese martial arts look about their stance. The weapons they have been trained to use predominate over the uniform in terms of dictating their bearing as gunners in action. We see this to be the case from the photograph in Chapter Four (Figure 4.3) and in Chapter Six from the evidence of foreign military attachés who witnessed Chinese artillery drill. Artillerymen in all armies at this time had a particular status. In the British army, for example, this status was that of a lower middle class technician who operated smelly noisy machines using precise mathematics; the very antithesis of the gallantry and dash of an aristocratic cavalry regiment.[171]

Now to an analysis of two last examples that illustrate the range from the most traditional of nianhua, colourful and full of symbolism and architectural conventions, to the xinwenzhi, a single news sheet. Such news sheets were put out by big printing houses where there was some likelihood of access to pictures drawn by artists who, if they had not been to that particular front themselves, had seen foreign soldiers drilling on ceremonial occasions. The news sheet telling of the victory at Liang Shan (Figure 3.3) again demonstrates the Chinese artist's ability to capture every minute detail of the body language resulting from the military training and cultural self-image of a French serving officer. The three groups of officers in attendance at the artillery pieces have adopted postures that we recognise as quintessentially those of European officers waiting for the appropriate moment to bring the artillery pieces to bear on the opposition.[172] The officer in the centre of the group in the foreground is standing with arms akimbo, not a stance to be adopted by dignified high-ranking Chinese officers wearing jackets with very deep sleeves. Interestingly, the group of Chinese artillery officers already discussed in the nianhua depicting captured foreign officers being brought before General Dong (Plate 3.20) as exhibiting a more characteristically Western stance, contains one artilleryman with an elbow on his hip. In 1917, Mao Zedong wrote that for Chinese men who wore the long traditional gowns "to stick out their arms and expose their feet, to extend their limbs and bend their bodies" would be shameful.[173] The rank and file soldiers, whether firing or at the ready, have the straight backs, upright heads, necks and shoulders of men firing volleys with repeating rifles. A few of the men have been drawn with their heads down so that their eyes are sighting along the rifle, also a characteristic posture.

The French are facing the troops of General Liu Yongfu. These troops were armed with modern weapons but fought largely using traditional tactics, particularly the hit-and-run guerrilla tactics of the banditry from which most of them originated. They had a high rate of success in battles with the French, regularly defeating them, and on two separate occasions capturing and beheading the French general commanding at the time. General Liu was a hero in the mould of *The Three Kingdoms*. Raised from his dubious state as a chief of a band of brigands, he was eventually honoured and decorated by both the Vietnamese and Chinese governments. He is an example of the type of hero discussed earlier who reached high official status through his military knowledge gained as a representative leader of the common people.[174] We cannot say that European cultural traditions gave rise to this type of military hero and leader. Neither Robin Hood nor Wilhelm Tell fit the model we see in Liu Yongfu and many other great Chinese military leaders. Liu came to be styled "the General of Three Provinces." In keeping with the stereotyping which was an essential part of the woodblock artist's way of communicating some kinds of meanings, the artist has depicted the stance of the troops of this great hero in the martial arts tradition, although they are deployed in similar formation to the French, possibly because the opposing Chinese forces are also armed with artillery. Unfortunately, the powder exploding does not allow the viewer a clear enough vision of the Chinese artillerymen and their stance. This picture makes it quite clear that two separate military traditions were inspiring the men on the field that day. It constitutes an accurate record of a military engagement drawn by a Chinese artist who has given as good a likeness of the French military as a French war artist might have done. Photography at the time was still primitive and unsuited to action-packed events such as war. This woodblock print of the Chinese army that eventually triumphed that day at Liang Shan, conveys the opening moments of the engagement more accurately than any photograph would have done.[175]

Turning to the second example, we see a nianhua showing the Imperial Chinese Army forcing the Boxers to confront the foreigners with knives at the battle for the cathedral in Beijing (Plate 3.16). This nianhua is drawn in the same tradition as the many representations of "The Ruse of the Empty City" from *The Three Kingdoms* (see Plates 3.1 and 3.2). Nevertheless, while the traditional conventions are applied to the drawing of the fortified walls and the cannons themselves, we see quite clearly that the artist has drawn the angles and towers of a Christian cathedral. Churches caused great offence in North China; the cathedral at Tianjin had been burnt down in 1870 and was to be burned again in 1900.

Offensive though it might have been, the cathedral and its angles have been faithfully re-created within the parameters of the artistic conventions of the nianhua. Similarly, the Western soldiers and their commanding officer have been embraced by the rubric of the nianhua tradition to the extent that the doll-like faces of those in the forefront make them look like painted lead toy soldiers. Their stance, though distinctive and different from that of the Chinese troops, is one of repetitive stylisation that characterises folk art as it represents soldiers in general (whether foreign or Chinese) as opposed to a news sheet purporting to describe particular soldiers. Nevertheless, the details of the foreign soldiers' uniforms are accurate — particularly considering that the cathedral in Beijing was defended by a motley conglomeration of foreign soldiers, mostly Italian, and civilians who withstood the siege with great courage.

This nianhua depicts battle as Chinese peasants would expect to see it. The Chinese soldiers and their commanding officers look like their counterparts in thousands of different nianhua depicting episodes from the great historical romances. The "balloon" device in this case, emanates from the semi-divine forces of the Red Lantern shining down to protect the Boxers who have been forced to the front. Paul Cohen interprets the "balloon" device differently and very plausibly as "The Red Lantern to the left rear … has flung a magical rope between the two sides, protecting the Red Lanterns in the middle from the cross-fire."[176] Such a nianhua would have contained strong symbolic messages for the rural and urban poor who bought it. The Boxers were thought to be invulnerable, hence they are drawn under the protection of the shining Red Lantern. (There were female groups of Boxers who trained separately and were known as the Red Lanterns.) The Boxers were obviously caught in the cross fire between the foreigners and the Chinese troops and armed with inferior weapons. The artist may have been attempting to indicate that the Boxers had been forced to take the hot seat with great courage, that they were being used as cannon fodder by the Qing, and that perhaps it is the Qing action which has broken the spiritual protection around them. While it is possible to have some ideas of total numbers of prints put out annually by various studios, it would be impossible to trace the numbers reprinted off a particular block. It would be very interesting, however, to know just how well this print sold.

Nianhua as Evidence of Military Weapons of the Day

The nianhua depicting battles may also be reliable sources of the use by all the armies involved of various kinds of military weapons or devices. Very often the nianhua would depict the Chinese forces as wearing old-style uniforms and using outdated weapons, whether or not this was actually the case in the battle concerned according to other documentary evidence. It is not suggested here that the nianhua should be used as they stand. Like any other primary source material, they need to be used with caution and in combination with other sources for a number of reasons. However, there are nianhua which give clear evidence, not only of the weapons and defence materiel involved in the particular action, but also of the fact that the Chinese had been Western drilled. The nianhua, "A Battle Between English and French Forces and Boxer Troops" (Plate 3.10), depicts a folk art rendition of Western-drilled troops. This nianhua, when viewed with the photographs of soldiers doing rifle drill taken by Auguste François between 1896 and 1904 (Figure 3.2), shows that folk artists were beginning to capture the distinctive military bearing of Western-drilled troops and their weapons. In this way, the nianhua were performing a vital function in showing the peasantry what Western-drilled Chinese soldiers looked like.

The nianhua showing the battle of Fuzhou (Plate 3.22) explicitly refers in the text to artillery mounted on the masts of fighting ships, both French and Chinese, and the artist has clearly depicted the guns in question. The nianhua showing the Chinese re-taking the city of Bei Ning (Bac Ninh) by assault in February 1884 (Plate 3.23) shows a French aerial balloon being used to report on the movements and dispositions of the Chinese troops. The Chinese are trying to down the balloon by firing arrows at it. One hundred years earlier, a French Jesuit, Jean-Joseph Amiot had tried without success to get the Chinese interested in the potential military value of balloons. In the 1780s, the Chinese thought that the expense involved did not justify the possible return.[177] In fact, balloons were not extensively used during the Napoleonic wars. By the 1880s however, the Chinese were extremely interested in the potential use of balloons in warfare, an informative article appearing in the *Dianshizhai huabao* about ballooning on page 6 of the first edition. By the army manoeuvres of 1908 (see Figure 6.20), the Chinese had their own ballooning corps as part of the engineering corps. It is quite probable that further research may establish the existence of a ballooning corps well before 1908.

This particular nianhua is a very exciting find as it is the only one uncovered by this research depicting real events that is used again, slightly altered, to describe another battle at a much later date. Re-using a woodblock was common practice in England and on the Continent. In China, certain blocks, such as those representing door gods for example, were also used again and again by the main studios until they wore out. However, the multiplicity and inventiveness of artists, their skill in colouration and fine detail as well as the discerning nature of their vast public meant that this was the exception in certain types of subject matter only, rather than the rule.

When the nianhua showing the capture of Bei Ning in 1884 reappeared as the recovery of Tianjin in 1900, all possible anachronisms had been removed, as was the balloon.[178] The French flag at the top of the corner "turret" had been replaced by a Japanese one. The soldiers pouring through the breach in the wall in the lower left hand corner now bore a Japanese flag rather than a French one. This nianhua was not carved expressly as a tribute to the courage and heroism of General Nie Shicheng.[179] However, it is notable that a picture describing events in the Sino-French War should have been chosen to represent the events in Tianjin in 1900 when so many other woodcuts of these events were being made. It is also notable that though the artist knew that there were French soldiers there that day, he wanted his audience to be clear that there were also Japanese soldiers there. After the re-issue several times of various prints of the Sino-Japanese War and the Sino-French War, and given woodblock artists' evident interest in providing correct detail for certain objects, this substitution of the French flag for the Japanese flag is interesting. Given the number of different nianhua of real battles that had already appeared and given this artist's specific intent to show that of all the eight countries involved, the Japanese were there in Tianjin, we may reasonably suppose that some of the people seeing or buying this nianhua now knew what a Japanese flag looked like. Flath has defined in a number of ways what "looking at a picture" meant in the context of the nianhua.[180] In the urban environment where these nianhua were posted up in public places and in the rural environment where they could also be seen and discussed at markets, it is the element of discussion that needs emphasising in the context of such details in nianhua of real battles rather than the element of learning new ways to see. If only one or two people looking at the Japanese flag knew that it was the Japanese flag, they would tell the others; if they also knew what the French or the Italian flag looked like, they would likewise explain this to the other people standing by.[181]

Foreign consuls and military attachés disliked these nianhua on the grounds that they allegedly systematically offered false accounts of the battles concerned. Mark Elvin gives as an example the fact that coloured prints were pasted up "showing the war of 1894 not as a national humiliation but as a Chinese victory not just over Japan but over all the other Powers as well."[182] According to these foreign observers, nianhua thus inflated the Chinese popular sense of national pride and patriotism whilst to Western commentators, the reality was that the Chinese were always being defeated. Western observers in the late Qing did speak of the fact that these military prints were re-issued at politically critical times[183] and there is evidence on some of the prints themselves as to the number of the edition of the particular surviving print. Some new ways we may look at these nianhua are to see them as evidence of a different cultural perception of victory; to see them as evidence of a battle that was actually won by the Chinese as agreed by contemporary Western military observers; and to see them as describing a decisive defeat as a victory and to postulate reasons why folk woodblock artists would produce a representation of a battle lost by the Chinese as a victory.

In its purest form the traditional folk art nianhua used symbols, plays on words and other devices to indicate good and evil. When folk artists drew woodblock pictures to depict the enemy, the aggressor, the "Other," the differences between this enemy, his buildings, his ways of fighting, were brought within the conventions of the folk tradition. Once inside those traditions, the enemy was drawn with the same kind of fidelity to acceptable folk art traditions, as were the heroes — in this case the Black Flags or Boxers — or the anti-heroes, the soldiers of one of the Chinese regular armies. These latter were supposed to support and protect the peasants and the urban poor, but very often they were the scourge of those whom they were sworn to protect. The Boxers were also responsible for the deaths of untold numbers of Chinese citizens and the destruction of their property even when it was quite clear that these people had never had the least contact with foreigners, let alone having been converted to Christianity. Thus there were particular differences singled out to describe the enemy and denote him as "Other," but there was no tendency to ridicule, to parody or to create the enemy as a grotesque monster. Within the tradition they worked, at this cataclysmic moment of Chinese history, Chinese folk artists depicted the action with an extraordinary faithfulness to the physical manifestations of an entirely different military culture. Like their counterparts in Britain, the artists drawing for the *Daily Mail*, the Chinese folk artists were emphatically not responsible for producing inflammatory pictures of foreigners despite the atrocious behaviour on the part of many of the troops in most of the invading armies.

Two Parallel Representations of War: Chinese Myths and Western Myths

We have examined extensive examples of the pictorial imagery of nianhua describing battles. It is evident that, to a high degree, these woodcuts give accurate information about the way foreign soldiers were dressed, the way they stood to give battle depending on the weapons they used and, occasionally, about unusual types of war materiel used by foreigners. On the issue of "reliability," "true and/or responsible representations of reality," we should note that this was not part of what the traditional artists nor the illiterate public expected of nianhua. Nianhua were about drama, action and heroic behaviour (that is, those pictures which fell outside the traditional category of good wishes). Thus as we move to a consideration of nianhua as purveyors of accurate factual information about real events, we will be evaluating the artists' ability to move outside tradition and assume a hitherto inconceivable and even possibly undesirable quasi-journalist role. Flath notes that:

> Changes in the practice of viewing intersect with changes in the subject to be viewed. This led to the development of a "media" in rural China which connected "event" to its representation as printed image.[184]

When the nianhua are examined together with their extensive captions, the issue of their reliability as descriptions of specific battles becomes more obscure. Overall, the captions divide into three categories. There are nianhua which were not objectively true in any possible sense. There are some that would have been seen to be true from the Chinese viewpoint at the time. Although the genre was savaged by contemporary Westerners for its inaccuracy, there are nianhua that did in fact convey a lot of correct factual information about the course of battles forming part of a chain of Chinese victories. Lastly, there are nianhua that can be validated as victories by recourse to parallel foreign sources but which neither foreign contemporaries nor posterity have accepted as reliable accounts of the military action in question. The existence of these three identifiable categories can be better understood if we accept that there are real cultural differences between what may be regarded as defeat and victory. These differences are highlighted by the nianhua themselves and by the reaction of foreigners to them.

The first category is relatively simple to identify; what then becomes interesting is the fact that at the time when there were examples of objective war reporting, in the *Shenbao* for example,[185] popular woodblock art was responsible for the wide dissemination of blatantly false accounts of battles. This raises the question of possible Qing intervention. Censorship in this context — that is the reporting of a defeat as a victory, the most notable example being Admiral Courbet's annihilation of the Chinese fleet and the recently French-built arsenal[186] at Fuzhou on 23 August 1884 (Plate 3.22) — would not, however, have impeded sales. Indeed, it would seem clear that the reverse may have applied. The second category of commentaries, those that may be seen to have appeared true to Chinese of the day, indicates the existence of a difference between victory as it appeared to the Chinese and as it appeared to their foreign enemies. The nianhua showing events of the First Opium War already discussed is an example of this. It is the third category that is the most interesting, that is, prints which contain written information that contemporary foreign observers and posterity have either obliterated from the record or refused to accept as true. However, as preliminary research into Chinese and foreign sources shows them to have been true; it is this category which merits some investigation.

The depiction of the events of the Boxer rising is the central focus of this book. In this chapter, the main concerns are to demonstrate that the nianhua brought new kinds of details about foreign soldiers to the rural and urban poor and that the nianhua are indicative of a difference between Chinese and foreign perception of victory and defeat. An important similarity exists between the reporting by Western contemporaries and posterity of the battles of the Sino-French War and the Boxer rising. Examples of other kinds of illustrations of the Boxer War are discussed throughout the book and we wish to take the opportunity here to examine nianhua of the Sino-French War to establish that the same themes can be followed through by a study of nianhua of another high-profile conflict between China and foreigners in the nineteenth century.

It cannot be sufficiently stressed that historians are notoriously blinded by outcomes. Outcomes are black and white to all but the most subtle of historians. Very few military historians assess the cost and consequences of victory, as does Kawano in his article "Allied Military Cooperation in the Boxer Rebellion and Japan's Policy."[187] In this study, Kawano postulates a reason for Japanese reluctance to send troops to the Boxer rising as being that the Japanese high command perceived that military resources had been over-strained by the Sino-Japanese War. Insofar as the Sino-French War and the Boxer rising are concerned, the long-term effects on China were that the country was not divided like a melon, as was Africa, for example. Neither did the French ever succeed in imposing a long-term presence in Yunnan in any way detrimental to China's interests.

One of the reasons for the inability of historians hitherto to acknowledge the fighting strength of the Imperial Chinese Army divisions involved in the fighting in 1900 is that both Chinese and Western historians have focussed on the Boxer rising as a peasant *rebellion*. However, it should also be perceived as a *war* between Chinese regular army forces and the invading armies of eight countries. Once the Boxer rising is discussed as a war, it naturally becomes impossible to dismiss the role of the Chinese regular soldiers who fought in that war in the way that all scholarly accounts of the events of 1900 have done so far. Similarly, authoritative recent accounts of the Sino-French War acknowledge the numbers of battles won by the Chinese. However, they tend to stress the irregular tactics of the troops under Liu Yongfu. There is a dearth of accounts that give a clear account of the military successes by Western-drilled Chinese troops over the years 1880 to 1885 or the qualities of tenacity, leadership, training, logistics, acquisition of materiel, military skill and judgment which gave rise to these successes.

Because of the evidence given by the nianhua describing events on Taiwan during the Sino-French War, it seemed imperative that French military accounts should be examined to ascertain the reliability of some of the statements made in the captions of the nianhua. As was the case in the Boxer War, during the Sino-French War, contemporary French military men had no difficulties in acknowledging Chinese military ability nor were they guilty in any way of minimising that ability. Captain Garnot's account, and others like it, presents details of every phase of every battle in the short-lived French campaign on Taiwan. Such accounts show that professional French soldiers fighting the Chinese were readily able to acknowledge their fighting strengths and were certainly not sources of the myths such as that the Chinese were afraid to fight in the dark. Instead of expressing incredulity of the "Sacré bleu!" type, on finding that the Chinese fought in the manner of Western-trained troops, Garnot noted this quite matter-of-factedly.[188] He also recorded such details as that the Chinese ability to ensure the forward supply of ammunition was superior to that of the French whose need for ammunition was great consequent on French wild, inaccurate and indiscriminate firing.[189]

It seems to this writer that there is a major historiographic fault-line running through Western scholarly accounts of battles between Chinese and foreigners in the nineteenth century. This fault-line consists of the perpetuation of negative myths about Chinese military capacity in any of its manifestations without recourse to the accounts — whether Chinese or Western — of the men who fought in the battles in question. Another crack in the fault-line arises because historians make assertions about the professionalism of the Chinese military in the absence of suitable comparisons with the contemporary Western military. An analysis that bases its concept of Western military professionalism on the self-image of the medieval knight is hardly appropriate to military conditions in the nineteenth century, particularly to the British or Prussian officer class.[190] Any serious evaluation of different military traditions requires an objective overview of comparable and differing factors in the same time period. The catastrophic consequences of the purchase of commissions in the British army lasted until well after the system was abolished in 1871. The snobberies of the British officer class which looked down on those officers who had earned their promotions through actual service in parts of the British empire, India in particular, were detrimental to the British army. The conservatism of the civilians in the British war office and the French ministry of war continued to have drastic consequences until the 1939–1945 War and, in the case of France, until the wars in Indo-China and Algeria.

As for the view held by Western intellectuals from the Enlightenment to the middle of the twentieth century that it is only underdeveloped cultures or subcultures that perpetuate myths concerning any aspect of military culture or performance, this is clearly untenable. This study adds to the work of those wishing to see "a conceptual break-through demonstrating not merely the importance but the centrality of myth [in particular in military contexts] in complex institutions and complex societies."[191] "Military culture, including the civil-military relationship, has been and continues to be of signal importance to a proper understanding of China."[192] All societies and all histories, popular, oral, fictional or scholarly, create myths surrounding specific wars, the image of the common fighting man, the image of the warrior hero, the great leader, courage itself and above all, victory and defeat. Myth in relationship to military endeavour can most usefully be understood as "epitomising and confirming a system's values and norms, producing models for emulation, and establishing the worth of specific behaviours."[193] With notably few exceptions, Western historians have not looked hard enough at the complexity of the myths created by the Chinese themselves about war and the fighting man,[194] neither have they examined the Chinese myths in the context of British or European, Japanese or American myths created about valour in war and greatness in military leadership.

A historian needs to evaluate the difference between the myths of the culture out of which he or she is writing and those of the culture he or she is describing. Obviously, the myths will not necessarily value any aspect of the military past in the same way. It would seem equally obvious that the myths of every distinct culture should be carefully evaluated in terms of the records of that culture itself. Records need not be written or pictorial records. An obvious form that has received little attention from historians in general and military historians in particular, is the folk song. Any physical symbol for which large numbers of men (sic) fight and die is of no greater or lesser intrinsic value as indicative of the courage of those men than any other physical symbol. Enough has been said on the subject of uniform to make this point quite clear. As Denis Showalter has pointed out with considerable insight, "Military events ... particularly invite transformation into myth and cultivation as social memory. They can be processed simultaneously as triumph and tragedy. Their complexity defies exact reconstruction."[195] We may add to this that military myths, whether processed as triumph or tragedy, are collectively understood as such by men, women and children at all levels of a particular culture at a particular time. The factor of the technological level of the society in question is immaterial. Acceptance of myths by any one society as triumph or tragedy may change but the cardinal point is that our view of change must embody the element of popular understanding of the day.

In order to attempt to provide another model for judging the relative merits of Chinese and foreign military performance as illustrated in conflicts between China and other foreign powers in the nineteenth century, a number of nianhua describing events of the Sino-French War and the Boxer rising have been selected. These nianhua have captions that constitute an accurate description of the battles they illustrate. In conjunction with other sources, these captions offer authoritative versions of those events which neither contemporaries nor posterity can dismiss as a type of propaganda appealing to the latent nationalism of primitive Chinese peasants in general, not merely those from Shandong and the North China Plain.

The Sino-French War

The course of the Sino-French War is as difficult to trace as that of any other comparable war, fought as it was intermittently over four years both on the island of Taiwan, at Fuzhou, Ningbo and on the China-Vietnam border, occasionally striking deeply into Chinese territory. Where difficulties arise is in finding Western scholarly accounts that give straightforward reasons for Chinese successes and detailed descriptions of successive Chinese victories, particularly those overwhelming victories of March 1885 which formed the unlikely prelude to the signing of a peace treaty. The fact of two weeks of hard fighting resulting in decisive Chinese victory after victory being a prelude to the signing of a peace treaty seemed unbelievable to Chinese contemporaries. Lloyd Eastman quotes the example of Bao Zhao, a front-line commander who wrote a Memorial telling of how his subordinate officers pleaded that they be permitted to continue the attack and that though he commanded them to, they would not leave his tent. They "... performed the kowtow without cease and they were so excited that they were in tears."[196]

Such a dichotomy might have reasonably been expected to be the subject of analysis by Western historians of the Sino-French War but this does not seem to have been the case.[197] There were some overall important defeats of the Chinese by the French, notably at Fuzhou where French victory was assured by violating international agreements concerning foreign warships.[198] There is a lot in the literature condemning the Chinese authorities for not honouring agreements. There is also a distinct Chinese military tradition that the victor is the one with the just cause. Thus there is a need for a dispassionate analysis of the numbers of Chinese victories, including where, as in Taiwan, the Chinese army encircled the French, gradually wore them down and drove them off the island. The actual military events of the Sino-French War would tend to suggest that the Chinese and foreign analysts of the day were right in their bemusement at the decision to sign a peace treaty when it seemed obvious that the Chinese were in the ascendant. The French public had already expressed its indignation at the disastrous course of the war with public opinion leading to the fall of Jules Ferry's government. Most of Denis Showalter's insights into the separate myths created by the French, the Americans and the Vietnamese about the different battles fought at Dien Bien Phu resound with eerie echoes of contemporary French public and military recognition of the disastrous performance of the French on the Indo-Chinese boarder and on Taiwan.[199]

This is not a verdict that emerges clearly from Western scholarship on the course of this war. When the Chinese did win, their victories were attributed to mismanagement or misjudgment by the French or to difficulties with the climate and the problems of logistics posed to the French. All these factors applied equally to some if not all the Chinese armies fighting the French. At various points during the war, various Chinese generals had to discharge men whom they could not feed. Lack of food and problems of sickness plagued Chinese troops not acclimatised to the region just as much as these discomforts affected the French. Hundreds of Chinese soldiers died of malaria.[200] Liu Mingchuan has been singled out by American scholars for his brilliant organisation and logistics when he had to fight both the French and the aboriginal people of Taiwan while simultaneously having to consider the very real threat from Japan.[201]

During the course of the French colonisation of Indo-China, two French generals lost their lives while fighting the Chinese. Francis Garnier was captured and beheaded by Liu Yongfu on 21 December 1873 as was General Rivière on 19 May 1883. Many senior French officers also lost their lives during the war, the disastrous course of which roused French public opinion to fever pitch. Chinese diplomats in Paris, London and Germany were well aware of the political consequences of this war for the home electorate and gave advice based on their accurate perception of the pulse of the French public. A careful reading of French sources, combined with the evidence of the nianhua, gives an accurate picture of the number of battles and engagements won by the Chinese. It also shows that in many instances, while French troops may have captured citadels, either in Vietnam or on Taiwan, they were unable to hold them and were obliged to leave after varying lengths of time. Such actions may have seemed to the French to have been indicative of victory while equally well appearing to the Chinese as clear evidence of French defeat.

The events in Taiwan between 1884 and 1885, including the blockade of the island and the attempt by Admiral Courbet's fleet to prevent the rice tribute coming to Beijing, are examples of action which could be seen by either side as indicative of victory. While the French mounted offensives with some initial success, like the British at Keelung in 1841, they never actually captured Tamsui. They were encircled by the Chinese who wore them down physically and psychologically. Even though desperately needed reinforcements were eventually sent from Algeria, these arrived too late to be of assistance.

As Garnot describes Admiral Lespès' difficulties in getting the Government to agree to vote him more troops and more supplies, we see that these problems were international; why did Gordon die in Khartoum? Only seventy years later, another French government was giving its military men similarly impossible orders:

> Increasingly, Dien Bien Phu became within the French army … a shorthand symbol for a paradigm in which politicians obsessed with the game of musical ministerial chairs and generals attuned to prevailing winds from Paris gave soldiers an impossible task, then befouled their sacrifices.[202]

To attribute Chinese losses to the particularly poor structure of the Chinese administration and a reluctance of military leaders in one area to send troops to the relief of another contested area, is to misunderstand the nature of perennial difficulties between the mentalities of soldiers and civilian administrators everywhere. These problems arise from what is perceived as necessary by the commander in the field, what is perceived as possible by the government of the day, what is acceptable to public opinion of the day and what is perceived as desirable by military leaders responsible for the defence of other areas of strategic importance.

Neither the metropolitan government in Paris nor his military superior in Tonkin would vote further men or supplies to Lespès in the struggle for Taiwan. This was a problem endemic in nineteenth century wars of empire. We need to advance a balanced assessment of China's ability to take into account the totality of the strategic threats during the course of an actual war. Such an assessment would incline one to the proposition that China's performance was little better or worse in the specifics of making decisions about the use of limited military resources than was, say, that of France in Indo-China or Britain in Africa and New Zealand.

The issue was not that "China's inability to defend herself on the sea in modern times was part of a larger failure to adjust her institutions to the Western impact."[203] It was, rather, that all military systems with new strains placed upon them, as was also the case with France and Britain in the nineteenth century, required some time before civilian policy and military exigencies aligned sufficiently to prevent disaster if, indeed, they ever aligned at all. Looked at from a broader perspective, China was by no means the only power to fail to obtain the sort of civilian and military coordination required to ensure success in the complex business of making war far from the metropolitan country itself, in the case of Britain and France, or the metropolis in the case of China.

Keelung was the site of three unsuccessful attempts by the British to scale the heights around the harbour and capture it in 1841, an episode in the First Opium War that receives scant attention in the literature. The occupation of Keelung by the French did not in any way influence the Court at Beijing on the frank admission of the French. They left, their members severely depleted by fever and the Chinese, six months after they had landed in Taiwan. From this brief account alone it is difficult to see how the French could have thought that they had obtained any kind of victory by their short stay on Taiwan and their unsuccessful blockade of the island and of Beijing.[204] However, on leaving Taiwan, Admiral Courbet set sail for the Pescadores and took the islands in one day. The French possession of the Pescadores was a matter of complete indifference to the Court[205] but the French saw it this way:

> In as much as the occupation of Keelung was useless, particularly in envisaging future eventualities, the occupation of the Pescadores could bring us advantages.[206]

In the wars of Empire it is true that barren insignificant trophies like Hong Kong could turn into thriving centres of profit for their new imperial masters. However, in the case of the Pescadores, this was not true for France, either in the short or in the long-term. A dispassionate analysis would appear to conclude that Admiral Courbet's efforts were either countered by Chinese military action or worthless as he had acquired points of insignificant strategic or commercial advantage. The captions on the nianhua showing the Chinese to have been victorious in action on Taiwan would thus appear to be accurate. (Figure 3.9)

The graphic style of the nianhua representing the military action on Taiwan is very similar to the style used in the early nianhua of the Opium War (see Figure 3.9 and 3.10, and compare with Figure 3.3). As with the nianhua already discussed, it may be seen that the woodblock artist has absorbed the difference in stance and body language of the European officers (see Figure 3.9) and military innovations, such as stacked rifles outside tents (see Figure 3.10). At issue is the wording of the text: is it accurate and does it contain inflammatory language used against the enemy?

At this point a distinction must be drawn between the wording of xinwenzhi and the style of nianhua. Xinwenzhi gave straightforward, if not particularly detailed accounts of the action depicted. Nianhua frequently had recourse to poetry, accounts or references to similar wars fought long ago or known in literary tradition, and occasionally had recourse to verbal symbolism very difficult to translate accurately today. This is particularly true of nianhua signed with a pen name.[207] It is for this reason that, of the nianhua with written captions describing actual battles referred to in this study, only those with straightforward verbal inscriptions will be selected for analysis.

In the case of Figure 3.9 "Liu's Troops Win Several Naval Battles One after the Other," the text is a completely accurate account of the French campaign in Taiwan as far as the action on land was concerned. The text of the nianhua goes on to give an example in which a French cruiser barred the way of the Chinese and was engaged by the Chinese vessel. According to the text of the nianhua, the French had run out of ammunition and in this engagement many French soldiers were killed. A reading of Garnot shows how often and with what disastrous effects the French land forces ran out of ammunition.[208] French accounts do not mention specific naval engagements but gloss over the details of Admiral Courbet's ineffectual blockade:

> For one convoy or two which our ships managed to intercept, twenty others got through. They were carrying more than 20,000 good fighting men, all well armed.[209]

It may be seen from this example that considerable research is required to validate the specifics of military history with relative certainty. As well, the point must be emphasised that in writing the history of wars between European and non-European peoples, particularly in the nineteenth century, insufficient weight has been placed on the evidence offered by non-European sources of any kind, not necessarily written. Historians in general have shown a reluctance to dissect campaigns battle by battle as Belich has done for the Maori Wars[210] and as has been done in the case of the battle of Dagu, the Seymour expedition and the battle of Tianjin in Chapter Seven. This nianhua serves as a starting point. Further research is required to elucidate whether or not there was one naval engagement between the Chinese and the French off the coast of Taiwan in 1884–1885 that was won by the Chinese. If Commandant Thirion wrote that for one Chinese convoy intercepted by the French, twenty got

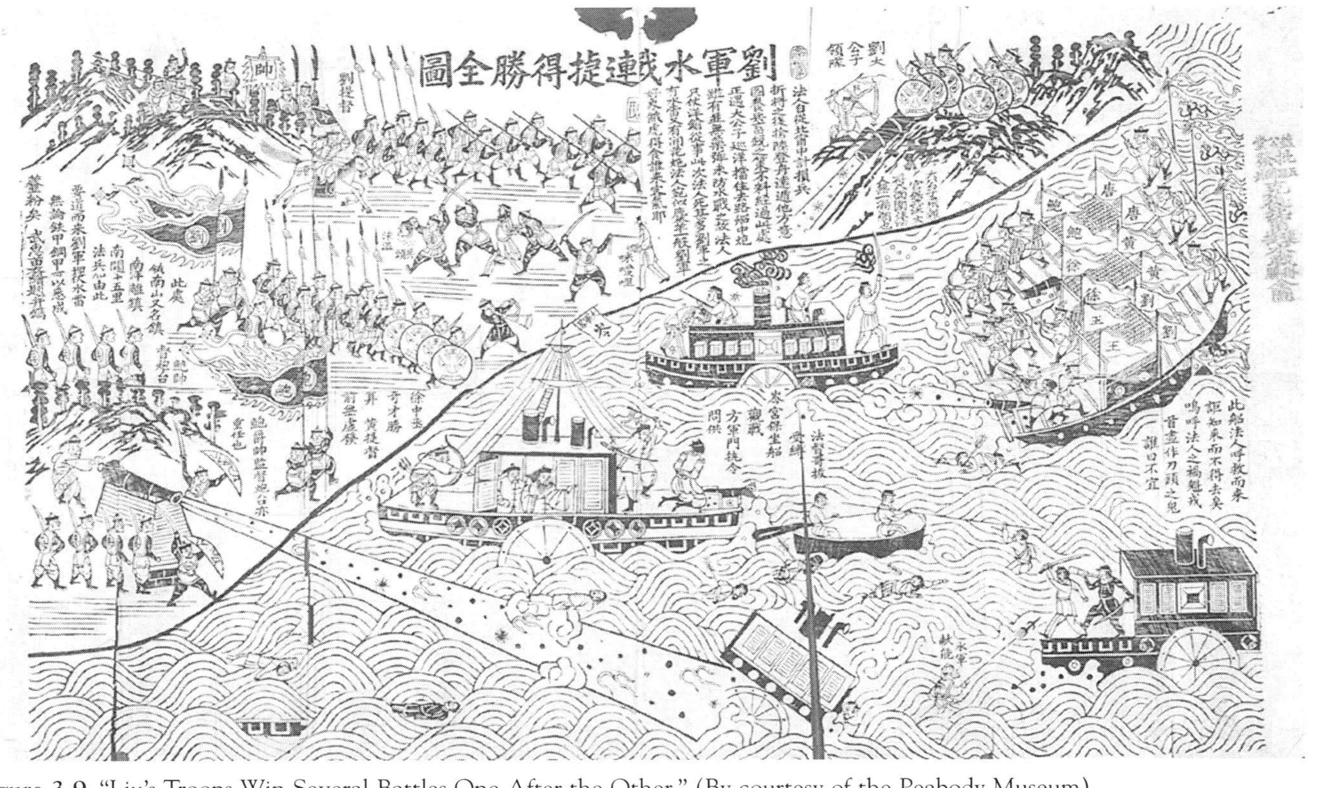

Figure 3.9 "Liu's Troops Win Several Battles One After the Other." (By courtesy of the Peabody Museum)

through, it is quite possible that there was an engagement along the lines described by the nianhua. Moreover, Thirion's account gives a lugubrious picture of the state of French rations and ammunition on Taiwan and makes it clear that their logistical backup was lamentable. In a note to the extract from Thirion's *Memoires*, Taboulet wrote:

> It is to be noted that during all these naval operations, it was the Chinese, supplied with the most recent equipment bought in Germany, who had the superiority in materiel.[211]

Given the almost complete consensus on the alleged inefficacy of the Chinese navy in the last twenty years of the nineteenth century, it must be stressed that on their own admission, the French were unable to sustain an effective naval blockade of Taiwan. Moreover, it is surely worth knowing whether — even if only on one occasion — the Chinese navy got the better of a more powerful foreign adversary.

Turning to the question of the degree to which emotive language was used in the wording of the text of the nianhua, there is a statement "French soldiers are just like sheep and Liu's soldiers are just like tigers. So when tigers see food, how can they be polite?" Night after night the under-nourished French guard was penetrated by the Chinese who exhumed the bodies of French soldiers and beheaded them, bringing back the heads as trophies to their commanding officers who paid a bounty of fifty taels for each head.[212] Under these circumstances, the metaphor of the French as sheep and the Chinese as tigers could hardly be said to be unjustified poetic licence.

The Sino-French War was in its fourth year when Admiral Courbet attempted to take Taiwan. The text of the nianhua says that "The French are at the top of the list of foreign enemies and they caused it [the war]. Who says it is not fitting that they become ghosts on the knives?" This is far from being torrid language designed to stir up the peasants who filled the ranks of the Chinese fighting men. The nianhua does in fact contain a marked moral tone in the cultural context of Chinese philosophy regarding just and unjust warfare.[213] The morality in question is that it is irresponsible to open hostilities for no good reason and if disaster follows, those who began the battle were seen by Chinese commentators in the nianhua tradition to have brought it on themselves. As Zhang Junbo and Yao Yunzhu comment "In a very real sense, Chinese traditional military theories place more emphasis on upholding 'justice' while Western theories focus on the gaining of interests."[214]

It is clear from the example of this nianhua that as sources, the nianhua invite further research and cannot be dismissed as vainglorious, emotive wildly inaccurate productions designed to delude the peasantry. That there were some which fell into this category is undeniable (see Plate 3.22).[215] However, a revised account of the Sino-French War would do well to examine actual performance in individual battles and to take into account the evidence of the nianhua.

Interestingly, the contemporary Western viewpoint has been preserved on a nianhua of the Chinese fighting the aboriginal inhabitants of Taiwan (Figure 3.10).[216] Written in barely legible English on two sides of the nianhua are the following words: "The war in Annam — note the want of perspective. The Chinese report universal victory for themselves when in reality it is the opposite." The reference to perspective may simply be a comment on the folk art style of the picture. The comment on the text is unequivocal despite the fact that the commentator has mistaken the theatre of war.[217] For the Chinese to report victories and disseminate them in nianhua was unacceptable to the Europeans. Even in the reasonably clear-cut case in which Admiral Courbet lost 1,400 men out of a total of 2,000 on Taiwan either in action or because of illness due to poor logistics — lack of food and medical supplies — and was obliged to abandon the island![218] Similar Chinese losses were reported during the same war. The difference was that these losses through illness were incurred in defending what the Chinese considered a tributary state to which China had obligations. In terms of aggression, this Chinese action was opposed to that of the French muscling in on a weak kingdom and setting out on a vainglorious attempt to capture an island which would have been of some considerable military burden to the French even had they succeeded. However, this writer has not found any evidence of scholarship in the English language that gives these details of massive French losses or other details of inept military performance on the part of the French. Even recent revisionist work perpetuates the myth that the French defeated the Chinese easily.[219]

The writing up of the Sino-French War affords an excellent example of Orientalism as Saïd would not hesitate to point out. The same military mistakes made by each of the opposing armies were on the one side (the French) glossed over or excused in a blatantly "Orientalist" fashion. Unless one looks for some kind of Orientalist mentality, how else can one possibly

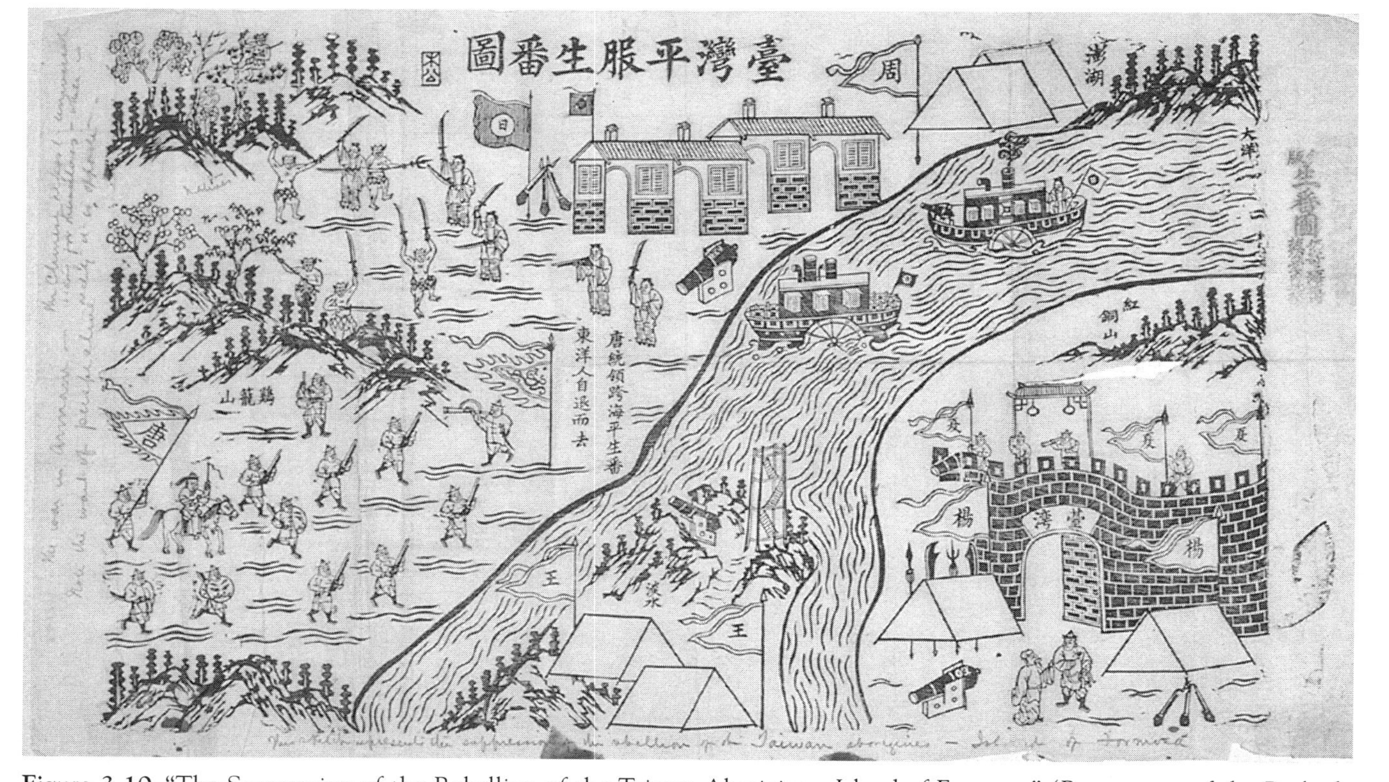

Figure 3.10 "The Suppression of the Rebellion of the Taiwan Aborigines, Island of Formosa." (By courtesy of the Peabody Museum)

interpret the fact that Admiral Courbet lost 1,400 men out of a force of 2,000 in just six months and earns no reproof in any of the histories? While on the other side (the Chinese), relatively minor setbacks — minor, that is for example, in comparison with Courbet's performance or the debacle in which General François de Négrier was wounded — have been condemned as demonstrating lamentable logistics and "poor leadership." If the Chinese won, this was because of "French indecisiveness, logistical difficulties, tactical errors and simple lack of preparation."[220] The Chinese never won because of any specified Chinese military skills. Accounts of these battles are consistently manipulated to make the French appear superior, certainly never definitely losing, while withholding credit for military initiative and prowess from the Chinese. What is most notable about the scholarly accounts of the Sino-French War is the consequences of the failure to look carefully at the results of every major engagement and the failure to use the first hand accounts of French officers who took part in the war.

The Boxer Rising

Turning to the nianhua of the Boxer rising, the same pattern emerges. The texts of the nianhua are brief. They can almost all be shown to constitute a fair description of the action at hand as far as can be ascertained by independent reference to European and Chinese sources, and they have been entirely ignored by scholars as accurate accounts of the individual pieces of action they describe. The nianhua "The English and the French Armies Engaged in Battle with the Boxers" describes the action on 28 June 1900. On this day the Boxers advanced and clashed with British and French soldiers as well as those of other countries. The text of the nianhua states that one of the commanders under General Nie Shicheng came to join the battle, as did the soldiers of General Dong and that it was an even match. In fact, the majority of skirmishes and artillery duels resulted in heavy losses and/or the withdrawal of the Allied forces during the first four weeks of the battle for Tianjin.

Having given a detailed analysis of nianhua and official military accounts describing the Sino-French War as well as a detailed analysis of photographic evidence and military accounts of the Boxer War in Chapter Seven, it is not proposed to give a detailed analysis of the texts of every nianhua describing the Boxer War. However, a few general points can be made about the military events described in the texts of the nianhua. With regard to casualty figures, for example, all the nianhua which give figures for enemy dead, give figures which are quite credible and certainly as credible as the figures given by Western sources during the first four weeks of the battle for Tianjin. Second, the types of strategies described in the texts of the nianhua are, in fact, the strategies described by the foreign military chroniclers of the action. They include mine-laying, bridge-building, trench flooding, the pressing of the attack from various quarters, the use of the element of surprise and the use of torpedoes in action against the Russian ships at Shanhaiguan. With regard to details of foreign soldiers and their uniforms, deployment and weapons, once again the nianhua are very faithful to these details. The nianhua "The Chinese Repulse 4,000 Japanese" (Plate 3.15) clearly shows very up-to-date cannon on modern gun carriages; there is one cannon quite unlike any of the others in the nianhua of the Boxer War that looks as if it may possibly be a gun that could absorb its own recoil — this would make it a Krupp cannon and the most advanced of the day. Though the Imperial Chinese Army certainly possessed some of these guns, (See photograph at Figure 7.8a) it is not absolutely clear whether or not the device the artist has drawn at the back of the gun carriage is an attempt to show such a gun.

In the surviving nianhua, General Dong Fuxiang is given more prominence as leading the action in Tianjin than was actually the case. Again, like Liu Yongfu, General Dong was a very charismatic leader. Even if he and his Muslim soldiers were greatly feared, certainly by the inhabitants of Beijing, his name resonated with heroism after the death of General Nie Shicheng and the withdrawal of Generals Ma Yukun and Song Qing. Overall, there are slightly more nianhua reporting victory than was really the case. However, once again, as in the Opium War and the Sino-French War, if victory is taken to mean that as the result of a particular engagement, the Allied forces withdrew, this is a realistic description of most of the military action around Tianjin in June and July 1900.

The texts of the nianhua describing the engagements of the Boxer War contain no vainglorious statements about the Chinese soldiers; they are described as fighting "with bravery" and the Boxers "with ferocity," descriptions with which all foreign military men concur. Finally, no scurrilous language is used to describe the enemy who is variously referred to as "the joint Allied forces" or "the Western armies" or "the foreign soldiers." In general, the neutral descriptive quality of the language of the nianhua corresponds to the accuracy of the artistic depiction of the action.[221]

Military Portraiture in China

Having exhaustively canvassed aspects of the Chinese and foreign military represented in the nianhua, there remains one extremely significant cultural difference with regard to the pictorial depiction of the military between China and Europe, Britain, Russia, America and Japan. In the thirty-volume Taiwan reprint[222] of the *Dianshizhai huabao*, China's "equivalent" to the *Illustrated London News* or any of the great European, Russian or Japanese illustrated weeklies, there are only sixteen full pages devoted to portraits; nine of foreigners and seven of Chinese. One unique woodblock print, neither in the xinwenzhi style nor the nianhua style, was found depicting a Chinese military leader, Liu Yongfu (Plate 3.24) Rather than go into the social, artistic and cultural reasons for this, its implications will be briefly discussed in the context in which a country is at war.

The latter half of the nineteenth century was the great age of the portrait of military heroes in European, British, Russian and Japanese weekly magazines. While some of these were photographs, many of them were drawings. These drawings formed a picture in the public eye of the hero whose military exploits they were following and made possible the passionate cult of a military leader.

> Here we have a soldier. Young though he is, he has earned the right to command; his bearing, his eye, everything about him, speaks of courage and manly pride.... It is clear how this subject should be treated. There must be a feeling of life, passion, movement.... An open-air effect, sharp shadows, no mysterious half-tones, the figure in a stable pose, an open and honest gesture, nothing vague; in the background a tumultuous array of suitably martial accessories.[223]

In gala uniform, in the field, on the quarter deck, mounted on horseback, the visual depictions of the European, British or American, Russian or Japanese military leader were infinite. Some interesting work has been done to show that after the Crimean War, the ordinary soldier too, received his share of space in illustrated magazines, whether as an individual or in groups.[224] The pictures resonated with courage, leadership, authority and the power to overcome difficulties: all these qualities were drawn for the Western or

Japanese public by professional illustrators in weekly magazines. There were often special editions with a particular general or admiral in full dress uniform that could be taken out and pinned on the wall.

The extraordinary contrast this forms with the Chinese case must be underlined. Research has uncovered one woodblock print (see Plate 3.24) containing a eulogy of Liu Yongfu. However, the picture itself is an insipid concoction and could not be said to resemble anyone in particular. Certainly it has not been ennobled by art as Western and Japanese culture conceived that painting or photography should invest a military man with glory. This woodblock print of Liu Yongfu made no attempt to impress on the public eye a striking image of that daring General, the Governor of Three Provinces. We have seen nianhua which show Chinese military leaders as most impressive figures within the Chinese nianhua tradition (Plate 3.19). The tradition existed in a very limited context and was not applied to this print. Moreover, as a proportion of the total print, the picture is insignificant, completely dominated by the text. The eulogy stresses that people from everywhere cherish the desire to see his likeness. The Chinese artistic traditions with regard to portraiture and the portrayal of human emotions on the human face and body were vastly different from those of the West. From its inception, that is, at roughly the same time as in the West, the Chinese were interested in portrait photography and had strong views on the subject.[225] Nevertheless, in time of war, the contrast between the Western (as well as Japanese) and the Chinese media approach to the pictorial depiction of military leaders played an enormous role in forming public opinion. In the Western and Japanese cultures, even if military leaders were occasionally exposed for culpable behaviour, their pictures, always in heroic military mode, were in the public eye all the time. During the Boxer War, the Germans and the Austrians published propaganda postcards showing naval officers resplendent in full dress uniforms, military decorations glittering on their breasts, keen blue eyes and thick golden beards completing the effect of the military man posed in all his glory. In the Chinese culture, the public was not attuned to identifying with a culturally created visual model of what constituted a heroic military leader. In China, the military leader in question might have behaved with extreme heroism or, like some of the English officers during the Crimean War or the General in command at Aldershot in the summer of 1900,[226] he might happen not to have been there on the day of the battle or the parade.

In either case, the military leader received no public media coverage comparable to the Western and Japanese newspaper and magazine articles with full portraits of military officers.

In China portraits of great military leaders (or any other important figures) were deemed unsuitable for illustrated magazines. This fact implies a great many interesting points about the role of illustrated magazines like the *Dianshizhai huabao* in creating images of important Chinese political, military and cultural figures. The *Dianshizhai huabao* contains a report on Feng Zicai, a poem and a portrait of Chen Yuying in honour of his sixtieth birthday (both generals had fought with distinction against the French) as well as pictures of Li Hongzhang and Zeng Guofan.[227]

A hero that one reads about is very different from a hero whose face and figure one has seen. It is very difficult to establish the cult of a hero whose face and figure one has not seen. As in the West, so in China, certain features were thought to indicate certain character traits. In China, private individuals had very strong ideas of how they wished their facial features to appear in daguerreotypes. Li Hongzhang had his picture taken together with Ulysses Grant on Grant's visit to China in 1878.[228] Photographic portraits of nineteenth century Chinese military leaders are extremely rare and were not widely disseminated at the time. In the West, media illustrators could and did slightly heighten certain facial characteristics of military leaders; as soon as the art of the daguerreotype was born, so was the art of retouching it.

Military men, as much as, if not more so than other professionals in the West and Japan, were photographed, painted, sketched and re-photographed endlessly. They were reproduced in every known technology. They were before the public eye as were their successes and failures. A magnificent portrait of Admiral Seymour in three quarter profile appeared very prominently in the *Daily Mail* on 28 June 1900. This was not the case in China. The names of great military leaders like Liu Yongfu were literally on everyone's lips, but until the twentieth century, their pictures were not before everyone's eye to be the more readily engraved on everyone's hearts. Incomplete heroes, their physical likeness was not public property in a culture as visually sophisticated as was the Chinese. This meant that the fighting careers of China's great military men were not followed in the same way as were the careers of the Lord Raglans, the Earl of Cardigans, the Gordons, the Lord Chelmsfords, the Kitcheners, the Seymours and other aristocratic British military leaders whose campaigns were often distinguished by their bumbling ineptitude even, in the case of Lord Kitchener in the Boer War, deliberate cruelty to women and children prisoners of war.

There was a particularly Chinese phenomenon of brilliant military leaders absenting themselves from active service just before victory was achieved. Outstanding Chinese military leaders commented openly on the deleterious effects of executing senior commanding officers in front of their men when the Chinese had lost a major military engagement. The distinguished nineteenth century Chinese civilian and military leader, Zeng Guofan is an example of the first phenomenon and he was one of those who raised his voice against the second. Another consequence of the British military tradition of glorifying failure is that soldiers would willingly fight again for a commanding officer under whom they had served and lost a major battle. Chinese soldiers rarely had this opportunity.

During the Crimean War, Lalumia has pointed to an abrupt about-face in the pictorial representation of general as hero to that of general as responsible for culpable defeat or general as shirker, betraying his men.[229] Those historians writing about the quality of leadership in the Chinese armies during the nineteenth century would do well to amplify their understanding of the nature of military leadership and its relationship to a given social structure by a study of the British system. In the British system it was the norm to buy a commission. This in turn lead to a high proportion of aristocratic, non-professional military officers[230] who nevertheless had enormous social and political clout viz à viz any of their fellow officers who might have been able to work their way up through the ranks.

If there was one factor that could mitigate public indignation at the repeated failures of British military leadership, it was a full page portrait of a military man. Admiral Seymour, for example: his uniform, his pose — all redolent of the heroism which the British public wanted to see in its military heroes despite their growing exposure in the press as culpable incompetents. China also had its great military leaders as well as its incompetent ones. The important difference was that these men were not continually before the public eye in illustrated newspapers and magazines, inspiring confidence and admiration by their portraits, whether or not, like their British counterparts, they sometimes betrayed or lost their men through their own incompetence.

There had been a time in Chinese history when an emperor had commissioned portraits of famous generals and had shown specific interest in European pictures representing military victories won by European sovereigns.[231] The absence of portraits of military leaders from Chinese pictorial traditions and media depicting war in the second half of the nineteenth century was not because there was a dearth of such leaders. The complete absence of the cult of the hero through frequent pictorial representations spoke of different cultural attitudes to portraiture. More importantly, it also indicated a tradition that had not as yet evolved to see the propaganda value of the charismatic military leader himself as opposed to the victory of the Emperor and his empire. In fact, personal valour and success in battle for a Chinese general often led to his downfall rather than brightening and lengthening his career. Nevertheless, the charismatic military leader did exist. He was rewarded, eulogies were written to him after his death, but in all the vastness of China, to most people he was just a name. That extra dimension, the visual, which allows people to create and others to identify with a military hero, was not present in any of the pictorial traditions of nineteenth century China.

Newspaper Illustrations

As so few newspaper illustrations in Chinese newspapers were found and as such illustrations are very rare in the non-missionary Chinese language press at this time, they will all be reproduced (see Figures 3.8, 3.12, 3.13, 3.14). These illustrations were originally drawn for a Shanghai newspaper, possibly the *Wenhu bao*. As we saw in the case of the *Daily Mail*, these drawings make no attempt to parody, to glorify, or to misrepresent their subjects in any way whatsoever. The Boxers destroying the railway look like any railway gang legitimately at work, the fleeing foreigners look as though they are taking part in a foot race at an annual picnic (Figures 3.12). The two pictures depicting really violent destruction, the firing of the church and the regulars of the Imperial Chinese Army fighting Boxers, are full of action but at a level quite in accordance with what is going on (Figures 3.13 and 3.14). The fifth picture showing the courageous men of the Chinese regular army in training having heard about the Boxer rising (Figure 3.8), is an interesting one as it gives irrefutable evidence of the modern headgear worn by Nie Shicheng's men and the modern weapons they were trained to use. This headgear also appears

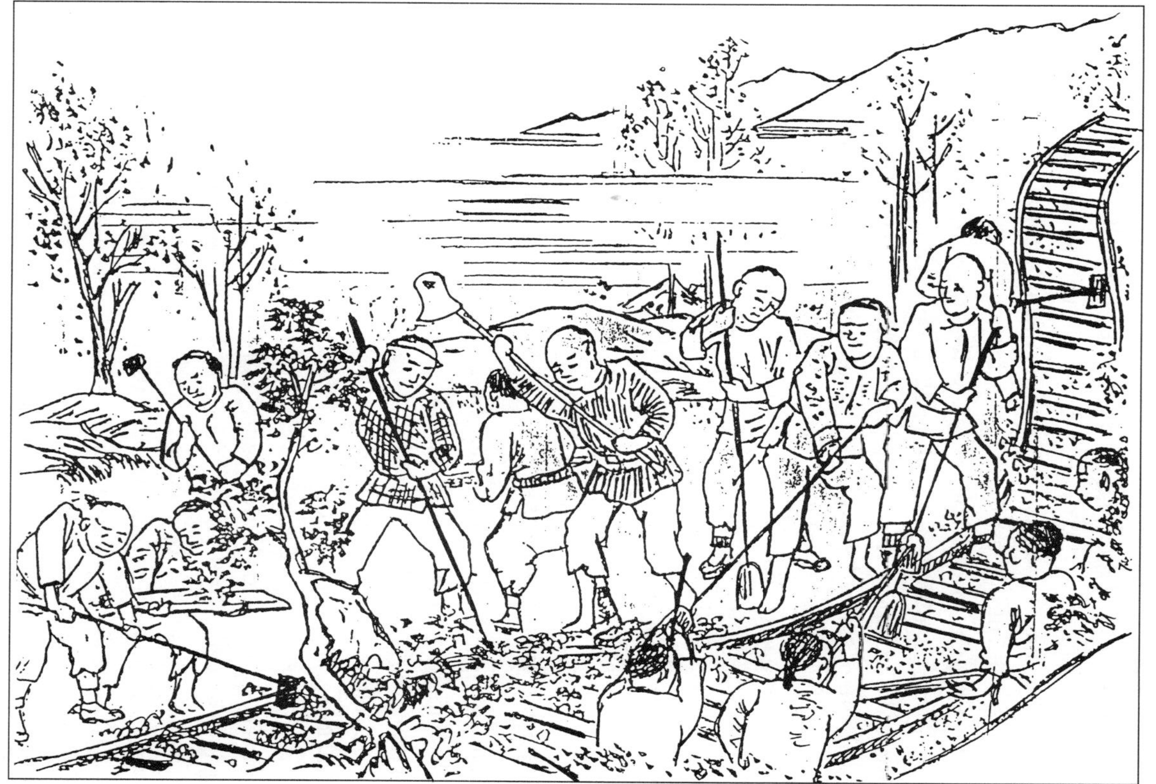

Figure 3.11 Chinese newspaper illustration showing the Boxers destroying the railway, *Manchoho*, 30 June 1900.

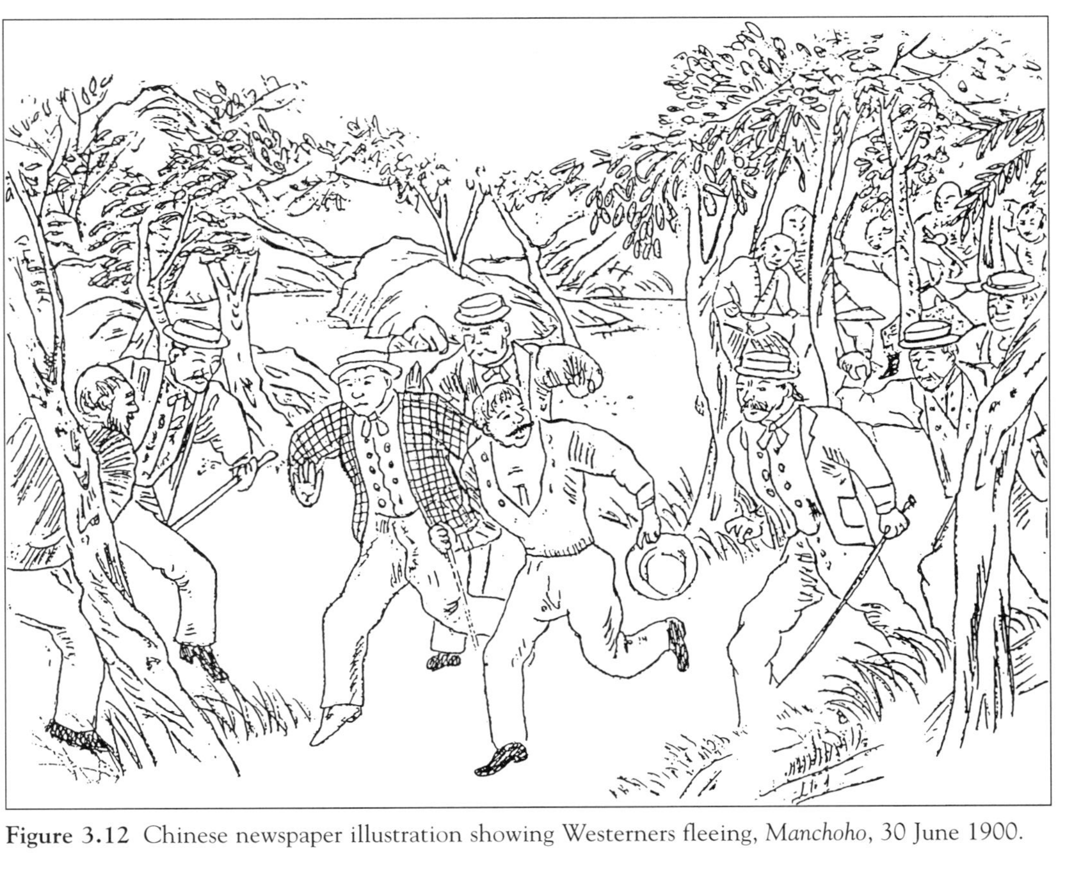

Figure 3.12 Chinese newspaper illustration showing Westerners fleeing, *Manchoho*, 30 June 1900.

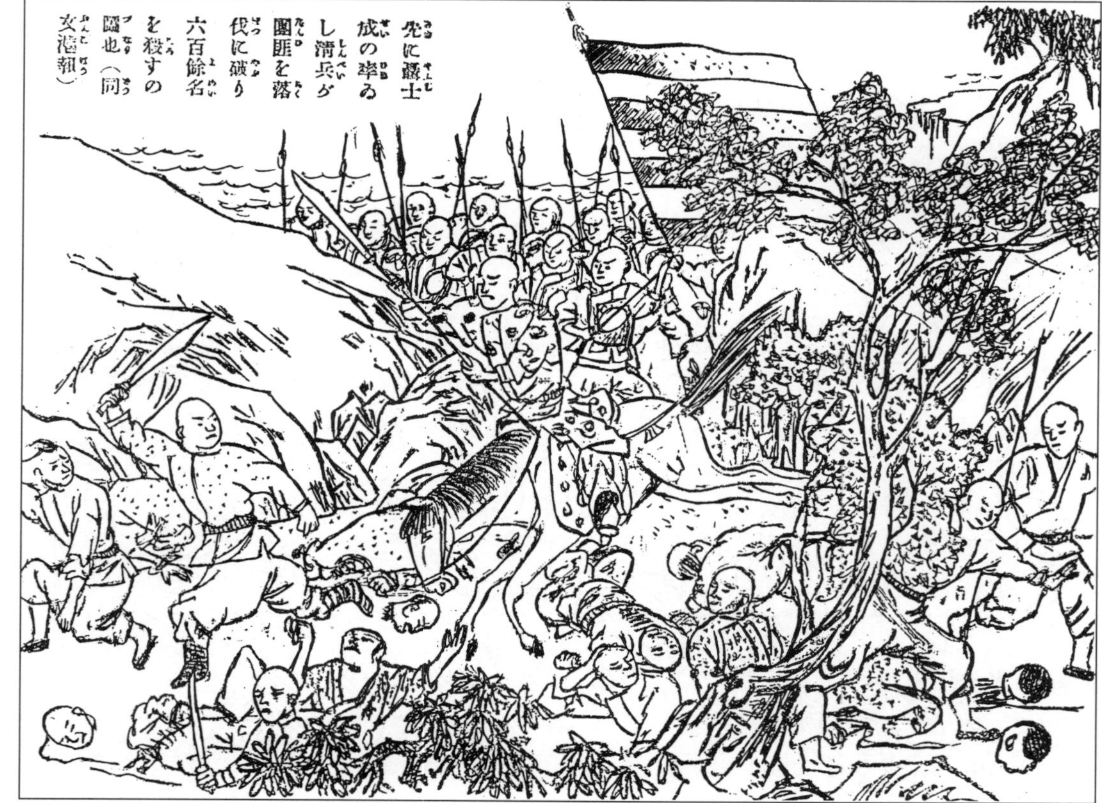

Figure 3.13 Chinese newspaper illustration showing the Imperial Chinese Army slaughtering the Boxers, *Manchoho*, 30 June 1900.

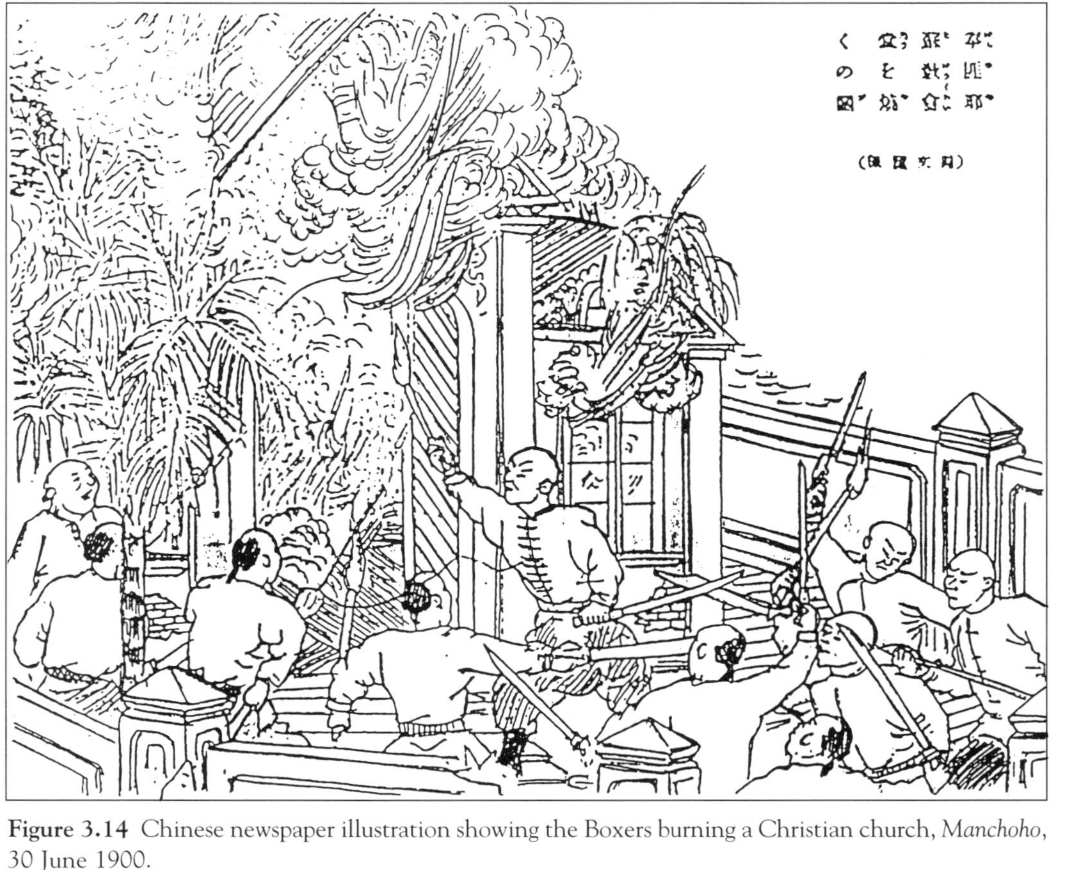

Figure 3.14 Chinese newspaper illustration showing the Boxers burning a Christian church, *Manchoho*, 30 June 1900.

in Savage-Landor's photograph (Figure 3.7). From photographic evidence, we can see that there was different summer and winter headgear and these Western boater-style hats worn by men of Nie Shicheng's army were summer uniform issue.

These five pictures, just like their counterparts in the *Daily Mail*, are — given the contexts — informative rather than sensationalist and give responsible pictorial information about the events being described. Similarly, the captions are not as inflammatory as one might expect under the circumstances. The picture showing the flight of the Westerners speaks of their "stupidity in their disorganised panic-stricken flight from our country" but none of these adjectives can be said to be excessive, given the hatred of foreigners that was inflamed by the Boxer rising. The picture showing General Nie Shicheng's men fighting the Boxers uses the verbs "battering," "killing off," "slaughtering." This is strong emotive language and it does indicate sympathy for the Boxers. However, even though this sample is very small, it is interesting that it reflects the same sorts and varieties of drawings and language we have seen used in middle class and working class papers in America and England. The question of the extent of the role of censorship under the circumstances of the Boxer rising in China with many telegraph lines being down is not one that can be readily addressed. Nevertheless, although the sample is too small to form the basis of a valid generalisation, it is interesting that the pictures from Chinese newspapers discussed here refrain from perpetrating a violent inflammatory sensationalist viewpoint, either pro or anti-Boxer. In fact, they are parallel to the commitment to responsible reporting demonstrated by the majority of the illustrated Western press.

Reflections

Chinese woodblock folk art representation of warfare is distinguished for its visual ability to encapsulate the action, the violence, the drama, the pace and the heroism displayed by men during battle. As well, the nianhua give an intense visual realisation of the enormity of war, the puniness of the individual soldiers and the distance men must place between themselves and their actions in order to fight, to destroy and to kill. They were cardinal in forming the conceptions of war and values as to what constituted a courageous fighting man in the minds of hundreds and thousands of rural and urban poor in China. There are important connections between the nianhua and religious and lay traditions of martial arts, between nianhua and the great Chinese romantic historical novels and between nianhua and Chinese opera. These heroes and battles were known intimately to every lad and his family in town or village in nineteenth century China.

Chinese nianhua of war are, above all, about the common soldier, the common soldier directed by his officer certainly, but the common soldier in all the multitude of postures, all the sound and colour of ordinary soldiers killing and being killed. Analogous with this is the fact that there are no nianhua depicting a great general on a battlefield in a particular pose with rank and file soldiers barely discernable in the distance as in the European folk woodblock tradition. This research uncovered one woodblock print celebrating the charismatic general, the Governor of Three Provinces, the hero Liu Yongfu. The *Dianshizhai huabao* was the monumental illustrated weekly reporting actual events at the end of the century in China. Over the years 1884 to 1898 there were four pictures in China's most celebrated pictorial whose only subject was a great military figure. Four pictures among an estimated 4,000 sheets of pictures extant from the *Dianshizhai huabao*.

Nianhua of real, fictional or operatic battles were a part of every peasant's daily life; they were to be found in or outside the homes of all the urban poor. The values they expressed regarding cultural traditions of valour, courage and skill in warfare were deeply imbued in the consciousness of the very men who fought those wars. The nianhua combined symbolism and conventions intimately understood by the peasantry and the urban poor. Thus they formed an ever-present visual stimulus to remind men, women and children of what war was all about. The art form itself allowed for layers of simultaneous action such as was the stuff of real war. It was ideal for conveying the intensity, the immensity, the confusion and the pace of war. Traditional artistic devices combined with the physical number of ordinary fighting men in each battle scene meant that by looking at a nianhua, one could almost hear the sound effects of the action. One feels the force of the fortress walls splitting open, the watch towers bombed to smithereens, the ships exploding, the men shouting and struggling in individual combat. The Chinese nianhua stood alone against all parallel traditions in the West at that time, as an art form which could depict the actions, struggles, destruction and death of the common soldier in war. Unlike Japanese woodblock prints (see Plate 3.25),[232] Chinese nianhua depicting war have not been discussed extensively in the literature and do not have any great intrinsic monetary value.

The artisans who produced these nianhua were extraordinarily accurate in their work, being able to incorporate into the Chinese tradition foreign soldiers and their completely alien physical movements, uniform and way of fighting. When one looks at the xinwenzhi of the victory at Liang Shan, it is with difficulty that one represses a sense of Monty Pythonesque exaggerations of the look of the nineteenth century British military man.[233] In this case the officers in question were French. Nevertheless, parallel European military traditions gave rise to a recognisable physical bearing and a particular mentality. Although Chinese folk art could and did use parody, the example of the clay French soldier at Figure 3.5 being a case in point, parody was never used in the nianhua. There was no tendency to ridicule or to create the enemy as a grotesque monster although grotesque monsters were very much a part of other Chinese visual and literary traditions.

In concluding, we return to the question raised earlier as to whether or not there was a difference of perception between European and Chinese artists and their audiences as to what constituted victory and defeat in warfare. This question is an important one for it breaks open the issue of whether or not the small wars of the nineteenth century between China and foreign countries really humiliated (as opposed to angered) the ordinary Chinese of the day. Before the Sino-Japanese War, the answer reflected by the nianhua and supported by our analysis of the nianhua, is that there was a difference of perception. This difference of perception was reflected in folk art. It is clear that the Chinese artists and their audiences perceived victory more than they perceived defeat in the nature of the military engagements with foreigners shown by the nianhua. The obverse of this view was the Western view which fulminated about the way in which the Chinese were arrogantly and willfully misrepresenting the outcome of minor wars, minor in the sense of their overall political and strategic long-term implications for the empire of China as a whole. The nianhua infuriated Westerners because it appeared that the Chinese were deliberately distorting the truth about wars in which various Western countries or Japan were involved. It seemed to the Westerners that the outcome of these small wars obviously indicated defeat more than victory. The war with Japan was not a small war in the minds of contemporary Chinese, the Chinese lost and yet nianhua — style prints appeared depicting Chinese victories.[234]

We have seen that there was little or no political censorship of pictorial representations of military events applied to the woodblock artists most of the time in the late Qing. They drew the pictures and wrote the commentaries on the basis of their understanding of the outcome of particular battles. As their understanding was so often one showing China victorious, we have to assume either that the artist was deliberately misconstruing the accounts he had heard of the action or that there was, in fact, another view which permitted the same events to be construed as a victory. This study suggests that there was another view, that artisans drew pictures incorporating that view and that the hundreds of thousands of ordinary Chinese who bought the pictures had grounds for seeing victory in those pictures and reading victory in those texts. The nianhua depicting war in the nineteenth century were more than a folk art form; they were the expression of a different but equally valid cultural tradition regarding defeat and victory in warfare.

Notes

1. My thanks to Professor James Flath, Professor Robert Harrist and Dr Frances Wood for their invaluable help in making detailed comments on an earlier version of this work.
2. James A. Flath, "Printing Culture in Rural North China," unpublished PhD thesis, University of British Columbia, 1996, discusses the work of two particular artists who also produced nianhua Qian Huian and Liu Mingjie.
3. Ibid.
4. Wang Shucun, *Ancient Woodblock New Year Prints*, Foreign Languages Press, Beijing, 1985, p. 8 and Zhang Dianying, *Yangjiabu muban nianhua* (New Year Woodblock Prints from Yangjiabu), Wenwu chubanshe, Beijing, 1990, p. 9.
5. Flath, op cit., p. 130 makes the important observation that "The introduction of event based narratives (narratives that describe events that occur in the present, and in relation to a fixed place) brought new configurations to the market."
6. Mark Elvin, *Another History. Essays on China from a European Perspective*, Wild Peony, Australia, 1996, "Mandarins and Millenarians: Reflections on the Boxer Uprising of 1899–1900," p. 201
7. For an incisive discussion of the Chinese response to foreign economic and military intrusion in Chinese affairs, see Joanna Waley-Cohen, *The Sextants of Beijing. Global Currents in Chinese History*, W. W. Norton and Company, New York, 1999, Chapter Six.

8. Flath, op cit., p. 139 and 172–173. Flath poses this important question "How the resilience of older standards of looking configured the understanding of war and whether the visualization of war as having a narrative independent of antiquity was involved in visualizing the conditions of nationalism. If so, how did the image influence the understanding of the nation?"
9. There is an extensive debate in the literature centred on the issue of whether or not an anonymous or even a known woodblock artist produces art or manufactures folk objects as an artisan. This debate ranges well outside the immediate world of scholarship concerning Chinese traditional folk art New Year paintings and is, perhaps, most usefully examined in Sally Price, *Primitive Art in Civilized Places*, University of Chicago Press, Chicago, 1989. In general, Japanese woodcuts, produced as they have been by well-known Japanese artists of various identifiable schools, have tended to be regarded by Western art historians as "high" art and command big prices in well-known galleries throughout the Western world. By contrast the anonymous productions of artisans in Chinese woodblock studios have not. Interestingly, since the flowering of the Chinese New Year print from studios in Suzhou in various periods, Japanese private collectors have recognised the artistic worth of these exquisite prints and have collected them extensively.
10. The amount and variety in the literature reflects the length and scope of the tradition of printed illustrations in China. Some useful works include: Sören Edgren, *Chinese Rare Books in American Collections*, China House Gallery, 1985; Max Loehr, *Chinese Landscape Woodcuts*, Belknap Press, Cambridge, Massachusetts, 1968. John Lust, *Chinese Popular Prints*, E. J. Brill, Leiden, 1996, p. 9, refers to Zheng Zhenduo's massive study of an old illustrated woodblock print book; Zheng Zhenduo, *Zhongguo suwenxue shi* (The History of Chinese Popular Literature), Beijing, 1954.
11. For a survey of European folk woodblock art, some useful references include Leonard S. Marcus (ed.), *An Epinal Album, Popular Prints from Nineteenth Century France*, D. R. Godine, Boston, 1984; Maurits de Meyer, *Imagerie Populaire des Pays-Bas. Belgique, Hollande*, Electra, Milan, 1970; Douglas P. Bliss, *A History of Wood-Engraving*, Spring Books, London, 1928; Robert Hutchinson (Introduction), *1800 Woodcuts by Thomas Bewick and His School*, Dover Publications, New York, 1962; Edward Hodnett, *English Woodcuts 1480–1535*, Oxford University Press, London, 1935; Paul Kristeller, *Küpferstich und Holzschnitt in vier Jahrhunderten*, Verlag von Bruno Cassirer, Berlin, 1922; Keith Moxey, *Peasants, Warriors and Wives. Popular Imagery in the Reformation*, University of Chicago Press, Chicago, 1989.
12. Edith Dittrich, *Glück Ohne Ende. Neujahrsbilder aus China*, Catalogue of the Exhibition of the Cologne Museum for East Asian Art, 1984. Dittrich provides a wealth of scholarship in her introduction to this exhibition as to the religious significance of all aspects of Chinese New Year prints. She provides detailed physical descriptions as to the religious significance of all stages of various rituals

involving New Year prints during the celebration of the traditional Chinese New Year as it was at the end of the Qing dynasty. The work of Maria Rudova is distinguished for its careful references to the most abstruse symbolism. See Maria Rudova, *Chinese Popular Prints*, Aurora Art Publications, Leningrad, 1988. Some of Professor Rudova's work is compiled from the notes of her teacher, the great Alexiev himself. I wish to acknowledge my particular gratitude to Professor Rudova for her invaluable assistance in giving extensively of her time to share with me her knowledge of nianhua. Thanks to Professor Rudova, I was able to see important and seminal Chinese art works from the Song dynasty onwards. Most of the works she showed me have never been on public display in the Hermitage Museum.

13. Bruce Doar, "The Boxers in Chinese Drama: Questions of Interaction," *Papers in Far Eastern History*, Vol. 29, 1984; see also Joseph W. Esherick, *The Origins of the Boxer Uprising*, University of California Press, Berkeley, 1987, pp. 45, 50, 54.
14. David Johnson, Andrew J. Nathan and Evelyn S. Rawski (eds), *Popular Culture in Late Imperial China*, University of California Press, Berkeley, 1985. See especially Robert E. Hegel, "Distinguishing Levels of Audiences for Ming-Ching Vernacular Audiences: A Case Study"; and Barbara E. Ward, "Regional Operas and Their Audiences: Evidence from Hong Kong."
15. B. J. ter Haar, review of Po Sung-nien and David Johnson, "Domesticated Deities and Auspicious Emblems: The Iconography of Everyday Life in Village China and Anne S Goodrich, Peking Paper Gods: A Look at Home Worship," *T'oung Pao*, Vol. 80, 1994, p. 437 quoted in Tanya McIntyre, "Chinese New Year Pictures: The Process of Modernisation, 1842–1942," PhD thesis, Melbourne University, 1997.
16. Moss Roberts (translator and editor), *The Three Kingdoms*, Pantheon Books, New York, 1976, Introduction, p. xix. This work is variously referred to as *The Romance of the Three Kingdoms* or *The Story of the Three Kingdoms*.
17. Wang Shucun has been the most prolific scholar and writer on Chinese woodblock prints. Some of his important albums include Wang Shucun, *Zhongguo minjian nianhua baitu* (One Hundred Chinese Folk New Year Pictures), Renmin meishu chubanshe, Beijing, 1958; *Sulian cang Zhongguo minjian nianhua zhenpin ji* (Compilation of Chinese Folk New Year Picture Treasures in Soviet Collections), Zhongguo renmin meishu chubanshe and Sulianafulia chubanshe, Beijing, 1989; *Zhongguo minjian nianhua shi tulu: Zhongguo meishu shi tulu congshu* (Illustrated Record of the History of Chinese Folk New Year Pictures; Collection of Records of Chinese Fine Arts), Shanghai renmin meishu chubanshe, Shanghai, 1991; and (with Li Zhiqiang), *Zhonguo yangliuqing muban nianhua ji* (Album of Paintings of Yangliuqing Woodblock New Year Pictures), Tianjin Yangliuqing huashe, Tianjin, 1992. Other works of interest include Bo Songnian and Li Bao-yi (eds.), *Zhongguo nianhua shi* (History of Chinese New Year Pictures), Liaoning meishu chubanshe, 1986; Hu Zhaojing (ed.), *Yangliuqing nianhua* (Yangliuqing

New Year Pictures), Wenwu chubanshe, Beijing, 1984; Lu Shengzhong, *Zhongguo minjian muke banhua* (Chinese Folk Woodblock Prints), Hunan meishu chubanshe, Changsha, 1990; McIntyre, op cit.; Yang Congsen, *Nafu yingxian* (Enjoy Good Fortune, Welcome a Suspicious Things), Guoli zhongyang tushuguan tecangzu, Taibei, 1991; Zhang Jinlan (ed.), *Weifang nianhua yanjiu* (Research on Weifang New Year Pictures), Xuelin chubanshe, Shanghai, 1991; Zhang Dianying, op cit.; *Collector's Show of Traditional Soochow Woodblock Prints in Taiwan, ROC*, Taipei Fine Art Museum, Taibei, 1987; John Lust, op cit.

18. On the impact of nianhua on women, see McIntyre, op cit., pp. 136–143.
19. These stories were also popular in Vietnamese woodblock prints well into the twentieth century. For a comprehensive discussion of the Vietnamese folk woodblock art traditions, see Maurice Durand, "Imagerie Populaire Vietnamienne," *Ecole Française d'Extrême-Orient*, Vol. 47, Paris, 1960. Barbara Ward's description of the audience of an opera depicting an unusually long sequence from *The Three Kingdoms* she saw in Hong Kong is worth repeating: "Kuan-Kong, T'sao T'sao and their companions posture endlessly about the stage, marching and counter marching their flag armies back and forth. There are few female roles, and little or no singing takes place. Curiously archaic performances, full of stylized but unpolished, movement, more like pageants than operas. There are no acrobatics. The audience is intent, following every move and usually silent. The seats are full, about half the spectators being males of all ages. An onlooker can have no doubt but that they are gripped by the drama."
20. Some foreigners found the nianhua amusing, see W. D. Bernard, *Narrative of the Voyages and the Services of the Nemesis from 1840 to 1843; and of the Combined Naval and Military Operations in China: Comprising a Complete Account of the Colony of Hong Kong and Remarks on the Character and Habits of the Chinese from Notes of Commander W. H. Hall R. N. with Personal Observations by W. D. Bernard*, Henry Colburn, London, 1844, p. 301; George Lanning, *Old Forces in New China, An Effort to Exhibit Fundamental Relationships in China and the West in their True Light: Together with an Appendix dealing with the Story of the Chinese Revolution down to the End of June, 1912: And a New Map showing the Natural Resources of China*, Shanghai National Review Office, Probsthain, London, 1912, p. 265 refers to "The amazing and amusing war pictures [which] call for far more notice than can be devoted to them, so curious and quaint are they"; and Edward H. Seymour, *My Naval Career and Travels*, Smith, Elder and Co., London, 1911, p. 366. Seymour writes of the forts at Shanhaiguan surrendering to the gun-boat *Pygmy*: "A comic paper at Shanghai — a sort of *Punch* — hit the situation off so ably with a cartoon, that I sent it to the Admiralty and think it helped to the officer's promotion!" Other military attachés and diplomatic personnel found the pictures galling as they very often described glorious victories whereas, in fact, the Chinese had suffered decisive defeats. The best example of

this is the French annihilation of the Chinese fleet and the arsenal at Fuzhou. A nianhua was published describing the debacle as a decisive Chinese victory. See Plate 3.22.

21. Zhang Jinlan, op cit., pp. 100ff; Lust, op cit., p. 173; Flath, op cit., pp. 56–57.
22. See Mason Jackson, *The Pictorial Press. Its Origin and Progress*, New York, 1969 (1885); de Meyer, op cit.; Marcus, op cit.
23. John Keegan, *A History of Warfare*, Hutchinson, London, 1993, p. xi.
24. Pierre Beglair, "OTAN; Doutes et Polémics," *Le Point*, 23 April 1999.
25. Zhang Junbo and Yao Yunzhu, "Differences Between Traditional Chinese and Western Military Thinking and Their Philosophical Roots," *Journal of Contemporary China*, Vol. 5, No. 12, July 1966, p. 217.
26. Nathan Chaikin, *The Sino-Japanese War 1894–1895*, Imprimerie Pillet, Martigny, 1983, p. 26.
27. Lust, op cit., p. 2, quotes Wang Shucun (1959) as saying that the famous studios at Yangliuqing brought out 2,000 titles in runs of 500 sheets each between 1860 and 1910. Lust gives production figures for other studios at different times, see pp. 69, 81, 90–91, 103, 107–109. Danielle Eliasberg, "Imagerie Populaire Chinoise du Nouvel An," *Arts Asiatiques. Annales du Musée Guimet et du Musée Cernuschi*, published by the Ecole Française d'Extrême Orient with the cooperation of the CNRS, 1978, p. 11, claims that "la production en Chine d'estampes populaires jusqu'au vingtième siècle a atteint des proportions colossales vraisemblablement inégalées dans d'autres cultures." See also Dittrich, op cit., p. 28 who says that by 1880 at Yangliuqing there were 20,000 people making nianhua and by 1927 there were still about 7,000. She says that the output of their workshops was 600,000 in 1958 and in 1959, two million. Flath, op cit., p. 37 notes that in many centres, production of nianhua was seasonal.
28. Evelyn Rawski, "Economic and Social Foundations of Late Imperial Culture," in Johnson et al., op cit., p. 24.
29. Rudova, op cit., p. 11.
30. Lust, op cit., p. 132 makes the point that the circulation of prints in backward regions may well have aided popular literacy as well as noting that visual and oral memory are extremely important in societies with a high proportion of illiterate people. Lust also comments on the high degree of visual literacy among the Chinese audiences of popular prints.
31. Flath, op cit., p 143, p. 158, pp. 172–173 focuses attention on the actual viewing of a nianhua and the implications of such viewing.
32. Paul A. Cohen, *History in Three Keys. The Boxers as Event, Experience, and Myth*, Columbia University Press, New York, 1997, pp. 104–109 and especially footnote 42, p. 326. See also Seiichiro Yoshizawa, "Tianjin yihetuan yundong yu difang shehui de jiyi" (The Tianjin Boxer Movement and the Memory of Local Society), unpublished working paper given at the centennial conference of Boxer Studies, Jinan, October 2000. Professor Yoshizawa mentions that

before the Boxer movement there had already been a local custom of young men praying in a state of possession at temple altars in Tianjin.

33. Ward, op cit., p. 186.
34. Elvin, op cit., p. 203
35. Lust, op cit., p. 106 gives a rare example of direct censorship when the Taiping forces occupied Yangliuqing in 1853. They permitted "only bird, insect and flower prints or landscapes to be run off, and [banned] figure drawings and the official values of Qing society." He also refers to censorship on pp. 39 and 130 and on p. 10, he notes that Alexiev admired the freedom open to the Chinese print makers.
36. See R. J. Goldstein, *Censorship of Political Caricature in Nineteenth Century France*, Kent State University Press, Ohio, 1989. For an example of pictorial censorship in Britain in connection with the Boxer rising see George Lynch, *The War of the Civilisations: Being a Record of a "Foreign Devil's" Experiences with the Allies in China*, Longmans, Green and Co., London, 1901, p. 309. Here Lynch writes of a picture of the Boxer rising by a Japanese artist that was published by the *Review of Reviews* but which Longmans refused to publish in his book. The Japanese government felt threatened by the comic periodical *Marumaru Shimbun*, and frequently tried to suppress it. See J. Iwasaki and K. Shimizu (eds), *Yomeru Nenpyo-Bekkan. Meiji Taisho Fushimanga to Seso-Fuzoku Nenpyo*, Dainippon Insatsu, Tokyo, 1982. My thanks to Genji Torii and Kazuyo Taguchi for this reference. Flath, op cit., p. 151 gives one example of censorship.
37. P. Cohen, op cit., pp. 227–229.
38. For details concerning the production and distribution of nianhua, see McIntyre, op cit., pp. 65–68 and Flath, op cit., pp. 52–58.
39. See, for example, Captain Arthur A. Barnes, *On Active Service with the Chinese Regiment: A Record of the Operations of the First Chinese Regiment in North China from March to October, 1900*, Grant Richards, London, 1902, p. xiii; Lanning, op cit., p 95; Anatole M. Kotenev, *The Chinese Soldier. Basic Principles, Spirit, Science of War and Heroes of the Chinese Armies*, Kelly and Walsh Ltd., Shanghai, 1937, p. 78.
40. Joanna Waley-Cohen, "Commemorating War in Eighteenth Century China," *Modern Asian Studies*, Vol. 30, No. 4, 1996, pp. 898–899.
41. See Chengxiao, "Shequ jiangying qun de lianhe he xingdong" (The Coalition and Movement of Elite Groups in the Community), unpublished paper given at the centennial conference of Boxer studies, Jinan, October 2000. Chengxiao asserts that by re-explaining exterior peril and interior trouble, the Boxer sects were displaying a local conception of nationalism. The present writer wishes to draw attention to the role of nianhua, drama and storytelling during times of social, economic or political stress, in giving peasants the basis for discussion and development of their own conception of nationalism. These cultural productions were not those of authority; whether gentry or Imperial. This writer

would strongly agree with Flath that "the construction of the peasantry as a simple consumer of the culture made available to it by higher order systems [is] especially problematic." Flath, op cit , p. 143.

42. P. Cohen, op cit., pp. 96–97.
43. Rudova, op cit., p. 134 and Zhang Dianying, op cit., p. 90.
44. Quoted in Ward, op cit., p. 183. See also McIntyre, op cit., p. 134.
45. Plate 3.3 comes from Zhang Dianying, op cit., p. 92, "Three Attacks on the Zhu Family Village," an episode from *Watermargin*; Plate 3.4 comes from Rudova, op cit., p. 130, "The Slopes of Chang Banpo in the County of Dangyang," an episode in *The Three Kingdoms*; Plate 3.5 comes from Wang and Li (eds), op cit., p. 38, "The Capture of Bai Juhua" (detail); Plate 3.6 comes from ibid., p. 95, "The Battle with Wuzhu at Aihua Mountain," an episode from *Shuo Yue quanchuan* (General Yue Fei: A Novel), the biography of the famous Song dynasty general, Yue Fei. My thanks to Mr C. C. Hsü for elucidating this reference.
46. Esherick, op cit., p. 64; Issei Tanaka, "The Social and Historical Content of Ming-Ch'ing Local Drama," in Johnson et al., op cit; Elvin, op cit.
47. Lust, op cit., p. 103.
48. Flath, op cit., pp. 56–57.
49. The process of deliberation involved was considerable with the male head of the household making the final decision and the oldest male child often pasting the picture on the wall. Information from Professor Wang Shucun to the writer, June 1994.
50. I am indebted to Professor Flath for drawing my attention to this point.
51. For those interested in the history of Chinese martial arts, the following articles by Stanley E. Henning are of interest: "Academia Encounters the Chinese Martial Arts," *National Physical Culture and Sports Commission Martial Arts Research Institute's Chinese Martial Arts History*, Vol. 6, No. 2, Fall 1999; "Chinese Boxing: The Internal and External Schools in the Light of History and Theory," *Journal of Asian Martial Arts*, Vol. 6, No. 3, 1997; "Observations on a Visit to Shaolin Monastery," *Journal of Asian Martial Arts*, Vol. 7, No. 1, 1988 and "Southern Fists and Northern Legs: The Geography of Chinese Boxing," *Journal of Asian Martial Arts*, Vol. 7, No. 3, 1988; "The Chinese Martial Arts in Historical Perspective," *Military Affairs* (now *Journal of Military History*), December 1981. My thanks to Dr Gerry Groot for drawing my attention to these references.
52. For a detailed discussion of these phenomena, see Winston S. Lo, "The Self-Image of the Chinese Military in Historical Perspective," *Journal of Asian History*, January 1997.
53. Joanna Waley-Cohen, "Religion, War and Empire-Building in Eighteenth Century China," *The International History Review*, Vol. 20, No. 2, June 1998, p. 337.

54. Ibid., p. 345.
55. P. Cohen, op cit., p. 108, quotes Wen-hui Tsai's research which shows that a sizeable percentage of the gods with historical backgrounds worshipped at temples in Taiwan, were also heroes in the three popular novels, *Enfeoffment of the Gods*, *The Three Kingdoms* and *Romance of the Sui-Tang*.
56. See Lo, op cit., pp. 6–7. Lo cites the story of Pan Chao.
57. For detail on the link between various rituals and the Boxer rituals and for amplification of the nature of Boxer leaders as "marginal" men who adopted a system of rituals containing political elements and approval of particular gallant men who were chivalrous and patriotic, see Zhang Ming, "Yihetuan de xiangzheng yinyu yishi wenhua yu zhengzhi" (The Cultural Symbols and Political Metaphors of the Boxer Rituals), unpublished working paper given at the centennial conference of Boxer studies, Jinan, October 2000. Interestingly Zhang Ming states that rebellious groups in *Watermargin* and non-orthodox groups in *The Three Kingdoms* were rejected by the Boxers. One notes that although we are discussing concepts of chivalry, gallantry, heroism and patriotism common to a group of mostly illiterate peasants and urban poor, this group nevertheless had specific opinions about the extensive Chinese romantic historical traditions of rebellion as described in these lengthy novels.
58. See Zhang and Yao, op cit., pp. 210–213
59. P. Cohen, op cit., p. 102, "at the village level, the sharp boundaries between the 'secular' and the 'sacred', to which modern Westerners are accustomed, simply did not exist."
60. See R. G. Tiedemann, "The Big Sword Society and Its Relations with the Boxer Movement, 1895–1900," unpublished paper given at the centennial conference of Boxer Studies, Jinan, October 2000. Tiedemann notes that "on the Shandong-Jiangsu boarder zone, the established pattern of traditional collective violence continued to prevail. Here people were accustomed to employing aggressive survival strategies while at the same time exercising reactive solidarity against outsiders." See also Elvin, op cit.
61. Wang and Li, op cit., pp. 82–83.
62. P. Cohen, op cit., pp. 100–101 also makes this point.
63. Wang Shucun, 1985, op cit., p. 28, Illustration No. 13.
64. Ibid., pp. 165–166.
65. P. Cohen, op cit., p. 106.
66. Ibid, p. 32.
67. Philip Kuhn, *Rebellion and Its Enemies in Late Imperial China. Militarization and Social Structure, 1796–1864*, Harvard University Press, Cambridge, Massachusetts, 1980 and Franz Michael, "The Military Organization and Power Structure of China During the Taiping Rebellion," *Pacific Historical Review*, No. 18, 1949. Pamela Kyle Crossley, *Orphan Warriors. Three Manchu Generations and the End of the Qing World*, Princeton University Press, Princeton, 1990, pp. 124–125.

68. Esherick, op cit., p. 60.
69. After the battle of Tianjin, Savage-Landor went to the Viceroy's yamen where he discovered drill books, ships' log books, scale models of ships, maps and charts, photographs of big guns and projectiles of every possible pattern and the latest artillery pieces, among other things. He watched as all this valuable material was swept into the canal and wondered why British military intelligence made no effort to preserve it. The pages out of the drill book that form the end pages of his two volume book, must have been re-copied by a non-Chinese speaking artist as many of the characters are gibberish. See A. Henry Savage-Landor, *China and the Allies*, William Heinemann, London, 1901, Vol. 1, pp. 226–227.
70. Plate 3.9 shows a page out of a Manchu drillbook, front end pages, Vol. 2, Savage-Landor, op cit.; Plate 3.10 shows "The English and French Armies Engaged in Battle with the Boxers," an unpublished woodcut held at the British Library; Figure 3.2 is from Dominique Liaboeuf and Jorge Svartzman (eds), *Auguste François en Chine (1896–1904)*, Musée Guimet, Paris, 1989, p. 61; Plate 3.14 shows "The Victory of General Dong at Beicang," an unpublished woodcut held at the British Library.
71. From Wang Shucun, 1985, op cit., p. 49.
72. Ibid., p. 169.
73. Lo, op cit., pp. 9–10
74. Joan W. M. Hichberger, *Images of the Army. The Military in British Art 1815–1914*, Manchester University Press, Manchester, 1988 gives a very interesting description and discussion of this process in Chapters One to Four.
75. Peter Paret, *Imagined Battles. Reflections of War in European Art*, University of North Carolina Press, Chapel Hill, 1997. This expression originated with the artist Benjamin West who felt that people would be morally uplifted seeing the death of a heroic commander surrounded by venerating officers but quite unedified by seeing such a commander "die like a common soldier under a bush." See Paret, pp. 50–51. Paret uses the expression of the common soldier, "dying under a bush," pp. 71ff, as he charts the emergence of the death of masses of ordinary men, or a specific ordinary soldier as a suitable subject for "high" art. I am indebted to Professor Robert E. Harrist for referring me to this work. For an important contribution to the politics of the appearance of the ordinary footsoldier as a suitable subject for Academy art, see Matthew P. Lalumia, *Realism and Politics in Victorian Art of the Crimean War*, UMI Research Press, Michigan, 1984, p. 134, the discussion of Lady Butler's painting "the Roll Call."
76. Marcus, op cit., (this work is not paginated) and de Meyer, op cit., p. 141, Picture No. 128, "Militaires," Grand, Musée de Folklore.
77. I am grateful to Dr Frances Wood for sharing with me her view that the major difference between a nianhua and a xinwenzhi lies in the manner of describing the picture. A typical nianhua will have, in addition to the major caption and

a sub-text, labelling of important places, people, armies, weapons and other information necessary to elucidate the action. Xinwenzhi, on the other hand, generally have a caption with a very short description and little or no descriptive labelling on the picture itself and are similar in the relationship between picture and text to the huabao format

78. Bibliothèque Nationale de Paris, Bureau des Estampes, Series Oe 173, unpublished nianhua "Estampes populaires relatives à la guerre franco-chinoise de 1885" (hereafter referred to as Series Oe 173).
79. See Chapter Six.
80. Bernard, op cit., pp. 277–278.
81. Series Oe 173, "The Second Defeat of the French by Liu Yongfu at Sontay."
82. Joseph Nathan, *Uniforms and Non-Uniforms. Communication Through Clothing*, Contributions in Sociology, No. 61, Greenwood Press, Westport, Connecticut, 1986, pp. 73–74. My thanks to Professor Robert E. Harrist for drawing my attention to this reference. Captain Garnot, *L'Expédition Française de Formose 1884–1885*, Librairie Ch. Delagrave, Paris, 1894, p 111, gives an interesting example of how the presence and use of flags in battle inflamed troops and made them act otherwise than they would have done in the same situation without the flags.
83. The Australian War Memorial in Canberra holds an excellent photograph of three of Dong Fuxiang's soldiers, No. AO5950, incorrectly labelled as "China 1900. Three Boxer Soldiers Pose for a Photograph During the Boxer Rebellion."
84. Wang Shucun, 1991, op cit., Vol. 1, p. 300, Picture 308.
85. Wang Shucun, 1989, op cit., No. 204.
86. Hu Zhaojing (ed.), op cit., Picture 15.
87. Series Oe 173, "The Defeat of the French at Bac Ninh by Liu Yongfu."
88. Ibid., the nianhua, "A Triumphant Military Report from Changmen" refers both in the text, and very clearly in the picture, to French guns mounted on the mast of the warship, a device the Chinese copied immediately.
89. Flath, forthcoming.
90. Hu Zhaojing (ed.), op cit., Picture 91.
91. Lust, op cit., p. 70, refers to the movement of artistic influence between the woodblock studios and the Court artists. See also McIntyre, op cit., pp. 40ff, 72–73, 79.
92. Ye Xiaoqing, "Popular Culture in Shanghai 1884–1898," unpublished PhD thesis, ANU, 1991, mentions that the *Dianshizhai huabao* regularly presented free reproductions of paintings by Ren Bonian and Sha Shanchun (p. 32) as well as free nianhua at the Chinese New Year. She also notes that the owner, Mr Major, sent the artist Zhang Zhiying to the front during the Sino-French War. Wu Youru also went (p. 33). Lust, op cit., pp. 4–36, gives examples of the snobbishness of literati attitudes to popular art that meant that the designers of

woodblock prints often remained anonymous. Nevertheless, it is interesting to note that "free art" was being distributed through newspapers in China well before Lord Harmsworth or W.T. Stead were doing this in Britain. Flath, op cit., refers to the work of two individual artists, Qian Huian and Liu Mingjie.

93. Wang Shucun, 1991, op cit., Vol. 2, p. 591, No. 602. See, also the print of "The Return of the Chinese Fleet to Xiamen (Amoy)" by Castiglione in the Library of Congress LC-USZ 6244387.
94. Rudova, op cit., pp. 130, 143–144, 146, 147, 157 and Wang Shucun, 1990, op cit., pp. 74, 95, 113, 118, 119, 121.
95. Asukai Masamichi et al. (eds), *Meiji taisho zushi*, Chikuma Shobo, Tokyo, 1979, Vol. 16, p. 222. My thanks to Margaret Hosking for drawing my attention to this reference.
96. See discussion in Chapter Six of the political context in which Chinese military leaders of modernised armies operated.
97. A good example of such a painting is the "Battle of Foshan Creek, 1st June, 1857" from a painting in the possession of General R. C. Boyle, in Colonel Cyril Field, *Britain's Sea Soldiers: A History of the Royal Marines and Their Predecessors*, Lyceum Press, 1924, Vol. 1, opposite p. 127. Paret, op cit., p. 56 asks the question, "Were naval battles more acceptable because images of the clash of great wood and canvas structures were less dependent on the presence of humans?"
98. De Meyer, op cit., p. 134, Picture No. 99, "La Galère", Haarlem, Collection Van Kuyck.
99. Paret, op cit., Chapters Six and Seven.
100. Lust, op cit., p. 172.
101. Paret, op cit., pp. 48ff on Benjamin West's paintings, "The Death of General Wolfe" and "The Death of Lord Nelson." It was West himself who wrote, "Wolfe must not die like a common soldier under a bush, neither should Nelson be represented dying in the gloomy hold of a ship, like a sick man in a Prison Hole." We have already noted the publication of highly sanitised photographs of members of the Royal Family carrying flowers and visiting injured soldiers on their pristine sick beds.
102. See Alexiev quoted in Lust, op cit., p. 5.
103. Flath, op cit., p. 36 (On prints that are so similar they must have been traced from another or taken from an unknown master copy), "There is a sense that the makers of the print felt a need to produce the print with some individual identity." See Plates 3.1 and 3.2 in this context.
104. See the very interesting discussion of the crossbow in Paulo Uccello's painting, "The Unhorsing of Bernadino della Carda," in Paret, op cit., pp. 24–25.
105. Ibid., pp. 38–39. In discussing the work of Jacques Callot, Paret notes that "some of the plates ... are marked by a distinct theatricality ... and pose ... [Callot] has men standing with the weight on their rear leg and the other leg thrust forward,

the foot pointed and slightly turned to the outside. The posture, which conveys the self-image of elegant masculinity often encountered in Baroque realism, is the same whether assumed by an officer or a musketeer; it is an element in the code of images by which the common brutality of the subject is raised to a level of formal drama."(See below discussion of Plate 3.19.)

106. Flath, op cit., p. 146 the case of Liu Mingjie "offers insight into how the changing conditions of trans-local experience in the late Qing contribute to changing perceptions of graphic art as something beyond the ritual, ethical, narrative and decorative configurations of Chinese domesticity."
107. Bernard, op cit., p. 215; Scott Dolby, "The Boxer Crisis as Seen Through the Eyes of Five Chinese Officials," unpublished PhD thesis, Columbia University, 1976, p. 280, telegram from the Commander-in-Chief Ronglu to General Nie Shicheng of 5 June 1990. *Dianshizhai huabao*, Ding 1, p. 5.
108. Flath, op cit., pp. 232–233.
109. Ibid., p. 58, "nianhua were not simple commodities; they were texts that carried complex cultural and social symbols, and when combined with a wider field of printed representation, became a wider carrier of human relationships ... [their] influence extended to formal and informal Confucian teachings, religious authority and countless other structures." A structure we can name here is that of the legally formed militias and armies and how battle and heroic death in battle were understood by the ordinary Chinese soldiers. One of the most reported, most often pictorially depicted and least understood human relationship is between a man and his enemy in battle or a group of men and their enemies in battle.
110. It is not suggested that illustrated anti-missionary literature had no influence at all on the peasantry. However, the present writer has seen little significant evidence of anti-missionary literature produced around the time of the Boxer War. Elvin, op cit., p. 201 notes the influx of anti-Christian broadsheets from Cangzhou in 1898. The writer acknowledges the existence of anti-foreign and anti-missionary literature but feels that it had comparatively little influence on the formation of the Boxer mentality when placed beside such factors as traditional Chinese influences, eg, theatre; social problems, eg, banditry, and specific regional phenomena, eg, unusual latent popular hysteria. Elvin himself makes the important observation that the various sects of the 1880s and 1890s incorporated Christians and foreigners "into a pre-existing framework of ideas" ibid., p. 212. The illustrated anti-missionary literature most commonly referred to in the literature and illustrated in Chapter One was produced in the very late 1880s and published in 1891. Original copies of these pictures are held in the Museum of Religion in Saint Petersburg. McIntyre, op cit., p. 35, note 18, relates these pictures to the violence of the Boxer rising and suggests that they "must certainly be read as something other than that of protest art" on the supposition that these pictures were a product of the Boxer movement.

111. I wish to acknowledge my great indebtedness to the generosity and scholarship of Dr Frances Wood of the Department of Oriental Antiquities at the British Library.
112. This research has uncovered nianhua depicting war in the Peabody Museum at Salem, in the Library of Congress, in the British Library, in the Bibliothèque Nationale, Paris, in the Tokyo Metropolitan Central Library and in the Tenri Library at Nara University in Japan. There are also important collections at the National Palace Museum in Taiwan and many in the hands of private collectors.
113. There is an interesting and rare nianhua at the front of A. Cunningham, *The Chinese Soldier and Other Sketches with a Description of the Capture of Manila*, Hong Kong Daily Press, Hong Kong, no date, possibly 1901. Facing p. 26 there is a nianhua showing a Chinese gunboat destroying a Japanese cruiser.
114. Exceptionally, Flath , op cit., pp. 147–148 discusses two nianhua of the war with Japan.
115. Marcus (ed.), op cit., Introduction, makes it clear that there were huge difficulties in getting government authorisation for certain prints and that censorship and surveillance were integral to the Restoration government's control of popular prints in France. In 1828, for example, Pellerin requested permission to distribute a print entitled "Napoleon on Horseback" but the government refused after a year's delay. In comparison, censorship in the late Qing was very mild indeed.
116. Lust, op cit., p. 148.
117. Lloyd E. Eastman, *Throne and Mandarins. China's Search for a Policy During the Sino-French Controversy, 1880–1885*, Harvard University Press, Cambridge, Massachusetts, 1967, p. 165.
118. Flath, op cit., p. 145 notes that in 1895 Liu "broke with standard forms of ... nianhua when he produced a series of prints with titles like 'World Geography', 'World Rulers', 'A Tourist Map of Taishan'."
119. Henrietta Harrison, "Justice on Behalf of Heaven," *History Today*, September 2000, convincingly invokes the feelings of country people about the Boxers and about foreign intervention in everyday small town and village life.
120. After the burning of the cathedral in Tianjin in 1870, "The Europeans were upset to find that thousands of fans containing pictures of the riot and the murdering of foreigners were being sold in Tianjin." The Chinese authorities were accused by the British of allowing this but met with an unsympathetic response from the responsible Chinese minister. See John Selby, *The Paper Dragon. An Account of the China Wars, 1840–1900*, Arthur Baker Ltd., London, 1969, pp. 160–161.
121. Flath speaks of the idea that "the present has a visuality distinct from antiquity ... emergent visualities and technologies of viewing were also influenced by existing understanding of what it meant to 'look at a picture'." Flath, op cit., p. 158. Flath rightly draws to our attention the need "to appreciate how these

... people looked at an image and used it to organise their environment," ibid., p. 233. In the context of nianhua, we need to add to this that pictures of new subjects gave rise to new elements in discussion as people stood and talked together looking at the pictures together in common public spaces. These new elements in discussions gave rise to new ways of thinking and feeling.

122. "The Battle of Foshan" can be seen in Field, op cit., Vol. 1, p. 144.
123. Bernard, op cit., Vol. 1, pp. 235–236.
124. Garnot, op cit., described the Chinese willingness to fight at night as something to be taken for granted. Much of the action during the fighting between the Chinese and the French on Taiwan was initiated by the Chinese at night. See Garnot, op cit., p. 133.
125. Keegan, op cit., p. 294.
126. Wang Shucun, *Zhongguo minjian nianhua shi lunji* (Collected Essays on the History of Chinese Folk New Year Pictures), Tianjin, Yangliuqing hua chubanshe, Tianjin, 1991, p. 201.
127. Bernard, op cit., Vol. 2, p. 52.
128. For details of the precision and accuracy (or lack of) of European firearms at this time, as well as the limitations on their use under any conditions of humidity, see Dorothy L Shineberg, "Guns and Men in Melanesia," *Journal of Pacific History*, Vol. 9, No. 4, July 1967.
129. Selby, op cit., p. 34.
130. Keegan, op cit., p. 216.
131. Zhang and Yao, op cit., pp. 213–217.
132. Denis E. Showalter, "Dien Bien Phu in Three Cultures," *War and Society*, Vol. 16, No. 2, October, 1998, p. 202. My thanks to Dr Gerry Groot for drawing my attention to this reference
133. Crossley, op cit., pp. 113 and 117–118 and John L. Rawlinson, "China's Failure to Co-ordinate Her Modern Fleets in the Late Nineteenth Century," in A. Feuerwerker, Rhoads Murphey, and Mary C. Wright (eds), *Approaches to Modern History*, University of California Press, Berkeley, 1967. See also James L. Hevia, "The Archive State and the Fear of Pollution: From the Opium Wars to Fu Manchu," *Cultural Studies*, Vol. 12, No. 2, April 1988, p. 249. In this otherwise seminal and thought-provoking article, Professor Hevia mentions "a series of military disasters" in which he includes China's defeat by the French in 1880–1885. See also Richard J. Smith and Kwang-Ching Liu, "The Military Challenge: the North-West and the Coast," in Dennis Twitchett and John K. Fairbank (eds), *The Cambridge History of China*, Cambridge Universiy Press, Cambridge, 1978 (1994), Vol. 2, Part 2, Chapter 4. It is this "disaster" school that the present work seeks to modify and the Sino-French War is an excellent example. No authoritative French contemporary sources known to this writer conclude that France won this war decisively; indeed, most give details of France's poor performance, loss of many important battles and death or capture of French

generals and high-ranking officers. This writer has not met any historians in China who would agree that China suffered a clear-cut loss in this war. A possible reason for his acceptance of the "disaster" school of thinking may be that Professor Hevia has read the sort of English-language account typified by that in the *Cambridge Modern History*. This work, details many (though not all) of the Chinese victories in the Sino-French War. It omits any reference to the very poor showing by the French. Most significantly, it does not mention the disastrous French performance on Taiwan or the sweeping Chinese victories immediately before the decision to stop fighting and go to the negotiation table. Nevertheless, it concludes that the French won decisively. It is this type of history that needs revision, modification and where necessary invalidation. It should not be thought that these attitudes on the part of historians of China refer only to her military engagements in the nineteenth century. Shu Guang Zhang wrote a detailed history of the Korean War from the Chinese side; *Man's Military Romanticism: China and the Korean War, 1950–1953*, Lawrence University of Kansas Press, 1995. "Zhang details exactly how Chinese forces adapted to and countered American technological and material supremacy in Korea to fight the war to what China's leaders viewed as a victorious conclusion" from John W. Garver, "Feature Review," *Diplomatic History*, Vol. 22, No. 3, Summer 1998, pp. 494–495. I am particularly grateful to Dr Gerry Groot for drawing this reference to my attention.

134. Crossley's and Rawlinson's work typifies the sorts of generalisations about China's inferior military technology which could be avoided by a close reading of Western primary sources written by military men who took part in the relevant action against the Chinese. There is a need for a broader understanding of the multifarious factors causing conflicts and contradictions in policies on defence expenditure as well in the West as in China at this time. More work like that of Allen Fung and David Wright needs to be done. See Allen Fung, "Testing the Self-Strengthening: The Chinese Army in the Sino-Japanese War of 1894–1895," *Modern Asian Studies*, Vol. 30, No. 4, 1996 and David Wright, "Careers in Western Science in Nineteenth Century China: Xu Shou and Xu Jianyin," *Journal of the Royal Asiatic Society*, Third Series, Vol. 5, No. 1, April 1995. My thanks to Dr Gary Tiedemann for drawing my attention to the latter reference.
135. Bernard, op cit., Vol. 2, p. 33.
136. Ibid., Vol. 2, pp. 226–227.
137. Ibid.,Vol. 1, p. 374.
138. Joanna Waley-Cohen, "China and Western Technology in the Late Eighteenth Century," *American Historical Review*, Vol. 98, No 5, December 1993, p. 1531.
139. Crossley, op cit. pp. 117–118.
140. Bernard, op cit., Vol. 2, p. 33.
141. Ibid., Vol. 2, p. 226.

142. Waley-Cohen, *Sextants*, op cit., pp. 145–146; "China and Western Technology," op. cit.
143. Waley-Cohen, *Sextants*, op cit., p. 144.
144. Ibid., pp. 204–205.
145. Lucien Bodard, *La Vallée des Roses*, Grasset, Paris, 1977, pp. 437–439, 448.
146. Zhang and Yao, op cit., p. 217
147. Figure 3.6 is an unpublished nianhua depicting the British and American bombardment of Nanjing in 1927. Held at the Library of Congress, LCUS 262 94972.
148. See Waley-Cohen, "Commemorating War," op cit.
149. See note 92 above.
150. *Dianshizhai huabao*, op cit., Jia 6, p. 42; Jia 8, p. 62.
151. Series Oe 173, "The Defeat of the French at Bac Ninh by Liu Yongfu."
152. Lust, op cit., p. 140 in discussing the accuracy of detail in the nianhua notes that "a horse, for example, will reflect the character and social status of the rider."
153. Series Oe 173, "Admiral Sun Junmen encounters Admiral Courbet while doing a night watch round."
154. Yang Congsen, op cit., p. 92.
155. Series Oe 173, "The Defeat of the French at Bac Ninh by Liu Yongfu."
156. Figure 3.7 is a hand-tinted photograph of Chinese soldiers (most probably men of Nie Shicheng's Divisions). See Savage-Landor, op cit., Vol. 2, p. 10. Figure 3.8 is a hand-drawn newspaper illustration from a Shanghai newspaper published in the Japanese paper *Manchoho* of 30 June 1900. My thanks to Ms Melanie Lowndes for the artwork necessary to bring a poor-quality microfilm copy up to publishable standard.
157. Victor W. Purcell, *The Boxer Uprising. A Background Study*, Cambridge University Press, Great Britain, 1963, p. 24. Ralph L. Powell, *The Rise of Chinese Military Power, 1895–1912*, Princeton University Press, Princeton, 1955, p. 31 in the passage beginning "the Chinese 'brave' appeared to be little more than a caricature" gives an inordinately Eurocentric, highly-coloured and very unfavourable picture of the Chinese soldier. Powell's description appears to be based on little more than the fact that Chinese uniforms of the day did not look like any kind of army uniform with which he felt culturally at ease. The same men he describes so deprecatingly for no other apparent reason than that they wore these uniforms, fought to the death in the First Opium War. The Chinese soldiers earned the highest admiration from their enemies for their courage. See Bernard, op cit., Vol. 2, p. 356 and pp. 402ff.
158. This nianhua may be found in the collection of the British Library and has been published in Arnold Toynbee, *Half the World: The History and Culture of China and Japan*, Thames and Hudson, London, 1973, p. 325.
159. This nianhua may be found in the collection of the British Library and has been

published in many collections; see, for example, Iwasaki and Shimizu (eds), op cit., p. 221 and Toynbee, op cit., p. 326.

160. Bodard, op cit., p. 333, "The English favoured [a uniform] squeezing them at the neck and stretched over their chests so stiffly and so heavily that the men appeared like statues, the more so as they were stuffed into their tunics so that their necks had disappeared, so tight were their tunics ..."
161. Ibid., p. 334, "The officers wearing their sabers were in fact imprisoned by the iron ring of their decorations, their badges of distinction, their bibelots and their equipment. So weighed down were they, that all they could display was the appearance, so much courted, of martial figures, especially their eyes and [their facial expression was] just the [minimum] necessary to express the refined and hereditary art of their war-like distinction." Bodard gives a brilliant literary evocation of the physical and cultural differences between French and British soldiers during the Second Opium War.
162. This was the impression of an elderly gentleman in Lin Yutang's novel *Moment in Peking* quoted from Robert E. Harrist, Jnr, "Clothes Make the Man: Dress, Modernity, and Masculinity in Early Modern China," unpublished paper, Columbia University, 1998, p. 9. I am extremely grateful to Professor Harrist for allowing me to read and make use of this paper.
163. Nathan, op cit., p. 65.
164. Ibid., p. 95.
165. Frederick A. Sharf and Peter Harrington, *The Boxer Rebellion. China 1900. The Artists' Perspective*, Greenhill Books, London, 2000. The American artist, Sydney Adamson had this to say "Some of the mandarins are fine-looking men, but their costumes are so theatrical, and their figures so old-womanish that I am always struck by a lack of apparent manliness and force."
166. The difference between the nianhua discussed in this chapter and those anti-missionary pictures shown in Chapter Two is striking (Figures 2.18a and 2.18b). The anti-missionary pictures are to be found in *The Cause of the Riots in the Yangtse Valley. A "Complete Picture Gallery,"* Hankow, 1891. This work has been attributed to Chou Han, "a native of Ning-Hiang." An example in colour of one of these anti-missionary pictures may be seen in Toynbee, op cit., p. 325. Ellen J. Laing mistakenly dates these pictures to the 1860s. See Ellen J. Laing, *The Winking Owl: Art in the Peoples' Republic of China*, University of California Press, Berkeley, 1988, pp. 9–10. Such pictures were reprinted frequently. These highly inflammatory pictures were collected by missionaries in the late 1880s. This makes it unlikely that they provoked immediate incentive to the peasants involved in the Boxer rising. See Bi Keguan and Huang Yuanlin, *Zhongguo nianhua shi*, (A History of Chinese New Year Pictures), Liaoning Fine Arts Publishers, Shenyang, 1986, pp. 23–24. See also McIntyre, op cit., p. 35 and for problems with dating prints, pp. 80–81.
167. There are several examples of Japanese prints of the Sino-Japanese War and the

Boxer War in which Chinese soldiers are depicted as looking ridiculous, overweight, confused, carrying antique weapons and wearing out-moded military uniforms. The Japanese soldiers, by contrast look strong and muscular and wear immaculate Western-style uniforms while their officers are invariably rapier thin, wearing uniforms closely approximating those of Western officers with rapier-thin trouser legs and they invariably sport a moustache. See Sharf and Harrington, front cover and Chaikin, op cit., Plate 20.

168. Nathan, op cit., p. 71, The British army regulations prescribe fourteen orders of dress for officers based on climate and occasion with numerous subcategories for each — six court functions and seventeen other occasions including reviews, investitures, balls, weddings, funerals and court-martials.
169. Bernard, op cit., Vol. 1, p. 205.
170. Dolby, op cit., p. 280.
171. Nathan, op cit., p. 94.
172. Bodard, op cit., pp. 371–372.
173. Harrist, "Clothes Make the Man," op cit., p. 14.
174. Waley-Cohen, "China and Western Technology," op cit., p. 1535, also mentions that for senior Manchus in the late eighteenth century, "military success was a surer path to political power than the civil service examinations in which they would have faced fierce competition from Chinese scholars."
175. See the work of the official American photographer, Captain Cornealius F. O'Keefe discussed in Chapter Four. The complete corpus of Captain O'Keefe's work taken when he accompanied the American contingent to the Boxer War may be seen in the National Archives in Washington DC.
176. P. Cohen, op cit., p. 140.
177. Waley-Cohen, "China and Western Technology," op. cit., p. 1537.
178. Wang Shucun, 1991, op cit., Vol. 2, p. 540.
179. Ibid., Professor Wang comments that this picture reflects the people's desire to do honour to General Nie Shicheng. This may well be so but it would appear unlikely as General Nie had earned popular disfavour for firing on the Boxers and, in addition, had been impeached by the Court. It is not likely that this print was re-issued for any particular person or reason associated with the events of 1900. On the issue of General Nie Shicheng's unpopularity with the people of Tianjin and the Boxers, see Liu Mengyang, "A Record of the Boxer-Bandits in Tientsin," manuscript translation by Mark Elvin, p. 8. I am extremely grateful to Professor Elvin for his generosity in allowing me to make use of this translation. On the Edict of July 12 censuring General Nie, see Robert Coltmann, *Beleagured in Peking. The Boxers' War Against the Foreigner*, Philadelphia, 1901, p. 239.
180. Flath, op cit., pp. 158, 172–173 and 232–233.
181. Nianhua artists did make mistakes occasionally. There is an uncatalogued nianhua at the Hermitage Museum in Saint Petersburg that shows a foreigner

waving a hybrid of the French and the Italian flag. The colours on the flag are green, orange and blue. The text of the nianhua recounts a running race for three year old children in France at which a large sum of prize money was given to the winner. The message of the nianhua is that foreign parents want their children to be strong and the nianhua deplores the fact that Chinese children are "listless and spiritless and cannot bear any hardship."

182. Elvin, "Mandarins and Millenarians," op cit., p. 201. See also Flath, op cit., p. 133.
183. Lust, op cit., p. 230.
184. Flath, op cit., p. 142.
185. Roswell S. Britton, *The Chinese Periodical Press*, p. 68.
186. Prosper Giquel, *The Foochow Arsenal and Its Results from the Commencement in 1867, to the End of the Foreign Directorate, on the 16th February, 1874,* translated from the French by H. Lang. Reprinted from the *Shanghai Evening Courier*, 1874. Giquel gives some very interesting details about rates of pay and relationships between Chinese and Western employees.
187. Teruaki Kawano, "Allied Military Co-operation in the Boxer Rebellion and Japan's Policy," *Revue Internationale d'Histoire Militaire*, No. 70, 1988, p. 101. My thanks to the author for drawing my attention to this article.
188. Garnot, op cit., p. 57.
189. Ibid., p. 162.
190. See Lo, op cit.
191. Showalter, op cit., p. 177.
192. Waley-Cohen, "China and Western Technology," op cit., p. 1526.
193. Showalter, op cit., p. 94.
194. Waley-Cohen, "China and Western Technology," op cit., p. 1527 and pp. 1543–1544 explains that the Chinese had a complexity of reasons for denying publicly that they were interested in military applications of Western technology in the late eighteenth century. Throughout this article, she gives detailed evidence delineating the various layers of Chinese thinking exteriorised in an obviously directed desire for the sort of mathematical and scientific knowledge that would have immediate military spin off while simultaneously denying any interest of or need for Western knowledge. In Chapter Six, we will discuss the head-on collision between Chinese military leaders trained as Western soldiers and Chinese conservative civilian leaders.
195. Showalter, op. cit., p. 94.
196. Eastman, op cit., pp. 194–195.
197. Neither Eastman nor Richard J. Smith and Kwang-Ching Liu, the authors of the chapter on the Sino-French War in *The Cambridge History of China* address this critical issue. However, Eastman does give an excellent overall account of the way this war looked in the eyes of a particular group of Chinese officials, the Qingliu (clear stream), and presents a fine analysis of the policy vacillations of

the Throne. See Eastman, op cit., and Richard J. Smith and Kwang-Ching Liu, op. cit.

198. Rawlinson, op cit. This work undoubtedly makes some useful points. However, it is plagued by a form of Eurocentrism which judges naval expenditure and co-ordination in the face of given long-term strategic concerns as well as short-term tactical considerations. The basis for assessment of these factors seems to be that of how a European naval power would have dealt with these problems. Moreover, the author shows no inclination to parallel his arguments about Chinese inefficiency with examples from contemporary British, German, French and Russian difficulties in the face of similar naval threats. It thus appears that in Rawlinson's mind, China's performance in the nineteenth century is to be judged by the criteria applicable to naval developments in the West during the twentieth century. While this is not the place to offer an extensive critique of this article, one example will suffice. The British navy was plagued by horrendous traditions regarding the commissioning of ships — and therefore, the command structure — still of such moment to the quality of leadership of the British fleets that Admiral Seymour discusses this at some length in his memoirs. Indeed a detailed reading of Admiral Seymour's memoirs would form an excellent counter-balance to Rawlinson's study. These memoirs provide extensive evidence from a professional serving naval officer that the problems experienced by China were in some respects paralleled by difficulties in the construction, disposition and leadership of navies in the West. The choice of Admiral Seymour's memoirs is particularly apt as he fought as a young midshipman in the action off Dagu in 1859. In this action, the British FAILED to take the forts either by sea or by land. They had to join forces with the French and return in 1860. It was Admiral Seymour who embarked on land operations in June 1900 using marines untrained for land-warfare simultaneously leaving the foreign naval ships off Dagu seriously depleted of fighting men in the event of enemy attack. See Seymour, op cit.
199. Showalter, op cit.
200. Eastman, op cit., p. 170 writes of the Chinese forces in Tongqing being decimated by malaria; 1,500 out of 2,000 men died in one unit alone.
201. Smith and Liu, op cit., pp. 257–265.
202. Showalter, op cit., p. 97.
203. Rawlinson, op cit., p. 105.
204. Garnot's account of the adventurers who ran the blockade to bring troops and weapons to the Chinese is a very interesting one.
205. Georges Taboulet, *La Geste Française en Indochine. Histoire par les Textes de la France en Indochine des Origines à 1914*, Librairie Adrien-Maisonneuve, Paris, 1955, p. 843. See also Commandant Thirion, *L'Expédition de Formose, Souvenirs d'un Soldat*, Paris, 1897.
206. Taboulet, p. 843

207. Professor Maria Rudova, a student of Alexiev and now curator of his collection of nianhua at the Hermitage Museum, has the notes of Alexiev's extensive field research. On many collecting trips throughout China, Alexiev asked the woodblock carvers themselves as well as educated gentlemen, about the visual and verbal symbolism, double-entendres and meanings in the nianhua. His notes show that he was able to get very few authoritative replies.
208. Garnot, op cit., pp. 55, 162.
209. Taboulet, op cit., p. 842.
210. See James Belich, *The New Zealand Wars and the Victorian Interpretation of Racial Conflict*, Auckland University Press, 1986.
211. Taboulet, op cit., p. 843.
212. Garnot, p. 96.
213. The French violated the treaty agreements in the lead-up to their attack on Fuzhou. In addition to the many strategic problems similar to those that would have cause identical difficulties for any European or Russian regional or central command, there was a specific Chinese attitude to justice as an element in considering whether or not to take up arms, see Zhang and Yao, op cit., pp. 210–213. Although the Chinese often blatantly disregarded treaties, in this case they did not expect the French to do likewise. Unpublished nianhua held at the Peabody Museum, Salem, Massachusetts Catalogue Number E64, 75O.
214. Zhang and Yao, op cit., p. 210.
215. Series Oe 173, "The Battle of Fuzhou."
216. Unpublished nianhua held at the Peabody Museum, Salem, Massachusetts, Catalogue Number E64,751, Accession number 22,091. I am particularly grateful to Ms Kathy Flynn for deciphering the almost illegible pencilled notes.
217. My thanks to Professor R. J. O'Neill for pointing this out. This striking geographical error lends greater depth to the point made in Chapter Two that the wars of Empire increased the geographical knowledge of citizens in Britain, France, Germany and other Western countries. Throughout the nineteenth century, Westerners harped on Chinese ignorance of world geography.
218. Taboulet, op cit., p. 842.
219. Waley-Cohen, *Sextants*, op. cit., p. 187; Hevia, op cit.
220. Smith and Liu, op cit., p. 225.
221. My thanks to Professor Chen Zhangfa for invaluable and extensive assistance with the translation of the nianhua of the Sino-French War and those of the Boxer rising. Working with a translator as gifted as Professor Chen was an intellectual delight.
222. Fang Shi (ed.), *Dianshizhai huabao*, Tianyi chubanshe, Taibei, 1978.
223. Michael F. Braive, *The Era of the Photograph. A Social history*, Thames and Hudson, London, p. 61. Braive is quoting Disdéri, *L'Art de la Photographie* (1862) in which Disdéri gave instructions for posing certain types.
224. Lalumia, op cit., pp. 64 and 80.

225. J. E. Elliott, "Why Western Cultural Inhibitions Prevented the Exploitation of a Technology for Over Half a Century. An Analysis of Photographic Portraits of the Chinese and American Photographs of the Boxer Rising," unpublished paper, Centre for Asian Studies, University of Adelaide, 1995, pp. 11–13. See also George Rowley, *Principles of Chinese Painting*, Princeton University Press, Princeton (1947) 1970.
226. At this parade at Aldershot, many soldiers collapsed with heat exhaustion and several died. The general in command at Aldershot was not there on the day of the parade and could not be located for several days after the incident occurred.
227. Fang Shi (ed.), op cit., Vol. 4, p. 81; Vol. 21, p. 73; Vol. 22, p. 1; Vol. 25, p. 57; Vol. 26, p. 60.
228. See Library of Congress no. LCUS262–706.
229. Lalumia, op cit., pp. 67 and 94.
230. Bodard, op cit., p. 338 gives a superb picture of the aristocratic unprofessional British commanding officer that is well supported by Cecil Woodham-Smith's witty portrayal of the eccentricities of the senior officers of the British army at the time of the Crimean War. Her characterisation of these senior British army officers is as amusing as it is alarming. See Cecil Woodham-Smith, *The Reason Why*, Penguin Books, 1958.
231. Waley-Cohen, "Commemorating War," op cit., pp. 871, 893–894 and "China and Western Technology," op cit., p. 1542, especially note 59.
232. This print is an unsigned news sheet print and interesting because, like its Chinese equivalent, it was considered to have little value, so very few of the cheap anonymous Japanese woodblock prints giving news of war have survived. The signed prints, however, are of great value. See, for example, Chaikin, op cit. My thanks to Ms Kazuyo Lee for allowing me to use this print from her private collection.
233. The British comedian, John Cleese, has parodied the British officer class and British NCO's in a number of his films, notably "The Meaning of Life."
234. A rare find has been two examples of nianhua depicting Chinese victories over Japan. See note 113 above.

Chapter 4

Why Western Cultural Inhibitions Prevented the Exploitation of a Technology for Over Half a Century[1]

Printing can only record what man knows and thinks; photography can record many things which man does not know and has not seen, much less understood … within limits it is an accurate statement of what was.

Kenyon Cox, *Scribner's Magazine*, 1898

The contention of this chapter is that up until 1900, photography could not, in fact, record things that people did not know and, more interestingly, was able to record ideas which men and women today no longer understand without the assistance of further interpretations. A study of the photography of the Boxer rising raises two issues. First, it is a test of the ability of photographers and editors to take and publish pictures showing something that was not known or generally accepted in the West. That is, that China was capable of fielding modern Western-trained armies with state-of-the-art weaponry. The second issue concerns the role of photography in conveying acceptable images of extreme physical violence at the turn of the century. The chaos, brutality and destructiveness of war form an excellent arena in which to examine this role. Both these issues will be discussed by reference to the work of American photographers in China in 1900.

American experience in photographing war was, by 1900, arguably the most developed in the Western world. The Crimean War and the American Civil War were almost contemporary events. The British and the French sent only a handful of photographers to the Crimea.[2] The Civil War was covered by hundreds of photographers from the most celebrated such as Brady, Barnard and Gardener to those anonymous tin type photographers who made a living on the fringes of the devastation of war.[3] The French experience was varied and interesting with some important photographs being taken in the Franco-Prussian War.[4] However, in the case of war photography, no developments occurred comparable to the work of American photographers.

The differences between the British and American adaptation to the photographic medium as a record of events could be shown by an analysis of the photographs of the Boer War and a comparison of these with the photographs taken by American photographers of the Boxer rising. Likewise, a survey of photographs taken by the French in the Mexican War of 1862 could serve to demonstrate the extent to which American photographers were developing unique responses to war. This chapter is mostly concerned with the work of the Americans for two reasons. First, there is a lot of photographic material that can be attributed to particular individuals. Second, in terms of factual knowledge and emotive connotations about China held by the American public, the events of the Boxer rising formed a powerful catalyst by which to test the nature of images made by Americans of China and its people.

An analysis of particular photographs will demonstrate that photographers were struggling to come to terms with the depiction of war itself. There were photographers who would not or could not, in fact, record things which people did not know and had not seen, namely the carnage of war. It was the particular events of the China crisis in 1900 that obliged the development of what we today would call the photo-document. By photo-document is meant a photographic image which, ambiguous or not, conveys a political message to its audience, whether or not the image is captioned. While there are many emotionally charged photographs of the Civil War, there are relatively few which have overt political content understandable as such today without the benefit of further textual explanations.[5]

There are few things that people understand less than death. It was fifty years before individual photographers could begin taking pictures that gave some feeling for the tragedy of war and for the indomitable nature of the human spirit in the face of war. It did not take so long because of the technological limitations of photographic equipment. The reason lay in the mind of the eye behind the lens and in the minds of the public as viewers of photographs. In order for photography to be able to "record many things which man does not know and has not seen, much less understood," individual photographers had to break free of the stereotyped vision of what constituted war. This stereotype was a creation not merely of the limitations of nineteenth century cameras and their users, but more importantly, it had evolved from the concept that editors had of what were suitable photographic images of war in conjunction with public response to such images. When we place the photograph next to the oil painting of war, we see at once that photographers had the same difficulties as artists in the nineteenth century. The subject had to be "suitable." What constituted "suitable" subjects of war as much for photographs as for oil paintings had nothing to do with the technical limitations of the camera or of oil paints and brush.

Western contemporaries and therefore to some extent posterity, accepted ill-informed clichés concerning the Chinese soldier and the nature of the Chinese armies in the late Qing. These clichés were fostered by one genre of military photograph taken by Westerners of Chinese soldiers; that of the exotic. The British concept of the photograph as contemporary document was little developed by 1900 in a tradition associated with the history of the illustrated press in Britain.[6] Photographs dating from as long ago as 1868 were being reproduced in 1900 in books, newspaper articles and illustrated magazines to give readers some background to the Boxer rising.

Thomson's photographs taken in the 1860s and 1870s appeared as late as 1937 as illustrations to Captain Kotenev's book *The Chinese Soldier*.[7] Appearing with other images showing the modern uniforms, weapons and training of the armies in North China before the turn of the century, such photographs might have given the impression that the Chinese military, like its Western European counterparts, was extremely proud of its traditions.[8] Appearing as they did, the exotic strand of photographs of Chinese soldiers served to give visual tongue to the clichéd generalisations about the outdated inefficacy of the Chinese armies (Figures 4.1 and 4.2).[9] The widely disparate nature of Chinese armies was not commonly understood in the West before the Boxer War. The way the Boxer rising was eventually digested and reprocessed by the West meant that the great differences between Chinese armies were still not particularly well understood after the Boxer War and have received no attention in the literature on the subject. The two photographs at Figures

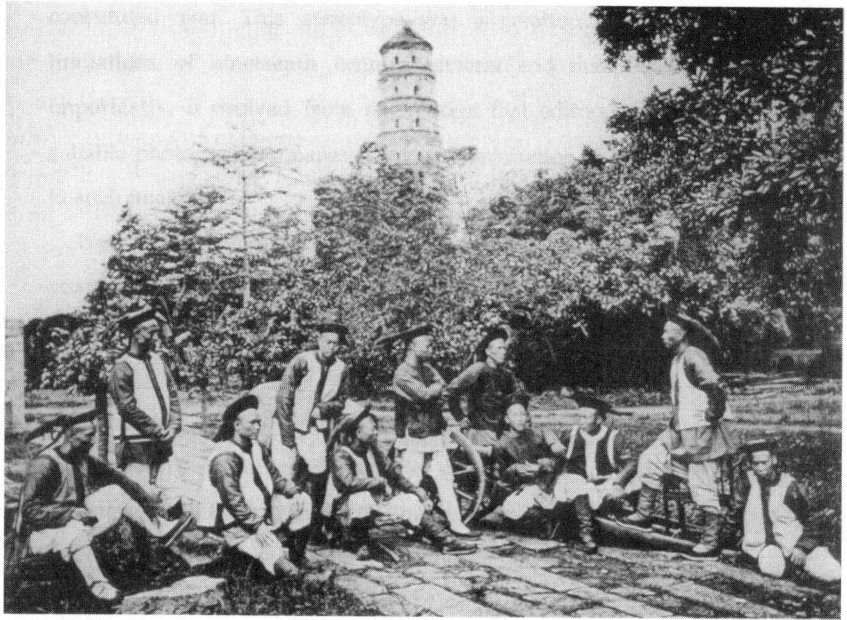

Figure 4.1 John Thomson, "Manchu Artillerymen" (1866–1870).

4.1 and 4.2 are the only two photographs this writer has seen illustrating scholarly works discussing any aspect of any Chinese army in the nineteenth century although Thomson did photograph foreign-drilled soldiers (see Figure 6.1). The significance of pictorial imagery cannot be underestimated. When we read extraordinarily inaccurate statements such as "the Qing army never really engaged with foreign troops,"[10] we understand just how much scholarship has suffered from the dearth of published photographs showing the modern-trained, modern-armed troops of the Imperial Chinese Army.

Group Photography — Chinese Soldiers Training and at War

There was also a second genre of military photograph taken in China before 1900; the group photograph. From its inception, photography was — and continued to be for at least two generations — an extraordinary phenomenon for contemporaries.[11] This means that enough evidence has survived to

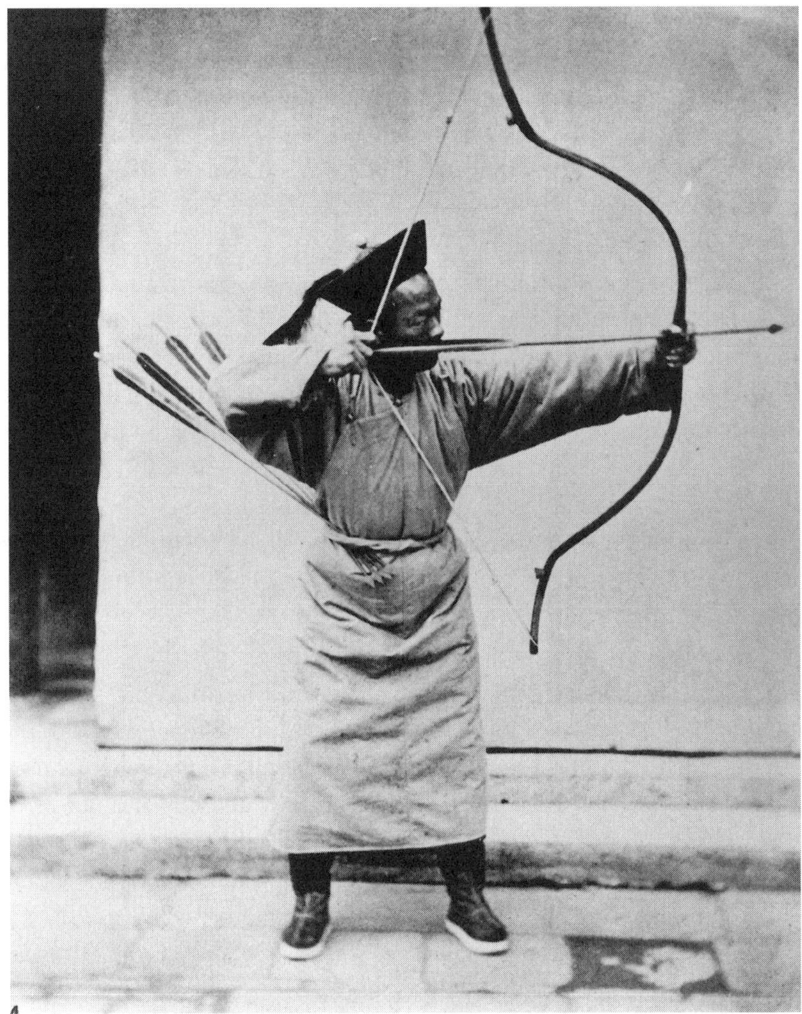

Figure 4.2 John Thomson, "Manchu Archer" (c. 1867).

allow us to answer some of the interesting questions about group photography posed by Marsha Peters and Bernard Mergen,[12] questions which have not yet been taken up in the literature.[13] An analysis of surviving group photographs of the military, Western or Chinese,[14] will make it possible to answer questions such as "Are people in the photograph aware of a group identity or cohesiveness?" "Does the photograph communicate this identity?" "Does the act of being photographed bring cohesiveness to the group?" "Does the photographer create stereotypes or capture already existing ones?" We may add to Peters' and Mergen's list, "What might the caption have added to the group's perception of itself as it was being photographed?" "What happens to the above questions when they are applied to a Chinese group which has solicited the taking of its photograph or allowed a Western photographer to take its image or been asked by a Westerner to stand in front of a camera?" Chinese photographic studios were producing good portraits by the late 1860s. Two last questions may therefore be put: "Did the Chinese military commander in question ask a Westerner or a Chinese to photograph his men and what was the photograph to be used for subsequently?"

All group photographs of Chinese soldiers uncovered by this research showing them to be a modern combat force and expressly taken as commercial ventures to sell to the general public, are either in American collections or have been taken by American photographers in a tradition which continued to 1911.[15] A number of these have never been published before.[16] Moreover, a discussion of them in relation to the questions concerning group photography and identity will demonstrate that the same sorts of preoccupations held by people in the West and Japan also led to group photographs of the Chinese military being taken at their request or with their consent. Furthermore, these photographs provide striking evidence of the rapid modernisation of the Chinese armies in the late Qing and not merely by illustrating superficial details such as uniforms and weaponry. They also provide material for consideration of the relationship between the caption and the photograph in the context of the group photograph.

Compare the two photographs of the "Artillery Class" (Figure 4.3)[17] and "Chinese Boys Defending Their Rights, China" (Figure 4.4).[18] In both these photographs it is clear that membership of a group has given the individual soldiers an identity and that the photographer has communicated this identity. Looking at the artillery class, it may be that the uniform itself functions in creating this identity as may the knowledge of belonging to an élite corps capable of manning the most modern Krupp gun in the world. This gun was a breech-loading weapon with an elevating mechanism so that it reared up on its trail to absorb the recoil.[19] In the British army, artillerymen were looked down on in the nineteenth century. They were a necessary evil; they knew too much about mathematics and often had dirty hands. These particular

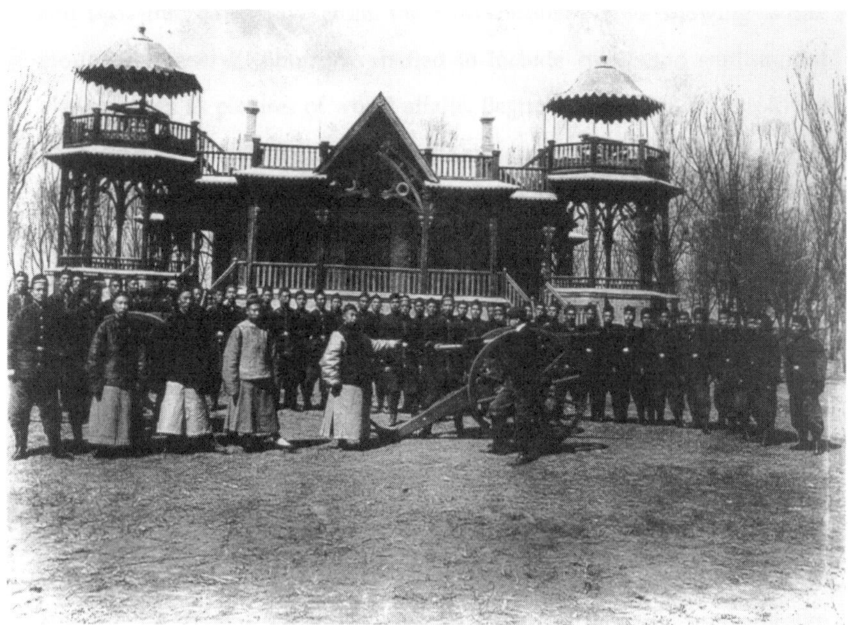

Figure 4.3 Anon., "Artillery Class" (no date — probably late 1890s). See also detail Figure 6.15. (By courtesy of the Library of Congress)

attitudes within a particular military tradition did not apply in the Chinese case at all. In China, the issue was rather, did one accept Western training and the modernisation it implied or not. There was no élitism associated with any particular branch of the military although Chinese emperors had had an interest in the mathematics of gunnery since the 1760s. Indeed, at any time, knowledge of Western military weapons, strategy and tactics could prove a liability for a Chinese senior serving officer.

Many of the soldiers in the photograph, the "Artillery Class" look "modern." The overriding reason for this comes from body language. The way they stand, the way they hold their heads, captures our attention because it is recognisable to us today as appropriate to a group of crack soldiers. These soldiers were Western-trained despite there being elements of Chinese tradition regarding the profession of soldiering which made such training difficult for Western instructors. However, this photograph is striking evidence that Chinese were Western-trained in every last sense of the concept. This training meant more than just learning how to march in a particular way or

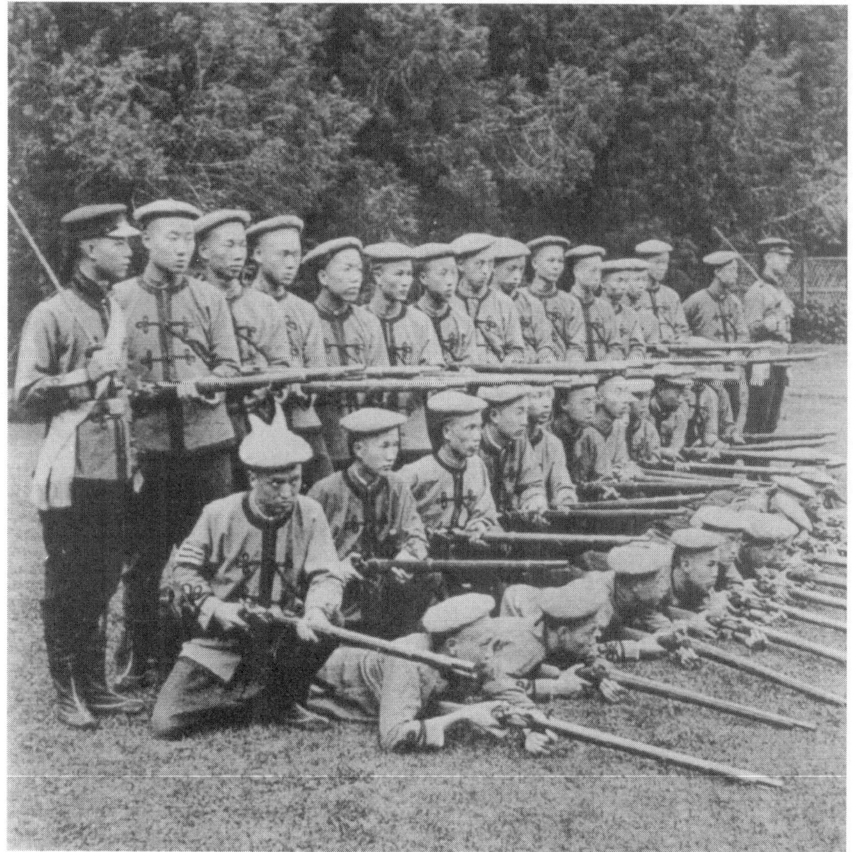

Figure 4.4 Ben W. Kilburn, "Chinese Boys Defending Their Rights, China" (1900). (By courtesy of the Library of Congress)

how to sight an artillery piece. The photograph shows us soldiers so well trained that some of the Western military culture inherent in such training is manifested in their bearing. They show an internalisation of Western values and expectations regarding the way in which soldiers should stand as a group.[20] No photographer could have taught these soldiers to stand like this. They stood like that because they were part of that group, because of their uniforms, their knowledge, and their training. We recognise this look as modern and it may well have come from the soldiers' sense of pride in who and what they were.

Had the photograph "Artillery Class" received wide exposure as evidence of the nature of Chinese soldiery, rather than Thomson's photographs of Manchu bannermen taken in the late 1860s, the image of Chinese soldiers in the visual data base of Western public opinion would have been very different. The pull of the exotic was still very strong in connection with Western perception of China in any of its cultural manifestations. Photographs of Manchu bannermen were reproduced over and over again. Photographs such as "Artillery Class" were not printed in newspapers, weekly magazines or books. Chinese soldiers looked like comic opera characters. Since Westerners "knew" this, they already "knew" that the Chinese army could not be a serious fighting force. The cultural significance of military uniform has been extensively discussed in Chapter Three. Thus in 1900, when the Chinese army performed well — in absolute terms or relative to its own performance against Japan only a few years before, this performance gained no recognition in the public or civilian official mind. In forming public and official attitudes, the weight carried by a picture cannot be overemphasised. The failure of Admiral Seymour's expedition to relieve the Legations, the success of the Chinese in repulsing three Allied attacks over a period of four weeks in the battle for Tianjin and the extent to which China had succeeded in modernising some of her armies despite — or because of — her defeat by Japan,[21] went unremarked by influential newspapers and illustrated weeklies.

Drawings and photographs are still being published showing Chinese troops wearing wildly atypical costume — the penchant for wanting to see the Chinese soldier as pantomime character seems to be deeply rooted, certainly in British mythologies of the Chinese soldier. Illustrations are still showing traditional uniform, or an inaccurate amalgam of the traditional and the modern being worn by soldiers adopting the stance appropriate to traditional training.[22] It is quite reasonable to publish these drawings and photographs if they are printed together with such photographs as those reproduced in this chapter and in Chapter Six showing evidence of modern uniforms, modern training and modern weapons. It also needs to be made quite clear that the Chinese were driving with all their resources to eliminate the traditional in favour of the modern. A balanced use of photographic evidence indicates that there were still some traditional Chinese armies by 1900 but the best of these, such as that of Dong Fuxiang, were unmistakably armed with the very latest military hardware. It was the modern armies with their training, logistical backup and infrastructure that had been concentrated in the most probable theatres of war by army reforms at the very end of the nineteenth century.

A second example shows just what power the caption had not only for the viewer and for the group being photographed but also when viewed together with the picture. At the turn of the century, there were still many cases indicating that the photographer himself had some power over the image and its verbal message despite the beginnings of editorial interference.[23] "Chinese Boys Defending Their Rights, China" (Figure 4.4)[24] was taken by or more probably for Ben W. Kilburn as a stereoscopic view. Stereoscopes were immensely popular from their inception in Europe, England and America for over eighty years.[25] The late nineteenth century equivalent of a slide-show in homes with a relative dearth of visual stimulus, stereoscopes were the focus of family group entertainment. They could be bought individually but were most often purchased as a series. They received even wider circulation through lending libraries and in schools. Military subjects were extremely popular.

With the war in China, the American stereoscope business saw an opportunity to do a good trade, with several companies sending photographers to cover it. The combination of the military theme with the exotic location and extensive newspaper coverage of the Boxer rising, often personalised to town and city dwellers through the emphasis on the presence in North China of a missionary from their very own town[26] — all ensured big sales of Boxer stereographs in America. Stereograph images of Chinese soldiery are therefore of cardinal importance in constructing a history of the influence of visual imagery of China and its people not only on the West, but on China itself. None of the photographs in this chapter or in Chapters Six and Seven appear in Chinese history books.[27] Ben W. Kilburn was a pioneer in opening up the stereograph business to a wider market by broadening the range of subjects photographed. He became not only publisher but also retailer of stereographs, engaging teams of door-to-door salesmen, first in America and then internationally. From the conventional views showing white mountain scenery, Kilburn diversified to include comic and sentimental views as well as pictures of world affairs. Beginning in 1890, he employed photographers to tour the world, but "the patriotic, moralistic and fanciful captions [for the stereo views] were mostly written by Ben Kilburn himself."[28]

The photograph "Chinese Boys Defending Their Rights, China" allows us to examine the question, "Does the photograph create stereotypes or capture existing ones?" This question is most usefully evaluated in the context mentioned above, namely, that of a stereotype being evolved in a process which took place between photographer and group. We know this photograph was taken for a company prepared to print it above this caption, and we see the posture and facial expressions of these young men. Kilburn has shown us a taut disciplined determination, uniforms foreign certainly, but immaculately turned out and approaching Western design. The cadets are armed with flint lock rifles, already obsolete weaponry. However, all over the world, military cadets are traditionally issued with dated weapons, even today.

It is not possible to look at this photograph and retain an image of Chinese soldiery as quaintly dressed extras for a Gilbert and Sullivan frolic. (Figure 4.1). Much about this photograph would have appealed to the American public. The extreme youth of the soldiers would have wrung chords in hearts that had just seen two generations of American boys go to war. Their raw, clean-shaven courage in defence of "their rights" would also have won sympathy. Kilburn, confronted with novel material out of which to make an image to sell to the American public, would have been aware of these clichés and set about planning this group photograph accordingly. While the Chinese soldiers would not have been aware of these American cultural and historical reference points, they had their own *esprit de corps*, their own national sentiments and professional ethos. Such a photograph above such a caption may not have sold as successfully in other Western European countries, particularly not Britain and Germany.[29]

The resulting photograph shows Kilburn to be one of the many of the new wave of photographers starting to mine the potential of photographic technology to produce the beginnings of the genre of photo-document as we know it. This photograph is posed, like any other military group photograph taken over the previous forty years. The difference is that an American took it with a particular caption in mind. Moreover, these Chinese military cadets were posed for the photograph in the very year of the war in which China kept the West at bay for nearly two months. In Western European historical experience, particularly in Britain, the Chinese as enemy in war occupied a very different place in the public eye, from, say, the Boers, the Filipinos, the Turks or the people of the Sudan.[30] Here we see a group photograph which has a group identity, which communicates this identity and which is an amalgam of stereotypes. Yet it is argued that the photograph itself, even thus captioned, is not recording something unknown either to Kilburn or to the young cadets.[31] Its success derives from its being able to communicate a fusion of that which was known to the photographer and to the group, thereby applying pre-existing stereotypes to a group which should have been "exotic," or "quaint"[32] or "ill-armed rabble"[33] but, through Kilburn's lens, turned out to be "Chinese boys defending their rights." There are unique photographs taken by Westerners of the Boxer rising as well as the thousands of clichéd newspaper images. The most striking point is that the fraction of the photographic evidence showing Chinese soldiers to have had the qualities that allowed them to fight successfully against combined Allied forces for four weeks, those photographs and therefore those qualities have been ignored by posterity both in China[34] and the West.

Central to the preoccupation of this study is Walter Benjamin's observation that "Every image of the past that is not recognized by the present as one of its concerns, threatens to disappear irretrievably." American newspapers recognised Chinese military gains in the first few weeks of the Boxer campaign but they did not print photographs such as "Firing a Volley from Shelter of Bank — Chinese Soldiers at Tien-Tsin, China" (Figure 4.5).[35] This photograph may have been posed. "Chinese Boys Defending Their Rights" was posed. If "Firing a Volley" was posed, using, for example, soldiers of the British-trained Weihaiwei regiment, it argues a photographer who recognised all aspects of contemporary Chinese military ability.[36] Telephoto lenses had only just been perfected so it is unlikely to have been taken during the battle for Tianjin. Thus there was an American commercial photographer at Tianjin in 1900 who had seen Chinese soldiers in action. He took a photograph not of bows-and-arrows or romantic Manchu bannermen draped around a gun as if on a picnic (Figure 4.1), but of appropriately uniformed men posed to look as if they were in action taking advantage of terrain in order to defeat their enemies.[37] These Chinese soldiers were armed with single-shot lever-action rifles that had a high rate of fire and were still being used by the Australian navy in the 1914–1918 War and by Australian naval cadets in 1959. They were wearing a field-type uniform rather than the "pyjama-style" uniform so often caricaturised in the Western press, this uniform was drab-coloured for camouflage and they were wearing effective headgear.[38] Their position and their weaponry were eminently suited to the terrain. These photographs were

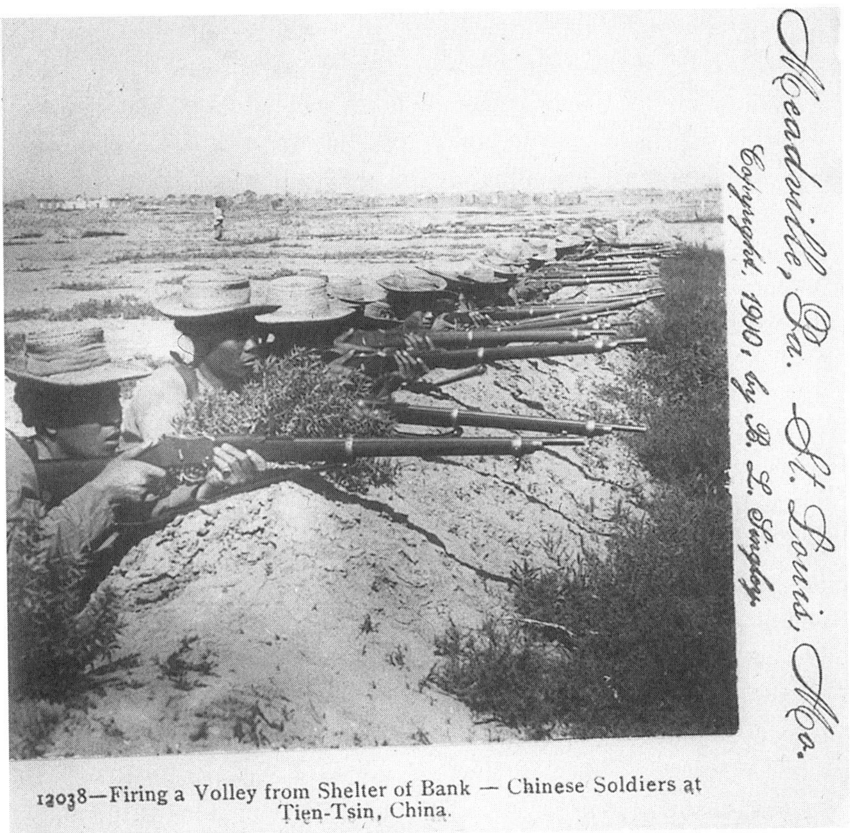

Figure 4.5 B. L. Singley, "Firing a Volley from Shelter of Bank — Chinese Soldiers at Tien-tsin, China" (1900). (By courtesy of the Library of Congress)

taken by a photographer who knew they would sell widely. To a public saturated with stereoscopes, photographs[39] and the primitive early beginnings of moving pictures depicting the military,[40] this picture was a close up of professional soldiers in action. The precision of the line-up, the modern weapons, the recognisable uniformity of headgear worn as it should be, hands grasping the weapons as they should do, all these elements added up to a picture of fighting soldiers. Other crucial photographic evidence from a Shanghai newspaper of June 1900, indicates that these men wore uniforms, or at least headgear, very similar to that of the men of General Nie Shicheng's army.

Yet this evidence, the images that did conform to Western notions of what was soldier-like, slipped through the fingers of the cultural and national hierarchies that determined which pictures would survive. They now lie forgotten in far-flung largely inaccessible library archives. However, Thomson's picture of the Manchu archer went on appearing in books and articles on the Chinese solider until 1937 illustrating texts which stressed — certainly in 1900 — that Chinese soldiers were primitive, poorly-trained, wore costumes suitable for a child's fancy dress party[41] and carried bows and arrows.[42] The élite of the French, German, British, Austrian, Italian and American armies still carried and used swords at the turn of the century.[43] Both their training and logistics left much to be desired as was shown by the performance of France in the Franco-Prussian War and again in the Sino-French War, the Americans in the Philippines, the British in New Zealand, the Sudan and in South Africa as well as the eight invading armies in 1900.[44]

The highly-coloured but inaccurate reporting of the Boxer rising in *The Times* came to be accepted as the true version of events. The more accurate, more informed but illustrated reporting of the American press lacked the credibility to override *The Times* in the minds of contemporaries and also therefore in the somewhat elusive but still definable eye of posterity.[45] So it was with the photographs. While the photographs analysed above constitute "an accurate statement of what was," they recorded what Western countries did not know. Hence they have been forgotten because they could not be understood and therefore could not be accepted by the most powerful image-makers of the time. Nevertheless, they serve as a reminder that representatives of Western nations reporting and photographing the Boxer rising were far from uniform in the images they produced of China, whether in words or pictures.

> If not only personality but nationality blocked objective statements about reality … a mechanical process had to be found, one which could effectively bypass the subjective responses and parochial training of all artists, or a reliable system of universal communication could not be developed.[46]

This brief survey shows clearly that until at least 1900, personality, nationality, and editorial views of what was acceptable to the public mind certainly could block the "objective statements about reality" made by photographers in China. Those photographs taken as stereographs were sold by the hundreds of thousands and reached an even wider audience than indicated by actual sales figures as they were also lent by libraries and constituted a very popular form of home entertainment. Yet the stereographs illustrated in this chapter and others like them were not printed in any major American or British daily. This survey also calls into question the very possibility that "a reliable system of universal communication," certainly not in operation by 1900, thanks to any "mechanical process," could ever be developed.

American Military Photographers — Captain Cornealius F. O'Keefe

Surviving American photographs of the Boxer rising can be divided into those taken by the military, those taken by professional photographers for subsequent sale as stereographs, those taken for or used in newspapers, and those taken by amateurs or professionals who happened to be in China at the time. This analysis will concentrate on the official American military photographs as well as the work of the gifted American photographer James Ricalton. Some photographs taken by French military men will be examined briefly for comparison in order to establish the originality or otherwise of particular themes and the element of individual talent in creating a photo-document.

The official photographer of the American contingent to the China Relief Expedition was Captain Cornealius F. O'Keefe. O'Keefe left for the mining towns of South America in 1882 when he was sixteen years old. Ten years later, he was established in Leadville, Colarado as a professional photographer. Here he established a reputation for photographing women. In 1898, he volunteered to join the American forces fighting Spain and was sent to the Philippines in June 1899. There he joined the Bureau of Military Information and worked full-time as a military photgrapher, covering the Insurrection battles in 1899. He returned to the US in July 1899 by which time he had become the official photographer of the Eighth Army Corps and was promoted to the rank of Captain. On 23 June 1900 he went with Colonel Liscum from the Philippines, arriving in Tianjin on 11 July in time for the battle of Tianjin on 13 July during which Colonel Liscum was killed and his men decimated by Imperial Chinese Army forces.[47]

O'Keefe's photographs of artillery in action show photography to have developed very little since the Civil War. What passed for action shots were neither intrinsically visually stirring nor comparable to the stirring work of the war artists still accompanying armies into the field.[48] Moreover, some of these photographs unwittingly show just how much the American and British armies had yet to learn in order to get optimum returns from artillery firepower.[49] Composed views of camp sites with well-pitched tents and neatly-stacked rifles abound in the tradition of the Civil War photographs[50] and do not approach the excellence of Beato's photograph taken in 1860 of the Anglo-French War against China.[51]

Tents, guns, tethered horses — these could be, and were, for most photographers, the unimaginatively repeated elements of their compositions, whether taken in Châlons in France, in Virginia or at Dagu. In fact, some of O'Keefe's photographs are nearly indistinguishable from those taken in America or in France forty-odd years before. Only an outstanding photographer like Beato could take those same elements and produce an unforgettable image that could not be improved on by more modern equipment or increased experience of the representation of reality which is a photograph. O'Keefe in China soon showed that he too possessed this outstanding ability. The "views," particularly of the Summer Palace, continue the tradition established by Thomson. They use the medium with great sensitivity to contrast the artifice of man in architecture and in landscape gardening, set against lines of distant hills, merging into empty sky in a fine Western mechanical imitation of the shanshui tradition of which Captain O'Keefe was probably entirely ignorant.

O'Keefe's photographs of the British Punjabi coolies closely approach a modern idea of the photo-document with one in particular showing these coolies filling water bottles and containing the arrested movement of activity that we recognise today as being an integral part of documentary photography. (Figure 4.6).[52] Only one of the coolies stands posed, aware that the photograph is being taken; the others are engaged in their tasks in a manner which suggests an understanding on O'Keefe's part of how to take such a photograph. This is no group photograph. The photographer is not exhorting the fillers of water bottles to go about their business in any particular way. To obtain such a photograph, Captain O'Keefe may have had a real affinity for the technical capacities of his camera and an eye capable of seeing and recording something much more extraordinary than the exotic, the exotic as mundane, as evidence of what he had never seen before. Or he did what professional

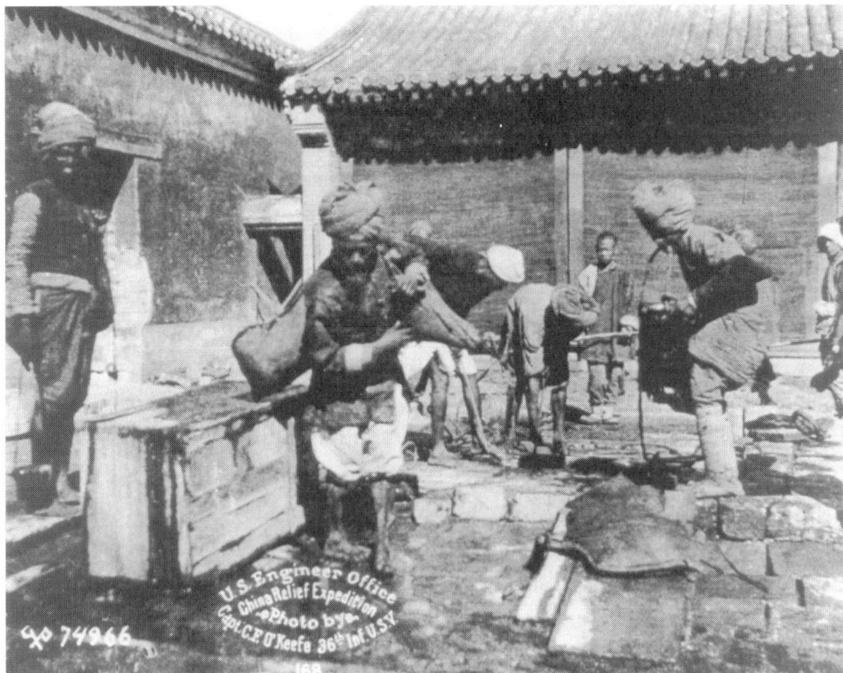

Figure 4.6 Captain Cornealius F O'Keefe, "British Soldiers Filling Waterbottles" (1900). (By courtesy of the National Archives, Washington DC)

photographers had barely begun to do; he took so many pictures of the same scene that this one became possible. The second alternative being unlikely because of the primitive nature of the art of photography and the excellence of O'Keefe's "views" of the Summer Palace having already been noted, it would seem no accident that the US contingent chose O'Keefe as its official photographer. This photograph reveals the potential of the technology, a potential that very few photographers had as yet grasped.

The filling of water bottles by the military had been the subject of photographs taken in France in 1864 and in 1895. Around 1864, Prévot had chosen this subject for his picture "La Corvée d'Eau. Jardin de l'Empereur. Camp de Châlons"[53] but this photograph is a stilted still-life with its subjects posed exclusively for a camera by a photographer only too conscious of the limitations of his equipment or dominated by a pre-conceived notion of what his subjects should look like. Around 1895, Lespieau took "Corvée dans la Cour de la Caserne: Grenoble"[54] and while this photograph has more spontaneity, it does not approach the work of O'Keefe. In the German illustrated weekly *Die Illustrierte Zeitung* of 25 October 1900, there is a photograph of British Indian soldiers fetching water in China.[55] This photograph, showing the identical subject to O'Keefe's, depicts a milling group of men barely distinguishable as Indian soldiers by their uniforms, photographed as they were from behind, engaged in an activity undiscernible to the viewer.

In the late 1860s Thomson had taken a photograph of Chinese itinerant tradesmen which shows evidence of his interest in and desire to produce a photo-document on a human theme, but the photograph is contrived. It is static information; people have been arranged by Thomson so that we can see how they go about their business. They are not going about their business.[56] In 1900, Commandant Corvisart, the French military attaché in Tokyo went to Tianjin to photograph the Boxer rising. His photographs, unlike those of Captain d'Amade,[57] are undistinguished, being typical, both in selection of subject and ability with the camera, of many amateur photographers of the time. Corvisart took a photograph of itinerant Chinese musicians, which shows a static group pasted onto a non-existent background, an exact replication of the work of Roger Fenton in the Crimea forty years before.[58] These are not people making music in the streets and drawing crowds of eager listeners.[59] Such a subject could have been taken by O'Keefe, but not by Corvisart. Even when photographing military groups, Corvisart's work is neither memorable nor informative. He took a photograph of mounted Siberian Cossacks in which these soldiers appear either from the back view or with the head facing away from the camera.[60] As a contribution to military intelligence or a striking image of world-renowned fighting men, this photograph leaves a lot to be desired.

There were enormous possibilities in the still life. Having as we do, the whole corpus of O'Keefe's work, we can see that he was definitely a product of the American tradition of war photography which concentrated on particular kinds of still-life scenes, so much an accepted part of Civil War photography and praised as such by contemporaries.[61] However, O'Keefe was able to bring out these possibilities in ways that showed innovative development in the mind that held a camera not significantly technologically advanced in such a way as would effect the taking of still-life scenes. These possibilities had been seen by Beato and to some extent by Brady, Barnard, Gardener, Kamiesch and Méhédin, contemporaries trying to photograph the challenging theme of war. It was these possibilities that had led from its inception to heated debate concerning the status of photography as an art.[62]

There is one photograph which, more than any other taken by any photographer at this time, reopens this debate. It shows Captain O'Keefe to have used the medium of photography to create a powerful work which as photograph and as document would have conveyed a socio-political message by its art. The phrase "Christianity at the mouth of the cannon" was endemic in speech making and newspaper reporting in America throughout 1900. It is improbable that Captain O'Keefe's photographs ever reached any but military eyes. However, this photograph, "Gun and Cathedral, Tientsin" (Figure 4.7),[63] was unarguably a deliberate creation. The cathedral so hated by the Chinese, burnt down for the second time, stands angular, taller and darker than the Chinese architecture it scornfully invalidates. Behind the dark embrasures in a pool of light, blacker but arguably less wicked than the upthrusting symbol of an unwanted God,[64] squats the cannon. The cannon, equally dark, equally alien, is trained on the cross. The photographer had an opinion about this war and by his artistry he has left us indisputable evidence of his opinion.

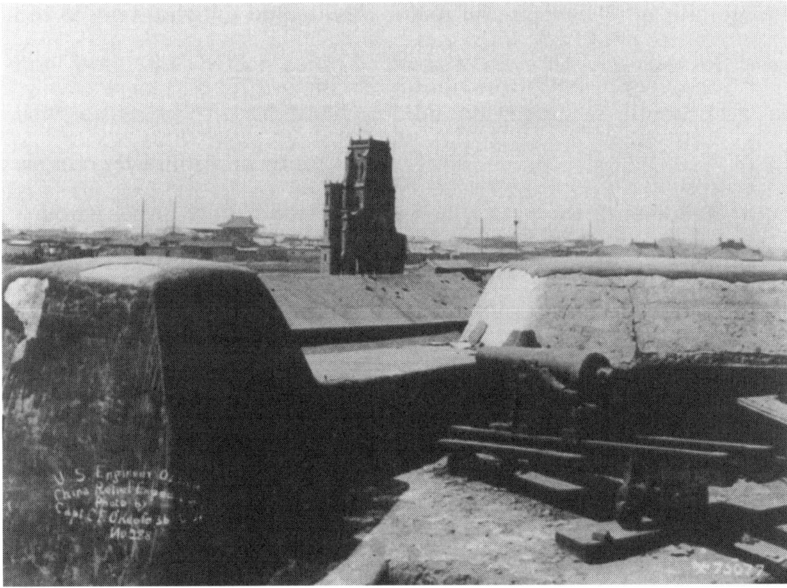

Figure 4.7 Captain Cornealius F. O'Keefe, "Gun and Cathedral, Tien-tsin" (1900). (By courtesy of the National archives, Washington, DC)

Without access to O'Keefe's personal papers, however, we are reminded of Ernst Gombrich's admonition that "images need much more of a context to be unambiguous than do statements."[65] Did O'Keefe take this photograph to provide a visual image fitting the oft-repeated phrase concerning the undesirability of presenting Christianity at the mouth of the cannon? Was he trying to show that the cross would rise triumphant over the heathen? In a more macabre vein, was he trying to show that for Christians there was life in the mouth of death? On the basis of the photograph alone, it is not possible to give a definitive response in respect of O'Keefe's intentions. At the least, he succeeded in taking a photo-document that contained complex ambiguities that could only be clarified by a caption. With the advent of such a photograph, the Pandora's box of describing an image with words was opened. The photograph had now been taken which could be made to have any number of meanings, irrespective of the intention of the photographer, depending on the caption given it by an editor.

Some have argued that photography as a medium offers universal visual communication, effectively bypassing the "subjective responses and parochial training of all artists."[66] In Captain O'Keefe's photograph "Gun and Cathedral, Tientsin" and Commandant Corvisart's cliché of the cathedral and the Black Fort (Figure 4.8)[67] discussed below, we have evidence that, by 1900, photographers of different national, cultural and historical backgrounds could not

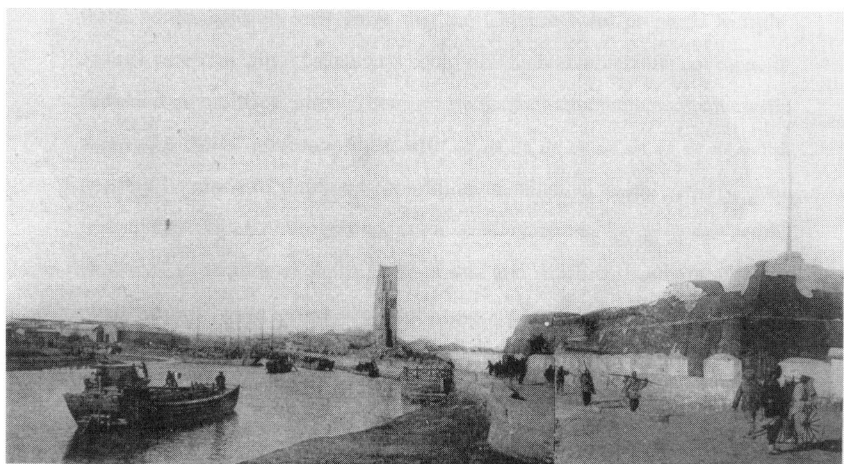

Figure 4.8 Commandant Corvisart, "Cathedral and Black Fort" (1900). (By courtesy of the Musée de l'Armée de Terre, Paris)

take photos alike one to another. Ivins had argued that a German in the fifteenth century could not draw like an Italian or a Frenchman;[68] by 1900, a Frenchman could not take a photograph like an American. Furthermore, the existence of a photograph like O'Keefe's shows that within the technical limitations of the medium, some individuals had begun to perceive that a photograph could be used to make a point. Having mentally conceived the point, they could then set about the planning and research that would produce the photograph to make that point, even if we today cannot pronounce definitively on the point on the basis of the image alone. This is another example of photography recording something that people already knew. But this time we are dealing with a different kind of "knowledge," the most difficult kind of "knowledge," socio-political views peculiar to a particular culture; a divided public; and an individual photographer who has deliberately used his camera to record his socio-political opinion and thus side with one sector of the public, inevitably — were his photograph to have been given prominence above a caption making clear his position — antagonising another.

What is new about O'Keefe's understanding of the potential of the camera is that he was successful in taking a picture of a complex socio-political idea. Many people had been exposed to these kinds of ideas. One photographer took a photo-document which using the elements of the still life, put these ideas into one image. O'Keefe had provided an image susceptible of being read in at least three opposing ways, depending on the caption. In this photograph we see that the camera could be made to take a picture of an idea, it could even endow that idea with ambiguity. And this without the need of a single written word. Although it has been argued that this was precisely what photographers did, take pictures of what they already knew, the kind of knowledge involved was less complex and it was generally shared by hundreds of photographers, editors and the public at large. As an individual, Captain O'Keefe may or may not have had an opinion on the issue of bringing Christianity to China before he arrived in Tianjin. The unique power of his photograph lies in its forceful demonstration that Captain O'Keefe was preoccupied with a different kind of knowledge. His service with the Expeditionary Force left him such a strong opinion that he reassembled all that was known about the medium to take a photograph that survives as a monument to the art of the photo-document.

The corpus of Commandant Corvisart's photographs taken in Tianjin and Beijing in 1900 provides material for comparison with the work of Captain O'Keefe. Corvisart's cliché of the cathedral and the Black Fort (Figure 4.8) exemplifies the eye of an amateur photographer and military man whose camera could take in two buildings in the one panorama. So the photograph depicts two edifices. Neither more nor less. Its limitations by comparison with Captain O'Keefe's striking photograph are obvious.

Captain O'Keefe showed an ability to use his camera to externalise his own feelings when confronted by the beauty of the Summer Palace; by an interest in men whose clothing and accoutrements were so different yet who did the same job as American soldiers were doing every day, filling water bottles; and perhaps by his knowledge that the Chinese were prepared to fight against accepting alien beliefs and could only be brought to accept them if subjected to military force. These photographs constitute a break with received pictorial tradition. Faced with death, the new medium could not possibly be made to duplicate the old, and the result could not achieve widespread popular recognition as an effective image of war and death. However, in striving to make sense of war and death, the camera and the photographer were forced into producing a photo-document. Death, the most problematic of all human experience, provides the ultimate challenge to the photographer and by 1900 we see that some photographers began to respond in a more complex way to that challenge.

Should we view Beato's camp in the Dagu forts, O'Keefe's Punjabi coolies filling water bottles and his gun and cathedral as occasional freak accidents in the practical application of a difficult technology[69] that otherwise showed little development over fifty years? Should we continue to labour the argument that photographers cannot take pictures which editors or the public refuses to recognise for what they are and hope to make a living? Or should we recognise that, as is the case with any art form, photography will throw up individuals who, confronted with the same compositional elements and using the same technology, will make images so far beyond the frontier of the possible for other contemporary practitioners and therefore, often, the public, that their work stands apart and becomes that debated excrescence of the human mind we call art? Whether or not, the viewer were conversant with the work of Gustav Doré, it would not be possible, for example, for anyone to look at John Thomson's photograph "Altar of Heaven Foochow, near Min River" taken about 1867[70] and dismiss this as a casual snapshot taken by yet another wealthy traveller eager to record a passage in wild remote places. That the elements of photography were so obviously chemical — that is, requiring "scientific" knowledge — made its status as an art no different. That it was such an expensive hobby, made it more likely that rich people who could afford the time, the accoutrements and the labourers to carry them would constitute the majority of travel photographers. In the nineteenth century, photography was still dominated by rich amateurs and a relatively high proportion of military men who did not necessarily have a particular affinity for the medium.

Some of O'Keefe's photographs show a break with the phenomenon of using the camera to take pictures of what was already known because O'Keefe himself was prepared to use the same technical apparatus with a different mind-set. With photographers like O'Keefe, we get the beginnings of the photo-document, the beginnings of the use of the camera to record things that people could not know, could not see and could not understand. In this way the photographer himself became the vehicle by which a new commodity and or new understandings were produced and accepted as such. Photographers like O'Keefe were rare. Rarer still, were the editors who would publish their work. The non-acceptance of the range of possibilities within the limitations of the technology of photography,[71] make it one of the slowest, least-willingly exploited to the full, of any of the technologies introduced into the West over the last one hundred and fifty years. Despite the ubiquity of its practice — by the end of the nineteenth century, comparatively as many people were taking as dreary and meaningless (to anyone else) snapshots as they do today — the greater potentials of the medium only showed occasionally in the work of a very few.

American Civilian Photographers — James Ricalton

James Ricalton was a school teacher and passionate amateur photographer. He spent his summer holidays visiting and photographing remote places quite unknown to small-town American citizens of the day. One notable summer, he trekked across the Russian taiga with his photographic gear in a handcart which he pulled along behind him. On another occasion, in defiance of the local Egyptian authorities, he climbed a pyramid in the dark just to be able to say that he had done it. Tianjin 1900 saw Ricalton extremely short of money.

What money he had went to buy photographic equipment. He told a story of how one day he saw a cart going down the street loaded with sacks of potatoes. One of the sacks had a hole in it and Ricalton was scrabbling down the street behind the cart to catch the potatoes as they fell. They became his staple diet for the next few days. He went on to distinguish himself for his extraordinary personal courage and his utter dedication to extending the bounds of the technically possible in photography during the Russo-Japanese War. He earned the unqualified admiration of the Japanese among whose lines he worked.[72]

In the work of John Thomson and James Ricalton, we have the benefit of their own written commentaries which give evidence about their personal frames of reference and how these could influence what the photographer saw and could write about but would not photograph. Because the primary concern in this chapter is to trace the evolution of American photographic images of China given a sudden and violent impetus by the Boxer War, we will conclude with a discussion of the work of James Ricalton. Ricalton's text and photographs, as with Thomson's work forty years earlier,[73] show evidence of the limitations imposed by the photographer himself — as opposed to his editors or his public — on the photographs he took. Ricalton was a man with boundless curiosity and an insatiable desire to see and record unusual or technically difficult phenomena. Yet he was heir to a tradition and willing member of a culturally accepted mind-set as to what constituted proper subjects for photography, particularly war photography. He could *write* of the horrors he saw:

> We were constantly passing dead bodies floating down, and, on either bank of the river, at every turn, hungry dogs from the deserted villages could be seen tearing at the swollen corpses left on the banks by the ebb tide. It was forty miles of country laid waste, deserted homes, burned villages, along a river polluted and malodorous with human putrefaction.[74]

He also expressly believed that knowledge of the horror of war "though it is repulsive, is also educative."[75] Yet, knowing when was the best time to capture the full horror of the bodies floating down river, a horror he was amply able to describe in words, he took an innocuous photograph which conveys relatively little of this horror and even pointed this out in his written commentary. By his own standards, Ricalton could have secured a more graphic depiction of the corpses in the river. The text accompanying this

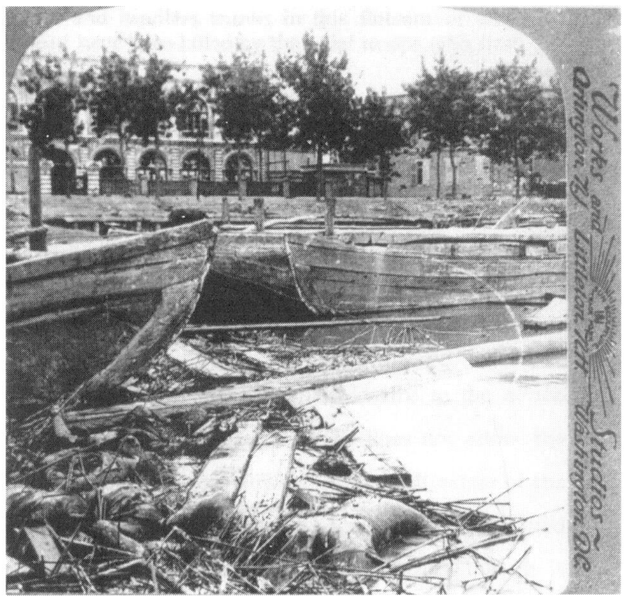

Figure 4.9 James Ricalton, "Horrors of War-Dead, Chinese Floating in the Pei-ho, Tien-tsin" (1900). (From the private collection of Mr R. Blum)

photograph entitled "Horrors of War-Dead, Chinese Floating in the Pei-ho, Tientsin" (Figure 4.9)[76] shows that despite what he saw, he was consciously or otherwise, unable to take the photograph which would provide full pictorial evidence of his verbal observations:

> several times a day coolies were sent to this place with poles to set free the accumulation of bodies and allow them to float down stream. [Why, asks the modern reader, did he not take a photograph of this?] At this moment, you see, there are only four or five in view, but at other times there are large numbers, especially in the morning, after a night's accumulation. At times I have seen heads and headless trunks in this flotsam of war. Many of these dead have been killed by the relief troops who first entered Tien-tsin ...[77]

He continues to describe this photograph in the same vein of "there were much worse things I could have taken a picture of, but I took this one instead":

> The shattered windows and pierced walls everywhere tell how the showers of shot swept everything at this point. You see the shell momentoes on this building

> at the right; there are other buildings along this Bund even more thoroughly scarred that [sic] those.[78]

Ricalton's willingness to attribute these civilian deaths to the action taken by the Christian and Japanese foreign troops does not allow the argument that he failed to take photographs showing the full extent of the carnage because he wanted to conceal the atrocities committed by the Allied soldiers. The reasons for his failure are more complex than this. Ricalton's personal and cultural experience, his conscious knowledge of and interest in photography, while enabling him later in his career to pioneer certain aspects of war photography and to receive huge financial and public recognition for so doing,[79] initially rendered his photography impotent before the horrors of war. Nevertheless, his experience as a photographer in Tianjin over a short time shows him to have found a way to internalise these horrors. In this process he crossed the boundaries of the known and began to make photography do what had been claimed for it: record "things which man does not understand." What do people understand less than death? What renders people more impotent than the excessive carnival of death which is war? Ricalton was cogniscent of this impotence and it had, as he expressed it, nothing to do with what an editor would print or a public would buy. Nor, it is argued, was Ricalton's impotence entirely to be attributed to his own explanation of the limitations of the camera itself:

> A hundred sights in Tien-tsin alone would give you a fuller conception but even the greatest number could not tell you all. It is impossible to picture the apprehension of faces on the street — the roar of bursting shells and deadly smaller missiles that filled the air. Subterranean housekeepers cannot be "sculptured by the sun" nor can pale, fear-stricken faces peering out of cellar windows; nor the measured tread of soldiers at all hours of day and night.... *These things cannot be portrayed by any cunning of the camera.*[80] [emphasis added]

Although "sculptured by the sun" was second nature by now to Ricalton, as far as technique was concerned, this passage shows that he was a reservoir of deeply rooted consciousness that this was still a new and developing technology. Yet this was the man who *took* the photograph "American Giving Water to Japanese Wounded after the Battle of Tientsin"[81] and *wrote* of it "Photography is merciful and does not portray the blood-smeared garments and the blood clots on the ground where the wounded have lain overnight."[82] Contemporary British pictorial or photographic rendering of the wounded left them out entirely, or showed them neatly bandaged posed in a group photograph or lying back in a pristine bed being consoled by a member of the British royal family.[83] Ricalton was the man who *took* a photograph of the South Gate at Tianjin when the Allied forces finally captured it and *captioned* it "Chinese Who Paid War's Penalty, South Gate, Tientsin,"[84] while *writing* of it:

> The number of dead along this wall was not great. You see the protection afforded by this loopholed defense rising on our left.... The greater number of dead are in the streets and houses near this gate, many of whom have been killed by common shells and the deadly gases of the lyddite shells.[85]

Ricalton's dilemma was no less than that of war itself. Ricalton was a well-travelled man who had faced personal danger many times. The shattering experience of war is so devastating precisely because it forces a sensitive observer to see so much more than mere personal danger. It is thus not surprising that a photographer of his technical excellence, personal sensitivity, visual acuity and conscious determination to master his medium,[86] should either take photographs with the "there was much worse to be seen this morning or round the corner" commentaries, or blame the camera for being unable to capture the totality of the destruction, the terror, the agony and the ultimately incomprehensible dislocation of war. Yet Ricalton was not so impotent as he described himself. He also took, captioned and wrote about images of war that very few photographers had as yet essayed. His photograph "Terrible Destruction Caused by Bombardment and Fire, Tien-tsin" (Figure 4.10)[87] is testimony to the savage extent of the bombardment and is accompanied by a text which begins:

> There is a sadness about a deserted home; there is a greater sadness about a deserted city or village. Before us lies a great city, not only deserted, but sacked, looted and in ashes by Christian armies.... Lilly-feet, which were so expensive at Shanghai, were here the appendages of mangled corpses that had no more consideration that [sic] the carcasses of dogs ... but the camera cannot portray nor the pen describe those heart-rending scenes along the narrow street after the battle. Now it is a pathetic scene of desolation.[88]

It is notable that the 202 photographs taken by Commandant Corvisart of the Boxer War contain no clichés of people, military or civilian, killed in battle.[89] The very few photographs taken by Corvisart of buildings destroyed during military action show the buildings as a background to a bustling street

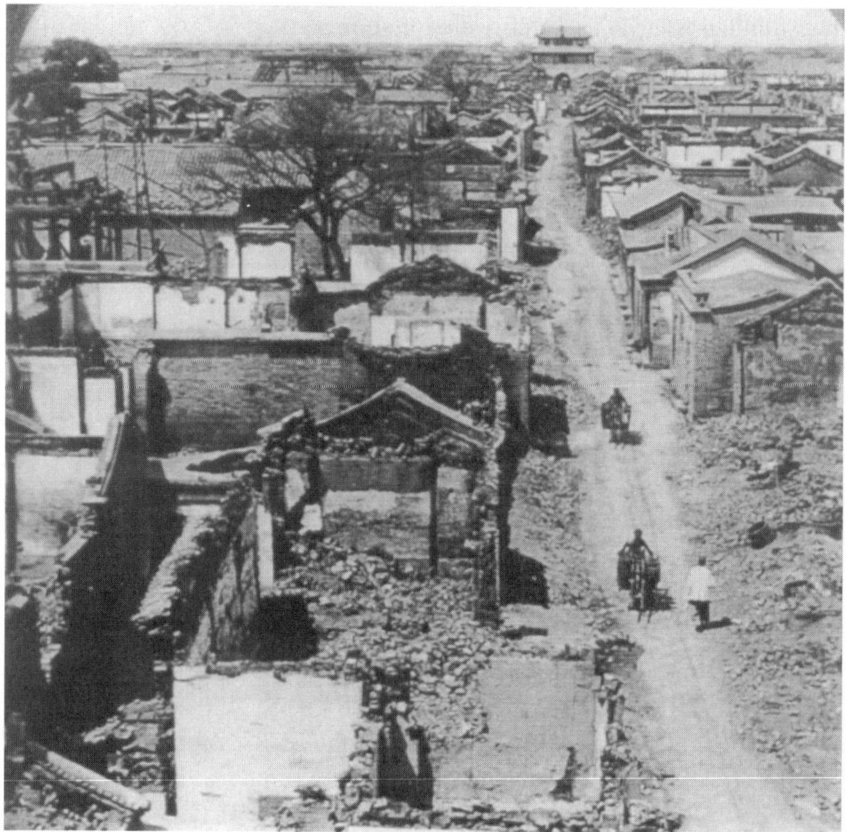

Figure 4.10 James Ricalton, "Terrible Destruction Caused by Bombardment and Fire, Tien-tsin" (1900). (From the private collection of Mr R. Blum)

scene, evidently taken after the re-building of life in Tianjin had begun. As such, the buildings stand as a neutral backdrop to a busy street on a sunny day, rather than looming as gaunt testimony to the destructive powers of modern shell-fire so much discussed by observers of this campaign. There were photographers in the Crimea, at the American Civil War and at the Franco-Prussian War who were able to use the eye of the camera to convey the desolation of war by taking pictures of demolished buildings. However, Ricalton's photograph of the destroyed city is unique, capturing these particular Chinese citizens, dwarfed by the scale of the destruction, pushing their pathetic barrows down the road. Looked at as a stereograph, this is particularly impressive. The three dimensional effect of the shadows cast by the figures emphasises their human stature and their living determination. With this image he achieved what he doubted possible; a photographic composition which would convey the effects of the ravages of war across cultural and temporal barriers.

The questions we must ask if we are to be able to assess Ricalton's photographs in a historical context are "Did anyone else at that time take pictures which better conveyed the horror of war?" "Do his pictures stand as powerful evocations of that horror without the benefit of the accompanying texts?" "How important are those texts in themselves?" "Was Ricalton able to use the medium of photography to record 'things which men did not know' or did he accept its limitations and continue to take photographs of camp sites, massed soldiers on parade, generals directing the troops and suitably arranged dead on the battlefield?" The camera and its technical limitations were a constant. The photographer, as a conscious vessel of received cultural preconceptions and traditions regarding visual imagery in general and the photography of war in particular, was also a constant. Was it then possible for an individual to mutate those constants into breaking with the received traditions by forcing new possibilities on to the technical limitations? Could an individual force his eye to make a camera create images which convey something of the horror of war to viewers with almost a century of further experience of visual imagery on this ultimately challenging subject?

Ironically, it is a photograph not of war, but of the banal everyday ritual of meal-taking, which shows that Ricalton did what he thought could not be done, make the camera convey the intangibles of the agony of war. Entitled "Family of the Lower Class in Their Home, Partially Destroyed During the Siege of Tien-tsin" (Figure 4.11),[90] this photograph and its caption do not require Ricalton's text to amplify understandings of the image. What this photograph does is show us how abnormal war is, how indomitable is the human spirit in the face of its havoc and, above all, that these factors apply equally to a ravaged poor Chinese family as they would to any other victims of war. A twentieth century reader may not know that from the inception of photography, there were strong taboos in the West against taking various kinds of subjects and debates on this issue grew fiercer as the century drew to a close. In the 1840s when the Langheim brothers at Philadelphia showed a daguerreotype of people eating at a table, it was withdrawn on the grounds that it was too vulgar for public display.[91] By 1900, then, we have a

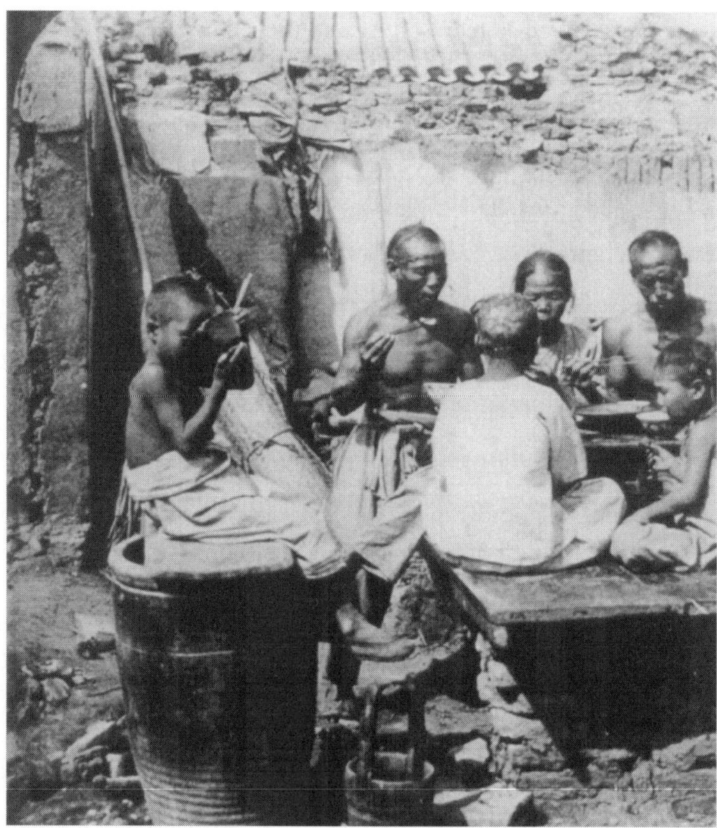

Figure 4.11 James Ricalton, "Family of the Lower Class in Their Home, Partially Destroyed during the Siege of Tien-tsin" (1900). (From the private collection of Mr R. Blum)

photographer prepared and able to break with irrational traditions generated by his own culture and in so doing, create the photo-document.

O'Keefe's consciousness of what he was seeing, what the Boxer rising was about, developed so that he went through the existing genres and found them inadequate to encapsulate his evidently strong feelings that this was a war happening in China to Chinese people. He synthesised what he heard, thought and saw and finally he took the photograph of the gun and the cathedral. So Ricalton, beginning with subjects already beyond the circumscribed, even if his attempts were self-confessedly limited, left as the high points in his oeuvre, the Chinese family eating lunch and the photograph of the narrow street, a band of desolation emphasised by the four figures toiling to an unknown destination down what was once a teeming thoroughfare, now flanked by the reason for the desolation. We do not need the text. It does not matter that Ricalton noted that the destruction was caused by Christian forces.

This is a photograph of war. No camp-sites, not even wounded soldiers or dead bodies; war is something that happens to civilians, even to civilian populations as controversially alien and exotic as the Chinese.

There was little or nothing in received tradition showing the destruction of masses of ordinary people's homes,[92] Civil War photographs showed the destruction of bridges, public buildings, factories, single magnificent Southern mansions. Similarly, it was rare that a photographer intentionally set out to record the effect of war on ordinary surviving civilian victims; during the Boxer rising, it was unique.[93] O'Keefe left evidence that he could deliberately make the camera take an image far exceeding contemporary pictorial conventions. In so doing, he left an image of his view of the war in China; a picture that remains to us today as an example of the power, the ambiguity and the artistry of photography. Ricalton, in choosing to take this family who survived the dislocation of war to be able to sit and eat a meal together in what is very literally a bombsite, had also broken through the limitations of the medium and produced a universally recognisable photo-document of war. War happens to everyone, rich and poor, old and young, Americans and even Chinese. This some of us know today, but whether or not anyone knew it in 1900, received tradition meant that it was not a subject for photography. With precious few glass plates left and no money, Ricalton *made* this a subject for photography. Like O'Keefe, his photographer's vision, confronted by the war in Tianjin, grew through the plates of corpses floating down the river, unsanitised images of the wounded and the dead, to culminate in this photograph of a family of Chinese, survivors of war, eating their midday meal.

In his outstanding study, *Reading American Photographs. Images of History*, Trachtenberg asks the questions "Is it possible for pictures ... to convey the 'earnestness of war' and its *form?*" [his emphasis] "Can any single photographic image bring home the reality of the whole event?" He rightly points out what Ricalton noted in the verbal imagery he chose to accompany his plates that "in the case of war, the normal gap between sense experience and mental comprehension is stretched to an extreme." Trachtenberg argues that the Civil War photographers produced images, the strength of which "lies in their mundane aspect — their portrayal of war as an event in real space and time ..."[94] The particular skill of the photographers whose work has been analysed here would seem to show otherwise. The work of Civil War photographers shows no development comparable to that manifested by the oeuvre of O'Keefe or Ricalton. When repeated fifty years later, much of this work was no longer recognisably relevant as a depiction of war. Its popularity when finally reprinted,[95] had more to do with a nascent American national identity consciously understood as the result of such a devastating historical experience as civil war. Some of O'Keefe's and Ricalton's photographs survive today as potent images of war, or the economic and cultural roots of war, irrespective of national mythologies which have grown up in the intervening years.

Ricalton's photograph of a poor Chinese family eating lunch around a makeshift table in the shattered remains of their home has the strength Trachtenberg claimed for the photographs of camp-sites and men on parade. It is mundane. It certainly does show war "as an event in real space and time." The twist is that Ricalton chose Chinese civilians as his subjects to show for all time the greatness of the human spirit demonstrated by the mundane. He did not photograph soldiers of any of the eight Allied armies comprising the Chinese Expeditionary Force or of any of the soldiers of the Imperial Chinese Army. Trachtenberg, in looking for a photograph which conveyed "the earnestness of war," meant the role of the battle in the political conflict at hand. In the history of war photography, O'Keefe's masterpiece of the gun and the cathedral is outstanding in conveying the political and cultural aspects of the Boxer rising as well as the form that rising took. Even for those unaware that the cathedral had been destroyed by Chinese people for the second time in thirty years, its truncated facade testifies to the physical force of political anger. The double entendres as it faces the cannon convey more about the nature of cultural and commercial imperialism when carried to its extreme in warfare, than could be achieved by volumes of history written from any viewpoint.

Reflections

What are we to make of the fact that Kilburn, O'Keefe and Ricalton, confronted by their experience of the Boxer rising, produced photographs which extended the frontiers of the possible in terms of subject matter and ways of seeing war while their work was ignored or quickly forgotten by the Western world? Civil War photographs were resurrected within fifty years and have enjoyed increasing popularity since then, as have photographs of the Franco-Prussian War. By contrast, photographers attempting to create a sense of the immensity, the grandeur, the timelessness of China, were having their work refused by American magazines before 1900.[96] So it is in the realm of China as it appeared in the Western mind, that we must look for an explanation first for the creation of photographs as unique in their exploitation of a limited technology as they are as photo-documents, and second for the fact that these photographs went unrecognised and thus have not remained easily accessible as evidence of the Boxer War.

This chapter has made clear that if photographs recorded what people already "knew," what those with the power to select and reject images had already seen and believed to be the "real" image, those photographs survived and came to constitute the accepted record of events. It has also shown that there were other photographs which, using the same technology, went beyond what people already knew or wanted to understand, to become works of art in themselves. Yet these were forgotten because they were unacceptable as a record of events. Their novelty, their accuracy, their conceptual innovation, these were the very factors that made them unacceptable.[97] Lastly, this analysis has shown that within the Western tradition at this time, photographers of different cultural backgrounds produced photographs as readily distinguishable evidence of their respective cultural traditions as much as their skill as individuals.

The fate of these products in the contemporary American context differed from that of the British or French context as much as the products themselves. China loomed in a controversial but by no means unified way in the Western consciousness. "An accurate statement of what was" was not only impossible for most photographers, it was unwanted by most editors and most publics. There was an ambiguous amalgam of what Westerners took to be the reality that was China. The Chinese had contributed to this as much as had Westerners.[98] In a very real way, China was also responsible for producing the state of affairs in which "Every image of the past that is not recognized by the present as one of its concerns, threatens to disappear irretrievably."

Perversely, images from the past — particularly Thomson's exotic antique soldiers — were taken to represent the present in a British historical tradition which paid little heed to the value of the pictorial image. Not only did this tradition with regard to the value of illustrated texts obfuscate major events in British history,[99] it continued to misrepresent events elsewhere. So this work has shown that we may reread Benjamin and see that where images of the past are taken to represent a present of which those images seem entirely unrepresentative, the present — not the image — disappears irretrievably.

Western culture with regard to the pictorial image was by no means uniform and the differences between the British and American views as they were applied to historical events in China, were quite apparent.[100] Thus it came about that among other factors, through different cultural attitudes to the relevance and value of the pictorial image, British, French and American photographers came to produce such strikingly different work.

Trachtenberg, when asking whether it is possible for photographs "to convey the [political] earnestness of war" may be answered in this way. Some Western photographers confronted with the war in China began to take pictures that broke with previous traditions. However, these photographs did not receive widespread publicity. No matter how sensitive or technically skilful the photographers were, this was not a war which editors and the American public could know a great deal about, "much less understand." It was another Chinese peasant rising against foreigners. The West knew something about Chinese peasant risings, some of its representatives began to take photographs which "within limits [were] an accurate statement of what was" but most of these particular pictures did not enter authoritative contemporary understanding of events in China.

In attempting to represent warfare, representatives of all cultures for different reasons will similarly bend visual images until the mirage of "an accurate statement of what was" dissolves in some cultures into nothing more than the coincidence of an individual who could distil the chaos into its one acceptable representative image. In another culture and on another social level, that of Chinese folk art, for example, there were individuals operating inside a tradition that was already able to represent the chaos of all warfare, in fiction or in life in the same, commonly acceptable way. It is, perhaps, only by detailed and culturally informed study of different visual traditions representing the same phenomenon that we can trace the nature of the struggle to depict warfare.[101] At no time can the artists divorce themselves entirely from the intended audience of their work, whether the work in question be an anonymous piece of folk art like the woodcut of the battle of Tianjin or Picasso's Guernica or Ricalton's photograph of a Chinese family eating a meal in their bombed-out home. There is a crucial symbiosis between artisan/artist, the public, the nature of the war being depicted and the perception of that war held by those in whose country the war is being fought. A historical description of the fate of the different images constitutes a statement of the geography of power. Like most of the nianhua of real battles discussed in Chapter Three, most of the photographs discussed in this chapter have not been republished.[102] In the case of the Chinese woodcuts, both Chinese and Western scholars see other functions and other subjects of folk woodcuts as being more representative than those whose goals were to awaken the minds of the illiterate to knowledge of unprovoked military action against their country by foreigners and to give them information about the outcome of such action. For different reasons, woodcuts of wars between China and foreign countries and photographs showing Chinese soldiers to constitute well-trained fighting men in the Western sense of the concept, were not acceptable representations of what was, so they have disappeared from the corpus of legitimate Chinese and Western images. The resurrection of particular images leads to the proposition that the geography of power was and is not now necessarily what contemporaries perceived it to be.

Notes

1. A version of this chapter was first published in *History of Photography*, Vol. 21, No. 2, Summer 1997. My thanks to Taylor and Francis for allowing me to make use of this material.
2. Matthew Lalumia describes the reasons for Roger Fenton's aims: first, to take commercially-appealing photographs and second, not to embarrass the sitting ministry. See Matthew P. Lalumia, *Realism and Politics in Victorian Art of the Crimean War,* UMI Research Press, Michigan, 1984, pp. 118ff.
3. "Tin type" was another name for ferrotype photography in which a positive image as opposed to a negative one was printed onto a tin plate. The process became popular around 1860 and was used by itinerant "while you wait" photographers (glass plates were more difficult to handle and took a lot longer to develop). The mother of Mr Ron Blum could remember tin type photographers

still taking photographs of young couples in the Adelaide parklands after the 1914–1918 War. Information from Mr Blum.

4. Photographs of the destruction of buildings were among the most common clichés taken to show the effects of war. As visual images, not even the best of these could convey the horror of war with the immediacy of the work of war artists. Michel Léon-Eugène Méhédin's photographs of Sebastopol showing the results of the bombardment of important public buildings are impressive. His work has a quality which manages to capture something of the desolation of the aftermath of war in a way that Corvisart's photographs of the destruction of Tianjin do not. For Méhédin's work, see the Catalogue of the 1994–1995 Exhibition by the Musée de l'Armée, *Crimée 1854–1856: Premiers Reportages de Guerre*, pp. 25, 88 and 89. Another French photographer who produced notable work was Kamiesch. His group photographs and panoramas have such a distinctive quality that they may be said to bear his signature by the nature of their composition. Kamiesch's photographs in particular are vastly superior to the work of the Englishman Roger Fenton whose group photographs may just as well have been taken in his London studio. Fenton was patronised by Prince Albert. By this early stage of the history of photography it was already clear that the camera could be used as the handmaiden of those in power or it could be made to produce what can be discerned today as the forerunners of the photo-document. There is an anonymous photograph in the Archives de l'Armèe de Terre, Château de Vincennes, Paris, No. 1195P27 which shows the destruction of the Fort de Vanves in 1871. This photograph is one of a very few which makes an unforgettable statement about the devastation of war. My thanks to M. Jean-Marie Linsolas for drawing this photograph to my attention. Even to the late twentieth century eye, matured by images of Hiroshima and Dresden, this is a powerful photograph. The contrast of massive ruined buildings with flattened empty space, a few ravaged trees and two minuscule gun carriages is riveting.
5. During the Civil War unsanitised photographs of the dead were taken, notably after the celebrated Battle of Antietam. A powerful and outstanding image taken at this time is an unattributed photograph of a dead horse said to have belonged to Colonel Henry Strong. The power of this image, however, comes rather from mystery and poetry than guns and politics. See W. C. Davis, *The Image of War 1861–1865, The Embattled Confederacy*, Vol. 3, Doubleday and Co. Inc., Garden City, New York, 1982, p. 35.
6. Mason Jackson, *The Pictorial Press. Its Origins and Progress (1888)*, Hurst and Blackett, New York, 1969, p. 141.
7. Anatol M. Kotenev, *The Chinese Soldier. Basic Principles, Spirit, Science of War and Heroes of the Chinese Armies*, Kelly and Walsh Ltd., Shanghai, 1937.
8. See Colonel Cyril Field, *Britain's Sea Soldiers: A History of the Royal Marines and Their Predecessors*, Lyceum Press, Liverpool, 1924. Vol. 2, p. 266 for an illustration

showing "Band Uniforms — Royal Marines" typically redolent with the panoply, pride and splendour of dress uniforms of bygone eras. During the Boxer rising photographs of Chinese soldiers on parade or in formations displaying their Western training and equipment were published in French, German and Russian illustrated magazines. Unique photographs, possibly taken by Auguste François show Chinese soldiers training in Yunnan province in the 1880s. See Figure 3.2. Photographs of Chinese soldiers training in Manchuria in the 1880s are held in the military archives in St. Petersburg. For developments in the Chinese military 1900–1911, there is a rich collection of manuscript albums in the Archives de l'Armée de Terre, Château de Vincennes, Paris.

9. John Thomson, *Illustrations of China and Its Peoples*, Vols. 1 and 3, Samson Low, Marston, and Searle, London 1869–1873.
10. Henrietta Harrison, "Justice on Behalf of Heaven," *History Today*, September 2000, p. 50.
11. R. Taft, *Photography and the American Scene. A Social History, 1839–1899*, Dover Publications, New York, 1938, pp. 39–40, "it was a matter of public interest when an individual was able to produce a daguerreotype. For example, the news is given in the *New York Sun* for 8 January 1840, that 'a gentleman in Wheeling, Mr. Mathers, has been successful in the construction and use of the Daguerreotype.' Try to imagine the condition of the press if, at present, it was thought necessary to record each successful snapshot of the multitude of amateur photographers."
12. Marsha Peters and Bernard Mergen, "'Doing the Rest': The Uses of Photographs in American Studies," *American Quarterly*, Vol. 29, No. 2, 1977, p. 295.
13. Neither Trachtenberg's illuminating study nor John Tagg's productive structuralist approach focuses on these sorts of questions, although these works do discuss some of the issues raised by group photography. See Alan Trachtenberg, *Reading American Photographs. Images as History. Mathew Brady to Walker Evans*, Hill and Wang, USA, 1989 and John Tagg, *The Burden of Representation. Essays on Photographies and Histories*, MacMillan Education, 1988.
14. In the West, the military was regarded as a proper subject for the photographer's lens. From the inception of photography, an increasing public interest and the relative ease with which photographs could be taken of all aspects of military life other than warfare itself, meant that proportionally, there was a huge percentage of photographs pertaining to the military world.
15. See Bain, "Chinese Soldiers in New York" (1911), collection of the Library of Congress. LC-B2-227.
16. See Jane E. Elliott "American Photographs of the Boxer Rising," *History of Photography*, Vol. 21, No. 2, Summer 1997.
17. Reproduced from the collections of the Library of Congress. LC-USZ62-33201.
18. Reproduced from the collections of the Library of Congress. Lot 12070-6, No. 14182.

19. On the occasion of Li Hongzhang's visit to Europe in 1898, he went first to Germany and then visited France. At this time, the French had as yet not perfected such an artillery piece and the French officer attached to Li's mission tried to get details of the German weapon from the Chinese. See manuscript *Rapport du Capitaine Meillet adjoint a l'Atelier de Construction de Puteaux sur son Voyage en Chine, 1896*, held at the Archives de l'Armée de Terre, Château de Vincennes Paris, Series 7N1674, pp. 16–17.
20. In his *l'Art de la Photographie* (1862), Disderi gave specific instructions for posing specific types. See M. F. Braive, *The Era of the Photograph. A Social History*, Thames and Hudson, London, 1966, p. 111, "Here we have a soldier. Young though he is, he has earned the right to command; his bearing, his eye, everything about him, speaks of courage and manly pride. In the last war he distinguished himself by deeds of exceptional bravery. It is clear how this subject should be treated. There must be a feeling of life, passion, movement.... An open-air effect, plenty of light, sharp shadows, no mysterious half-tones, the figure in a stable poise, an open and honest gesture, nothing vague; in the background a tumultuous array of suitably martial accessories." This passage makes it clear that a Western photographer did not take a picture of a soldier; he took a picture of a received idea of a soldier. This idea could be but was not necessarily transferable from one culture to another.
21. Allen Fung, "Testing the Self-Strengthening: The Chinese Army in the Sino-Japanese War of 1884–1885," *Modern Asian Studies*, Vol. 13, No. 4, 1996.
22. Ian Knight, *Queen Victoria's Enemies (4): Asia, Australasia and the Americas*, Osprey, London, 1990, p. 8 and coloured drawings A and B. My thanks to Professor Joanna Waley-Cohen for giving me a copy of this work.
23. P. B. Hales, *William Henry Jackson and the Transformation of the American Landscape*, Temple University Press, Philadelphia, 1988, p. 245 notes that the power of cropping, layout and editorial choice over the idiosyncracies of photographer or even subject — not only message but style as well — had been appropriated by the power of the journal. With all this divested of him, Jackson himself became a sort of ghost, a byline that contributed to the homogeneous product constituting *Harpers* but without the power to explode the formulae that determined, ordered, and limited the meaning and effect of his pictures.
24. From the collection of the Library of Congress. Lot 12070-6, No. 14182.
25. See Taft, op cit., pp. 184–185 and Trachtenberg , op cit., p. 17.
26. In the Hoover Institute for War and Peace, Stanford University, there is an interesting collection of newspaper cuttings from the *Topeka Daily Capital*, the *Topeka State Journal*, the *Kansas City Star*, and the *Emporia Gazette* (Kansas) which makes this connection very clear.
27. A version of Jane E. Elliott, "American Photographs," op. cit., containing three photographs (as opposed to eight photographs in the original article) was published in *Lao Zhaopian*, Vol. 7, October 1998, Jian Ailüete, "19 shiji waiguoren

paishe de Zhongguo shibing" (Nineteenth Century Foreign Photographers' Pictures of Chinese Soldiers).

28. W. C. Darrah, *The World of Stereographs*, Darrah, Gettysburg, PA, 1977, p. 46.
29. Jane E. Elliott, "Who Seeks the Truth Should Be of No Country. The British and American Press Report the Boxer Rising, June 1900," *American Journalism*, Vol. 13, No. 3, Summer 1996. As a consequence of his notorious brutality, Baron von Ketteler, the Minister at the German Legation in Beijing was executed by a Chinese soldier acting on his own initiative. This outraged the Kaiser and provoked him into making a famous speech expressing his anger and contempt for the Chinese. This speech was universally reported in the German press and a celebrated illustration depicting Germany as an avenging angel also received widespread publicity.
30. Ibid.
31. Trachtenberg, op cit., p. 84, points out that "Not only do staged compositions enact unstated ideologies and betray unconscious wishes; their motifs often clash with countervailing ideas." He continues, "The photographs often transmit contradictory messages, the idea of history as heroic action at odds with sheer mundane event." The photographs analysed in this study are examples of images which succeed in conveying history by portraying "sheer mundane event" because it is argued that the men who took them in China developed different ideas about how to portray war itself. It would seem to be the case that the Civil War photographs about which Trachtenberg is writing here certainly did "enact unstated ideologies and betray unconscious wishes" but that the "transmission of contradictorary messages" has more to do with the limitations of the mind-set of the photographer and the expectations of the viewer than the actual content of the photograph — intended or otherwise.
32. Ralph L. Powell, *The Rise of Chinese Military Power, 1895–1912*, Princeton University Press, Princeton, 1955, p. 31 gives a highly-coloured picture of the Chinese soldier, stressing the quaint and "unmilitary" aspects of his uniform. In 1900 there were some armies still uniformed as Powell describes. However this passage creates a powerful comic image of the Chinese soldier, the "neglected son of Mars," which bears little relation to the numerous professional armies in the North and the Southwest. Some of these armies had been wearing Western-style military uniforms since the 1860s. As uniform creates such a powerful cultural stereotype of what is soldierly, it would seem important to take care to describe the whole gamut of Chinese response to Westernisation of the military in respect of uniform.
33. *The Times*, 12 June 1900, leading article.
34. There are complex national, cultural, social and political reasons behind the various styles of pictorial depiction of the Boxer rising by Chinese artists, see, for example, *Yihetuan tongsu huashi*, Cilian chubanshe, Shanghai, 1954. This book contains caricatures of situations including missionaries fighting Chinese for

loot and Western traders losing money over delayed goods drawn in the style common to comic strips all over the world in the 1950s. None of the illustrations are based on any contemporary illustrations. There is a paucity of published or unpulished photographs in China documenting the Chinese armies of the late Qing. One recently published source shows some rare photographs of northern Chinese soldiers training. See Liu Beisi and Xu Qixian (eds), *Gugong zhencang renwu zhaopian huicui* (Selection of Photographs of People Kept at the Imperial Palace), Forbidden City Publishing House, Beijing, 1994, pp. 225–231. Extensive discussions with historians in Shandong, Tianjin and Beijing indicate that there is no material in China comparable to that which forms the research base for this paper. My thanks to Ms Irene Cassidy for providing me with copies of photographs held in the Imperial War Musem in London and to Mr Teruaki Kawano of the National Institute of Defence Studies, Tokyo for sending me copies of photographs held in the archives there. One significant source of photographs of the military in the late Qing not covered by this chapter is the material held in German archives.

35. From the collection of the Library of Congress. Lot 12070-8, No. 12308.
36. See Figures 3.7, 3.8 and 6.2. By 1900, there was a striking similarity between British and Chinese ideas regarding uniform. There was little difference between the headgear of the soldiers of the Weihaiwei Regiment and those of Generals Nie and Yuan.
37. This photograph was taken very close to the Dagu forts. My thanks to Professor Chen Zhenjiang, for this information. Dagu and surrounds are at present part of a military zone closed to foreigners.
38. Several Chinese scholars have expressed to me their incredulity that soldiers in the late Qing would have been prepared to wear such headgear. Figure 3.7 and the drawing of General Nie Shicheng's soldiers which may be seen at Figures 3.8 and 3.13 provide indisputable evidence of the headgear worn by soldiers of the Imperial army in the North at this time. There is a wealth of photographic evidence concerning the Chinese army manoeuvres of 1903, 1907 and 1908 showing the full extent of the Westernisation of military uniforms in the North. An excellent collection of these can be seen in the Archives de l'Armée de Terre, Château de Vincennes, Paris. In view of the extent of the commentaries on the issue of Westernisation of clothing in huabao into 1912, it is interesting to note that Chinese soldiers had adapted to Western uniform and headgear as early as 1900. See *Mingquan huabao*, Shanghai, 1912. See also Robert E. Harrist, Jnr, "Clothes Make the Man: Dress, Modernity and Masculinity in Early Modern China," unpublished paper, Columbia University, 1998. I am deeply grateful to Professor Harrist for allowing me to read and make use of this paper.
39. See Taft, op cit., p. 61 for a table giving the number of photographers per head of population in the USA from 1840 to 1930. On p. 63, Taft notes that by 1853

the *New York Daily Tribune* estimated that three million daguerreotypes were being produced annually. (The population of America was twenty-three million in 1850.)

40. The earliest moving pictures held in the collection of the Library of Congress include the re-enactments of events in the Boxer rising and the earliest "heart-throb" telling of a young soldier returning from the war in the Philippines.
41. See the artist's coloured impression of a tigerman in Knight op. cit., Figure A.
42. This myth has been perpetuated in modern writing. See Pierre Lorain, "Les Armes de la Guerre des Boxeurs 1900–1901," *Gazette des Armes*, No. 76, 1980, p. 29.
43. During the Sino-French War, in fighting on Taiwan, the French officers had to abandon their sabres because of obstruction by tropical vegetation. They used instead long bamboo sticks tipped by the iron point of a lance. See Captain Garnot, *L'Expédition Française de Formose, 1884–1885*, Librairie Ch. Delagrave, Paris, 1894, p. 120.
44. There was an enormous scandal following a parade of the Reserve Guard at Aldershot in 1900 at which several soldiers collapsed and one died of heat exhaustion. Commenting on this, the *Daily Mail* wrote on 20 June 1900, "we now hear that chaos prevails at Aldershot ... and that the general who should be in command is not at his post." During Admiral Seymour's forced retreat to Tianjin, British and Russian artillary was lost by being loaded into junks too light to bear the weapons or simply abandoned in the fields. A contingent of British troops coming from Hong Kong to reinforce the invading army arrived in Tianjin to find that its ammunition had been left behind. The forces of the eight armies besieging Tianjin were short of ammunition for the wide variety of weapons being used even within each separate national military group. See Chapters Six and Seven.
45. Elliott, "Who Seeks the Truth," op. cit.
46. H. E. Jussim, *Visual Communication and the Graphic Arts. Photographic Technologies in the Nineteenth Century*, R. R. Bowker & Co., 1974, p. 103.
47. This biographical material has been taken from Frederick A. Sharf and Peter Harrington, *China 1900. The Eyewitnesses Speak. The Boxer Rebellion as Described by Participants in Letters, Diaries and Photographs*, Greenhill Books, London, 2000.
48. There is an interesting woodcut by Shunsai Toshima (1866–1908) which shows a group of Japanese war artists in the field during the Sino-Japanese war. See N. Chaikin, *The Sino-Japanese War 1894–1895*, Imprimerie Pillet, Martigny, 1983, p. 129.
49. See O'Keefe's photographs of "Artillery in Action at Peitsang," 5 August 1900, and "Artillery in Action" on the march to Peking. This latter differs hardly, if at all, from O'Sullivan's photograph of Battery D, Fifth US Artillery in action

at Fredericksburg, Virginia, May 1863 in Taft, op cit., p. 236. Both of O'Keefe's photographs are held in the National Archives, Washington DC, Numbers 111-SC-84910 and 111-SC-88856 respectively.

50. See O'Keefe's photographs 111-SC-75010 and 111-SC-75011, National Archives, Washington DC.
51. The best reproduction of this celebrated photograph is to be found in Nigel Cameron, *The Face of China. As Seen by Photographers and Travelers, 1860–1912*, Aperture Inc., 1978, pp. 16–17.
52. This photograph is held in the National Archives in Washington, DC, No. III-SC-74966.
53. J. Humbert, L. Dumarche and M. Pierron, *Photographies Anciennes, 1848–1918, Regards sur le Soldat et la Société*, Collections Historiques du Musée de l'Armée, Paris, 1985, p. 21, photograph No. 34.
54. Ibid., p. 70, photograph No. 144.
55. *Die Illustrierte Zeitung*, 25 October 1900, pp. 610–611.
56. See Cameron, op cit., p. 65 and also p. 91 which shows an anonymous photographer's picture of a Western businessman in a rattan factory, c. 1875. This latter photograph is a posed photograph that succeeds neither as a photo-document nor as a group photograph, because of the contrived compositional elements of the group.
57. Capitaine d'Amade, *Vues Diverses Provinces du Sse-Tchouen, Yunnan et Youang-si. Voyage du Capitaine d'Amade de Pékin aux Frontièrs du Tonkin* (1889), Tientsin, May 1890. Manuscript album held at the Archives de l'Armée de Terre, Château de Vincennes, Paris.
58. "Photographies prises en Chine par le Commandant Corvisart, Attaché Militaire à la Légation de France au Japon, 1900," manuscript albums held at the Musée de l'Armée de Terre, Château de Vincennes, Paris, Album No. 1, p. 22, photograph No. 40.
59. The photograph of the audience of a public storyteller is the one exception in Corvisart's work in which he captures the expressions on the faces of the spectators and in which the photograph gives a clear idea of the activity in which its subjects are engaged. See "Photographies," op cit., Album 2, p. 20, photograph No. 136. In general, Corvisart's photographs of soldiers or Chinese civilians are posed and static; see Album 1, p. 35, No. 61 and p. 39, No. 69.
60. "Photographies," op cit., Album 1, p. 21, photograph No. 38.
61. Trachtenberg, op cit., p. 84 quotes *The Times* review of Brady's 1862 publication in which, predictably, the reviewer noted "the easy groups … creditable to the skill of the artist," but commented on how "slovenly" the Federal soldiers looked, "men with un-buttoned coats and open collars and all sorts of head-gear … their overalls gathered half-way up the leg." "Slovenly" looking men could not constitute material for good soldiers. Interestingly, the present writer has

seen no denigration of the Boers based on the clothing they wore when fighting the British. See Chapter Three for extended discussion of the culture surrounding military uniform.

62. The controversy in France is well canvassed in R. A. Sobiezek's "Photography and the Theory of Realism in the Second Empire," in Van deren Coke (ed.), *One Hundred Years of Photographic History — Essays in Honor of Beaumont Newhall*, University of New Mexico Press, Albuquerque, 1975, see also Braive, op cit., pp. 113–125.
63. This photograph is held at the National Archives, Washington, DC, No. III-SC-75077.
64. In his article, "Catholic Images of the Boxers," *The American Asian Review*, Vol. 9, No. 3, 1991, p. 52, Jean-Paul Wiest refers to "old faithful Catholics who traced the conversion of their families to the early part of the Qianlong reign." There is ample literature on the reasons why Chinese people of all backgrounds disliked Christianity. A study of those Chinese families who retained their Christian beliefs over several generations would seem worthwhile.
65. Ernst Gombrich, "The Evidence of Images," in C. S. Singleton (ed.), *Interpretation Theory and Practice*, Johns Hopkins Press, 1969. In this essay, Gombrich makes a number of important statements about "the bearing which our interpretation may have on the way we actually see and experience a picture" (p. 73). His masterly analysis of a medieval painting of Herod, shows him putting into practice his ability to yield to "The temptation to think that the landmarks which interest the historian today loomed equally large in the lives of people of the past … images need much more of a context to be unambiguous than do statements." (p. 97)
66. Jussim, op cit., p. 103.
67. Covisart, op cit., Album 1, p. 38, photograph No. 68.
68. Jussim, op cit., p. 103.
69. In his historical commentary to *The Face of China*, op cit., Cameron gives an excellent resumé of the technology and its difficulties in the mid to late nineteenth century. See pp. 152ff.
70. Ibid., p. 117.
71. A vital taboo on the subject of a photograph as far as war photography was concerned was that which shunned the photographing of corpses of soldiers or civilians. During the American Civil War, corpses were generally arranged before a photograph was taken. Nineteenth century attitudes to photography of the dead are extremely complex and lie beyond the scope of this study. Nevertheless, it is worth emphasising that neither Captain O'Keefe's nor Commandant Corvisart's work contains images of dead or wounded soldiers or civilians.
72. These biographical details are taken from C. J. Lucas (ed.), *James Ricalton's*

Photographs of China During the Boxer Rebellion. His Illustrated Travelogue of 1900, Edwin Mellen Press, New York, 1990.

73. Thomson frequently described in ghoulish detail the fate of lunatics or criminals in the Chinese system of justice. Yet his photographs of criminals in the cangue did not constitute comparably vivid pictorial images of the horrors he was able to create with words. As with Ricalton, Thomson's mastery of the technical aspects of photography had gone beyond mere image-making to become art. The cameras he used were, in point of technical capacity, able to take the sorts of pictures which would have provided the images conveying to the viewer the horrors he described in his accompanying text. As was the case for Ricalton, one is obliged to see in Thomson's personal and cultural attitude to the depiction of human suffering the reason for his inability to capture this with his lens. Another eye behind the lens of that same camera could have taken a picture of those horrors. The camera was technically able to take a photograph of what Thomson could write about but could not bring his eye to see.
74. Lucas, op cit., p. 163.
75. Ibid.
76. Reproduced by kind permission of Mr R. J. Blum. I am greatly indebted to Mr Blum for sharing with me his extensive knowledge of stereographs, his collection of stereographs and stereographic cameras as well as his own photographs taken with stereographic cameras.
77. Lucas, op cit., p. 164.
78. Ibid.
79. Ibid., pp. 48–50. Ricalton was the first photographer to capture a shell leaving an artillery piece during the Russo-Japanese War. Newspaper rights alone for this plate sold for $5,000.
80. Ibid., p. 166.
81. From the collection of Mr R. J. Blum.
82. Lucas, op cit., p. 173.
83. Lalumia, op. cit., pp. 62 and 78. The *Illustrated London News* contains a number of such photographs.
84. From the collection of Mr R. J. Blum.
85. Lucas, op cit., p. 174. Lyddite was a high explosive manufactured in England mainly consisting of picric acid; it was not deliberately used for its poisonous qualities and when these were discovered, the use of lyddite as an explosive was phased out.
86. See Rudisill, R., Mirror Image. The Lure of the Daguerreotype on American Society, University of Mexico Press, Albuquerque, 1971, p. 195, for an evocation of photographers' conscious involvement in the technical mood of the era and p. 238 for their view of themselves as professionals.
87. From the collection of Mr R. J. Blum.
88. Lucas, op. cit., p. 176.

89. There is one exception and these men were not killed in battle. It was Commandant Corvisart who took the well-known photograph of the heads of executed Boxers suspended on the wall of the East Gate at Tianjin. See "Photographies," Album I, p. 15, photograph No. 25.
90. From the collection of Mr R. J. Blum.
91. G. MacDonald, *Camera, A Victorian Eyewitness*, B. T. Batsford, London, 1979, p. 179. My thanks to Mr Blum for drawing my attention to this work.
92. A notable exception is a photograph which was as unique in subject matter as in the technical ability to capture the movement of flying debris. This picture of the destruction of a Boer farmhouse was taken by an anonymous British officer and published in William T. Stead's *Review of Reviews*, December 1900, p. 543. On p. 542 there is a photograph captioned "Boer Farmhouse about to Be Destroyed — Soldiers Looting Chickens." There were problems of military security which arose when serving military personnel took photographs as private individuals. Such problems were legislated for differently in different countries at different times.
93. Wilbur Chamberlin of the *New York Sun* was remarkable for his interest, sympathy and respect for the Chinese at a time when written accounts of the events of the Boxer War abounded but were notably lacking in these qualities. One story exemplifies the man and the people and makes Chamberlin a verbal witness in the same outstanding way as Ricalton was with his camera. In war-torn Beijing, Chamberlin thought he saw some toys. "A China boy who was looking at one of the stands more or less wistfully, pulled my coat and asked for a cash. This is the tenth of a cent. He could say a word or two of English (pigeon), and I gathered from what he said that he did not have any father or mother, and he did want to buy a toy. I was in a hurry to get to camp, and I gave him the cash without stopping to investigate further." See Wilbur J. Chamberlin, *Ordered to China*, Methuen, 1904, p. 245. A family gathered to eat lunch, a boy wanting a toy; the kind of vision that sees and transmits these cross-culturally understood needs and wants on the part of the people of a country embodying a wealth of powerful images — many negative — for Westerners; this vision made Ricalton and Chamberlin men ahead of their time.
94. Trachtenberg, op cit., p. 74.
95. Brady had difficulty selling his Civil War photographs and they were eventually bought by Congress in 1869.
96. Hales, op cit. William Henry Jackson's monumental photograph taken in 1895 of the Wu Men gateway to Peking was not used by *Harper's Magazine*.
97. This incredulity has persisted. The present writer's work on the modernisation of the Qing armies in the North of China was criticised by anonymous readers for the Journal *Modern China*. Their view in their critique of the work which is the basis of Chapter Six, was that China could not possibly have fielded weapons more modern than those used by the eight armies of the China

Expeditionary Force. These scholars did not deem it necessary to provide evidence for their negation of evidence and assertions based on the most rigorous application of the requirements of historical method. It has thus become clear that extensive photographic evidence of the weapons, uniforms and training manoeuvres used by the Chinese as well as tables detailing the armaments of the invading forces need to be published. Written evidence from the manuscript or published journals of the Western military men who took part in the action or from the military attachés whose job it was to report on these matters is apparently insufficient.

98. For a lucid exposition of Chinese reasons for appearing to reply on several conflicting levels to the introduction of aspects of foreign technology and thought, see Joanna Waley-Cohen, "China and Western Technology in the Late Qing," *The American Historical Review*, Vol. 98, No. 5, December 1993.
99. Jackson, op cit.
100. Elliott, "Who Seeks the Truth," op cit.
101. H. B. Chipp, *Picasso's Guernica. History, Transformations, Meanings*, Thames and Hudson, London, 1989 is a work which describes the context of the genesis and subsequent public influence of one painting inspired by a single horrific act in war. As such it makes an important contribution to understandings of the struggle to represent warfare.
102. The exception is Paul A. Cohen, *History in Three Keys. The Boxers as Event, Experience and Myth*, Columbia University Press, New York, 1997, p. 179 and p. 183 showing two superb reproductions of Ricalton's Boxer War stereographs.

Chapter 5

Many a Truth Is Spoken in Jest: An Analysis of Cartoons of the Boxer Rising[1]

It is in the oeuvre of its cartoonists that the true soul of a nation is most definitively and starkly displayed.

Frédéric Régamey[2]

Any reader of political cartoons[3] will have noted that the laugh is almost always at the expense of the individual or event concerned. Moreover, this kind of humour can be very hard-hitting, making statements and connections that are rarely put so bluntly in editorial pages. Because of the peculiar nature of graphic humour it is even possible to make revealing statements about a political situation and its protagonists without the use of a single written word (Figure 5.1). This means that as a form of mass communication, cartooning is unique. It is able to suggest and attribute motive and meaning in such a way that the majority of readers understand and laugh or are stirred to indignation, anger, pity, horror, even to abandon old attitudes and take up new ones.[4] The cartoonist is primarily concerned with provoking readers in the sense he wishes to direct his comment. It is not therefore, in his interest to make use of symbolism which is too abstruse for the audience he[5] hopes to target. Neither does he focus on inconspicuous people. A part of the political cartoonist's function has always been to attack the status quo; as such, cartoons provide an alternative fulcrum for public opinion and their power lies in their function of giving voice to a minority or non-official view while whittling away at the majority. Cartoonists are not a subgroup of journalists. They stand unique.

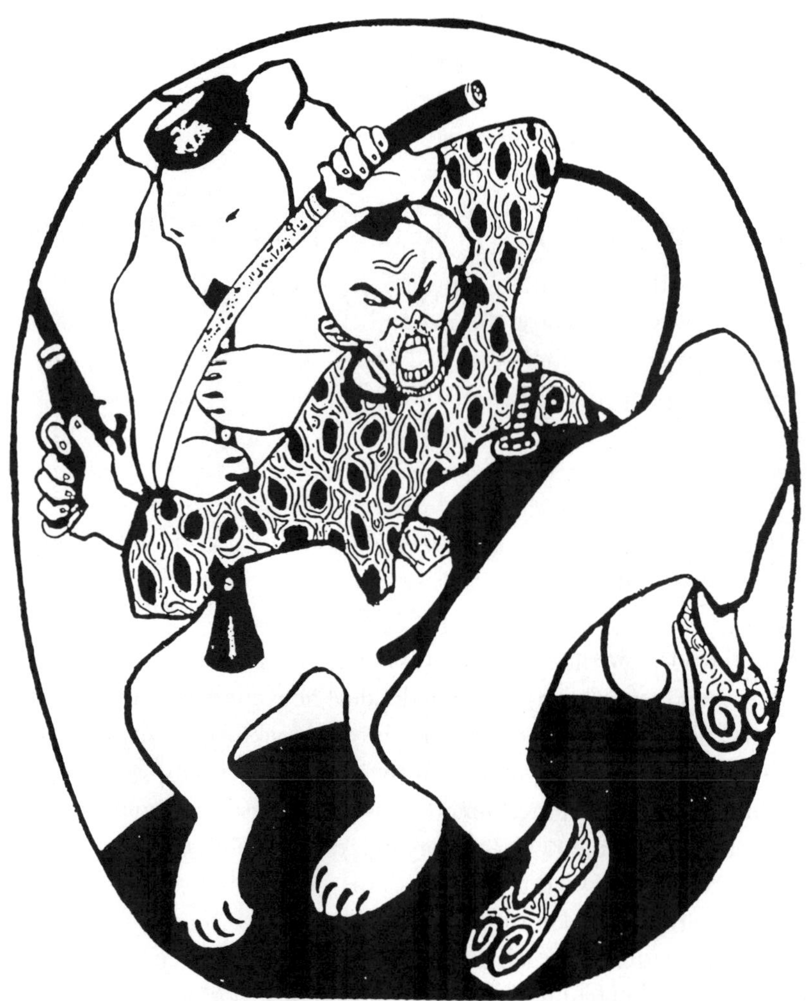

Figure 5.1 *Simplicissimus.*

In the nineteenth century, cartoonists were feared more by governments than were journalists. Throughout Europe, in Russia and in Japan, the frequent fining and jailing of cartoonists, editors and even printers indicated the depth of official fear of the image as cartoon. In Britain and in America on occasion, cartoonists were bribed by those in power. Political cartoons were seen as having more impact than the written word and being more effective in transmitting a message.[6] There was a strong link between a cartoonist and his mass audience.[7] Interestingly, cartoonists all over the world respond in a very similar way to an outrageous or shocking event in public life, most particularly to war.[8] It is thus notable that cartoonists do "betray the true soul of a nation" as Régamey put it when describing German cartoons of the 1914–1918 War.

Against this background one would expect the Boxer rising of 1900 to have provoked an explosion of wrath against the "heathen hordes"[9] who had risen in their thousands killing missionaries, burning foreign property, destroying railways and telegraph lines and effectively bringing to a standstill foreign commerce in North China. As well, the advent of the Boxers and eventually the Imperial Chinese Army, laying siege to Beijing for nearly two months was an event both unprecedented and highly provocative. Furthermore, some writers have pointed to the depth of anti-Chinese feeling already existing in America.[10] There was a markedly negative attitude to the Chinese in Britain on the part of the ruling classes and their press. As the crisis worsened, the German ambassador was shot in the street as was a counsellor of the Japanese Legation. German indignation, expressed roundly by the Kaiser,[11] was particularly intense. The French had been severely trounced by Liu Yongfu in the vicinity of Indo China only fifteen years before and Franco-Chinese relations were still strained.

Cartoonists "betray the soul of the nation," that is, they have a particular ability to stir mass opinion by their drawings. There was to some degree a background of anti-Chinese feeling and the beginnings of explicitly stated yellow-peril fears in Germany, the United States and Britain. One might anticipate a burgeoning of cartoons depicting wild, pigtailed, slant-eyed men savagely mutilating innocent Western women and children, foreign soldiers and even Christian Chinese, in an excess of rampant fanaticism. In over 340 cartoons examined, only two were found showing bestial Chinese killers of European women and children. This reflects a markedly different pattern concerning the depiction of the enemy as beast or Other from that which has emerged in studies of cartoons and propaganda posters during the 1914–1918 European War and the 1939–1945 War.[12] This difference is so marked that it requires explanation.

The cartoons chosen for this study either came from the most famous cartoon weeklies of the day or were chosen from newspapers to reflect a broad spectrum of readership in terms of the social class background of readers.

Given that many newspapers with an upper class readership still printed no kind of graphic material at all by the year 1900, there were fewer newspapers in this category to choose from. Nevertheless, as far as the English language was concerned, *Punch* was catering to the upper middle and upper classes in Britain by 1900.[13] *Simplicissimus*, *Le Rire* and *Marumaru Shimbun* were celebrated periodicals that had a wide circulation and received continuous publicity by attracting government harassment.

In the case of the British, French and German illustrated weeklies publishing cartoons, they were well-known in Europe and even in America and Japan. A number of cartoonists from Britain and Germany went to America to work in the late nineteenth century, a sign of the internationalism in the cartoon world.[14] These periodicals retain their interest for historians of cartooning and were included in the survey because of their contemporary notoriety, the lasting fame of some of their cartoonists who have remained household names in their respective countries until today. Other periodicals were selected because of the fame of their cartoonists; Sokolovsky (pen name Coré) who drew for *Novoe Vremya* was an internationally recognised cartoonist of his day.

The American press provides the greatest opportunity to survey cartoons from newspapers with a wide circulation in terms of the class background of its readership. Because of the number of cartoons, the fact that they come from fourteen distinct cultural traditions, and the representative breadth of the audiences of the periodicals selected for the survey, the results are indicative of national and international response to the China crisis as well as international recognition of a Chinese statesman, Li Hongzhang.

The international interest in the work of cartoonists can be seen by the fact that many cartoons were translated and reprinted into foreign periodicals. It is notable that the translations were sometimes very free indeed. European cartoons reached Japan in translation, as much a reflection of Japanese interest in political cartooning as in the particular events of the Boxer rising.[15] Russian cartoons were reproduced in Britain, Europe and Japan, and British and European cartoons were reprinted in the United States. This osmosis in the nascent international political cartoon scene points to editorial awareness of the cartoons being produced in other languages. Significantly, it also suggests editorial opinion that foreign cartoons of the China crisis were so apt or provocative that they should be translated or reproduced. This in itself is a significant indication of the international interest and similarity of response to the China crisis on the part of those periodicals that did print cartoons.

The cartoonists did not directly experience the Boxer War. None of those whose work has been included in this survey ever went to China. Nevertheless, their acuity and the art of cartooning itself gave them status as a particular kind of "experiencer." Their testimony has much to reveal about China itself and about public feeling concerning China and the Boxer War. It has even more to reveal about views editors would publish in the form of a cartoon but would never allow to be included in the published form of the reports sent back by those journalists who were firsthand "experiencers."[16] The copy of the latter was pre-edited in their own minds, often consciously, and then frequently edited again in the head office in London, Paris, New York or Berlin. Even drawings from artists in China were redrawn in newspaper offices in London.[17] Not so cartoons. They remained the unique product of unique minds. The importance of this study is to show that right around the world those unique minds produced common responses to many political themes evoked by the Boxer War.

A survey of 344 cartoons, the majority from the British, American, French, German, Russian and Japanese press shows that cartoons drawn to elicit anti-Chinese sentiments are distinctly in the minority. Of the political points being made by cartoonists depicting the Boxer rising, virulent anti-Chinese sentiments in the "yellow peril" vein constitute by far the smallest percentage. If it is true that during the early decades of the twentieth century, the Boxers were widely viewed as "the Yellow Peril personified" and that "the very word Boxerism conjured up visions of danger, xenophobia, irrationality and barbarism,"[18] the international corps of cartoonists drawing in the summer of 1900 was certainly not responsible for fuelling these "Yellow Peril" fears. The material presented in this chapter is powerful testimony to the acute awareness of the cartoonists of the day. They were contemporaries whose profession required them to be able to reinterpret for broad public consumption all currents of all kinds of experience as well as all kinds of politicians and heads of state. In the events of the Boxer rising, they had the most provocative material to hand. We are brought up short by their testimony. They did not see the Boxer rising in terms of Chinese barbarism. The consensus was that any barbarism singled out by their pens was emphatically that displayed by the armies of the invading Allied Powers. The tables below break down the cartoons surveyed according to the broad subject they treated and the main political point each cartoon was making.

The cartoons of the Boxer rising thus form an exceptional corpus and are inexplicable unless one agrees with the hypothesis that many cartoonists from completely different cultural and historical traditions saw the invasion of China as unjust and even inhumane, uncivilised and un-Christian. Furthermore, cartoonists did reflect at least a section of popular opinion, they did confirm prevailing attitudes, and they did wish to attack current main-stream thinking[19] on China. However they were unable to stray too far out of the editorial line of the periodical for which they worked.[20] Thus we may postulate widespread editorial and popular sympathy for the Chinese during an unprecedentedly explosive international situation. Far from being con-veyed as ridiculous, venal, bestial fanatics, the Chinese were frequently depicted as justly repelling the advances of the civilised Christian world (see Tables 5.1 and 5.2). As the voice of their day, we cannot ignore the testimony of the cartoonists.

> It is the pride of PUNCH that the "Cartoon of the Week," in which for so many years he has regularly crystallised his opinion of the week's chief idea, situation, or event, is truthfully representative of the best prevailing feeling of the nation, of its soundest common-sense, and of its most deliberate judgement — a judge-ment ... seriously formed, albeit humorously set down and portrayed ... the record of how public matters struck a people ... at the instant of their happening is surely not less interesting to the future student of history, of psychology, of sociology, than the most official record of the world's progress[21]

The body of cartoons discussed is indicative of the repository of knowl-edge that existed about China in the West. The cartoonists of the day used existing knowledge to explain or to condemn their fellow countrymen, not to savage or belittle the Chinese. This unexpected revelation of a genuine current of sympathy for China arises as much from the general refusal by cartoonists to savage the Chinese or their leaders[22] as from a general consensus to attack various aspects of individual and national Allied politics revealed by the events of the Boxer rising. This leads to an alternative explanation of the scarcity of anti-Chinese cartoons during a sensational war[23] in which China had the rest of the world at its knees begging for information concerning the fate of the entire foreign population of Beijing. There was an element of

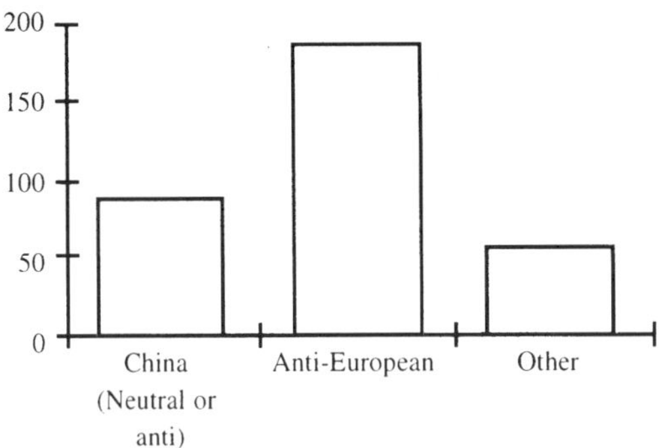

Table 5.1 Relative number of cartoons by main subject.

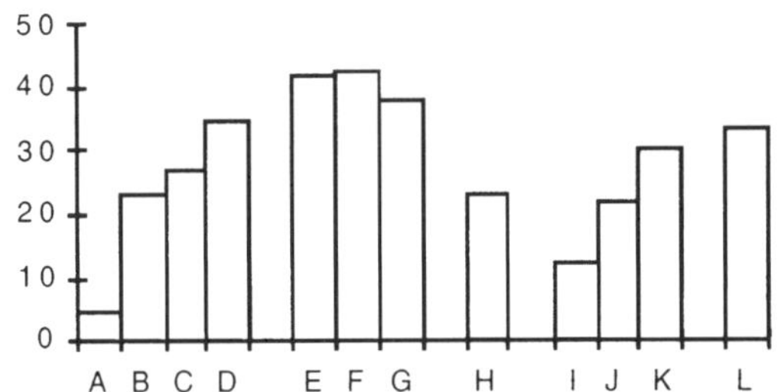

Table 5.2 Relative number of cartoons by main political point being made.

A Chinese cruelty/"yellow peril"
B Satire at the expense of the Chinese
C Li Hongzhang
D Chinese political moves
E Allied discord/anti-imperialism
F European greed/unwarranted invasion
G Satire at the expense of "Christian civilised humanity"
H Chinese symbols as a commentary on American politics
I Anti-Russian
J Anti-English
K Anti-German
L Other

sympathy for China, even containing echoes of the perceived injustice of the Opium War.[24] However, many cartoonists were preoccupied with the events in China more as they reflected great power rivalry than as they were going to influence China's very survival as a nation and the future for relations between China and the invading Powers. These cartoonists used events in China to produce anti-Russian, anti-German and anti-British cartoons. China as a whole, and possible outcomes of the Boxer rising in particular, were seen as occupying an essential position in international politics.

In the case of the United States, preoccupation with great power rivalry and the balance of world power was replaced with a parochial tendency to use the events in China as a commentary on contemporary American politics. In what may be seen superficially to be supreme examples of Orientalism, the abbreviated identity tag symbols,[25] the trademark of the political cartoonist, were applied by American cartoonists to internal American political situations evolving at the same time as the Boxer rising. Thus pigtailed men, the cangue, Chinese clothing and shoes, the setting of an enemy head on a stick, all these symbols which the public had learned to equate with China were worn by American politicians to depict their particular characteristics to the American public. Overall, however, as can be seen by reference to Table 5.1, the number of anti European/pro-China cartoons was greater than the number of cartoons depicting China in world or national politics not of its own making.

Ouriel Reschef has done a convincing study showing the similarity of French cartoonists' response to the German invasion of France in 1870, despite their widely differing backgrounds.[26] In the case of the Boxer rising, we see an even more interesting phenomenon; that of the similarity of response by cartoonists representing fourteen cultural traditions in Europe, Britain, India, Russia, America, Australia and Japan. In addition to demonstrating this similarity of response by analysing selected cartoons, we may also use the cartoons as an indication of the extent of public knowledge about China or its leading statesmen in the countries concerned at the turn of the century. While there are many cartoons which are intrinsically amusing, shocking or provocative, there are many more which require a certain level of knowledge about Chinese culture and Chinese politics in order for the reader to grasp the point. In concluding, we will examine the proposition that cartoons can depict a truth which is not or cannot be revealed by words, drawings or photographs.

Cartoons of the Boxer Rising as Commentary on Allied Politics

Two strands of commentary emerge from cartoonists of all nationalities including the Japanese. The first is the theme of discord among the Allies and great power rivalry. While the majority of these cartoons constitute a perception of international relations solely from the viewpoint of the major powers involved in the China crisis, there were some cartoonists who viewed China as an essential force in preserving the balance of power. The second political theme seized on by cartoonists was anti-imperialism. Cartoonists saw the China crisis as a manifestation of European greed and an unwarranted invasion of China as a sovereign state and participant in the discussions leading to the "Convention with respect to the laws and customs of war on land" of 1899 resulting from the Hague Peace Conference held in 1899.[27] Again, cartoons on this theme were drawn by nationals of all the major powers involved.

Turning to the theme of discord among the invading Powers, this was present from early in the crisis with the appearance of the cartoon "A Legacy of Discord" in *Punch* on 27 June 1900 (Figure 5.2). The caption reads: "CHINAMAN: 'You allee chop-chop me now, but welly soon forrin devil chop-chop forrin devil!'" While this cartoon depicts a Chinese soldier in full traditional panoply with primitive sword and grotesque shield, the viewer must be careful about making assumptions that the Chinese are hereby singled out for ridicule. In the same cartoon, the Russian, French, German, Japanese and American warriors are also depicted in dated or exaggerated versions of their national military uniforms and weapons, in order to distinguish them readily to the public and perhaps, to make some kind of comment on the military. One of the techniques in the cartoonists armoury is manipulation of the size of the human figure; exaggeratedly tiny or huge figures conveying an immediate message to the viewer.[28] In this cartoon, the Chinese soldier, while he wears pantomime costume, is clearly the main figure. He stands alone, large and solid with his back to a sketched-in version of a Chinese Great Wall. The six representatives of the invading Powers are shown further to the foreground of the cartoon,[29] clearly delineated but nevertheless being held at bay by the solitary Chinese warrior.

Some of the cartoons depicting disunity make the Allied forces look ridiculous. An example of such a cartoon was published in the *World* on 5 August 1900. It showed a rowboat labelled "relief" riding low in choppy seas manned by unskilled soldiers wielding uncoordinated oars bundled up in cumbersome caricatures of their respective national uniforms. They are being

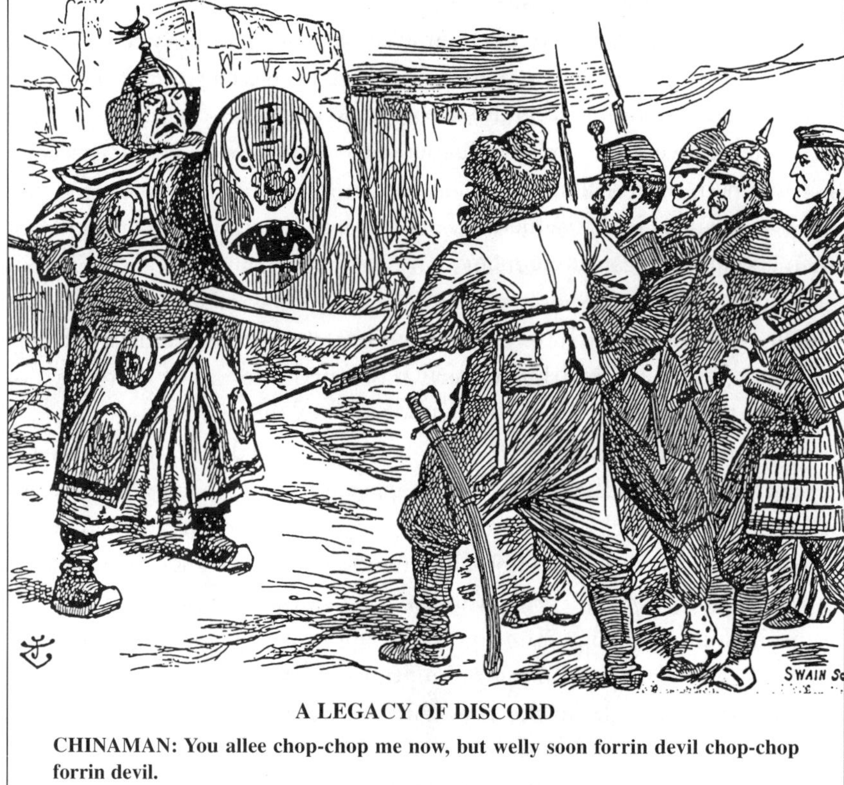

A LEGACY OF DISCORD

CHINAMAN: You allee chop-chop me now, but welly soon forrin devil chop-chop forrin devil.

Figure 5.2 *Punch.*

exhorted by a figure of stern and manly bearing standing in the prow shouting "For God's sake, pull together boys." Charles Green Bush, the *World* cartoonist, had the view that America was a disinterested party playing a role essential alike to the interests of China as to the interests of the other powers. Although the leading figure is the only one whose oar is unlabelled, aspects of his clothing and body language indicate that he represents America. Other cartoons show the great powers as a monstrous but ineffectual hydra or as ridiculous Roman warriors mounted on tortoises arriving at a locked gate in a wall manned by modern guns (Figure 5.3). A German cartoon expressed the extreme mutual distrust between the Allied invading forces. It shows a group of staff officers around a table on which there is a relief map of China. The caption reads "Each says to the other: 'You may look at everything but touch nothing'."[30] Another German cartoon sums up the fragility of the alliance between the invading Powers and their inherent distrust of each other (Figure 5.4).

The perception of mutual distrust was also shown in cartoons depicting differences between the individual countries. Japan against the rest (Figure 5.5), Germany against the rest, England against Germany, Russia against the rest, Italy against Germany, Germany, France and Russia against England and Japan and France against Germany. There was also a view that this disunity was causing military ineffectiveness. A Viennese cartoon showed diminutive soldiers representing each power huddled in a group in front of a giant rock blocked in with a craggy fist and oriental features. Each little soldier has his forefinger to his forehead. This cartoon was reprinted in the *Review of Reviews*

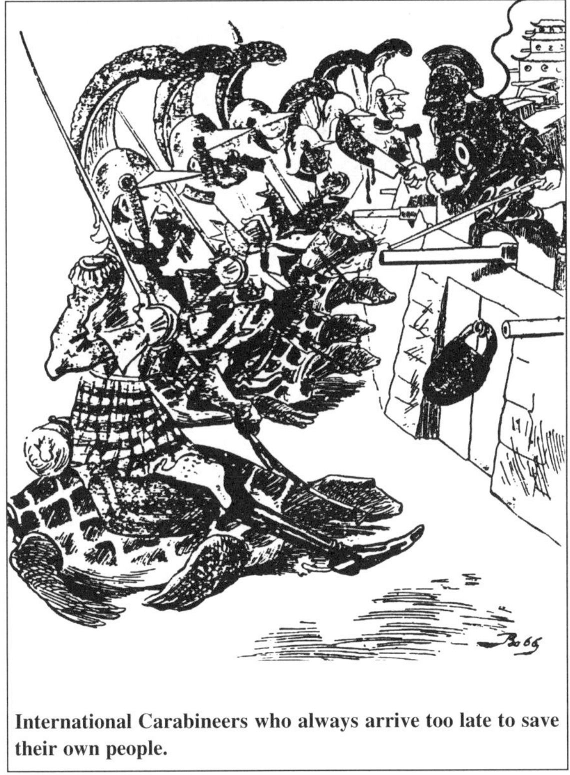

International Carabineers who always arrive too late to save their own people.

Figure 5.3 *La Silhouette.*

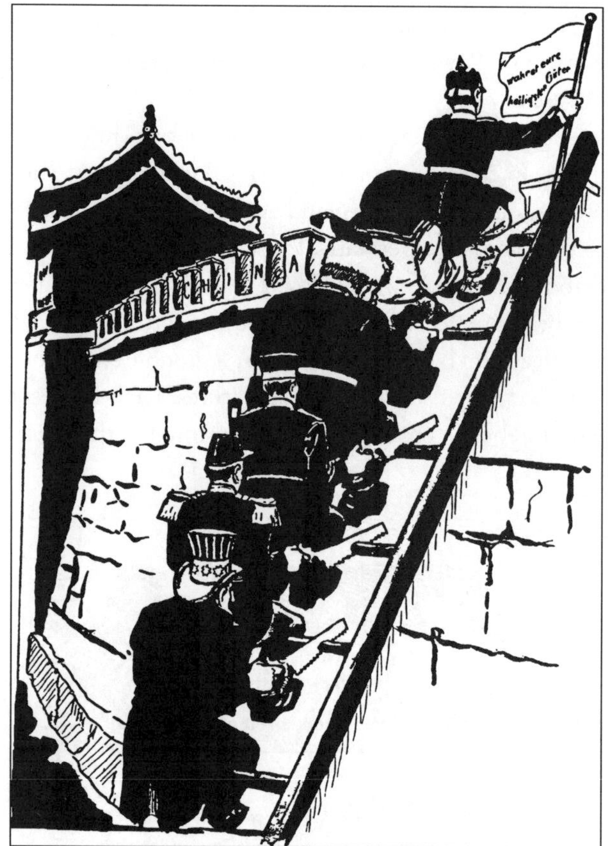

Unity is a good thing, but one gets further without it.

Figure 5.4 *Ulk.*

and *Le Rire* with slightly different translations of the caption. The French version reads "The Powers consult at the foot of the wall" and the English version is "The Great Powers have now come to the mountain." The cartoon is another example of the use of exaggerated size to make the point. The quaint little mannikins stand non-plussed, over-shadowed by the vast bulk of the rock roughly hewn into the shape of the waiting China.[31]

There were two related aspects of the great powers' view of China as a weak country that needed to be divided for its own sake and for the sake of maintaining the balance of power. These either showed China, like Turkey,

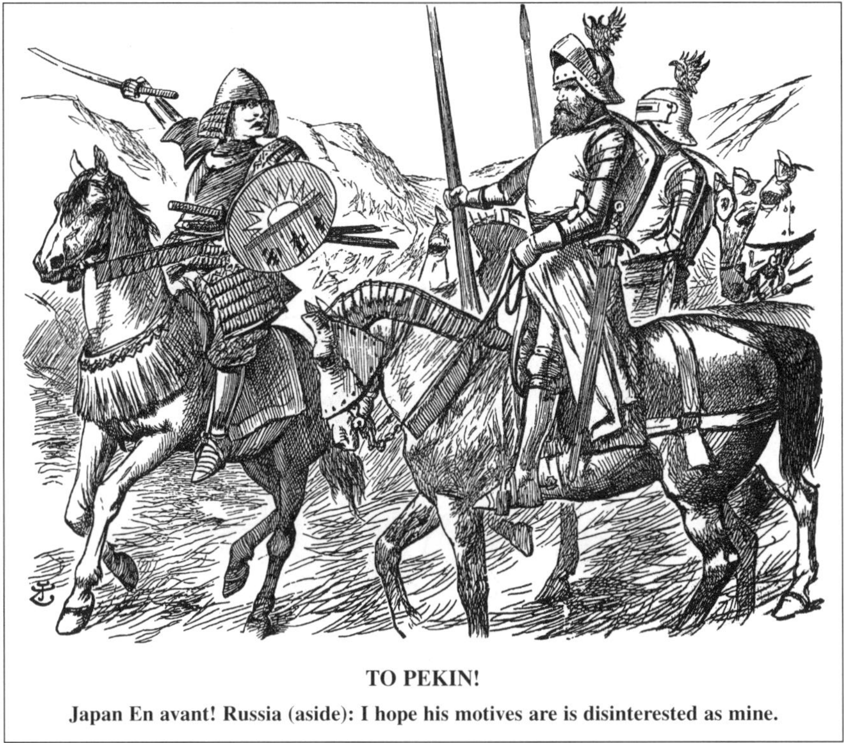

TO PEKIN!

Japan En avant! Russia (aside): I hope his motives are is disinterested as mine.

Figure 5.5 *Punch.*

as a sick man whose weakness needed to be cured by the powers or they represented China as a prize to be divided among the powers (Figures 5.6, 5.7 and 5.8). This latter view was current among the great powers and maps were even produced showing China as it would be when divided.[32] Knowledge of this view and such maps predated the Boxer rising and was widespread in China, enraging those sections of the Chinese public that were aware of it.[33] The sick man metaphor was carried through a series of four cartoons in the Saint Petersburg illustrated weekly *Novoe Vremya* on 4 October. A cartoon from *Kladderadatsch* related the sick man phenomenon to disunity among the Powers. It showed an old man wearing a Turkish fez sitting up in a hospital bed speaking to the terrified Chinese man in the bed next to him. Dim military figures representing the great powers stand in the background. The caption reads, "The Sick Man (the Turk): 'Don't worry yourself! They

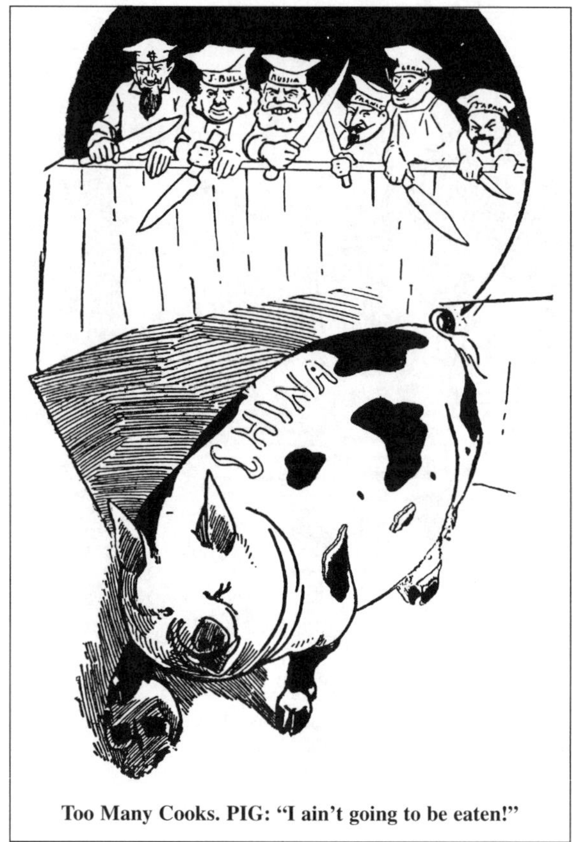

Too Many Cooks. PIG: "I ain't going to be eaten!"

Figure 5.6 *Sydney Bulletin*, N.S.W.

will not harm you. I have been here for several years and am feeling very well, because the doctors never agree'."[34] Japanese cartoons also used the image of the sick man, in one case, more appropriately, considering the role and the power of the Empress Dowager, the sick grandmother, with the Powers disputing which was the best cure.[35] The celebrated German weekly *Simplicissimus* published a cartoon expressing the fear beneath the surface of the late nineteenth century scramble for imperial power. Headed "The Powers in China," the caption reads "Our relations are now at their warmest, world war can begin."[36]

Even a "sick man" was seen to have a role in preserving the power balance. If the Chinese dragon/sick man died, this would precipitate real

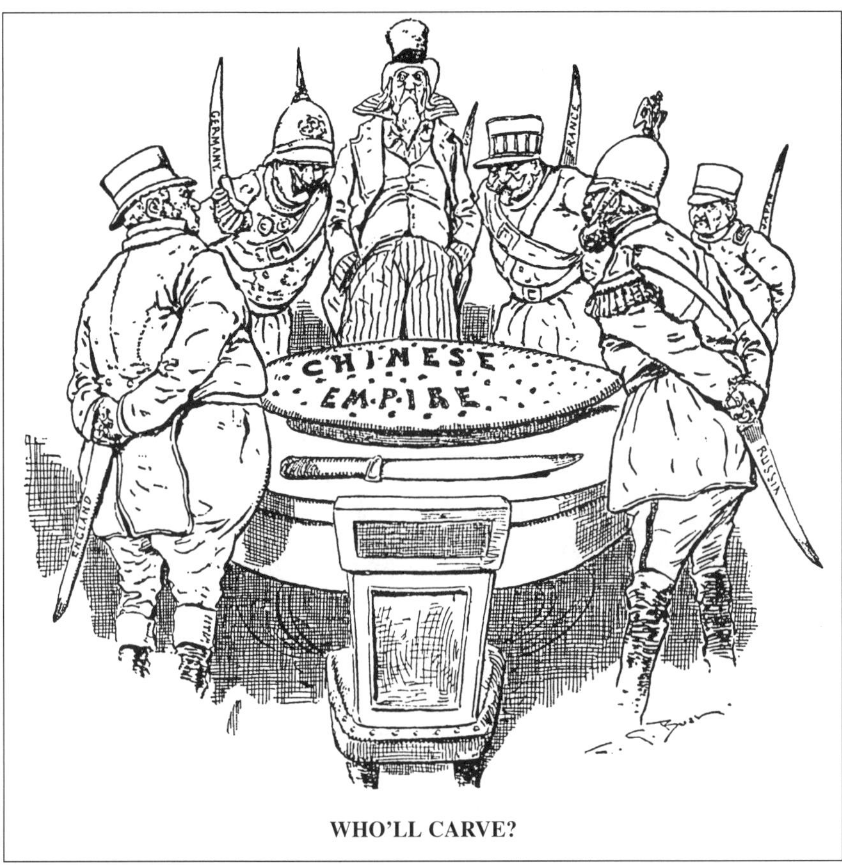

Figure 5.7 *New York Evening Journal.*

problems. A Viennese cartoon accorded China a place in preserving the balance of power and portrayed a gleeful, very much living China falling to the ground while the great powers attacked each other over his prostrate body (Figure 5.9). Several cartoons forecast inevitable disunity if the great powers won and showed China dancing triumphantly or laughing fit to split his sides at the spectacle of the great powers warring to establish their rights after victory (Figures 5.10 and 5.11).

Anti-Imperialism

Twenty four per cent of the cartoons in the survey illustrated the themes of

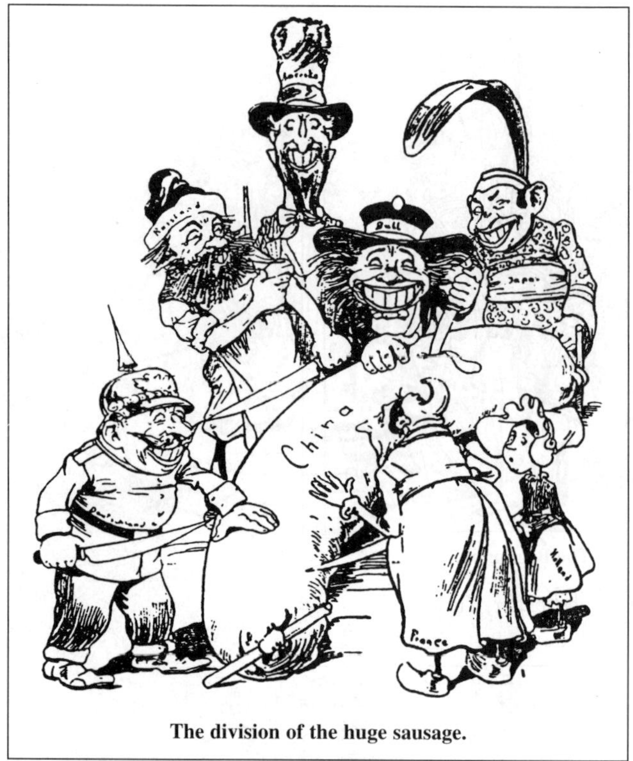

The division of the huge sausage.

Figure 5.8 *Nebelspalter*, Zurich.

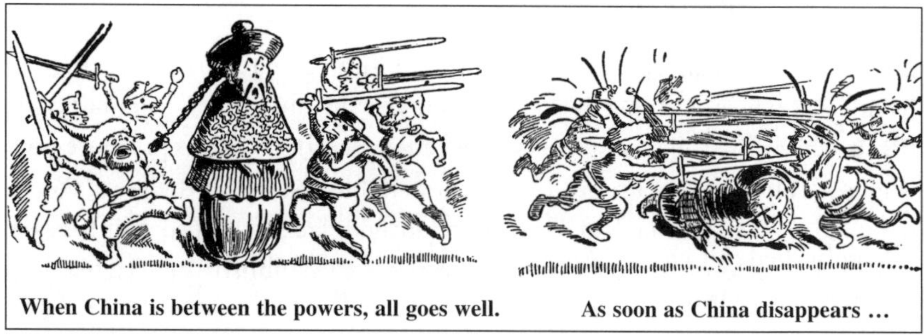

When China is between the powers, all goes well. **As soon as China disappears …**

Figure 5.9 *Fischietto*.

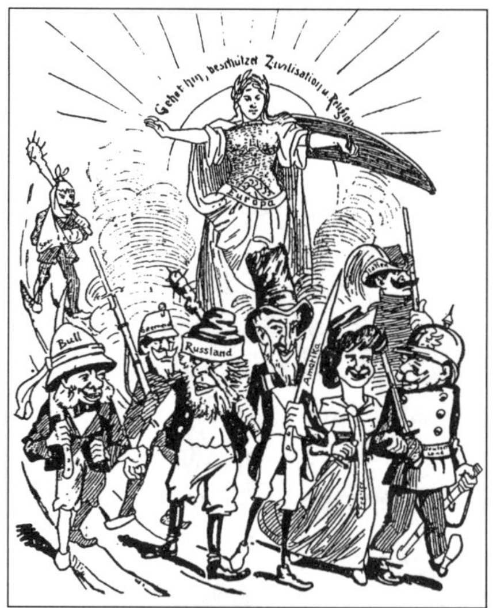

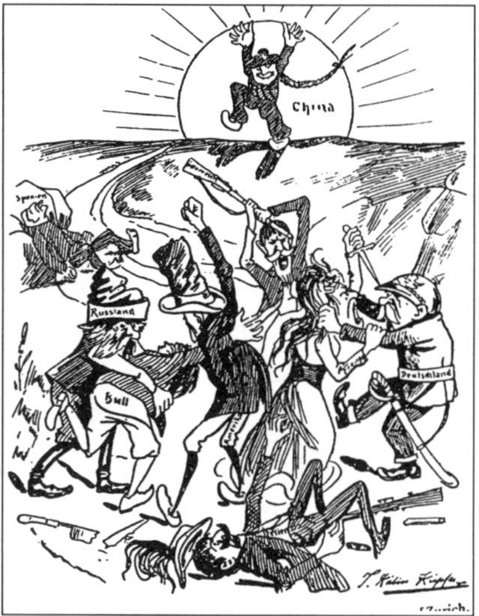

I. The Beginning. **II. The Finale.**

Figure 5.10 *Nebelspalter*, Zurich.

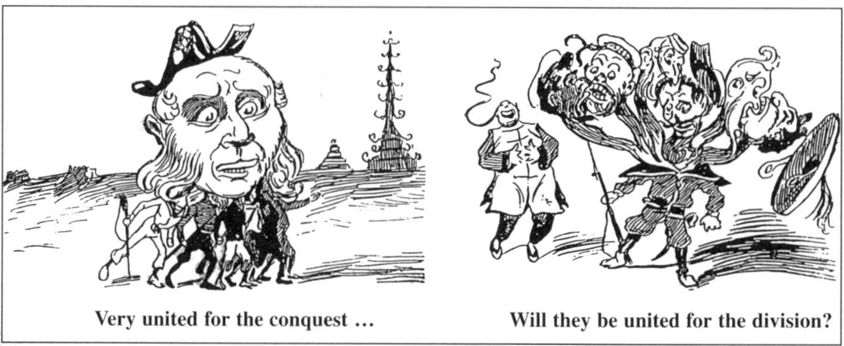

Very united for the conquest ... **Will they be united for the division?**

Figure 5.11 *Fischietto*.

anti-imperialism, European greed and unwarranted invasion; of these, most were published in German periodicals. The great powers' view of China as a weak country to be divided and the cartoonists' perception that this division would provoke disunity among the victorious powers, is closely related to the perception of European greed. In all these cartoons, China is shown as some succulent or delectable type of food that the greedy powers are sharpening their knives to attack (see Figures 5.6, 5.7 and 5.8).

The significance of the role of the political cartoonist as serious commentator whose work could set the tone of a publication[37] is demonstrated by the German cartoonists' graphic opposition to Kaiser Wilhelm's violently expressed views about China and the Chinese. The Kaiser's savage brutality surfaced in his speech to the departing German contingent and was the subject of critical editorial comment in the British, French and American press as well as many anti-German cartoons (Figure 5.12). Moreover, within Germany itself, there was a strong perception among German cartoonists that the Allied invasion was unwarranted and that military intervention stemmed from European greed. As far as Germany's participation was concerned, *Simplicissimus* published an article on the war in China under a picture of German officers headed "Die moderne Hunnen"[38] and many of the

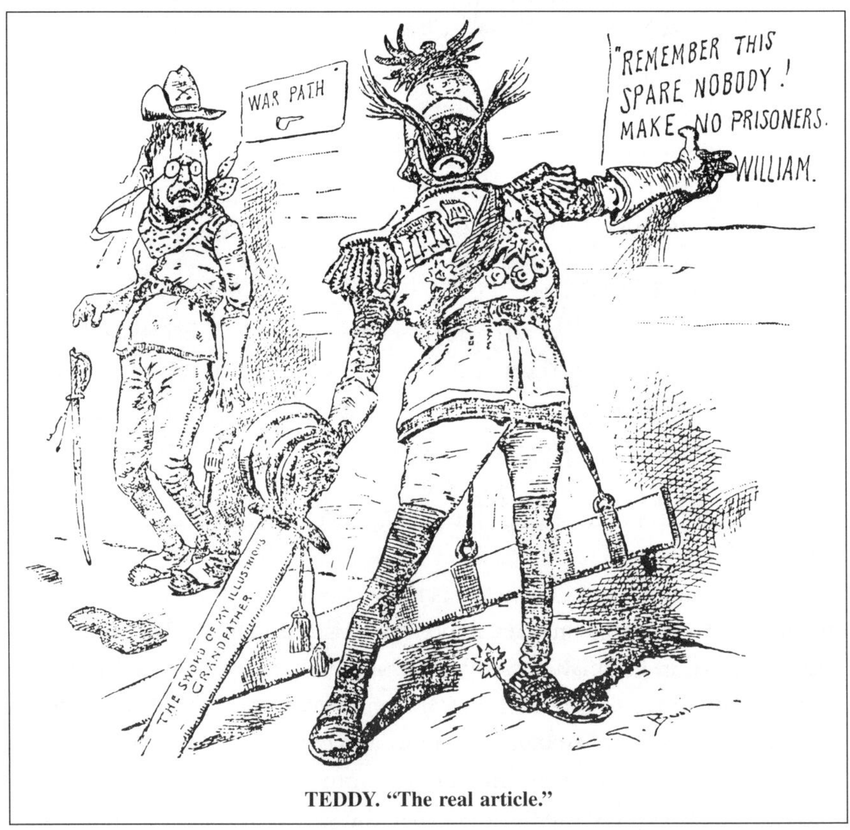

TEDDY. "The real article."

Figure 5.12 *New York Evening Journal.*

anti-German cartoons were drawn by German cartoonists for German periodicals.

The role of *Simplicissimus* and the cartoonist Thomas Theodor Heine predominated in savaging European greed.[39] Heine's powerful graphics made strikingly clear his view that European intervention in China was unwarranted, unjustified and unwelcome. Indeed, of all the cartoonists whose work is discussed in this survey, Thomas Heine's boldness and originality is outstanding. In Figure 5.13, "The Chinese Empress's Dream," we see a giant knight in armour, his visor shut, his legs astride the globe discharging effluent from a conch shell. The cartoon originally appeared in colour and it was clear that the knight was pouring blood over the globe. This knight is no gallant of King Arthur's court; he is a precursor of some deadly Darth Vader. Heine's view that the European drive to disseminate its culture was undesired and undesirable is made clear in this cartoon. The size of this blind armoured automaton adds to our perception of the inappropriate and unjustified use of force to "pour the blessings of European culture over the globe" as the caption tells us. The portion of the globe receiving the blessings in question is China. This cartoon has been reproduced in the original colours to give the reader a better idea of the power the cartoon would have had in an era when coloured plates were relatively rare (see Plate 5). In his cartoon "The Chinese Wasps' Nest" (Figure 5.14), Heine again makes it clear that the motley collection of attacking dogs have no place trying to settle down in China.

Another striking cartoon attacking the German trader in China appeared in *Simplicissimus* (Figure 5.15). The powerful figure of the Chinese dominates the frame, indeed almost steps out of it. Below him grovels the German trader whom he has just ejected. There is nothing monstrous about the size of the Chinese colossus standing in his doorway. He has a right to be there. It is the ejected German trader who looks pathetic and the school boy retort of the vanquished comes to his lips as he clutches his aching posterior "Anyway I'll tell my big brother, the one with the armoured fist." This alludes to an expression used by Kaiser Wilhelm when he gave a stirring speech exhorting the navy to go to China and "smash into them with an iron fist" because German interests were threatened.[40] German greed is depicted again in *Simplicissimus* by a cartoon showing a group of German officers looking through a telescope for the advent of the treasure ship bringing back profits from China.[41]

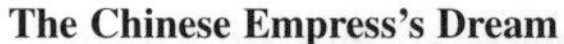

Figure 5.13 *Simplicissimus.*

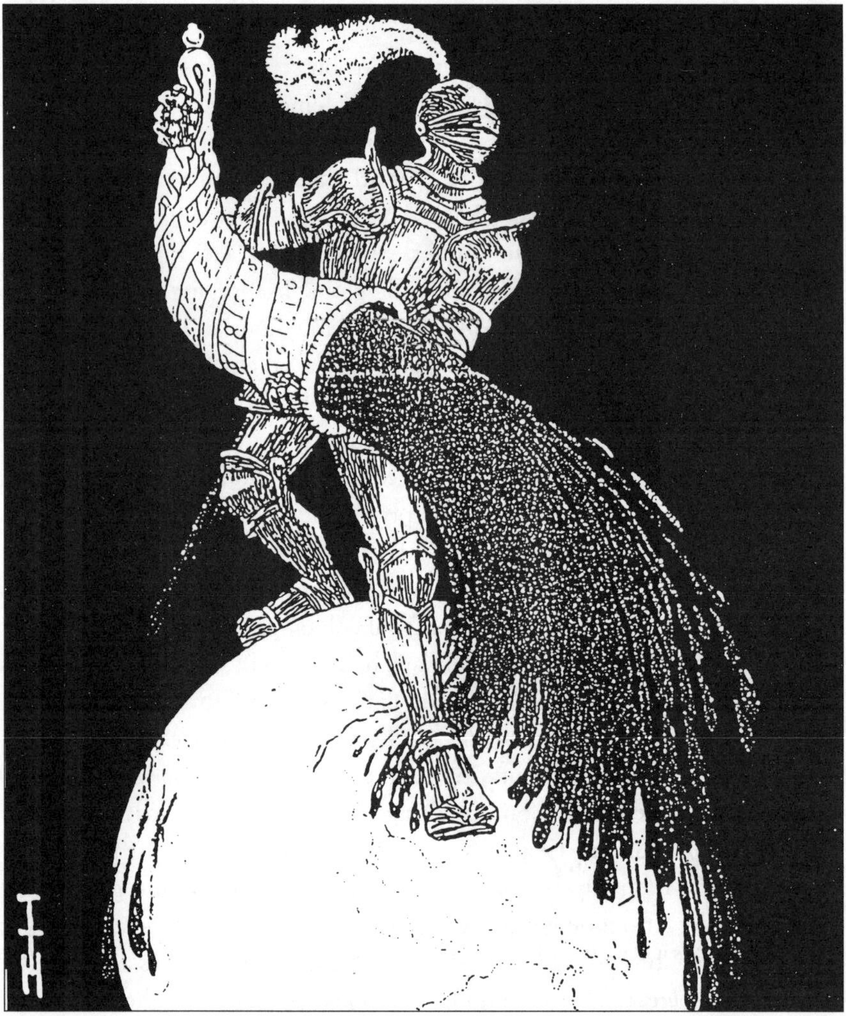

As for the unwarranted nature of German military intervention, this is shown in a cartoon illustrating an encounter between some German soldiers before their embarkation for China. The caption reads "Well you Bavarian morons, do you have any idea what great national tasks we have to undertake in East Asia?" "We're allowed to brawl and we won't be punished."[42] In this

The Chinese Wasps' Nest

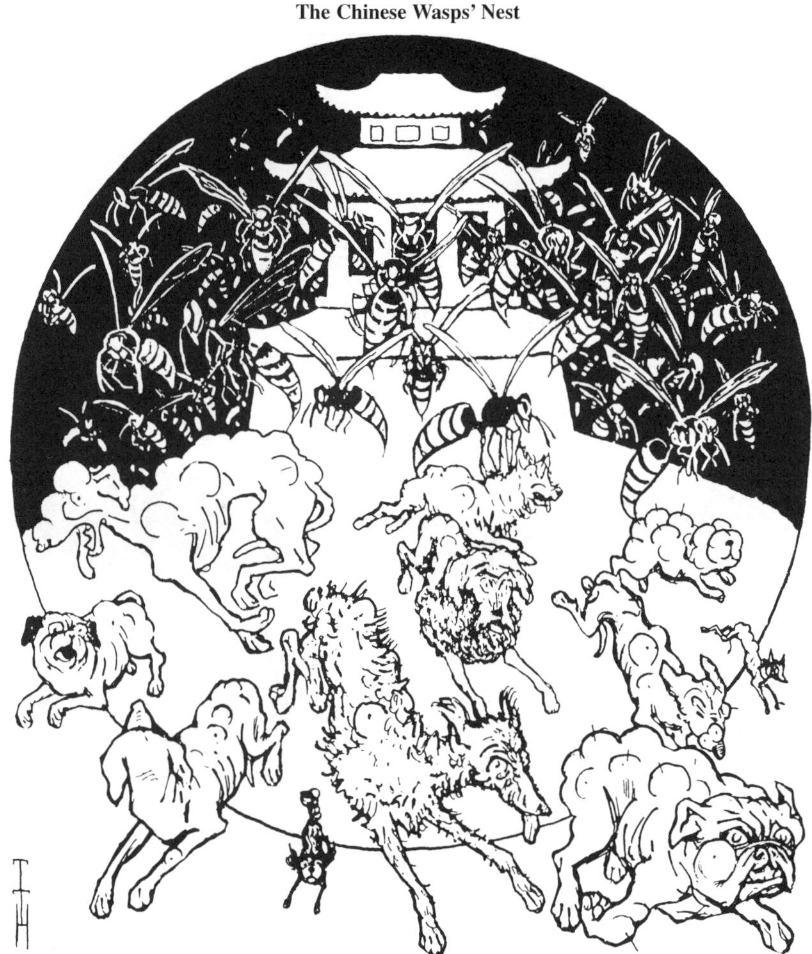

"As a place to settle, this doesn't seem to be quite suitable."

Figure 5.14 *Simplicissimus.*

cartoon the Bavarian half-wits in question are drawn as the archetypal moronic soldiers but the caption itself is cardinal in making the impact on the reader. Anti-Bavarian jokes were a common genre and Bavarian yokels who loved fighting were a standard theme of *Simplicissimus*. However, in this particular case, the cartoonist was drawing to the viewers' attention the international phenomenon of faintly surprised ignorance as to the real motives for intervention in China. The phenomenon of surprised ignorance

German Trade in China

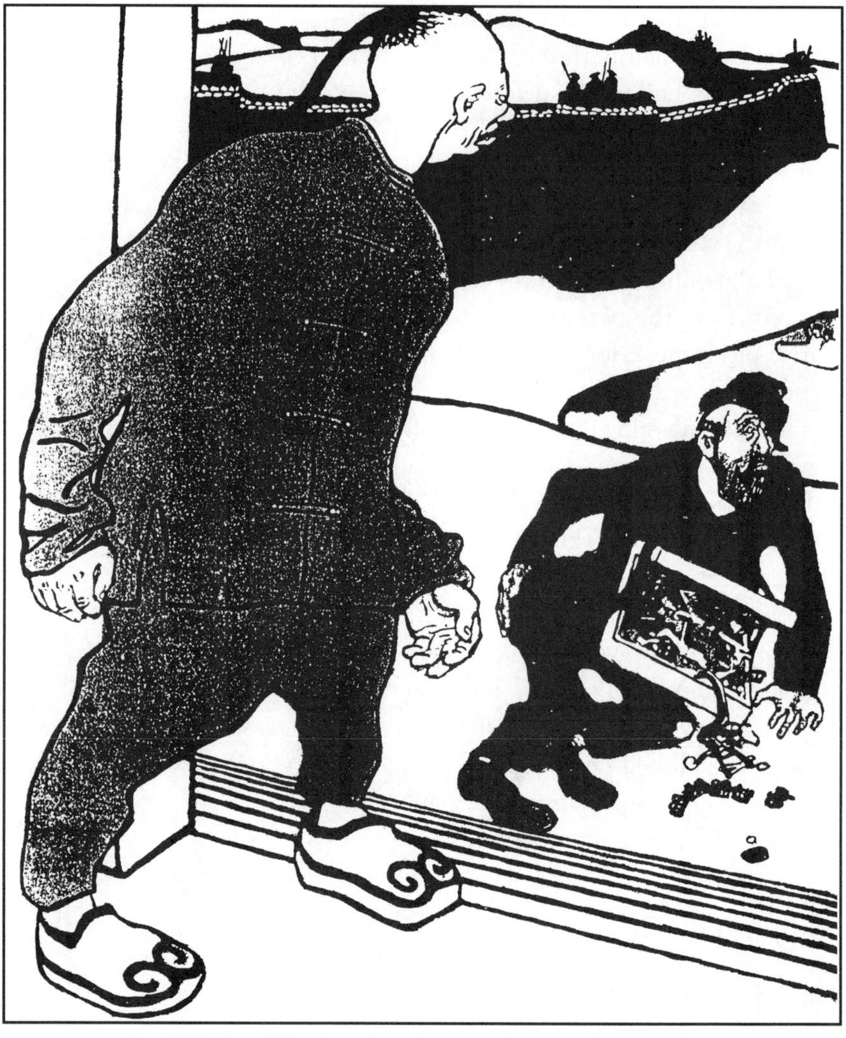

Well then, I'll tell my big brother, the one with iron fist.

Figure 5.15 *Simplicissimus* (1900).

regarding military intervention in little-known places in the East continued until the 1950s.[43] This same theme appeared in the work of French and British cartoonists. The other four German cartoons from Berlin and Munich periodicals while making the same point, lack the up-front visual brilliance of the graphics published in *Simplicissimus*.[44] It is an unfortunate fact about "Orientalism" that in the main, the Western world acquires new data about other cultures mainly through war or lesser types of aggressive action, eg, enforced dam building or deforestation. The twentieth century has shown that the motives making technologically advanced Western countries use military aggression have not been significantly more complex than those behind the nineteenth century wars of Empire.

In the case of the United States by contrast, cartoonists followed the official and military line on the China crisis. The official line was strikingly different from the personal attitude of the Kaiser or the attitudes of the British or Japanese, for example. At a meeting of the representatives of the eight invading Powers on 16 June 1900, the American Admiral Kempf abstained from voting to initiate hostilities with China when the other seven powers demanded the handover of the Dagu forts.[45] Furthermore, Admiral Kempf did not participate in the battle of Dagu on the grounds that there was no justification for making war on a fellow delegate to the Hague Peace Conference of the year before. Although there was some debate in the American press about whether Admiral Kempf should be censured for this decision, events proved it to have been a wise one and both public opinion and government policy moved to stand firmly behind him. The *Chicago Tribune*, the *New York Evening Journal*, the *Morning Oregonian* and *Harper's Weekly* all published cartoons decrying the use of naked force or deploring the onward march of imperialism (See Figures 5.16 and 5.17). A Spanish cartoon also made the point about the use of unjustified force (See Figure 5.18).

China: The Conscience of the "Civilised" World

Thirty-eight cartoons in this sample (12%) were drawn to make a point about the respective civilisation, humanity and cultural worth of China and the invading Powers. Only one of these depicts China as in such a desperate case internally that the "civilised" powers should intervene.[46] Reference to Table 5.1 indicates that cartoons drawn on this theme constitute the second largest group in the sample. These cartoons were drawn during a crisis in which Chinese peasants and officials did kill foreign men, women and children, a crisis in which at one point, owing to an erroneous telegram, the entire world believed that every foreigner in Beijing had been killed. At this point,

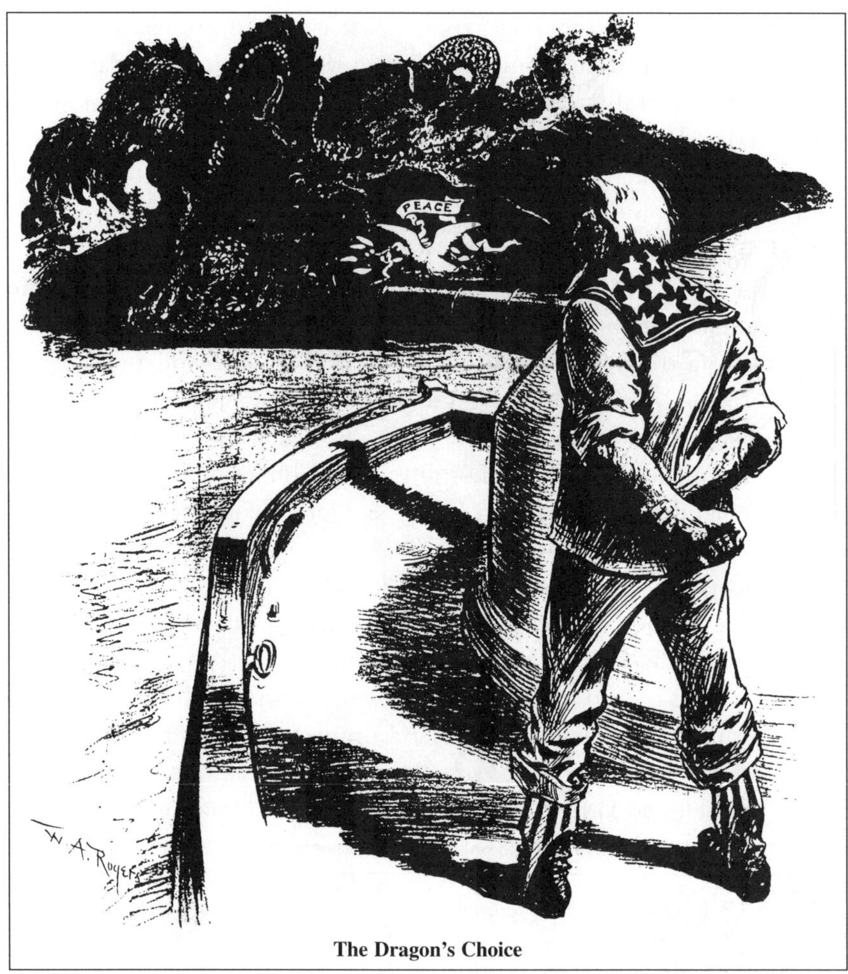

The Dragon's Choice

Figure 5.16 *Harper's Weekly*.

headlines in newspapers all over the world were screaming out horrific — if entirely manufactured — details about the killings which, had they actually happened, would have constituted the most outrageous event of modern diplomatic history. They did not happen. What happened instead was that the Imperial Chinese Army held back the eight invading armies for four weeks at Tianjin. The result of the strength and military excellence displayed by the Chinese army deterred the Allies from marching on to Beijing immediately. Military records reveal that the reason for stalling

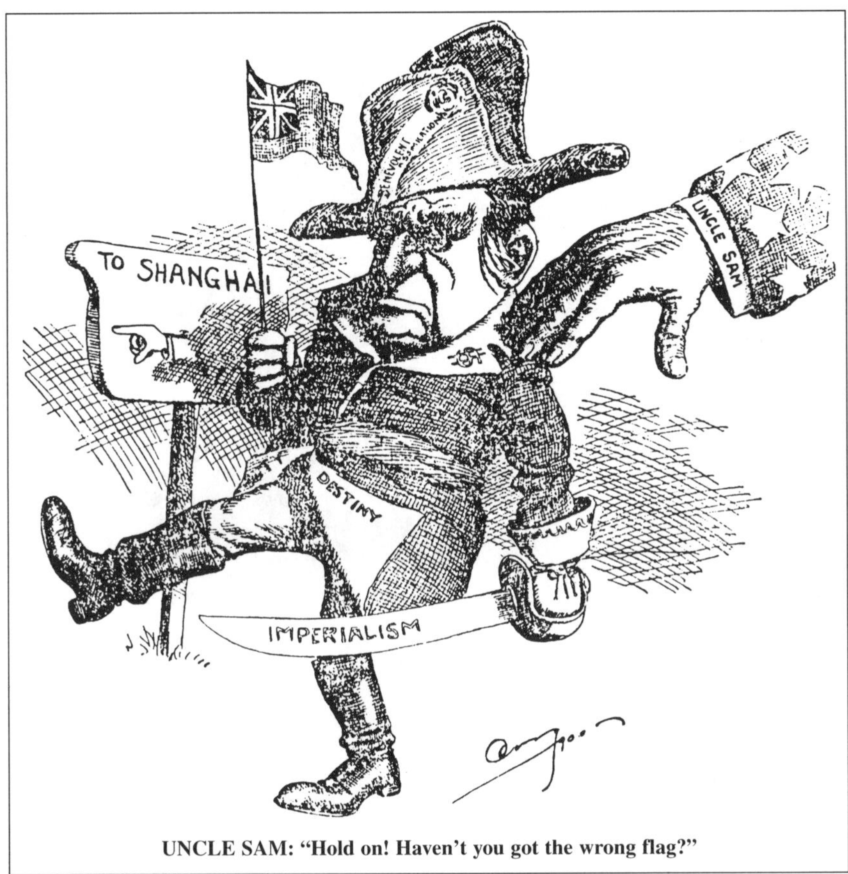

UNCLE SAM: "Hold on! Haven't you got the wrong flag?"

Figure 5.17 *New York Evening Journal.*

was primarily a perception of the need for reinforcements. This perception directly reflected the excellence of the performance of one of the five wings of the Imperial Chinese Army posted to defend Beijing. Disputes as to who should lead the contingent do not appear in written memos of discussions by the senior officers representing the invading Powers, though they were a factor. Scholarship on the Boxer War has emphasised that it was the disunity between the various nations that was the prime factor in the delay in marching on Beijing. As the Allies did not march on Beijing until they had what they considered sufficient re-inforcements, it would seem that the

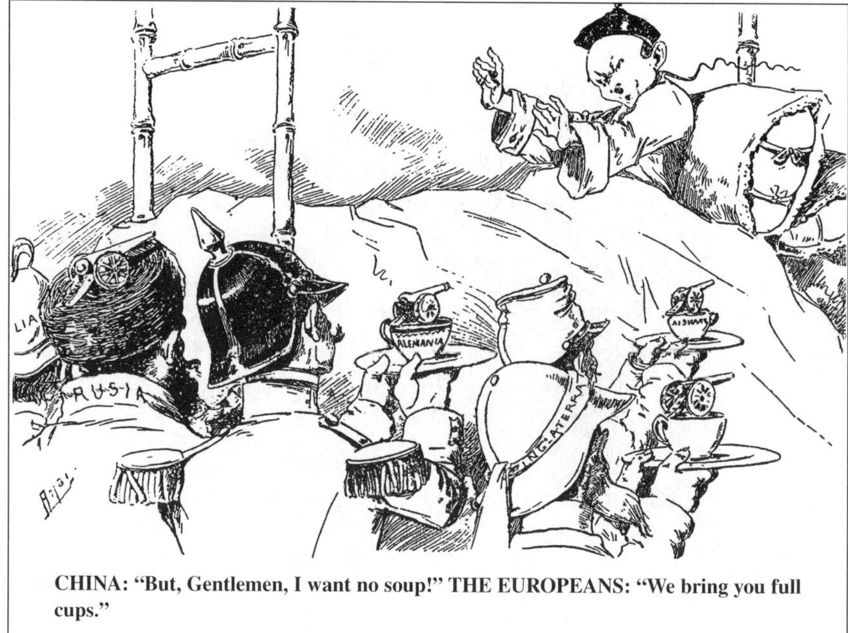

CHINA: "But, Gentlemen, I want no soup!" THE EUROPEANS: "We bring you full cups."

Figure 5.18 *El Cardo.*

superb performance of the one wing of the Imperial Chinese Army to engage the eight invading Powers was the most important factor.

When the eight invading armies finally obtained sufficient reinforcements, they marched to Beijing. After capturing the city, the foreign troops gave themselves to indiscriminate looting, raping and killing of the Chinese population. While the killing and raping was confined in the main to the efforts of soldiers,[47] foreigners of all callings from missionaries to ambassadors took part in the looting, observers being particularly shocked by the activities of ambassadors' wives in this respect.[48] Punitive military expeditions into the countryside took place for months after the capture of Beijing. On these expeditions, uncounted innocent Chinese were killed, their homes and belongings, meagre or otherwise, destroyed.[49]

The measure of civilised conduct in war is difficult. However, whether by number or degree of intensity of atrocities committed in 1900, the invading countries and some of their nationals already resident in China, came out clearly ahead of the Chinese. This fact elicited no major response in Western newspapers, let alone from the governments of the invading Powers. As far as journalists were concerned, although some wrote of these atrocities in their memoirs, they also noted that their copy on these incidents was refused. Their respective governments were busy trying to negotiate a settlement with the Chinese government, whereby the Chinese should pay reparations for damage done by the Boxers. In this climate, journalists writing about wholesale massacres of Chinese coolies,[50] village wells along the route to Beijing choked with women jumping in to escape rape — and as often, being pulled out half-living to be gang-raped anyway, the burning of the priceless Hanlin library, and the mass looting of private and government wealth, received little or no space for such copy in the columns of their respective papers. Examples of such behaviour may be found in copious detail in the published memoirs of journalists who accompanied the invading armies to Beijing.

The testimony of the "experiencers" was acceptable by contemporary society in some arenas but not in others. That is, all the journalists saw the same things and some of them wanted to report what they saw. However, this was not always possible. The same newspapers publishing savage anti-European cartoons refused copy from journalists on the spot who described the atrocities committed by the soldiers — and even some officers — of the invading Powers. Being an "experiencer" did not necessarily give a person the right to an uncensored public voice. Paul Cohen notes that "historians' evidence [is] insufficient in a purely quantitative sense [and] it is almost always stacked qualitatively."[51] By allowing voices to speak who have never spoken on the Boxers before, cartoonists as well as journalists, military men instead of officials or diplomats or Boxers, Chinese woodblock artisans as well as American photographers, this study goes some way towards diminishing the degree to which evidence on the Boxer War and its impact has been "stacked qualitatively."

In Chapter Three, the official accounts of the French military were combined with the pictures and the texts of Chinese peasant folk art — Chinese folk artists, then as now, do not rate highly as "experiencers" in the eyes of scholars. The result was that we saw a clear need to question and reopen for debate some widely accepted outcomes of conflict between foreigners and Chinese in the nineteenth century. This process of "reading backwards" through the records of the powerful to hear the voices of the powerless is possible because of the different mindset, values and cultural background of various categories of people as "experiencers." It is also possible because with hindsight, historians can establish the "experiencer's" production of a version of what happened in terms of the values of the audience the "experiencer" was intending to target. The historian also takes cognisance of the "experiencer's" cultural and professional background. Missionaries, traders, military men, wives and young women, and journalists, were all present at the sacking of Beijing; many representatives of these groups also experienced the events which took place on the march to Beijing. Some deliberately excluded some kinds of information, some presented information to one type of audience but withheld it from another, yet others presented information to have it be refused by those controlling the content of information destined for a particular audience. For these and many more reasons, "firsthand observers" are not necessarily privileged over those who never saw what happened; the work of the cartoonists analysed in this chapter is ample testimony to this. Firsthand experiencers often have conscious or subconscious reasons for failing to portray truthfully what they see, or at the very least for lying by ommission. Written records are not necessarily privileged over pictures or statues or songs. The written records of women have been conspicuously under-privileged by some historians of the Boxer rising for their value as "experiencers."[52]

The cartoonists' work on the Boxer rising was deemed suitable for publication, not only in their own countries or even merely within the same language group. Editors in other countries found their work so apt, they had it reprinted — and if necessary — translated and reproduced in their daily, weekly or monthly newspapers or magazines. The cartoonists were not "experiencers" yet they were able to distill the experience of others with their own vast store of knowledge of human, social and political behaviour. The result is a form arguably more influential at the time than that of any group of "experiencers." They could draw searing cartoons depicting the atrocities committed by the troops of the invading armies while journalists were having their copy or their photographs of the same events refused by editors. Sometimes, when the journalists wrote up such events as memoirs in book form, the same information was deemed acceptable. A notable example was provided by George Lynch who wrote acidly that his editor — a man devoted to blood sport — had refused to publish a picture that had been published elsewhere.[53] Cartoonists used combinations of graphics and words far more pungent and stinging than any other category of "experiencer" and this work was published. At this time, the name of a great cartoonist such as Thomas Heine or Caran D'Ache or Sokolovsky was often the only catalyst for a member of the public to buy a particular paper rather than another one. As some of these cartoonists savaged European values so mercilessly, we may postulate editors whose perception of the public was that readers would still buy these papers despite the violent attacks on European behaviour or pitiless humour at the expense of the "civilised" world.

It is here that we must draw attention to a vital function of political cartooning, one that has not been developed in the literature.[54] We have already noted that cartoonists can act as the conscience of a nation by taking en masse a stand against the contemporary political line. In the case of the cartoons drawn to show how the "humane," Christian, "civilised" world was actually behaving in China, we observe the vital role played by cartoonists in depicting what would otherwise not have been able to appear in any other form in their papers. Both in France and Germany as well as in Russia and Japan, cartoonists working for periodicals included in this survey were frequently jailed.[55] In Japan, cartoonists working for *Marumaru Shimbun* came to be honoured by such government attention.[56] Some writers have emphasised the way in which political cartoons use humour and ridicule as an aggressive weapon.[57] Others have typified cartooning as having quite a different function, that of "persuasive communication" by which it is not necessarily understood that "persuasive" and "aggressive" are interchangeable.[58] What we see in the cartoons drawn to criticise the behaviour of the "civilised" nations in China is that they constitute a voice which would not have appeared in mass print at all without the vehicle of the cartoonists' art. The cartoonists fulfilled a vital function by voicing truths that could not be revealed by any other combination of words, drawings or pictures in the newspapers and periodicals of the day.

Turning to specific cartoons, once again criticism of the barbarity of the invading nations came from the pens of cartoonists of all nationalities. Thomas Theodor Heine of *Simplicissimus* made his point by the savage daring of his conception (Figure 5.19) and the stark brilliance of his graphics (Figure 5.20). Heine was savage in his treatment of the Prussians, the children playing "China War" in imitation of their elders are drawn perpetrating the same atrocities which were being committed by the invading armies in

As the adults sing, so do the children chirp.

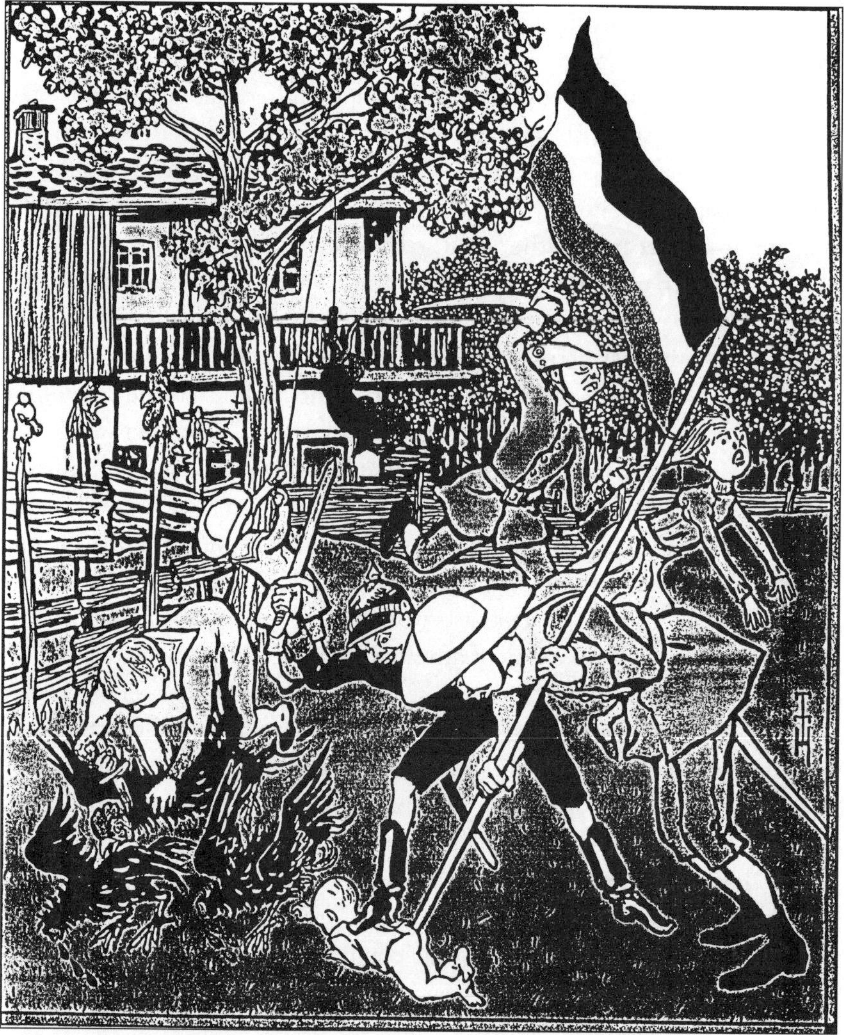

The Major's children play a game of China war and spread Prussian culture in the fresh summer air.

Figure 5.19 *Simplicissimus* (1900).

China. Heine's use of events in China as yet another poisoned arrow to shoot into the image of Prussian Germany in no way diminishes the point the cartoon is making about the behaviour of the foreign armies in China.

Reckoning

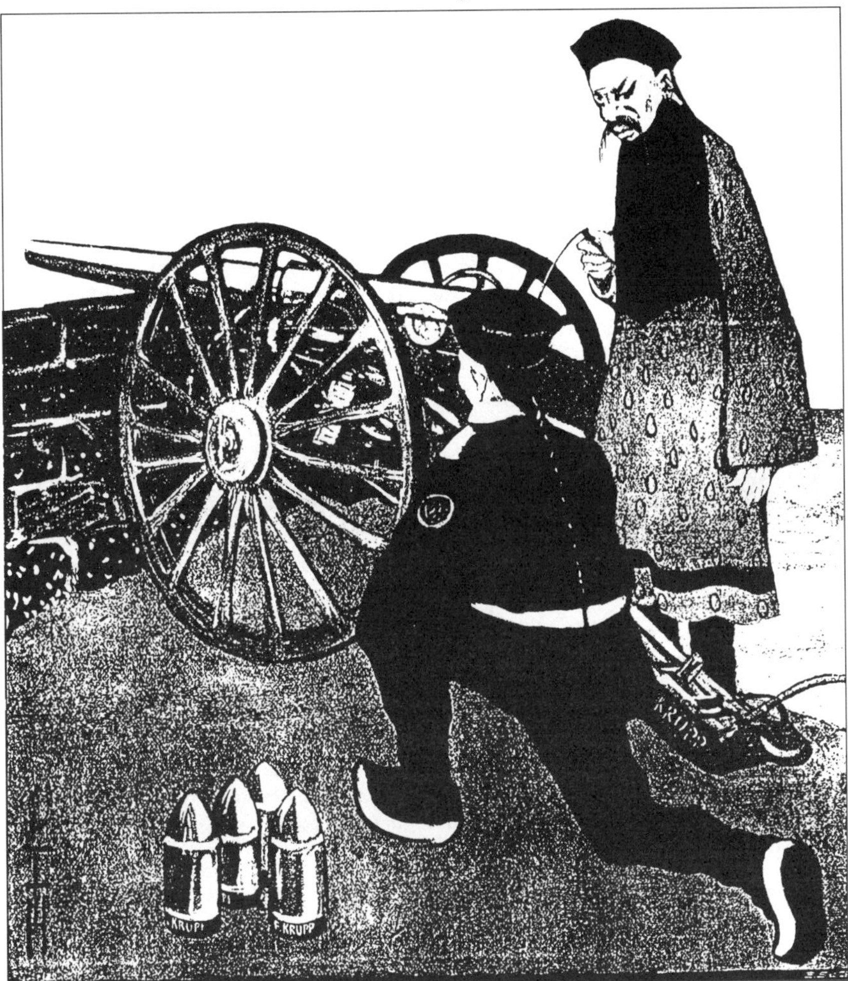

"Peoples of Europe, here are your sacred goods returned."

Figure 5.20 *Simplicissimus* (1900).

American cartoonists working for *Puck* and *Life* were merciless in pointing to the connection between the Christian nations, their traffic in arms and their unjustified use of these arms (Figures 5.21, 5.22 and 5.23). In a highly provocative cartoon, Confucius and Christ are shown holding hands in heaven above their respective warring disciples (Figure 5.24). Given the

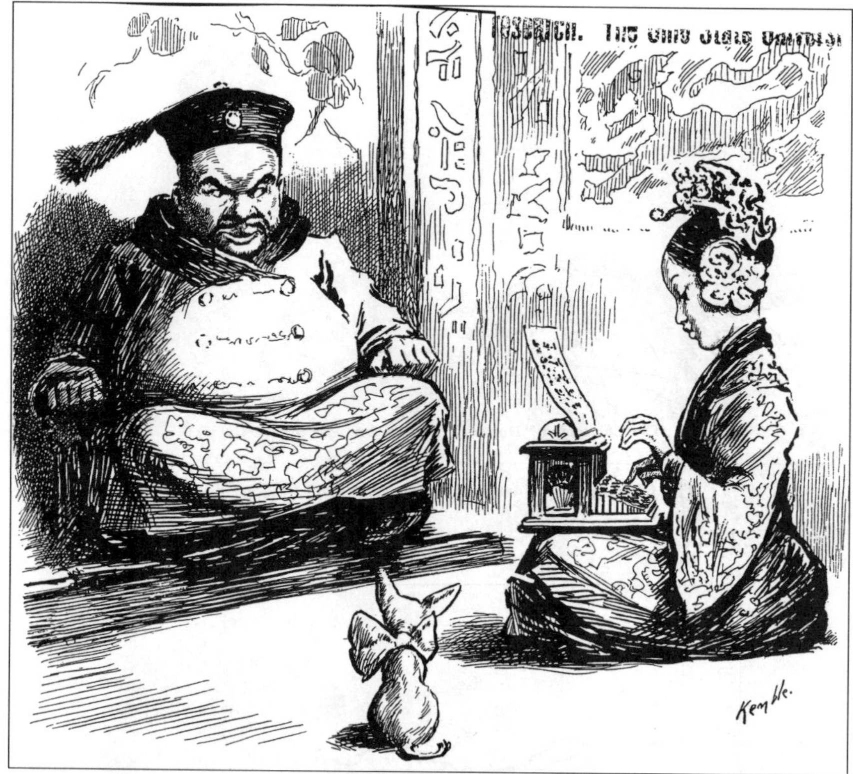

The Viceroy: **Say to the Christian nation that another Christian nation has declared war against us, and when it sends the next batch of missionaries, to send also ten thousand rapid-fire guns and two hundred thousand pounds of Lyddite Shells. We, being a heathen nation, do not make them.**

Figure 5.21 *Life.*

strength and widespread influence of the missionary lobby in America at this time, this *Puck* cartoon would have scandalised large sections of the American community. The dominance and pointedness of American cartoonists' sympathy for China during the most heated moments of press response to the Boxer rising, calls into question the analysis of those writers who have argued that Americans became increasingly China-phobic by the end of the century.[59] It also compells us to reiterate and further refine our understanding of the unique power of the art of cartooning.

A cartoonist for the Viennese periodical *Der Floh* saw the behaviour of

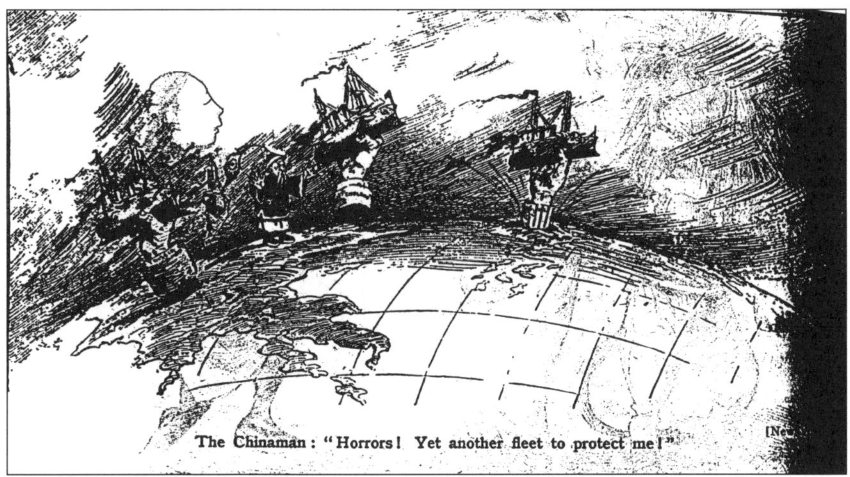

The Chinaman: "Horrors! Yet another fleet to protect me!"

Figure 5.22 *Life*.

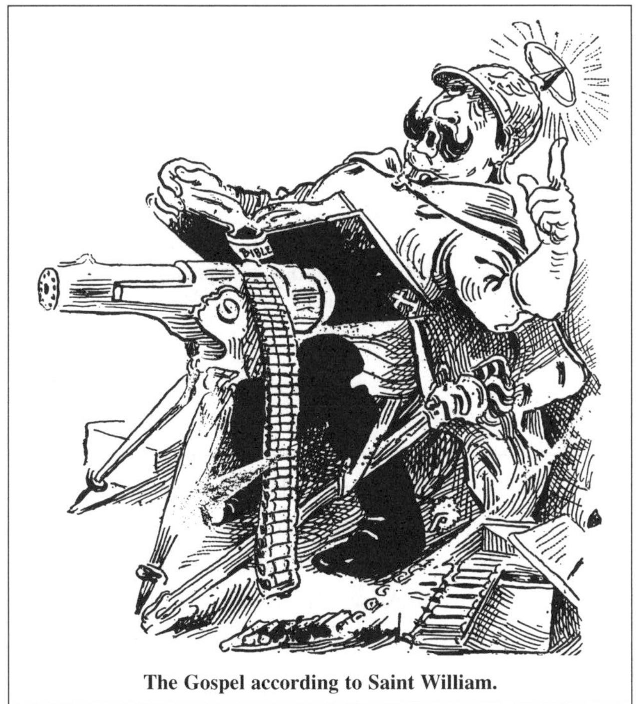

The Gospel according to Saint William.

Figure 5.23 *Puck*, New York.

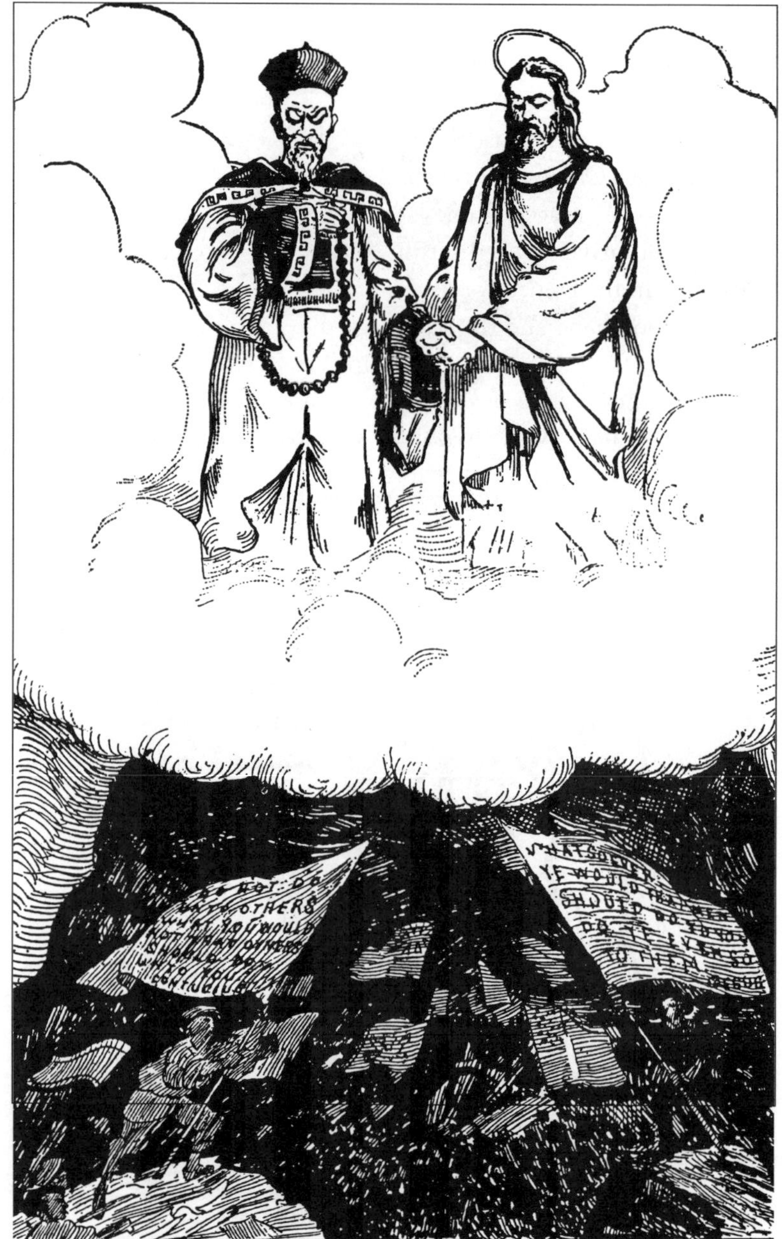

Jesus Christ and Confucius — What use has our teaching been?

Figure 5.24 *Puck*, New York.

the Huns in former times as an improvement on what was happening in China in 1900.[60] The Italian paper *Fischietto* published cartoons condemning Russian and German behaviour in the name of civilisation (Figures 5.25 and 5.26). The Russian cartoonist Sokolovsky who worked for *Novoe Vremya* showed an enraged Chinese spitting on Europe, "a sinister missionary" (Figure 5.27) and the same enraged Chinese figure with a huge fist thumping a top-hatted representative of civilisation and saying in French "down with civilisation."[61] In the French weekly *Le Rire*, two full-page cartoons appeared showing Li Hongzhang and his entourage in a munitions factory with the caption "When the Chinese buy arms in Europe, it is called: CIVILISATION" and on the other page, a battle scene captioned "When they use them against her, it is called: BARBARISM"[62] (Figure 5.28). The last word on the labels of "barbarism" and "civilisation" comes from *Le Cri de Paris* (Figure 5.54). There is no difference between the behaviour of those above the label "civilisation" and those above the label "barbarism", that is, there was no

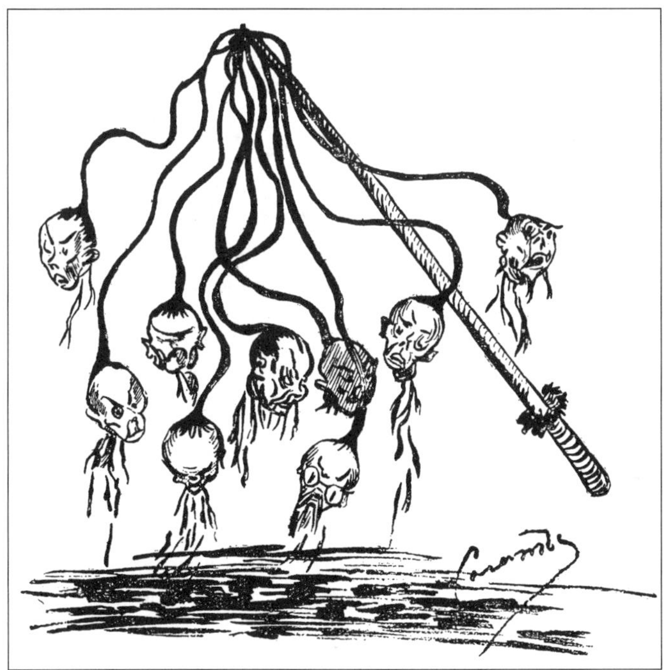

The Russian whip has become the great teacher of civilisation in China.

Figure 5.25 *Fischietto*, Turin.

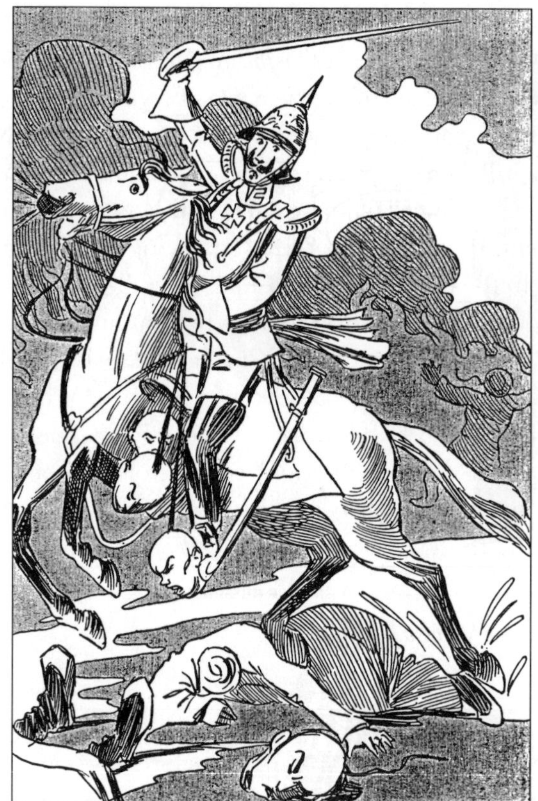

The modern Attila leaves for war in the name of civilisation

Figure 5.26 *Fischietto, Turin.*

difference between the behaviour of the Boxers and the invading foreign soldiers. The cartoonists' understanding on this point was rare among any group of professionals in any era. They refused to fall into the trap characterised by Lévi-Strauss "In refusing the status of humanity to those who appear the most 'savage' or 'barbaric' … all people are doing is borrowing one of their own typical attitudes. The barbarian is first and foremost the man who believes in barbarism."[63] This cartoon makes an apt conclusion to the discussion of the contribution made by the world's cartoonists in obliging a wide reading public to see the hypocrisy and inhumanity of foreign behaviour in China. It bears repeating that many of the cartoonists were celebrated men and readers bought the periodicals they worked for solely to look at their

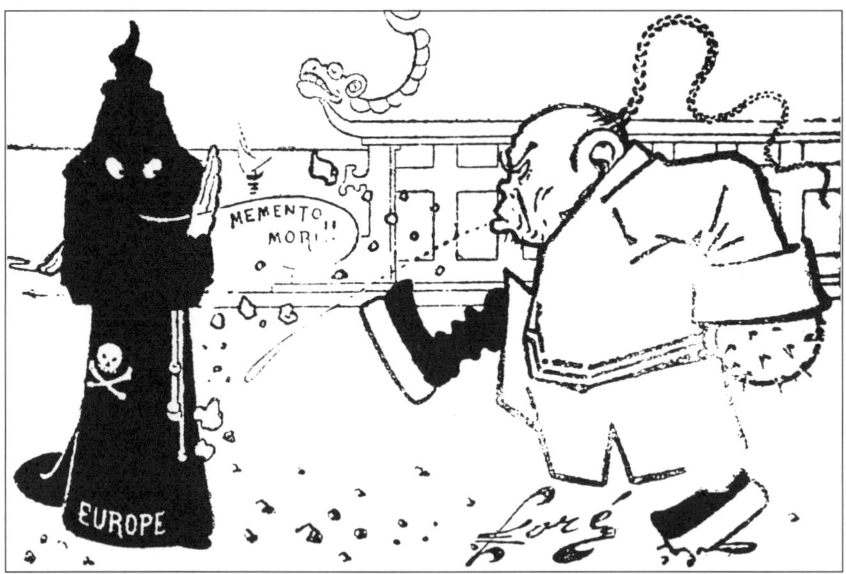

A sinister missionary

Figure 5.27 *Novoe Vremya.*

(a) (b)

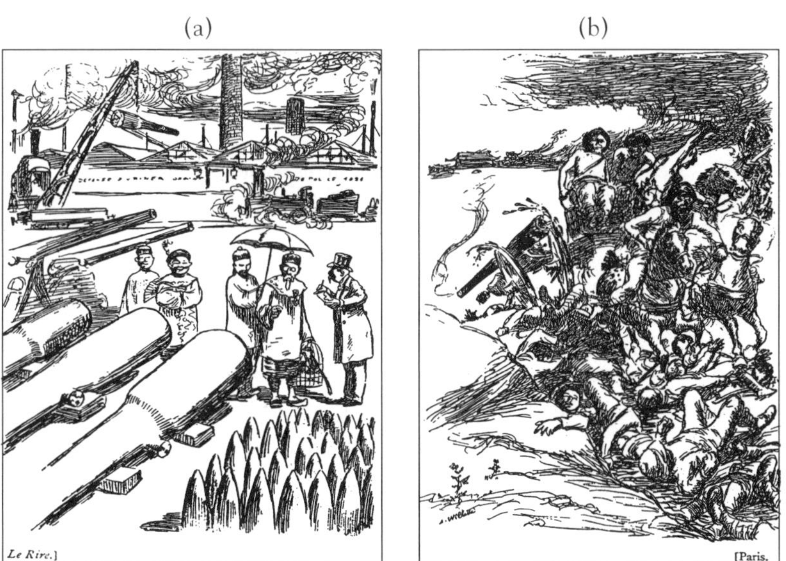

(a) When the Chinese buy arms in Europe, it is called: CIVILISATION
(b) When they use them against her, it is called: BARBARISM

Figure 5.28 *Le Rire.*

work. We must therefore assume that if those readers did not initially have some sympathy for China, such powerful graphics and hard-hitting captions would have generated at least some doubt in the public mind about the rectitude of foreign behaviour during the China crisis.[64]

China the Enemy

The cartoons preoccupied with the image of China as a major political protagonist can be divided into several groups: those depicting the political moves made by China in her own interests and those which illustrate Chinese cruelty, refer directly to the "yellow peril" threat, or contain lighter anti-Chinese satire. In this group of eighty-nine cartoons (26% of the sample), there are only two which shock by their bestial representation of Chinese cruelty. One of these, a cartoon by Cadel drawn for the French weekly *Le Sourire* appeared in colour on the front cover of the 25 August issue. The cartoon appeared well after the news of the relief of Beijing had reached the outside world and it is difficult to assess its impact. It must be emphasised that this was *the only* cartoon on China printed in *Le Sourire*. It was also the only cartoon in the entire sample to make use of oral imagery. It portrayed Prince Duan as a preternaturally enormous head and slavering mouth with his bloody claws clutching the body of one of his female victims; a cartoon appealing to our earliest associations of oral aggression. Such cartoons became commonplace in twentieth century propaganda as images of the insatiable enemy. Sam Keen writes of this enemy:

> He bites, chews and swallows his victims. His eating habits are not the civilized tasting of the gourmet but the gluttonous gorging of an animal. He is the toothy monster of fairy tales and nightmares.[65]

This cartoon is one of a sample of 344; it is clearly atypical of representations of the Chinese as enemy. As such, it is felt that the morality of reproducing it is questionable.[66] Out of dozens of cartoonists from fourteen different countries, one cartoonist produced *one* sickening image that shows the enemy as beast. In terms of the relative influence of this cartoon on the public mind, we may conclude that this representation of the enemy as slavering monster had little impact relative to the totality of depictions of the Chinese in general and leading Chinese military and political figures in particular. As a cartoon it does, however, have historical interest as the precursor of the twentieth century propaganda posters produced in all countries showing the enemy as lustful, aggressive beast.[67]

The other cartoon in the sample of 344 showing the Chinese as cruel, blood-lusting enemy was printed on the front page of the *World* on 17 June 1900 (Figure 5.29). Drawn above a quotation from Kipling, this enemy, with blood-dripping sword between his teeth, reaching across the globe with relentless claws, personified the fears of China the "Yellow Peril," the bloodthirsty fanatic given to mutilating his foes in indescribable ways. While the circulation of the *World* at nearly nineteen million copies per month was the largest in the world, this was the only cartoon published by this paper

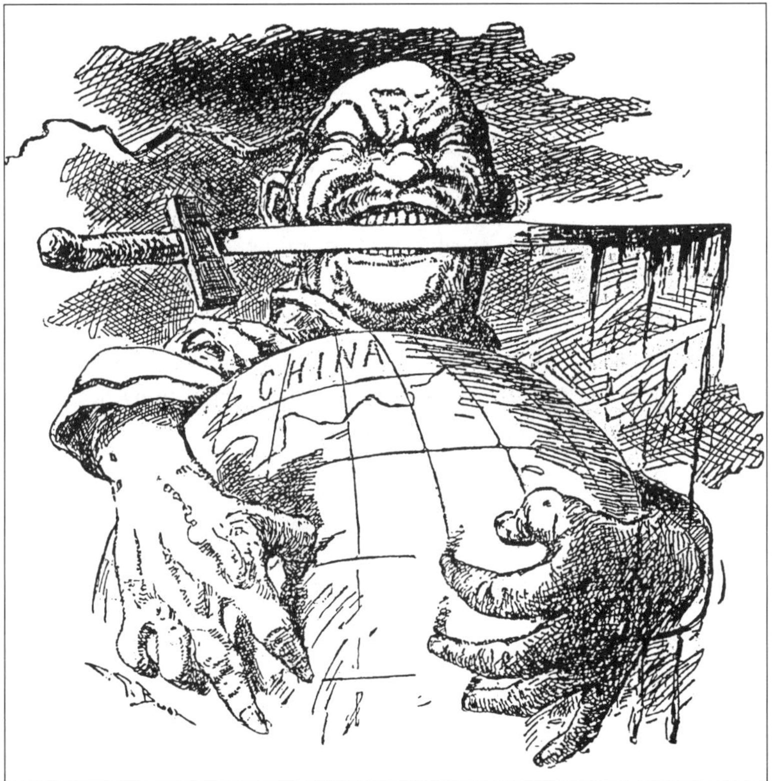

When the dawn comes up like thunder, Out o'China crost the bay — *Kipling*

Figure 5.29 The *World*.

which would have fuelled the image of the Chinese as barbaric fanatical enemy. More typical of the cartoons published by the *World* and of the cartoons of the Chinese as enemy, was a cartoon that appeared on 17 July 1900 (Figure 5.30). By this date, the world had heard of the final capture of Tianjin after its siege by the eight invading countries for four weeks. The fate of the foreigners in Beijing was still unknown. This cartoon portrays the Boxer as a ferocious enemy but one who will inevitably be swept off the face of the globe by the intervention of the Allied Powers.

A common theme among cartoonists was of the Chinese enemy as more or less sophisticated liar.[68] In one of these cartoons in the *World* of 27 July, the duplicitous character of the enemy was seen as a legitimate weapon in the Chinese armoury. The archetypal lying mandarin is depicted with six

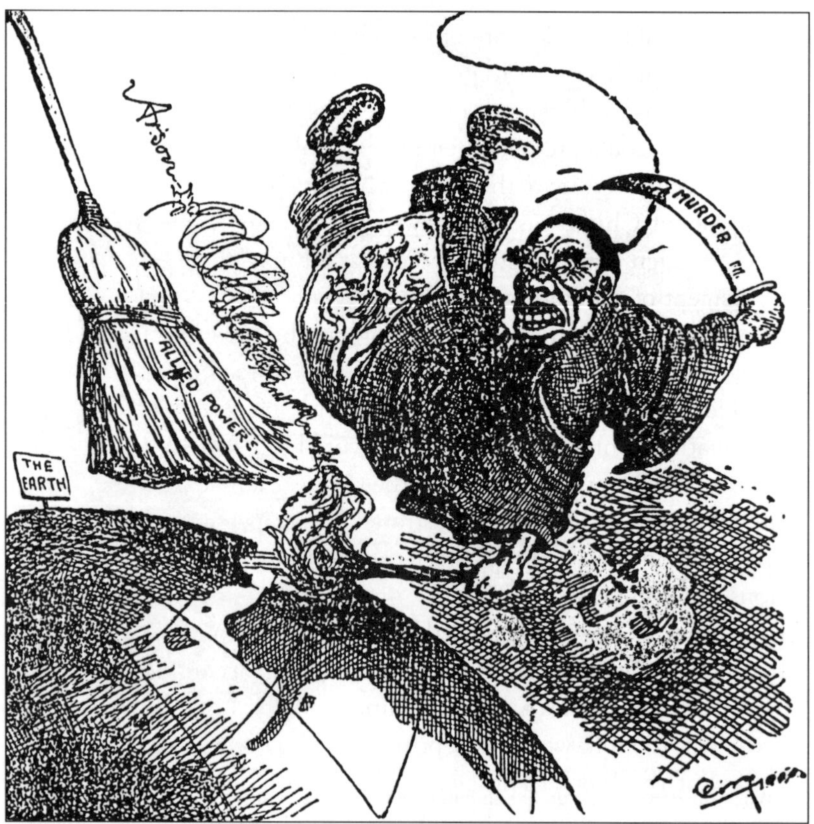

Figure 5.30 *New York Evening Journal*, "The Yellow Devil."

diminutive representatives of the major invading Powers swinging from his queue. The cartoon is captioned "Bamboozling the Powers." Seven cartoons made direct reference to the Chinese as incompetent in military terms. One Japanese cartoon went so far as to satirise Chinese soldiers as cowards so accustomed to fleeing from battle that they wore their medals on their backs and invented a reversing cart to which they could harness a horse backwards and thus escape in style.[69] Another Japanese cartoon lampooned Chinese military prowess by depicting a satirical map giving advice to the Empress Dowager and her court as to how they could best escape. Most of the suggested avenues of escape were through gates labelled "coward gate," "fleeing gate." "weakness gate," "failure/flight gate." These satirical punning maps were a favourite with the cartoonists of *Marumaru Shimbun*, others appearing on 21 July and 11 August. Two Japanese cartoons showed the Chinese enemy as a figure well able to take care of himself and his country, an enemy who used the means in his power to preserve his integrity.[70]

The cartoons in this survey provide evidence of the amount of knowledge cartoonists could presume their audience already had about China. An unfortunate characteristic of the way in which foreign countries accumulated new data about China was that newspaper readers learned more during periods of foreign armed aggression against China. There had also been a strong element of admiration for some aspects of Chinese culture since the first flowerings of the fashion for Chinoiserie in the early eighteenth century. These two modes of coming to terms with China, through military clashes or fashionable interest in selected aspects of Chinese culture are both present in the information contained in cartoons devoted to Chinese political initiatives during the Boxer crisis. As far as the Chinese were concerned, Chinese woodblock prints and Chinese illustrated newspapers provided means for more data about foreigners to enter the worlds of the lower and middle echelons of Chinese society. As the nineteenth century drew to a close, armed conflict likewise prompted the publication of pictorial information about various foreign countries and identified them according to the extent of their intervention in China and Chinese affairs. In terms of the public they reached, the folk woodblock prints (nianhua) were equivalent to the *Daily Mail* or the *World*. The *Dianshizhai huabao* did not really have an equivalent outside China. By the turn of the century, the British, American and Chinese illustrated press — and the folk woodblock equivalent in China

— distinguished itself by steadfast refusal to print illustrations deliberately designed to inflame public opinion. Missionary newspapers published in China aimed to educate the Chinese about important data outside their world by, for example, extensive articles on the walrus, the penguin, the Eskimo and other denizens of the Arctic world. Such publications were short-lived and appeared in very small editions, an indication of their attraction for the Chinese public. Missionary newspapers published in France and America in particular, cannot be regarded as representative of European or American public opinion at large.

> No traits whether physical or psychological in nature, can be *totally* manufactured by the cartoonist. The trait must exist to some extent in popular consciousness or graphic tradition before it can be amplified and caricatured by the artist (author's emphasis)[71]

Cartoonists could rely on quite a large repository of information about China in the public mind in Britain, Europe and America. In a direct antithesis of the broom metaphor, which showed the Allies sweeping China off the globe, a German cartoonist drew a powerful Chinese warrior dressed in traditional garb sweeping the foreigners out of China. The caption read "What do you expect my good friends. This is my revenge for Qingdao, Wei-hai-Wei, Tonkin and Port Arthur."[72] This cartoonist was reminding his audience that the Boxer War occurred in a historical context in which the Chinese would inevitably take revenge for the concessions which had been forced out of them by foreign powers. For this point to reach even a fraction of readers, they would have to have had some associations with these Chinese geographical references and to have been able to make the connection implied by the cartoonist. This theme of retaliation as a motive for Chinese political manoeuvring during the Boxer crisis occurred in other cartoons that also showed the Chinese reaction as inevitable.[73]

A unique drawing came from the pen of Hermann-Paul cartoonist for *Figaro* (Figure 5.31). Captioned "China for the Chinese," this powerful drawing is a political statement. It is not meant to amuse the reader or satirise the subject. It is also extremely ambivalent which adds to its impact. The following remarks are not proposed as a definitive interpretation. Surprisingly modern, the Chinese figure exudes a sullen dangerous force, the force of unleashed naked power in the shape of an aggressive and doubtless ignorant,

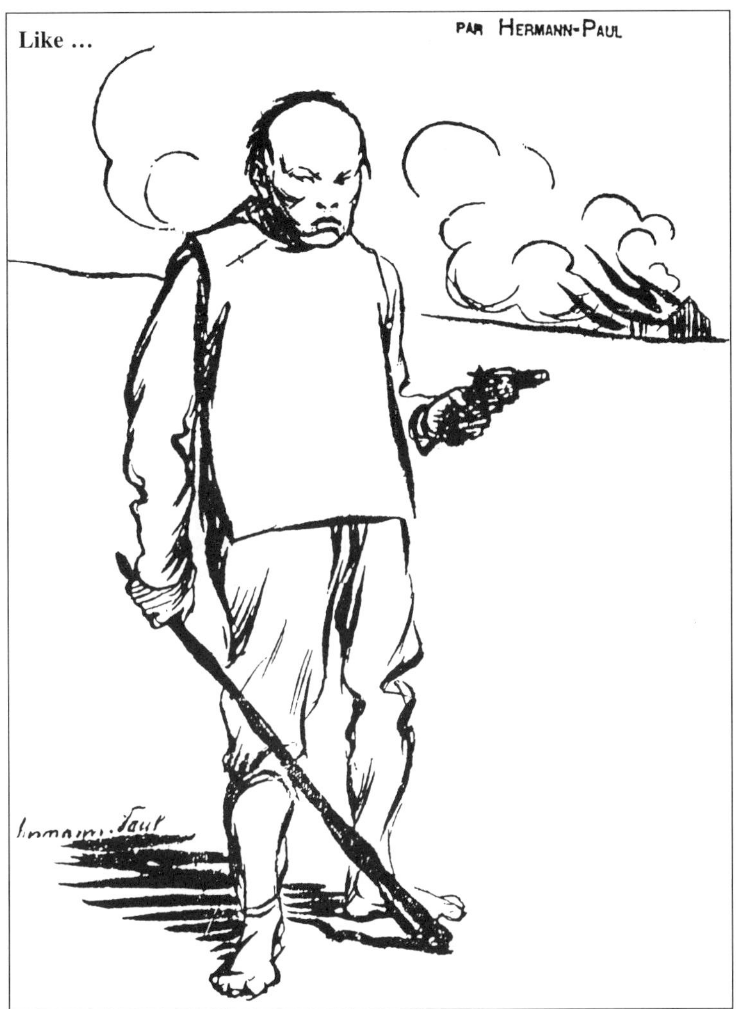

China for the Chinese!!

Figure 5.31 *Figaro.*

peasant. His clothes are plain, there is no ridiculed queue in evidence, rather we see the power of a man stripped and waiting on his strong bare feet to reclaim his country. This is a man who will shoot to kill — note that he carries a pistol in one hand, not some antique Chinese opera weapon. With such an extensive consensus in the literature regarding the primitive weapons used by the Boxers, we may note Mark Elvin's evidence that "Both Suquain in northern Jiangsu and Lingling in western Shandong were famous for the sale of rifles and revolvers for personal protection" (p. 205).

One of the points being made in Hermann-Paul's cartoons is that rebellions and revolutions, while not bloodless affairs, are nevertheless, based on the simplified mass emotions of justice and patriotism. These emotions could — and did in the case of the Boxer rising — become ugly and destructive. Nevertheless, they had their origins in the patriotic sentiments recognisable as the likely reaction of the populations of any country threatened, as China was, by foreign invasion and dismemberment. There was a real sense in which the cartoonists of 1900 saw that this kind of patriotism had a justifiable basis, though such patriotism was belittled by later writers, "it was not possible for an ignorant mass of superstitious peasant youths" to have "a true sense of nationalsism"[74] — and even thought by foreigners living in China at the time to be non-existent.[75] To best understand this cartoon, we might apply Gombrich's insight — that many cartoons are neither humourous nor propagandistic. They satisfy us simply because they reduce a complex situation to a formula which sums it up neatly.[76] There must have been an audience in France who could have sympathised with Hermann-Paul's cartoon.

Ridicule was certainly an element in the cartoons depicting Chinese political initiatives during the Boxer crisis. But this ridicule was aimed as much at the invading Powers as at the Chinese. Methods of Chinese torture received widespread graphic coverage during the crisis. *Figaro's* celebrated Caran d'Ache employed these symbols, by this time intimately associated with Chinese life, in a cartoon of the Emperor with his head in a cangue captioned "I would be happy to have it communicated to the powers that, for my part, I would give them my hand with pleasure" (Figure 5.32). Another delightful cartoon from the *Chicago Daily Tribune* of 25 July depicts a little short-legged Chinese emperor above the caption "Yesterday was the Emperor's Birthday." The exotically costumed little fellow says "Wonder what I'm going to get." Here we see diminutive size used to ridicule but we note that even Chinese Emperors like English Queens had birthdays. As for ridicule directed at the great powers, an Italian cartoon depicts Li Hongzhang juggling the representatives of the major powers. The cartoon is captioned "Chinese customs and traditions. How they play shuttlecock and battledore in China" (Figure 5.33).

In all these cartoons, the details of Chinese costume are correct. Much

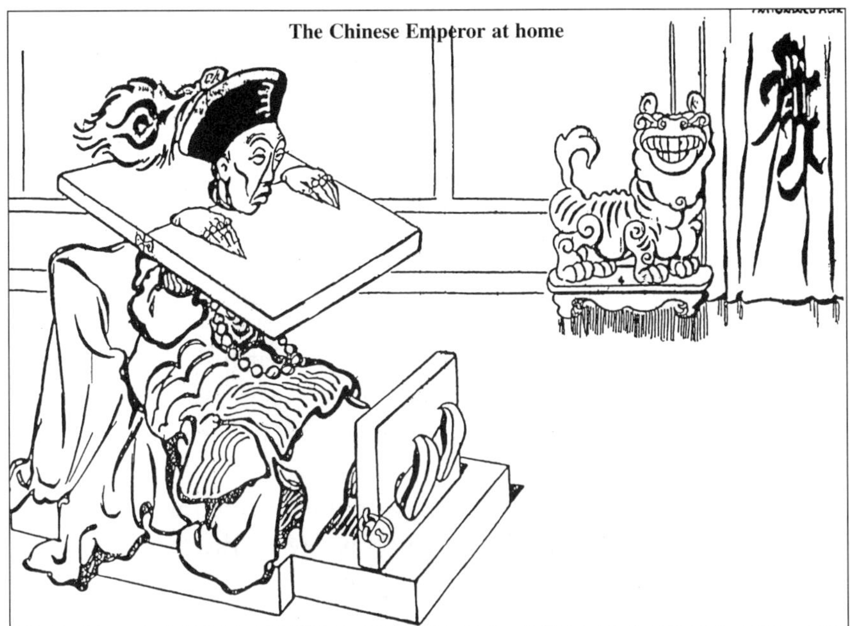

I would really like to say to the Powers that as far as I am concerned I would give them my hand.

Figure 5.32 *Figaro.*

has been written about negative stereotyping in cartoons and propaganda.[77] It should also be said, however, that stereotyping has a hidden positive function; it gradually conditions people to accept the different as the norm. Chinese dignitaries wore unusual hats and long robes but when one of them, Li Hongzhang, appeared in America in 1896, he was received with open arms and given lengthy sympathetic coverage by American journalists. The popularity of the Chinese Ambassador to America at the time of the Boxer crisis was such that he was invited to give the 4 July address in Philadelphia in 1900.[78] Although he wisely declined, Ambassador Wu and his family went everywhere in their national dress and were dear to the American public; Madame Wu gave an interview to the *World* in the middle of the Boxer crisis.[79]

In concluding, we note that despite a minority of frightening depictions of the Chinese as enemy, the overwhelming majority of cartoonists drew pictures above captions aimed at showing the political justification of

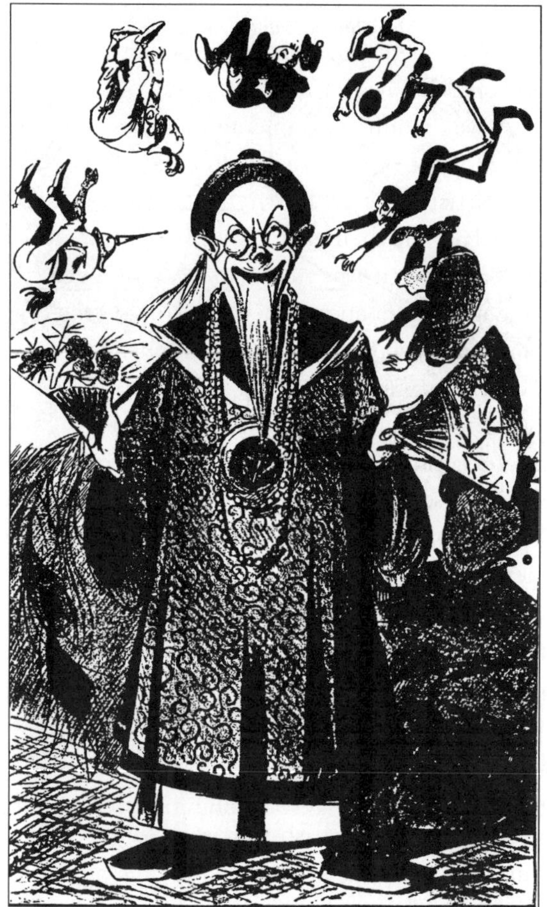

CHINESE CUSTOMS & TRADITIONS. How they play shuttlecock and battledore in China.

Figure 5.33 *Fischietto*, Turin.

Chinese actions. As such, it cannot be said that in the minds of cartoonists in 1900, the Chinese were enemy in the way that Japan or Germany appeared as enemy in 1939–1945, or Japan as enemy in 1937–1945, or Germany in 1914–1918. It is suggested that this abstention on the part of the international corps of cartoonists from any consensus that China was monstrous beast, is congruent with the cartoonists' view that China was the victim of uncivilised inhumane treatment by the "civilised" world. In Chapter Six it is emphasised that the Boxer rising was not just another peasant rebellion, it was the occasion of a war between China and eight foreign countries. However, as the cartoonists of 1900 saw it, there was an important sense in which this was not a war. A war requires an enemy but the enemy has not always necessarily been thought of as barbaric and inhumane. From 1914–1918 onwards, graphic artists created horrifying images to make it certain in readers' minds how barbaric their enemy was. In the history of war, it has not always been the case that it was necessary to formulate a concept of the enemy as barbaric and inhuman in order to justify killing him. A great deal more than a change in weapons technology and the class base of the fighting man changed on Saint Crispin's day if we are to believe Shakespeare's characterisation of what King Harry expected of his troops with regard to their treatment of a conquered populace.

This study would seem to show that the process of dehumanising the enemy had not, in fact, begun in 1900 as far as the illustrators of Western and Chinese newspapers was concerned nor as far as the cartoonists were concerned[80] (see Chapter Two). If the enemy was not barbaric or inhuman but responding in kind to unreasonable provocation, a process of dehumanisation did not necessarily have to occur. The illustrated press was not responsible for instigating this process. The process of dehumanisation may have been evolving but it would seem that it was not yet universally accepted by all strata of Western society. The year 1900 is a particularly interesting year to test this hypothesis as the British were simultaneously involved in war against the white Protestant Boers, the yellow heathen Chinese, and the black heathen Ashanti. The revelation of inhuman treatment of Boer women and children put in concentration camps by the British caused consternation in Parliament. There were still debates in Parliament at this time about whether or not it was appropriate to use certain kinds of lethally destructive bullets against racially different foes. That is, that there remained vestiges of the rules that had governed the proper manner of waging war at least since mediaeval times in Britain and Europe. Further work needs to be done on this hypothesis but it would seem that the racial and cultural background of the enemy modified considerably the enemy's entitlement to be treated according to more humane rules of war.

Once the enemy is dehumanised, it becomes justifiable for "us" to treat "them" with barbarity because "they" are barbarians. This process undoubtedly happened in China. The raping, looting and indiscriminate shooting of ordinary civilian Chinese by the invading Allied armies was extensively described in the diaries or memoirs of scores of people. The cartoonists of the world reached a consensus that the Chinese were not barbaric in the circumstances in question. They were also the only group to come to this conclusion and to be able to air the unjustifiable atrocities of the invading Powers directly in the press.

It is remarkable that cartoonists from fourteen different countries should independently have produced cartoons on this theme and that their work should have been published and republished. They unambiguously produced cartoons showing that "they" were more than justified in using whatever means they had in "their" power to retaliate. The other theme they drew on again and again was that "we" behaved like greedy hypocrites, even barbarians, using force when there was no other option to sate "our" greed and justify "our" hypocrisy. This is not to say that the Boxers themselves were innocent; however very few writers have noted that the number of foreigners killed by the Boxers was miniscule in comparison with the number of Chinese killed by Boxers.[81] It was certainly not the cartoonists of 1900 who provided further ammunition for the "Yellow Peril" fears that were beginning to emerge particularly in America. Research has amply demonstrated the means used by graphic artists to create an enemy during and after the 1914–1918 War. In this survey there were only two cartoons depicting China as enemy; the picture of Prince Duan as slavering monster and the huge Chinese head with a sword dripping blood clenched in its teeth and claw-like hands reaching out to clutch the globe (Figure 5.29). As a whole, Hermann-Paul's powerful cartoon "China for the Chinese" (Figure 5.31) represents most characteristically, the view of European, British and American cartoonists. Notably Japanese cartoons of the Boxer War demonstrate a marked lack of sympathy for the concept "China for the Chinese". Hermann-Paul drew a man defending his country with the only means at his disposal, not a bestial Other.

Li Hongzhang — the Most Cunning Mandarin of Them All or Respected International Figure?

Much has been written about China's isolation and the refusal or inability of its leaders to absorb Western ideas.[82] These two elements of interpreting China's relations with the rest of the world are being eroded by revisionist scholarship.[83] Cartoons depicting Li Hongzhang as the central figure constituted the third largest group in the sample studied (see Table 5.2). A brief glance at aspects of the career of Li Hongzhang show him to have been adept at making friends with celebrated Westerners and agile in manipulating the Western press both when at home in China and on his tour of Russia and the West in 1896 at the age of seventy-two. As a politician, Li understood the importance — both domestic and international — of creating a well-equipped, well-drilled army. He began moves towards this end under the patronage of Zeng Guofan in the 1850s. The Taiping Rebellion brought him into contact with both English and American soldiers and mercenaries. When General Ulysses Grant visited China on his world tour in 1878, he and Li developed mutual respect and friendship based on their common experience as soldiers and politicians in countries torn by civil war. All over the world, the 1870s was the decade for the fashionable to have their photograph taken. The Chinese were not at all behind in this regard and Li and Grant were photographed together on this tour.[84] There were far fewer leading statesmen and soldiers who were keen to be photographed in China than in the West. Li was an exception in this respect. He was the subject of two early films made during his tour of America.[85] In this, Li was in advance of most other politicians on the international stage. Moving pictures (films) made around 1900 made a striking impression on the American public and Li's willingness to appear on the earliest form of celluloid gives him a totally different image from that accorded him by *The Times*.

On his American tour, Li endeared himself to the public by shedding tears on a visit to the tomb of Ulysses Grant. After Li's visit, in a tribute to General Grant, Chinese soldiers marched to his tomb and laid a wreath on the anniversary of his death every year until 1911.[86] Much has been written about the fear engendered in the American working class by the threat of competition from Chinese labour. However, it needs to be emphasised that gestures like this and the men and women who made them, endeared themselves to all classes in all countries.[87] Li Hongzhang was such a widely known figure to the American working class that he appeared on a huge coloured advertising poster showing him reading the paper and bearing the caption "Li Hung Chang Never Misses the *Sunday Journal*."[88] In Britain, Li had visited and been photographed with workers in the cotton mills in Lancashire and had his photograph taken with Gladstone at Howarden. Li must have had a particular regard for Gladstone as by 1896, Gladstone was eighty-six years old and had long retired from politics having been four times elected Prime Minister of England.[89] In Germany and France, Li attracted less publicity, possibly because he sought less publicity, his visits to those two countries being in connection with the purchase of arms and ammunition.[90]

This thumbnail sketch shows Li as a political figure recognised and respected in the West. The sketches, photographs and films made during his visit reveal a Chinese leader able to command positive media coverage, attention and sympathy outside China. In this respect, Li Hongzhang stands out from any other Chinese political figure before or since 1900. Although Li came from a culture in which the desirability of gaining positive media coverage was a non-factor, it is interesting to note that he not only recognised the need to have such coverage but was also notably successful in gaining it. He also managed to re-integrate himself on his return without attracting too much adverse attention from conservative Chinese officials because of his experience in the West. Some of the other early Chinese ambassadors to the West were less fortunate and were relegated to insignificant posts after their overseas tour of duty. In considering the ability of leading political figures in China to adapt to Western institutions even when such adaptation could cost them dearly on their return home, we may note again the way Ambassador Wu and his family endeared themselves to the American public at the turn of the last century. International cartoonists were familiar with Li, with his physiognomy, his dress, his politics, his achievements and his difficulties and most of them accorded him quite some respect. Coupe has observed that:

> Even when a cartoon inclines to punitive satire, a certain sympathetic process is often at work. The constant repetition of a given politician's features establishes him as a person in our minds and the familiarity inevitably breeds that measure of sympathetic contempt.[91]

Coupe has also pointed out that as well as contributing a vehicle for aggression, caricature can equally well convey grudging admiration, even affection and he cites some cartoons of Charles de Gaulle as an example.[92] We see Li as a well-known leader on the international stage, not as some nameless, faceless, conniving mandarin, despite *The Times* characterisation of him as "one of the most astute instruments of reaction [in] command of the methods of Oriental negotiation."[93] As *The Times* would have it, there was something devious and underhand about "the methods of Oriental negotiation" rather than something to be admired in the way Li managed to maximise many difficult, if not impossible foreign policy situations for the benefit of China. In a lengthier description of Li, a leading article in *The Times* of 20 June 1900 described him as follows:

> He is, if possible, below the average of his brother Mandarins in falsehood and in corruption, but though his ignorance of the true meaning of Western civilisation is in many respects profound, it is at least less gross and palpable than that of his rivals and colleagues ... In the meaner arts of Oriental diplomacy, Li Hung Chang enjoys a bad pre-eminence. Falsehood, evasion, double-dealing, and intrigue are his familiar tools, and of all of them, he has repeatedly proved himself a master.

The article goes on to refer to this internationally respected dignitary as "the wily old Chinaman," displaying a thoroughly contemptuous tone to the end.

Against this background, a brief evaluation of the attention paid to Li Hongzhang by cartoonists during the Boxer rising shows two factors of interest. First, the number of cartoons with Li as subject, 27 or 8% of the sample, show him to have been an internationally recognisable figure. Indeed there are more cartoons referring specifically to Li and his role in the crisis than there are cartoons drawn of a generalised mandarin whether depicted as lying and duplicitous or as standing firm for China. Second, the cartoonists taking Li as their subject reflect the same pattern already noted in so far as the demonisation of China is concerned. That is, only one cartoon out of the sample portrays Li as a Chinese leader seeking to do evil to the foreigners and even this cartoon, entitled "Dr Jekyl and Mr Hyde" with all the connotations thereby implied, also shows Li as "our great and good friend" (Figure 5.34). While there is obvious irony in this cartoon and its caption, in his Dr Jekyl persona, Li was truly perceived as a good friend by the American public and by American statesmen. Taken together with the other cartoons, it would seem that the Mr. Hyde transformation was prompted by the pressure of the war. Another cartoon of Li by Sokolovsky appeared in the *Novoe Vremya* of 3 August (Figure 5.35). Evidently a caricature, it must be said that the beast revealed by Sokolovsky's pen is a very benign one indeed, indicative rather of

Dr. Jekyl and Mr. Hyde

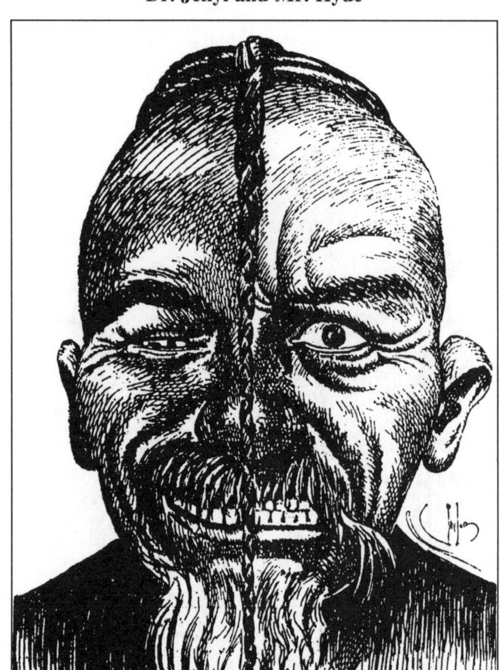

Cover each half of the picture alternately and see "our great and good friend" Li Hong Chang in his great transformation act.

Figure 5.34 *Sunday Tribune.*

an international perception of Li as an aged learned statesman using the last of his waning powers in the service of his country.[94] Comparison of a person with a fox was insulting in both China and Japan. However, the Russians shared the European view that a cunning old fox was to be admired for his repertoire of tricks and skill in outwitting his foes.

Known and respected internationally for his role in attempting to wrest the best possible deal for China after the Sino-Japanese War, Li's skill as a negotiator was also the subject of cartoons (Figures 5.33, 5.36, 5.37 and 5.38). A cartoon appeared in *Marumaru Shimbun* of 4 August depicting Li with a

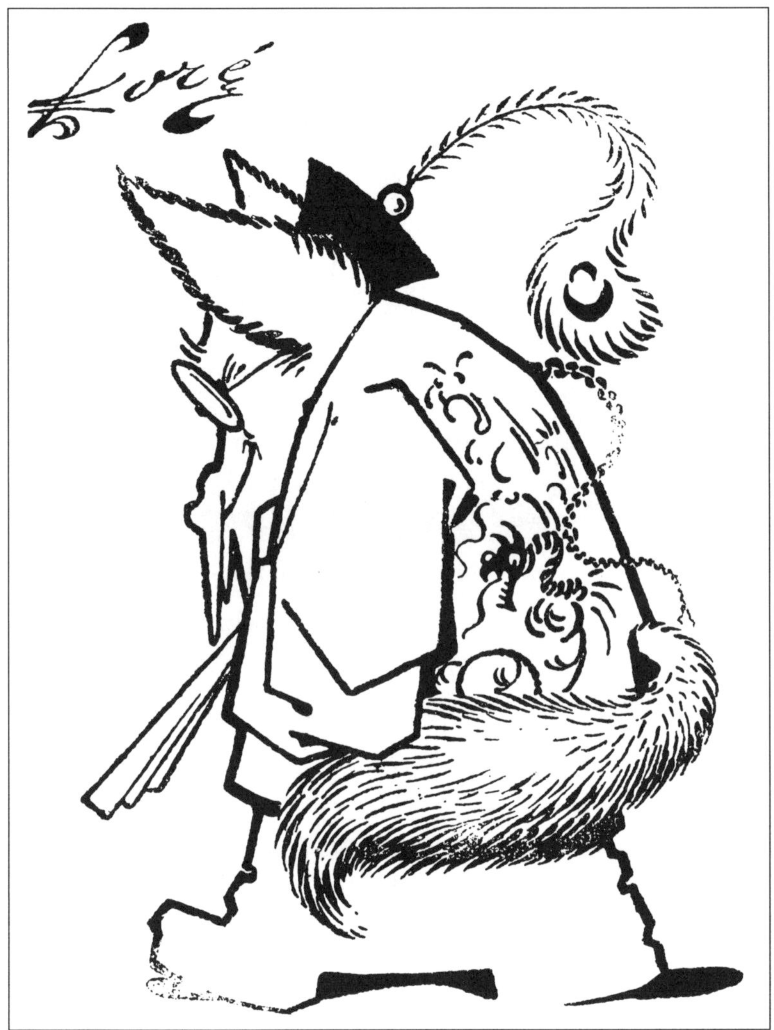

Li Hongzhang

Figure 5.35 *Novoe Vremya.*

long exaggerated tongue; his prowess in negotiation was wryly acknowledged by the ridiculous but nevertheless effective "talking shield" representing Li's face. *Marumaru Shimbun* also published a cartoon showing the evolution of Li Hongzhang's face into a pear (Figure 5.39). The character for "Li" is also the character for "pear" so there is a pun here in Japanese, although the slang

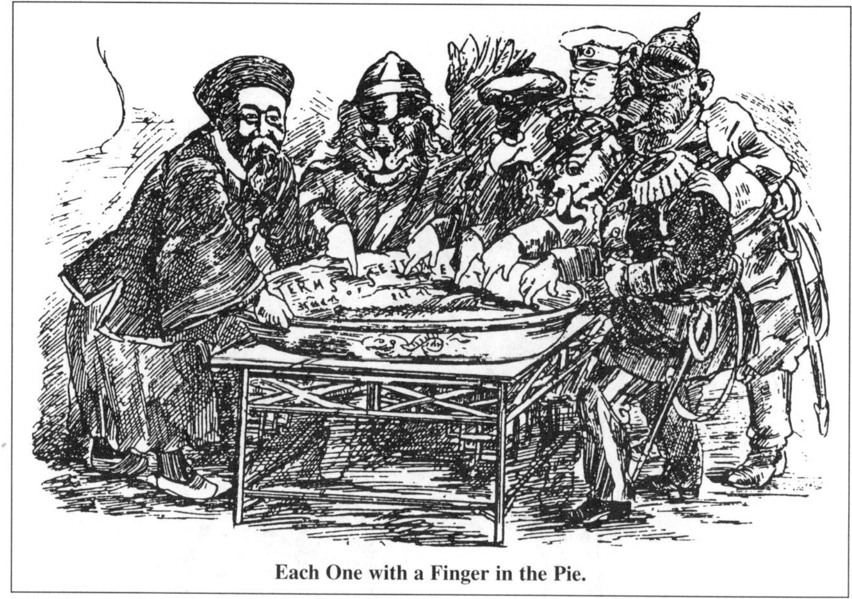

Each One with a Finger in the Pie.

LI HUNG CHANG: Come on, friends, put your finger in the pie and — then chop, chop , chop each others throats.

Figure 5.36 *Hindi Punch.*

meaning "fathead" in French had no equivalent in Japanese. It is impossible to dismiss entirely the likelihood of a connection with the enormously celebrated cartoon of King Louis-Philippe as a pear drawn by Honoré Daumier in 1831 (Figure 5.40). Daumier and his editor were imprisoned for this drawing. Nevertheless, the lasting fame of this cartoon was indicated by the fact that in 1906, the French caricature expert Paul Gaultier wrote "We are no longer in the time in which the drawings of Daumier could (cause) a band of frenzied caricaturists (to) lead a mad dance around the 'pear'."[95] Although it had its own long-standing traditions, Japanese cartooning was immensely influenced by European, particularly British, cartoons and periodicals such as *Punch.*[96] Japanese art students had been studying European traditions since the advent of the Dutch.[97] This influence was a two-way exchange; Thomas Heine, for example, was greatly influenced by Japanese woodblock prints.[98]

Li Hongzhang's vacillation during the Boxer crisis, or rather his attempts to keep away from Beijing, the centre of the storm, were depicted with

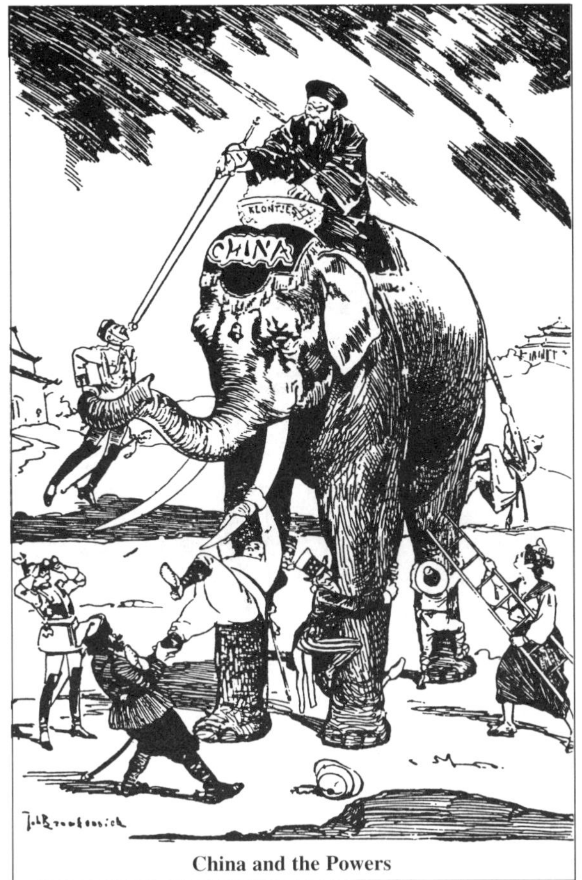

China and the Powers

LI HUNG CHANG: "You may all come: I have sugar for everyone."

Figure 5.37 *Amsterdammer.*

evident sympathy by American, British and Japanese cartoonists. The *Westminster Gazette* portrayed Li's dilemma very nicely with a cartoon of Li as Hamlet bearing the caption "To box or not to box, that is the question."[99] In the 22 June edition of the *Chicago Daily News*, a cartoon appeared showing that his calculated self-interest was a characteristic he could as well have acquired from American politicians on his recent tour as developed home-grown for political survival (Figure 5.41). A Japanese cartoon from *Marumaru Shimbun* of 7 July shows "The Hesitation of Grandpa Li." It depicts the aged Li standing on Southern China and looking at Northern China saying "I

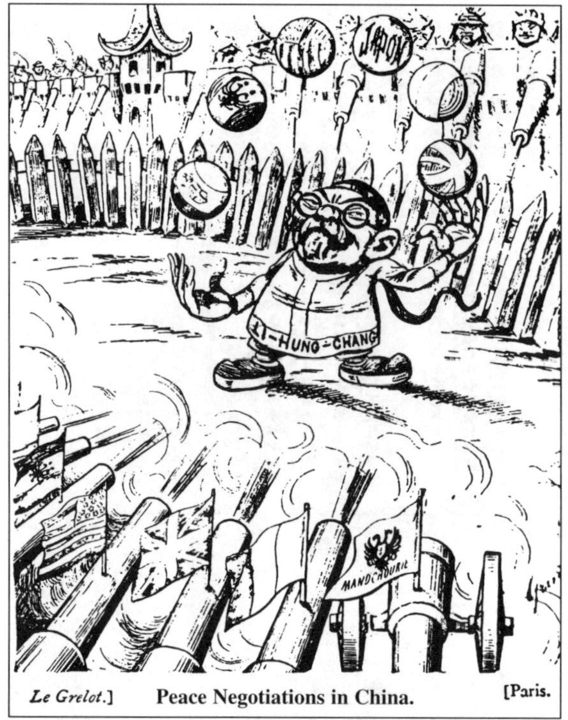

Le Grelot.] **Peace Negotiations in China.** [Paris.

Figure 5.38 *Le Grelot*, Paris (1900).

heard all the commotion and hurried to this point but considering my own safety it seems that its better to observe the situation from where I am" (Figure 5.42).

Other aspects of Li's manoeuvring characterised with sympathy rather than antagonism were his desire to make the most for his country when playing at a disadvantage for very high stakes (Figure 5.43) and his capacity for avoiding action and publicity when expedient. A cartoon by Henri Somme of *Le Rire* shows Li at his writing desk under the caption "What Li Hung Chang is doing at this very minute." It reads "How pleasant it is to come back to the avocation of belle lettrist after the tumult of politics: at the moment I am translating Monsieur Octave Mirbeau's *Le Jardin des Supplices*." Somme's choice of this author was particularly interesting; the work was a topical one distinguished by its bloodthirstyness. Mirbeau was a

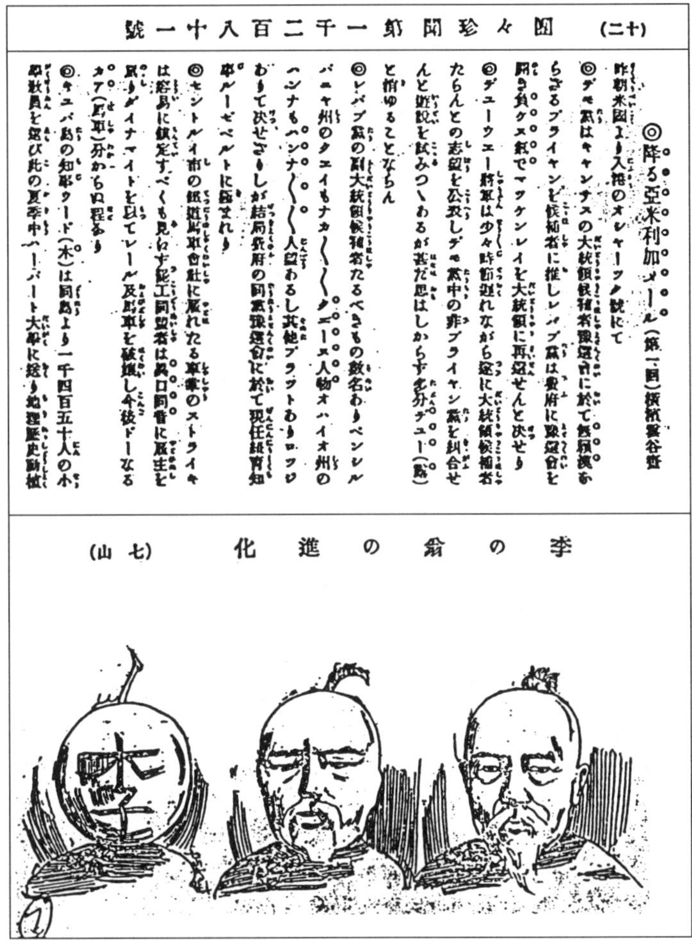

團々珍聞 第一千二百八十一號 (十二)

◎降る亞米利加メール(第一回)横濱鬱谷杏

昨朝米國より入港のオレヤーツク號にて

◎デモ黨はキャンサスの大統領候補者撰擧會に於て無頼漢あらざるブライヤンを候補者に推しレパブ黨は費府に撰擧會を開き負ケヌ氣でマツケンレイを大統領に再選せんと決せり

◎デユーウエー將軍は少々時節遅れながら遂に大統領候補者たらんとの志望を公表しデモ黨中の非ブライヤン黨を糾合せんと遊説を試みつゝあるが甚だ思はしからず名分デユー(駄)と消ゆることならん

◎レパブ黨の副大統領候補者たるべきもの數名ありペンシルバニヤ州のクエイもナカ〳〵クエー〳〵人物オハイオ州のヘンナもヘンナ〳〵人物あるし其他ブラツトありロツジありて決せざりしが結局費府の同黨撰擧會に於て現任紐育知事ルーゼベルトに極まれり

◎セントルイ市の鐵道馬車會社に雇れたる車掌のストライキは容易に鎮定すべくも見えず罷工同盟者は異口同音に雇主を罵りダイナマイトを以てレール及馬車を破壊し今後ドーなるカア(馬車)分からぬ程あり

◎キユバ島の知事ウード(木)は同島より一千四百五十人の小學教員を選び此の夏季中ハーバート大學に送り地理歴史動植

李の翁の進化 (七山)

The transformation of the character for "Pear" into its homonym "Li," being the family name of the Chinese statesman Li Hongzhang.

Figure 5.39 *Marumaru Shimbun.*

misogynist with a horror of the deception and lying of social and political life and a marked curiosity for innovations.

We now live in an era in which at least for the last ten years, European and English-speaking politicians have been so conscious of their image that they employ special make-up artists and advisors for their major television appearances. Such media image-consciousness is slowly beginning to be taken

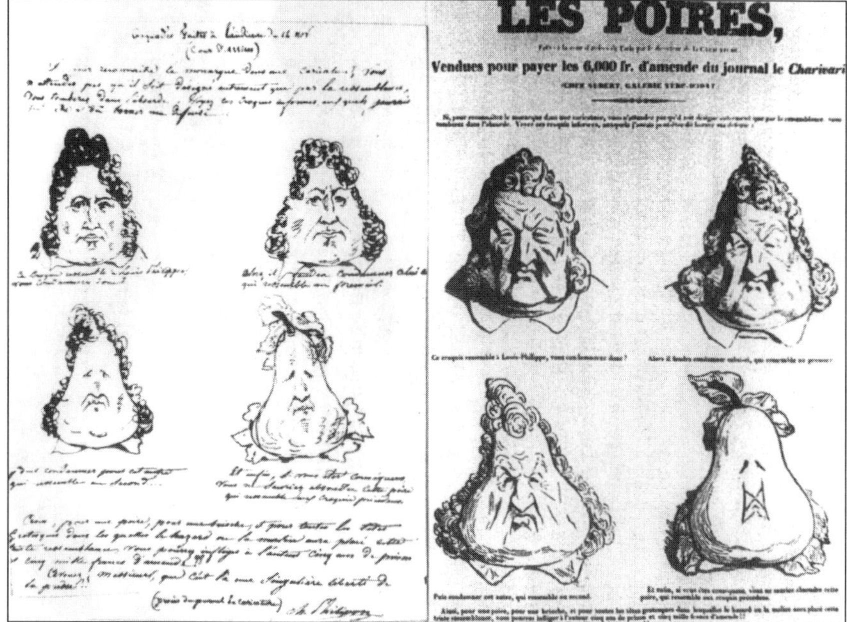

The celebrated cartoon by Daumier showing the features of King Louis-Phillipe transforming into a pear.

Figure 5.40 Daumier, "Les Poires" (1831).

up by Chinese politicians. In capturing sympathetic press coverage during his overseas tour, Li Hongzhang showed himself to be a statesman and politician far ahead of his time. The impression he left behind him after his 1896 tour was so favourable that when the Boxer War erupted, he and his initiatives were portrayed with sympathy by many cartoonists. One of the major objectives of Li's tour was to buy arms and ammunition. He was interested in all aspects of weapon manufacture as well as in various possibilities of financing weapons acquisition. His interest was remembered by a French cartoonist in the weekly *Le Rire* (Figure 5.28).

The editor of *The Times* and *The Times*' correspondents in China showed a lamentable ignorance about the political leanings and the political power of important Chinese statesmen. By contrast, the cartoonists in Japan, Russia and the Western world had followed the career and achievements of Li Hongzhang closely enough to appreciate his skill as a negotiator in the face

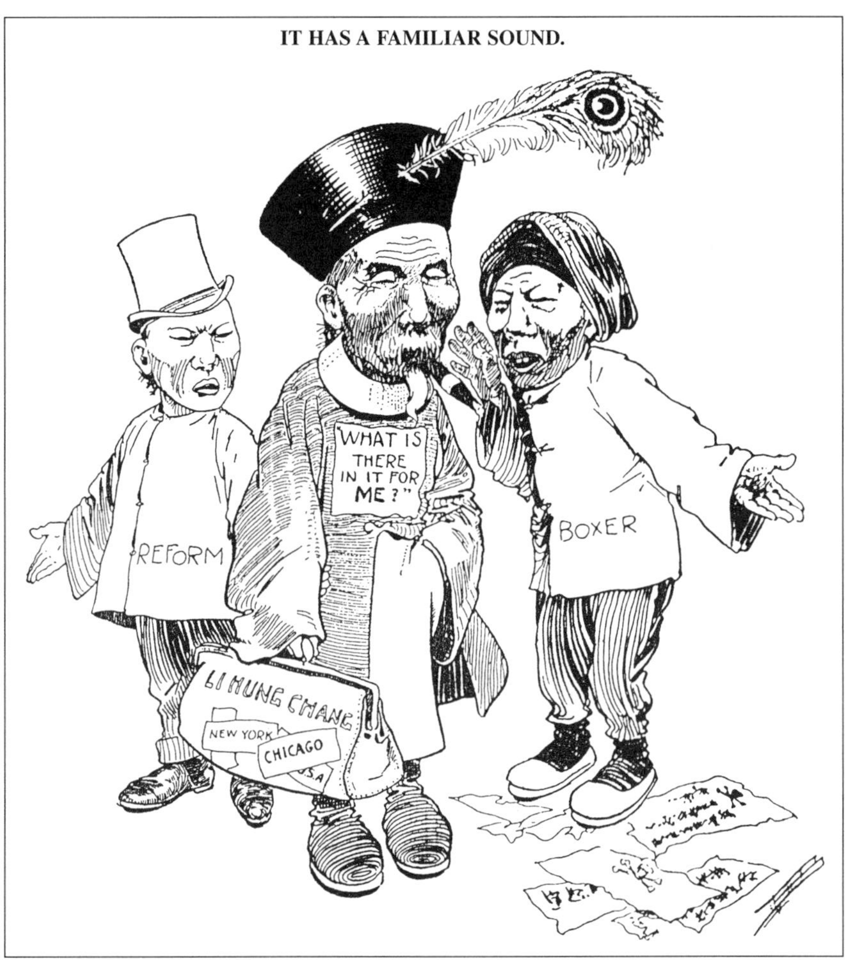

Now we are told that Li is a mercenary fraud. But we must remember that he recently made a study of our own politicians.

Figure 5.41 *Chicago Daily News.*

of apparently impossible situations for China. The cartoonists of the world went so far as to portray Li as skilful at being able to set the foreign powers against each other in the interests of China; in so doing, he was following an age-old principle of Chinese statecraft: that of setting barbarians to control barbarians. Li obviously followed Western politics and statesmen closely enough to have a real relationship with men such as Grant and Gladstone,

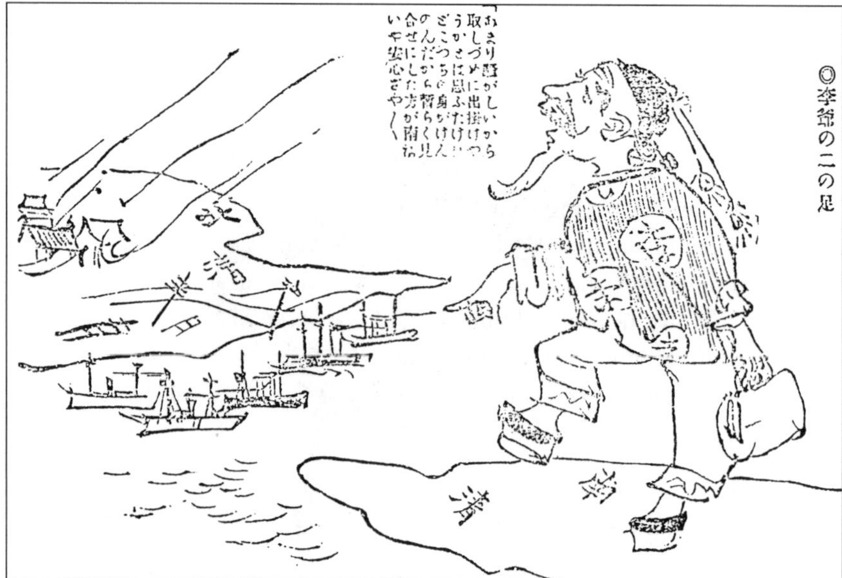

"I heard all the commotion and hurried to this point but considering my own safety it seems that it is better to observe the situation from where I am.

Figure 5.42 *Marumaru Shimbun*, "The hesitation of Grandpa Li."

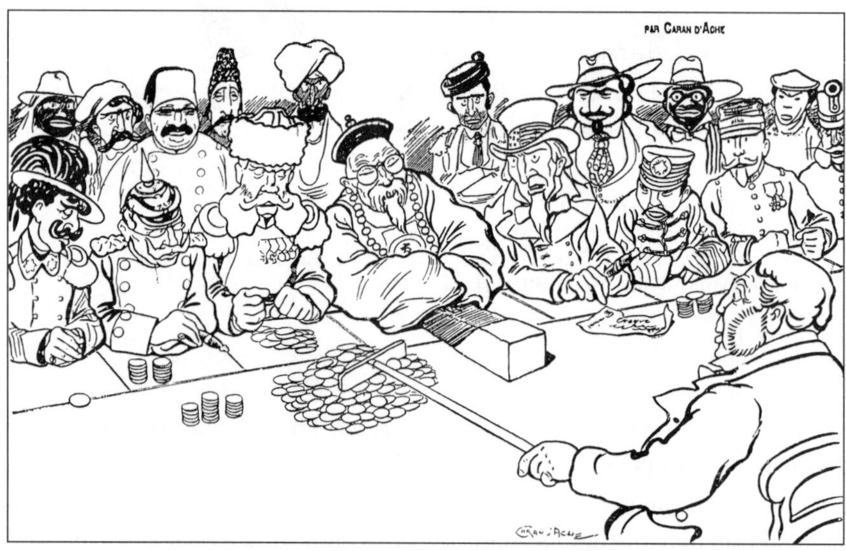

The Players: "Come, pull up your sleeves Your Excellency."

Figure 5.43 *Figaro*, "High Stakes."

not to mention the German arms manufacturer, Krupp. Despite enormous cultural and linguistic barriers, Li was able to recognise and appreciate leadership qualities in individual foreign statesmen.

The cartoonists of the day portrayed Li Hongzhang with admiration rather than following the lead of *The Times* and talking of his "profound" "ignorance" and asserting that "Falsehood, evasion, double-dealing and intrigue" were his familiar tools.[100] The readers of *The Times* included the British ruling classes and their representatives and *The Times* published no political cartoons. In terms of number and class base of people exposed to a view of Li Hongzhang showing grudging admiration, the cartoons discussed above show that at the time of the Boxer War, as China's leading statesman, Li had earned the esteem of the cartoonists of the Western world.

America: A Different Tradition, Another Response

The China crisis was used by cartoonists to display their view of international politics and — in the case of the United States — national politics. Of the cartoons in this survey, one was specifically anti-Japanese, twelve were anti-Russian, twenty-two anti-British and thirty anti-German. Interestingly, no specifically anti-French cartoons were found. The cartoonists of the United States, while contributing their perceptions of the international scene, also created a unique body of cartoons by using the China crisis as a commentary on American politics or by acting as spokesmen for specifically American public opinion on the China crisis. With hindsight, this breakdown of cartoonists' opinions on world or national politics is very revealing. It would seem that the cartoonists of the world in the year 1900 not only had the capacity to reveal the true soul of their respective nations, but had an unerring sense of the direction of international power politics which was proven accurate by the alignments of the 1914–1918 War.

The anti-Japanese, German, Russian and English cartoons typically voice the opinion that each of these countries was attempting self-aggrandisement through claims on Chinese territory. With the exception of the anti-Japanese cartoon, predictably drawn by Sokolovsky of the *Novoe Vremya*,[101] the other common factor was that cartoonists of the nation concerned were also responsible for drawing cartoons savaging that nation's imperialist ambitions in China. This was notably the case with the anti-German cartoons, 20% of which were drawn by German cartoonists for German periodicals. This critical perception of great power imperialist ambitions in China was a common one shared by cartoonists of all nationalities. Indeed, in a negative sense, it expressed the perception of the importance of undivided China in maintaining the status quo in the international balance of power. The atypical group of cartoons were those drawn with Chinese themes to reflect uniquely American national political concerns.

The attitude of American statesmen, diplomats and newspaper editors towards China was qualitatively different from that of any other Western power. There was a perception that the US was the power that would keep peace in China, that the US would not consent to the cutting up of China,[102] that the American people had no imperialist interests in China,[103] that the US had "no more right to send troops to China than Queen Victoria has to send her soldiers to St Louis if Englishmen's lives are imperiled in riots there"[104] and that the US was not really at war with China. It has already been noted that Admiral Kempf would not join the other powers in initiating hostilities against China. Although initially censured in the press for this stand, within three weeks he earned official and public support for his decision. Furthermore, the *Chicago Daily News* reported that the Admiral had refused a captured Chinese torpedo boat, which was, offered him by the British.[105] By such actions, Admiral Kempf was reflecting American recognition of China's status as a sovereign state with the right to handle its own internal affairs and its status as a fellow delegate to the Hague Peace Conference of 1899. However, as the crisis progressed, another side of American opinion began to assert itself, namely that if China refused or was unable to control the Boxers, the Americans would step in (Figure 5.44). 1900 was an election year and the Philippines War, although officially over, was still dragging on. We see in official statements, newspaper articles and cartoons the development of two strands of thinking. Imperialist involvement was undesirable but if any country had the right to step in and sort out an international crisis, it was America (Figures 5.44 and 5.45).

American journalists, cartoonists and advertisers were preoccupied with the puns on the word "Boxer" in a way that was not notable in the press of any other country involved.[106] Particularly in New York City, the summer of 1900 saw a lot of controversy about boxing as a sport. A number of deaths in the ring,[107] disputes over the considerable profits among those organising fights[108] and police fear of rowdy behaviour at fights where liquor could also be obtained, led President York of the New York Police Board to say that the board "would refuse to grant licenses for public matches when the present licenses expire on 1 May."[109] The *New York Times* published an article on 9 September showing how promoters of boxing matches planned different strategies to get around the Lewis law. What is clear from this article is that boxing was a controversial form of athleticism legislated for differently in different states. What is also clear from a survey of the pages of the *New York Evening Journal* is the immense popularity of the sport. In the month of June

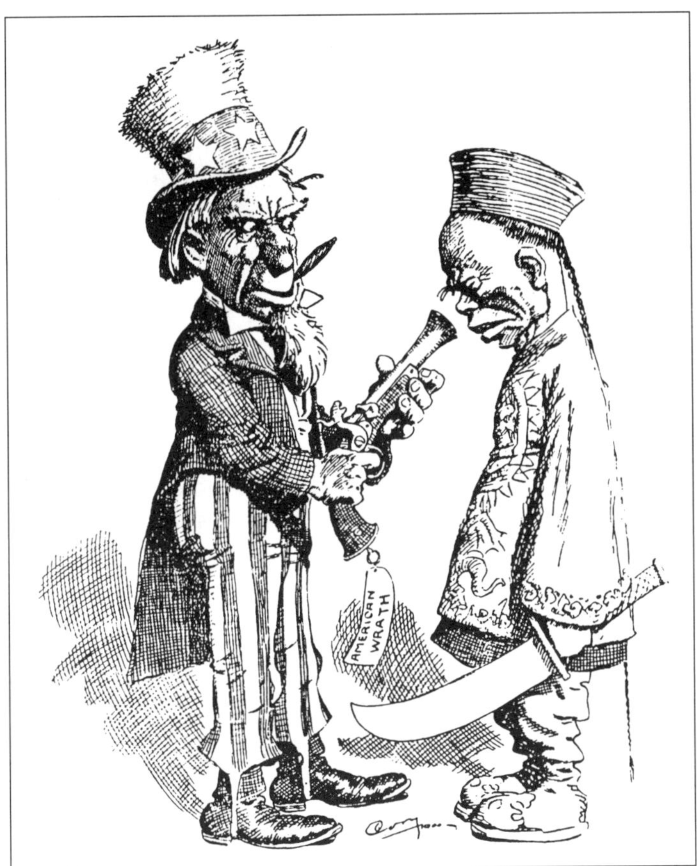

UNCLE SAM — "No, John, I don't b'leeve she's ludded, but folks do git shot up sometimes a meddlin' with empty weapons."

Figure 5.44 *New York Evening Journal.*

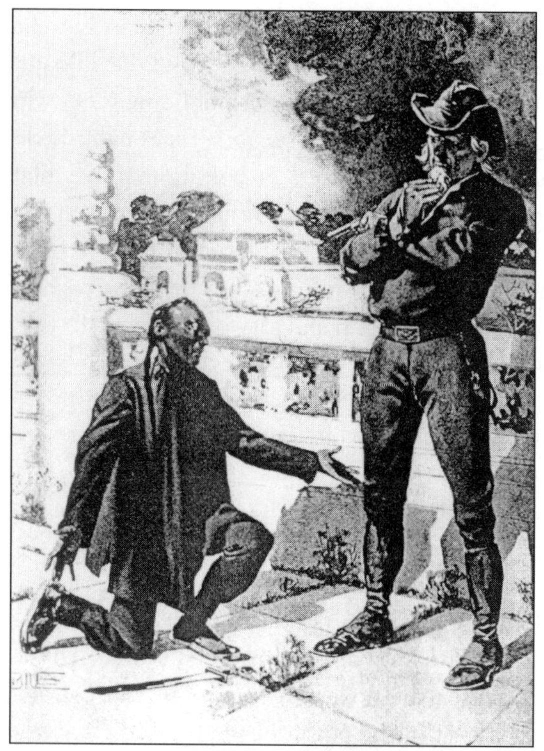

Cartoon of a Boxer at the feet of Uncle Sam, entitled "Justice or Mercy"

Figure 5.45 *Leslie's Weekly* (1900).

1900, thirteen full-column articles each illustrated and extending right across the page and two single column articles both also illustrated, gave boxing the overwhelming predominance in the sporting pages. Horse racing and rowing received similar coverage in terms of space devoted and size of illustrations but in only four issues each as opposed to the thirteen issues on boxing. The next most popular sport was cycling with three issues covering this sport on a similar scale to boxing coverage.

Reading the sports pages on the reports of fights that ended in death for one of the contenders, the clear impression is that pugilism was regarded as a manly sport and perceived by its proponents as the brightest gem in the crown of athleticism. Into this manifestation of huge public sporting interest exploded the Boxer rising. Unsurprisingly, the American press, particularly the New York press and its cartoonists, leaped at the chance to make puns on the China crisis.

Some examples from the American press:

> Chinese Foreign Office signifies its intention of handling the "Boxers" without gloves.[110]
>
> It will take a large number of muscular Christians to put the Chinese "Boxers" in a box.[111]
>
> The Chinese "Boxers" are hitting below the belt.[112]

The *Chicago Daily News* commented ruefully on 3 July that the "Chinese Boxers are on the front page every day while American heroes of the ring are lucky to get fourteen lines in an obscure corner" (Figure 5.46). The American press had reported realistically on Chinese military successes, including those of the Boxers and had even reported the links between the Boxers and other Chinese secret societies. However, it was not evident at this stage that American commentators were aware of the aspects of Boxer drill which derived from Chinese martial arts traditions or were intended to imbue its practioners with spiritual or magical powers. Nonetheless, the American press was reporting that the Boxers were winning to a culture deeply imbued with a sporting interest in the power of the fist at a contentious moment in the history of boxing. It is thus not surprising that cartoonists were quick to pit Uncle Sam against the Boxers in this sporting context. As observed on the editorial page of the *World* "Li Hung Chang has great faith in the Americans. And the Americans have considerable faith in themselves."[113] The cartoonists had no doubt that if Uncle Sam donned his gloves, he would win (Figures 5.47 and 5.48).

More than half the American cartoons present the symbols evoked by the Boxer crisis in American political contexts. Many of these were of ephemeral importance and as such, contain meaning only for those experts who have an in-depth knowledge of the American presidential campaign of 1900 or some of the great public scandals uncovered at that time by the "muckraking" "yellow press." These cartoons contain references to very specific scandals of the day such as references to the trusts, particularly to the ice trust, to the Ogden Gas company and to individuals such as Mark Hanna, leading Republican figure and political "boss"; Zebulon Reed Brockway, superintendent of the Elmira New York reformatory; President McKinley,

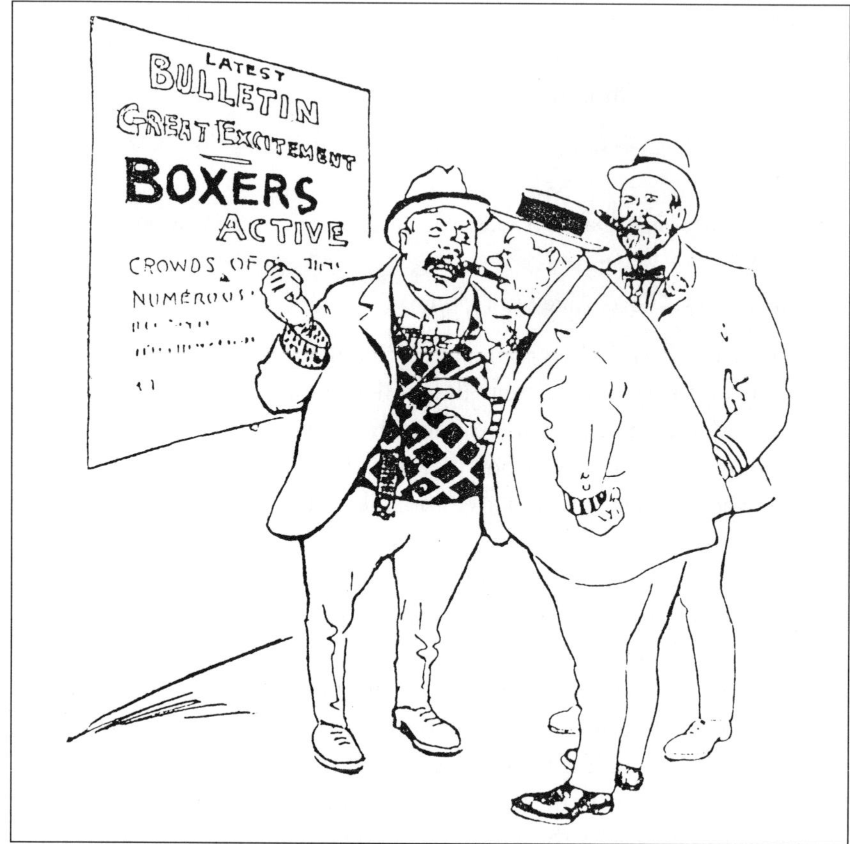

City Father to Brother Alderman — "What's dis? Somebody giving a boxing show in town without sending us any passes?"

Figure 5.46 *Chicago Daily News.*

David Bennett Hill, Senator of New York and Boss Croker of Tammany Hall.[114]

Why should this be so, why were American cartoonists the only group to present ephemeral events and personalities of national politics in the context of the symbolism associated with the Boxer rising, remains a complex question. To see in this a form of Orientalism, would be to charge the issue with elements alien to the motivation of the cartoonists of the day. We have noted the penchant of cartoonists for looking for powerful identity tag symbols. We

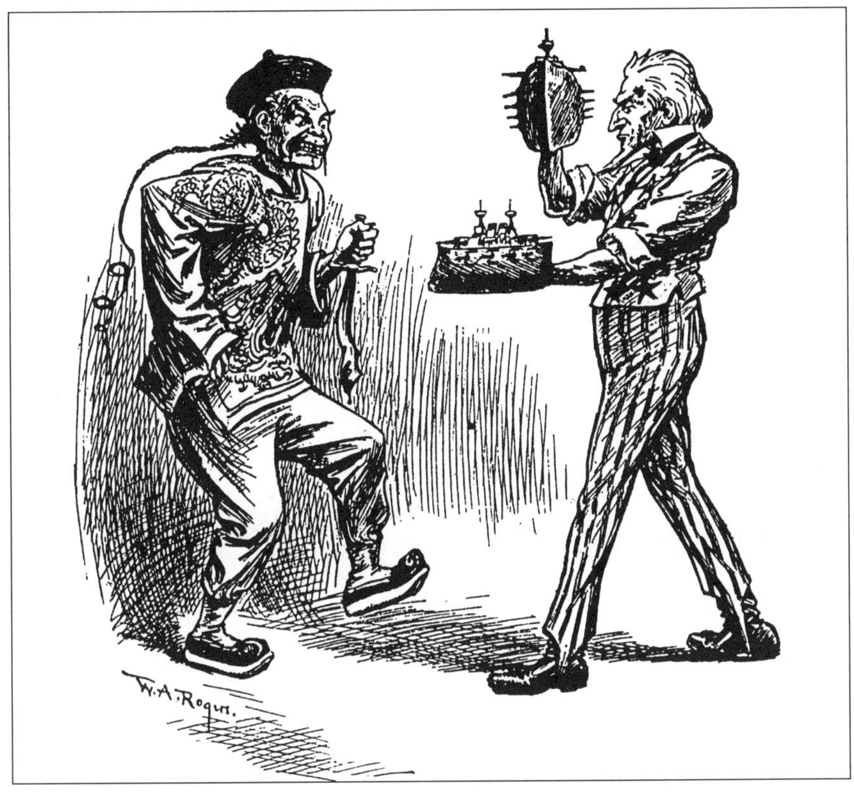

THE BOXERS

UNCLE SAM (to the obstreporous Boxer). "I occasionally do a little boxing myself."

Figure 5.47 *Harper's Weekly.*

have also noted a similarity of response to the China crisis by international cartoonists. However, to explain this particularly parochial trend in American cartoons, we must look to the differences in American official policy and public opinion with regard to China. The history of America's relations with China until 1900 contains about-faces quite unlike the parallel history of any European power in the same period. Whatever negative factors there had undoubtedly been,[115] a notable characteristic of American trade relations with China was an evident respect for its status as a sovereign power relative to the very evident lack of such respect on the part of Britain, Germany and France. In marked contrast to the leading newspapers in Britain, American

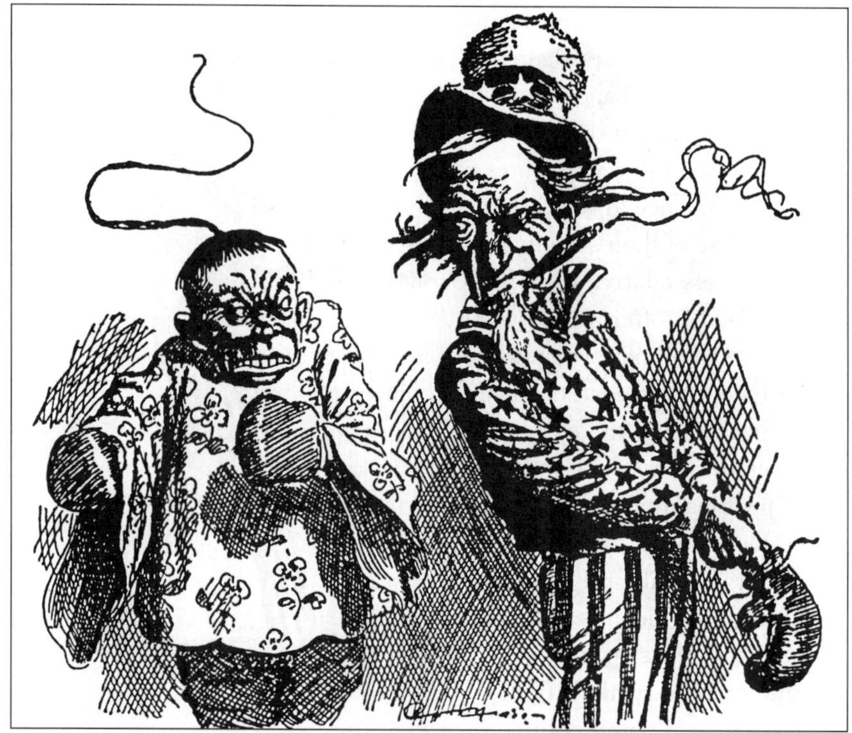

UNCLE SAM: " 'Boxer,' hey! Well, don't forget that we don't raise nothin' but heavy-weight champeens in Ameriky."

Figure 5.48 *New York Evening Journal.*

newspapers showed an ability to analyse the Chinese political situation in terms of Chinese political figures and their influence and other factors in the Chinese domestic situation. Such analysis was factual and unaccompanied by any form of emotive language. At the same time, we have noted a peculiarly Yankee tendency to seize on the sporting puns associated with the Yihetuan, commonly translated as the Society of the Righteous or Harmonious Fists. This reflected a perceived unity of symbolism in the coincidence of the Boxer rising with the contention surrounding an extremely popular American sport that same summer.

Politics is about power. The Americans as a nation were still defining themselves in opposition to the "older" "imperialist" nations whose problems they saw as being a consequence of the injustice of those nations' territorial ambitions. At the same time, American politics itself was as well represented by ruthless and corrupt figures in power as by those embodying truth and justice. Those newspapers containing cartoons at the turn of the last century were by no means in the majority. Many conservative newspapers were still refusing to publish any pictures of any kind. Thus in addition to their eye catching influence as we know it today, cartoons were the more striking in 1900 because of their scarcity and the scarcity of any graphic material at all in newspapers relative to the case today. The Boxers were responsible for foreign deaths, often in most unpleasant circumstances. Despite this, the cartoonists of all nations drew more cartoons showing China as a victim of unjust European greed in the name of humanity and civilisation than cartoons showing China as the evil beast. Thus the graphic symbols of the Boxer rising; clothing, weaponry, the figure of the Empress Dowager who had fought to keep China intact, the dragon, even the cangue, a Chinese instrument of punishment similar to the stocks used in Britain, all these symbols came ready to hand to describe the use and abuse of power in the domestic American political scene. Violence, corruption and the abuse of power in America were equated with the same factors in China. For the cartoonists to be able to use specific graphic symbols from the Chinese context to make these points about American power politics, they knew they could also rely on a reservoir of knowledge about China in the mind of the American public.

Figure 5.49, for example, captioned "The Boxer of Politics" drawn by T. E. Powers for the *World* shows the defeat of David B. Hill's plans and hopes to dominate the New York State Democratic Convention in September 1900 by Boss Crocker of Tammany Hall. Crocker's ruthless outmanoeuvring of Hill typified a type of American politics and this very type could be conveyed by reference to the parallel ruthlessness of the Boxers who beheaded their victims and carried the heads on sharpened poles.[116] David Bennett Hill was unpopular with the cartoonist W. A. Rogers and Figure 5.50 shows Hill made to look anguished and rather sheepish at the same time wearing the clothing of a humbler Chinese (as opposed to the well-known Mandarin's gown) and carrying a cangue.[117] A cangue looked just as Rogers has illustrated it. Another characteristic of the cangue was that the offender had to parade the streets wearing it and that the crime for which the wearer was being punished was written clearly on the cangue itself. Readers of *Harper's Weekly* were so familiar with illustrations of Chinese life that they would have seen at least

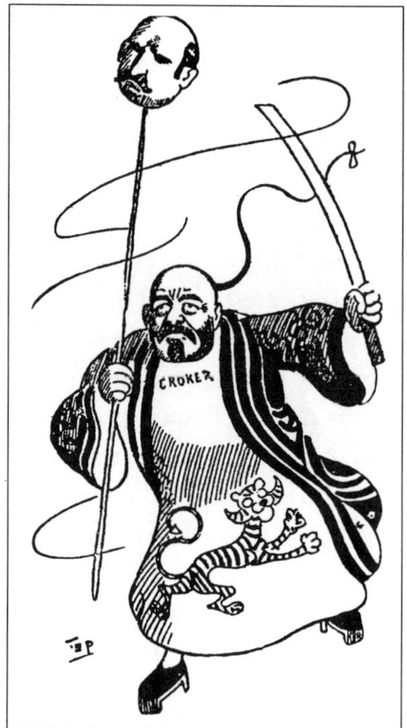

The Boxer of Politics

Figure 5.49 *New York World.*

some of these associations in Rogers' cartoon otherwise the cartoon would have been meaningless and therefore unacceptable qua cartoon. A last example of the international political scene related to national American interests, shows a number of international political leaders pulling at Mark Hanna, Republican boss and asking him to get them another term of office (Figure 5.51).

In summary, America was unique at this time in respect of the politics surrounding the sport of pugilism and in respect of public, official and military recognition of China as a sovereign state. American cartoonists had proven the extent of their power when they blighted the careers of Tweed and Hanna, among others. Despite the ferocity and efficacy of the cartoons drawn in the heat of savage political campaigns, freedom of the press for these cartoonists in America was a reality as it was not in contemporary France, Germany, Russia or Japan. Moreover, American cartoonists came from a

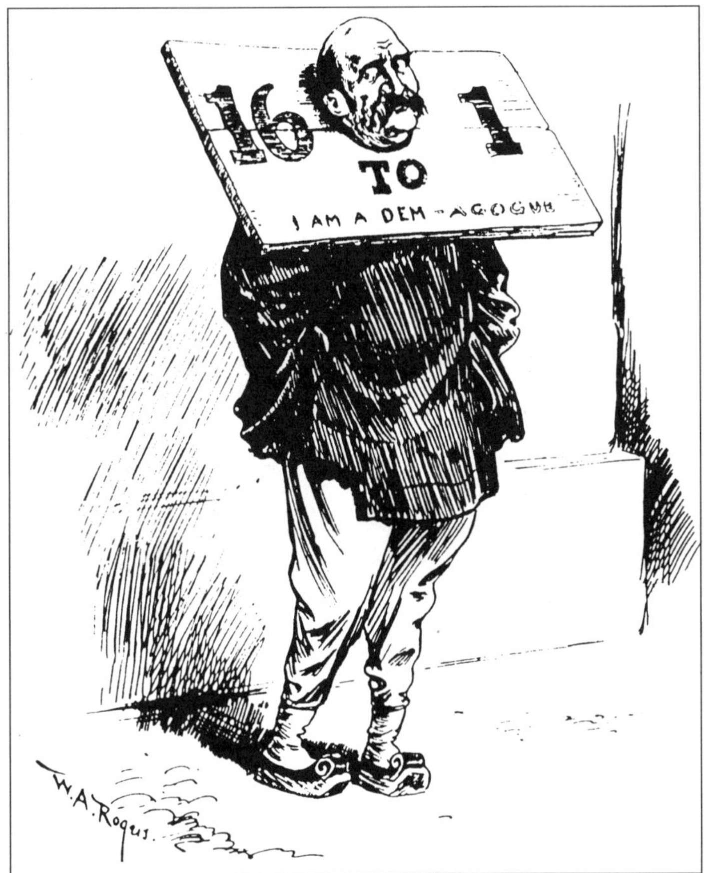

A Victim of Circumstances.

Figure 5.50 *Harper's Weekly.*

younger tradition looking to all kinds of sources for symbols sufficiently powerful to arm their drawings of the domestic political scene, a scene so different from European political life that it did require innovations in the armoury of the cartoonist. American missionary involvement in China had attracted a huge following, a public unlikely to view China over-favourably. In these contexts then, American cartoonists could expect a resonance from their public when they used symbols evoking the situation in China. British, French, German, Russian or Japanese cartoonists with their respective

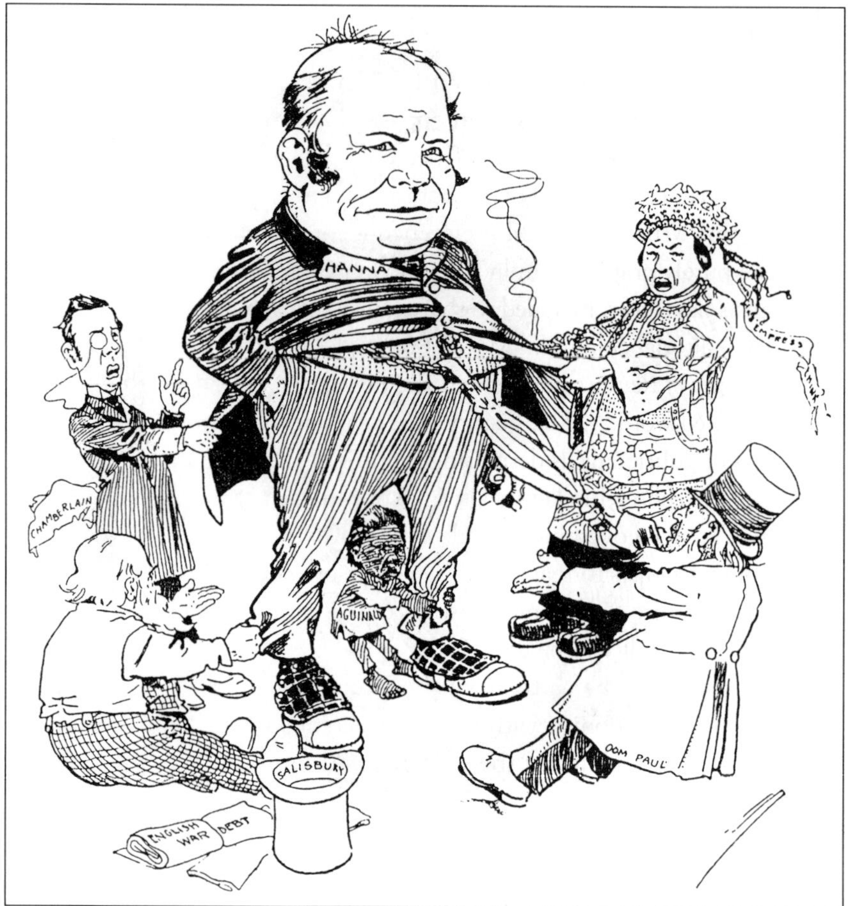

CROWD (in unison) — "Can't you do something in the way of another term for me, too?"

Figure 5.51 *Chicago Daily News.*

differing official and public attitudes to China, to the sport of boxing and to the tradition of domestic political cartooning and its relationship with authority, could not and did not attempt to use the graphic symbols brought onto the page by the Boxer rising as commentary on domestic power politics. Thus we see that while the cartoonists had some attitudes in common irrespective of their nationality, they also reflected some variations in official and public conceptions of China generally and the Boxer rising in particular.

Cartoons as Art

For the purposes of this discussion, it is not necessary to analyse the cartoon as a form of graphic art in itself, in opposition to the fine arts[118] or as a new direction in the "appreciation of the common man."[119] This survey has covered a great cross section of cartoonists working at the turn of the century. Though this writer's personal preference is for the work of Thomas Heine from the purely graphic standpoint, enough examples of the work of other cartoonists have been included so that readers may make up their own minds.

In an editorial column in May 1900, W. T. Stead the controversial editor of the *Review of Reviews* pointed out the power of a political cartoon relative to the printed word.[120] The history of American cartooning contains many examples of politicians as despairing victims of the cartoonist's pen.[121] The history of the censorship laws relating to drawings in print testifies to the fear successive French governments had of the power of the political cartoon. The ability of cartoonists to teach us to see a person anew and then see him as a ridiculous creature[122] is a unique aspect of the cartoonist's art. However it is not this aspect that will be discussed.

In his study of the cartoons of the Franco-Prussian War, Reshef shows how a group of cartoonists with nothing in common reacted similarly to the shock of war. Coupe linked the fact that cartoons were "consumer goods" published for their sales appeal with the proposition that cartoons thus constitute a valuable guide to the climate of contemporary public opinion. As an extension of this, he wrote that cartoons "do speak with a surprisingly unanimous voice."[123] What is of interest is that there was a consonance between the corpus of cartoons discussed in this chapter and the tastes, ideas and sentiments of the time, not merely appreciable as such in the work of a group of cartoonists of one nationality, but globally.

The unique ability of the political cartoonist as an artist lies in the production of graphic comments on political events which are remarkable in being so closely in tune with the feelings of the societies in which they live. The critical sting of the cartoonists' pens was such that, despite their being sent to jail in Japan, Germany, Russia and France, they reached a public which showed its accord with them directly in buying the newspapers or periodicals for which they drew. Whether or not this public had views on China, the cartoonists whose work they chose to read were advocating consistent and strong views on the China crisis. This same public, whether in America, Germany, France or Japan, contained many people who could not or did not vote for the government of the day. These governments feared the power of the political cartoon, but even when bribed, jailed or working for suppressed publications, the cartoonists continued to draw and the periodicals continued to sell. Thus whether the cartoonists reflected already existing public opinion or moulded that opinion on specific issues, there was a demonstrable consonance between them and their publics in respect of the sales figures of the newspapers and periodicals for which they worked. This consonance was so marked that, as we have seen, cartoonists in 1900 were drawing national sentiments in such a way that analysed as a whole, the remarkable fact emerges that the cartoons of the China crisis in 1900 presaged not only the outcome of the China crisis but also the Russo-Japanese War and the great power alignments in the 1914–1918 War — or in the case of the United States, its initially non-interventionist policy in that war.

It is this ability to fit the spirit of the times into a pungent unity of words and pictures with such prescience that is the most unique and interesting aspect of the cartoonist's art. As immensely popular, even notorious celebrities, the cartoonists operating in 1900 had a national and international reputation. Their feel of the political pulse was unerring, the expression of their art had the power to make governments tumble and individual politicians quail. How did they see the issues involved in the Boxer rising? How did they use this unerring political instinct, considered by this writer as the most powerful expression of their art, to create an image of China during a confrontation unprecedented in the history of any country as it faced the unwanted advances of the West? We have seen that their overwhelming response was to savage the behaviour of the invading powers; to ridicule their hypocrisy in using the words "civilisation" and the ideas of Christianity while selling arms to China; to attack the greed which was the basis of imperialism; and to represent Chinese political moves and a particular Chinese leader, Li Hongzhang, with sympathy. There was an overwhelming consensus that great power rivalry would lead to eventual self-destruction while the smiling Chinese figure looked on knowing that he would eventually be rid of the invaders. As it turned out, the cartoonists of the world had predicted correctly. China, unlike Africa, was never sliced like a melon, carved up like a pie or offered to an inferior European power as a tasty morsel of sausage.

In exercising that aspect of their art which kept so close to contemporary public sentiments or which moulded public opinion, cartoonists drew what would eventually come to pass. As W. T. Stead said, "a caricaturist with his pencil employs a language universally understood."[124] Stead also pointed out the power of caricaturists to inflame bad feeling. Insofar as China was concerned, only two savagely inflammatory anti-Chinese cartoons were found in the course of this study. The headlines of the newspapers in which these cartoons appeared began to scream for vengeance when it was thought erroneously that all the foreigners in Beijing had been killed. The dissonance between these headlines and the cartoons appearing on the same day show the cartoonists' art to be the ability to seize on the events of the moment singled out by journalists and to remark on the political behaviour of their own nationals in a wider and longer arena. At the turn of the century there were exceptional cartoonists plying their art. Faced with the moral challenge posed by the nature of the war with China, they showed themselves to be artists of genius. Not for them a superficial explosion showing hordes of heathen beasts savaging helpless Europeans. Rather they gave a deeper penetrating glance at the motives of the European powers and showed some understanding of the way Chinese politicians would have to deal with those powers. In the ephemeral political cartoon often seen as of slight importance, we observe that degree of serious analysis which gave cartoonists the status of political seers. In the summer of 1900 they reached the apogee of their art.

Cartoons and War

The cartoons drawn of the clash between China and the eight invading Powers in 1900 are atypical, resembling neither those of the Franco-Prussian War nor those depicting the great twentieth century wars. Unlike the frequent use of the ape as beast by American cartoonists to depict the Japanese after Pearl Harbour, there is not one instance of the Chinese being portrayed as bestial apes or monkeys. While there are a number of cartoons using the dragon as a symbol for China, the majority of these are drawn if not with sympathy for the dragon, with at least some understanding that the dragon having been stirred, it is natural and inevitable that it will awaken.[125] In any case the dragon was the symbol of Imperial China as the lion was of royal

Britain. There are no cartoons depicting Chinese giants in the sense of relentless hulks tearing to shreds everything in sight.

Talking of the propaganda which appeared on both the American and Japanese home fronts in 1941–1945, John Dower wrote:

> The war did not create the image of superman, but rather brought it to the surface — conjured it up, not from some pool of past impressions of the Japanese, but rather from the great Western reservoir of traditional images of the Other. For like the mark of the beast, in times of fear and crisis, "superman" qualities too are commonly ascribed to despised outsiders.[126]

The summer months of June, July and August 1900 were certainly times of crisis. For fifty-five days the whole world lived in fear that all the foreigners in Beijing had been killed. Why is it then that the cartoonists of this war unanimously eschewed the belittling categories of "the primitive, the child, the mentally and emotionally deficient enemy ... [those] formulaic concepts, encoded in the Western psyche and by no means reserved for [one particular enemy]"?[127] By mid-July the newspapers of the world were screaming for revenge but no corresponding cartoons evoking the barbarian image were spawned in their pages.

The cartoons of the Boxer rising represent a remarkable manifestation of the rarely heard and even more rarely publicised sentiments that this was not a just war and that "we" behaved dishonourably towards "the enemy." Cartoonists have always been the hardest hitting and often the only commentators in the vanguard, whether of domestic or international political situations.[128] In 1900 no editorials commented on the particular brutality of the Russian soldiers as we see in Figure 5.25. In 1900 no editorials spoke out in words against looting and rape the way Thomas Heine savaged the behaviour of the invading armies particularly concentrating on Germany (Figures 5.19 and 5.52). To some extent Heine was using the China crisis to criticise tendencies in Imperial Germany which he had been attacking consistently. While he was making the point that looting was the very shabby downside of the behaviour of the armies of the "civilised" world, he was also using the dog to berate the servile nature of the German public.[129] Russian cruelty was notorious during the campaign and is described in detail in the memoirs of journalists and the military men of the other Allied invading Powers. But the cartoonists hit much harder and reached a far wider audience than a passing

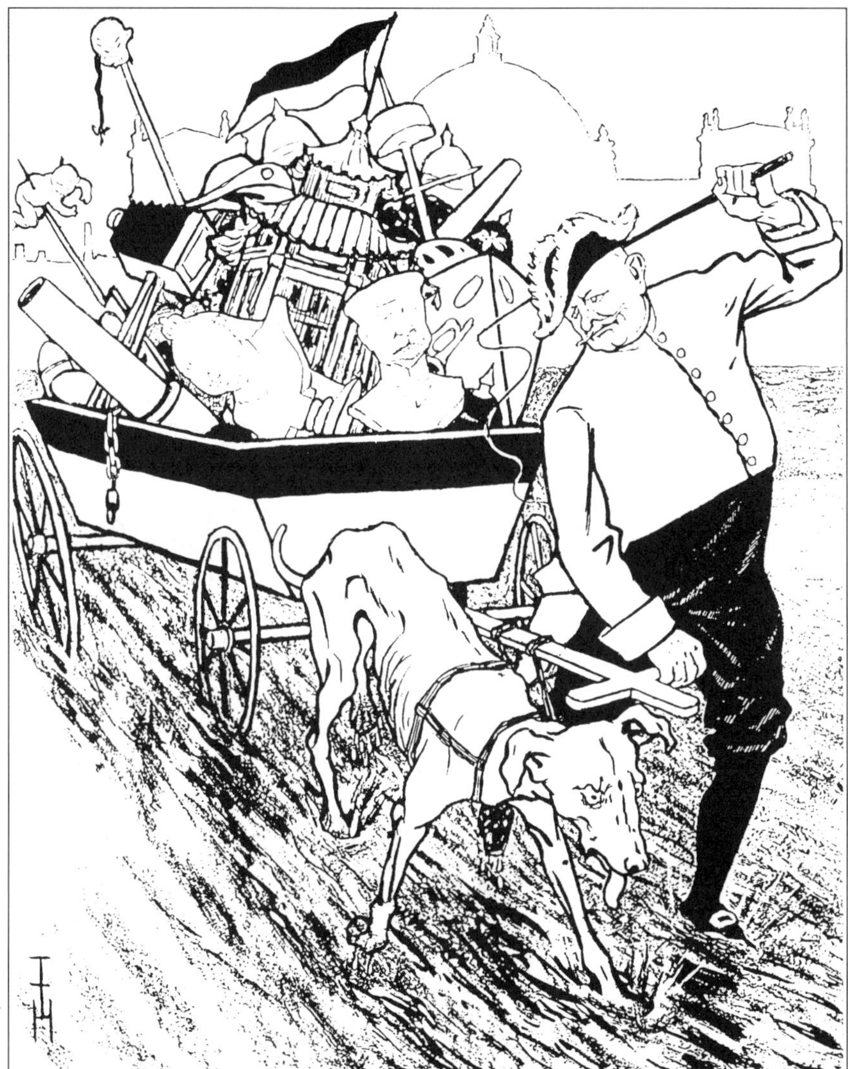

Of all dogs, the German hound is best suited as a transport animal. Burdened with the heaviest load, he will yelp a bit but quickly settle to glad service and pull the cart patiently through the thickest muck.

Figure 5.52 *Simplicissimus.*

sentence in a journalist's memoirs. Christian cruelty overshadowed them all (Figure 5.53).[130] There was one stereoscope which bore the caption "Sikhs a-lootin"[131] but no lengthy newspaper coverage of the extent of the looting and violence after the fall of Peking.[132] This brings us to another vital function of these political cartoons; their creators managed to use the cartoon to make unequivocal statements about behaviour in war, statements which would not have been permitted at that time if expressed in any other way.

A common complaint in diplomatic correspondence and in the press as the nineteenth century drew on, was that Chinese leaders refused to

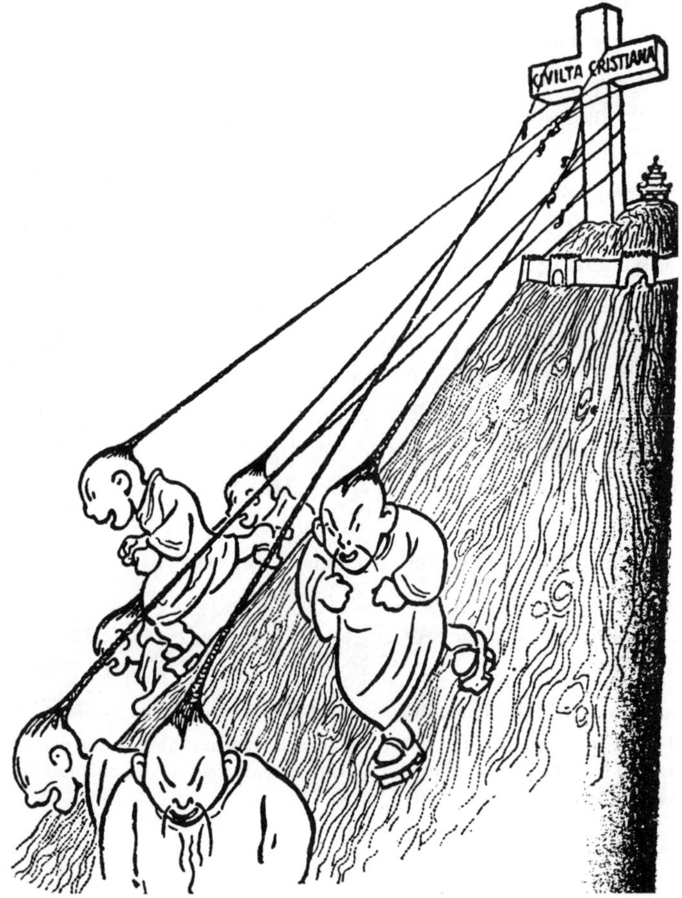

The good little Chinese make great workers!!!!!!!!

Figure 5.53 *Italia-Ride.*

acknowledge military defeat and to comport themselves at the negotiating table accordingly. One good reason for this was that in terms of the overall Empire, minor clashes won by Europeans here or there could not be taken by the Chinese as the defeat of China. Other reasons as discussed in Chapter Three were that the same events regarded by Westerners as victory, were in fact not perceived as such by the Chinese and that there were real differences between Chinese and Western military philosophy as to what constituted defeat and victory in warfare. In the case of the Boxer rising, when the invading Powers reached the Forbidden City, they found that the persons of the Emperor and the Empress Dowager had eluded them, a point that the cartoonists were quick to seize on.[133] Thus instead of being outright conquerors, the invading Powers then had to continue to negotiate with the Empress Dowager and her advisers. They were still operating undisturbed as rulers of the country and the Empress Dowager succeeded through her able advisors in moderating, to some degree, some clauses in the foreign demands for settlement after the war.

We have already noted that prescience is the most remarkable quality of a political cartoonist's art. It is suggested that the most difficult test of such prescience is the turmoil and fear engendered by war. It is further suggested that cartoonists owe the accuracy of their forecasts to the ability to use their unblinkered pens to criticise the behaviour of politicians and soldiers of their own nation or that of fellow allies. A maxim of those who would depict war more truly may be said to be "know the extent of your own inhumanity as well as that of your enemy." The cartoonists who had such knowledge were the same cartoonists who could pen drawings explaining Chinese political motivation. It is perhaps to these two qualities, the ability to see one's own defects and the ability to accept the motivation of one's enemy, that these cartoonists owed the accuracy of their judgements on the international situation as it effected China and as it was to effect Europe and America in 1914–1918.

It is also possibly because of such knowledge that these cartoonists drew cartoons not propaganda. An analysis of these cartoons does not involve the description of the words and images conjured up to transform the enemy into Other. In this sense the cartoons of the China crisis relied on already existing knowledge of China and the Chinese and added to that knowledge. By using existing knowledge to *emphasise* rather than to savage or belittle Chinese behaviour, cartoonists produced new and controversial images of foreign behaviour in China. This was art, not merely the production of propaganda in which any enemy could be substituted for the enemy now under attack by the propagandist's pen. Sam Keen wrote:

> wars come and go, but the hostile imagination has a certain standard repertoire of images it uses to dehumanize the enemy. In matters of propaganda, we are all platonists; we apply eternal archetypes to changing events.[134]

It could be argued that the extraordinary speed of an international situation in putting eight such unlikely bed-fellows together was responsible for a form of Orientalism in which the context of the China crisis gave cartoonists sufficient information to expose deeper and older antagonisms in the European arena. While this is one manifestation of their work, it is not the most important. Knowledge is power. It has been amply demonstrated that the cartoonists of the world in 1900 were able to use the entirety of their knowledge of the Boxer crisis to draw savage commentaries on the behaviour of their own compatriots. In this war, at least, the enemy was seen as having political leaders motivated by the same degree of national and self-interest as politicians anywhere in the world. In this war, knowledge of Chinese usages was transported into other political cultures as expressions of power. In this war, far from being depicted as monstrous barbarians, the Chinese were shown as being identically motivated in respect of weapons purchasing policy without the hypocrisy of the Western Christian nations (Figure 5.21). Insofar as the labels of "barbarism" and "civilisation" were concerned, there was nothing to choose between them (Figure 5.54). As for the justice or otherwise of the war, one country refused to join initial hostilities. American behaviour was consistent throughout, the Americans being the first to withdraw their troops from Beijing and the first to waive reparation payments. Thus to the attitude of the international corps of cartoonists, that in this war at least, China was a country led by people with comprehensible motivations, we can add the fact that such graphic idealism was mirrored by the actual behaviour of America.

Reflections

In the late nineteenth century, cartoonists were regarded as serious commentators whose work could set the tone of a publication. As well, cartoonists,

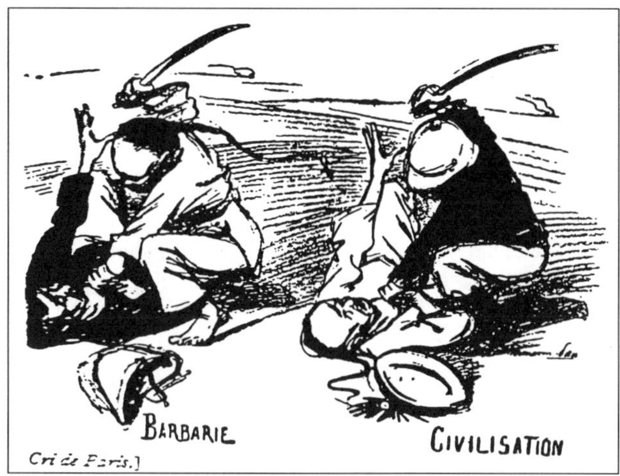

Barbarism and Civilisation

Figure 5.54 *Cri de Paris.*

editors and even printers risked heavy fines and/or jail sentences or the suppression of their periodicals in many of the countries producing cartoons included in this survey. There is a tension between the cartoonist as "betraying the spirit of the nation" and as an individual with the power to stir the conscience of the majority by representing a minority view. This tension is particularly evident in the cartoons of the China crisis. It is remarkable that the huge body of auto-critical cartoons appeared during a war in which many headlines and editorials voiced very different opinions about the Chinese. In 1900 the phenomenon of the political cartoon reaching a mass audience was a relatively recent one. It is thus probable that a proportion of the public was influenced more by cartoons, particularly those on the front page of newspapers, than was influenced by editorials. As there was still controversy over printing any pictures at all in newspapers, editors of the day had strong views about graphics.[135] As editors had more to risk, they were unquestionably highly sensitive to the power of the political cartoon.

Not only were pro-China cartoons printed right around the globe, but also editors considered some cartoons from other publications and even other languages, of such importance that they had them translated and put in prominent places in their publications.[136] The cartoonists, the "men in the truth" as they have been called,[137] were supported in this way by their own

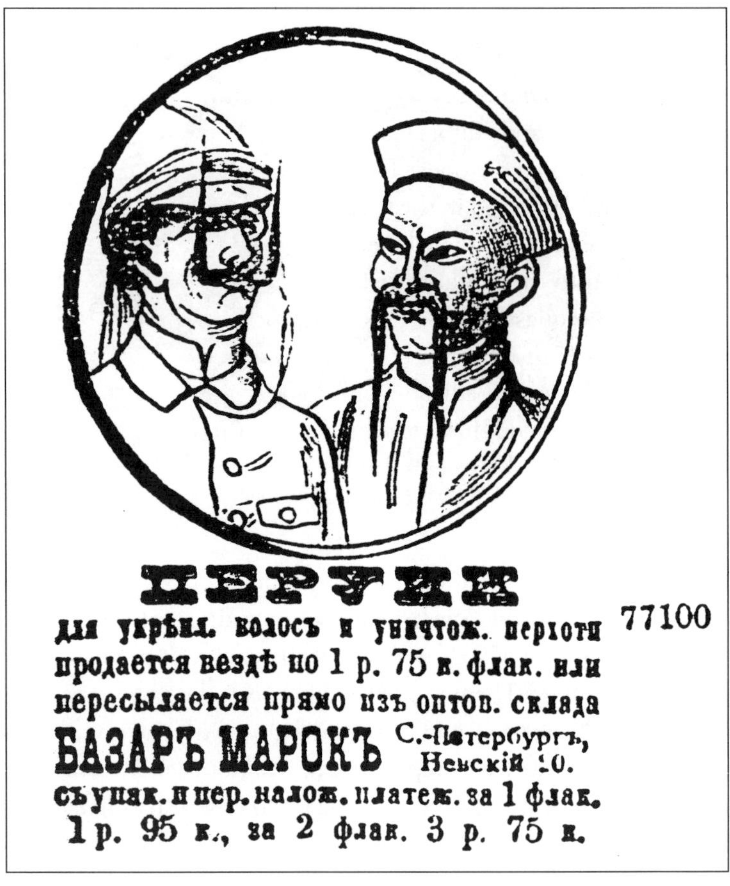

Figure 5.55 This Russian advertisement for men's hair lotion to strengthen and thicken hair appeared in the *Novoe Vremya* three times in the month of July. It is of extreme interest to see such an advertisement appearing at the height of the Boxer crisis. There were many other advertisements connected with the Boxer War (see, for example, Figure 2.10) but none of them made such a clear and witty point as this one. Chinese gentlemen used the right brand of hair oil and their moustaches were immaculate. English gentlemen had yet to see the light and use the right product and their moustaches stood on end. There may have been only one such advertisement but it underlines the point made throughout this chapter that all round the world there was a current of sympathy for China which enabled cartoonists — and it would seem — some advertisers — to portray the Chinese in a sympathetic light or even as fellow human beings.

editors and by unknown editors of other publications. It remains to be explained why these same editors wanted to publish pro-China cartoons in a paper containing inflammatory anti-China headlines. Acting in unspoken collusion, cartoonists and editors may have had different reasons for drawing or publishing pro-China cartoons. They may have done so because they were anti another power involved in the China crisis, because they were anti some aspects of European behaviour, or because they felt that a cartoon had a different function to the unillustrated written word.

Insofar as the question of where the truth lies between the cartoon and the news sheet or editorial column, what needs to be highlighted is that cartoonists drew and editors published opinions on the China crisis which would otherwise not have appeared in mass print at all. It is notable in the history of relations between China and the West that at a time when public interest and even hysteria was focused on China as never before, a body of artists and their editors working separately in completely different cultural traditions produced a commentary on events in China in which criticism of the invading Powers was a dominant voice. Whatever anti-Chinese feeling appeared in the West as a result of the Boxer rising, it is to the credit of the cartoonists of the day as well as their editors, that a majority of cartoons appeared exercising the function of expressing or moulding public opinion to portray a wronged China, the conscience of the "civilised" world.

At this point of the history of political graphics depicting war, to be enemy was not to be beast or Other. To be enemy meant simply to refuse the advances of another culture and to be self-selective of its products. The Chinese bought and used Krupp guns and they did not wish to buy and use Protestant Bibles. It is true that a part of the art of the cartoonist is to reduce the issues to shorthand symbols readily identifiable by most readers. That they bought and used Krupp guns while rejecting Christianity was not perceived by the cartoonists as inappropriate. The ultimate test of the cartoonists' vision was that these actions by China being logical choices for the Chinese, were also the very actions that saved China from being divided by the European powers. We learn from the cartoonists of the day that China was saved from such division by Allied discord. We also learn that China owed her salvation to the actions of her own politicians, armies and peasants.

Notes

1. My thanks to Professor William A. Coupe for his punctilious reading and critique of this chapter. To Professor Lucy Shelton Caswell, I am deeply indebted not only for her comments on the chapter as a whole but also for her erudition in elucidating many obscure points related to American and British history of cartooning.
2. Frédéric Régamey, *La Caricature Allemande pendant la Guerre*, Berger-Lerrault, Paris, 1921, p. 7.
3. There has been a great deal written in the literature on the difference between cartoon and caricature. See, for example, L. H. Streicher, "On a Theory of Political Caricature," *Comparative Studies in Society and History*, Vol. 9, No. 4, July 1967, p. 431; I. R. Stuart, "Iconography of Group Personality Dynamics: Caricatures and Cartoons," *The Journal of Social Psychology*, Vol. 46, 1964, pp. 147 and 155, W. A. Coupe, "Observations on a Theory of Political Caricature," *Comparative Studies*, op cit., Vol. 11, 1969, pp. 87–88. For the purposes of this study, Goldstein's definition of political caricature is apt. See R. J. Goldstein, *Censorship of Political Caricature in Nineteenth Century France*, Kent State University Press, Ohio, 1989, pp. ix–x.
4. There is a difference of opinion in the literature about the degree to which readers do actually grasp the cartoonist's message. See D. Brinkman, "Do Educational Cartoons and Editorials Change Opinions?" and L. M. Carl, "Educational Cartoons Fail to Catch Many Readers," *Journalism Quarterly*, Vol. 45, No. 4, 1968. On balance, I would agree with T. M. Kemnitz, "The Cartoon as a Historical Source," *The Journal of Inter-disciplinary History*, Vol. 4, No. 1, 1973, p. 84 who notes that because cartoons convey their messages "quickly and pungently" they are "more likely to get (their) point across than other printed means of communication." I would also agree with Kemnitz's assertion that more people understand the cartoon than read the editorials. For a view of the relationship between interpretive skills of the reader and the intention of the cartoonist see M. J. Medhurst and M. A. Desousa, "Political Cartoons as Rhetorical Form: A Taxonomy of Graphic Discourse," *Communication Monographs*, Vol. 48, September 1981, pp. 217–218 and p. 205 for a view of the relationship between the effectiveness of a particular cartoon and audience ability to comprehend and participate.
5. While the twentieth century has seen the emergence of women cartoonists, noted particularly for their commentaries on social and personal relationships, at the turn of the last century there were no women cartoonists publishing political cartoons in major national newspapers.
6. Goldstein, op cit., p. ix.
7. Ouriel Reschef, *Guerre, Mythes et Caricature. Au Berceau d'une Mentalité Française*, Presses de la fondation nationale des sciences politiques, Paris, 1984, pp. 128–

147 has written a particularly thought-provoking chapter on the relationship of the individual cartoonist to the collective spirit of his time.

8. Sam Keen, *Faces of the Enemy. Reflections of the Hostile Imagination*, Harper and Row, San Francisco, 1986 and John W. Dower, *War Without Mercy. Race and Power in the Pacific War*, Pantheon Books, New York, 1986, both rely heavily on graphics and propaganda posters as well as the work of cartoonists to explain how perceptions of the enemy were formulated.
9. As shown in Chapter One, this was the emotive language used by the leading British newspaper *The Times* in its editorial columns during the China crisis.
10. S. C. Miller, *The Unwelcome Immigrant. The American Image of the Chinese 1785–1882*, University of California Press, California, 1969. R. McClellan, *The Heathen Chinee: A Study of American Attitudes Toward China*, Ohio State University Press, Columbus, 1971.
11. Virginia Coutes, *The Kaiser*, Collins, London, 1963, p. 177. On 27 July 1900, the Kaiser made a speech to the marines departing for China. He exhorted them to open the door for culture, "You must know my men that you are about to meet a crafty, well-armed, cruel foe! Meet him, beat him! Give no quarter! Take no prisoners! Kill him when he falls into your hands! Even as, a thousand years ago, the Huns under their king Attila made such a name for themselves as still resounds in terror through legend and fable. So may the name of Germans resound through Chinese history a thousand years from now."
12. See Keen, op cit. and Dower, op cit. See also R. A. Berger, *Myth and Stereotype: Images of Japan in the German Press and in Japanese Self-Representation*, Verlag, Peter Lang, Frankfurt am Main, 1990.
13. D. Kunzle, "Between Broadsheet Caricature and 'Punch': Cheap Newspaper Cuts for the Lower Classes in the 1830's," *Art Journal*, Vol. 43, 1983, p. 343.
14. L. P. Curtis, *Apes and Angels. The Irishman in Victorian Caricature*, Smithsonian Institute Press, Washington, 1971, pp. 62 and 96, points out that many cartoonists were marginal to the society in which they lived and worked in the sense that they were Germans in America or Scots in London. The celebrated Caran d'Ache (Emanuel Poiré) whose nom de plume means "pencil" in Russian and whose work will be discussed below, was born in Moscow in 1859. He died in Paris in 1909.
15. A Viennese cartoon was reprinted in *Nichiroko shinpo* of 1 November 1900 and other unattributed foreign cartoons appeared in the same newspaper on 22 July and 17 August 1900.
16. Paul A. Cohen, *History in Three Keys. The Boxers as Event, Experience and Myth.* Columbia University Press, New York, 1997, pp. xi–xviii.
17. Frederick A. Scharf and Peter Harrington, *The Boxer Rebellion. China, 1900. The Artists' Perspective*, Greenhill Books, London, 2000, contains many pictures published in newspapers re-worked from sketches sent by artists in China.

18. Jeffrey Wasserstrom, "The Boxers as Symbol: The Use and Abuse of the Yihetuan," unpublished paper 1984, quoted in Cohen, op cit., p. xii.
19. W. A. Coupe, "The German Cartoon and the Revolution of 1848," *Comparative Studies*, op cit., Vol. 9, No. 2, January 1967, p. 160.
20. A number of writers have made the point that as cartoons gained a wider and larger audience, they sacrificed something of the impact of their art as the cartoons had to be acceptable to this bigger buying public. See Kemnitz, op cit., p. 88; see also J. J. Appel, "Ethnicity in Cartoon Art," *Cartoons and Ethnicity*, The 1992 Festival of Cartoon Art, Ohio State University Libraries, 1992, p. 24 and p. 40. My thanks to Professor Lucy Shelton Caswell for drawing my attention to this reference. I would like to add that cartoons had to be not only "acceptable" to this wider audience but also understandable.
21. M. H. Spielmann, "Cartoons from 'Punch'" (1906) quoted in Kemnitz, op cit., p. 81.
22. There were only three cartoons depicting the Empress Dowager, Cixi, in this sample. All three showed her repelling the advances of the foreign countries trying to grab a slice of China.
23. In the summer of 1900 news of the Boxer rising supplanted news of the Boer War. It gave rise to screaming headlines and immense coverage of China in terms of space, variety of articles and pictorial material in all the dailies, weeklies and monthlies in Britain, Europe, America, Russia and Japan. Many papers issued special China supplements.
24. See cartoon in *Novoe Vremya*, 4 October 1900, p. 10 depicting a physician in a dunce's cap administering to a reclining Chinese patient from a huge bottle marked "opium." The caption reads, "The first physician: It's the stomach. Take opium, as much as possible. Buy it only at John Bull's drug store."
25. Streicher, op cit.
26. Reshef, op cit., p. 128. He notes that "la question méthodologique majeure réside dans le passage de l'individu au collectif, de l'inconscient de l'artiste aux répresentations collectives. L'artiste n'est pas le seul à projeter dans l'ouevre désirs refoulés et fantasmes: cette même projection, si l'on en croit certains psychologues de l'art, est aussi l'une des raisons profondes de la jouissance du spectateur," p. 131.
27. See Roger R. Thompson, "Military Dimensions of the 'Boxer Uprising' in Shanxi, 1898–1901," pp. 294–297, in Hans van de Ven (ed), *Warfare in Chinese History*, Sinica Leidensia, Brill, Leiden, 2000.
28. On the image of Superman as beast, see Dower op cit., p. 116. On the relative size of objects within the frame see Medhurst and Desousa, op cit., pp. 213–214.
29. On the significance of placement in the frame see Medhurst and Desousa, op cit., p. 216.
30. This cartoon comes from *Ulk*, Berlin and can be seen in the *Review of Reviews*, "History of the Month in Caricature," July 1900, p. x.

31. This cartoon comes from *Der Floh*, Vienna and can be seen in the *Review of Reviews*, "History of the Month in Caricature," July 1900, p. x and in *Le Rire*, 4 August 1900.
32. See, for example, *Harper's Weekly*, 7 July 1900, p. 619.
33. For evidence of the Chinese reaction to discussions in the Western press and widely-read accounts of China such as Lord Charles Beresford's *The Break-up of China*, Harper Brothers, New York, 1899, see George Lanning, *Old Forces in New China*, the National Review Office, Probsthain, London, 1912, p. 148 and Chester Tan, *The Boxer Catastrophe*, Octagon Books Inc., New York, 1967, p. 14.
34. This cartoon can be seen in the *Review of Reviews*, "History of the Month in Caricature," July 1900, p. x.
35. *Marumaru Shimbun*, 15 September 1900.
36. *Simplicissimus*, volume 5, No. 14. This periodical has an unusual system of numbering beginning from its first edition. It is therefore difficult to give the date and the month and often difficult to give the page number but the cartoons can be found readily by reference to volume and issue number.
37. Kemnitz, op cit., p. 81.
38. *Simplicissimus*, volume 5, p. 168.
39. See R. Christ, *Simplicissimus 1896–1914*, Rütten and Loenig, Berlin, 1972, p. 75 for a brilliant piece of graphic work by Heine on the front cover of a special edition on China. The cartoon is headed "The Chinese Automaton" and depicts a piggy-bank in the shape of a Chinese person being kicked by a German wearing a night-cap who is tugging at the handle marked "pull." The caption reads "Now I have put so much money in the damned thing and it is not coming back out." The Chinese automaton stands immovable and it is the German trying to get his money back whose movement is invested with ridicule by Heine's drawing.
40. My thanks to Professor W. A. Coupe for drawing my attention to this connection.
41. *Simplicissimus*, volume 5, p. 201.
42. Reproduced in colour in Christ, op cit., p. 77.
43. L. S. Stavrianos, *Lifelines from Our Past. A New World History*, Pantheon Books, New York, 1989, p. 7.
44. These cartoons can be seen in the *Review of Reviews* "History of the Month in Caricature," a cartoon from *Kladderadatsch*, Berlin, June 1900, p. v, and a cartoon from *Jugend*, Munich, July 1900, p. x. The other two can be seen in *Le Rire*, 15 September and 29 September.
45. See letter from John D. Long, Secretary of the State Department of 28 July 1900 to the Secretary of War enclosing copies of letters from the Senior Squadron Commander, US Naval Force, Asiatic Station (eighteen enclosures). See especially enclosure No. 8, letter 33-D, 22 June 1900, containing the final statement of the reasons for not joining in a demand for the capture of the Dagu forts. See

State Department Papers on China Station, National Archives, Washington DC.

46. *Chicago Daily Tribune*, 12 June, front page.
47. G. Lynch, *The War of the Civilisations. Being a Record of a "Foreign Devil's" Experiences with the Allies in China*, Longmans, Green and Co., London, 1901. Lynch's account is the most candid in respect of atrocities committed by foreign troops. See pp. 36, 39, 46, 299–300. Lynch was conscious of the fact that his work had been the object of censorship by his publisher "a most terribly humane man, although I have only yesterday discovered the redeeming feature in his character, that he is a master of the fox hounds." See also Mary Hooker, *Behind the Scenes in Peking*, Oxford University Press, Hong Kong, 1987 (1910), pp. 190–191.
48. For a reference giving an idea of the complete sang froid of educated foreigners regarding looting, see Lancelot Gile's *The Siege of the Peking Legations. A Diary*, edited L. R. Marchant, University of Western Australia Press, Nedlands, 1970, p. 178 "Every day looting parties go out and get what they can. I have done some splendid looting already." For ambassadorial looting see Lynch, op cit., p. 153 and Hooker, op cit. pp. 189–191, For the scale of looting see B. L. Simpson *Indiscreet Letters from Peking*, Arno Press, New York, 1970 (1907). Recent authoritative and important work has been done by James Hevia "Loot's Fate. The Economy of Plunder and the Moral Life of Objects," *History and Anthropology*, Vol. 6, No. 4, 1994. See also Frederic A. Sharf and Peter Harrington, *China, 1900, The Boxer Rebellion as Described by Participants in Letters, Diaries and Photographs*, Greenhill Books, London, 2000, pp. 120 and 236.
49. R. Nicholls, *Bluejackets and Boxers, Australia's Naval Expedition to the Boxer Uprising*, Allen and Unwin, Sydney, 1986, p. 85, extract from Able Seaman Bertotto's diary, 13 October 1900, which describes the looting of a large old house in a manner reminiscent of the traditional story, The Tinderbox.
50. Russian soldiers massacred 300 Chinese coolies hired by the British to unload ships at Dagu at the beginning of the campaign, provoking some comment as to the morality of this act. The coolies were told to swim back to land and then shot as they were swimming. Some of the commentary by members of other nationalities was of the more utilitarian kind, noting that as a result of this act by the Russians, it would be very difficult to obtain labour. For a reference to this incident, see Lynch, op cit., pp. 299–300 and p. 307.
51. Cohen, op cit., p. 11.
52. Susanne Hoe, *Women at the Siege, Peking 1900*. The Women's History Press, Oxford, 2000.
53. Lynch, op cit.
54. Streicher, op cit., p. 439 made the point that the more the newspaper avoids truth, the more cartoonists' special function becomes important. He refers to cartoonists aptly as men who are "in the truth" and associates their "production

of meanings through image-making" with "the value-neutrality of the news write-up." However, there is a more complex process at work. In any era, no matter what freedom of expression may be employed in newspaper columns, there are always subjects which remain taboo or off-limits. One of these has notoriously been the atrocious conduct of one's own nationals in war. A more extensive survey would reveal how typical or otherwise was the case of the Boxer rising in terms of concentration by cartoonists on the inhumane and barbarous behaviour of the foreign troops in China. A comparison of a similar cross-section of cartoons of the Boer War, for example, would be instructive.

55. S. Appelbaum, *Simplicissimus, 180 Satirical Drawings from the Famous German Weekly*, Dover, New York, 1975, p. x. Heine was jailed for six months in 1898. *Simplicissimus* was viewed officially as immoral, revolutionary and socialistic.
56. By 1879, 15,000 copies of *Marumaru Shimbun* were being printed weekly. The then government felt threatened by its influence and frequently tried to suppress it. Eventually it was considered the highest honour when the periodical was banned because of the political content of its cartoons. See J. Iwasaki and K. Shimizu (eds), *Yomeru Nenpyo-Bekkan. Meiji Taisho Fushimangato Seso-Fuzoku Nenpyo*, Dainippon Insatsu, Tokyo, 1983. My thanks to Ginga Torii for this reference.
57. Michael Cummings, "How a Political Cartoonist Views His Profession" foreword in W. M. Jones, *The Cartoon History of Britain*, Tom Stacey, London, 1971, p. 13, "A political cartoonist is a weapon of attack, a warmonger in pictorial aggression." See Stuart op cit. for a discussion of the way group hostility focuses on individuals as an outlet for group frustration resulting in cartoons which can be described as "scurrilous, malicious and disgusting" pp. 147–152. Victor Alba, "The Mexican Revolution and the Cartoon," *Comparative Studies in Society and History*, Vol. 9, No. 2, January 1967, p. 127, notes that readers of cartoons "will be pleased that someone has expressed their own desire to attack." Coupe "Observations," op cit., pp. 87–88, by contrast, observes that "the modern cartoonists who use caricature as an act of outright aggression are in a distinct minority."
58. Medhurst and Desousa, op cit., p. 198.
59. This study would seem to point to flaws in Professor Miller's thesis that all over America anti-Chinese feeling was endemic and pre-dated the advent of Chinese coolie labour on the West coast. A careful reading of Miller's study shows that a more plausible interpretation lies in his own observation that American attitudes towards China reflected (and still reflect) "the swing in American consciousness from unreasonable optimism to unreasonable pessimism." See Miller, op cit., p. 6. In this he follows Harold Isaacs, *Images of Asia. American Views of China and India* (originally *Scratches On Our Minds*) Harper and Row, New York, 1972. Isaac's six point characterisation of the swings in American views of China from the eighteenth century to 1949 is quoted in Miller pp. 9–10.

60. See the cartoon from *Der Floh* in *Le Rire*, 18 August 1900.
61. *Novoe Vremya*, 8 June 1900.
62. *Le Rire*, 4 August 1900.
63. Claude Lévi-Strauss, *Race et Histoire*, Denoël, France, 1995 (1952), p. 22.
64. Medhurst and Desousa, op cit., p. 202.
65. Keen, op cit., p. 48.
66. Given that most readers only retain a small percentage of what they read and given the visually shocking and highly memorable nature of this cartoon, it would constitute a disproportionate part of what most readers would retain from this chapter. For those readers who are nationals of the People's Republic of China or Taiwan, it would be unacceptable to give them the impression that this cartoon was in any way representative of foreign conceptions of the Chinese in 1900. For the historian of the depiction of the enemy in war, a copy may be seen at the reference given.
67. See Dower, p. 9, pp. 84–92 and Keen, op cit., pp. 76–77.
68. *Marumaru Shimbun*, 9 June 1900; The *World*, 36 July, 6 August; *Novoe Vremya*, 7 July; *Le Rire*, 11 August 1900.
69. *Marumaru Shimbun*, 18 August, p. 387.
70. Ibid., 27 October, p. 730.
71. Medhurst and Desousa, op cit., p. 202.
72. Published in *Le Rire*, 8 September 1900. The image of the broom was also used in a Japanese cartoon where the inverted broom meant "go away." See *Marumaru Shimbun*, 18 August, p. 383. My thanks to Kazuyo Taguchi for her help in translating and elucidating the Japanese cartoons examined for this survey.
73. See "The Chinese Retaliate" from *La Silhouette* in *Review of Reviews* "Caricature of the Month," p. xi, June 1900 and "The Metamorphosis of the Open Door" from *Lustige Blätter*, in *Review of Reviews*, op cit., July 1900, p. xiii.
74. William J Duiker, *Cultures in Collision: The Boxer Rebellion*, Presidio Press, Cambridge, Massachusetts, 1967, pp. 203–204.
75. Lanning, op cit., p. 95; Captain Arthur A. S. Barnes, *On Active Service with the Chinese Regiment: A Record of the Operations of the First Chinese Regiment in North China from March to October, 1900*, Grant Richards, London, 1902, p. xiii; *Hong Kong Daily Press*, editorial, 10 May 1900.
76. E. Gombrich, *Meditations on a Hobby Horse and other Essays on the Theory of Art*, Phaidon Press, London, 1963, p. 131.
77. Both John J. Appel and Lucy S. Caswell have pointed to more complex ramifications of stereotyping. See Appel, op cit., pp. 14–15 and Caswell, "Illusions: Ethnicity in American Cartoon Art," in *Cartoons and Ethnicity*, op cit., p. 51. "Stereotypes in cartoon art allow cartoonists to communicate complicated ideas efficiently."
78. The *World*, 3 July 1900.
79. The *World*, 12 August 1900.

80. It may be true that "Boxerism" "in the twentieth century West, became in the minds of many, emblematic of the savagery and barbarism specifically of the non-Western world" but we cannot see any evidence of this idea being widely promulgated in the press of the day. Again, it should be emphasised that the missionary press was not examined for the purposes of this study. The fifteen English-language newspapers forming the research base of this work represent a broad cross section and a very large percentage of the newspaper-reading public in Britain and America or the English-language newspapers in China and Hong Kong. For those interested in the missionary press and its influence, James Hevia's study is most useful. See James Hevia, "Leaving a Brand on China: Missionary Discourse in the Wake of the Boxer Movement," *Modern China*, Vol. 18, No. 3, July 1992. This writer would not agree with the assertion that at all times in all societies during wars "all human beings ... have the capacity ... to define their adversaries as less than human and then treat them accordingly" See P. Cohen, op cit., p. 186. There have been long periods in the history of warfare among literate and illiterate peoples during which very specific rules for the conduct of war were laid down and obeyed with the precise objective of making warfare a conscious act between two groups of human beings who shared common values as adversaries. Highest among these values, was a sense of honour and the conduct proper in war. This sense actively prevented opponents dehumanising each other and behaving accordingly.
81. See Mark Elvin's review of Jonathan Spence's *The Search for Modern China* in *The National Interest*, Fall 1990, p. 88.
82. Mary C. Wright, *The Last Stand of Chinese Conservatism. The T'ung Chih Restoration 1862–1874*, Stanford University Press, Stanford, 1957.
83. Joanna Waley-Cohen, *The Sextants of Beijing. Global Currents in Chinese History*, W. W. Norton and Co., New York, 1999; Joanna Waley-Cohen, "China and Western Technology in the Late Eighteenth Century," *American Historical Review*, Vol. 58, No. 5, 1993; David Wright, "Careers in Western Science in Nineteenth Century China: Xu Shou and Xu Jianyin," *Journal of the Royal Asiatic Society*, Third Series, Vol. 5, No. 1, April, 1995. My thanks to Dr Gary Tiedemann for drawing my attention to this last article.
84. From the collection of the Library of Congress LC US262-706.
85. Li was the subject of several motion films on his visit to America in 1896 although only one of these has survived and can be seen in the Library of Congress, Motion Pictures Division. There is also a film of Li taken by Ray Ackerman for the American Mutoscope and Bioscope Company showing him being presented with a parlour bioscope on 14 January 1901 at his summer residence. This film can also be seen at the Library of Congress. China was an extremely popular subject for early motion pictures. The American Mutoscope and Bioscope Company of New York City alone had produced twenty-eight China titles by November 1902.

86. Library of Congress, Bain Collection, LC-BZ 2279-13 "Chinese Sailors With Admiral's Wreath for Grant's Tomb."
87. *Punch*, 5 September 1900 carries a cartoon captioned "Praise a Frenchman, Find a Friend" and refers to Admiral Seymour's gallantry in acknowledging the fighting ability of the French troops who fought a losing battle under his command. A similar acknowledgement by Admiral Seymour of the valour of the Italian soldiers when read to the Italian parliament brought tears to the eyes of many delegates. In view of the way in which women were supposed to remain secluded from public life as much in the West as in China at the turn of the century, it is interesting to learn through the columns of the *World* how much Madame Wu was respected and admired during the time her husband was Chinese Ambassador to America due to her sensistivity in her public appearances.
88. L. Ghiglione, *The American Journalist. Paradox of the Press*, Library of Congress, Washington, 1990, p. 7. My thanks to Frank Carroll for drawing my attention to this reference.
89. *Review of Reviews*, September 1898, p. 202.
90. The reports written by French military personnel well acquainted with Li Hongzhang during his visit to France give a strong indication of Chinese awareness of the security implications of concealing from the French details concerning the extent and nature of their purchases in Germany. See especially "Rapport du Capitaine Meillet adjoint à l'Atelier de Construction de Puteaux sur son Voyage en Chine, 1896," manuscript held at the Archives Militaires de l'Armeé de Terre, Château de Vincennes, Paris, Series 7N1674.
91. Coupe, "Observations," op cit., p 89.
92. Ibid., p. 92.
93. *The Times* leading article 12 June 1900.
94. A number of writers following Gombrich have noted that the function of the cartoonist in reducing a person who is the object of public hatred to something ridiculous, means that people in laughing at the cartoon, can put their fears in perspective. See E. Gombrich and E. Kris, *Caricature*, Penguin, London, 1940, pp. 12, 14–15, and Coupe "Observations" op cit., p. 91. At the beginning of the twenty-first century, one has difficulty seeing in Sokolovsky's cartoon of Li Hongzhang any of these processes at work. Li had also visited Russia for the coronation of Nicholas and Alexandra. Even on his visit to Japan in 1896 to conduct negotiations after China's defeat by Japan, Li's personal courage, competence and negotiating skills won him sympathy from a wide cross-section of the Western press. None of the cartoonists drawing Li during the Boxer War produced images matching any of the words used by *The Times* to describe him.
95. Goldstein, op cit., p. 236.
96. F. I. Schodt, *Manga! Manga! The World of Japanese Comics*, Kodansha International, Japan, 1983, pp. 38–41.
97. M. Sullivan, *The Meeting of Eastern and Western Art from the Sixteenth Century to*

the Present Day, Thames and Hudson, London, 1973.

98. W. Killy (ed.), *Literatur Lexicon. Autoren und Werke Deutsche Sprache*, Vol. 5, Bertelsmann Lexicon Verlag, Munich, 1990, p. 154.
99. This cartoon was repeated on the front page of the *Chicago Daily Tribune*, 21 July.
100. *The Times*, 20 June 1900.
101. *Novoe Vremya*, 2 September 1900. The cartoon shows a Japanese soldier with his long legs hanging over the side of a cradle. The caption reads "A grown-up person needs a bigger bed."
102. See The *World*, 8 June 1900. Report of interview with John Barrett, former US Minister to Siam and an authority on China.
103. The *World*, 25 June 1900.
104. Article from the *Philadelphia Times* reprinted in the *World*, 28 June 1900.
105. *Chicago Daily News*, 30 June 1900. In the event, the British kept one themselves and gave the other three to the Russians, Germans and Japanese.
106. The only other cartoons in this survey which made a pun on the word "boxing" in connection with the sport appeared in the *Westminster Gazette* of 20 and 22 June. Both of these cartoons also came into the category of being a commentary on other political events (British politics and the Boer War) but they were atypical of British cartoons and they appeared very early in the crisis when little or nothing was known about the Boxers, particularly in Britain.
107. The *New York Times* reported six deaths in the ring by August 1900.
108. See the *New York Times*, 26 August 1900. Among other points of interest, the article mentions that $80,000 profit was to have been realised by the three fights, the organisation of which was in dispute.
109. *New York Times*, 18 April 1900. I am particularly indebted to Professor Caswell for this reference which enabled me to connect the manifest popularity of the sport as seen in the pages of the *New York Evening Journal* with the events in China.
110. *Chicago Daily News*, 30 May 1900.
111. The *World*, 30 May 1900.
112. Ibid., 6 June 1900.
113. Ibid., 29 June 1900.
114. See the *Chicago Daily News*, 1 June, 21 June, 22 June and 26 June; *Chicago Daily Tribune*, 19 July; *New York Evening Journal*, 21 July; *Chicago Sunday Tribune*, 5 August; *Harper's Weekly*, 23 June. My thanks to Professor Caswell for assistance in interpreting a number of these cartoons.
115. See Miller, op cit., Isaacs, op cit.
116. W Murrell, *A History of American Graphic Humor, 1865–1938*, Cooper Square Publishing, New York, 1976, p. 143.
117. My thanks to Professor Caswell for the information about Rogers' attitude to David Hill. See W. A. Rogers, *Hits at Politics*, R. H. Russell, New York, 1899.

118. Aimeé Brown, "Official Artists and Not-so-official Art: Covert Caricaturists in Nineteenth Century France," *Art Journal*, Vol. 43, 1983, p. 365.
119. Anne McCauley "Caricature and Physiognomy in Second Empire Paris," *Art Journal*, No. 43, 1983, p. 359.
120. *Review of Reviews*, May 1900, p. 431.
121. See caption and cartoon "Mark Hanna as he is and as Davenport made him" in Ghiglione, op cit., p. 32. Thomas Nast was bribed to stop his attack on William Macy Tweed, boss of New York's Tammany Hall, op cit., p. 43. George III reputedly spent £12,000 trying to buy off artists so that they would not publish scurrilous caricatures of him. See *English Caricature 1620 to the Present: Caricaturists and Satirists, Their Arts, Their Purpose and Influence*, Victoria and Albert Museum, London, 1984, pp. 19–20. My thanks to Professor Caswell for pinning down this latter reference.
122. Gombrich and Kris, op cit., p. 12.
123. Coupe, "The German Cartoon," op cit., p. 160.
124. *Review of Reviews*, May 1900, p. 431.
125. The *Chicago Daily Tribune* reprinted a cartoon on this theme from the *Westminster Gazette* on 28 July 1900.
126. Dower, op cit., p. 116.
127. Ibid., pp. 145–146.
128. Coupe, "The German Cartoon," op cit., 140–144 describes the degree of lewd salaciousness with which cartoonists savaged King Ludwig I of Bavaria and his mistress Lola Montez.
129. My thanks to Professor W. A. Coupe for this insight.
130. Although the details of Chinese costume were reproduced with great accuracy, there were some exceptions. In this cartoon the Chinese are depicted wearing Japanese clogs and in another cartoon in *Le Rire*, 8 September 1900, a Chinese mandarin is shown wearing Dutch clogs while speaking to a diminutive rebel. In general, however, if there were inaccuracies, these tended to consist of confusing Chinese and Japanese costume or hair styles. Such confusion was the exception rather than the rule.
131. Commercial slide by Underwood and Underwood. From the private collection of Mr R. J. Blum, Adelaide.
132. Such details as there were about foreign looting may be gleaned from the journals and diaries kept by those who lived through the siege. Mark Twain started a furore when he wrote to the American press on the subject of missionary looting. His letter and the letters in reply may be seen in the collection of the Hoover Institute for War and Peace, Stanford University. See also Hevia, op cit.
133. *Chicago Daily Tribune*, 18 August 1900 and *Punch*, 29 August 1900.
134. Keen, op cit., p. 13.
135. See R. Taft, *Photographs and the American Scene. A Social History, 1839–1889,*

Dover Publications, New York, 1938, p. 421 for Pulitzer's thinking on the value of illustrations in his newspaper in the 1890s.

136. For further background on the attitude of editors to the value of their news as commercial property and the development of the view that copyright laws should be extended to protect this property, see Barbara Cloud, "News: Public Service or Profitable Property?", *American Journalism*, Vol. 13, No. 2, 1996.

137. Streicher, op cit., p. 439.

Chapter 6

Chinese Military Capabilities in 1900: Myth and Reality[1]

The stress on gaining the victory without fighting is not a utopian fancy but part of a larger view that seeks to maintain the established order without the use of violence.... In the old China, war was too complex a matter to be left to the fighting man, however well trained he may be. Its object was not victory but the reestablishment of order, and for this the arts of peace were equally necessary.

John King Fairbank

Chinese preparations for war in the last thirty years of the nineteenth century were intensive and impressive. The Sino-French War of 1880–1885 and the Sino-Japanese War of 1894–1895 acted both as learning experience and as spur to those military and civilian leaders whose objective was to prepare China for war against increasingly aggressive Imperialist powers. Their task was greater in magnitude than that facing any Western power or that of Japan. There were four factors unique to China in terms of decision-making concerning defence policy and budgetary priorities. These were: first, the physical size of the country; second, the probability of war breaking out simultaneously at widely disparate geographical locations and involving various combinations of possible enemies; and third, ever-present large scale internal rebellions which continually drained the defence budget as well as requiring manpower organised and trained in ways not necessarily suitable for meeting modern-trained armies in the field. The fourth factor was that China was ruled by the Manchus, an alien dynasty. The age-old imperial fear of the rise in power of great military leaders was accentuated under the rule of the Manchu emperors who kept constant vigil over the power base of its greatest generals, splitting them and or their armies when they perceived potential threat. This may have been an important factor in preserving Manchu rule but it was detrimental to the national interest when individual generals could not continue to lead the men they had commanded so gloriously. Western military men trained in traditions venerating heroic generals like Napoleon or Wellington, could not understand or identify with the continuous deliberate reduction of the image of the charismatic military leader. Historians writing of the military in the late Qing have not commented on or even raised this as a problem.

There is a wealth of detailed evidence concerning China's military modernisation programmes in the latter half of the nineteenth century. This evidence is to be found in the reports of those who were in the best position to comment at the time; the foreign military attachés resident in China, quite a few of whom spoke and wrote Chinese and all of whom were professional soldiers. Analysis of the reports of the military attachés, the photographs they took, the maps they drew, the training they witnessed and the arsenals they visited, creates a very different picture of the Chinese armies in the late Qing from the one still dominating the literature. Western preoccupation with technology is but one factor in assessing military performance. The use of human resources, military and civilian, forms a significant part of a distinctively Chinese philosophy of war. The Chinese had also begun to learn to acquire and emphasise certain relevant aspects of innovative technology as soon as they were seen to be necessary.[2] By contrast, it does not seem that the various Western-trained armies fighting in China from the First Opium War onwards looked back on their experience and reflected that they might have anything to learn from the Chinese.

Conservatism in military thinking is an international and understandable phenomenon. The most cursory glance at British and French performance in the various small wars of empire in the nineteenth century or American experience in the Philippines in the Spanish-American War, would seem to show such a high level of conservatism that very little useful innovative data entered the Western military mind. Officers and their men may have been forced to learn from their experience in remote jungles and deserts but this knowledge did not become a part of mainstream military training. Another interpretation of the inability of Western military thinkers to learn anything from their engagements with non-white Western European foes during the nineteenth century might be that for specific cultural reasons, they did not think it was possible that such enemies could teach them anything. A major reason for this inability to learn was the deep-rooted conviction that ultimately, the superiority of Western military technology would win the day. This conviction has gone on to dominate the writing of Western scholars although there is evidence of revisionist thinking on the subject.[3] Those writing about the performance of China in international conflict right up to and including the Korean War would do well to enlarge their criteria from the narrow field of the relative technological capacity of the armies concerned.

Works are still being written that give as the major reason for Chinese defeat in the various small wars of the nineteenth century, Chinese technological inferiority in comparison with the technologically advanced West. In addition, there was — and still is — a very strong myth current in the West which portrayed the Chinese as:

> ... those heathen Chinamen with their barbarous ways and comic-opera methods of campaigning. Some of them were so queerly dressed that you might have thought they had come out of the Ark itself.[4]

This type of colourful language and the mentality behind it has been echoed in serious literature on the subject of the Chinese army:

> The Chinese "brave" appeared to be little more than a caricature of a soldier. The typical Chinese enlisted man had little resemblance to his Western counterparts. His uniform consisted of baggy trousers and a brightly coloured but ill-fitting jacket, topped by a turban or conical bamboo hat. This unmilitary appearance was often accentuated by the addition of a fan or an umbrella ... this neglected son of Mars [had antiquated weapons] but in rare instances he was armed with a modern breech-loading rifle.[5]

Previously unpublished photographs taken by foreign military observers show this kind of colourful prose to be an unrepresentative description of soldiers in the armies stationed in the strategically important areas of China from the 1870s to 1900. There has been a tendency on the part of those writing about Chinese military modernisation to see in the Chinese military

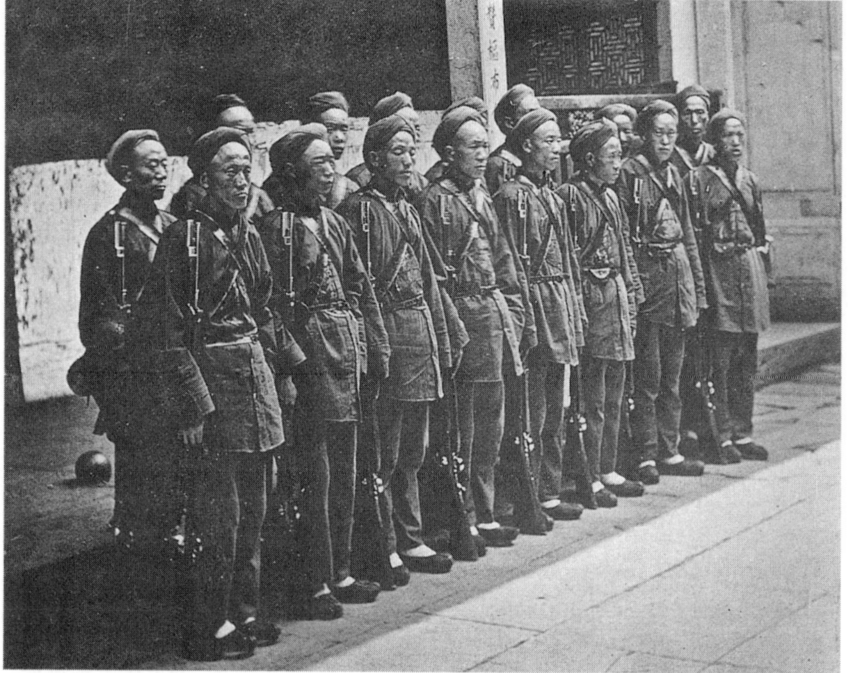

Figure 6.1 John Thomson, "Foreign-drilled Troops," c. 1867–1868.[6]

the archetypal losers and to look only for evidence supporting this presupposition.[7] The identical sources used by those writing in the "loser" school of thought may profitably be re-examined to yield precise evidence concerning successful implementation of modernisation. Because the "loser" school arose largely from the writers' cultural perceptions of what constitutes military threat and what constitutes the "correct" response to this threat, it is vital to weigh into the debate the entire body of evidence of foreign military attachés in China. Writers who analyse Chinese military ability and responses in terms of internal and external strategic threats other than those actually facing China in the nineteenth century will not come up with a balanced view of the success or otherwise of the Chinese response.

Symptomatic of the cultural preconceptions of those writing in the "loser" school, is their attitude to uniform exemplified in the passage quoted above describing the Chinese soldier as "this neglected son of Mars." Attitudes to military uniform seem to be tenaciously culture-specific.[8] Those who have contributed to the "loser" school regarding the nineteenth century

Chinese military do not provide any photographic evidence showing the uniforms worn by the modern Chinese armies. Where there is pictorial evidence it shows, without exception, endlessly repeated photographs of Qing bannermen taken in the late 1860s by John Thomson (see Figure 4.1).[9] In the absence of other photographic evidence, writers in the "loser" school have shown themselves unable to shed their cultural perceptions of what a fighting man should look like.

A uniform is undeniably the ultimate symbol to those wearing it and to their civilian countrymen. The attitude to uniform constitutes a powerful example of Orientalism in that there has been a view that a fighting man should be dressed like his Western counterpart and only then will he deserve to be evaluated in depth for his performance as a fighting man. Almost all the photographs presented here for the first time show that the Chinese soldiers in the modernised armies of the late Qing were in fact dressed in uniforms similar to those worn by Western soldiers. A problem seems to have been that the cultural notions of many historians whose work has touched on the Chinese military at this time have been so strong that they have prevented them from looking for such photographs. Cultural blinkers regarding uniform are as strong in the minds of Chinese scholars as of foreign scholars. Some Chinese scholars on being shown photographs of soldiers of the Imperial Chinese Army in 1900 informed the writer that no Chinese soldier would have consented to wear headgear as shown in Figure 3.7, for example. It is for this reason that the Chinese newspaper illustrations uncovered in the Japanese press of the day are of such supreme importance. (See Figure 3.8, also Figure 6.2) There can be no reason to doubt contemporary evidence regarding Chinese regular army uniform as shown by a British photographer, nor can there be any reason to doubt a drawing by a Chinese or British newspaper illustrator. Culturally conditioned attitudes as to what constitutes appropriate military uniform and what this uniform connotes as to the qualities of soldiers as fighting men, persisted well into the twentieth century.

Studies have been produced which, by concentrating on defects in the Chinese command system or rearmaments programmes, give the impression that China was hopelessly behind the West.[10] Looking at Chinese efforts to cope with the internal and external threats to the Empire and to modernise its defence establishment accordingly, is something that cannot be usefully undertaken in a vacuum. To assess China's progress in the last thirty years of the century, we must also examine briefly the forces of conservatism and the inadequate military command structures of selected Western countries. Too many historians of China's military system display a startling ignorance of the conservative forces in British and European military thinking in the nineteenth century. Civilian leaders have never liked spending money on defence and the question of the defence budget is still a major political issue in most countries. Once again, however, in looking to see how the Chinese managed, the evidence of those most in a position to know, the foreign military attachés who were watching each other as jealously as they watched the Chinese, is the most valuable.

In order to form a realistic assessment of China's progress in building herself a modern military machine, precise examples of improvements in Chinese capacity to manufacture her own weapons will be given; changes in policy with regard to weapons acquisition will be documented; the adoption of Western drill by certain armies and the results thereof will be discussed; and the preparation of the North as one of the most probable theatres of war will be described. Examples of these innovations must be plentiful and detailed as, with few exceptions,[11] historians of conflict between China and the West have been somewhat facile in adopting the view that Chinese defeats were inevitably linked to and caused by the clash of superior Western technology with inferior Chinese technology. The reasons why nations win and lose wars are infinitely more complex than this black and white approach. Indeed, as one historian pointed out in the case of Saddam Hussein, a leader and a nation might well refuse to accept what seems to their enemy as an obvious defeat.[12] This theme was discussed in some detail in Chapter Three. More recently an observer noted with respect to NATO intervention in Serbia, "NATO had to adapt its strategy and redefine its military goals [in the face of] Serbian response to NATO bombing."[13] We may add to this that some cultures win victories that they prefer to forget.[14] That there is more than one possible attitude towards the acceptance of a defeat as dictated by a victor, is a cultural fact with regard to military philosophy which certainly applies in the Chinese case.

Historians need to go beyond the simplistic "we won," "they lost" approach to scrutinise what the winners gained by their victory and what the losers learned from their defeat. An excellent study has been done on this in the case of the Franco-Prussian War.[15] Moreover, the very notions of "defeat" and "victory" can be shown to be cultural ones.[16] The case of China in the nineteenth century is redolent with the remarks of indignant foreign plenipotentiaries or traders or military men who inveighed against the fact that the Chinese did not behave as a defeated nation should behave. A simple answer to this was that in many instances, what the foreigners regarded as a decisive defeat was regarded by the Chinese as an insignificant peripheral engagement of no real military, political or economic consequence or even, a victory. The war in China in 1900 demonstrated that, militarily, the Chinese had learned a great deal from their defeat by Japan in 1895. They were able to put up an impressive military resistance at Dagu and Tianjin by a standing army in the sense understood by the invaders as constituting full-scale modern warfare.

Both Western and Chinese historians have written of the Boxer rising from the perspective of the Boxers themselves. Far more was involved, most notably the question of the performance of the Chinese regular army. The Boxer rising was not just another, albeit spectacular, rebellion by untrained peasant insurgents. The resistance by the Imperial Chinese Army was of a calibre that made the armies of eight nations sit in Tianjin for four weeks before they had what they felt to be sufficient reinforcements to march on Beijing. Allied understanding of what constituted "sufficient reinforcements" was dictated by the nature and extent of the performance of the Imperial Chinese Army during the battle of Tianjin, a battle that has not received in-depth attention in the English-language literature[17] and is, astonishingly, still being written out of the literature.[18] Politically, foreign cries for slicing China like a melon[19] which had been shouted stridently in the Chinese press from 1898 onwards, were silenced after the Boxer War. Economically, although the reparations were a heavy burden,[20] it was these very reparations burning into the Chinese psyche at all social levels, which formed an important role in helping her in the ongoing task of determining herself as a nation state.

The objective here is not to explain why the Chinese did not win the Boxer War. The most cursory reading of Sun Zi, coupled with Li Hongzhang's realisation that if the foreigners were defeated, they had but to retire and regroup, reappearing in crushing strength which China could not hope to match, should suffice to explain the Chinese military response. This response was one of furious defence against which the Allied armies were initially powerless, and subsequent dispersal with only pockets of fierce resistance being offered as the Allies marched on Beijing. The result of this response was that China's modern-trained armies that had been grouped in the strategically vital areas around Beijing were left intact. However, a glance at the question why did the Chinese not win the Boxer War might seem to uphold Fairbank's assertion that "war was too complex a matter to be left to the fighting man." In order to evaluate what actually constituted a Chinese fighting man, the correspondence of a Chinese general in the field will be discussed and analysed below. For those interested in a more comprehensive discussion of Chinese strategic culture over several dynasties, Alistair Iain Johnston's book, *Cultural Realism. Grand Strategy in Chinese History*, provides a detailed study of elements in Chinese strategic thought and their application under varying circumstances. It would seem to be the case as Johnston contends that in Chinese military thinking, there is a strong expectation that violence inheres in human social processes, and that preparations for, and the use of violence are vital for self-preservation.[21]

There is a need for another study of Li Hongzhang's writings, policies, personal alliances, attitude to the West and specific Westerners (it is well to bear in mind that two of Li's greatest personal friends were Ulysses Grant and the German arms manufacturer Krupp). His performance as international representative and negotiator, and as national figure behind the immense leap forward made by China between 1870 and 1900 in the manufacture of armaments and the training of armies would be worth analysing as a specific case study in the terms of Johnston's work. The late Qing provides an example of a dynasty in decline and Li's behaviour fits in with Johnston's analysis that although there was a preference for "offensive over static defensive and accommodationist strategies," this was in periods when a dynasty saw itself "with a relatively large advantage in capabilities." The last forty years of the Qing was not such a time and Li and other leaders were obliged to use "less coercive" strategies at this time.[22] The Qing had to deal increasingly with greater exposure to Western thought and Western military culture than had previous dynasties. Johnston's description of the general cyclical tendencies of Chinese empires with regard to strategic thinking when in growth and when in decline, fits very well with the attitudes towards the building of a modern military machine *and its use*, displayed by those in control in the late Qing.[23] Johnston quotes Lo Jang-pang who saw in the Chinese mind a tendency to place:

> ... great stock on the guidance of history. In the conduct of foreign affairs, as in social intercourse, there are maxims and precedents that were so constantly quoted that they became clichés and, like political slogans, exerted an influence in the shaping of policy and the making of decisions.[24]

A key to understanding the behaviour of Li Hongzhang and the immense effort made to modernise the Chinese military machine observed in all vital strategic areas by foreign professional soldiers, is to see him as a product of the strategic culture set out by Johnston. Li was very well able to prioritise and control goals during conflict. Li was over-ruled many times so that his understanding of "a strict hierarchy of goals during conflict"[25] (and the surrounding diplomacy) was blurred by the policy decisions of others. However Li's thinking and that of other outstanding military leaders of the late Qing is well described by Johnston:

> One solution to this escalation dynamic [in which conflict is viewed as zero-sum, where the prospect of partially unmet goals is viewed as an absolute loss] is to hold, consciously or not, to a long-term vision of the value of different strategic outcomes. The value of future goals is sustained in the face of short-term setbacks, making these more palatable. This reduces the pressure to escalate violence in the present.[26]

Johnston's view of Chinese thinking probably best describes the actual course of China's military build-up from 1840 onwards and her diplomatic and political attitude to small-scale conflicts with Westerners in different parts of the Empire. It also explains the attitudes and behaviour of those statesmen and military men who saw the need to modernise China's armies. They understood that her industrial base was insufficient to make the desired leap forward on the scale required. They expressly realised that traditional views of the military and the profession of soldiering and of training great military leaders could not be changed overnight and would have to be changed gradually.

The war resulting from the Boxer rising has in common with the Sino-Japanese War and the Sino-French War, the fact that Chinese military ability and outstanding fighting qualities have been written out of the histories. In writing these military skills back into the account, we are concerned with demonstrating military preparedness of a high order. Granted that conservative forces in every nation were reluctant to increase defence spending, China's case was a special one. In China, such preparations were tied to the contentious issue of "modernisation" and accepting foreign ideas, foreign instructors, and foreign-style education. As well, China lacked an industrial base comparable to that of the West. General Yang Mushi who fought under General Nie Shicheng in the battle of Tianjin was able to assess the performance of his army quite dispassionately.[27] The aim here is to explain as General Yang did, why and how an army which crumbled when pitted against the Japanese only five years before,[28] was able to put up such redoubtable resistance for four weeks against the armies of eight invading nations in the battle for Tianjin. Looking at the performance of one of the five armies responsible for the defence of Beijing and its approaches, we can understand how this Chinese army seemed both to its own generals and to its enemies from eight different military traditions and experience, as an army worthy of its name. General Yang's assessment is a fair one:

> Some days ago I defended Tianjin and other places and although I gave up defence of these places only little by little, the troops never measured up to the quality of the foreign armies. But for the soldiers of our side to hold the defence of Tianjin ... against the soldiers of the foreign powers for whom they are no match, shows them to be as battle worthy as the great armies of our past ...[29]

The hydra-headed eight power invading army contained men who were superbly led and who fought courageously. (See Figure 5.11) It also contained men whose performance left a great deal to be desired. The behaviour of these latter, while recorded in handwritten journals, never became part of the official histories although there is no lack of accounts of Chinese soldiers who broke and ran when confronted by the enemy. Nevertheless, the primary sources, the accounts written by professional soldiers all, to a man, acknowledge the many highly-developed military skills and the tremendous courage of their opponents. Their evidence forms the basis of an account which shows how in a very short time, all aspects necessary to the modernisation of the Chinese defence capability had improved to such an extent as to offer resistance noted by officers and men of all the invading countries as skilful, tenacious, and courageous. The collapse of the Chinese armies after the fall of Tianjin is rightly the subject of another study. Such a study would need to take into account the problems of training and leading a modern army in a military environment pervaded with the philosophy of Sun Zi, not Clausewitz and a civilian culture steeped in the great historical romances such as *The*

Three Kingdoms and *Watermargin* while operating under the command-chain of the traditional Qing court. These problems were exemplified by the performance, death and posthumous rehabilitation of General Nie Shicheng.[30] Such a study would have to take into account the problems and perspectives of the highly-placed military leaders and their power bases as well as the high civilian authorities and the factions to which they belonged at Court. As well, such a study would have to take into account the tenacity of the hatred of the common people for foreigners.[31]

Myth-making

> The govt. [sic] have proclaimed peace to be established but a more rediculous [sic] thing cannot be imagined.... Heke [a Maori leader] the principal boasts and indeed with truth that he never asked for peace and that the [British] Government have left off attacking him because they were tired of getting their soldiers killed without any advantage ... anyone to read [Colonel] Despard's despatches would think that we had thrashed the natives soundly whereas they really have had the best of us on several occasions. I really begin to think that it was perhaps all a mistake about us beating the french [sic] at Waterloo. I shall for the rest of my life be cautious how I believe an account of battle.[32]

In China in 1900 as well as in New Zealand during the Maori Wars, participants and many contemporary observers were well aware of the real outcome of trial by military strength. There was also a realisation that there were discrepancies between actual military events and their subsequent portrayal. In the above quotation, the New Zealand settler F. E. Manning further relates his experience of these discrepancies to the probability of their being a constant factor in the official record of war. One writer has pointed to the ability of several British governors to turn British defeats into victory by skilful propaganda.[33] The concept of propaganda involves a degree of conscious intent on the part of those disseminating information. As it is not possible to demonstrate this conscious intent in the context of the Boxer campaign, it is preferable to use the term "myth-making."

There is still much interesting work to be done in uncovering the elements surrounding the making of myths in the specific context of war between Western Europeans and their non-white foes. The discussion below of the initial action during the Boxer War forms part of a global re-examination of nineteenth century wars of Empire and contributes as much to that re-examination as it does to an understanding of the military events of the Boxer rising. The military writers constituted yet another group of contemporaries who were able to form realistic images of China and the Chinese. However, not only has the substance of these images slipped out of collective memory and been forgotten, but the images have even been replaced by contradictory ones.

The making of the myths regarding the Seymour expedition and the respective capacities of the Allied and Chinese military throughout this campaign, differed according to origin.[34] The Western military myths had as their primary object the glorifying of Admiral Seymour's courageous failure to rescue the foreigners besieged in the Legations in Beijing. The myths created by some foreign observers and journalists are quite different in character. They produced accounts which had as their objective the demonstration of superior Western training, leadership and weapons technology which must inevitably defeat the corrupt, disorganised, antiquated Chinese forces. The military writers were all able to record new information about their Chinese antagonists without detracting from the power of the myth they wished to uphold. Indeed, had they consciously analysed their accounts, they may have had no problem recognising their own characterisation of the Chinese military as it ultimately increased the stature of the hero they were making.

Some journalists and other observers, missionaries, travellers and diplomats constituted quite a different body of myth-makers. The majority of them already "knew" that the Chinese were treacherous, corrupt, badly-trained and poorly-equipped and that Western Europeans and their allies were well-drilled and in command of the latest communications and weapons technology. They approached the Boxer campaign with this "knowledge," thus bringing no new information about Chinese military or para-military forces into the Western database. The appeal of this latter mythology has influenced both popular images and much of the scholarly evaluation of the relative military merits of China and the West as exemplified by the Boxer War. This is not to say that journalists were not aware of the pressures on them to provide sensational copy,[35] or that they all succumbed to these pressures. Wilbur Chamberlain, correspondent for the *New York Sun*, wrote a remarkable series of letters to his wife in which his determination to get views from a variety of Chinese sources stands out as a recurring theme.[36]

Both strands of myth-making have proved powerful. The ultimate statement of the glorification of Admiral Seymour's failure lay in his promotion and the honours and extraordinary ceremonial privileges conferred on him as a result of his performance as Commander of the China Station, notably his unsuccessful attempt to relieve the Legations during the Boxer rising.[37] The French military attaché at Tianjin summed up Admiral Seymour's thoughtless foray with the mots justes:

> Admiral Seymour who threw himself like a sub-lieutenant into the foolish adventure of the march on Peking, came out of it with glory ... he is the most loved and most esteemed leader among us.[38]

"A heroic battle to the death against hopeless odds [is a type of myth that] exist[s] in all military cultures."[39] It can be shown to be more powerful in some cultures than others. Admiral Ding Jucheng's performance in the Sino-Japanese War showed supreme heroism as this quality is understood in Western military cultures. His was a courage that, had he been an Englishman, would have put him beside Nelson in the British pantheon of heroes. One wonders how much we would know about what Admiral Ding actually did aboard his crippled flagship in the midst of a ferocious naval battle had there not been a foreign witness who survived the battle. It is not the case that all military cultures emphasise the same qualities in their myths. It may be argued that the heroic-battle-against-hopeless-odds myths are more powerful in some military cultures than in others, or at some periods of history rather than others:

> They are unusually powerful in a West that has evolved a distinctive way of war that emphasises stand-up slugging matches at the expense of cleverness. Clausewitz continues to shape military education; Sun Zi is an afterthought.[40]

The military men taking part in the Seymour expedition did not resort to denigrating the performance of their enemy in order to mythologise their hero. They did not have to. Theirs was a military culture with a tradition in which the failure of Admiral Seymour's unplanned sortie could be viewed as glorious courage. Some examples of the way military writers went about creating the myth include Captain Barnes' reference to 26 June as "a great day because Admiral Seymour's brave men returned from their unsuccessful attempt to reach Peking"[41] and the remarkable contribution by the American Captain Taussig who wrote that Admiral Seymour:

> would never have *succeeded* had not Captain Bowman H. McCalla been in command of the American battalion which led the allied *advance* on that memorable retreat.[42] [emphasis added]

This kind of language is as powerful as the rewriting which omits reference to enemy successes and the failures of one's own troops. It is difficult to read into Captain Taussig's description any of the material discussed below regarding Chinese and Allied military performance in this minor episode of an internationally riveting campaign. Minor episode it may be today, but it serves as a clear example of how myths get written into accepted history. At the time, the fate of Admiral Seymour's expedition, which had vanished from Western view despite the superiority of Western communications technology (the Chinese, in fact, controlled the only operable telegraph lines during the Boxer rising) was more anxiously discussed than the fate of those besieged in the Legations. While some contemporary newspaper accounts eventually made it clear that Admiral Sir Edward Seymour had failed to reach Beijing and relieve the Legations,[43] none gave any detailed reasons for the rout of the Allied force involving Chinese military or para-military activity. Similarly, the battle of Dagu and the siege of Tianjin as reported in some contemporary papers[44] and by many subsequent historians, became such non-events in the Western histories that the military performance of the Imperial Chinese Army and Boxer insurgents has not emerged as an indication of the capacities of those forces at that time.

Contemporary military writers were more than capable of doing justice to the Chinese as enemy; the picture of the Chinese soldier as described by Captain McCalla bears no relation to a caricature in an opera ditty. Glorification of one's own heroism was not, thus, incompatible with describing the courage and ability of one's enemy, at least in China in 1900.

> I have seen fighting in many parts of the world, but never saw harder than we had with these untutored Chinese. We just got over the wall or barrier when the Chinese opened fire. Our men dropped like flies, and were obliged to take shelter. They lay and fought for ten hours. The Chinese shot so well that it was with difficulty the hospital corps could get in to do its work.[45]

It is to the other source of myth-making, the newspapers and some published accounts by journalists and other civilians, that we must look to find the material which denigrated the Chinese military. It was these accounts that gave rise to an interpretation of the campaign which stressed the sweeping victories of superior Western technology over the weak, corrupt, ill-disciplined, poorly-equipped, badly-paid Chinese forces. Another strand of this type of writing simply made no reference to Chinese military resistance whatever. These two strands have influenced all subsequent histories both of the military action during the Boxer rising and many general works on the capabilities of the military in the late Qing. In a book, *The Chinese Soldier*, published in 1937, Captain Anatol Kotenev published John Thomson's photographs of Manchu bannermen and Mongolian archers taken in the 1860s without any visual evidence of the rise of modern-trained armies in the nineteenth century. He also described the events of 1900 as follows:

> Boxerism ... meant very little to modern warfare. It was unable to produce anything more than cold blooded cruelty and contempt of death shown equally by the highest military commanders and officials and the lowest men under their command, which was considered in China as patriotism and nationalism.[46]

Kotenev and more recent writers[47] linked military prowess to nationalism while defining the validity of the latter in accordance with Chinese performance in the field. It is therefore important to note that these writers were factually inaccurate and applied different standards to China concerning the relationship between valid expressions of nationalism through military means from those they applied to Western nations. Kotenev, for example, erroneously asserted that the Chinese regular army did not join the Boxers in fighting the Allies.[48] He also characterised the army as follows: "armed with modern guns they displayed a complete lack of the necessary resistibility and incapacity to bear loss under artillery fire."[49] The fact was that in the battle of Tianjin, Chinese artillery fire power was so accurate that the Allied soldiers were not even able to mount their guns before their positions were sighted and blown to pieces. Of all the heroism displayed by the Chinese regular army during the siege of Tianjin, the courage of the military cadets in dying to a man to defend their academy, struck the contemporary American mind as supremely courageous.[50]

The propriety of the actions of the Western military powers was notably and publicly questioned by cartoonists, some observers and even some military leaders. Admiral Kempff refused to take part in the battle of Dagu. On 16 June 1900 seven powers provoked hostilities with China, a fellow delegate to the Hague Peace Conference of 1899. After the capture of Beijing, senior officers of several of the invading armies officially authorised the holding of auctions of loot. The problem of looting was so bad that it broke down authority between officers and men.[51] These two military initiatives if linked to nationalism in the same way as some writers have made the link for the Chinese, would produce a most unflattering characterisation of the meaning of nationalism in the West at the turn of the century.[52] If a Chinese soldier or peasant died for his country, this was not, somehow, true patriotism or nationalism. May we ask the question does this mean his manner of dying was perceived as culturally inappropriate? Was it culturally appropriate for Sikhs or Tonkinese troops to die in North China in 1900? Breaking international peace conventions and organising official military auctions of loot have not been rated by writers on the Boxer War in terms of their perceived demonstration of the sentiments of patriotism and nationalism.

Some sections of the Western media at this time proved largely unable to break out of the bondage of popular "knowledge" and bring to their readers accounts of a war which involved a Chinese soldier other than as a quaintly dressed fellow with a pigtail carrying a bow and arrow or the ludicrous object of comic opera ditties. As a corollary, some newspapers in the West were unable to write of China as a nation with valid political entities, rights and responsibilities in the wider community of nations. Those newspapers which *were* able to thus portray China formed a minority voice or were directed to a working class audience and were soon forgotten. Many photographers were unable to take photographs of "things which man does not know and has not seen" or if they did succeed in taking such pictures, editors did not print them. Yet photography and the Western press were regarded at this time as the ultimate embodiment of the determination to search for the truth and lay it before the public. The truth in the case of the Chinese military, it would seem, remained deposited in the writings or photographs of Western military men. Their verbal or pictorial imagery confounding popular mythologies as they did, never became part of mainstream knowledge or representation of China. It is their accounts that may be trawled to discover traces allowing the resurrection and introduction of another heroic protagonist taking part in the Boxer rising: the soldier of the modern Imperial Chinese Army.

The Build-up of a Military Machine and Its Culmination in the Application of Western Training by a Chinese General in the Early Stages of the Boxer Rising

The evidence of the men who fought against the Boxers and the Imperial Chinese Army shows marked professional respect for the performance of the Chinese army and in many specific instances, for the military performance of Boxers some of whom were also proficient in the use of state-of-the-art weaponry. Scholars have noted that Western soldiers admired the Boxers but the examples given are restricted to instances demonstrating their physical courage in fighting with extreme bravery using antiquated weaponry.[53] Inasmuch as the writings of the foreign invaders oblige the resurrection of the reputation of the regular soldiers of the modernised Imperial Chinese Army so do they expressly refer to Boxer skill in organised military strategy and in the use of modern weapons.[54] Western soldiers and some civilian Westerners, for example, Herbert Hoover, Roland Allen and Arnold Savage-Landor, acknowledged the fighting skills of both the Boxers and the regular Chinese army. Their assessments stand out in marked contrast to some contemporary newspaper reporting and to the judgements made by many subsequent historians. This professionalism was reciprocated by the writings of the Western-trained members of the Chinese High Command in the field as exemplified by the detailed discussion below of General Yang Mushi's confrontation with the Boxers.

A reason why these sources have been largely ignored by subsequent historians may stem from a reluctance to grapple with the actual sequence of the battles themselves.[55] It has been possible for historians to perpetuate generalised myths about Chinese military inefficacy because they have ignored or misread the sources that describe the actual battles in question.[56] One eminent historian went so far as to say that the battle of Dagu never happened; that the Chinese just tamely handed over the forts some time before the expiry of the Allied ultimatum demanding that they do this.[57] It makes a very great difference to Western perception of Chinese fighting ability during this campaign — and, indeed, to Chinese perception of their own performance — if a savage, hard-fought, blazing artillery duel starting at about one in the morning and lasting for seven hours should be written out of any history of the Boxer rising. The Charge of the Light Brigade became glorious myth. The Battle of Dagu "never happened."

Any realistic assessment of the performance of the Imperial Chinese Army in fighting the eight invading Powers in 1900 must address precise questions of training, armaments, logistics, strategic planning and actual performance in specific battles. An examination of China's achievements in all these respects leads to the question as to why so many historians writing about the Boxer War have failed to acknowledge some fighting ability on the part of the Imperial Chinese Army. There are strong racial and cultural reasons lying hidden behind apparently objective assessments of skill in warfare and the attribution of strengths and weaknesses to non-white Western European foes. Newspaper accounts and letters to the editors of many Western newspapers at this time spoke of Boer military ability and courage in tones often bordering on admiration. The Chinese, however, rarely received this kind of press. British soldiers coming straight from South Africa to Tianjin all stated that the Chinese were fighting better than the Boers in some respects, notably in their artillery work. While contemporary soldiers had no difficulties acknowledging the skills of their enemy, some contemporary journalists and many subsequent writers have ignored or rewritten the battles of the first four weeks of the war provoked by the Boxer rising.

In assessing China's moves to purchase or manufacture arms and ammunition and in training soldiers to form modern armies drilled in the Western manner, the French military accounts have been selected for in-depth analysis for two reasons.[58] Following the defeat of France in the Franco-Prussian War and the defeat of France by China in several important battles in Indochina in 1880–1885, the French became highly sensitive to military developments in China just as much as in Russia and Europe. While some French attachés complained that the Chinese would not let them see troops drilling or observe major army manoeuvres,[59] this if anything increased their assiduity and vigilance. Added to France's particular interest in developments in the Chinese army because of sensitivity over the Yunnan Indochina border, was the fact that the Chinese chose German, Russian and to a lesser extent British military instructors in preference to the French increasingly over the years 1870 to 1900. The events of the Franco-Prussian War did not pass unnoticed by Chinese observers. French military observers were thus watching Chinese troops drilled by representatives of countries with which the

French felt considerable rivalry. Under these circumstances it might be expected that the French would make derogatory remarks about training and belittling comments about the end result. While this was the case occasionally, the overwhelming consensus was to note the very high degree of skill in the handling and maintenance of Western arms displayed by Chinese soldiers in the North over the years 1870 to 1900.

Any discussion of the armies in China in the late nineteenth century should stress that there were enormous variations between them in terms of weaponry, training, military preparedness and combat experience. There were, for example, great differences between the armies trained and equipped by Zeng Guofan, Li Hongzhang and Yuan Shikai in the North and the armies of the South West which had fought several outstandingly successful campaigns under Liu Yongfu against the French in the 1880s. However, the detailed reports and other evidence in the correspondence of the French military attachés make it quite clear that both the civil and military arms of the state in the late Qing saw the need to strengthen areas of strategic importance and were buying or making weaponry and training troops to this end. The Yunnan Indochina border was obviously sensitive but the approaches to Beijing had the greatest priority in terms of preparations for defence. Moreover, the Boxer rising mainly involved the Northern armies so the discussion of equipment acquisition and training will be limited to these armies.

With regard to Chinese capacity to manufacture weapons, once again the French military attachés had a keen interest in this subject, among other reasons because German and French arsenals were in direct competition for the growing Chinese market. The French attachés also sent back a steady flow of reports on other military establishments such as officer training schools, naval dockyards, mine and torpedo capabilities, the accuracy of Chinese mapping and, of course, detailed reports on the various armies in terms of troop strength, estimation of the capacities of each arm, of fortifications, logistics and assessments and personal impressions of the individual members of the Chinese High Command. These reports covered the areas of strategic importance: Port Arthur, Zhili, the Yangtze Valley, the southern coastal areas and Yunnan. With the object of providing background to a detailed discussion of the action in the first four weeks of foreign military intervention in the Boxer rising, only the reports on the troops of Zhili will be examined in detail along with reports on Chinese arsenals and official weapons procurement policy.

Chinese Acquisition of Modern Weaponry 1860–1900

Some contemporary writers saw that by 1900 the Chinese were showing evidence of having learned some important lessons from the Sino-Japanese War. Actually, development of thinking favouring modernisation in the Chinese army had begun no later than China's defeat in the Opium Wars and defeat by the Japanese gave it further impetus.[60] China's drive for military modernisation in the second half of the nineteenth century came as much from big internal rebellions — the Taiping, the Nien and the Muslim rebellion in Chinese Turkistan, to name a few of the significant ones — as from a perception of a maritime threat from the West, Russia or Japan. Chinese policy makers were faced with momentous decisions about allocation of defence funds in the 1860s, the 1870s and the 1880s, particularly in competition with disaster relief funds; failure to allocate such funds could only too easily lead to further rebellion. These were priorities peculiar to China and experienced in no comparable way in any Western country at the time.

As early as 1842, that is, right after the Opium War, Lin Zexu wrote recommending the purchase and manufacture of Western ships and guns. In 1855 Zeng Guofan established small arsenals in Jiangxi and in 1861 he established a large arsenal and a shipyard at Anqing and at Jiangnan. In 1861 Prince Gong started a Western-trained Manchu army using Russian guns and Feng Guifen wrote, "What we then have to learn from the barbarians is only one thing, solid ships and effective guns."[61] By 1863 Li Hongzhang, noting that different Chinese military leaders had different attitudes to learning about foreign military methods, had himself nevertheless fully internalised the superiority of artillery. He was to learn a great deal from the sight of the destruction of Fuzhou by French cannon on 23 August 1884. By 1864 Li Hongzhang ordered his assistants in Fuzhou and Shanghai to instruct officers and soldiers of the government troops in Beijing in the manufacture and handling of modern weapons.[62] While the Chinese could not as yet cast guns, they could make the shells.[63] The arsenal in Fuzhou was begun in 1867 under French auspices. By 1876 the Tianjin torpedo school had the capacity to manufacture electric mines.[64] This torpedo school was soon to become the Tianjin Military Academy. In an undated report from the Belgian Legation about the time of the Boxer rising, it was stated that the Tianjin arsenal was capable of manufacturing rapid firing rifled Nordenfelt pattern cannon and ammunition.[65]

There was vigorous debate and criticism among the Chinese ruling class and intellectuals concerning army training and recruitment.[66] A unique characteristic of Chinese military life was that there were several military systems operating concurrently. There were the Manchu bannermen, a hereditary caste descended from the original invading Manchu forces whose function was to fight external foes. There were the troops of the Green Standard whose function was to maintain internal order — their function was akin to that of a police force. There were also legally constituted trained local militia groups called on for minor action against bandits. Finally, there were large armies trained and loyal to particular civilian officials or generals directly responsible to the Head of State. It is this last group which is under discussion, particularly the armies in Zhili province strategically placed to protect the capital.

By 1864 each battalion of Zeng Guofan's Hunan army had several squads armed with foreign rifles, two light mortars, forty-eight gingals, matchlocks, swords and spears.[67] By 1876, forces of the Qing army in Xinjiang were using repeating rifles, twelve and sixteen pounders, Krupp needle guns and a "European cannon that could hit as far as several *li*" (one kilometre equals approximately two *li*).[68] There is a Japanese report on the military forces in China dated 1882 which covers all military arms, personnel strengths, dispositions, weapons and strength of fortifications. Its specific focus is on the modernised armies.[69] A secret Russian report of 1884 on the Chinese army has a section on troops and weapons in Zhili. This report lists all the latest weapons and describes the artillery as being composed of 586 Krupp pieces of various calibres, as well as a small number of Armstrong, Bokhous and Vavassern guns.[70]

A report on the defence of the Northern zone in the Zhili region was compiled in 1892 by Captain de Fleurac who also wrote a report on the mines and torpedoes in the ports of Zhili listing all the relevant equipment.[71] While he noted that he had no information about the artillery in some locations, wherever he had information, the artillery was mostly Krupp cannons from

120 mm to 210 mm although there were some Armstrong 120 pounders. He also noted mortars and Gatling guns as well as Maxim guns.

Captain d'Amade had compiled a series of five reports on the equipment, organisation, training and disposition of the troops in the military camps between Tianjin and Shanhaiguan in 1888.[72] Of the fourteen cavalry, infantry and artillery units he saw, only two were armed with obsolete weapons and only three were not Western-trained. In one camp alone did he observe incompatible weaponry: in Shanhaiguan the German-drilled troops had Mausers, Berdan and Winchester rifles and some still had muzzle loaders. Captain d'Amade's comment was that he could not understand why these men were not issued Mausers from the extensive stock in Tianjin. The reason may have been that these particular units had not yet been trained to use modern rifles. Thus, eleven out of fourteen of the units in this strategically important area were Western-trained and twelve out of fourteen were drilled in the Western manner on modern Western weapons. In the North of China there were crack armies raised by leading Chinese statesmen and trained by foreigners or foreign-trained Chinese, paid regularly by their Chinese commanders and proficient in the use of modern weaponry by 1900. General Nie Shicheng's army, for example, which had to fight both Boxer insurgents and the combined Allied forces, was equipped with Maxim machine guns, Krupp artillery and Winchester repeating rifles.[73] Stationed in Shandong, Yuan Shikai's army which did not join the fighting in Tianjin, was similarly equipped and equally well-trained (see Figure 6.2).

Extensive purchase of foreign weapons was in full swing by the 1890s. A scientific military research capacity had also developed with the work of Xu Shou and Xu Jianyin.[74] What is particularly notable about the careers of these two scientists is how quickly they came to the attention of Zeng Guofan and Li Hongzhang. They were co-opted and redirected into defence-related work very early in their careers, thus having little time for the pure research they were so obviously capable of doing. Just how intensive and far-reaching were Li's efforts in modernising every aspect of the military was discovered by the British journalist and writer Arnold Savage-Landor after the fall of Tianjin. He went to see the Viceroy's palace and offices as it was from here that much of the military operations had been directed. He thought it would have been the first place visited by British Intelligence. He got permission from the Russians to visit the part of the building that had been used as the War Office. He found:

> drill-books for the Chinese army, some for the artillery, some for the infantry, others for the cavalry. The various exercises and drills were fully demonstrated in coloured pictures.... Further on was another neat pile of small volumes. They were the log books of the various men-of-war, kept in the most accurate fashion day by day, according to European fashion, and up to the day of the capture of Taku [sic]. There were also foreign scientific books on explosives, on navigation, on gunnery, on chemistry, on machinery of all kinds, and endless photographs of big guns, rifles and projectiles of every possible pattern. Maps and charts in Chinese were lying pell-mell everywhere, and beautiful models of war-ships were smashed and thrown into one corner.... A number of coolies entered and began to sweep all these valuable papers into the canal.[75]

Chinese Arsenals

There is a dearth of studies which give precise details of Chinese capabilities in weapons production in the nineteenth century. There has been some excellent work done in quantifying Chinese manufacture of and imports of ordnance towards the close of the nineteenth century and relating this to political and military developments in China. Unfortunately this work has not received the attention it merits.[76] In the face of continued and persistent reiteration of the degree of Chinese technological backwardness in the military sphere, there is still a requirement for a precise description of the extent of Chinese acquistion and mastery of military technology. Responsible officials were well aware of Chinese technical limitations and shortcomings so they tailored their weapons buying and weapons and ammunition manufacture accordingly. Over the thirty years from 1870, these officials learned to adapt and modify their policies because they had a realistic understanding of the speed of modernisation possible for the defence industry in China.

There were major arsenals in Fuzhou, Jiangnan (Shanghai), Nanjing, Jinan, Hanyang, Tianjin and Hankou. There were also shipbuilding yards at Anqing, Weihaiwei and Fuzhou as well as steel and gunpowder plants at Hanyang, Tianjin and Longhua. In addition, the events of the Boxer rising were to reveal a previously unknown arsenal in the military camp at Xigu outside Tianjin. The map at Figure 6.3 shows the extent of development in the arms and munitions industry in China by 1895.[77] At the time of the Boxer rising, despite the efforts of the military attachés, Western military intelligence showed a complete unawareness of the extent of China's rearmament programme.[78] The attachés had certainly written the reports but — as

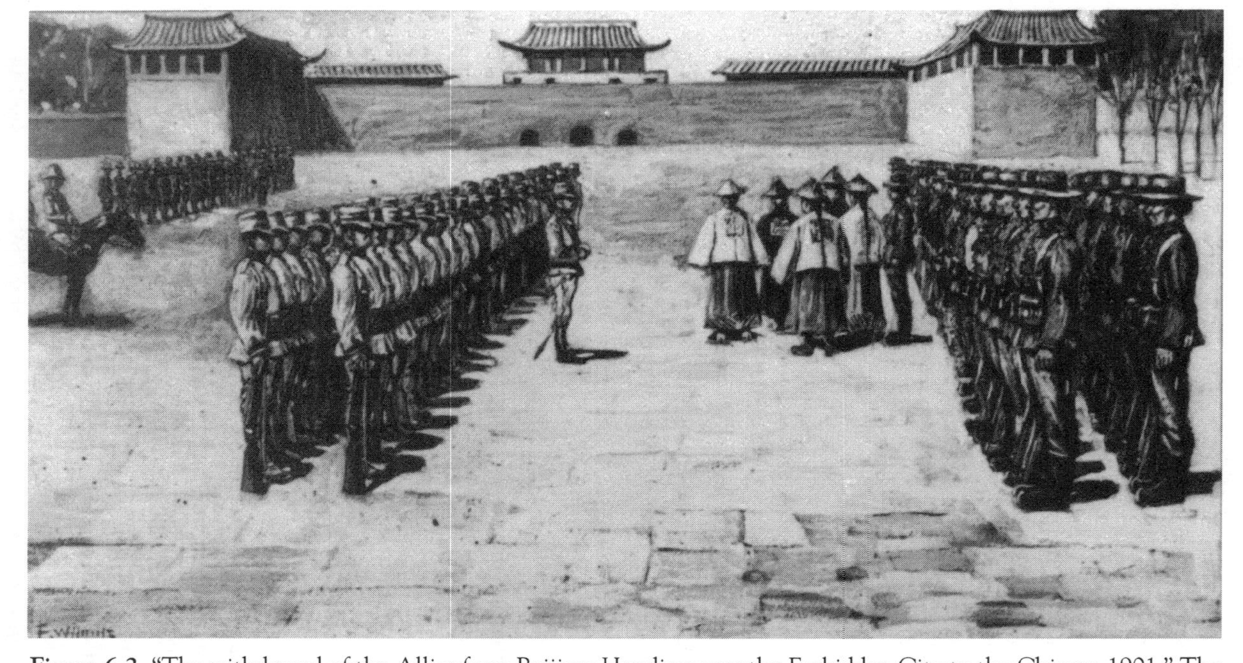

Figure 6.2 "The withdrawal of the Allies from Beijing: Handing over the Forbidden City to the Chinese 1901." The troops on the right are troops of Yuan Shikai. Those on the left facing the Chinese troops are Japanese soldiers.[79] (By kind permission of Greenhill Books, London)

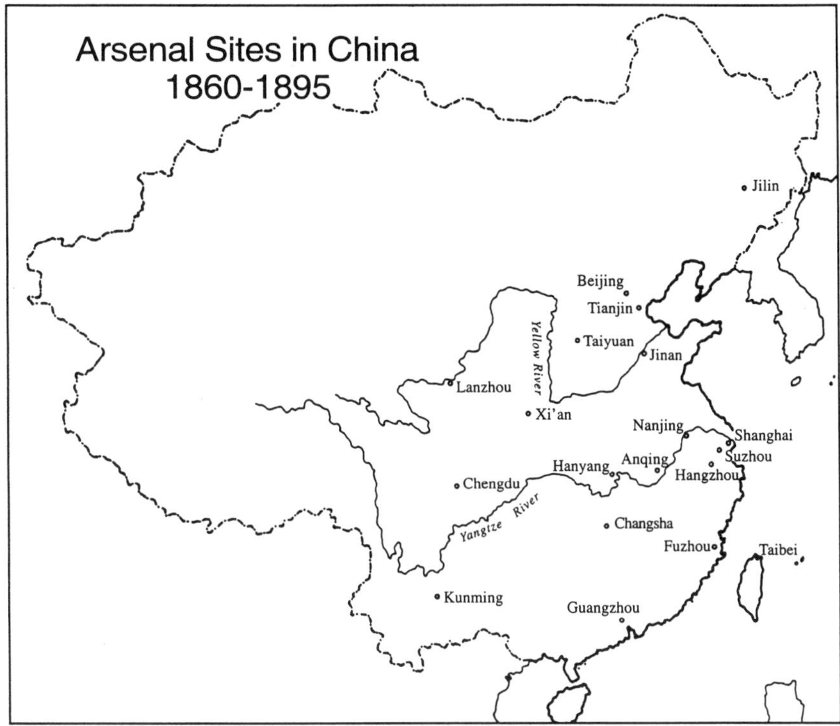

Figure 6.3 Arsenal sites in China 1860–1895. From Thomas L. Kennedy.[80]

was the case with state-of-the-art Japanese fighter planes downed in China in the 1930s[81] — these reports were not widely disseminated.

There is total disagreement among the experts who visited these arsenals in the years between 1872 and 1900. Nevertheless, all experts record China's entry into the modern arms race and her performance therein. Just as Western arms manufacturers were sensitive to showing foreign visitors particular processes or capabilities,[82] so the Chinese were selective about what they allowed foreigners to see for obvious reasons. The size of the Hanyang arsenal, covering sixty acres in 1876[83] as indicated by Figure 6.7, makes it clear that specific workshops and their products could be kept secret from foreign visitors. Nevertheless, the reports of the French military attachés and engineers provide reliable evidence in that the writers were all experts and their views ranged from enthusiastic to condemnatory. More significant than individual impressions, was the evidence that all observers commented on the fact that the arsenals were being augmented all the time with their capabilities continually being extended.[84] They also noted a drive to replace Western managers, instructors and engineers by Chinese ones.[85]

One of the earliest reports by foreigners on Chinese arsenals comes from a French military attaché, Captain de Contenson and was written in 1872. His lament regarding accessibility was echoed until 1896 when Captain Meillet noted that although he was allowed to go almost everywhere and take notes, the Chinese would not answer his questions either because of "ill will or even out of ignorance."[86] In 1872 Captain de Contenson had fewer illusions: "The Chinese refuse to give information when asked or deliberately give false information."[87] In attempting to evaluate the output of these arsenals, it is too simplistic to say that because the Chinese were defeated by Japan in 1895, Chinese attempts to become self-sufficient in arms manufacture had failed.[88] A factor remarked on by the military commentators was that after being defeated in 1860 and 1895, the Chinese continued weapons acquisition and weapons manufacture without faltering:[89]

> The exchange of ratifications of the Treaty of Shimonoseki (in March 1895) has given complete reassurance to the European arms traffickers who are supplying China with arms and ammunition. The *Tzéne* charted by Mandl reappeared at the bar [at the mouth of the Baihe river] on 29 May [1895]. There she discharged several thousand rifles and revolvers and more artillery batteries for which the cost amounts to more than 30 million taels [120 million francs]. On the other hand, 15,000 soldiers from Shandong are marching to reinforce the garrison of Shanhaiguan and Messrs von Spitz, Heckmann and Schnell patiently instruct their recruits.... Has China really made peace? She has signed the treaty; for other countries that would be enough; for China it means nothing.[90]

The events of 1860 which, as in 1900 saw the Chinese forces fighting on two fronts against the Taipings as well as the Westerners, and the Sino-Japanese War of 1894–1895 did not at all impede the forward march of all aspects of China's weapons acquisition policy.

One Japanese scholar gives as a reason for Japanese government caution over the issue of sending troops to fight with the Western troops against China during the Boxer crisis, the fact that:

> As Japan had almost exhausted her national resources owing to the Sino-Japanese war of 1894–95, it was not wise to further waste her resources by sending out a large army when the situation was essentially uncertain.[91]

This view, together with the fact that China's rearmament programme continued without missing a beat, would appear to invalidate any simplistic interpretation of the Sino-Japanese War as "revealing China's rottenness to the world"[92] or as an indication of China's failure "to build a modern military industrial complex."[93] Such explanations fail to take into account the complex of reasons for which any nation loses a war. They also ignore the fact that for both the Chinese and the Japanese civilian and military authorities, the war was a learning experience in just the same way as was the Franco-Prussian War, the Boer War or any other war involving European protagonists.

Throughout the Boer War, letters were written to the editor of *The Times* indicting various British authorities for carelessness or irresponsibility in military matters, some of which resulted from exactly the same military situation as was happening in China, namely "allowing the land forces of the Queen to be launched against a formidable enemy in possession of an equipment of field guns superior in type and efficiency to those supplied to our own land forces." The writer of this particular letter felt that "some one or some body ... are to be indicted for this"[94] Needless to say, nobody was indicted for it. However, fighting the white Protestant Boers was perceived to be a learning experience for the British army and the British public in a way that fighting the heathen Chinese was not. Certainly Britain had much more at stake in South Africa and the Boer War lasted far longer than the Boxer War. However, the congruence between readers' letters, editorial policy and reports from journalists on the spot in their views of the Boers as enemy and the Chinese as enemy is remarkable, notably in *The Times*.

There is evidence that in terms of acquiring capabilities at the same time as Western countries, in terms of being able to manufacture weapons not known in the West, in terms of numbers and range of output, in terms of the recognition of the need to develop a research capacity as well as the ability to keep up with the relevant Western developments by an extensive translation programme, and in terms of a gradual move towards an express policy realistic for the existing conditions in China, the Chinese arsenals showed a capacity to produce and adapt which has not been recognised in the literature.[95]

A photograph by John Thomson taken about 1868 is accompanied by a text designating one of the weapons illustrated as a "mitrailleuse." (See Figure 6.4) On the left of the "mitrailleuse," the photograph shows a torpedo and rocket tube, a pile of shells, a howitzer, a rocket-stand, and a field-gun

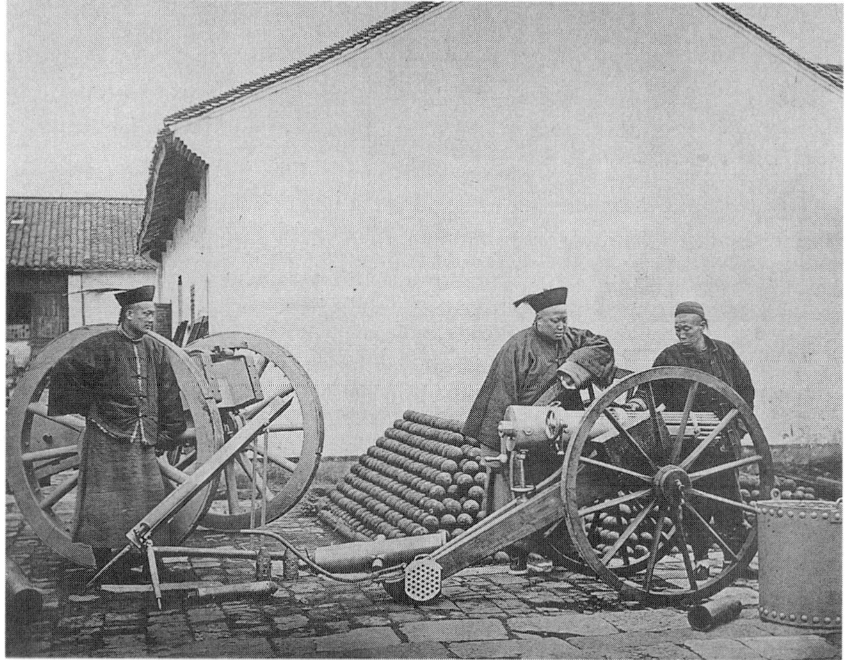

Figure 6.4 John Thomson, "Nanjing Arsenal," c. 1873.[96]

carriage. Prototype machine guns (Gatling guns) were invented in 1862 and first used in the American Civil War at Petersburg in 1864 by General Ben Butler who purchased four of these weapons at the inordinate sum of $1,000 each. They were adopted by the US army in 1866. *The Oxford Dictionary* notes the first use of the word "mitrailleuse" in 1870 by which date there was still not an English equivalent to the French word. In 1874 Gatling guns were first produced at Nanjing arsenal.[97] In 1875 Xu Jianyin and John Fryer translated a manual on the Gatling gun.[98] Thus the Chinese were neither behind in weapons technology nor in the dissemination of literature describing the technology.

On the occasion of his visit to the Nanjing arsenal in 1868, John Thomson wrote:

> The departments most interesting to me were the ones where rifle caps were being punched and filled by machinery and another where the guns were being cast with such solidarity and perfection as to rival the finest work of the kind I have seen anywhere in Europe.[99]

In another book published some years later, Thomson wrote:

> These instructors [at the Fuzhou Arsenal], all of them, remarked to me on the wonderful aptitude displayed by the Chinese in picking up a knowledge of the various mechanical appliances employed in the arsenal … There are indeed many admirable specimens of complicated work carried out solely from drawings; the whole betokening an advanced degree of skill or knowledge on the part of the workmen … the mandarins connected with the arsenal look with pardonable vanity at the steam gunboats that have been built under their own eyes and sent into commission from their own naval and shipbuilding yards.[100]

An observer at the Nanjing arsenal in 1892 saw naval artillery, Hotchkiss, Maxim and Nordenfeld guns being manufactured:

> I look at one of the models which is being used to make reproductions and I read, Hotchkiss, Paris, 1886. It is no more difficult than that.[101]

According to Monsieur Bryois, the Chinese could copy any weapon they wanted by the time of his visit in 1892. This ability to copy weapons and more complex mechanisms in relation to defence materiel has already been noted with Bernard's observations during the First Opium War being quoted extensively.[102] Bernard had observed important modifications to artillery pieces, gun carriages and the mechanism by which the war junks were propelled. These took place in "real time," that is, while the Chinese were actually engaged with the British in this war. Relevant technical military literature was republished in time for the end of the war.[103] The very earliest instance of Chinese reproduction of a foreign piece of ordnance to which they had been exposed in war, was the appearance of Chinese copies of Portuguese guns. These Chinese weapons were manufactured from 1520 onwards, only six years after the arrival of the Portuguese at Macao.[104]

In terms of range of output, the arsenal at Tianjin was already making Dahlgren prototype bronze guns and Remington rifles at a rate of 10,000 rifles a month in 1872. Under Li Hongzhang's supervision, the Tianjin arsenal continued upgrading so that in the 1890s it was able to manufacture Maxim machine guns, 42 and 60 mm machine guns, rapid firing rifled Nordenfelt pattern cannon and ammunition, Krupp pattern guns and guns with a pneumatic system for closing the breach by 1896. In respect of these latter guns, the Chinese were, in fact, ahead of the French, probably due to Chinese familiarity with German weapons research and production. From the outset, arsenals had manufactured ammunition for the weapons they produced.[105] As the Westernisation of the Northern armies speeded up, there was a move to the policy of manufacturing ammunition in China for weapons produced abroad. On his visit to the workshops of Le Havre in 1896, Li Hongzhang repeated insistently to the director:

> Hurry on the manufacture of a new rifle and you can then sell us all the stock you have at present.[106]

For Captain Meillet this was an indication that because the Chinese had difficulty in making weapons themselves, it was still preferable to buy them in Europe.[107] This is a possible, and in some cases a likely interpretation. Another interpretation might suggest that as China's arsenals were capable of producing sufficient ammunition for her own needs, buying recently outdated weapons saved her the expense of upgrading machinery and allowed the procurement of effective weapons at bargain prices. Such a policy would be

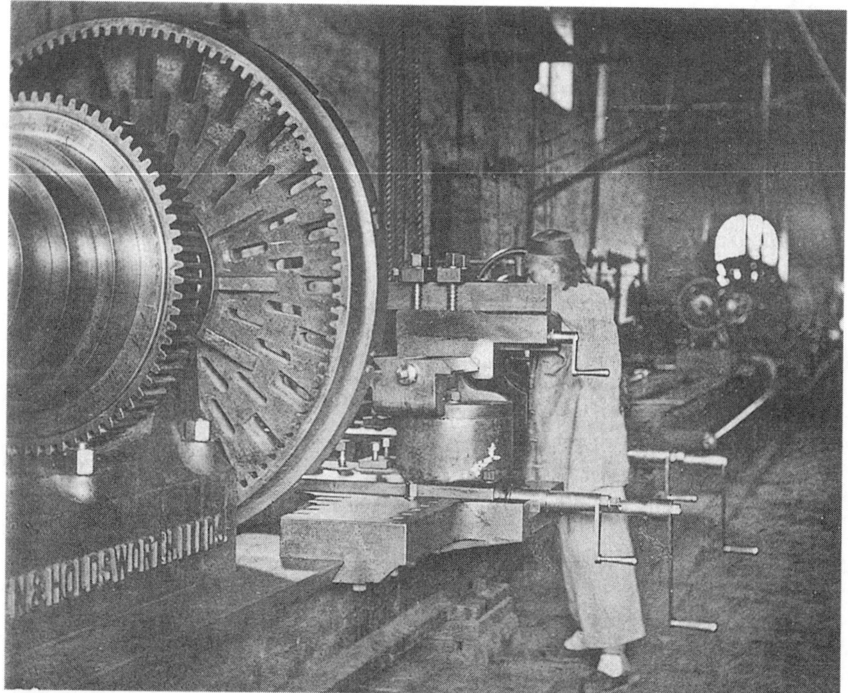

Figure 6.5 John Thomson, "Interior of Workshop, Nanjing Arsenal," c. 1873.[108]

disastrous only in the event of a huge jump in technology. Although there was a very strong move to make China independent from the West, statesmen like Li Hongzhang and Zhang Zhidong had sufficient technical knowledge and experience to know just how far such ambitions were practicable and possible.

There is also evidence of Chinese initiative in the production of weapons that were observed and tested by foreigners and found to be superior to any other comparable weapons of the time. Test production began in 1891 at the Jiangnan arsenal of an 8.8 mm calibre magazine rifle based on the Mannlicher but considerably modified. It could fire a five round clip without pausing to reload after each shot as necessary with the Remington. The striking force of the bullet was greater when smokeless powder was used rather than black gunpowder. The rifle was subject to overheating and required cooling after ten rounds if black powder was used and fifteen rounds if smokeless powder was used. Liu Kunyi suggested employing a higher grade of steel to overcome this problem. Li Hongzhang was impressed with the weapon and it was tested in 1892 by troop commanders and foreign instructors at Tianjin.

In 1893 General Kawakami of the Imperial Japanese Army visited Li in Tianjin. He was favourably impressed with the Jiangnan rifle and said that the Murata rifle, which the Japanese regarded as better than contemporary German and French models, could not compare with it. The weapon did not live up to its promising reputation, however, and new weapons began to be produced in China that outshone the reputation of the Jiangnan rifle. By 1901 production of this model had ceased. Nevertheless, it is notable not only that the rifle attracted such favourable attention, but also that the defect initially observed, namely the rapid heating of the weapon, had in Liu Kunyi a technically competent official able to suggest a reasonable remedial proposal. Unfortunately, we do not know whether or not Liu's suggestion was tested. There may well have been corrupt and ignorant Chinese officials associated with the Jiangnan arsenal over the years, but evidently there were also some competent individuals involved in its oversight.[109]

As for production of modern weapons unknown to Westerners, the testimony of Captain Meillet makes it clear that the Chinese refrained from showing him everything. It is also apparent that he did not understand everything he saw. At the arsenal at Hankou, he was shown some extremely light 40 mm guns of a type he had never seen before. He was told that these weapons were highly sought after in China as being very suitable to a variety of commonly arising military situations. However, he was unable to get any information as to their firepower or their ammunition. His assumption was that these guns would just be used to make a noise rather louder than could be produced by fire-crackers.[110] However, the fact that he was told that these guns could be easily carried by donkeys and small horses, together with the fact of their popularity, may suggest another interpretation of the deployment of these weapons. Banditry on land, on rivers and on the sea was endemic in China. Meillet's discovery of a weapon unknown to him and highly desired by the Chinese, in combination with the few facts he was able to glean about this weapon, may indicate that it was used in the sort of action required to surprise and eliminate small fast-moving bandit groups on land or on the water.[111] Another military situation commonly arising in China in which such a type of weapon would have been useful, would have been against small-scale peasant insurrections or insurrections by minority groups.

The reports of de Contenson, Meillet, de Fleurac and Henri Bryois contain enormous discrepancies in the evidence concerning the personnel and upkeep of the machinery in the arsenals they saw or more accurately, in

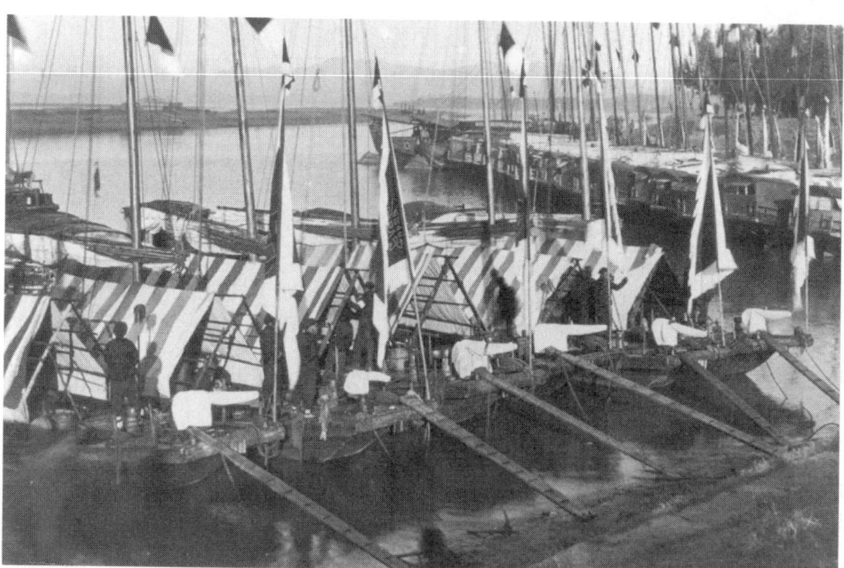

Figure 6.6(a) Armed War Junks. From the Album of Laribe, 1908. (By courtesy of the Musée de l'Armée de Terre, Paris)

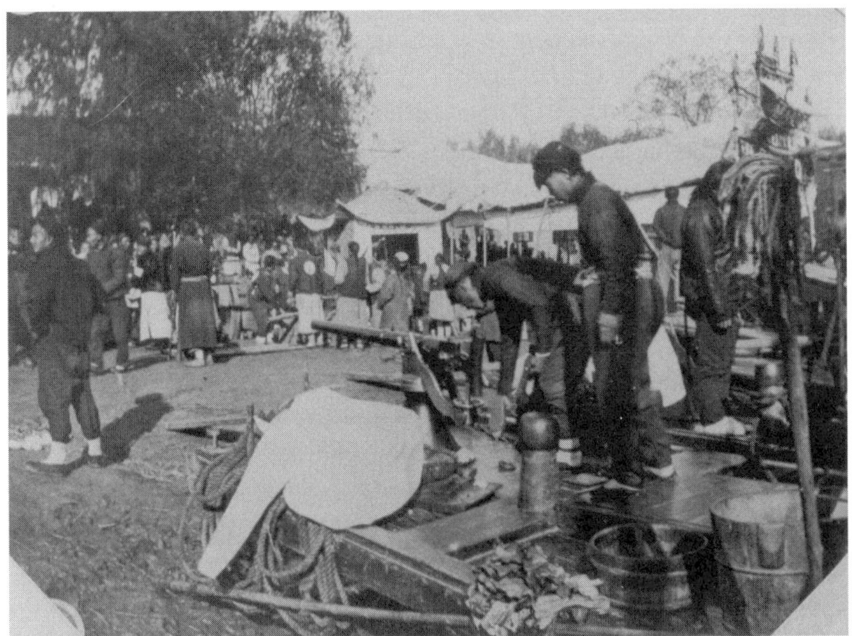

Figure 6.6(b) Armed War Junks. Laribe, 1908.[112]

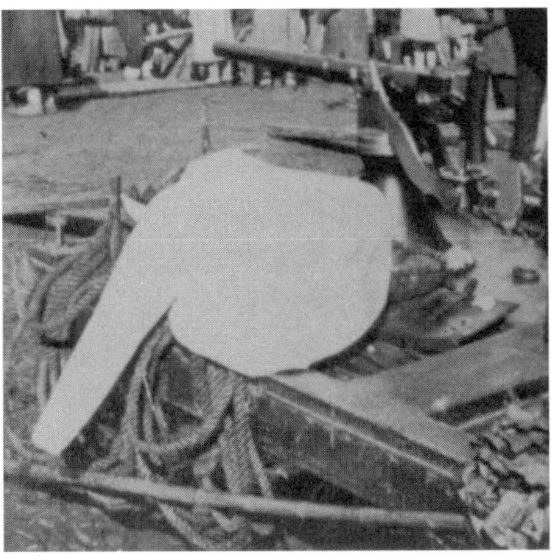

Figure 6.6(c) Armed War Junks (insert).

the parts of the arsenals which they were allowed to visit. All sources agree in respect of the type of weapons manufactured and the output of ammunition. De Contenson's reports were detailed and factual with regard to amount and type of production. He also observed in connection with the arsenals at Tianjin, Shanghai and Fuzhou that they were all being refitted and augmented continuously. His assessment of the arsenal at Tianjin was that it would become "extremely important."[113]

Captain Meillet had little use for the cliché that the Chinese people had an in-built traditional dislike for progress

> The people hold on to traditional usages as a matter of routine but willingly accept all reforms concerning administration or improvements facilitating every day life and commerce as can be seen by the usage they get out of the telegraph and steam boats.[114]

However, Meillet felt that in general, mandarins would not favour progress and he observed corruption in respect of the production of the arsenals he visited.[115] Although he was not permitted to go everywhere on his visit to Nanjing, and although he documented an impressive range of weapons made at the arsenal, he thought the arsenal was in such a state that it could not possibly produce anything regularly.[116] This same arsenal had been visited four years earlier by Henri Bryois:

> There I found the most modern equipment, enormous steam hammers, the widest variety of hydraulic equipment, machinery for cutting wood and metal. In numerous on-going building sites, work is intelligently portioned out in accordance with the best rules of efficiency with the result that guns and rifles come from the workshops at Nanking which can abundantly supply the army of the Viceroy Li Hongchang.[117]

Bryois was struck by one singular fact in his travels in China:

> ... the incredible activity deployed by the highest authorities in this country in perfecting military organisation.[118]

In 1892 de Fleurac had the opportunity to watch the manufacture, testing and laying of mines and torpedoes at Tianjin. He observed that despite the fact that laying was done carelessly, all the work in this domain had been successful.[119] In a letter to the Minister of War of 21 December 1892[120] de Fleurac, with his experience of Chinese manufacture and testing of weapons, expressed his extreme dissatisfaction that a sample of French

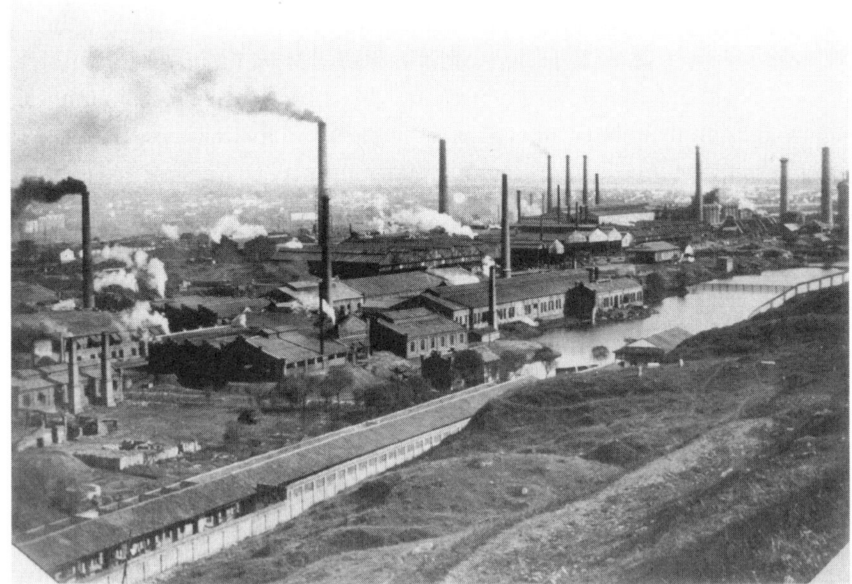

Figure 6.7(a) The Hanyang Arsenal from the Photograph Album of Laribe 1908. (By courtesy of the Musée de l'Armée de Terre, Paris)

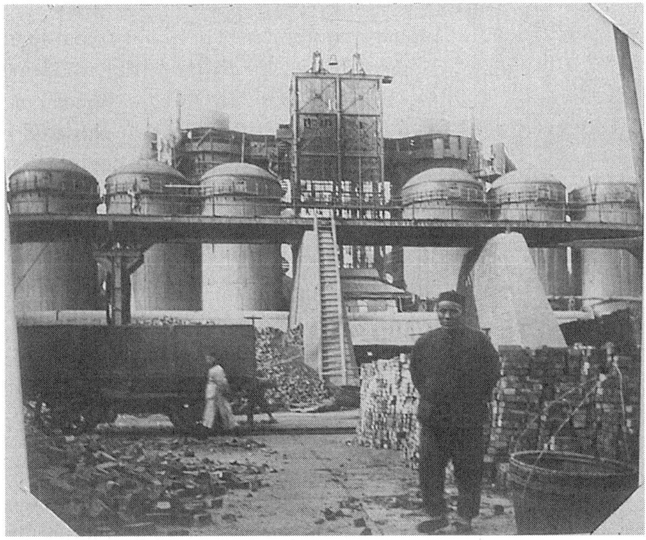

Figure 6.7(b) The Hanyang Arsenal. From Laribe 1908.[121] (By courtesy of the Musée de l'Armée de Terre, Paris)

smokeless powder from the National Manufactory at Sevrons-Livry should have been given to the director of armaments at Tianjin and to Li Hongzhang by a representative of R. Telge and Company of Hamburg. De Fleurac's opinion was that Chinese weapons research was of such excellence that it was the height of folly to have allowed this sample to get into Chinese hands. An early example of Western copying of Chinese military technology occurred in 1788 when the French Jesuit Amiot sent a sample of Chinese gunpowder to

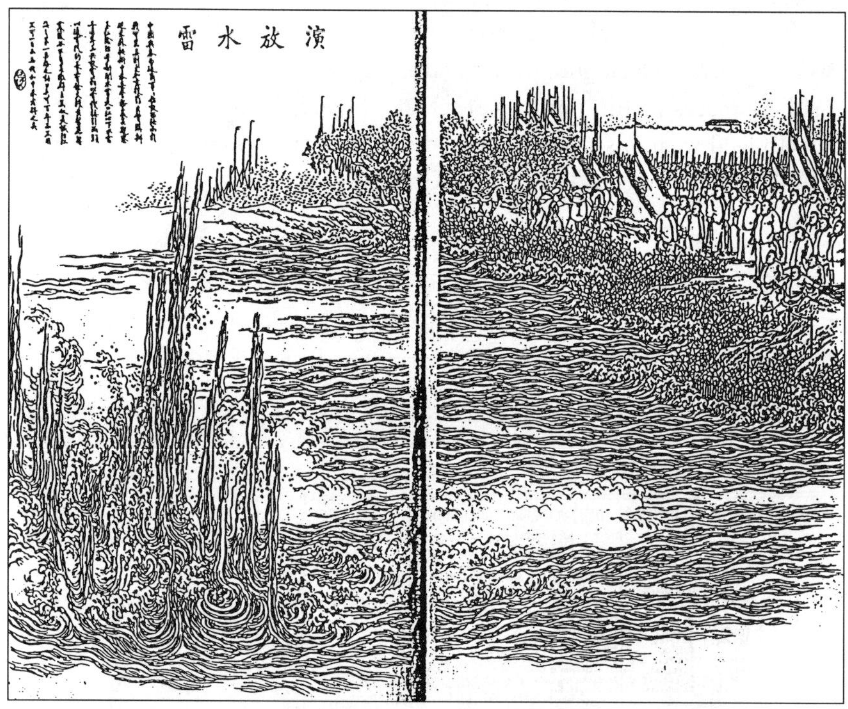

Figure 6.8 *Dianshizhai huabao*. Testing Mines, 1884.[122]
Testing the performance of water mines.... Recently, the Commander-in-Chief of Jiangsu Province sent observers to the Yu River to inspect the performance of water mines. The soldiers put three mines in the central part of the river, installed the electric box on the bank and connected wires about three kilometres long to the water mines to ignite them. As soon as the soldiers started the generator, the mines exploded. The explosion caused terrifying thunder and the waves smashed at the cliff of the river bank, reaching an astonishing height. They are surely the best defensive arms for borders of seas and rivers.

the French official Henri Bertin for analysis. Amiot wrote in some detail about the chemical composition of gunpowder which suggests that he "grasped the greater sophistication of Chinese knowledge."[123] Xu Jianyin was noting properties of German smokeless powder in 1881.[124] A translation of a work on gunpowder manufacturing machines was produced in 1881 and the first smokeless gunpowder was being produced in Shanghai in 1894.[125] The Tianjin arsenal concentrated particularly on the production of gunpowder and by the late 1880s had the largest and finest gunpowder-making works in the world.[126] The action in the first four weeks of the Boxer rising saw the Chinese using smokeless gunpowder to great effect while the Allied forces were still using black gunpowder and in consequence, having to move their artillery pieces within minutes of setting them up.

Indeed weapons research was given priority. It may well have been a "noble but neglected side-stream of Chinese culture,"[127] but men with highly

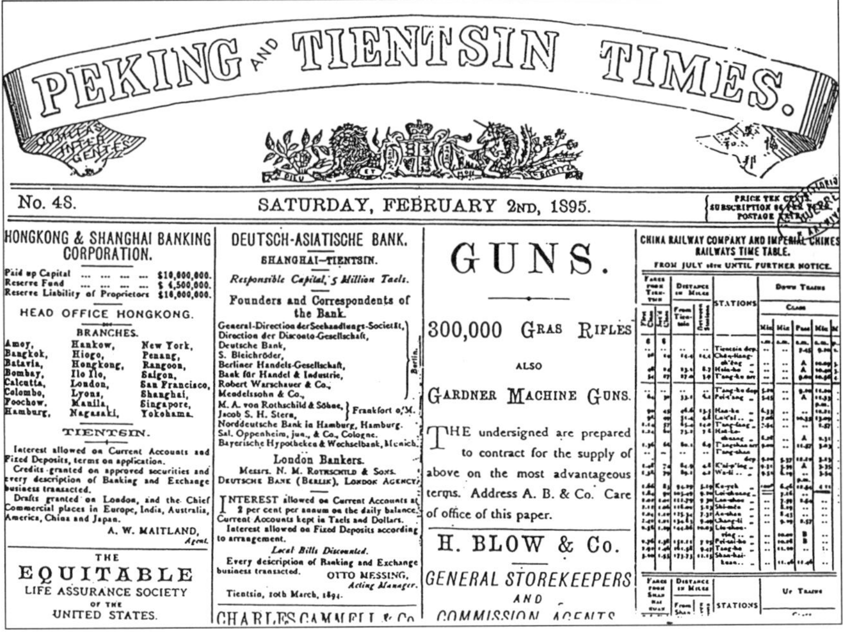

PEKING AND TIENTSIN TIMES.

COMMEAS INTER GENTES

No. 48. SATURDAY, FEBRUARY 2ND, 1895.

PRICE TEN CENTS
SUBSCRIPTION PER YEAR
POSTAGE EXTRA

HONGKONG & SHANGHAI BANKING CORPORATION.

Paid up Capital ... ... $10,000,000.
Reserve Fund ... ... $ 4,500,000.
Reserve Liability of Proprietors $10,000,000.

HEAD OFFICE HONGKONG.

BRANCHES.

Amoy, Bangkok, Batavia, Bombay, Calcutta, Colombo, Foochow, Hamburg, Hankow, Hiogo, Hongkong, Ilo Ilo, London, Lyons, Manila, Nagasaki, New York, Penang, Rangoon, Saigon, San Francisco, Shanghai, Singapore, Yokohama.

TIENTSIN.

Interest allowed on Current Accounts and Fixed Deposits, terms on application.

Credits granted on approved securities and every description of Banking and Exchange business transacted.

Drafts granted on London, and the Chief Commercial places in Europe, India, Australia, America, China and Japan.

A. W. MAITLAND,
Agent.

THE EQUITABLE LIFE ASSURANCE SOCIETY OF THE UNITED STATES.

DEUTSCH-ASIATISCHE BANK.

SHANGHAI—TIENTSIN.

Responsible Capital, 5 Million Taels.

Founders and Correspondents of the Bank.

General-Direction der Seehandlungs-Societät, Direction der Disconto-Gesellschaft, Deutsche Bank, S. Bleichröder, Berliner Handels-Gesellschaft, Bank für Handel & Industrie, Robert Warschauer & Co., Mendelssohn & Co., } Berlin.
M. A. von Rothschild & Söhne, Jacob S. H. Stern, } Frankfort o/M.
Norddeutsche Bank in Hamburg, Hamburg.
Sal. Oppenheim, jun., & Co., Cologne.
Bayerische Hypotheken & Wechselbank, Munich.

London Bankers.

Messrs. N. M. Rothschild & Sons.
Deutsche Bank (Berlin), London Agency.

INTEREST allowed on Current Accounts at 2 per cent per annum on the daily balance.
Current Accounts kept in Taels and Dollars.
Interest allowed on Fixed Deposits according to arrangement.

Local Bills Discounted.

Every description of Banking and Exchange business transacted.

OTTO MESSING,
Acting Manager.

Tientsin, 10th March, 1894.

CHARLES CAMMELL & Co.

GUNS.

300,000 GRAS RIFLES

ALSO

GARDNER MACHINE GUNS.

THE undersigned are prepared to contract for the supply of above on the most advantageous terms. Address A. B. & Co. Care of office of this paper.

H. BLOW & Co.

GENERAL STOREKEEPERS AND COMMISSION AGENTS

CHINA RAILWAY COMPANY AND IMPERIAL CHINESE RAILWAYS TIME TABLE.

FROM JULY UNTIL FURTHER NOTICE.

Figure 6.9 The front page of the *Peking and Tientsin Times* advertising military hardware, banking facilities and the train timetable. The prominence given to the advertisement for guns is striking.[128]

inventive and creative intellects were co-opted to work in arsenals early in their careers and sent to Europe with the express purpose of studying the Western manufacturing base. Under the patronage of Li Hongzhang, Xu Jianyin was sent to investigate European factories of all kinds and to purchase armour plated warships. It was obvious that this trip and the resulting reports contributed to the high degree of technical expertise displayed by Li during his 1896 visit. Xu Jianyin's visit to Europe impressed upon him some precise reasons for the gulf between China and the industrialised countries.

> In gunpowder manufacture (Xu) noted that the machinery used in Germany was not as advanced as that in Shanghai, Tianjin or Jinan, but the quality of the product was higher, because the Germans were constantly improving the process. His experience in Europe ... made him markedly more pessimistic than he had been before, and more aware of the enormous technological gulf which now lay between China and the industrial states [and also] Japan.[129]

Setting Xu Jianyin's pessimism in a wider context, his translation work was of great service to those wishing to modernise China. His pessimism reflects the thinking of the pure scientist rather than that of a statesman soldier. Li Hongzhang who sought Xu's advice and then combined this advice with his own expertise as a civilian and military official, forged ahead to adapt the reality of China to the possibilities Xu saw in the West. For Li to be able to disseminate knowledge and understanding of these possibilities, Xu's translation work was invaluable. Some titles available in Chinese included *New Types of Steam Engines* (1872), *The Engineer and Machinist's Drawing Book* (1872), *Essentials of the Steam Engine* (1873), *Manoeuvring Steamships* (1874), *Electricity* (1880), *Record of a Visit to the Krupp Gun Factory* (1881) and *Methods for Manufacturing the Outer Shells of Mines* (1881).[130]

Another factor in the rapid modernisation of a small but significant proportion of armies in the North was the personal interest of Chinese statesmen-soldiers such as Zeng Guofan, Li Hongzhang, Yuan Shikai and Zhang Zhidong. Zeng and Li had to resort to extraordinary finesse and financial manoeuvring in order to equip and train modern armies. At times they had to use their own personal funds.[131] Li's efforts to establish arsenals put him on a level with any great leader on the world stage of the day. "The superiority of the Huai-chün weapons which made the Huai-chün the strongest fighting force in the land, was largely a result of Li's control over the [Jiangnan] arsenal."[132] In building such arsenals, shipyards and factories, Li "accustomed a whole generation of Chinese to these important aspects of modern culture."[133] He demonstrated an extraordinary view of the breadth and depth of the issues involved. He appointed men to all aspects of work required to bring a country onto a modern war footing; from finance to science, from factory production to parade ground drill. He played a cardinal role in purchasing state-of-the-art weaponry and employing military instructors to train various armies in the use of this weaponry. He was zealous about the need to dispense with foreign instructors as soon as possible so as to have the soldiers trained by Chinese officers. His interest began as early as his association with foreign military men during the Taiping Rebellion and a photograph taken by John Thomson in *c.* 1867–1868 shows Li Hongzhang's Western-drilled Chinese troops. According to Captain Meillet, the French engineer who met Li in March 1896, Li:

> ... had precise opinions on most questions relating to weapons, finance and industry as a result of the extensive relations he had had over many years with Europeans ... long before the war with Japan, he had pointed to the danger of not acquiring European weapons.[134]

One might also add that Li's opinions were, in part, the result of the translation work done by gifted young Chinese scientists who collaborated with John Fryer (director of the department for the translation of scientific books in the Jiangnan arsenal)[135] as well as Li's perspicacity in employing such men and familiarising himself with their work.

On his visit to France, it was the issue of finance which most preoccupied Li and he even visited the French bank, Credit Lyonnais, to try and organise a loan.[136] During these discussions, it became obvious that Li had detailed information about Russia's financial strategy in funding weapons acquisition.[137] Chinese-speaking Captain d'Amade accompanied Li during his 1896 visit to France and noted that the Chinese had already organised an effective weapons procurement system. They had their requirements translated into English and French and distributed to all the Consulates in Tianjin and Shanghai. Their orders were for those defensive weapons for which Chinese arsenals could make ammunition. Captain d'Amade wrote of this as though the Chinese policy was somewhat ridiculous and that the Chinese should be acquiring more up-to-date weaponry[138] but such an approach would seem ideally suited to the economic, technological and political climate of China in the last decade of the nineteenth century. We see in d'Amade's opinion, the dominant influence of the Western military view that the capacity to harness powerful technology is the best way to win wars. In the Chinese response to the arms race as exemplified by Li Hongzhang's careful decisions regarding purchase viz á viz manufacture, the dominant thinking was clearly that the "human factor" could be harnessed to overcome slight obsolescence in the "weapons factor."[139] From Li Hongzhang buying recently obsolete rifles for which his arsenals could manufacture ammunition, to the sergeant majors barking out separate commands in different languages to Chinese soldiers armed with different weapons on the same parade ground, we see a distinctive Chinese adaptation to the arms race.[140] The talented young scientist Xu Jianyin came to see that sophisticated military hardware should be bought from foreigners and that Chinese arsenals should "make items for which they had the raw materials."[141] Xu's association with Li dated back to 1874 when they worked "to set up a gunpowder factory and a process for acid manufacture which made acid said to be 'better and cheaper' than any that could be imported."[142]

Li was well aware of the market value of the weaponry he was shown on the tour and informed d'Amade that the Belgians were asking less for a particular small calibre gun he saw at the arsenal at Creusot.[143] His questions on the handling of the 1886 rifle manufactured at Saint Etienne were noted by d'Amade as "highly precise."[144]

> Li examined a cavalry carbine, being particularly interested in the automatic self-closing mechanism; he understood perfectly the function of the charger. He examined the officers' revolver model 92 ... he examined in considerable detail the organization of the distribution of power by electricity, the distribution of lighting and the installation of water tanks for reducing the temperature in the condensers.[145]

D'Amade was also impressed that Li Hongzhang already knew that France was selling these weapons to Russia. On his visit to Saint Etienne, Li's technical expertise with regard to electrical appliances regulating machinery at the arsenal was evident as was his interest in experiments in the nature of the explosion of weapons loaded with ammunition containing impurities. One is reminded of the extreme technical precision of the Qianlong Emperor's (reigned 1736–1795) knowledge of and interest in military matters.[146]

Li also spent some time questioning the director of Saint Etienne on details concerning the employees, their contracts, the relationship between these and maximum daily production; on the source of all primary materials used in production, and on the methods of procuring these. While no evidence has been found to show the slightest irregularity in any aspect of the running of the arsenal at Tianjin under Li Hongzhang, it is undeniable that there were irregularities in employment procedures at Jiangnan, for example.[147]

The French in their turn, knowing that Li and his party had already visited Krupp's workshops, questioned members of Li's entourage on several occasions to try and get precise details about the latest Krupp guns which could absorb their recoil. The French and the Chinese had been fighting in Indochina/Yunnan only eleven years before. It thus comes as no surprise that Captain Meillet was unable to get the technical information he wanted about these weapons, the Chinese aides de camp being rather vague about such details as the exact diameter of the guns, the weight of the shells or their velocity.[148] D'Amade observed that on the question of this particular weapon, he was able to get some reasonably accurate information from the Chinese "although in general the Chinese lack precision in their ideas."[149]

For those looking for evidence of extreme precision in the ideas of the Chinese as evidenced by the action in 1900, there is plenty, most particularly with reference to the deadly accuracy of Chinese artillery. Chinese interest in the mathematics related to gunnery dated from the early eighteenth century.[150] In addition, "the Chinese had been well aware of the military significance of cartography .... The great strategist Sun Zi had stressed the importance of 'knowing one's terrain'."[151] Foreshadowing the detailed discussion of the battle of Dagu and the rout of Admiral Seymour's expedition to relieve the Legations, it is in this historical context that we note that Chinese gunners were able to locate their targets in the dark or at a distance of up to three miles away. At Dagu, the artillery duel lasted all night. The Chinese gunners were using tidal charts, flares and searchlights. Their feat in hitting every attacking vessel, while largely leaving the considerable amount of merchant shipping untouched, was extraordinary and will be discussed in detail in Chapter Seven.The Chinese had built the Xigu arsenal outside Tianjin without the knowledge of foreign military intelligence. They obviously had precision maps locating the arsenal in relation to their guns in Tianjin. In the British military culture, gunnery was long considered to be a dirty noisy affair requiring a chap to have a good head for figures and was not, in consequence, as highly esteemed as was service in a cavalry regiment, for example.

In addition to the production of weapons in China, there was a huge official and unofficial acquisition programme aimed at buying weapons in Europe. Krupp regarded China as an important customer and he had a photograph of Li Hongzhang above his bed.[152] Military attachés observed both the official and the unofficial trafficking in arms.

> At this moment on the docks at Tianjin there are more than thirty enormous cases containing German guns.[153]

Captain Chambry was told that these guns were destined for the forts in Manchuria but as, like his predecessors, he was unable to get into the Dagu forts, he speculated anxiously as to the true destination of these weapons. Captain de Fleurac wrote to the Minister of War on 13 August 1892 that the troops of Zhili were to be rearmed on a massive scale:

> It appears that their [the troops of Zhili] armament will grow by 30,000 Mauser rifles which, according to telegrams coming from Europe would have been sent from Hamburg to Tianjin in the last days of June.[154]

Evidence of private arms trafficking may be seen in the startling front page newspaper advertisement pictured at Figure 6.9. That 300,000 rifles could be advertised for sale on the front page of the only English-language paper in Tianjin, wedged between the train timetable and banking notices, should give some idea of the scale and openness of private arms dealing with China at this time. During the Boxer rising, Li Hongzhang had an official beheaded for his part in gun trafficking.[155] Although arms trafficking was common knowledge, Qing officials were supposed to put their orders through the official channels and certainly not to be caught openly smuggling arms.

The outstanding features of China's initial attempts to modernise her armaments production were the building and continual updating of modern arsenals, some of which had more modern equipment than some of their European counterparts; the development of a research, analysis and education base including a systematic translation programme; the ability to manufacture large quantities of arms particularly suited to Chinese requirements; the systematic training of research and executive personnel by sending them to Europe; the gradual realisation that China lacked the financial resources to compete in the production of state-of-the-art weaponry and the apparent consequent policy decision to adopt an arms acquisition programme on the basis of Chinese capacity to supply ammunition for the weapons they were buying; the development of self-sufficiency in some areas such as the production of mines and electric torpedoes; and the personal interest and in-depth knowledge of some of China's most influential statesmen. However, in China, just as in Western cultures, there was also an immense weight of conservatism among other civilian and military men.

In this last respect, any assessment of China's attempts to modernise after 1860 should take cognisance of the conservatism among civilian and military men in all cultures. As Lévi-Strauss reminds us, "The diversity of human cultures ought not to invite us to make observations which are divisive or dividing."[156] Studies of Chinese military history have tended to concentrate far too much on the different rather than pointing to the similar. The differences in the types of government in Britain, France and China in the second half of the nineteenth century were less important than the fact that the ruling classes of all these countries produced a majority of the high-ranking military officers[157] and a majority of civilian men who were opposed to military innovation and the expenditure consequent thereon. Only a minority of men in power, whether civilian or military, saw the need for change, in response to external — and in the case of China — internal threat as well. Any assessment of China's attempts at military modernisation, to be at all balanced would thus also, have to include a brief description of the conservative forces in the French and British High Command during the same period.

To take two examples; the Secretary of State for War, Cardwell (1813–1886) broke his health trying to abolish flogging and the purchase of commissions in the British army, resigning shortly after he finally secured the passage of the Army Reform Bill in 1871. The Army Reform Bill, though passed three times by the Commons was blocked in the House of Lords by men such as the Duke of Richmond, the Marquis of Salisbury and the Earl of Dalhousie. These leaders were all of "those pure Conservatives whose Conservatism is never so intense as when allied to military habits of thought."[158] The system of purchase of commissions was finally abolished by Gladstone circumventing the House of Lords, going to Queen Victoria and recommending that she terminate the practice through a royal warrant. George Trevelyan wrote an

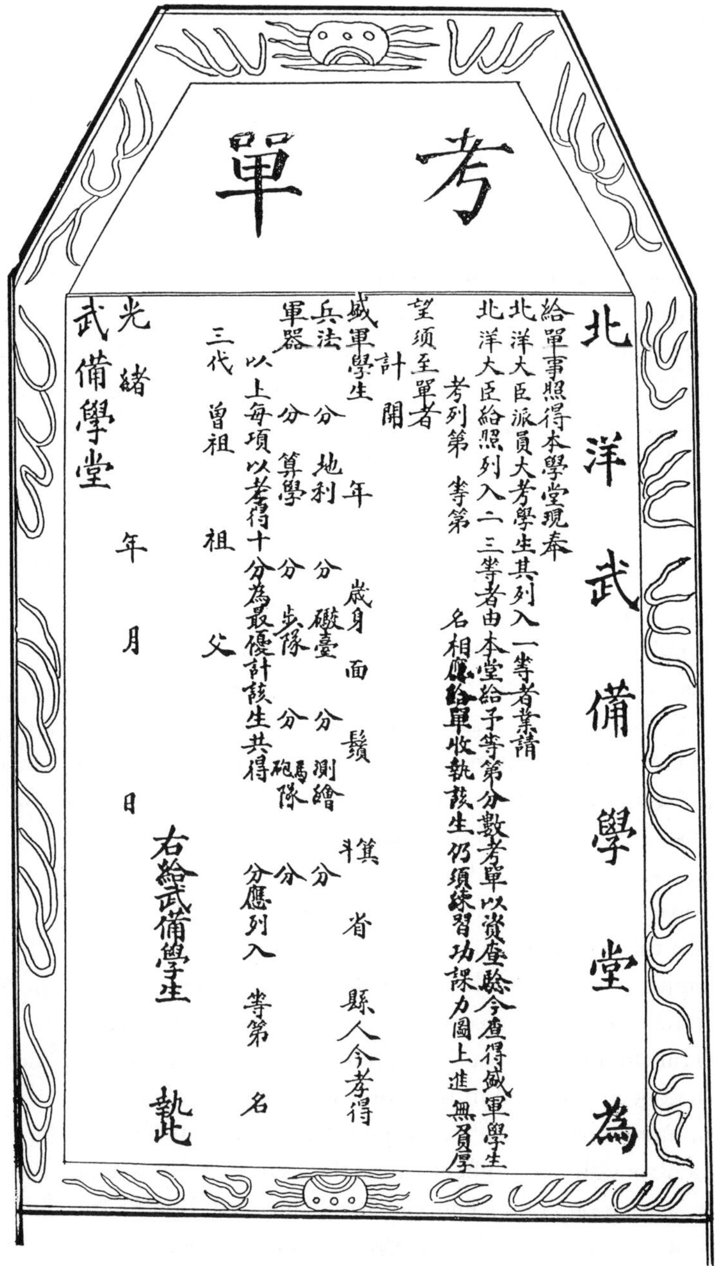

考單

北洋武備學堂為

給單事照得本學堂現奉

北洋大臣派員大考學生共列入一等者業請

北洋大臣給照列入二三等者由本堂給予等第分數考單以資查驗今查得威軍學生

考列第　等第　名相應給單收執該生仍須練習功課力圖上進無負厚

望須至單者

計開

威軍學生　年　歲身　面　鬚　斗箕　省　縣人今考得

兵法　分　地利　分　礮臺　分　測繪　分

軍器　分　算學　分　步隊　分　馬隊砲隊　分

以上每項以考得十分為最優計該生共得　分應列入　等第　名

三代　曾祖　祖　父

右給武備學堂學生　執此

光緒　年　月　日

武備學堂

Figure 6.10 Northern Sea Naval College Certificate, *c.* 1890.[159] (By courtesy of the Musée de l'Armée de Terre, Paris) essay restating the case for army reform: "The Purchase System in the British Army," 1867 which ran into four editions (1869). In it he inveighed against the absence of middle-class officers in the British army.[160] As the purchase of commissions was only stopped in 1871, by 1900 there would have still been many high ranking British serving officers who had bought their first commission. Flogging was not actually abolished until 1879 in the Navy and 1881 in the Army.

The purchase of military and civilian rank in China has received attention from historians in the context that this was not always conducive to the country's best interest. How many parochial livings were bought by wealthy English families for their sons, thinking that a career in the Church was at least worth a try? Perhaps buying the right to take charge of people's spiritual lives might be seen to be less harmful than buying the right to command men in war. However, the effect on the British officer corps of the institution of buying commissions was not always salutary. The details of the military career of the Earl of Cardigan and his performance in battle remain a stunning example of the ultimately undesirable military consequence of this practice. As for weapons and training, the Armstrong breech-loading gun was only introduced experimentally in the British army in 1858 and it was two decades before breech-loaders became standard. At the time of the Boxer rising, muzzle-loaders were still in use, as were pikes and tomahawks. While it may be argued that combat conditions may make some more primitive weapons ideal, this argument would have to be applied as well to the Chinese fighting on two fronts during the Boxer rising, as to the Allied forces.

Conservatism as an element in military thinking was also an important factor in the organisation, training and equipping of Western armies in the nineteenth century. One historian of the Chinese army offers the view that the Chinese army contained a "vast officer corps which was sunk in ignorance, conservatism and nepotism."[161] From the 1860s British and American soldiers had been involved in training various Chinese armies. We have seen that military schools were established in Shanghai and Tianjin in the 1870s at which time the first officers were also being sent overseas to study. The officers' mess rooms of the élite cavalry regiments in Britain in the 1870s were still dominated by men who had purchased their commissions. Almost all of them were excellent on horseback, reflecting the social significance attached to fox hunting by the British country gentry. However, there were a great

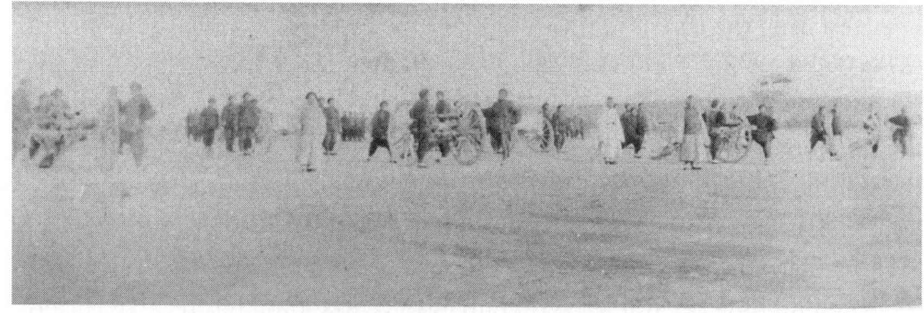

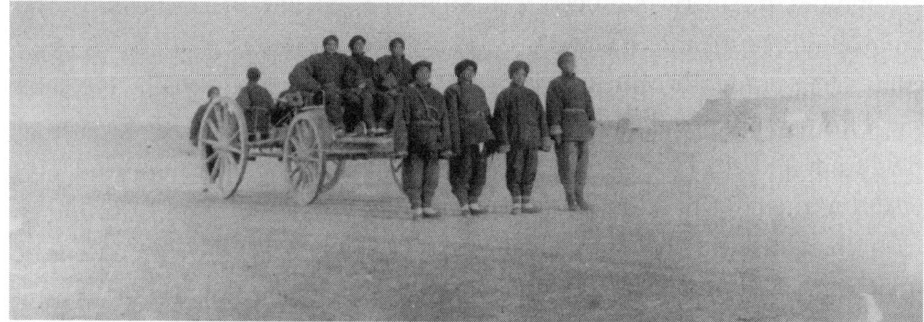

Figure 6.11 Artillery on the Parade Ground of the Junliang Cheng, 1888.[162] (By courtesy of the Musée de l'Armée de Terre, Paris)

many whose conception of their rôle as cavalry officers was indistinguishable from their fetishism over the cut of their breeches or the curve of their moustaches. (See Figures 5.55 and 2.12) A comparison with the British navy shows that on the officer level, the Royal Navy "was still a ragged, unfinished profession" until reforms of the hierarchy began to take effect in the 1870s.[163] As for the men, it was not until 1853 that the British government inaugurated the first-ever system of long-term service, replacing the press-gang or short-term volunteers. Admiral Seymour observed in his Memoirs that he remembered naval ratings receiving up to one hundred pounds at one time, indicating just how long the men had been serving without pay.[164] The pay of an ordinary rating at this time rarely exceeded ten pounds a year. Insofar as change itself was concerned, Michael Lewis wrote of the British navy:

> Neither Government nor people welcomed it. Every change was grudgingly accepted and sometimes dangerously delayed.... Britain did not lead the new trends, but only accepted them as compelled by threats from the outside. The pioneers were the French and the Americans.[165]

One is struck by the parallels between Britain and China in respect of a conservative approach to change in the armed forces. Scholars have laboured the point about the inappropriateness of some aspects of traditional Chinese military examinations as preparation for modern warfare. To take but one parallel example from Western military training institutions — and that of a relative newcomer to a type of education steeped in tradition — the second-year cadets of West Point in 1900 were required to study Molière's *Don Juan* in the original seventeenth century French. With the ongoing war in the Philippines, if American officers were to have some familiarity with a second language, Spanish might have been considered more appropriate than the study of seventeenth-century French drama.

Photographic evidence of the annual manoeuvres of the Chinese army held from 1902 to 1908 suggest that the Boxer War was also instrumental in ensuring the continuation of efforts to modernise China's armed forces. (Li Hongzhang had first held army manoeuvres in the 1870s.) (See Figures 6.12, 6.19, 6.20, 6.21 and 6.21[a])

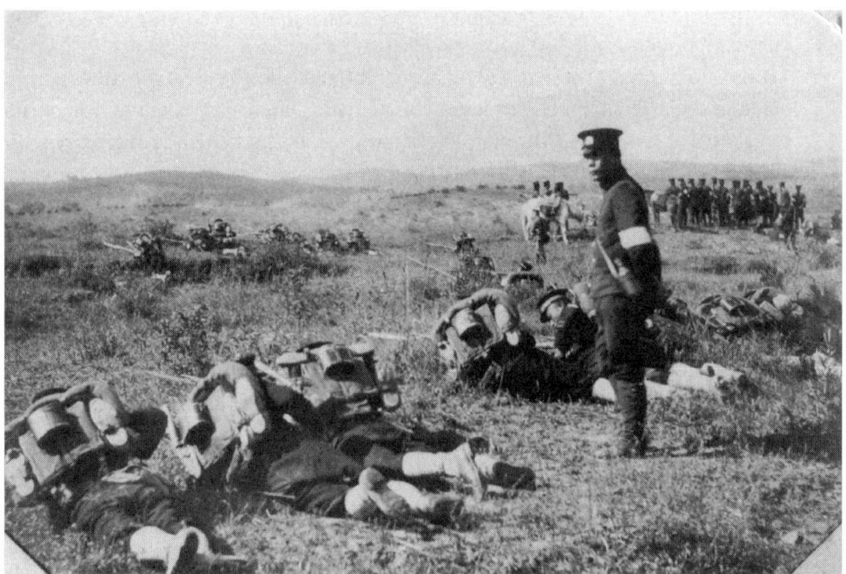

Figure 6.12 The army manoeuvres of 1908 showing infantry exercises. Army manoeuvres similar to those of 1908 had begun in 1901 though Li Hongzhang's Huai army had held annual manoeuvres since the early 1870s.[166] (By courtesy of the Musée de l'Armée de Terre, Paris)

A representative of the "loser" school, states that:

> By 1894, too, there were "arsenals" — or at least machine-shops in nine centres. Yet at some factories where modern arms were, or could be made the Chinese continued to manufacture gingals and muskets![167]

This represents a distorted underestimation of China's weapons manufacturing capability before 1900. The eyewitness sources used by scholars to describe the Chinese arsenals are notable by their absence. A complete reading of Beresford's chapter on arsenals shows him to have been impressed by all the arsenals he was taken to visit. His only rider was that they could have been making greater quantities of ammunition in the same amount of time. At Shanghai arsenal he saw the work in hand:

> Two 9.2 guns to be mounted on hydro-pneumatic disappearing carriages
> Two 9.2 guns for garrison batteries
> Eight 6" guns, Q. F.
> Twelve 4.7" guns, Q. F.
> Twelve 12-pounders, Q. F.
> Twenty 6-pounders, Q. F.
> Fifty 3-pounders, Q.F.
> These guns were of the latest Armstrong pattern. All the steel for these guns is made in the arsenal, chiefly from native ore. The gun factory does not accept this steel until it has passed through the same tests as the British Government use and each gun is proved by the tests the British use before it leaves the arsenal. I saw machinery for making guns of every calibre up to the 12" 50-ton gun. Several of these last-named guns have been manufactured in the arsenal, and I saw some of them mounted in the forts I visited.[168]

Beresford's account contains a great deal of positive information about the capacities of the Chinese arsenals he visited, notably their ability to turn out good Mauser-pattern rifles. He also commented on the waste of machinery as he saw a lot lying around not as yet set up. His main negative observation concerned the manufacture of gingals[169] at arsenals capable of making modern weapons. One notices a reluctance on the part of some scholars to report on the positive as well as the negative aspects mentioned in primary sources they have consulted.[170]

None of these writers from Lord Charles Beresford to recent historians have taken into consideration the fact that the vast non-Western-trained bulk of the widely different branches of the Chinese army could not be armed simultaneously with modern weapons. Nevertheless, a Japanese intelligence report of 1882 estimated that by this date an impressive three fifths of the Chinese army was armed with modern weapons. This report specifically refers to the modern armies.[171] Lengthy and expensive training in the use of such weapons is a prerequisite capability. Without such training it would be pointless to issue men with modern weapons. While some armies in the North were completely armed with modern weapons, others had only some units thus equipped and still others had no modern weapons at all. It is therefore logical in a situation in which only gradual modernisation could be envisaged, that Chinese arsenals should concentrate on equipping the most strategically important armies with modern weapons. At the same time, arsenals could continue to equip those armies that had not as yet been modernised and they could be issued with Chinese ammunition for familiar weapons on which they had trained.

The assumption of contemporary writers, like that of Beresford and d'Amade, was that if the Chinese continued to manufacture outdated arms in arsenals capable of producing modern weapons, this implied some kind of blind adherence to tradition on their part. Modernisation of Chinese armies and the concomitant necessary extensive Western training and drilling, began in selected armies which had been raised by statesmen-soldiers in areas of strategic importance. China's achievement in equipping and training these armies, based on her own resources as far as possible, was impressive. However, political, social and economic factors made it impossible to extend this modernisation at greater speed to the rest of China's armed forces. The problem of providing the Western training needed for Chinese soldiers to be able to use modern weapons was as great as the problem of financing weapons acquisition. In this context, it was expedient to continue to produce obsolete weapons to replace those in the sections of the army still trained to use them.

Training

There is a wealth of detailed evidence concerning the training of the Northern armies. European instructors first began drilling Chinese troops in the mid-1860s under the direction of Li Hongzhang. During Li's tour of France in 1896, Captain d'Amade noticed Li's keen interest in an infantry combat exercise and an artillery display that was put on for him at his request at Saint

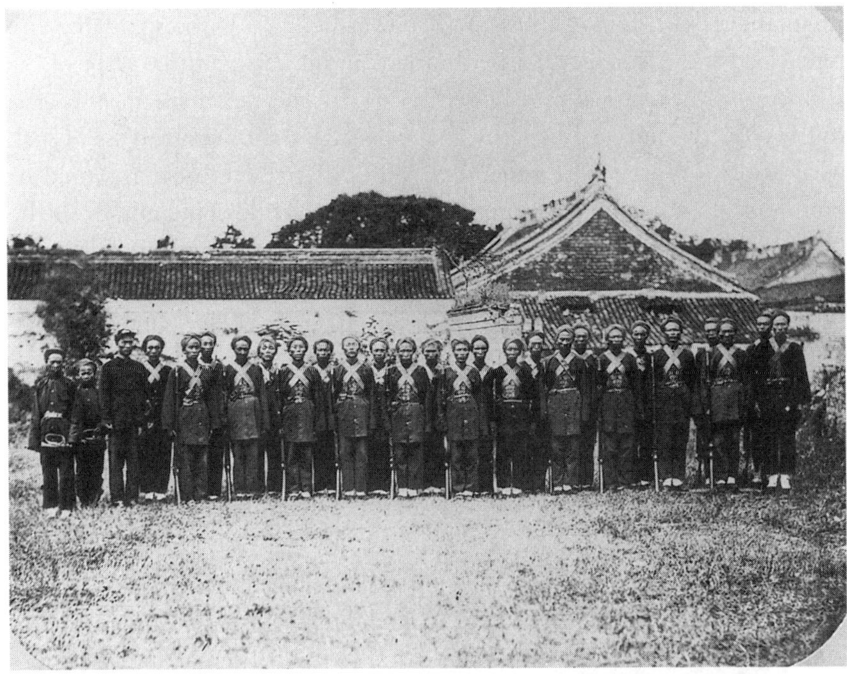

Figure 6.13(a) Men of Li Hongzhang's Huai army, *c.* 1870s. Note the polished belts and immaculate turnout.[172] (By courtesy of the Library of Congress)

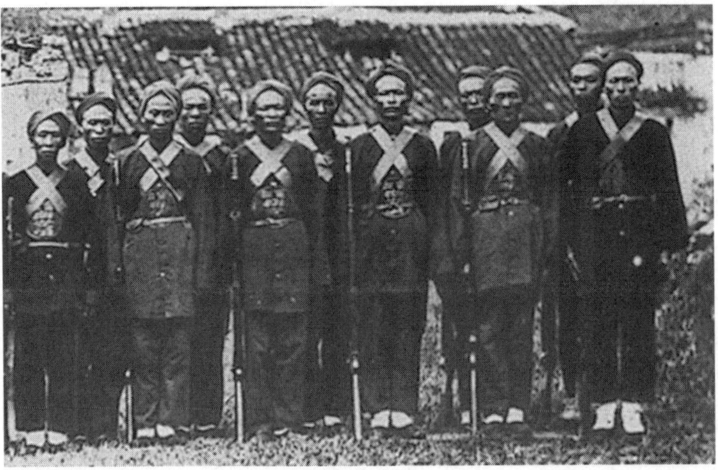

Figure 6.13(b) Men of Li Hongzhang's Huai army (insert).

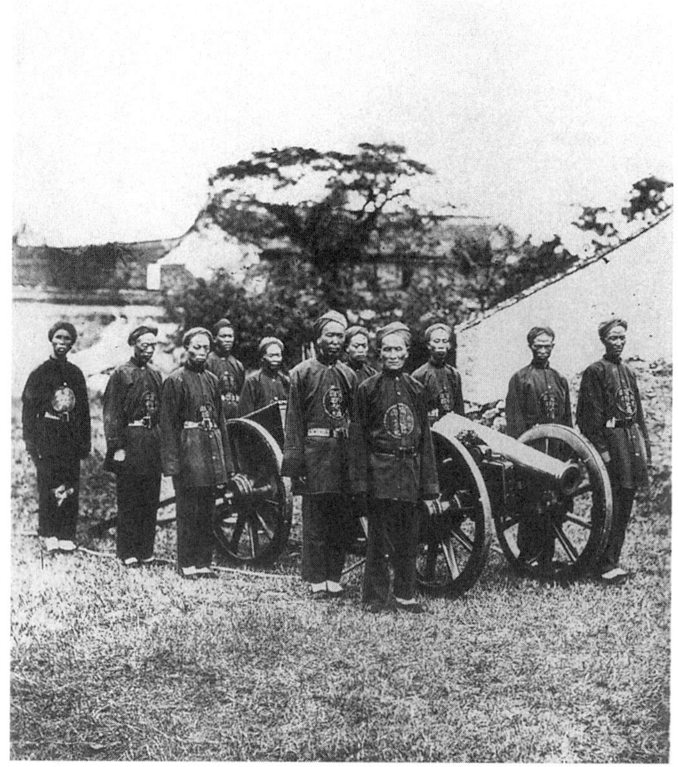

Figure 6.14 Artillery troops of Li Hongzhang's Huai army, c. 1870s. Their position with respect to the gun shows the adoption of Western artillery drill.[173] (By courtesy of the Library of Congress)

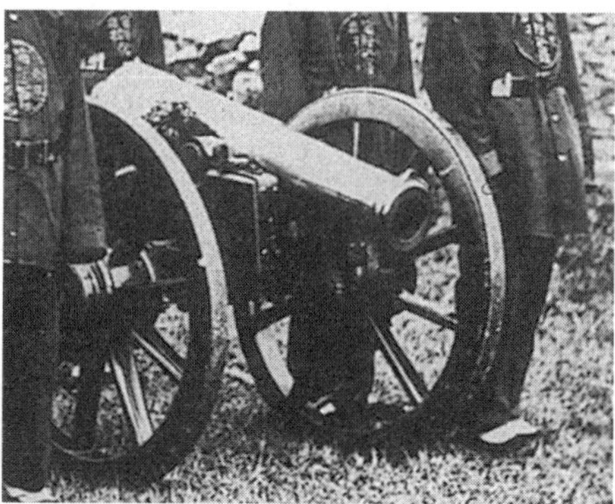

Figure 6.14(a) Artillery troops of Li Hongzhang's Huai army (insert).

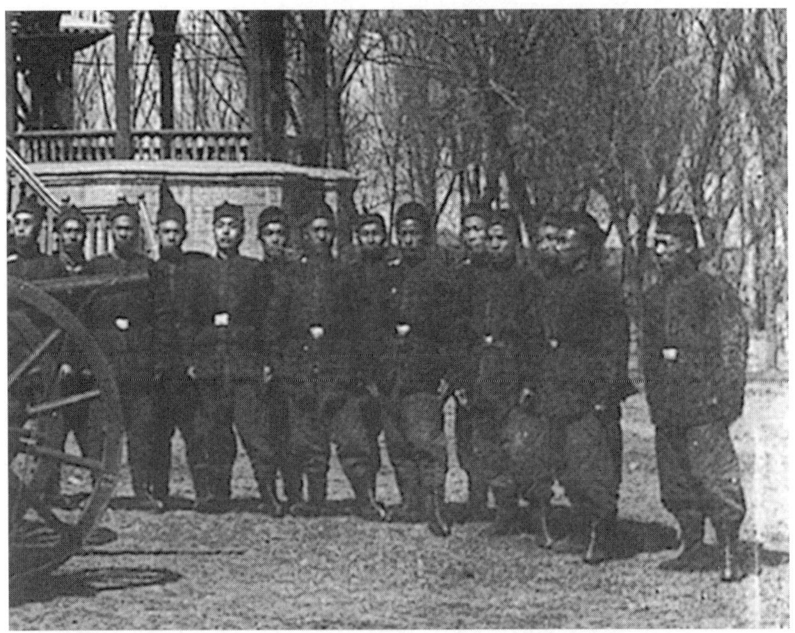

Figure 6.15(a) "These Untutored Chinese" (insert). Artillery class (anon) possibly late 1890s.[174]

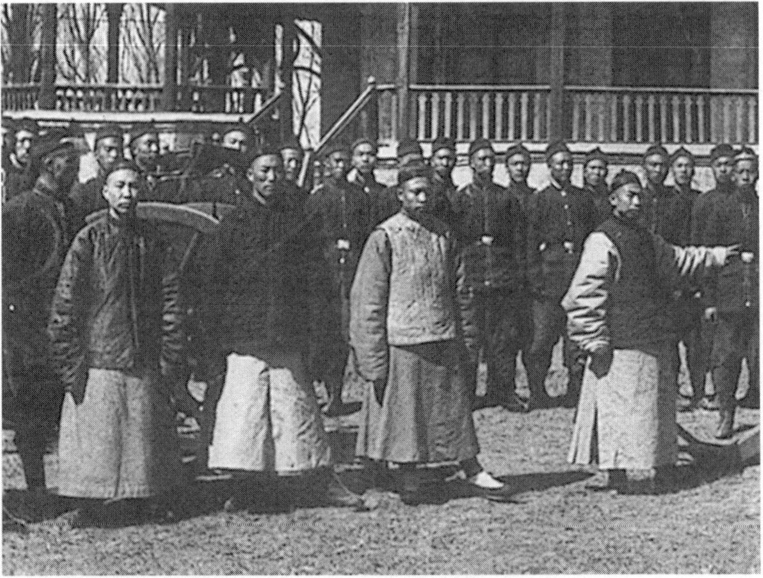

Figure 6.15(b) "These Untutored Class" (insert).

Cyr. At that time, a member of Li's entourage, the director of the military school at Tianjin, Zhang Yu, asked for details concerning the forward supply of ammunition during battle and the evacuation of the wounded.[175]

In 1882 the French Captain Chambry saw a review of Li's personal guard and his troops who had been trained by a Mr Schnell, a former Non-Commissioned Officer (NCO) in the German army. Schnell had been employed by the Viceroy of Shandong who had found him too strict and had sacked him in 1879.[176] Chambry also saw a division of Li's troops that had been trained by the English. The review Chambry saw was the second annual review since Schnell's appointment. Chambry observed that all the troops were immaculately and uniformly dressed. Those using English weapons responded to English directions and commands in English; those using German weapons responded to directions in German and commands in Chinese.[177] This is fascinating evidence of Chinese ability to overcome problems posed by patchy rearmament programmes. There was contemporary and subsequent belittling of the Chinese because they used incompatible weapons.[178] It would seem from this example that, where necessary, individual Chinese generals could evolve workable solutions to immediate problems of incompatible weaponry, training, tactics and logistics in armies where these posed difficulties. It would also seem that the soldiers training together and responding correctly to two different languages were intelligent men. As can be seen from a comparison of Figures 6.2 and 6.16, even troops drilled by foreign instructors from the same country were markedly different. This element introduced a further complication in the factors that resulted in extreme variations in China's modern-drilled armies.

Whether English or German, Chambry emphasised that the weapons were maintained to perfection and of top quality. The troops he saw were armed with Mauser rifles and Krupp guns and Martini rifles and Armstrong guns. He thought that the gun carriages were old-fashioned and was told that they had been made in China but once again, he emphasised that they were in perfect condition. Chambry's report went on to describe in detail the exercises he saw executed. These corresponded exactly to the way British and German troops were being drilled at this time. There was, however, a difference between the way British and German troops were drilled and what Chambry saw was the German manner of drilling. Chambry concluded his report:

> In summary, the German exercises executed at this review by their extremely remarkable precision from beginning to end, would have done honour to the soldiery of any European nation.... I was permitted to observe target range firing at which what surprised me most, I must say, was the perfect maintenance of the weapons. At a range of one hundred metres, the accuracy could pass for satisfactory. The men were armed with Mauser rifles.[179]

A report of 12 April 1886 by General Chanoine described the principal reforms in tactics and training he observed in a corps of 18,000 to 19,000 men that had been raised in Beijing between 1862 and 1869 and trained in the European manner by the English. That is, the men he saw and on whom he commented favourably were part of a group that had received its training for seven years, seventeen years before General Chanoine watched them drilling. By the time he saw them, their drill had been modified, most notably to take account of the updated weapons with which the troops were being issued. General Chanoine also recorded that an infantry battalion had been trained by French instructors in Shanghai during the 1860s. Since 1876 he noted that German instructors, never less than twenty at one time, had begun training Li Hongzhang's troops in Zhili. They had created a school for NCOs near Tianjin and were training the artillery batteries using German weapons. General Chanoine reported that there were forty trained artillery batteries and that there would be forty more within two years.[180] Captain d'Amade had reported that in Zhili by 1888 twelve out of fourteen of the cavalry, infantry and artillery units he saw in this strategically important area were Western-drilled on Western weapons.[181]

Other French military attachés tried to witness Chinese military manoeuvres or training during the 1890s but recent hostilities between the French and the Chinese in Indochina meant that it was difficult if not impossible for the French to watch Chinese military training. However, Captain de Fleurac wrote a report on the organisation and training of Li Hongzhang's troops in 1892. He reported that artillery training took place daily, morning and evening and gave a detailed description of the types and duration of the exercises.[182] Captain de Fleurac also compiled valuable reports on the organisation, training and weaponry of Chinese troops in other strategically important parts of China, showing that they were drilled and armed in Western fashion, used rapid firing rifles and were "more or less well-drilled."[183] In view of the belittling characterisation of Chinese soldiers by some contemporaries, repeated without evidence by subsequent writers, it is interesting that in 1890, units of the modern-trained Chinese armies refused to use Chinese-manufactured Remington rifles. These particular rifles manufactured at Jiangnan had a serious fault in that they frequently emitted breech blast when fired owing to a defect in the breech mechanism. The director of the arsenal proposed a safety modification to be made at negligible cost but the rifles ended up being used for peace-time training when newer and better rifles were manufactured at Jiangnan.[184] The Chinese soldier we glimpse here is a trained professional who thinks and acts as part of a highly disciplined, highly organised unit. Presented with potentially dangerous weapons, such soldiers would naturally stand to a man until they were issued with suitable weapons. He is certainly not the one described in the Chinese adage as being made from a useless nail, nor is he the one described by *The Times*, Kotenev, Duiker, Purcell or Powell.

Another important indication of the extent to which the Imperial Chinese Army was modernised was their uniform. Uniforms require upkeep; soldiers must present themselves immaculate on parade; uniforms embody pride in the wearing, comradeship, bearing; uniforms are the external sign to outside observers of the soldierly qualities of their wearers.

On 5 June, General Nie had received a telegram from the Commander in Chief of the five armies, Ronglu:

> The uniforms of your troops make them look like foreigners, and the ignorant villagers may mistake them for foreign troops. The Boxers are the children of China. You should earnestly explain to them and make every effort to disperse them.[185]

The symbolism of uniforms was rightly perceived to be important. In 1900, the Japanese were very much admired for their smart uniform and turn-out by the military writers representing the other Powers. None of them happened to know that in the Sino-Japanese War of only five years before, Japanese infantrymen wore straw sandals with tragic consequences for hundreds of men who had to reconnoitre in deep snow.[186] This writer has seen no evidence of any Chinese infantrymen, whether in modernised or traditional armies, wearing straw sandals in the nineteenth century. Some contemporary Westerners derided Chinese traditional military uniforms. Others commented on how smart they were. This probably indicates that the contemporaries in question had seen soldiers of different Chinese armies. It was General Nie's experience that the wearing of Western uniforms excited hostility from conservatives at Court as well as simple villagers.[187] When soldiers must spend hours each day polishing their leather belts to pass inspection on parade, this presupposes a kind of communal discipline and group culture. Such discipline culminates in pride, among other sentiments. The photographs reproduced throughout this chapter show soldiers wearing polished leather belts which would have satisfied the most stringent of sergeant majors at Sandhurst, Saint Cyr or West Point. The observations of Western military attachés on standards of discipline[188] together with the photographic evidence show that the men of the Western-drilled armies had indeed reached such a standard on parade as to be compared favourably with soldiers of the Guard in Berlin or St Petersburg.[189] Attention has not been focused in studies of the military in the late Qing on this simple but fundamental emblem, the uniform. While Chinese soldiers were being trained and eventually fighting and dying beside their comrades in Western-style uniforms, these same uniforms were provoking criticism and hostility from their countrymen.

The issue of uniforms has been canvassed in Chapter Three. We shall see in the discussion below of the military performance of General Yang Mushi,

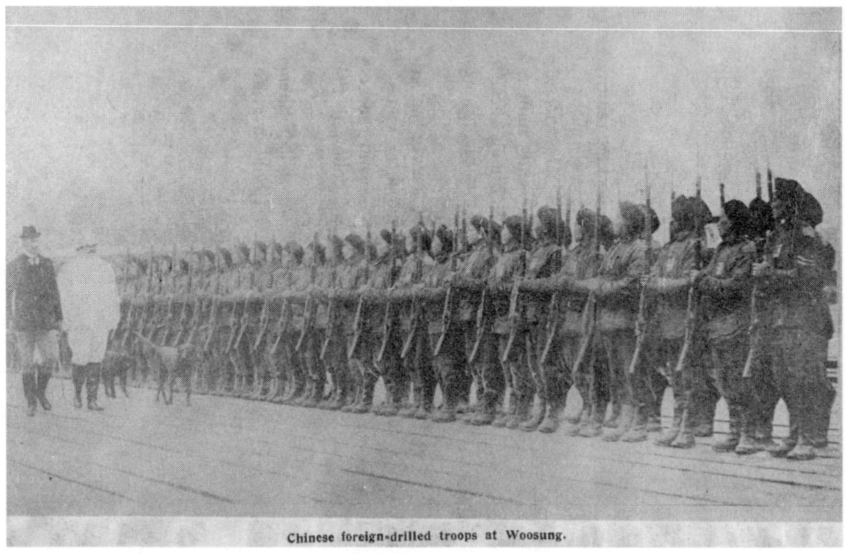
Chinese foreign-drilled troops at Woosung.

Figure 6.16 German-drilled troops at Shanghai, 1898.[190]

his officers and his men, that his men were trained and prepared to die for their country obeying orders under the most difficult of circumstances. The Imperial Chinese Army, particularly the soldiers of the former Huai army fighting in 1900 under General Nie Shicheng, owed its whole ethos to the forces of modernisation and all of this was symbolised by the uniform. Soldiers of the Huai army had begun wearing a semi-Western-style uniform in the late 1860s (see Figure 6.1) and had begun to perform Western-style annual manoeuvres in the early 1870s.

A last point needs to be made about training. In all military establishments after a major defeat there is a strong push to review military structures, training and strategic thinking. After the Sino-Japanese War, the Imperial Chinese Army adopted changes in all these three areas. With regard to training, during Li Hongzhang's visit to France in 1896, he showed particular interest in demonstrations put on for his benefit at Saint Cyr. One of the officers of his entourage spoke to Captain d'Amade about the effect of the Sino-Japanese War in changing the thinking of Chinese military and civilian leaders. The Chinese officer indicated that now the main idea was to send greater numbers of promising young Chinese to study in European military academies. Nie Shicheng adopted new training programmes and so did other leading Chinese officers all over the country. In Arthur Cunningham, we have an ideal witness to the success of this training.

In his book *The Chinese Soldier*, Arthur Cunningham shows himself to be an example of one of those writers who was heavily satirical about the Chinese military. His account of a Chinese Red Cross hospital at Weihaiwei during the Sino-Japanese War drips with irony at the expense of the Chinese. As a journalist, Cunningham uses savage mockery to describe what he saw of the Chinese military and its organisation during the 1894–1895 War. It is therefore of great interest to read his description of foreign-drilled troops putting down a rebellion of 6,000 Manchu bannermen in their camps at the mouth of the river above Shanghai. Cunningham wrote that:

> During the period when the foreign-drilled brigades were being formed, these petty rebellions were frequent, because the old troops of bannermen were disbanded, and finding their occupation gone, used their military knowledge in terrorising and robbing the peasantry. Especially … in the Yangtze region.[191]

We note here another problem consequent on the modernisation of the military in the late Qing that bears further investigation. What was to be done with the hundreds of thousands of people, the men and extended families of the hereditary Manchu bannermen, now made superfluous because of the rise of modern-trained Western-style armies?

Cunningham noted that by May 1897 outside Shanghai there were ten companies of foreign-drilled infantry each 250 strong, a squadron of cavalry and two artillery batteries, all German-trained. They had been training for over a year and had recently been reviewed before the Chinese civilian mandarin and the British and Russian military attachés who found them most commendable. They were commanded by Chinese and German officers.[192]

It is worth quoting Cunningham at length as a journalist who had seen the action in the Sino-Japanese War and subsequently witnessed this minor rebellion which began two years later on 9 May 1897:

> The Chinese soldier had never previously impressed me with a display of horsemanship, but the dash of these troopers on that wretched slippery path, guiding their ponies with reins in one hand and gripping their lance with the other was a revelation … [When] I made my entry on the scene of conflict … the foreign-drilled troops were having it all their own way [one of three camps was still resisting]. Drawn up in extended order fifty yards in front of the "camp" was a company of foreign-drilled troops, who, notwithstanding that they were facing death … were eager, grim and steady. Not a man moved until a sharp order was given — a number in Chinese — and up went their rifles at the ready! [The bannermen immediately capitulated and the cavalry were back in the saddle within twenty minutes]. One incident was very gratifying to witness, as an instance of good comradeship. A soldier dropped unconscious and his three immediate fellows picked him up and carried him in turn … eight miles to the barracks. The foreign-drilled soldiers were universally cheerful and polite and seemed in high glee at their victory, although it had been won by effect and not by fighting.[193]

This drive to continue to institute better training programmes continued throughout the country. In August 1905, well after the Boxer rising and after the representatives of the Powers had been invited to several annual Chinese army manoeuvres not substantially different from those illustrated in this chapter, Auguste François, French consul in Yunnan where he had lived and worked since 1896, wrote to the Minister of War. His object in this letter of 10 August was to put:

> in your hands proof that the transformation of the Chinese army has reached

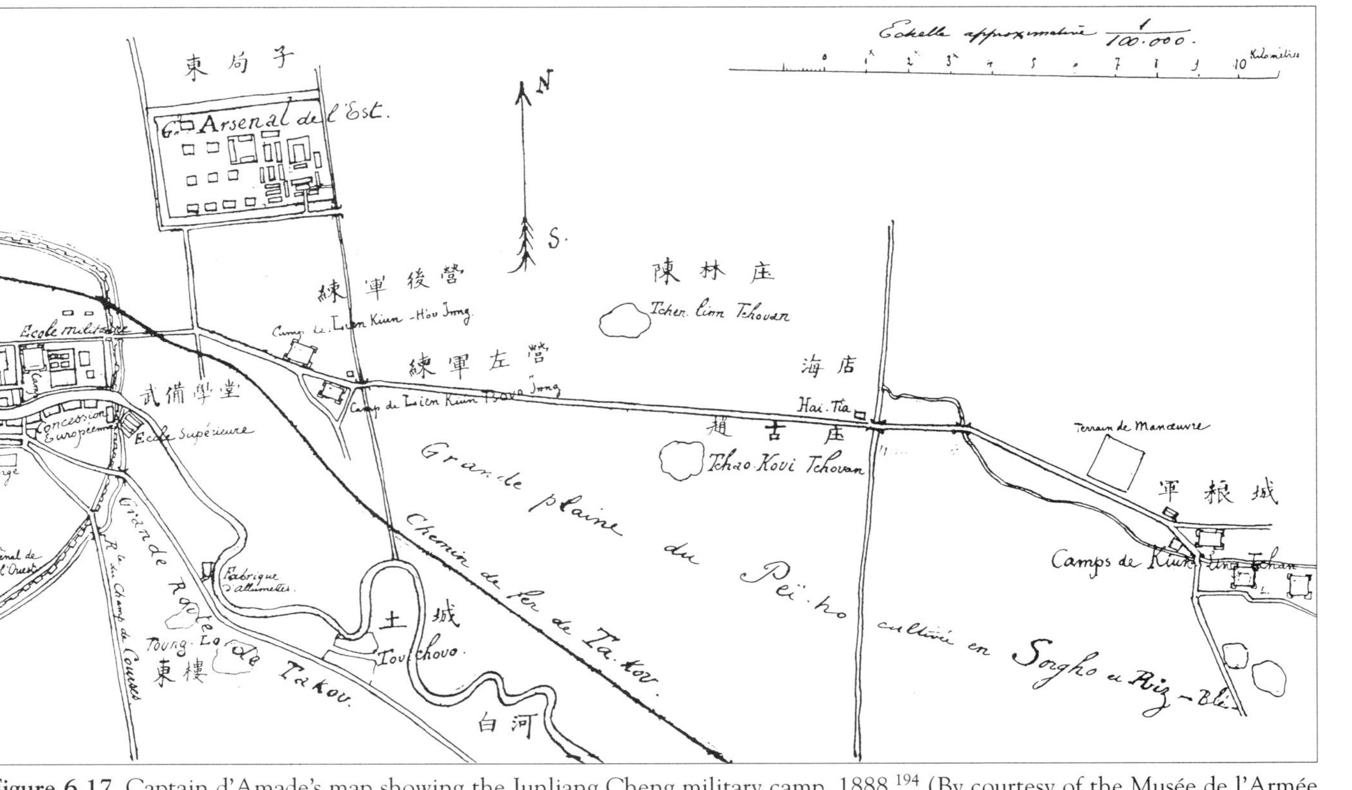

Figure 6.17 Captain d'Amade's map showing the Junliang Cheng military camp, 1888.[194] (By courtesy of the Musée de l'Armée de Terre, Paris)

> right out to Yunnan, the most backward place in the Empire. This is why I am attaching a copy of the rules for the organisation of army reserves instituted for attack and defence.[195]

Chinese forces had already fought many successful engagements against the French in Indochina in the 1880s and François's judgement of further improvements in the organisation of the Chinese army is in line with that of other observers who noted marked improvements in the training and organisation of the Chinese army following defeat in 1895 and 1900. Looking back on the Boxer rising, Colonel Brissaud-Desmaillet's assessment of the results of this training described above echoed the judgement of the soldiers taking part in action against the Chinese in 1900:

> the Chinese infantry sometimes executed offensive action [the contemporary belief was that the Chinese were incapable of taking the offensive]; numerous gunners were killed on their weapons.[196]

Chinese Strategic Preparations

The fragmented nature of the military structure and changes in Court politics with regard to the value or otherwise of modernisation could justifiably be thought to have impeded the development of unified strategic thinking in the closing decades of the nineteenth century. To the traditional threats of Russia in Manchuria had been added the threat of France in Yunnan and Japan in the North. There was also the consciousness of an impending partition of China by the European Powers that had already gained lucrative concessions in important parts of China.[197] However, it was clear to military observers that the Chinese were making a concerted drive to enhance military defences in two theatres, Port Arthur and the province of Zhili. Once again the discussion will centre on military preparations and installations in Zhili immediately before the outbreak of the Boxer rising.

We are fortunate in having an overall view expressing the thoughts of a European military man in the five reports by Captain d'Amade written in January 1888. D'Amade was impressed firstly by the quality of the roads that, throughout the region, were all strategically well-placed. These roads had been built by the soldiers stationed in the camps of the region between 1876 and 1883. The roads were constructed in straight lines like Roman roads with no attempt to be of any use to surrounding civilians. Some roads ran through

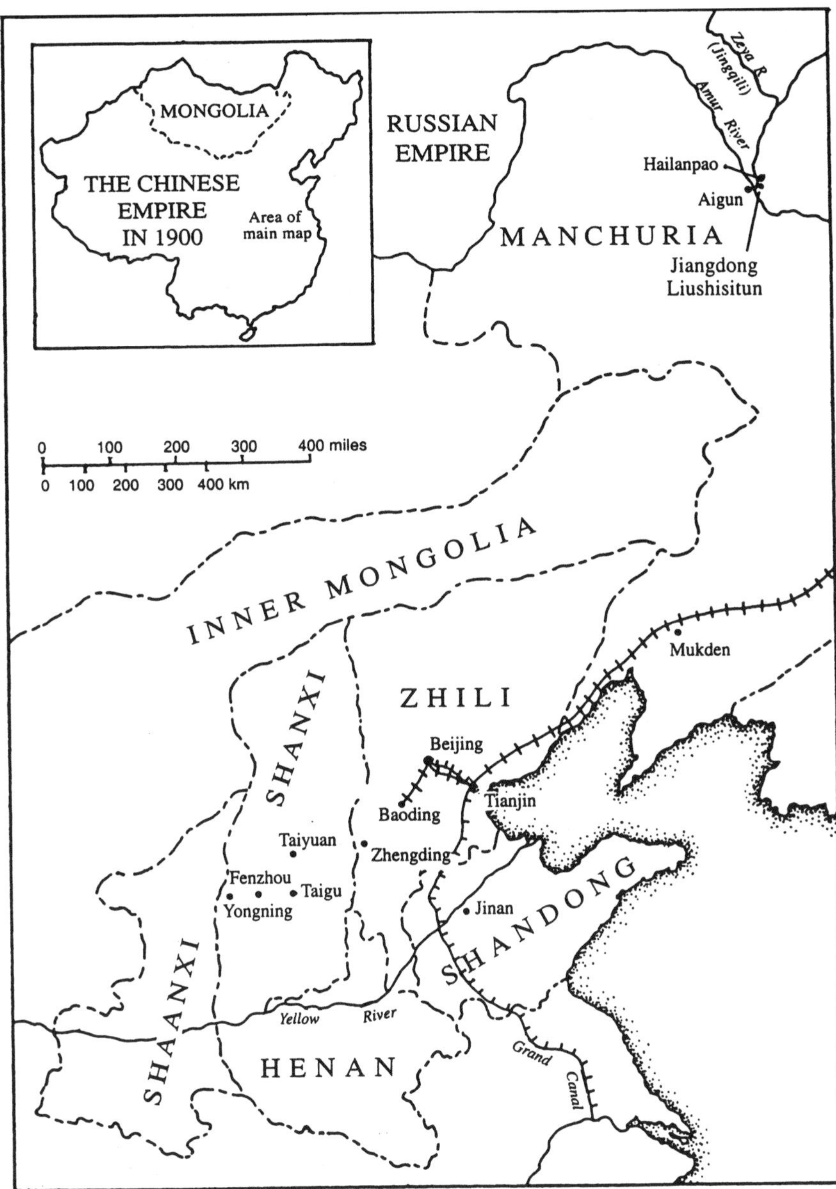

Figure 6.18 Map showing the location of Zhili and Shandong. From Paul A. Cohen.[198]

no villages at all and on others, villages were very rare. All roads were lined by telegraph and served by rail. The roads were doubled by canals. Thus when they became impassable in the rainy seasons, the adjacent canals allowed for troop movement. Furthermore, d'Amade had occasion to make a crossing by barge of a 500 metre wide river. He observed that the barge could take four Chinese carts with twelve animals, that the loading and unloading was the responsibility of the bargemen, the drivers only having to harness and unharness their animals, and that the crossing was done with precision and no waste of time in ten minutes.

With regard to the railway, this had been funded and built by the Chinese. The trains were manned by Chinese drivers and the Europeans were carefully kept away from all direct interference in the business of layout, exploitation and financing. D'Amade noted that the railway had modified the strategic importance of Beitang, making it more significant because reinforcements from all the camps of the Bei river area could be brought there by train. Furthermore, the rail assured the protection of its flanks because in the event of an attack on Beitang, the troops could be detrained at any point of the line, south or north to mount a counter offensive. As well, he noted that the only place at which the rail line was vulnerable was eight kilometres south of Lutai where it crossed the river on a 220 metre long iron bridge but that this point was more than fifteen kilometres from the coast. We note with hindsight that he was not contemplating a peasant insurrection in which it would be in the peasants' interests to prevent the Chinese regular army moving quickly and easily by rail through the region. It does not seem to have occurred to those writing about the Boxers' activities, that they destroyed the railway as much to immobilise soldiers of the Imperial Chinese Army as foreign troops.

Other points bearing on logistics noted by d'Amade were the two-wheeled vehicles for transporting artillery or infantry. These were built on the Western model but were much smaller and with Chinese modifications, an important consideration for all vehicles required to use Chinese roads. In d'Amade's experience, these Chinese vehicles could move on any road because the flagstones were closer together in contrast with the situation in Europe where so many big vehicles were unable to get by. On the adjacent canals, d'Amade observed large, broad-bottomed sampans being used for transportation of food and ammunition. In point of logistics, Commander

Vidal also carefully noted costs of transport for the various types of provisions in peace and in wartime.[199]

D'Amade's conclusion, after visiting the area and noting that the headquarters of the highest military authority had been moved from Gubeikou to Lutai, was that all these preparations were in line with the new military preoccupations of the Court. D'Amade's analysis was that in the Chinese view, the zone of probable attack was the area between Dagu and Shanhaiguan. By moving the provincial commander of the Green Standard troops to Lutai, they were placing him at the centre of the perceived threat.[200]

Furthermore, the Chinese were planning to lengthen the railway from Kaibing to Shanhaiguan and to push it on towards Manchuria. In d'Amade's view:

> This is a military conception of very great value as it will link the theatre of operations of the Pei [sic] river where the main forces of Li Hongchang are stationed with a quite different theatre of operations which has as its objective Peking with its axis the great Mandarin route from Mukden to Peking via Yung Pingfou with the region of Shan Haiguan as the zone of disembarkation.[201]

According to d'Amade, plans had already been drawn up for this railway with the Russian threat in mind.

These five reports also contain detailed descriptions of troops stationed permanently in the region, their training and weaponry, detailed descriptions of points of military value and detailed descriptions of the fortifications at Shanhaiguan. It should be born in mind that d'Amade's view was that not only of a Western military man but a French military man. As such, his interpretations of what he saw on this tour were necessarily coloured by his training and his national heritage with regard to war and methods of warfare. However, even without the parallel evidence of the Russian and Japanese reports, there are some objective military truths which emerge from his report. The road-building programme, the railway construction, the network of canals, the types of boats and vehicles he saw, the type and armament of fortifications he described, the deployment of European-trained and armed troops in a zone of maximum strategic importance; all these factors point to a deliberate concentration of military resources in an effort to protect the capital.

Beyond these factors were d'Amade's interpretations; the reason for the re-positioning of the provincial commander, the reason for the extension of the railway to Shanhaiguan and into Manchuria, his supposition that the Chinese perceived the Russian threat as influencing their thinking. It might be argued that without access to corresponding reports and documents in Chinese, it is not possible either to validate d'Amade's interpretations or to determine whether or not they were congruent with Chinese military thinking. However, this is not pertinent to the present discussion. It is clear from d'Amade's reports that the Chinese were making intensive military preparations in areas where they perceived the highest likelihood of military threat and that as a professional Western soldier, these preparations were immediately obvious to d'Amade.

Key Chinese figures had had extensive contact with Europeans and the European military. Both Li Hongzhang and Zhang Yu, director of the military school at Tianjin, had been in the position to learn whatever they wanted about any aspect of the Western military machine.[202] Moreover, they were indirectly responsible not only for the equipping and training of the armies in Zhili province but also for determining overall policies with regard to the degree and pace of Westernisation, of the manufacture of weapons, and training in their use. The interpretations of a professional like d'Amade arrived at as specific observations in the context of his awareness of the new

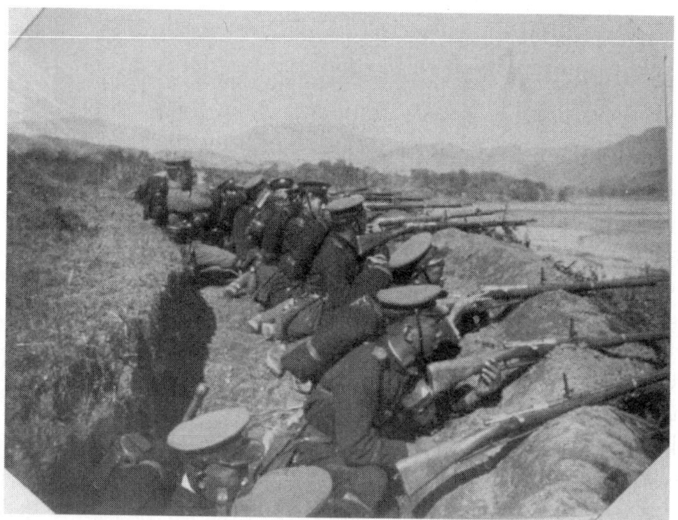

Figure 6.19 Infantry in a trench for firing at the knee or seated. 1908 manoeuvres from the Album of Laribe.[203] (By courtesy of the Musée de l'Armée de Terre, Paris)

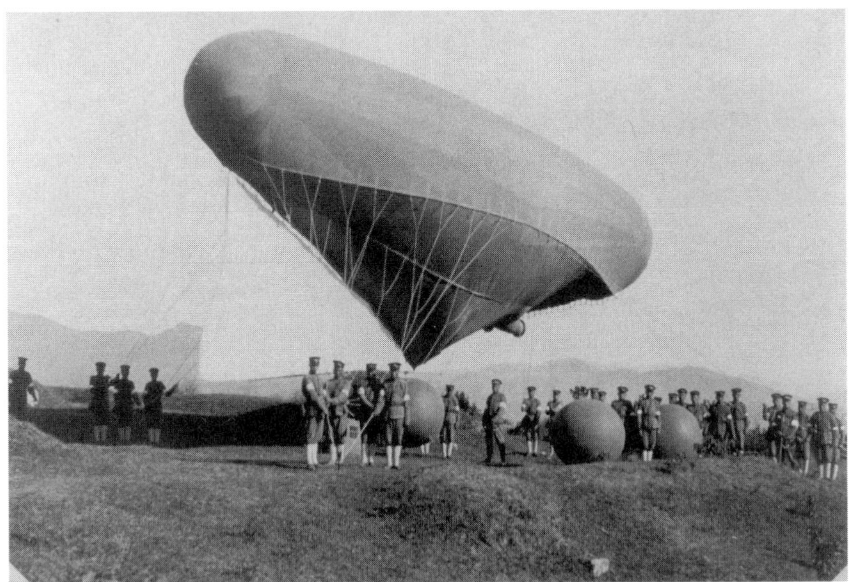

Figure 6.20 The Balloon Detachment attached to the Engineering Corps, 1908 manoeuvres.[204] (By courtesy of the Musée de l'Armée de Terre, Paris)

military preoccupations of the Court, reflected to an important degree some of the impetus behind the nature of the military build-up in Zhili province.

Like many military men, within the confines of his profession, d'Amade had the soul of a poet:[205]

> I travelled in this region from 14 to 17 of January. I left the inn every day at 4 am, three hours after the convoy of vehicles had left. I was on horseback; for five minutes every quarter of an hour I had to walk, this was the only concession that I made to a temperature of 29–30 degrees below zero. The journey was made as on a French road, the rivers crossed without any indications other than the humps of pebbles revealing their presence, so well had the ice been hidden by the layers of dust brought by the North winds. The road was bustling with many travellers using all types of transport; carriages, sleds, horses, donkeys, mules; the mandarins in sedan chairs, the peasants going on foot to the nearest market. The road drained and absorbed all the life of the region. All the passers-by were so noisy and happy under a perfectly clear sky. The traffic was so busy and continuous that one might think, closing one's eyes, that one could hear an army moving by.[206]

None of his reports contain belittling remarks about the Chinese. On one

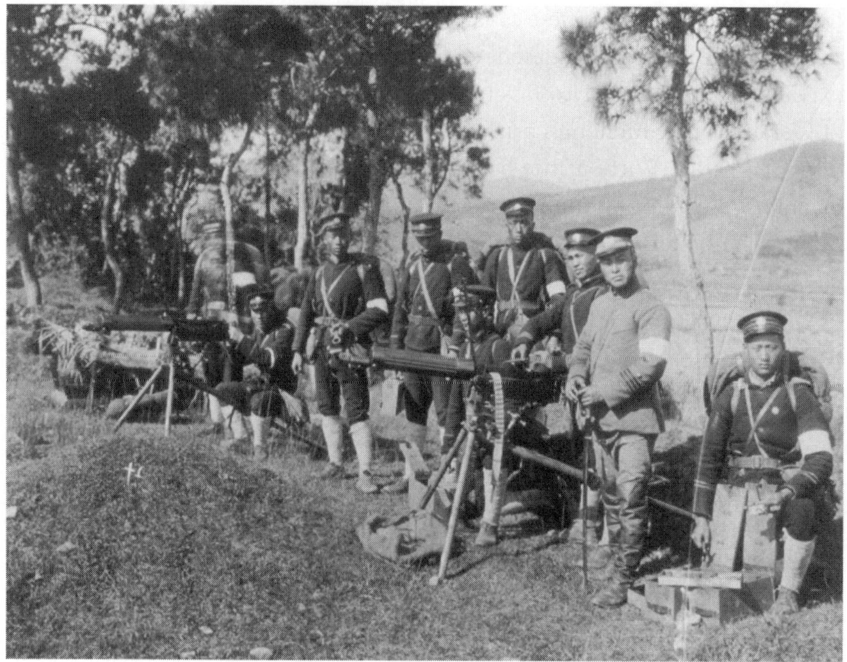

Figure 6.21(a) Machine Gun Detachments in the 1908 army manoeuvres.[207] (By courtesy of the Musée de l'Armée de Terre, Paris)

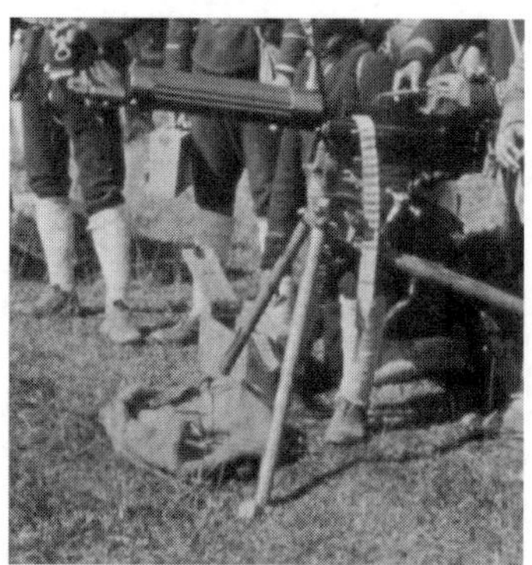

Figure 6.21(b) Machine Gun Detachments (insert).

occasion he observed Chinese cavalry and infantry drill which seemed pointless to him but he nevertheless described the drills with punctilious detail including explanatory diagrams. Those very same manoeuvres were used by battalions of General Nie Shicheng's army in action against the Boxers, and will be discussed below. Without the benefit of d'Amade's description illustrated by diagrams, a reading of the reports of the Chinese officers describing action against the Boxers does not in itself give sufficient idea of the nature of the cavalry manoeuvres involved. It is notable that d'Amade concluded his observations of the — to him — pointless manoeuvres as follows:

> However, the good execution of these complex movements shows that if training were given over to competent instructors and directed in a practical sense the results would be very good.[208]

Chinese peasant insurrections and Chinese banditry called for handling outside Western military experience. There had been no time in recent European military history in which well-armed units of as many as 500 men and as few as forty had been surrounded by determined, variously-armed countrymen in their thousands whom the soldiers had had orders to treat as "children of the Imperial house."[209] The British had agreed that it was de rigueur to use certain weapons, for example, the dum dum bullet, generally regarded as inhumane, against frenzied natives. However, the correspondence of officers of Chinese Western-armed and drilled troops makes it very clear that they were ordered by Imperial Decree in the context of the Boxer rising to treat the Boxers as "the children of China."[210] As well, the Chinese officers themselves wished to do everything possible to allay the fears of the common people.[211] The "people" also impressed various foreign military writers by their implacable hatred of foreigners and constituted a significant though voiceless force in the calculations of both Chinese regular army officers and men and soldiers and officers of the invading forces.

This study is leading us towards an understanding of the immense range of images made of the Boxer rising. It is thus appropriate to conclude this survey of the modernisation of the Chinese armies, a piecemeal process, certainly, but in places very thorough and deliberately ordered, with the thoughts of d'Amade. D'Amade was quintessentially French but also a soldier able to come to terms with much of what he saw and heard during his extensive travels in China. As well, he spoke and wrote Chinese.

> In the event of a war, the military efforts made by China to increase its standing army and perfect its armaments will be beyond all rational forethought. The enemy to be fought, the theatre of war, financial resources are all factors which can influence China in so many different ways that this power will always adapt its pace to that of its adversary; our European ideas of the size of the standing army in peace time or on mobilisation would not be applicable in China:[212]

Written in January 1888, this assessment is remarkably prescient in terms of the war of resistance against Japan (1937–1945). Apparently a Western military man could find words to describe what warfare might mean in Chinese history and culture.

A Modern Army, a Great Leader, a Fine Soldier: General Yang Mushi

This study has canvassed a wide range of impressions of China which were already extant in Western minds when people opened their newspapers to read about the most electrifying news of the day: the Boxer rising. Surviving Chinese popular picture of wars with foreigners indicate an increased audience for information about real wars. In the West, various groups — the press, illustrators, photographers, cartoonists, the military — provided material which either reinforced pre-existing impressions about China or obliged people to form new impressions. In both China and the West, two types of information were produced: information reinforcing existing stereotypes and new information describing what was happening in China. Of the many impressions, those on which most attention has been centred in this chapter have been impressions of the Chinese soldier. The reasons for this are twofold: first, the work of those who produced the image of the inept, the ridiculous, the comic-opera is still being cited in serious scholarly studies of the Chinese army.[213] Second there has been an even longer lasting myth about the extent to which Chinese military technology was responsible for its defeats, a myth that has continued into the 1990s. For different reasons, these myths are widespread in both China and the West.

In 1900, there was a dominant strand of thought that Chinese soldiers were ridiculous and this gave rise to all kinds of misconceived impressions. They were afraid to fight in the dark, their uniforms and equipment were designed for flight rather than attack and their weapons were antiquated. The

Chinese soldier was the subject of belittling comic opera ditties at the turn of the century:

> Chinese Sojer-man
> He wavee piecee fan
> He shoutee Hip, hoo-lay for Empelor,
> He makee hollid yell
> Bangee drum and lingee bell
> When Chinese sojer marchee out to war![214]

The correspondence of General Yang Mushi from 26 May to 18 July 1900 reflects the thinking, motivation and leadership qualities of a particular Chinese soldier. General Yang's correspondence from the field shows that, confronted with the Boxers, he faced exactly the same military problems as Admiral Seymour but that because he was a serving officer of the Imperial Chinese Army, the problems involved were far more complex for him and his men as they contained a serious political component. It also demonstrates that the men of the Wu Wei army which had only existed as such for seven years, fought for many of the same reasons as the Allied invaders and displayed the same qualities of professionalism, loyalty and courage as the men in the best of the Allied armies. In addition, General Yang's letters reveal the devastating effect on Western-trained professional soldiers when conflicting orders came through the civilian arm of authority. In judging the performance of the Imperial Chinese Army, it is of great importance to note the effect of vacillations in Imperial policy concerning the Boxers on soldiers of the Imperial army serving in the field. These policy changes made it difficult and eventually impossible for the Imperial Chinese Army to carry out their orders to fight the Boxers. This in turn affected their morale as well as their physical condition. Some battalions were completely exhausted from trying to disengage with the Boxers when they met the invading armies. The Qing soldier rates so poorly in the dominant mythologies of Western and Chinese scholarship that no attempt has been made to evaluate his actual performance in the field or his particular difficulties in that summer of 1900.

Before there was any thought of war breaking out between China and any foreign powers, General Yang had been sent with three battalions to protect the railway and telegraph in an area approximately fifty kilometres southwest of Beijing (See Figure 6.22). For his commanding officer, General Nie Shicheng, and for General Yang himself it was clear that this railway was imperial property, along with the railway stations and bridges, and it was the paramount duty of the army to protect the railway from destruction by Boxers. For their part, the Boxers and sympathetic villagers all along the line were determined to destroy the railway, setting fire to it, stealing tools and removing sleepers, to this end.[215] Their understanding of the mechanisms involved was such that they would remove the pins from moving joints in locomotives and rolling stock[216] to disable them, if they were unable to destroy them. The degree of precise mechanical understanding required to do this complements the addition made by this study to our understanding of the Boxers. Not only were they determined to acquire and able to use modern weapons, they also displayed sophisticated knowledge in disabling railway equipment.

Scholarship on the Boxers has not addressed the issue that the Boxer's aggressive behaviour in mid-May may not have been *primarily* anti-Christian.[217] According to Sawara Tokusake, there were White Lotus bandits in Beijing at the same time as the Boxers.

> They took regicide, execution of Government officials and the taking of the throne as their doctrine. The White Lotus bandits were caught by soldiers and seventy were killed.... These bandits dared to make a paper effigy of the Emperor and other High Officials and they beheaded the effigies in the food market.[218]

This passage throws new light on the extent of the turmoil and confusion caused by rebellious elements in Beijing during the siege of the Legations and the difficulties inherent in recognising and dealing with more than one rebellious element. As well, Lu Yao, the international expert on sects around the time of the Boxer rising, mentioned that a Buddhist monk put himself forward, volunteering his expertise to destroy the foreign warships by magic. Though his attempt was unsuccessful, he was accorded honours by the Court.[219] This attitude of the Court towards religious sect practitioners is striking when compared with its attitude to its Army as we will see in discussing the performance of Generals Yang Mushi and Nie Shicheng.

The taking of Zhuozhou and the destruction of large sections of the Beijing-Baoding railway line indicate more probably that the Boxers were trying to gain a power base for their rebellion while trying to prevent the Imperial Chinese Army from moving rapidly by rail. There is, certainly, an argument that the railway was hated by peasants and coolies for a number of good reasons but we need to balance into this argument the fact that the Boxers were conducting a guerrilla rebellion and that it was likely that military reasons weighed in largely when they first began destroying the railway. The actual sections of rail they attacked initially were of prime strategic importance to their own military position. If their motives were simple Luddism, the areas chosen for destruction and the length of rail plus supporting equipment destroyed, would not have been geographically the same, nor would the destruction have been as thorough. In June, the Boxers' objective changed and they wanted to prevent Admiral Seymour from moving. Again descriptions of the nature of the destruction they wrought and their determination in so doing fits more closely with the idea that their objective was a military one and superstition, primitivism or Luddism were not primary motives.

Railways were relatively new as objects to be guarded in military operations and guarding them against an enemy using guerrilla tactics[220] was extremely difficult as the British had just been discovering in South Africa.[221] General Yang was confronted with the problem of protecting about thirty kilometres of railway against a rapidly appearing and disappearing enemy. This enemy had the complete loyalty of the people in the surrounding countryside, to the extent that in some places the population clearly favoured the Boxers against the regular soldiers.[222] At any time large groups of Boxers appeared, their numbers were immediately swollen by villagers. In the eyes of the Boxers, it was as important to deprive Chinese regular army troops from freedom of movement as to prevent foreign soldiers — or any foreigners at all — from moving by rail in the vicinity of Tianjin and Beijing. If posterity sees the Boxers as heroes and the soldiers of the Chinese regular army as villains, judgement may need to be modified when it is considered that the military initiatives taken by the Boxers directly reduced the fighting ability of the regular army by the time the Chinese had to face the invading foreign armies.

On 17 May the Boxers attacked a troop of Imperial Chinese Army cavalry and infantry led by Colonel Yang Futong. The regular troops withdrew to a small hill and fired on and killed some fifty or sixty Boxers. This incident made the Boxers vow to have revenge on Colonel Yang.[223] Although Imperial Chinese Army troops were in the area initially at the request of foreign missionaries, then at the request of Chinese magistrates, it is quite clear from

Chinese sources that the original anti-Christian activity of the Boxers had given way to a desire to fight Chinese regular troops. On 22 May Colonel Yang leading a cavalry squadron of thirty men and forty infantry was ambushed by armed Boxers northwest of Gaoluo village. One of his men seeing the nature of the ground criss-crossed by irrigation ditches and ideal for potential ambush, advised Colonel Yang not to cross it.[224] Colonel Yang replied that as an officer, it was his duty to lead his men as appropriate.[225] Because the ground the Boxers had chosen was unsuitable for cavalry, Colonel Yang ordered his men to dismount. The number of Boxers increased rapidly. Colonel Yang initially wanted to try to disperse them and was reluctant to give the order to open fire. Eventually he was forced to do so.[226] Pressed on all sides by Boxers, Colonel Yang's horse was hurt in the mêlée. It reared, he was thrown and hand-to-hand fighting broke out. Colonel Yang was severely wounded and his two personal aides tried to persuade him to remount but he refused and continued to fight, killing several Boxers until, exhausted from his wounds and from fighting, he fell.[227] Presumably Colonel Yang had refused to mount and thus be relatively safer because he was leading thirty cavalrymen who had had to dismount and were now fighting the Boxers while having to ensure the safety of their horses. The Boxers hacked him to pieces. Three other soldiers were also cut to pieces but the rest of his men managed to fight their way out and disperse the Boxers.[228]

> The body of the loyal sub-commander was wounded in more than one hundred places so that no part of his skin was left intact. His face was unrecognisable, his innards lay open and the thumb and index finger of the right hand were cut off. He was killed with such viciousness that it was terribly painful even to look at him.[229]

It would seem that Colonel Yang led his men with extreme determination and personal valour of the highest degree, providing an exemplary figure of leadership qualities by a commanding officer in the most dangerous of combat situations. His personal courage was mentioned by Magistrate Zhu Zhaotang. The fact that his men were devoted to him is indicated by their expressed determination to take revenge on the Boxers for his death.[230] Boxers were gathering in the vicinity of Dingxing, Xincheng and Laishui in such numbers that it would appear unlikely that their target was merely Christians or foreigners. It would seem more likely that they wanted to establish a base — which they did a few days after the death of Colonel Yang — and that they were spoiling for a fight with the Imperial Chinese Army. According to an account by Sawara Tokusake, "the Court blamed this incident on the army and the people found this quite strange."[231] We may infer from Tokusake's observation that already the Court had no sympathy at all with General Nie's army and far from seeing the army as the group of professionals trained to protect China and hence the Court, actually published unsympathetic edicts concerning individual officers of the army; we may further infer that there were people in the region who did not see the Boxers as "Knights of Righteousness" but as "bandits." These people found it surprising that the army should be blamed because it had been attacked by the Boxers and a senior officer was killed.

The Chinese Weihaiwei regiment trained and led by the British had been involved in the identical type of skirmish with the Boxers on 5 May 1900. Major Penrose was severely wounded, two other British officers and two Chinese soldiers were also wounded. The party was a smaller one of twenty-two men and its ammunition was running out when it was rescued by a sortie from the camp.[232] There was extensive contemporary criticism by Westerners of the Chinese officer class that has been echoed by posterity. It is interesting to see that in the two parallel incidents, the men of the Chinese regular army were able to fight their way out and drive off the Boxers. The Chinese regulars were perhaps spurred on by the death of their commanding officer, whereas the British-trained Chinese soldiers with all their officers wounded had to be rescued by a sortie. It is not acceptable to build a large case on two parallel incidents. However, it is equally unacceptable to make generalisations about the fighting qualities of men and their leaders without any specific instances at all being given.[233] The other notable point about this incident is that Boxers mutilated their enemies, whether they were regular soldiers of the Chinese army or foreign invaders. Mutilation was greatly feared by the men of Admiral Seymour's expedition. However, Zhu Zhaotang's letter makes it clear that mutilation was equally horrific to the Chinese and had exactly the same effect on morale because of their Confucian beliefs about preserving the body intact after death in order to return it whole to the ancestors.

In a postscript to his letter describing this incident and requesting a pension and benefits for Colonel Yang and the three soldiers who died, Magistrate Zhu wrote:

> I have time and again requested guidance for dealing with the Boxers and I am always ordered to disperse and disorganise them but never to suppress them mercilessly.… Even though the Boxers were awed into submission by the threat of military force … they hate me very deeply [and they may] return and cause me trouble.[234]

Thus before hostilities with the Allies had broken out, Chinese military men with clear orders to protect the railway were operating in the districts of civilian magistrates who had equivocal orders regarding the Boxers. Yet as General Yang wrote in a notice to villages along the railway from Zhuozhou to Dingxing:

> I am wondering how you Boxers, who talk about righteousness, can do harm to your country? The railway was built by the Court so when you burned several tens of *li* of it you threw away several hundred thousand taels, rebelled against the government and defied the laws. What is the difference between you and traitors? Sub-Commander Yang was officially appointed by the government. When you dared to kill him, didn't this amount to rebellion? It is quite impossible for me to be lenient with you, for my only aim is to destroy you.… And since I have to destroy the Boxers, I will likewise gun down all those who join them.[235]

In this notice, General Yang specifically appealed to the Boxers in the context of harming their country. It was a commonly-held view by Westerners in China at this time that the Chinese had no concept of patriotism and some scholars writing about the Boxers have belittled the possibility that they were motivated by some form of national sentiment.[236] As the leader of three battalions of Western-trained professional soldiers, General Yang unmistakably used his military authority to point out to the rebels the connection between their country, its lawfully-appointed leaders, its property, its well-being and his own obligation to uphold these connections. He clearly believed that ordinary villagers would understand this point and respond to an appeal to their patriotism. The problem was that the Boxers' anti-foreign platform created conflicting views about what constituted appropriate patriotic action, both among the villagers, the soldiers, the local and the Court officials. For General Yang in the field, there was no such conflict. At this point, war had not broken out between China and the invading Powers, nevertheless General Yang was fully engaged with the Boxers and losing men and officers in action against them.

General Yang realised that he did not have enough men to pursue Boxers caught sabotaging the railway and at the same time continue to protect it. He was also thoroughly familiar with Boxer tactics of moving rapidly from place to place, striking unexpectedly and then withdrawing. It was quite clear to him that the priority was the protection of the railway.[237] In an incident on 29 May, he tried using blanks to disperse the Boxers, to no effect. This may have been because of Boxer belief in ritual protection. It may equally well have been because there were enough ex-soldiers among them who knew what blanks were.[238] When General Yang was forced to fire on them, he used the extreme moderation of a well-trained professional:

> They still advanced on us and resisted. I had to fire on them with loaded guns and I ordered three rounds to be fired which killed or wounded ten or more of the Boxers.[239]

At the time he "was afraid this would cause trouble" and in fact, he was temporarily relieved of his commission at the end of June for his conduct in this incident.

On 31 May General Yang received a telegram from the Commander-in-Chief in which General Nie stated that he had been telegraphed an edict concerning the Boxers' destruction of the railway. At this point, it will be remembered, there had still not been an outbreak of hostilities with the foreign Powers.

> It is now urgently necessary to punish and suppress [the Boxers] vigorously. Yulu [Viceroy of Zhili province] is ordered to instruct Nie Shicheng specially to dispatch a column of troops to protect properly the Lu Bao and Jing Lu telegraph lines and railway.[240]

General Nie added that it was his duty to tell the commanders in the field to obey this edict "and in turn to order each battalion and platoon to carry out orders obediently. There must be absolutely no negligence."[241] The next day General Nie telegraphed Generals Xing and Yang giving them instructions on where and how to deploy their men to protect the rail and all supporting constructions.[242]

By 31 May it was clear that the insurrection was becoming uncontrollable:

> Chochou (sic) [Zhuozhou] has not fallen and yet it is lost to us. The Boxers now control the opening and the closing of the city gates so that administrative persons cannot enter the city [the power of] the military and civilian officials

> in the city exists in name only [the Boxers] are as reckless and as cruel as before.[243]

General Yang had the men, the weapons and the logistic support to crush the Boxers. To this point he had killed or wounded ten. His view was that he was confronted with a dangerous insurrection that could only be dealt with by decisive military force but he was hampered by temporising or directly contradictory instructions from the highest civilian authorities in Beijing. He was constantly being told to refrain from firing on the Boxers lest he kill some of the common people by mistake. General Yang's professional opinion was that he should first put down the Boxers by force and only then would it be possible to conciliate the local population. The point to be remarked is that for the Court, for the civilian and military authorities and for the soldiers themselves, the common people were an important factor. Moreover, the Court was heavily divided in its view of the common people. There were those who saw the Boxers as dangerous undisciplined rabble and those who saw them as: "Knights of Righteousness." The former tended to be moderates, the latter reactionaries. General Yang's own view was unequivocal:

> Even though our policy is to disband and to let [the Boxers] go peacefully, it can be effectively executed only when the military operation of suppression has been basically successful.[244]

In this he was supported by General Nie who had had experience fighting in the Nien rebellion in 1862, had led the Taiwan expedition in 1871, had fought in the Muslim rebellion in Chinese Turkistan in the 1870s, had crushed a rebellion in Mongolia in 1891 and had fought with distinction in the Sino-Japanese War of 1894–1895. General Nie, like General Yang, was under no illusions about the difference between putting down internal insurgencies and fighting foreign troops.[245]

General Yang's task was made difficult in many ways that Admiral Seymour's was not. He was ordered to protect the railway and ordered not to shoot Boxers. He was well aware of the political implications of these orders in terms of the attitudes of the moderates and reactionaries at Court and thus was under a psychological pressure as a Commanding Officer that was quite alien to the military in any of the eight invading armies. As an indication of just how dangerous it was for an officer of the Imperial Chinese Army at this time, the British Royal Navy Captain Edward Bayly noted in his journal on 12 June that:

> A special train brought a Chinese General, prisoner, who was at once conveyed to the Native City in a covered cart, said to be a prisoner of war on account of not suppressing Boxers!?[246]

The difficulty of protecting the railway was insuperable because the villagers were helping the Boxers. Local support became an increasing theme in Yang's letters:

> The Boxers do not have to be a large rushing band because when they come the people from the villages gather on both sides of the railway and start fires which we are helpless to prevent.[247]

The Boxers succeeded in capturing seventeen of Yang's cavalrymen. One need hardly ask about the manner of their death or the effect of this on their comrades. He began to see that in order to protect the railway and deal with Boxer attacks on his forces, he needed reinforcements. He asked General Nie for two battalions. He also requested 57 mm guns. He had with him two pound cannon and sixty-two rounds of shot but he envisaged a need for more ammunition. As a further indication of General Yang's moderation, in the same letter to General Nie in which he expressed his view that the Boxers should be put down by force, he reported an incident on 31 May when villagers had torn up the railway:

> In places far removed from our battalions ... I led twenty cavalry troops and twenty personal guards ... to make arrests. I saw several tens of persons on both sides of the railway tearing up tracks and road bed and using three carts to tow away the pieces. The cavalry and the guards arrested *seven* of them.[248] [emphasis added]

It could be said that in the face of apparently contradictory orders, namely to protect the railway at all costs and to disband actively aggressive insurgents and let them go peacefully, General Yang was carrying out a difficult mission with exemplary foresight, attention and restraint. His correspondence gives no indication that any "Chinese Sojer-man [was] waving piecee fan."

The pressure on Yang and his men increased. Every day they heard unfounded threats of attack and by 3 June the men of his battalions had been unable to bed down for three nights. Moreover, their position was in the very centre of strong Boxer activity and Yang wrote to Nie that in the event of his battalions being annihilated by Boxers, "they will become a force none can stop."[249] Yang repeated his request for reinforcements adding "Should you be able personally to lead our crack troops here, you would greatly strengthen our prestige."[250] By 5 June General Nie received a letter from the military secretariat, saying that troops were needed to prevent the Boxers gaining control of the provincial capital and at the same time to prevent the Boxers from blocking the railway.[251] General Nie's dominant concern remained the railway.[252] When he did lead his troops against the Boxers, he had no trouble dispersing them.[253]

> It is my duty to protect the railway, I am now leading my army to attack them [the Boxers] along the railway. After the crisis is resolved, I shall not evade whatever blame may be laid on me.[254]

Eventually on 6 June there was a major battle between the Boxers and General Yang's men. The Boxers withdrew after an hour of fighting, leaving over one hundred killed. A telegram from the military secretariat to the Viceroy appraised him of this incident and asked Yulu to order "15,000 rounds of Mauser rifle shot and 1,000 rounds of two pound shot for Nanjing cannon to be released to Battalion Commander Wang in Fengtai for safe escort."[255] Nevertheless, despite this show of force, General Yang still considered that he was "pinned into a corner where I can neither eliminate the Boxers nor protect the railway."[256] The Boxers continued to build up pressure and by 8 June he was surrounded. On this day he received his first explicit orders from the Imperial Commissioners that he was to take no steps against the Boxers.[257] The Empress Dowager had sent three Commissioners to report on the Boxers. Their report was a positive one saying that the Boxers constituted a useful force for the throne. General Yang perceived the situation as any Western soldier might have done:

> If they attack me in full force and I destroy them, then I shall act counter to the wishes of my superiors. If I do not fight, I fear that my three battalions will be destroyed ... to let all of these weapons fall into the hands of the Boxers is a very ill-considered plan.[258]

Later that day, 8 June, General Yang received a telegram containing instructions from Grand Secretary Gangyi ordering him to withdraw his troops immediately "and by every means possible to avoid further fighting

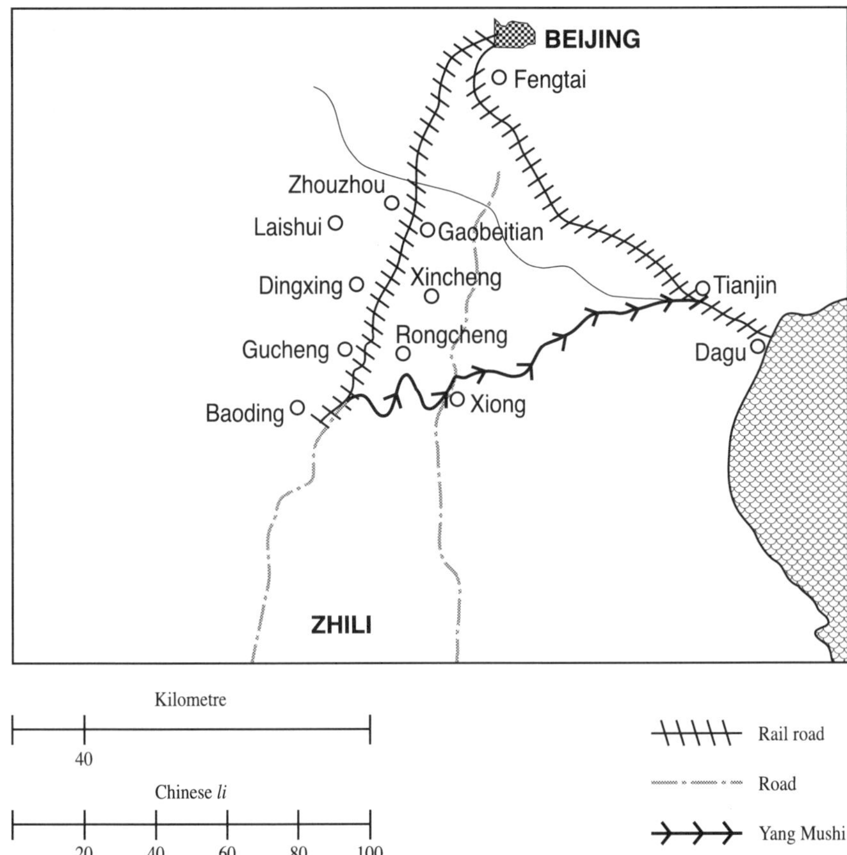

Figure 6.22 Sketch map showing the route taken by General Yang Mushi on his way to regain Tianjin. Adapted from Scott D. Dolby.[259]

with the Boxers." This telegram was from General Sun Shoujing and concluded: "I request that you withdraw your battalions without the slightest delay. This is essential. Otherwise I fear that the Grand Secretary will reprimand and embarrass you."[260]

General Yang replied to Gangyi saying that it would "have been a crime to have been defeated and destroyed [by the Boxers].... Moreover, I have the responsibility to obey imperial instructions to protect the railway."[261] General Yang went on to ask Gangyi for clear instructions as to whether he should withdraw and for these instructions to be issued through the proper chain of command. Gangyi and the two other Commissioners had been sent by the Empress Dowager. She was now swinging to a policy of supporting the Boxers. This letter shows General Yang as a courageous professional responsible for his men, his equipment and imperial property. Gangyi was extremely powerful at Court and a rabid reactionary. In a climate in which it was common for high-ranking officers to be cashiered, dismissed or executed by a single order from the Court, General Yang revealed himself as a man prepared to push the civilian authority to limits dangerous for his personal and professional survival, in order to protect the wider interests he saw himself as serving. He took the ultimate step of writing to the Viceroy of the province as follows:

> As long as I am in Gaopeitien [sic], I will not abandon the lives of my men in my three battalions or their equipment to the Boxers because I am worried that such action would cause deterioration of the general situation. If the bandits attack us, we will fight. If they do not attack, then we will not.[262]

General Nie saw the problem of the Boxers in the same light. On 9 June, that is, the day after Gangyi's telegram ordering immediate withdrawal of troops and the avoidance of further fighting with the Boxers, General Nie sent a telegram to the Viceroy informing him that:

> The Boxers intend to attack my army from the rear. Having no time to wait for a decree, I have directed my cavalry and infantry forces to attack and stop them and then proceed to suppress them all so as to save the general situation.[263]

General Yang received a telegram on 13 June from the Viceroy through General Xing and another on 15 June from General Nie through the financial commissioner, ordering him to bring his men to Tianjin. Neither of these telegrams mentioned the threat of the Allied initiatives; indeed, Yulu's telegram made it clear that he was ordering General Yang to move his troops for "fear [that they] will create an incident,"[264] that is, take action against the Boxers. It took General Yang five days of constant marching while fighting the Boxers to reach Tianjin. On the night of 18 June there was heavy rain and wind.[265] Rain would have been seen as an extremely auspicious sign by the Boxers. General Yang's men camped in a square formation and "throughout the entire night our cavalry attacked in rapid sorties."[266] By morning the men were unable to sit down and eat, being rushed by Boxers in a surprise attack from two directions. As well, the villages in the area sent all their armed men against the Chinese regular troops. All along their line of march, the villages had Boxer associations and everyone of these moved to obstruct General Yang's troops. "From two p.m. of the 19th until 5 p.m. of the 20th of June, we could not eat and could not water our mouths."[267] At midnight on 20 June they were surrounded by Boxers. "By morning we were still surrounded and attacked from four sides, but we fought our way forward step by step."[268] General Yang was complying with General Nie's orders to return to Tianjin but to do this he was having to kill Boxers. He had been told by Gangyi:

> ... Since the people who are Boxers are not all equally bad, one should also make distinctions between leaders and followers. Moreover, the common people are the children of the Imperial house and I have not spared either a worn out tongue or parched lips in patiently and clearly instructing and analysing the problem and communicating the love and virtue of the court to them. [Then I found out that you — Yang — decoyed and attacked the Boxers][269]

It was widely recognised that Gangyi had great faith in the Boxers. "When [Gangyi] heard the news of Colonel Yang Futong's death he observed 'It is not right to harm the Knights of Righteousness'."[270] Liu Mengyang, a reformist scholar living in Tianjin at the time of the Boxer rising, expressed the generally-held view that "Gangyi favoured and trusted those at Court who believed in the bandits; and gave bitter hatred to those who did not believe in them."[271] Mark Elvin observed that what we see here as bitter faction fighting at Court, became "virtual civil war" between pro-and anti-Boxer officials in Zhili province.[272] Moreover, the effect of the hostile initiative by the Allies was to give the ultra-conservative reactionaries a stronger voice at Court. "Denunciations of military officers who had been trying to suppress the Boxers grew more vociferous."[273] General Yang and the men he led were fighting knowing that he could be denounced and removed from his post at at any moment. This was even move true of General Nie. General Nie's superb performance in leading troops both in internal rebellions and foreign wars extended back for nearly forty years. Many of the soldiers fighting in his battalions had fought with him before and those who had not would certainly have heard stories of General Nie's past performances. What did it feel like being an officer or a rank and file soldier fighting under General Nie Shicheng when he finally was impeached? It is suggested that this created a vast difference in morale between the soldiers of the Imperial Chinese Army and those of the eight invading armies by the time of the Battle of Tianjin. This is indicative of extremely complex attitudes to the military on the Chinese side, both age-old, related to the accumulation of power in the hands of a great general and very recent, related to modernisation of the armed forces.

In following orders to return to Tianjin, General Yang had had to fight continuously for five days and nights. He estimated that his troops had killed or wounded between two and three thousand Boxers.[274] Under the circumstances, it was detrimental to General Yang's interests to kill even ten Boxers; it is therefore unlikely that he would have exaggerated these figures. He knew that he had incurred the displeasure of a highly placed court official whose political interests were diametrically opposed to everything Yang stood for and he also knew that once he withdrew his platoons from the railway, Boxers and villagers would destroy it. His was not an enviable position: "I have learned that there are Boxer leaders … who have gone to Peking to make charges against me and I can do nothing but accept the outcome."[275]

The charges made against General Yang and General Nie involved them denying their very profession. In 1900 any association with foreigners was dangerous. To lead foreign-trained armies using foreign weapons and foreign military tactics was to invite the same sort of reaction from the Court as was seen during the anti-Rightist campaign of the late 1950s and early 1960s or the Cultural Revolution. The important difference is that General Yang was a soldier fighting for China, not a university professor, a writer or a musician. He was fighting not only with his own life, but also with the lives of the men in his battalions against the Boxers and their highly-placed supporters at Court. Moreover, he was fully cognizant of the professional, political, and economic problems involved in using his military skill to do his duty and protect the railway.

His letter describing his march to Tianjin and the battle at the Xigu arsenal shows that for Yang, his fellow Generals and the Commander-in-Chief, at this stage (26 June), their greatest preoccupation was with the Boxers. Roughly 3,000 men of Nie's army of 10,000 were engaged in protecting the railway in the area from Baoding to Zhuozhou. With all his experience, General Nie was being forced to deploy his forces with the Boxer threat in his mind rather than the threat from the Allied invaders.[276] Shortly after this battle, General Yang was temporarily relieved of his commission in personally unpleasant circumstances.[277] In his letter of self-defence, his entire case is based on the decision he had made with regard to action against the Boxers.

This letter contains no reference to the foreign invaders or the loss of the Xigu arsenal.

For General Yang, the main problem was the Boxers. A fortnight before news of the Boxers hit the Western press, in mid-May, he had posted notices telling them that they would cause a foreign invasion. In this he showed the broad political sense and prescience to be expected of an outstanding soldier. By the day of the fight for the Xigu arsenal on 23 June, two groups of professional soldiers, each exhausted after seven days non-stop fighting the Boxers, met to do battle. They were equally matched in every possible way, Admiral Seymour's men having been able to exchange their outdated weapons for the more modern ones they found in the Chinese arsenal. The only difference was that of morale. General Yang knew that in having obeyed some of his orders and having been unable to obey others, he risked being relieved of his commission and possibly worse. Admiral Seymour had preserved most of his men from Boxer attacks and knew that if he could hold out a little longer he had a chance of regaining his base.

During the fight for the Xigu arsenal, General Yang had three mounts shot under him but his insignia flags were the first to be raised over the arsenal roof. His troops had an insufficient hold, other Chinese battalions held back and would not advance together with his troops. General Nie required the troops of Generals Yang and Hu as he feared that any delay would bring trouble with the Boxers and so General Yang had to retreat from Xigu. His fellow officers, Battalion Commander Xu, Assistant Commander Lu and Company Commander Wang died at Xigu along with 120 men and 130 wounded.[278] In the Imperial Chinese Army, as in most of the invading armies in 1900, there were undoubtedly ignorant conservative officers who owed their position to family interest. A reading of General Yang's correspondence does not show any such officers to have been under his command. Yang Mushi's account of this fight at the Xigu arsenal tallies exactly with that of Ruffi de Pontèves. The only difference was that de Pontèves did not know why the Chinese fell back and did not press the attack:

> And here is a Chinese officer on horse back, superb; he leaps the rampart and hurls himself forward at the head of his troops. The enemy is on the assault. One leap of ten metres and he is on us. Fire at will! The Chinese officer is killed and his horse shot dead; around the officer the ranks are falling. Nevertheless the blue multitude throws itself forward … it's all up with us.[279]

In his personal courage, his restraint, his foresight in deploying his troops and assuring his lines of supply, General Yang performed as well as Admiral Seymour. In the case of numbers lost, killed or wounded fighting the Boxers and the Allies and in the case of logistics, of course, his performance was better than that of Admiral Seymour. However, as soldiers, he and his Commander-in-Chief faced difficulties of a different order to those experienced by the Western and Japanese soldiers on this campaign. It is technically difficult to control a large well-armed group of men being threatened by a far larger group of poorly-armed men. It was not until the Boxer War gained momentum that the Boxers procured or were given modern weapons; at this stage they were still using weapons such as steel-tipped lances which were nevertheless lethal in the kind of engagements taking place. The restraint shown by General Yang in skirmishes and in longer engagements with the Boxers was only possible because his men were highly disciplined and personally loyal. Chinese soldiers fighting their own countrymen and led by Chinese officers did their duty with restraint, intelligence and courage. They did this even when their "duty" involved firing on men from their own counties, men who far from always behaving as the "Knights of Righteousness," had burned the shops and homes of innocent Chinese citizens and slaughtered and plundered Chinese men, women and children who were neither Christians nor related to foreigners in any way. They did their "duty" knowing that whatever the Boxers had done, they were not allowed to use the full force of the weapons or the training at their disposal to decimate Boxer bands. General Yang had described the animosity of the Boxers towards his troops and the troops of General Nie:

> The rise of the Boxers in Tianjin could certainly not be prevented because they killed on sight both the men who belonged to my troops and men who did not. As soon as they killed someone, they disappeared leaving us no way to discover who had done it.[280]

> [The Boxers] take the authority of the Court upon themselves and they feel absolutely no fear about killing officials, people and soldiers [I am] unable to estimate the numbers of those who were killed by the Boxers in the various Routes of the Army of the Vanguard and Provincial Commander-in-Chief Nieh [sic] and Governor General Yu did not dare make any enquiries.[281]

"Anti-Boxer officials were murdered legally by decrees and illegally by assassins, either at their own whim or at the urging of pro-Boxer officials."[282] Elvin also referred to the fact that "regular troops from pro- and anti-Boxer factions fought with each other as well as foreigners."[283]

Political views affecting scholarship as they do, there was a great oral history project undertaken in the 1960s to find out more about the Boxers. No oral history project was undertaken to find out what the Chinese soldiers thought when their comrades were killed by Boxers or when their commanding officers were publicly disgraced. There was a chance to know more about the ordinary soldier in the Imperial Chinese Army back in the 1960s but the opportunity was not taken.

General Yang was obeying orders knowing that he was going to incur the displeasure of the highest civilian authorities and he was commanding a group of men who had every reason to hate and fear the Boxers. At no stage did he order indiscriminate infantry or artillery fire, nor did his men decide for themselves that they would put a stop to Boxer harassment with their superior weapons. General Yang used tactics of decoy, envelopment, encirclement, ambush and the traditional Chinese cavalry tactics that were precisely described with diagrams by Captain d'Amade in his Report on his visit to Zhili province in January 1888. Such tactics were ideally suited to conditions in which a small number of well-armed mounted men supported by infantry and artillery were being surrounded by a hostile force, less well-armed but vastly superior in numbers.

Moreover, General Yang knew that, far from being appreciated, his own reputation was being destroyed at Court by pro-Boxer elements. Even worse, he knew that his Commanding Officer, General Nie Shicheng had been impeached. General Nie had been ordered to give his command to General Ma Yukun who had slighted General Nie publicly on a number of occasions.[284] Men whom Nie had reprimanded, damaged his standing at Court by saying that General Nie's army had to be weeded out as it contained Christian converts and those who had collaborated with foreigners.[285] These accusations infuriated General Yang:

> Now if there were persons in the Army of the Vanguard who converted to Christianity and who collaborated with foreigners, then how did it come about that it fought a month long violent, bloody battle in which so many men were killed and wounded?[286] [he is referring to the siege of Tianjin]

The result of these accusations was that General Nie Shicheng was fighting for his country knowing that he had been impeached and that if he lived he and his entire family would be disgraced and ruined. As for General Nie's personal reputation, Liu Mengyang reported that:

> The people of the city cursed him among themselves as "Devil Nie." The reason for this was that the Commander-in-Chief had been sparing no effort to wipe out the Boxer bandits in the hinterland. Those who were on the Boxers' side concocted the rumours that Nie Shicheng was sympathetic to the foreigners, and had taken bribes from them, undertaking to attack the Boxers. This accusation was on everyone's lips ... with the result that the Commander-in-Chief was smeared with a slander from which his name has not yet been cleared.[287]

Gangyi was displeased with Yang Mushi but even more displeased with Nie Shicheng:

> Although the General and his fellow officers found it all but unbearable, since their superiors tolerated and believed in Boxers, they did not dare to fight them without authorisation. All they could do was to withdraw. Even the General had to suffer their insults patiently, unable to do anything about them.[288]

There was even an incident in which, when General Nie, riding in the streets of Tianjin, came face to face with a group of over a hundred Boxers; he was obliged to dismount and escape through the back alleys.[289] And this was the city which Elvin assessed as having possibly the only effective official leadership of the Boxers under Circuit Intendant Tan Wenhuan.[290] General Yang Mushi wrote bitterly that the Court showed neither distress nor sympathy on hearing the news of the death of General Nie:

> Provincial Commander-in-Chief Nie, as part of the routine command of his troops, often imitated Western methods, for which measures the Boxers called him "Foreign" soldier ... the Court itself believed the charges. It rejected and ignored [the Council of] loyal and conscientious officials. And now the army weeps bitterly for this.[291]

We can perhaps more fully appreciate General Yang's bitterness if we imagine for a moment what would have been the official and popular attitude in Britain had Admiral Seymour been killed in action.

General Yang's overall perspective on the battle of Tianjin needs highlighting and is worth quoting at length:

> The Army of the Vanguard of the Wu Wei armies ... has existed as an army for seven years.... Although it is not superior, yet it does not stand behind others in

> the five armies of the Wu Wei. Some days ago I defended Tianjin and other places and, although I gave up defence of these places only little by little, the troops never measured up to the quality of the foreign armies. But for the soldiers of our side to hold the defence of Tianjin for an entire month against the soldiers of the foreign powers for whom they are no match, shows them to be as battle worthy as the great armies of our past … to battle hard for a month and to calculate losses to be one hundred men killed or wounded in each battalion is, of course, no small number. *But one cannot say the whole army was defeated and broken*.… During the time that Provincial Commander-in-Chief Nie was stationed in and defended Tianjin, he held back the foreigners for twenty distressing critical days. Tianjin remained protected without mishap. On 9 July he was killed in battle and 14 July the city was lost.… Although General Nie had little talent, yet for every day he was able to remain in Tianjin, for that day the city was protected. He held the city by means of determined battle and gave it hope by [fighting to] certain death. This distinguished him from the other generals who over and over again retreated.[292] [emphasis added]

This moving letter written to Li Hongzhang who had formerly commanded the army, shows the sentiments of a great soldier and a true patriot. Yang had heard that the troops under General Ma Qingshan had been tricked by the Boxers and suffered "an unbearable disgrace." As he saw it, the Boxers were the greatest threat to China. "The basic security of our country is collapsing, our armed forces are hard-pressed and I, being a person at present charged with serious crimes, do not dare recklessly propose a remedy."[293] For Yang Mushi, the patriot, steeped in the traditions of *The Three Kingdoms*, *The Watermargin* and the Taiping Rebellion just as much as the losses of the two Opium Wars and the Sino-Japanese War; the Boxer rising, backed as it was by the populations of entire countrysides in the vicinity of the strategically vital cities of Tianjin and Beijing, seemed to him a more serious threat to China than the foreign invasion. Very early on, he had foreseen that one would lead to the other;[294] Yang's judgement was influenced by the power of the common people. These brief excerpts show this power to have been a very real one indeed. This was a kind of power quite out of the military experience of the commanders of any of the eight invading armies. Dynasties ruled when they held the Mandate of Heaven and when they were perceived by the common people to hold that mandate. Thus General Yang's brief campaign against the Boxers was militarily more complex and more difficult to execute as a professional Western-trained Chinese soldier than was Admiral Seymour's reckless foray.

To the points in common between General Yang and his Western counterparts, one last needs to be added. It arises from his moving letter to Li Hongzhang. Soldiers fight for a flag, an insignia, a name; these are tangible exteriorisations of the complex of feelings that lead men to fight, kill, destroy and die for their countries or their beliefs. General Yang was trained in the Western mould. He believed that it was essential for orders to be sent and received through the appropriate chain of command. His letters show him to have been intensely loyal to General Nie, and to his fellow divisional commanders and officers. For soldiers like General Yang, personal loyalty, loyalty to a flag and service to his country were the main motivating forces of his professional life. So we can empathise with his concern when he asked Li Hongzhang to restore the name of the Huai army to the army that used it. The Empress Dowager had reorganised the Northern armies on 7 December 1898. Yang saw that by changing the name of the Huai army when it was incorporated into the Wu Wei army, Li Hongzhang lost the men of his former command; some of them went to General Nie, the others to General Yuan Shikai. It then became difficult to weld the men together and urge them to action under the name and the flag of a new army. Twenty battalions were now fighting as the Vanguard of the Wu Wei army and Yang asked that these twenty battalions be referred to as the Left and Right Wings of the Huai army. What's in a name? A great deal for officers and soldiers who drill together every day preparing for the time when they will fight relying on the loyalty and comradeship of the men carrying their colours, bearing their flags, their name. Any Western-trained soldier of that day would understand the importance of belonging to a given regiment, of fighting under regimental colours, of dying if need be for the name and the colours of the regiment. What else is in a name? A name can be seen as a location in a slippery political environment.

In the first section of this chapter, we examined tangible signs of modernisation of the Chinese army. In this section we have closely followed General Yang Mushi in action, we have seen his three mounts shot away from under him during the battle of Xigu and we have seen his courage in being prepared to disobey orders though he knew this would cause him personal disgrace and possible ruin. We have seen him temporarily removed from his commission by General Nie and then go on to write a moving tribute to his army and his Commander-in-Chief. One should not be misled by his

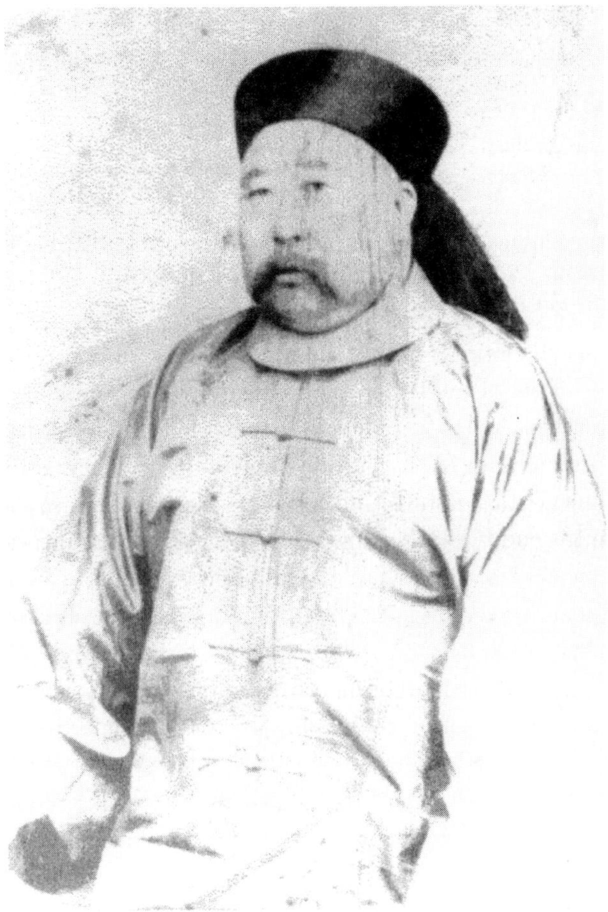

Figure 6.23 General Nie Shicheng.[295]

understatements; General Yang was proud that he fought under great leadership to keep the foreigners out of Tianjin for a month. General Nie, far from being a man "of little talent," was the man whose prestige he had called upon to smash the Boxers. General Nie was the man with the leadership qualities and military experience enabling him to be Commander-in-Chief of an army containing Generals like Yang Mushi. General Nie was the man who held Tianjin for China every day he lived despite being maligned by calumny and forces at Court out of touch with the realities by which and for which men such as Colonel Yang Futong and Battalion Commander Xu had fought and died. It is fitting to let General Yang conclude this description of the qualities of the modern Western-trained Chinese soldier fighting for China in 1900.

> I am an insignificant general in the Huai army who recently suffered defeat. But I have been able to restore my former outlook and I am more content than one could hope for. There is nothing which I want to request of you [Li Hongzhang] for myself.... But the catastrophe of the Boxers and the grief of my army gives me an inner disquiet which I cannot dispel in eating, drinking, sleeping or dreaming.[296]

What was important for such a man? A Chinese soldier and a patriot, he saw that the nature of the Boxer rising threatened the fabric of his country. He knew that the Boxers were being manipulated by the conservative factions at Court. He was perfectly aware that with the men and the weapons at his disposal he could smash this insurrection. He was also fully conscious of the fact that his hands were tied by orders coming through the very chain of command he was sworn to obey. He saw that men whom he held in the highest esteem had been disgraced by fellow nationals and unjustly treated by the Court. Above all, he saw that his army suffered the worst nightmare of any professional soldier; conflicting orders from the highest civilian authorities who had no appreciation of the skills, the courage and the patriotism of the greatest officers and the well-trained rank and file in their best armies. These were the concerns of General Yang, these were the challenges, successes and failures of a professional Chinese soldier in 1900. These challenges and this professionalism were evaluated in precisely the same way by an American officer of the day, a product of military traditions quite alien to those of traditional Chinese soldiery, but whose definition of an experienced officer fitted Generals Yang and Nie precisely. Brigadier General Daggett wrote of the differences between an experienced and an inexperienced officer:

> The former, exercising self-restraint, looks to the interests of his Government; the latter, impulsive, excited, looks for personal glory; the former, his reputation for personal courage being secure, bends all his energies to the best methods of gaining victory; the latter, having no reputation for personal courage, exerts all his energies to get one[297]

The performance of Generals Nie Shicheng and Yang Mushi on various battlefields against widely differing foes showed them to be truly experienced officers as defined by an enemy professional fighting against them. General

Yang and his fellow commanding officers preferred to abandon Xigu after a valiant attempt to retake it, because as they saw it, any delay in deploying their troops "would bring trouble with the Boxers." At this stage the foreigners weighed little in the balance of the concerns of General Yang Mushi. He had demonstrated his understanding that a large-scale peasant insurrection would bring trouble with the foreigners and, to the last, it was his concern with the insurrection, with his commander, with his army, which dominated his record.

Here perhaps it may be appropriate to look beyond a mental framework that sees Boxers either as heroes or as harbingers of barbaric, yellow-peril filled hordes, beyond the idea of the Qing dynasty as an alien or corrupt dynasty, to the mental framework that sees China as a whole country. The division of China was an option being openly discussed by many foreigners in the 1890s. Many modern-trained Chinese officers and soldiers had either trained in foreign countries or faced foreign armies in the field. It is possible to postulate on the basis of this brief outline of General Yang's performance and attitudes, that he and selected fellow senior officers fought not primarily as willing agents of the Qing Court but for a clear concept of their country in an international context. If the Qing had fallen in 1900, China would have been entirely at the mercy of the Powers. Its fate may have been like that of Africa, at least for some time. If some officers thought in terms of their country, it is possible that some soldiers thought like this as well. If Boxers saw their country as menaced by foreigners, how much more would soldiers have understood this, particularly those veterans of the Sino-Japanese War? It is a pity that we do not know how the regular soldiers serving in General Nie Shicheng's army thought although we get a fleeting glimpse from a Chinese source that commented on the Qing government's continual criticism of General Nie Shicheng and said that "all his soldiers were depressed."[298] Their memories of why they held together and why they thought they were fighting are a lost heritage. Their discipline when ordered to fight against fellow-countrymen or, in a complete turnaround, to fight with them, is a quality that has not been evaluated.

When we attempt to appraise the character of Chinese military leadership as it appeared during the events of 1900, we should reflect on the differing responses of Generals Nie Shicheng and Yuan Shikai. The British public had been told that General Nie had established his reputation during the

Sino-Japanese War.[299] The letters of one of his commanders in the field give ample testimony to General Nie's ability to evoke leadership qualities in his officers and men and to command their absolute loyalty. He had a clear concept of his duty to obey orders and to serve his country. Moreover, when these two concepts led to conflict, he accepted responsibility and under humiliating circumstances went on to fight and die for his country, inspiring his men to the last. This would appear to be almost the copybook picture of a model Western-trained soldier.

Turning to Yuan Shikai, despite being ordered three times to bring his troops up to Beijing, he made no move to leave Shandong. He was to become the President of China in 1912. The question remains as to which of the two men best represented the Western training they had received. As posterity in China and the West remembers Yuan Shikai and has largely forgotten Nie Shicheng, one answer may be that professional soldiers in China needed more than the techniques and ideals of Western soldiering. Another answer may be that in the cultural tradition of some military annals the ultimate heroism is forgotten and is not a match for the tradition glorifying surviving heroic failures such as Admiral Seymour or the surviving astute tacticians who disobeyed orders and did not appear when called on to fight for their country.

The question may reasonably be asked, how representative was a leader like Yang Mushi? Having asked this question, we may also reasonably ask, how representative was a leader like Admiral Seymour? In answering these questions we must acknowledge two entirely different military cultures in the matter of what is considered heroism. The French military attaché at Tianjin summed up Admiral Seymour's contribution as "glorious folly." The history of British nineteenth century wars of Empire is littered with Seymours whose glorious failures elevated them to the stature of public heroes. We need look no further than Gordon of Khartoum, formerly "Chinese Gordon." In nineteenth and twentieth century British military history, spectacular military failures became the subjects of poetry by the Poet Laureate (again, the "Charge of the Light Brigade" comes to mind), poetry that was chanted in every school classroom throughout the British Empire. Alternatively such glorious failures became public holidays when thousands turned out to watch the heroes who lost on that day so long ago. The group of heroes dwindled every year but nevertheless went on gripping the imagination of the British themselves as well as the inhabitants of those small outposts of what was once Britain's far-flung Empire. Seymour's right to fly an insignia when he was in his base, an insignia uniquely reserved for use by members of the Royal Family, may be seen as a sign to every officer and man under his command, that he and his countrymen could be beaten not only once, but twice by the Chinese, and remain heroes.

In China there was no such cult of the heroic defeat. As far back as the fourth century of the Christian era, officials given military command preferred to retire early rather than risk banishment or execution.[300] In some cases it was as dangerous to win as to lose. As the Taiping Rebellion came under control, Zeng Guofan progressively took a back seat. Countless Chinese admirals and generals committed suicide rather than face impeachment, banishment or worse. General Song Qing is one of the better-known Chinese officers cashiered despite his solid performance in the Sino-Japanese War.[301] Much has been written on the subject of military leadership in China but there has been little comment on the devastating effect on morale that occurred when senior commanding officers were executed in front of their men for failing to win a battle. Of the untold numbers of unfortunate cases, that of General Su Yuanchun (1845–1907)[302] serving in Yunnan was particularly tragic. After the debacle at Fuzhou during the Sino-French War, Zeng Guofan protested that such stringent disciplinary measures as executing ships' captains in front of their crew would do incalculable damage to naval morale.[303]

While there were obviously corrupt and inefficient generals and high-ranking officers in the Chinese army as in most armies that have ever been raised, the price paid for failure by men who fought gallantly and often to the death was that they and their families were frequently publicly disgraced, even exiled, banished or executed. A wounded man who had fought with Seymour and survived would die willingly for his Admiral in another campaign. In Chinese military culture, Divisional-Commanders like Yang Mushi often did not have the option of retaining the personal loyalty of their men. Western military tradition is not replete with examples of brilliant generals being asked to take command and save their country knowing that they and their entire families have been condemned in advance to dishonour or worse. Nie Shicheng was publicly reinstated in his office posthumously through the intervention of Yuan Shikai who inscribed in his own hand a memorial to

General Nie which can be seen in Tianjin today. However, his experience, his ability to inspire and lead men; all that died with him when he chose to face death from enemy artillery fire that July in Tianjin. He felt that he could no longer fight as he had been impeached at Court and his career was in ruins. Kotenev's dismissal of "Boxerism" as being "unable to produce anything more than .... Contempt of death shown ... by the highest military commanders [and] considered in China as patriotism and nationalism"[304] does little justice to men like General Nie Shicheng. It ignores the whole complexity of factors facing Chinese generals trained on Western models but operating in a political and social environment in which traditional Chinese values often dominated or could be made at any moment to dominate. Given the stakes, such a military tradition which could also embrace modernisation to produce Generals like Su, Yang and Nie was a military tradition bound to produce the very finest leaders absolutely dedicated to their men and to their country. That modernisation of selected Chinese armies was more than skin-deep by 1900, is shown by the superb discipline and courage of the rank and file serving under Generals Yang and Nie.

Notes

1. My deepest appreciation to Professor R. J. O'Neill for his detailed critique of an earlier draft of this chapter, enabling me to direct my research to cover all significant aspects of Chinese military modernisation from 1860 to 1900.
2. Joanna Waley-Cohen, "China and Western Technology in the Late Eighteenth Century," *American Historical Review*, Vol. 98, No. 5, December 1993. See also the discussion in Chapter Three of the observations of William Barnard during the First Opium War.
3. A forerunner of the revisionist school of thought regarding Chinese military capacity in the nineteenth century is Allen Fung, "Testing the Self-strengthening: The Chinese Army in the Sino-Japanese War of 1894–1895," *Modern Asian Studies*, Vol. 30, No. 4, 1996.
4. "With Gordon in China: The Storming of Canton. From the Narrative of Private John Clarke of the 59th Regiment," in Walter Wood, *Marvellous Escapes from Peril As Told by Survivors*, Blackie and Son, London, no date.
5. Ralph L. Powell, *The Rise of Chinese Military Power, 1895–1912*, Princeton University Press, 1955, p. 31.
6. John Thomson, *Illustrations of China and Its People. A Series of Two Hundred Photographs with Letterpress Descriptive of the Places and People Represented*, Sampson

Low, Marston, in 4 Volumes, London, 1869–1874, Vol. 1, Plate 12, photograph No. 21.

7. Ian Knight, *Queen Victoria's Enemies (4): Asia, Australasia and the Americans*, Osprey Publishing, London, 1990. This work is intended for High School students and very clearly perpetuates the "loser" school mentality with regard to the Imperial Chinese Army especially in connection with the Boxer War. The hand drawn illustrations are particularly notable as they recreate the exotic pantomime image with a picture of a Chinese "Tigerman" and do not show a soldier in the modern uniforms typical of the armies stationed in the strategically most important areas of China. By contrast, the hand drawn illustrations of the Maori warriors depict them as real fighting men complete with dead English soldiers at their feet. The Maori purchased modern weapons for their wars with the British. So did the Chinese. The Chinese also learned to manufacture modern weapons but their image of exotic hopeless fighters using antiquated weapons is still being actively perpetuated. I am greatly indebted to Professor Joanna Waley-Cohen for giving me a copy of this book.
8. See Chapter Three for a discussion of the cultural connotations of military uniform.
9. The most recent work to use this photograph with great prominence is Pamela Kyle Crossley, *Orphan Warriors. Three Manchu Generations and the End of the Qing World*, Princeton University Press, Princeton, 1990. Crossley's description of the action in the First Opium War contains some breathtaking quotations from a contemporary British eyewitness of courageous but hopeless last stands on the part of the Chinese. However, it is notable that she does not use these same sources in assessing the contribution of this war to the immediate upgrading of Chinese naval technology. See discussion in Chapter Three.
10. John L. Rawlinson, "China's Failure to Coordinate Her Modern Fleets in the Late Nineteenth Century," in Albert Feuerwerker, Rhoads Murphey and Mary C. Wright (eds), *Approaches to Modern History*, University of California Press, Berkeley, 1967. Those reading Rawlinson would do well to read the accounts of French military men stuck on Taiwan with inadequate forces and supplies as they begged for reinforcements from the Commander-in-Chief in Tonkin and the Government in France during the Sino-French War of 1880–1885. The difficulties faced during the nineteenth century by British generals in the field in obtaining reinforcements are too numerous to detail. Suffice it to say, that the reluctance of various Chinese military men cited by Rawlinson as being unwilling to send their ships and other reinforcements to Fuzhou, is a reluctance which has an international character. The military problem in question was one that was being faced by Western armies constantly during their various nineteenth century wars of Empire. On occasion, Western performance was as disastrous as that of the Chinese in Fuzhou. The fate of Gordon in Khartoum comes to mind, not to mention some of the debacles in

New Zealand and Africa, all caused by the same factors that resulted in the annihilation by the French of all the important Chinese military installations in Fuzhou.

11. The work of Allen Fung and David Wright combines careful scholarship with the data and approach required to begin a revision of the actual nature of China's performance in war and scientific research capacity relative to developments in military technology. See Fung, op. cit., and David Wright, "Careers in Western Science in Nineteenth Century China: Xu Shou and Xu Jianyin," *Journal of the Royal Asiatic Society*, Third Series, Vol. 5, No. 1, April 1995. My thanks to Dr Gary Tiedemann for drawing my attention to this latter reference.
12. John Keegan, *A History of Warfare*, Hutchinson, London, 1993, p. xi.
13. Pierre Beglair, "OTAN. Doutes et Polémiques." *Le Point*, 23 April 1999.
14. Michael R. D. Foot, *Art and War. Twentieth Century Warfare as Depicted by War Artists*, Headline, London, 1990, p. 28, "Haig and Foch were the joint victors in the late summer of 1918 over Hindenberg and Ludendorff, a crushing victory the British would have been reluctant to add to the nationally remembered battle-honours because it came after the slaughter of Passchendaele."
15. Ouriel Reschef, *Guerre, Mythes et Caricature. Au Berceau d'une Mentalité Française*, Presses de la fondation nationale des sciences politiques, Paris, 1984.
16. See Chapter Three for an extensive discussion of this phenomenon.
17. The Chinese language authorities are Li Dezheng, Su Weizhi and Liu Tianlu, *Baguo lianjun qinhua shi* (A History of the Eight-Power Allied Forces Agression Against China), Shandong University Press, Jinan, 1990; Shi Yuceng, *Yihetuan yundong yibai zhounian jinian: Yihetuan yundong he baguo lianjun qinhua zhanzheng* (Commemoration of the Centennial of the Boxer Movement: The Boxer Movement and the Eight Allied Forces War of Aggression), Chuzhong Huiguan, Tokyo, 2000; Sun Qihai, *Tiexue bainianji: Baguo lianjun qinhua zhanzheng jishi* (Commemoration of the Centennial of the War Against the Eight Allied Forces Aggression), Huanghe, Jinan, 2000; Mo Anshi, *Yihetuan dikang lieqiang guafen shi* (The History of the Boxers' Struggle Against the Foreign Countries Who Wanted to Divide China), Jingji guanli, Beijing, 1997; Zhao Jianli, *Yihetuan baguo lianjun, xingchou tiaoyue. Gengzi zhi bian tuzhi* (The Boxers, the Eight Invading Powers, the Boxer Protocol. Illustrated Records of the Changes That Happened in the Year 1900), Shandong huabao, Jinan, 2000.
18. Henrietta Harrison, "Justice on Behalf of Heaven," *History Today*, September 2000, p. 50: "The Qing army never really engaged with foreign troops."
19. Joanna Waley-Cohen, *The Sextants of Beijing. Global Currents in Chinese History*, W. W. Norton and Company, New York, 1999, pp. 168–169.
20. Paul A. Cohen, *History in Three Keys. The Boxers as Event, Experience, and Myth*, Columbia University Press, New York, 1997, p. 56. This writer could not agree with Professor Cohen's assessment that the Chinese military made "a poor

showing" nor with those historians both Western and Chinese, who see in Cixi's flight to Xi'an some sort of "humiliation." In fact, it kept her out of the hands of the Allies and allowed her to keep issuing decrees and have an important impact in diminishing the severity of the claims made against China by the Allied Powers. However, his point that "The draconian nature of the settlement" most certainly did "[energise] the forces of both reform and revolution in Chinese society" is one that emphatically dominated in the courte durée. In the minds of ordinary folk and intellectuals any possible humiliation or otherwise either because of the performance of the Chinese army or because of the flight of the Empress Dowager weighed far less than the economic consequences of the fiscal demands of the Boxer Protocol.

21. Alistair Iain Johnston, *Cultural Realism. Strategic Culture and Grand Strategy in Chinese History*, Princeton University Press, Princeton, 1995, p. 72. My thanks to Professor Joanna Waley-Cohen for drawing my attention to Johnston's work.
22. Ibid., p. 31.
23. Ibid., p. 57. See also Allen Fung, "Chinese Failure Reconsidered: An Analysis of the Defeat of the Chinese Army and the Chinese Military Culture During the Sino-Japanese War (1894–1895)," unpublished BA thesis, Oxford, 1990, p. 33. Fung gives his opinion that one of the reasons for Chinese defeat by the Japanese was deficiencies in Chinese military strategy as applied in Chinese tactics in specific contexts during this war. I am particularly grateful to Professor Mark Elvin for drawing my attention to this reference.
24. Johnston, op cit., pp. 51–52.
25. Ibid., p. 66.
26. Ibid.
27. See below for a detailed discussion of General Yang's correspondence.
28. Nathan Chaikin, *The Sino-Japanese War 1894–1895*, Imprimerie Pillet, Martigny, 1983. Chaikin's purpose is to write an art book about the magnificent woodcuts produced by Japanese artists who went to the front during the Sino-Japanese war. He also gives some details about the horrendous mistakes — or should they be called "learning experiences" — consequent on the uneven nature of the modernisation of the Japanese army. Two examples will suffice; during this war, the Japanese footsoldier wore straw sandals. In February 1895, a Major Saito took his men on a reconnaissance at 0200h and returned at 2300 hours through two feet of snow. More than 1,500 men suffered severe frostbite and were removed from the front, many to be amputated and crippled for life (p. 38). A second example: during the Seikan campaign, Major-General Oshima took his men south to Asan. It was a tedious and harassing march and "the desertion of the coolies on the very first day drove Major Koshi to suicide, through sheer exasperation." The Japanese decided on a night attack. "In the excitement, Lieutenant Tokoyama and twenty men jumped into a deep pond

and drowned." (p. 63) There are too many black and white histories which see the victors as (in this case) successfully modernised Western-type armies and the vanquished as hopelessly corrupt, inept and incapable of modernisation. Thus we get the histories of the Sino-Japanese war which recount only the successes of the Japanese and the failures of the Chinese. Chaikin's account of the last stand of Admiral Ding Jucheng in the battle of Yalu is the very last word in the account of a hero (p. 75). Where are the histories which recount the heroism of the defeated or do only certain cultural groups have the right to such histories?

29. Scott Dolby, "The Boxer Crisis as Seen Through the Eyes of Five Chinese Officials," unpublished PhD thesis, Columbia University, 1976, p. 177. Letter of 18 July 1900 from Yang Mushi to Li Hongzhang.
30. There is a monument in Tianjin dedicated to the memory of Nie Shicheng and inscribed in Yuan Shikai's calligraphy.
31. A useful study on anti-foreignism is Judith Wyman, "The Ambiguities of Anti-foreignism: Chongqing, 1870–1900," *Late Imperial China*, Vol. 18, No. 2, December 1997. My thanks to Dr Gerry Groot for drawing my attention to this reference.
32. James Belich, *The New Zealand Wars and the Victorian Interpretation of Racial Conflict*, Auckland University Press, New Zealand, 1986, p. 69. Belich is quoting the New Zealand settler, F. E. Manning.
33. Ibid.
34. See Denis E. Showalter, "Dien Bien Phu in Three Cultures," *War and Society*, Vol. 16, No. 2, October 1999. Showalter gives a clear exposition as to what Dien Bien Phu meant to the French, the Americans and the Vietnamese in terms of myth and the effect of myth on military action
35. Frederick Brown, *From Tientsin to Peking with the Allied Forces*, Charles H. Kelly, London, 1902, p. 29.
36. Wilbur J. Chamberlin, *Ordered to China*, Methuen, London, 1904.
37. Rear-Admiral Bowman H. McCalla, "Memoirs of a Naval Career," typed manuscript held in the Marine Archives, Quantical, Virginia, USA, undated, Ch. 27, pp. 46–47 and Chapter 26, p. 13. Typed manuscript given to me by Mike Miller of the Marine Corps library, Quantical, Virginia. I am indebted to Mr Miller for this and other references.
38. Archives Militaires de l'Armée de Terre, Château de Vincennes (hereafter referred to as "Armée"), Paris, Series 7N1668, 3 July 1900. Despatch No. 97 from Vidal to the Minister of War.
39. Showalter, op. cit., p. 95.
40. Ibid.
41. Captain A. A. S. Barnes, *On Active Service with the Chinese Regiment: A Record of the Operations of the First Chinese Regiment in North China from March to October 1900*, Grant Richards, London, 1902, p. 31.

42. Paolo E. Coletta, *Bowman Hendry McCalla, A Fighting Sailor*, University Press of America, Washington, DC, 1979, p. 120.
43. Among the British press, the *Daily Mail* stands out as giving accurate coverage of the first four weeks of the Boxer campaign as did American papers such as the *World* and the *Chicago Daily News*.
44. See Chapter One.
45. "An Officer," quoted in Brown, op cit., p. 37
46. Anatol M. Kotenev, *The Chinese Soldier. Basic principles, Spirit, Science of War and Heroes of the Chinese Armies*, Kelly and Walsh Ltd., Shanghai, 1937, p. 78.
47. William J. Duiker, *Cultures in Collision: The Boxer Rebellion*, Presidio Press, California, 1978, pp. 203–204, "How could an ignorant mass of superstitious peasant youths rally the nation against the full power of Western imperialism.... The resentment of the illiterate peasant against the Western missionary and of the village scholar against Western ideas and scientific innovations did not result from a clear consciousness of Chinese national identity. A true sense of nationalism implies an awareness of the world and the place of one's homeland in it." Dying for one's homeland obviously rated differently on the scale measuring consciousness of national identity if one was a Chinese fighting to defend his city or his village and if one was a Sikh, a Punjabi coolie or a Tonkinois fighting to defend British or French views of "the place of their homeland in the world."
48. Kotenev, op cit., p. 177.
49. Ibid.
50. *Consular Records, Tientsin, January 1900–30 June 1903*, Department of State, held in the National Archives, Washington, M114, Despatch from US Consul Ragsdale to Secretary of State, "The Uprising in North China," 16 July 1900. Chinese historians saw this incident as the one that really sparked off indignation and the decision to act on the part of forces of the Imperial Chinese Army. See Liu Tianlu et al., op. cit., pp. 126–127.
51. Barnes, op cit., p. 95. George Lynch, *The War of the Civilisations. Being a Record of a "Foreign Devil's" Experiences with the Allies in China*, Longmans, Green and Co., 1901, describes ambassadorial looting, p. 153 and p. 223 notes that American soldiers' loot was auctioned and the proceeds given to the poor of Beijing. For other references to looting see ibid., pp. 137 and 238, A. H. Savage-Landor, *China and the Allies*, Vol. 2, William Heinemann, London, 1901, pp. 192–195 and Brown, op cit., p. 101. Mark Twain provoked a violent response by writing to the American press about missionary involvement in looting. Simpson's account of French soldiers looting is highly evocative, see Bertram L. Simpson, *Indiscreet Letters from Peking*, Arno Press, New York, 1970 (1907), pp. 342–346. See also p. 415. Lieutenant Bernard Frederick Roper Holbrooke describes the British army's organisation of looting in Beijing and Captain Edward Bayly mentions Allied and foreign looting in Tianjin. See Frederick A. Sharf and

Peter Harrington, *China, 1900. The Eyewitnesses Speak. The Boxer Rebellion as Described by Participants in Letters, Diaries and Photographs*, Greenhill Books, London, 2000, pp. 130 and 236. The recent authority on looting during the Boxer rising is James Hevia whose careful and provocative scholarship takes a difficult social by-product of war and traces both its physical and metaphysical origins and results. See James L. Hevia, "Loot's Fate. The Economics of Plunder and the Moral Life of Objects," *History and Anthropology*, Vol. 6, No. 4, 1994. See also James Heria, "Plundering Beijing, 1900–1901," unpublished paper given at the Conference "1900. The Boxers, China and the World," London, June 2001.

52. The relationship between Western perceptions of military ability and nationalism as defined according to these perceptions has been pointed out by Belich in the context of the Maori war effort. See Belich, op cit., p. 132.
53. Cohen, op. cit., pp. 187–188.
54. Knight, op. cit., p. 7, "The Boxers had no means of acquiring modern arms and in any case their philosophy rejected all things Western." "All things Western" fell short of Krupp guns and repeating rifles which they used to great effect. See discussion in Chapter Seven.
55. Mistakes are still being made in the chronology of events after the foreigners attacked China on the night of 16–17 June. See Sharf and Harrington, *China, 1900. The Eyewitnesses Speak*, op cit., p. 15.
56. See discussion in Chapter Three.
57. Joseph W. Esherick, *The Origins of the Boxer Uprising*, University of California Press, Berkeley, 1987, pp. 302–303; Cohen, op cit., p. 50 follows Esherick and omits any reference to the battle. Roger R. Thompson follows Cohen so we do not learn anything from him about the part played by the Imperial Chinese Army in the battle of Dagu, see Roger R. Thompson, "Military Dimensions of the 'Boxer Uprising' in Shanxi, 1898–1902," p. 303 in Hans van de Ven (ed.), *Warfare in Chinese History*, Sinica Leidensia, Brill, Leiden, 2000.
58. The reports of the Russian, British, German and Japanese military attachés are all of extreme interest and merit further detailed study. These reports are easily accessible in the archives of the respective countries. The French archives contain Japanese reports and secret reports translated from Russian which can both be found in Armée, Series 7N1679.
59. See, Armée, Series 7N1666 Annex No. 6 to report No. 54, 28 November 1892 by Fleurac. See also Series 7N1674, "Rapport du Capitaine Meillet adjoint à l'Atelier de Construction de Puteaux sur son Voyage en Chine, 1900," p. 70.
60. Waley-Cohen, "China and Western Technology," op cit., shows deliberate acquisition of elements of Western thinking applicable to the development of military technology to have begun as far back as the late eighteenth century.
61. Ssu-Yu Teng and John K. Fairbank (eds), *China's Response to the West*, Harvard University Press, 1961, p. 53.

62. Ibid., p. 72.
63. Ibid., p. 70.
64. Stanley Spector, *Li Hung Chang and the Huai Army. A Study in Nineteenth Century Chinese Regionalism*, University of Washington Press, 1974, p. 163.
65. US Department of State. Documents on the Chinese Crisis (hereafter referred to as *China*), National Archives, Washington, undated letter from the Belgian Legation describing the location and capabilities of the Chinese arsenals.
66. Teng and Fairbank, op cit., pp. 137–138. Spector gives an interesting account of the dominant considerations in the training of the "trained armies" (*lian-jun*), Spector, op cit., pp. 165–170.
67. Powell, op cit., p. 24. Powell's authority here is W. C. Bales, *Tso Tsungt'ang, Soldier and Statesman of Old China*, Shanghai, 1937.
68. Richard J. Smith and Kwang-Ching Liu, "The Military Challenge: the North-West and the Coast," in Dennis Twitchett and John K. Fairbank (eds), *The Cambridge Modern History of China*, Chapter 4, Cambridge University Press, Cambridge, 1978 (1994), p. 239.
69. Armée, Series 7N1679, "Forces militaires de la Chine en 1882 d'après des Renseignements Japonais."
70. Armée, Series 7N1679. A confidential report of 1884 translated from the Russian with a section on the militia and the levied troops of Zhili province.
71. Armée, Series 7N1666, de Fleurac, "Report on mines and torpedoes in the ports of Zhili." Tianjin, 18 February 1892.
72. Armée, Series 7N1665, Captain d'Amade, Fascicule 1, "Chine, Armée du Pei-Tchi-Li, Voyage d'hiver 1888"; Fascicule 2, "Les troupes stationnées au Nord du Pei-ho"; Fascicule 3, "Les camps de Kuin-Ling-Tchang"; "Les troupes stationnées au Nord du Pei-ho"; Fascicule 4, "Troupes et fortifications de Pei-tang"; "Troupes stationnées au Nord du Pei-ho"; Fascicule 5, "Chann hai kuann."
73. Most of the military accounts note with precision the quantity and type of arms and ammunition possessed by both regular army soldiers and Boxer insurgents. Having detailed the modern weapons being used in the siege of Tianjin and found in munitions depots and arsenals in prodigious quantities, Colonel Pélacot observed wryly, "What should we thus think of the information we were given at the beginning of the siege by European officers, former instructors of the Chinese army, according to which the Chinese only had *one battery of Krupp guns* with *eight shells* apiece?" [emphasis added]. Colonel Pélacot, *Expédition de Chine de 1900 jusqu'à l'arrivée du Général Voyron*, Henri Charles-Lavauzelle, Paris, 1901, p. 120.
74. Wright, op cit.
75. Savage-Landor, op cit., Vol. 1, pp. 226–228.
76. Thomas L. Kennedy, *The Arms of Kiangnan: Modernization in the Chinese Ordnance Industry, 1860–1895*, Westview Press, Colorado, 1978. It is notable that Ralph Powell's book is most often cited as the authority on the development of

the Chinese army and includes details on arms manufacture, training and logistics. Powell, op cit., pp. 108–109 gives figures for the imports of foreign weapons showing a tremendous increase in the figures for Tianjin — a more than eight-fold expansion — between 1898 and 1899. The major points Powell draws from these figures are that these imports were necessary because of the "corruption and inefficiency of [Chinese] ordnance plants" and that foreign agents were often dishonest when supplying China with weapons. Kennedy stresses that under Li Hongzhang, the arsenal at Tianjin was smoothly and efficiently run with no trace of corruption. Other points could be made about the figures. They reflect a strong perception of the potential threat in the North; hence the figures for imports in Tianjin 1899 are more than five times those for Hankou, the next largest importing city in Powell's figures. Figures given by Kennedy reflect changes in policy with regard to attempts to keep up in the arms race as opposed to developing a deliberate policy of staying one step behind and manufacturing ammunition, gun carriages and light guns in China while importing weapons from Europe. Typical of Powell's negative assessment of all aspects of China's attempts at military modernisation, he mentions the fact that "large numbers of rejected and even condemned weapons were sold to Chinese officials by agents of foreign firms." (See Note 167 below). He does not mention the very special relationship between China and Germany through Li Hongzhang's connection with Friedrich Krupp who took a personal interest in the Chinese market. There is a photograph of a clay statue of Li attached to Annex 2 to de Fleurac's report of 16 June 1894. See Armée, Series 7N1665. The Krupp works at Essen were to cast this statue. Krupp had a portrait of Li Hongzhang hanging over his bed. See Wright, op cit., p. 80, Note 189.

77. Kennedy, op cit., frontispiece.
78. Colonel Pélacot, op cit., p. 120 and Rear-Admiral Bowman H. McCalla, op cit., Chapter 26, p. 13.
79. Frederick A. Sharf and Peter Harrington, *The Boxer Rebellion. China, 1900. The Artist's Perspective*, Greenhill Books, London, 2000, p. 73.
80. Kennedy, op cit., frontispiece.
81. John W. Dower, *War Without Mercy. Race and Power in the Pacific War*, Pantheon Books, New York, 1986, p. 104, notes that both British and American intelligence had prepared full reports on Japanese fighter planes downed in China in the 1930s. Dower observes that it was not Japanese secrecy that kept Western military men from knowing about these planes but "the blindness of most high-ranking officers who simply could not conceive of Japan independently designing and manufacturing an aircraft of this calibre."
82. See Wright, op cit., p. 80, Note 191. When Li Hongzhang was visiting the Atelier des Forges et Chantiers de la Mediterranée, he wanted to see a 254mm cannon which was being built for the Swedes. The French asked for Swedish government authorisation for his request by telegram. See Armée, Series 7N1674,

"Extrait du Rapport du Capitaine d'Amade, détaché auprès de l'Ambassadeur Extraordinaire Li Hong Chang pendant le séjour en France de la mission chinoise, 13 July-1 August 1896."

83. Kennedy, op cit., p. 73.
84. Armée, Series 7N1665, Report No. 2 by Captain de Contenson, 13 August 1872. See also Kennedy, op cit., passim for meticulous details.
85. See *North China Daily News*, 22 October 1892, "L'Industrie militaire en Chine," see Kennedy, op cit., passim.
86. Armée, Series 7N1674. Report by Captain Meillet, op cit., pp. 101–102.
87. Armée, Series 7N1665. Report No. 3 by Captain de Contenson, 10 September 1872. De Contenson also tried to get inside the Dagu forts in 1873 but was not permitted. He sent a translation of a German report on the forts instead. The military build-up he observed around Tianjin may have been prompted by Chinese anticipation of reprisal for an incident in 1870 in which the cathedral in Tianjin was burnt and some European nuns and missionaries were killed. See Series 7N1665. Report No. 4 by Captain de Contenson, 10 June 1873.
88. Fung, "Testing the Self-Strengthening," op cit., pp. 10008–10009.
89. Armée, Series 7N1665. Report No. 2 by Captain de Contenson, 13 August 1872.
90. Armée, Series 7N1666. Report No. 206 from Captain de Fleurac to the Minister of War, Tianjin, 1 June 1895.
91. Teruaki Kawano, "Allied Military Co-operation in the Boxer Rebellion and Japan's Policy," *Revue Internationale d'Histoire Militaire*, No. 70, 1988, p. 101.
92. P. H. Clements, *The Boxer Rebellion: A Political and Diplomatic Review*, New York, 1967 (1915), p. 35.
93. Wright, op cit., pp. 50–51.
94. *The Times*, 1 January 1900.
95. Powell, op cit. and Victor W. Purcell, *The Boxer Uprising. A Background Study*, Cambridge University Press, Great Britain, 1963, whose source on Chinese arsenals is Powell, offer a one-sided view of Chinese armaments developments. Purcell's assessment of the arsenals stresses the negative owing to the limitation of his sources. While he relies on the *North China Herald*, he does not cite the report in that newspaper which quoted Mr Bryois as saying that the plant at Hanyang was capable of turning out 400,000 rifles a year with European workmen and half that with Chinese workmen. According to Bryois, the Jiangnan arsenal "has succeeded in producing steel which is acknowledged at home to rival the product of the great European foundries, and is importing the great hydraulic presses for compressing it." See *North China Herald*, 21 October 1892. This was confirmed by Admiral Lord Charles Beresford's visit seven years later.
96. Thomson, *Illustrations of China*, op cit., Plate 12, photograph No. 22.
97. Kennedy, op cit., p. 68.

98. Wright, op cit., p. 77.
99. Thomson, *Illustrations of China*, op cit. There are no page numbers but Thomson's observations on the arsenals can be found in the texts relating to the photographs "Nanking Arsenal" and "Foreign-Drilled Troops."
100. John Thomson, *Through China with a Camera*, A. Constable, Westminster, 1898, pp. 144–145.
101. *North China Daily News*, 22 October 1892, Henri Bryois "L'industrie militaire en Chine."
102. See Chapter Three.
103. Waley-Cohen, "China and Western Technology," op cit., p.1531.
104. Kennedy, op cit., p. 10.
105. Armée, Series 7N1665. Report No. 2 by Captain de Contenson on the Tianjin Arsenal, 13 August 1872.
106. Armée, Series 7N1674. Report by Captain Meillet, op cit., p. 16.
107. Ibid.
108. Thomson, *Illustrations of China*, op cit., Plate 10, photograph No. 18.
109. Kennedy, op cit., p. 133.
110. Armée, Series 7N1674, Report by Captain Meillet, op cit., p.16.
111. Armée, Series 7N1665, Report by de Contenson on Fuzhou, Shanghai and Tianjin Arsenals, No. 3, 13 August 1872 mentions the Chinese drive to get suitable vessels for deployment against pirates.
112. "Albums de Photographies faites par le Commandant Laribe pendant les Manoeuvres de l'Armée Chinoise en 1908," Musée de l'Armée de Terre, Château de Vincennes, Paris. pp. 96–97.
113. Armée, Series 7N1665, Report No. 2 of 13 August 1872 by Captain de Contenson on Tianjin arsenals.
114. Armée, Series 7N1664, Report by Captain Meillet, op cit., p. 18.
115. Ibid., p. 89.
116. Ibid., pp. 75–76.
117. *North China Daily News*, 22 October 1892.
118. Ibid.
119. Armée, Series 7N1666, Report No. 25 from Captain de Fleurac on the mines and torpedoes in the ports of Zhili, 18 February 1892.
120. Armée, Series 7N1666, Report No. 59 from Captain de Fleurac to the Minister of War, 21 December 1892.
121. "Albums de Photographies faites par le Commandant Laribe," op cit., pp. 75–76.
122. My thanks to Professor Lei Yi and Mr C. C. Hsü for help with translating this caption.
123. Waley-Cohen, "China and Western Technology," op cit., p. 1536, footnote 35.
124. Wright, op cit., note 208, p. 83.

125. Ibid., note 212, pp. 68 and 85.
126. Kennedy, op cit., p. 142.
127. Wright op cit., p. 49.
128. Armée, Series 7N1679. Unattached document.
129. Wright, op cit., p. 81.
130. Ibid., pp. 77–78.
131. Spector, op cit., pp. 75–82 and 195–233. Odoric Y. K. Wou's work on Yuan Shikai's financing of the Beiyang Army is a model of useful scholarship. See *Asian Profile*, Vol. 2, No. 4, August 1983, "Financing the New Army: Yuan Shi-k'ai and the Peiyang Army, 1895–1907," pp. 339–356.
132. See Spector, op cit., pp. 164 and 157–167.
133. Ibid., p. ix.
134. Armée, Series 7N1674. Report by Captain Meillet, op cit., pp. 4 and 5.
135. Wright, op cit., pp. 76–78.
136. Armée, Series 7N1674. Report by Captain Meillet, op cit., p. 10. See also "Extrait du Rapport du Capitaine d'Amade" op cit., p. 16.
137. Armée, Series 7N1674. Report of Captain Meillet, op cit., p. 10.
138. Armée, Series 7N1674. Report of Captain d'Amade, op cit., p. 16.
139. Zhang Junbo and Yao Yunzhu, "Differences Between Traditional Chinese and Western Military Thinking and Their Philosophical Roots," *Journal of Contemporary China*, Vol. 5, No. 12, July 1966, p. 213.
140. Armée, Series 7N1665. Report by Captain Chambry to the Minister of War, 29 November 1882.
141. Wright, op cit., p. 79.
142. Ibid.
143. Armée, Series 7N1674. Report of Captain d'Amade, op cit., pp. 24–25.
144. Ibid., p. 27.
145. Ibid., p. 28.
146. Waley-Cohen, "China and Western Technology," op cit., p. 1534.
147. Kennedy, op cit., pp. 124–125.
148. Armée, Series 7N1674. Report of Captain Meillet, op cit., p. 16.
149. Armée, Series 7N1674. Report of Captain d'Amade, op cit., p. 34.
150. Waley-Cohen, "China and Western Technology," op cit., p. 1532
151. Ibid., pp. 1529–1530.
152. Wright, op cit., Note 189, p. 80.
153. Armée, Series 7N1665. Report No. 40 of Captain Chambry to the Minister of War, Tianjin, 29 November 1882.
154. Armée, Series 7N1666. Report No. 37 from Captain de Fleurac to the Minister of War, 13 August 1892.
155. *China*, op cit. Letter from Consul McWade in Canton, 9 July 1900, to the Secretary of State, Hill.
156. Claude Lévi-Strauss, *Race et Histoire*, Denoël, France, 1995 (1952).

157. Matthew Paul Lalumia, *Realism and Politics in Victorian Art of the Crimean War*, UMI Research Press, Michigan, 1984, p. 130.
158. Ibid, p. 133.
159. See Series 7N1665, Attachment to Report No. 63 of 13 March 1890 by Captain d'Amade.
160. Lalumia, op cit, p. 134.
161. Powell, op cit., pp. 41–42.
162. See Series 7N1665, Part I of d'Amade's report on the army of Zhili, "Troops stationed to the north of the Pei-ho river."
163. Michael Lewis, *The History of the British Navy*, Pelican, 1957, p. 232.
164. Sir Edward H. Seymour, My *Naval Career and Travels*, Smith, Elder and Company, London, 1911, p. 76.
165. Lewis, op cit., p. 223.
166. "Albums de Photographies faites par le Commandant Laribe," op cit., p. 40.
167. Purcell, op cit., p. 26. Purcell's source for this statement is Powell, p. 42. Although Powell did not cite Admiral Lord Charles Beresford in this particular instance, he had used Beresford as a source. Powell's sources do not include eye-witness reports by military or engineering experts.
168. Admiral Lord Charles Beresford, *The Break-up of China, with an Account of Its Present Commerce, Currency, Waterways, Armies, Railways, Politics and Future Prospects*, Harper Brothers, London and New York, 1899, pp. 295–296.
169. Ibid., p 297 this is the only part of Admiral Beresford's report that may have been referred to by Powell.
170. Kennedy, op cit., p. 140. Kennedy's work makes the same negative point as Powell based on Beresford's account and similarly omits to mention the positive observations detailed by Beresford.
171. Armée, Series 7N1679, "Forces militaires de la Chine en 1882 d'après des renseignements Japonais."
172. Library of Congress, Still Pictures Division, Lot 6374, No 55H. My thanks to Professor Chen Zhenjiang for his assistance in identifying the soldiers in this photograph and in Figure 6.14.
173. Library of Congress, Still Pictures Division, Lot 6374, No. 63H.
174. Library of Congress, LC-USZ62-33201.
175. Armée, Series 7N1674. Report by Captain d'Amade, op cit., p. 18. Allen Fung, "China's Failure Reconsidered," op cit, pp. 24–25 concluded that the performance of the Chinese during the Sino-Japanese War, showed marked deficiencies in training and the culture associated with military training and drilling. It is quite obvious by the performance of the Imperial Chinese Army in 1900 that both the learning experience of the Sino-Japanese War and the impetus given by this war to Chinese responsible for decisions about training and drilling were significant in producing an overwhelming improvement in battle performance.

176. Armée, Series 7N1665. Report by Captain Chambry to the Minister of War, 29 November 1882.
177. A direction is an utterance of the order of "soldier Wang, realign yourself with the man in front of you" while a command is of the order of "By the right, quick march!"
178. Armée, Series 7N1665. Report No. 63, 13 March 1890 by Captain d'Amade, Armement et Troupes du Vice Roi du Pei-Tchi-Li, p. 10 and Powell, op cit. p. 47.
179. Armée, Series 7N1665. Report by Captain Chambry to the Minister of War, 29 November 1882.
180. Armée, Series 7N1665. Report No. 21 by General Chanoine on a mission to China, 12 April 1886.
181. Armée, Series 7N1665. Captain d'Amade's report on the army in Zhili in the winter of 1888, op cit.
182. Armée, Series 7N1666. Report No. 54, Annex No. 6, 28 November 1892, de Fleurac to the Minister of War.
183. Armée, Series 7N1666. Report of 3 May 1892 "Effectifs des troupes chinoises exercées et armées de fusils européens à tir rapide." From de Fleurac to the Minister of War.
184. Kennedy, op cit., p. 109.
185. Chester C. Tan, *The Boxer Catastrophe*, Octagon Books Inc., New York, 1967, p. 66.
186. Chaikin, op cit., p. 38.
187. A well-known Chinese Boxer scholar, on seeing photographs of Chinese troops wearing Western headgear in 1900, informed the writer that in the late Qing "no Chinese troops would have consented to wear hats like that." Cultural expectations about uniform are very strong. See Nathan Joseph, *Uniforms and Non-uniforms. Communication through Clothing*, Contributions in Sociology, No. 61, Greenwood Press, Westport, Connecticut, 1986.
188. Armée, Series 7N1655. Report by Captain Chambry to the Minister of War, 29 November, 1882.
189. Armée, Series 7N1679. Letter from Commander Vidal to the Minister of War, Report No. 68, 4 January 1899.
190. Arthur Cunningham, *The Chinese Soldier and Other Sketches with a Description of the Capture of Manila*, Hong Kong, Daily Press Office, no date, possibly 1901, p. 55.
191. Ibid., pp. 50–60.
192. Ibid., p. 61.
193. Ibid., pp. 63–66.
194. Armée, Series 7N1665. Captain d'Amade's Report on the army of Zhili in the winter of 1888, op cit., Vol. 1, p. 2.
195. Armée, Series 7N1679. Letter from Auguste François to the Minister of War, 10 August 1905.

196. Armée, Series 7N1680. Report on the 1905 manoeuvres of the Chinese army by Colonel Brissaud-Desmaillet. See Introduction.
197. George Lanning, *Old Forces in New China*, Probsthain, London, 1912, p. 148, "maps were prepared showing the Empire parcelled out into spheres of influence, and copies of these were sent out throughout the provinces with Chinese explanatory letter-press which lost nothing of its significance when translated."
198. Cohen, op cit., p. 37.
199. Armée, Series 7N1668, 30 July 1900. Letter by Commander Vidal to the Minister of War on types, cost and quantities carried by each type of transport from a Japanese, Chinese or Korean coolie to a horse or a buffalo cart.
200. In the Manchu system, the troops of the Green Standard were for keeping order — as do today's policemen – while the bannermen were the troops who went to war.
201. Armée, Series 7N1665. Report No. 3, "Troops stationed at the North of the Pei-ho at Lutai by Captain d'Amade, Winter 1888."
202. Spector, op cit., p. ix.
203. "Album de Photographies faites par le Commandant Laribe," op cit., p. 40.
204. Ibid., p. 48.
205. D'Amade's Report from Zhili, op cit., No. 5, 7 June 1888, p. 25.
206. Ibid.
207. "Album de Photographies faites par le Commandant Laribe," op cit., p. 71.
208. D'Amade's Report from Zhili, op cit., No. 1.
209. Dolby, op cit., p. 276. Letter from Gangyi to Yang Mushi.
210. Tan, op cit., p. 66.
211. Dolby, op cit., p. 280. Telegram from General Nie Shicheng to the Financial Commissioner and the Provincial Judge.
212. D'Amade's Report from Zhili, op cit., No. 5.
213. Ralph Powell who espoused many belittling "beliefs" about the Chinese soldier, the Chinese officer and the Chinese capacity to manufacture arms, all of which "beliefs" are cited on the basis of little or no evidence, is still being cited in scholarly articles published in 2000. See Roger R. Thompson, op cit.
214. Purcell, op cit., p. 294. See also Spector, op cit., p. 53. Westerners openly derided Li Hongzhang's Huai and Xiang soldiers when they were quartered in Shanghai.
215. Dolby, op cit. Letter from Yang Mushi to Nie Shicheng, 31 May, pp. 248–249.
216. Barnes, op cit., p. 119.
217. Sharf and Harrington, *China, 1900. The Eyewitnesses Speak*, op cit., p. 24. Account of Charles Davis Jameson, American mining engineer, "The cause of the uprising which followed cannot in any way be laid to the missionaries; it was an anti-foreign uprising, not an anti-Christian one." Mark Elvin, *Another History. Essays on China from a European Perspective*, Wild Peony, Australia, 1996, "Mandarins and Millenarians: Reflections on the Boxer Uprising of 1899–

1900," op cit., p. 212, "we find the Christians and the foreigners being worked into a pre-existing framework of ideas." Jon Guttmann, Editorial, *Military History*, June 1900, "In the countryside, Christian missionaries, who had come to be seen by the Boxers as more proselytizers of Western culture than of religion, also came under little attack." Many thanks to Dr Gerry Groot for drawing this latter reference to my attention. In putting forward this viewpoint the writer wishes to stress that a particular time-frame and particular locations only are to be considered in this context.

218. Jian Bozan et al. (eds), *Yihetuan* (The Boxers), 4 Vols., Shenzhou guoguang she, 1953 (1951), Shanghai, Vol. 1, p. 256.
219. Lu Yao, "Minjian mimi jiaopai" (The Boxer Movement and the Secret Sects), unpublished paper given at the conference "1900. The Boxers, China and the World," London, June 2001.
220. Dolby, op cit., p. 231. Letter from Yang Mushi to Nie Shicheng 27 May. Not only Yang himself but the civilian officials "were ... thoroughly familiar with the Boxer [tactic of] moving rapidly from place to place." See also p. 254, Letter from Yang to Nie of 3 June.
221. *The Times*, 16 June 1900, carried a report condemning the military negligence which had allowed the Boers to cut off Lord Roberts by cutting the railway.
222. Dolby, op cit., p. 255. Letter from Yang Mushi to Nie Shicheng of 3 June; p. 283, letter from Yang to Zhang Yuzhu of 5 July.
223. *Yihetuan shiliao* (Historical Materials on the Boxers), 2 Vols. Ed. Zhongguo shehui kexueyuan jindaishi yanjiusuo "Jindaishi ziliao" bianjizu ("Modern Historical Materials" Editorial Group of the Modern History Institute of the Chinese Academy of Social Sciences), Zhongguo shehui kexue chubanshe, Beijing, 1982 (hereafter referred to as *Yihetuan shiliao*), Vol. 2, p. 126.
224. Jian Bozan et al., op cit., Vol. 4, p. 390.
225. Ibid.
226. Ibid., p. 376.
227. Ibid., Vol. 1, p. 376.
228. Liao Yizhong, Li Dezheng and Zhang Xuanru, *Yihetuan yundong shi* (History of the Boxer Movement), Renmin chubanshe, Beijing, 1981, p. 129 are unclear about the outcome of this skirmish, saying at one point that the Boxers destroyed the whole of Yang Futong's cavalry and infantry and at another point that some wounded soldiers fled. Magistrate Zhu who had to write for compensation for the families involved was clear that apart from Colonel Yang, only three men were killed and five wounded. See *Yihetuan*, op cit., Vol. 4, p. 317. This account of Colonel Yang's death is at variance with Paul Cohen's account. See Cohen op cit., p. 284 and Liao Yizhang et al., op cit., pp. 125–129. The present account is based on *Yihetuan*, op cit. and *Yihetuan shiliao*, op cit. My thanks to Situ Danian for extensive help with translating these materials.

229. Dolby, op cit., pp. 221–222, 26 May 1900. Letter from Zhu Zhaotang to two Chief Commissioners of the Provincial Government Concerning Pension and Benefits for the Late Sub Commander Yang.
230. *Yihetuan*, op cit., Vol. 1, pp. 370 and 376.
231. Ibid., Vol. 1, p. 257. I am singularly grateful to Professor Mark Elvin for drawing this reference to my attention and to Situ Danian for translating this material.
232. Barnes, op cit., pp. 6–8.
233. Powell, op cit., p. 42, "However, a few scattered Western-trained officers could make little impression on the vast officers' corps which was sunk in ignorance, conservatism, and nepotism." The sources on which Powell bases this assertion are unclear. Photographic evidence of Western-drilled troops and their officers in this chapter and in Chapter 4, as well as the correspondence of General Yang, would appear to conflict with Powell's generalization. It seems unlikely that after twenty-five years, the Tianjin military academy should not have produced some fine officers. As it was, the Allies were impressed by the officer cadets in Tianjin in 1900 who died to the last man, defending the military academy.
234. Dolby, op cit., pp. 228–229. Letter from Zhu Zhaotang to his cousin Li Jusheng, 27 May.
235. Ibid., p. 239, 30 May. Notice from Yang Mushi to villagers along the railway from Zhuozhou to Dingxing.
236. Lanning, op cit., p. 95; Barnes, op cit. p. xiii; *Hong Kong Daily Press*, editorial, 10 May 1900. Duiker, op. cit., see pp. 203–204.
237. Dolby, p. 236, 26 May. Letter from Yang Mushi to Financial Commissioner Ting and Provincial Judge Ting.
238. Mark Elvin, "Mandarins," op cit., p. 205. "We may note in passing that military primitivism, sometimes ascribed to the Boxers, was usually a symbolic act on the part of anti-foreign officials rather than the result of popular taboos." In his footnote 37, Elvin gives some excellent examples, including Governor Yuxian's purchase of bamboo shields and spears in June 1899 and Li Bingheng's "loathing of foreign clocks." Elvin also notes that Suqian and Lingqing (in northern Jiangsu and Western Shandong respectively) were famous for the sale of rifles and revolvers for personal protection.
239. Dolby, op cit., p. 241, 30 May. Letter from Yang Mushi to Nie Shicheng.
240. Ibid., p. 243, 31 May. Telegram from Nie Shicheng to Generals Xing and Yang in Baoding and Commander Hu in Tianjin.
241. Ibid.
242. Ibid., p. 245, 1 June. Letter from Nie Shicheng to Generals Xing and Yang.
243. Ibid., pp. 245–246, 31 May. Letter from Yang Mushi to Nie Shicheng.
244. Ibid., p. 247.
245. Ibid., p. 245, 1 June. Letter from Nie Shicheng to Generals Xing and Yang.
246. Sharf, *China 1900. The Eyewitnesses Speak*, op cit., p. 104.
247. Dolby, op cit., p. 248, 31 May. Letter from Yang Mushi to Nie Shicheng.

248. Ibid., p. 249.
249. Ibid., p. 254, 3 June. Letter from Yang Mushi to Nie Shicheng.
250. Ibid., pp. 256–257.
251. Ibid., pp. 262–263, 5 June. Letter from Zhang in Military Secretariat to Nie.
252. Ibid., pp. 260–261. Telegram from Nie to Yang, sent 2 June, received 3 June.
253. Ibid., p. 264, 4 June. Telegram from Governor General Yu to Nie.
254. Tan, op cit., p. 99.
255. Dolby, op cit., p. 266, 6 June. Telegram from Zhang in Military Secretariat to Governor Yulu. Letter from Yang Mushi to Nie Shicheng.
256. Ibid., p. 268.
257. G. Gipps, *The Fighting in North China Up to the Fall of Tientsin City*, Sampson Low, Marston and Company, London, 1901, p. 16.
258. Dolby, op cit., p. 268.
259. Map adapted from Dolby, ibid., p. 210.
260. Ibid., p. 270. Telegram from General Sun Shoujing to Yang Mushi, received 8 June.
261. Ibid., p. 273, 8 June. Letter from Yang Mushi to Gangyi.
262. Ibid., p. 275.
263. Ibid., p. 279, 10 June. Telegram from General Nie Shicheng to Governor General Yulu.
264. Ibid., p. 280. Telegram from Governor Yu for General Xing to transmit to Yang Mushi. Sent 12 June, received 13 June.
265. A part of Boxer beliefs was that sacrilegious foreign behaviour had angered the gods and caused the drought. Hence rainfall would be seen as a positive sign by the Boxers. The Allied soldiers were also conscious of this. See Ruffi de Pontèves, *Souvenirs de la Colonne Seymour*, Librairie Plon, Paris, 1903, p. 121.
266. Dolby, op cit., pp. 282–283, 5 July. Letter from Yang Mushi to Zhang Yuzhu.
267. Ibid., p. 283.
268. Ibid., p. 284.
269. Ibid., p. 276. Letter from Gangyi attached to a letter of 8 June from Yang Mushi to Gangyi.
270. Liu Mengyang, "A Record of the Rebellion of the Boxer Bandits in Tientsin," manuscript translation by Mark Elvin, p. 8. I am most grateful to Professor Elvin for his generosity in allowing me to make use of this translation. The original may be seen in *Yihetuan*, op cit., Vol. 2.
271. Liu Mengyang, op cit., pp. 8–9.
272. Elvin, "Mandarins," op cit., p. 219.
273. Ibid.
274. Dolby, op cit., p. 285, 5 July. Letter from Yang Mushi to Zhang Yuzhu.
275. Ibid.
276. Ibid., p. 287.
277. Ibid.

278. Ibid.
279. De Pontèves, op cit., p. 219.
280. Dolby, op cit., p. 209, 5 June. Letter from Yang Mushi to Zhang Yuzhu.
281. Ibid., p. 292.
282. Elvin, "Mandarins," op cit., p. 219.
283. Ibid.
284. Dolby, op cit., p. 295, 18 July. Letter from Yang Mushi to Li Hongzhang.
285. Ibid., p. 294.
286. Ibid.
287. Liu Mengyang, op cit. , p. 8.
288. Ibid., p. 10.
289. Ibid.
290. Elvin, "Mandarins," op cit., p. 225.
291. Dolby, op cit., p. 295, 18 July. Letter from Yang Mushi to Li Hongzhang.
292. Ibid., pp. 296–297.
293. Ibid., p. 290, 5 July. Letter from Yang Mushi to Zhang Yuzhu.
294. Ibid., p. 233, 27 May. A Notice to the Boxers by Yang Mushi.
295. By courtesy of the Tianjin Yihetuan Museum.
296. Dolby, op cit., p. 298, 18 July. Letter from Yang Mushi to Li Hongzhang.
297. Brigadier-General A. S. Dagett, *America in the China Relief Expedition*, Hudson-Kimberly Kansas City, 1903, p. 33.
298. *Yihetuan*, op cit., Vol. 2, p. 154.
299. *How to Read Chinese War News. A Vade-Mecum of Notes and Hints to Readers of Despatches and Intelligence from the Seat of War, with a Coloured War Map and a Glossary of Military Technical Terms, Local Titles, Places, Phrases, etc.* T. Fisher and Unwin, London, 1900, p. 41.
300. Robert E. Harrist, "A Letter From Wang Hsi-Chih and the Culture of Chinese Calligraphy," in Robert E. Harrist and Wen C. Fong (eds), *The Embodied Image. Chinese Calligraphy from the John B. Elliott Collection*, The Art Museum, Princeton University, 1999, p. 241.
301. Allen Fung, "China's Failure Reconsidered," op cit., p. 21. "… one has no reason not to rely on the opinion of General Song Qing who was widely regarded as a conscientious and honest general. On 25th April, 1895, Song recommended to the court that China should fight on … because he thought if the Chinese army 'regrouped itself with the best elements remaining and continued to fight patiently and practically,' there was every chance that the Chinese army could hold up the Japanese onslaught."
302. Su Yuanchun (1845–1907) joined the Xiang army in 1863 and was involved in putting down the Taiping Rebellion and also a rebellion by the Miao. He fought with distinction against the French in Indochina winning the battle of Zheng Nan Guan. In 1902 he was impeached and banished on the grounds that his men were poorly disciplined and that he had embezzled their pay. He was exiled

in 1903 to Xinjiang province and died just as he was released in 1907. I am indebted to Situ Danian and Zhang Dongsu for these biographical details.

303. Dominique Liaboeuf and Jorge Svartzman, *L'Oeuil du Consul. Auguste François en Chine (1896–1904)*, Musée Guimet, Paris, 1989, pp. 193–197.
304. Kotenev, op cit., p. 78.

Chapter 7

The Battles

During the time that Provincial Commander-in-Chief Nie was stationed in and defended Tianjin, he held back the foreigners for twenty distressing critical days. Tianjin remained protected without mishap ... for every day he was able to remain in Tianjin, for that day the city was protected. He held the city by means of determined battle and gave it hope by [fighting to] certain death.

Yang Mushi

Despite a large and growing literature on the Boxer rising, there has been no thorough evaluation of the nature of Chinese military resistance to the Allies in 1900 in the English-language accounts. Writers have evaluated the Boxer rising as a peasant rebellion rather than as a war involving the trained regular soldiers and officers of nine armies. In his superlative study of the Maori Wars, James Belich points out that too often historians take the military action as given and proceed from an inaccurate basis to discuss larger issues. In the case of the Maori Wars, he instances the British dominance of the historical record which makes it difficult to reconstruct Maori motivation, attitudes, tactics and strategies.[1] Insofar as the Boxer War is concerned, there is an unusual number of errors regarding the most basic aspects of the war. These errors continue to proliferate in even the most recent publications, varying from the fact that the "Qing" army did not fight at all, that the Chinese did not give battle at Dagu, that battles occurred on different dates from those on which they actually happened, to analysis of individual

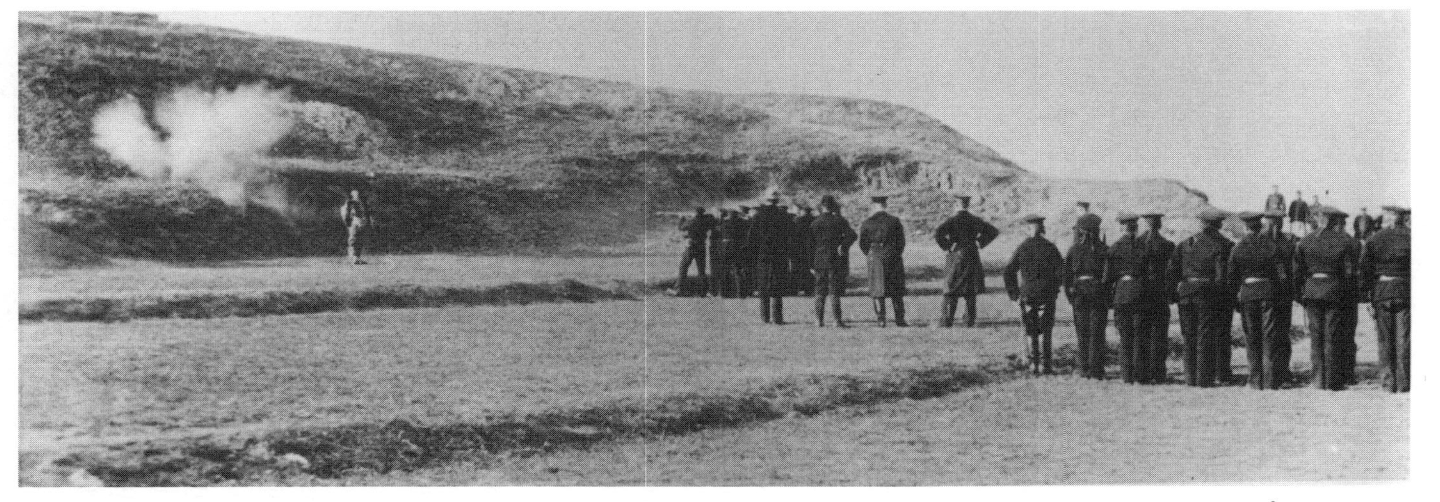

Figure 7.1 Soldiers of the Imperial Chinese Army — probably German-trained — assisting at the execution of a Boxer.[2]

skirmishes which do not correspond to the description given in Chinese sources. On this basis as it happens, historians have not, in fact, gone on to discuss what happened in the Boxer War let alone document regular and irregular Chinese resistance after the fall of Beijing.

It is not necessarily the case, that a study of the writings of those "dominating" the historical record as winners of a war makes it difficult to reconstruct the military performance of those who lost. Recent literature on the Boxer rising continues to stress the origins and motivations of the peasants without offering any assessment of the nature of the fighting qualities of the soldiers of the Imperial Chinese Army. Either ignored entirely or discredited by posterity in Chinese scholarship as "oppressors" of the Boxers and by Western scholarship as weak, poorly-armed, badly-led and ineffectual, the Chinese soldier of the modernised armies finds his champions in the writings and photographs of his enemies. Enemy assessment of Chinese regular and irregular forces involved in the Boxer War constitutes a reliable professional assessment of their fighting qualities.

As far as the Chinese regular army was concerned, action against the Boxers had already begun in May 1900 and was fraught with difficulties. An integral part of the definition of a "modern" soldier trained in the Western military tradition is that he obeys the orders of the government he serves. Much earlier in the Qing dynasty, commanders serving in the field against insurgents reputedly endowed with magic powers just as the Boxers claimed to have, had experienced major problems of desertion.[3] Despite the technical and political problems posed by government orders related to the Boxers throughout the month of May, desertion was not a significant element in the thinking of commanding officers as exemplified by the correspondence of General Yang Mushi or highly-educated Chinese civilian observers like Liu Mengyang.

An unauthorised Allied expedition led by the British Admiral Seymour had left Tianjin to relieve the besieged Legations on 10 June. On 16 June, seven of the eight Allied naval commanders presented the Commander of the Dagu forts with an ultimatum to the effect that he should hand over the forts within twenty-four hours. From 17 June to 14 July, there was a bitter struggle between the invading Powers and Chinese forces, regular and irregular, to capture Tianjin.

A detailed examination of these events from the point of view of the invading soldiers taking part gives rise to a number of new insights into the military capacity and preparedness of both the Chinese regular army and the peasant Boxers. These insights come from the observations of trained military men fighting against one another and the remarkable congruity of their opinion testifies to their professionalism in recognising the respective strengths and weaknesses of their opponents. It also constitutes irrefutable evidence of the impressive degree to which some sections of the Chinese regular army had interiorised the outward form of Western training. They had mastered the use of this training in combat situations as well as retaining elements of traditional Chinese military tactics necessary for dealing with peasant insurrections.

Following the failure of the reform movement of 1898 in which Yuan Shikai played a vital role,[4] the Empress Dowager ordered Ronglu, Governor-General of Zhili and President of the Board of War, to reorganise the troops of several traditional and Western-trained armies with a view to sharpening the defence of Beijing. This was seen to be necessary as a consequence not only of the Sino-Japanese War but of increasingly open discussion concerning the partition of China[5] particularly following Lord Charles Beresford's visit in 1898. The defence of Beijing was to be assured by the Wu Wei army. The Centre division was led by Ronglu as Commander-in-Chief. During the first four weeks of the Boxer rising, the Centre division took part in some action against the Boxers around Toutian in early June but was thereafter stationed in Beijing and took no part in the battle of Tianjin. Dong Fuxiang led the Rear division and after participating in action against Admiral Seymour's forces at Langfang, took no further part in the action outside Beijing.[6] His army, together with that of Ronglu and an indefinable number of Boxer irregulars was occupied in besieging the Legations in Beijing itself. Yuan Shikai had commanded the Pacification army from December 1895, reputedly, with the army of Zhang Zhidong, China's crack Western-trained army. In Ronglu's reorganisation, Yuan Shikai led the Right division of the Wu Wei army, but took no part at all in the Boxer War. The Left division led by General Song Qing was divided into two battalions, and stationed at Shanhaiguan. Led by General Ma Yukun, one battalion arrived in Tianjin on 9 June. The other battalion was not ordered to Tianjin until 3 July and arrived on 10 July. It was the Front or Vanguard division, the former Tenacious army of General Nie Shicheng stationed at Lutai near Tianjin and commanded by General Nie, which bore the brunt of attacks by Boxers from May 1900 and from the invading Powers from June 1900. General Nie's division consisted of 10,000 men equipped with Winchester repeating rifles, Maxim machine guns, 57mm Krupp artillery and mortars. Of these forces, 3,000 men had been diverted to fight against the Boxers since early May. By 23 June, the eight Allied nations had 14,000 troops in the field although they were hampered by inferior artillery and insufficient ammunition.

Opposing General Nie and the invading foreigners was an ever increasing group of peasants, the redoubtable Boxers, most of whom had no military training but some of whom were discharged soldiers or had served in militia groups. Insufficient attention has been given to the role played by the Boxers in attacking the forces of the Chinese regular army. Boxer attacks on the Chinese regular army in the vicinity of the strategically crucial area around Tianjin, divided its forces and weakened its ability in action against the invading forces. The Boxers attacked General Nie's army with exactly the same ferocity, unpredictability and overwhelming numbers with which they fell on Admiral Seymour's expedition. Admiral Seymour was defeated by Boxer tactics in combination with regular army initiatives, renounced his attempt to relieve the Legations and retreated to Tianjin. General Nie, officially censured for taking effective action against the Boxers as he was initially ordered to do, was impeached and cashiered but reinstated temporarily to be able to lead Chinese regular forces in the battle of Tianjin. He deliberately exposed himself to Allied artillery fire and died fighting on 9 July. Tianjin fell late on 14 July. It was not until 4 August that the Allied Powers had sufficient reinforcements and felt confident enough to march on Beijing. Estimates of required reinforcements went as high as 120,000 men.[7] The time gap and the perception of the need for such considerable reinforcements reflects the respect that the eight invading Powers had come to feel for the Chinese regular army as a consequence of its performance in the battle of Tianjin as much as it does the disagreements concerning order of precedence and the choice of the Commander-in-Chief of the army to march on Beijing.

The Battle of Dagu

To complete an understanding of the complexity involved in assessing the degree of success in modernising China's armies, we now turn to a detailed discussion of the battles of the first four weeks of the Boxer campaign. The significant action was fought at the battle of Dagu (Taku), the rout of the Seymour expedition and the battle for Tianjin. The battle for the Dagu forts illustrates the nature and degree of Chinese preparedness for attack on this vital strategic point.

On 16 June, the Allied naval commanders presented the commander of the Dagu forts with an ultimatum to the effect that he should hand over the forts within twenty-four hours. The American Admiral Kempff abstained from joining the other Allied commanders in their decision to present the ultimatum. The grounds for his abstention were that first, there was no justification for what amounted to an act of war on a country which had been a fellow delegate to the Hague Peace Conference of 1899. Second, such an ultimatum would endanger the lives of all Europeans then in North China.[8] The ultimatum was taken by a Russian officer to the Commander of the Dagu forts who, to de Pontèves surprise, far from torturing the bearer,[9] offered him a glass of champagne. He then explained that the twenty-four hour period was insufficient for him to communicate with the Viceroy at Tianjin as rail and telegraph had been cut.[10]

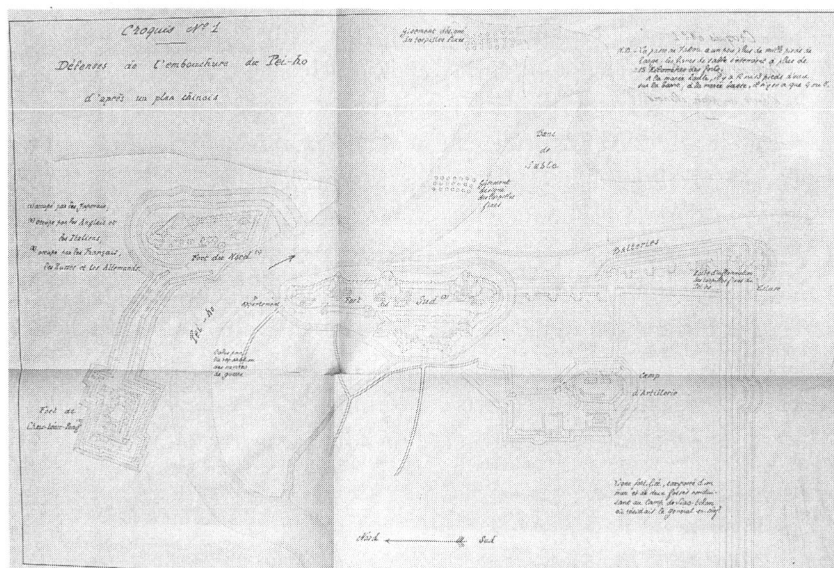

Figure 7.2(a) Diagrams of the Dagu Forts made from Chinese drawings. No. 1 — Defences of the Beihe River from the Album of Corvisart, 1900. (By courtesy of the Musée de l'Armée de Terre, Paris)

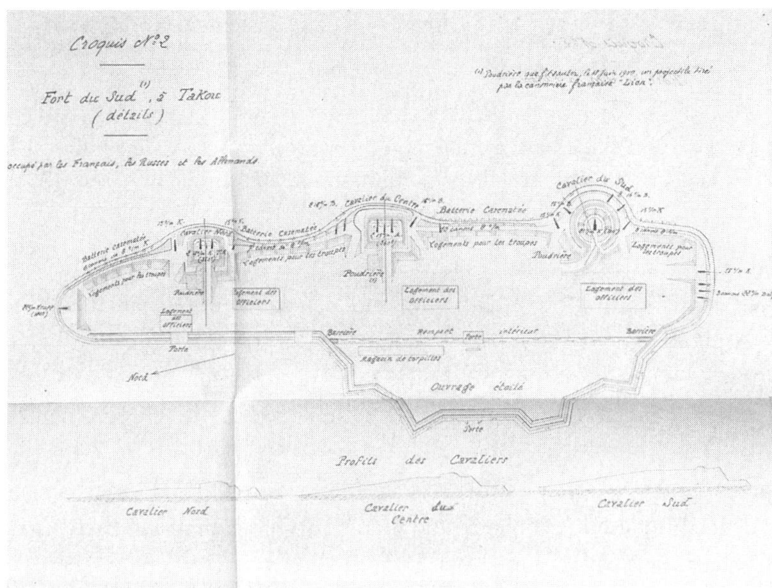

Figure 7.2(b) Diagram No. 2 — South Fort, Dagu, from the Album of Corvisart, 1900. (By courtesy of the Musée de l'Armée de Terre, Paris)

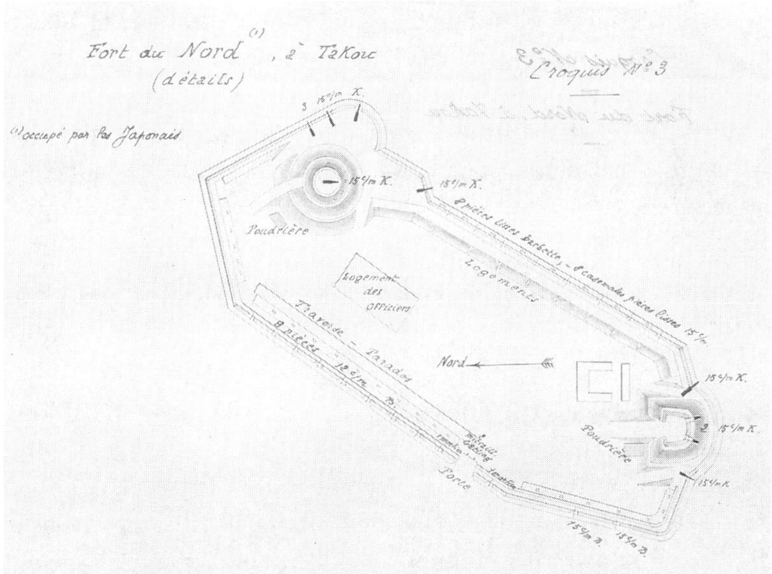

Figure 7.2(c) Diagram No. 3 — North Fort, Dagu, from the Album of Corvisart, 1900.[11] (By courtesy of the Musée de l'Armée de Terre, Paris)

One account by the Chief Officer of a coastal steamer, J. Gordon, states that:

> Some of the naval officers went to see the General [in command of the Dagu forts] at 12 o'clock on Saturday night, to ask what he intended doing. The General replied that he meant to fight, and a bombardment by the fleet was arranged for 2 o'clock that morning.[12]

On the basis of this account, we must assume that some, at least, of the senior naval commanders of the Allied fleet off Dagu were aware that the Chinese were going to fight and that therefore it was not a complete surprise when the Chinese took the initiative and opened fire around 1 am.[13]

Admiral Seymour had left Tianjin on an expedition expressly unauthorised by the Chinese government on its sovereign territory, to relieve the besieged Legations on 10 June. On 13 June an Imperial decree had been issued to General Nie Shicheng and Luo Rongguang directing them to stop this expedition.[14] By 13 June some Boxer bands were acting in concert with the Imperial Chinese Army.[15] Together, the regular and irregular Chinese forces had taken possession of the walled city of Tianjin, cut off communications with Admiral Seymour's expedition and were threatening communications with the Allies' base at Dagu.[16] Against this background of mounting hostilities, Chinese regular forces had the prescience to take the initiative of protecting the mouth of the Beihe river by laying electric mines on 15 June, that is, the day before the Allies delivered the ultimatum. After the presentation of this ultimatum, Captain Bowman McCalla of the US Marines wrote in his memoirs,

> It was surprising to all Foreign Naval Officers off the Pei Ho [Bei He], that the Chinese should have taken the initiative. During the afternoon, the Chinese in the Forts had been very busy, drilling successive squads at the guns in plain sight of the officers and men on the gunboats.[17]

Despite the evidence that the Chinese were anticipating an outbreak of hostilities, there was general confidence among the Allies that though the fortifications were strong and extensive and armed with modern artillery,[18] Dagu would easily be captured. Captain McCalla recalled that the Commander of the German gunboat *Ilitis* thought it would be an affair of twenty minutes: "It was a clear case of underrating one's enemy."[19] In the American official military report of the action, it was noted that an unsuccessful attempt was made at 0300 hours to land troops but that they were unable to get within 1,000 yards of the North West fort:

> ... little damage had so far been done to the fort, all its guns were still in action, and the commanders agreed that an attack, if delivered then, would result in serious and unnecessary loss.[20]

In the event, the action lasted for seven hours with the Chinese gunners hitting the nine vessels taking part and some others. The commander of the *Ilitis* lost both his legs and over sixty men killed.

At 0145 hours on 17 June — the Allies had said they would take over the forts at 0200 hours — the Chinese took the initiative and opened fire "simultaneously from every gun in the forts which could be trained on the ships."[21]

As the battle continued, three more Allied gunboats joined the six that took part in the initial attack. No sources give a complete list of the Allied vessels hit by the gunners of the Dagu forts. A number of published and unpublished journals, written by those who took part in the action, provide evidence of eleven Allied vessels being damaged during the action. These vessels were the *Guilak* — McCalla said this Russian gunboat was sunk and that sixty-seven officers and men were killed and wounded; the *North China Herald* refers to the "unlucky Russian," "we are informed that she had four holes alone in one side, three of them very near the water line,"[22] a description of a target decisively located by Chinese gunners rather than one which was the object of a "lucky" hit; the *Bohr* (Russian); the *Koreetz* (Russian) — the German Captain Schlieper admired the Russian warships as the "most imposing" of the Allied demonstration fleet;[23] the *Algerine* (British), the *Whiting* (British); the *Alacrity* (British); the *Barfleur* (British); the *Atago* (Japanese; this may have been already disabled owing to engine trouble and moored within reach of the guns in the Dagu fort[24]); the *Lion* (French); the *Ilitis* (German); and the *Monocacy* (an American vessel on which women and children from Tianjin were taking refuge). Only two merchant vessels, the *Yongping* and the *Tianxing* were hit, giving further evidence of outstanding Chinese gunnery, the anchorage holding a lot of merchant shipping at the time.

Naval action off Dagu was complicated by natural factors; the larger Allied war vessels were unable to get within five miles of the shore and only the vessels with the smallest draught were able to approach the forts.[25] Thus all Allied warships could not take part in the action. That is, the Chinese were fortunate in the physical geography of this commanding position but had taken every possible step to take advantage of their asset. It was McCalla's opinion that "the gunboats alone could not have driven the Chinese from the forts; although 15,000 rounds of ammunition were expended without making any appreciable impression on the fortifications ..."[26] The much-vaunted naval superiority of the West was thus not immediately evident in this decisive action over the strategic key to Beijing. After two hours of continuous Allied bombardment, little damage had been done to the fort and all its guns were still in action.[27] In his report, Admiral Kempff noted that when the forts were captured at 0700 hours,

> The forts, being of thick mud and grass adobe, were but little damaged by the gunfire, although they had received a host of projectiles. The guns and gun shields as a rule were not damaged. Two or three of the modern guns were destroyed.[28]

Two land assaults were made on the North East fort, the first being unsuccessful and the second being led by Japanese marines. In his report the Japanese naval officer Captain M. Nagamine referred to the heavy fire kept up by the Chinese when a party of foreign soldiers eventually made it to shore for an assault on the forts. Captain Hattori was killed during the bayonet charge.[29] The South fort was captured when a powder magazine exploded after a chance hit by a shell from the *Algerine*. There is disagreement about which of the attacking enemy warships fired the lucky shot but all Western military accounts agree that it was a lucky strike.[30] The artist F. C. Dickinson claimed that:

> When one of the batteries on the north side of the river had been stormed and carried by a British, Italian and Japanese landing party, the guns in it were immediately turned onto the forts on the south side of the river. At 6 a.m., a shell from this battery entered the magazine of the South Fort, causing a terrific explosion.[31]

Dickenson was not present at the battle and his account does not agree with British, French, German, American and Japanese accounts all written by officers who took part in the battle of Dagu.

In summary then, this action shows that both the Chinese and Allied forces possessed modern artillery and that Chinese gunnery was superior. Firing in the dark using flares and searchlights, the gunners of the Dagu forts hit every attacking foreign warship, seriously disabling four of the six which took part in the initial action, while largely avoiding non-combatant vessels. The accuracy of their artillery fire was ensured by their precise knowledge of tidal levels. Sightings would have been taken in daylight, presumably while McCalla and others watched the Chinese gunners drilling and reference to tidal charts would have enabled the Chinese gunners to perform such feats as hitting an attacking vessel three times on the water line when firing at night. If this still seems today an incredible feat in the age of radar, we need to stop and acknowledge that it *was* an incredible feat. The fact is that the Chinese gunners *did* hit or disable every attacking ship. On the benefit or otherwise of state-of-the-art technology as opposed to men who were outstanding in their ability to handle whatever weapons they were trained to use, in February 2001, an American submarine surfacing off the coast of Hawaii hit and sank a Japanese vessel killing nine people. In his initial statement, the commander

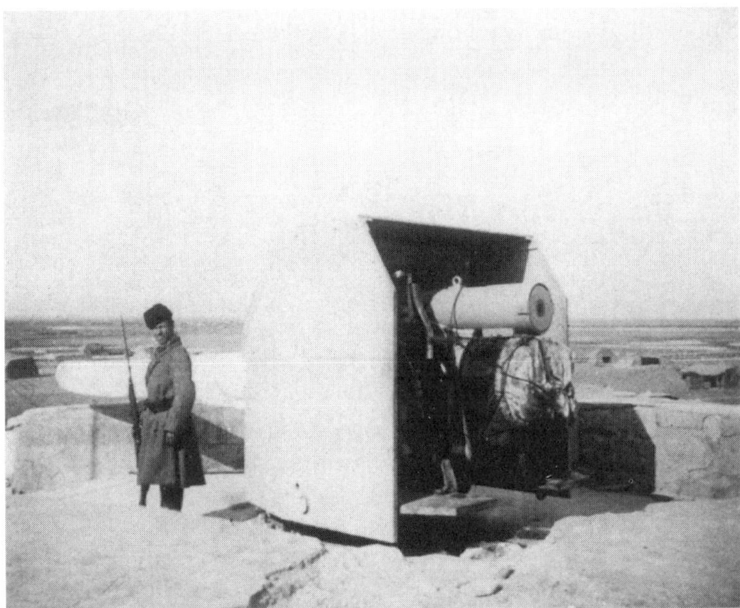

Figure 7.3 The South Fort at Dagu after the battle of the night of 16–17 June 1900. Note that the gunshield is entirely intact.[32] (By courtesy of the Musée de l'Armée de Terre, Paris)

of the submarine said he was using "passive sonar" instead of the more accurate "active sonar."[33] The gunners at Dagu used extant technology and aids to a point where we can safely say their performance was brilliant. The use of flares and signal fires was an age-old Chinese military tool, dating at least from the third century of the Christian era. To this, they added searchlights using the benefit of recently introduced military applications of electricity. The belief that Chinese soldiers could not fight in the dark was not only far from the truth, but ran counter to ample historical evidence that campaigning in the dark was a long-established, highly-developed skill of the Chinese military. Chinese gunners in 1900 took the limits of the possible and utilised their equipment almost beyond the limits of the credible. An American submarine commander using sonar, surfaced, hit and sank a ship in 2001. With the best equipment, military men can make mistakes; with the same equipment, some can outperform others. Those foreign military observers who watched the Chinese gunners doing preparatory training on the afternoon of 16 June and saw them dying and being replaced on their guns throughout the battle of Tianjin, had no hesitation in saying that the artillery fire power they met with in China was hotter and better directed than any they had met before.[34] By contrast, on the written evidence of McCalla and Rear Admiral Kempff and the photograph taken by Commander Corvisart (See Figure 7.3), Allied guns did little or no damage to the Chinese fort or its artillery.

Whence then the myths that the Chinese preferred defence to attack, used antiquated weapons, were afraid to fight at night and were badly trained on what few modern weapons they possessed? Turning to the contemporary press reports of this action, there are two notable phenomena. Either the battle of Dagu is not mentioned at all or dismissed in two or three lines,[35] or it is described in terms such as:

> The Chinese guns seem to have been pluckily worked but their shooting was poor. An eyewitness says that had the forts been manned by Europeans, not one gunboat would have escaped.[36]

The same two techniques for describing Chinese military action have resurfaced in the literature ever since.[37] Omission of any description of Chinese military action in the Boxer crisis in this short, but to contemporaries, high-profile conflict,[38] has remained a dominant mode with the myth of the superiority of European arms technology and total military ineptitude of the

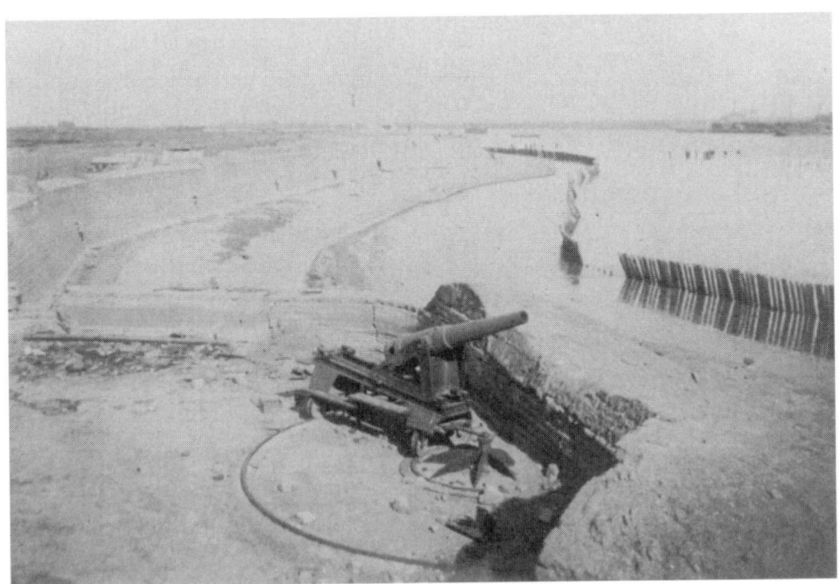

Figure 7.4(a) The South Fort, Dagu, 1900.[39] (By courtesy of the Musée de l'Armée de Terre, Paris)

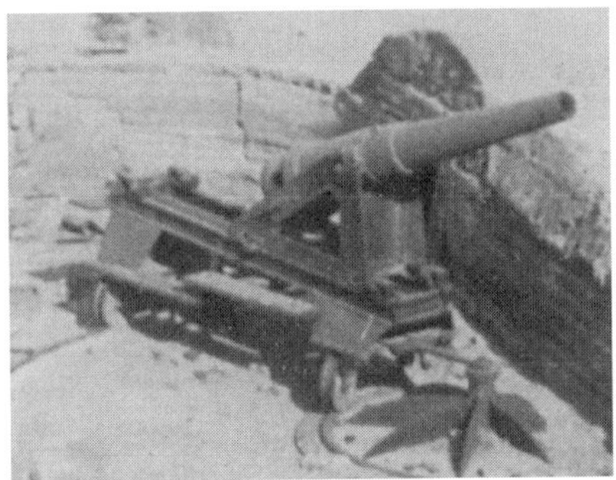

Figure 7.4(b) The South Fort, Dagu (insert).

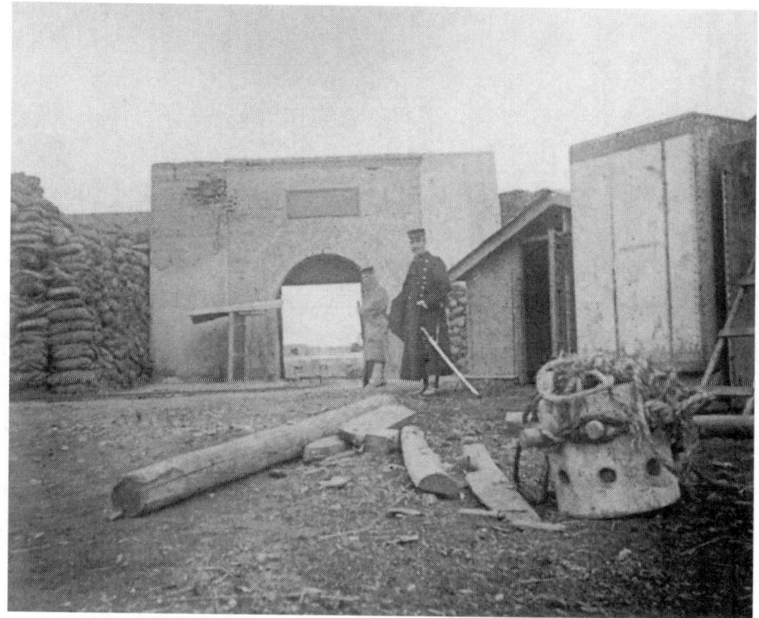

Figure 7.5 Entrance to the North Fort Dagu, 1900. Note sandbagging[40] (By courtesy of the Musée de l'Armée de Terre, Paris)

Chinese becoming accepted explanations for Chinese defeat.[41] A third factor emerging at the time conflicted with these first two. That was to admit that the guns at Dagu were ably manned and thus to assume they could not have been fired by Chinese gunners but must have been operated by Russians forced to man the guns.[42] The reality was that the Chinese had guns as modern as those of the attacking forces and had been superbly trained on those guns.[43] That is, in point of weapons technology and training, the Chinese were superior to their enemies. As for fighting courage, they were at least equal to the best of their enemies, numerous enemy officers having described with admiration how new gunners immediately replaced their dead or wounded comrades. We have to look to the actual course of the battle to find out why the Dagu forts fell, despite the courage and outstanding performance of the gunners.

The capture of the Dagu forts then was not a result either of superior modern weaponry or superior European ability in the use of that weaponry. Enemy guns had neither located and silenced the Chinese guns, nor had they

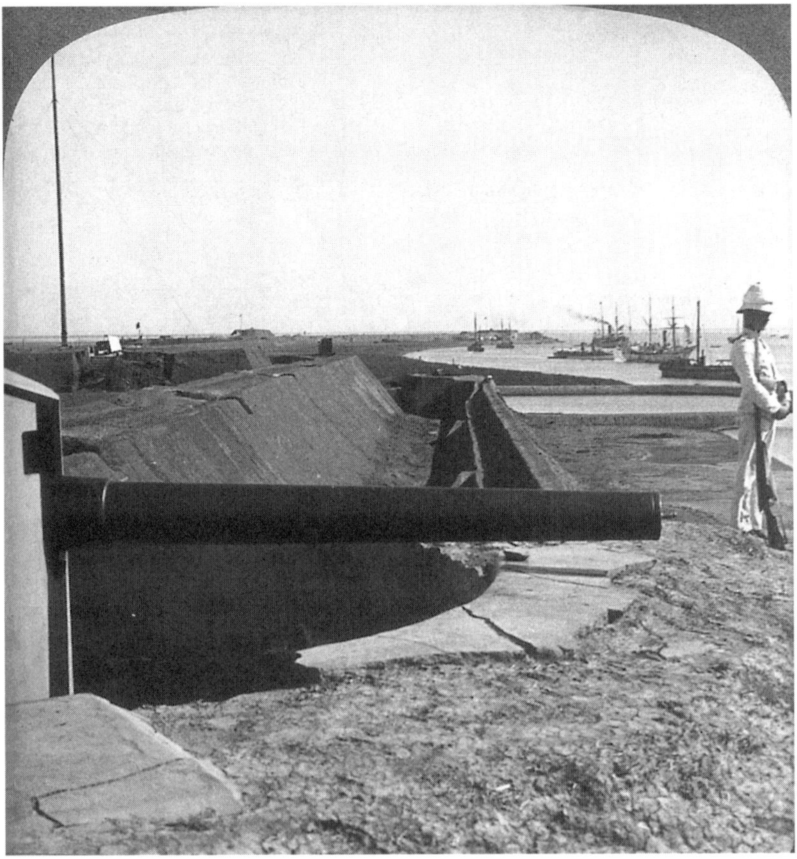

Figure 7.6(a) Gun at the Dagu Forts, commercial stereograph.[44] (From the collection of Mr R. Blum)

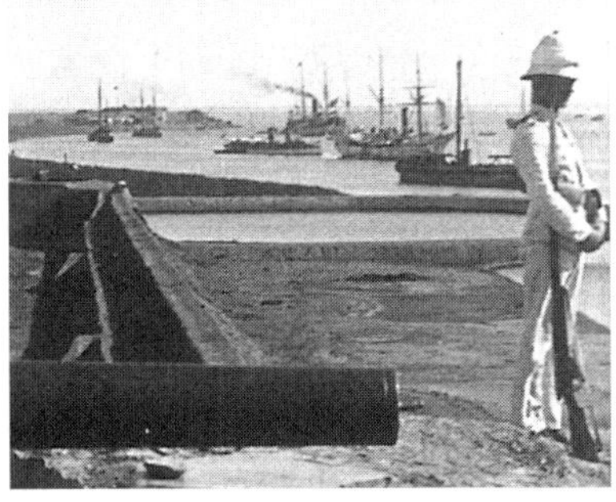

Figure 7.6(b) Gun at the Dagu Forts (insert).

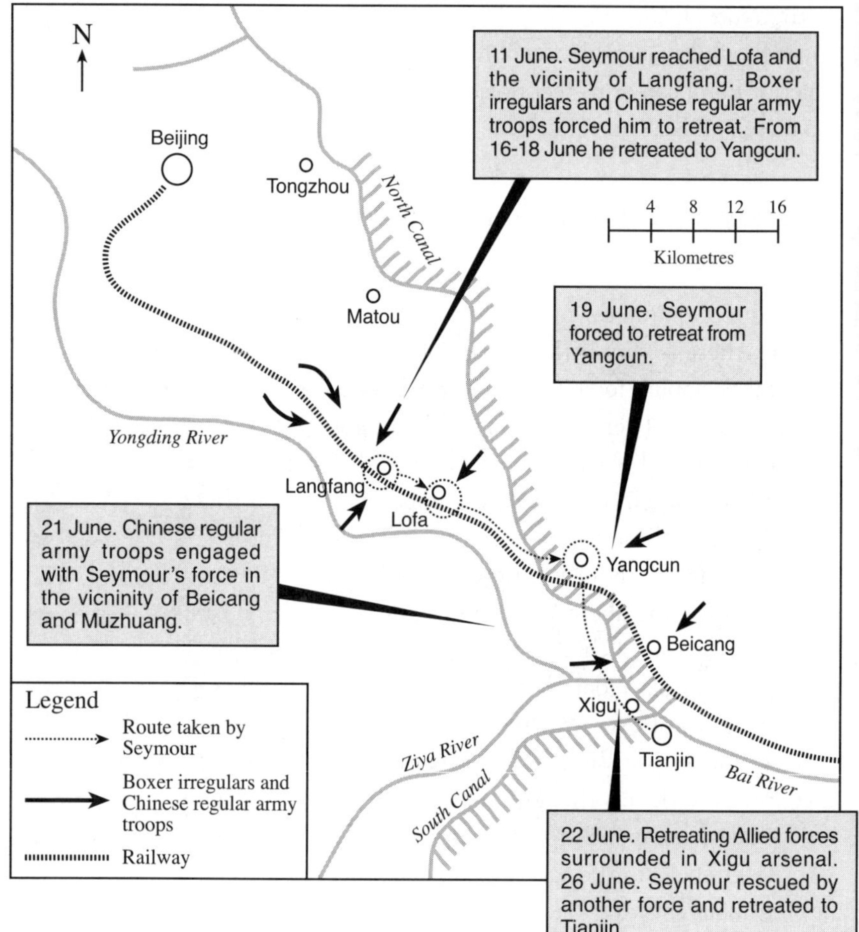

Figure 7.7 Map showing the route of the unsuccessful Seymour expedition to relieve the Legations. From Liu Tianlu, Su Weizhi and Li Dezheng.[45]

made any impression on the forts. The journals of the European and American officers all admit to the "chance hit" on the magazine in the South fort. This would have severely affected Chinese morale and nullified their ability to continue manning the guns. After the gunboats had failed to make any impression and the Chinese in the South fort had been rendered hors de combat, the North fort was taken by storm. The Japanese and Russians bayoneted all the Chinese soldiers they found. According to a correspondent of the *North China Herald*, "the pools of blood [lay] a foot thick."[46] The bayonet, while a suitable weapon in the context, was not a clear example of superior European arms technology or training, particularly in the hands of Japanese and Russian soldiers.

The Seymour Expedition — Boxer Strategy, Weaponry and Tactics

Turning to Admiral Seymour's abortive attempt to relieve the Legations in Beijing, there is very little in the literature which attributes the defeat of Admiral Seymour's force to Boxer or combined Boxer and Imperial Chinese Army activity.[47] There is nothing in the literature that clearly delineates the extent of Admiral Seymour's military irresponsiblility, nor discusses the extent of his failure in terms of the number of men and the valuable artillery lost. However, those writing out of the Western military culture had been writing in detail about Chinese losses in these two repects since 1840. Historians writing about the military lessons of the Boxer War emphasise specific criticisms of the Chinese army which the accounts of those taking part decisively invalidate but seem unable to take the step of describing in detail what the Boxer War showed about the successful aspects of China's drive to modernise some of her armies. Those writing about the military actions of the Boxers themselves do not indicate the extent to which they used modern weapons or the tactics suitable to the use of such weapons. There is strength in the reasoning and validity of Allen Fung's arguments as he sets about showing "How scholars [need not have] unwittingly engaged themselves in a witch-hunt for the inadequacies of the Chinese army and navy." He is referring to the Sino-Japanese War during which many Japanese officers made horrendous errors of judgement,[48] but the same reasoning applies to the way the Chinese military action during the Boxer rising has been ignored or belittled.[49]

The Boxer rising was a war. Moreover, it was a war in which at times, all three groups of protagonists were fighting on more than one front. Evaluations of the performance of the forces involved need to take into account all the details of how the irregular bands of peasant insurgents fought as well as how the regular Chinese or Allied soldiers fought. Any approach that takes the military action as given and proceeds to discuss the larger issues is unlikely to come up with a well-balanced assessment. Such an approach was begun by *The Times* and adopted by writers describing the Boxer action from George Nye Steiger to Joseph Esherick. None of these writers engaged with the full *military* implications of the fact that unarmed peasant rabble deliberately destroyed bare-handed over 140 kilometres of rail tracks[50] and all supporting railroad equipment. This was no primitive Luddism[51] nor was it initially conceived by the Boxers as heroic defenders of China in order to prevent the movement of Admiral Seymour's troops.

The Boxers had begun destroying the railway more than two weeks before the Seymour expedition set out and the Allies had opened fire on the forts at Dagu. Moreover, Boxer activity in destroying the railway in late May was centred around Gaobeitian, some sixty kilometres due west of Tianjin, not an area of strategic significance if their goal was to prevent foreign invaders from marching on Beijing. It would seem clear that the Boxer bands in this area wanted to strengthen their control of this area. To do this they had to prevent the movement of Imperial Chinese Army troops. By 12 June, Boxers had begun destroying the railway line between Tianjin and Beijing. Reinforcements had been sent to Beijing and the foreign Legations were asking for further reinforcements. By this time, it may be said that the Boxer goal was definitely to prevent the movement of foreign troops. Language can be used to deprive an enemy of victory or to minimise recognition of the enemy's military effectiveness in using successful tactics. When used by another enemy, the same tactics could be positively attributed to the military savoir faire of that enemy. In the year 1900 and in the case of cutting rail communications for the same reason, the white Protestant Boers acting in the same way as the yellow heathen Boxers with the same objective, were praised by influential sections of the British media specifically for their military acumen. The Boxers whose military objectives were more complex, did not rate a mention at the time or since for their actions as indicative of their military acumen.

The Boxers showed extraordinary determination in destroying the railway, returning under fire to the tracks which had just been re-laid by Admiral Seymour's coolies.[52] Popular superstition had it that the Lantern Bandits could protect the Boxers, "from the skies they can use their magic to cause fires, and what is more they can steal the screws [or perhaps "firing pins"] from the foreigners' artillery."[53] That is, popular knowledge contained understanding of what screws or firing pins were. In 1900, the peasants of the North China Plain may not have epitomised the acme of technological knowledge but they were like illiterate people in all cultures at all times. When exposed to another technology of immediate consequence to their working lives, they were very quick to embrace it. Naturally they took this knowledge straight into the context of warfare. The Boxers had been dedicating their energy to destroying the vital rail communications link days before Admiral Seymour's relieving force had even left Tianjin. Admiral Seymour was aware of this, yet he and many of his fellow officers packed their dress uniforms in total confidence of being able to wear them on their arrival in Beijing on the night of 16 June.

Admiral Seymour obviously did not conceive of Boxer activity as a serious military threat. As well, although he had been told clearly by Chinese civilian authorities that he was not to proceed to Beijing, he did not allow for any contingency that forces of the Imperial Chinese Army might be sent against him. By contrast, General Yang's correspondence showed him to have been acutely alive to the disastrous consequences of allowing the Boxers to isolate his forces by cutting the railway. In order to control neighbourhoods, towns and cities, the Boxers had to stop troop movement by rail. Their conduct in this respect shows them to have been as determined to isolate battalions of the Chinese regular army as the invading Seymour expedition. Operating as guerrilla bands with popular support, appropriate technical knowledge and great courage, they were equally successful in cutting the railway to isolate both Chinese and foreign regular troops. General Yang described the Boxers as "undisciplined rabble" and on one level his correspondence shows that he did not take them seriously as a military force.[54] Unlike Admiral Seymour, General Yang did express his sharp awareness of the fact that Boxer tactics were preventing him from carrying out his orders, namely to protect the railway. Moreover, General Yang internalised the military implications of the increase in Boxer numbers and determination as well as their popular support base. These factors, in conjunction with Imperial orders not to fire on them meant that Yang Mushi had to take the Boxers seriously. Rabble they may have been, but their numbers, popular support and the nature of their military objectives required the diversion of a large number of troops to deal with them. They were a problem for General Yang as they were not for Admiral Seymour because General Yang had orders to disperse the

Boxers using the least amount of force possible. Thus, while he characterised them as militarily insignificant, he also asked for reinforcements of troops and ammunition to deal with this "undisciplined rabble."

One wonders whether the officers commanding the Allied invading force thought that the military principle of isolating their enemies from supplies and reinforcements was a tactic too complex for primitive Chinese peasant insurgents to grasp. The Boxers cut the railway in front of Admiral Seymour's advancing force so that he never got more than half way to Beijing and then they cut it behind him so he was unable to get back to Tianjin by rail or to send for further supplies and reinforcements. They destroyed the water towers so that the locomotives could not take on water and burned all the stations and guard houses.[55] In accordance with age-old Chinese military strategy, the Boxers cleared provisions from the countryside surrounding the Allied advance.[56]

There is an almost complete consensus in the literature to minimise the Boxers' *military* perception of the value of destroying the railway when fighting.[57] Thus the Boxers' military capacity as demonstrated by their part in defeating Admiral Seymour's expedition may be described in terms of the effectiveness, persistence and precise technical knowledge demonstrated by the nature of their attacks on the railway.[58] Boxer sabotaging of the railway in the region of Gaobeitian had also had the effect of forcing the Imperial Chinese Army troops back on Tianjin. The destruction of the railway connecting the invading Allies to their objective and cutting them off from their base was a deliberate military initiative conceived of by the Boxers to prevent Admiral Seymour from reaching Beijing. Questions arise as to the nature of the relationship between Boxer and regular army forces during the retreat of the Seymour expedition. It is clear that both forces harried Seymour and his men; that the Boxers had modern weapons; and that Chinese regular troops could take up commanding positions at will and had cavalry forces at the ready throughout the retreat of the Allied expedition. It is thus less clear whether or not officers of the Imperial Chinese Army were able to persuade the Boxers to contain rather than annihilate the Seymour foray.

When General Yang engaged with Admiral Seymour's forces at the Xigu arsenal, both sides were battle weary and under intense strain from at least ten days of fighting the Boxers — and, in the case of Admiral Seymour's forces, the Imperial Chinese Army as well. With evidence from the German naval Captain Schlieper, in addition to the observations of General Yang, concerning the secreting of railway materials in villages and on junks, it is obvious that the Boxers commanded a significant level of military and social organisation. By nature the uprising was leaderless,[59] but the successful military initiatives taken by the Boxers were such that it is misleading to refer to this admittedly widely disparate rising as "the most primitive in terms of organisation of any agrarian uprising in history."[60] The peasantry may have been "averse to discipline by its very nature"[61] but the systematic and determined destruction of the railway as well as Boxer military initiatives during the siege of Tianjin show the concepts of "discipline" and "organisation" to be capable of wider interpretation than that applied, for example, to a regular army trained on the Western model. Landlords constituted 22.5 per cent of Boxer leaders in Shandong.[62] Many of such people had experience in militia organisation, if not training and leadership. Some of them would have been accepted as leaders by some Boxer groups along with the demobilised soldiers whose military knowledge of modern weaponry would have been valued and very likely passed on.

Insofar as Boxer weaponry is concerned, while many Boxers were "only" armed with bamboo lances tipped with iron (often described as "spears"), some observers noted that "these were the most effective [weapons] of all."[63] In hand-to-hand fighting more than one Allied officer tasted the quality of the steel in Boxer swords or lances.[64] Colonel Yang Futong died in a most gruesome manner at the hands of Boxers armed with these primitive weapons. Other observers noted that Boxers had been issued with Winchester repeating rifles and Mannlichers[65] and some Boxer forces possessed and used with proficiency two Krupp field cannon.[66] Financial problems had obliged civilian authorities like Li Hongzhang to pay off large numbers of foreign-trained soldiers after the Sino-Japanese War.[67] Some of these men were certainly among the ranks of the Boxers and were most probably able to use any modern Western weapons they were given by sympathisers[68] or managed to capture. In late June the Court told governors and governors-general to levy and arm Boxer militias.[69] One of General Yang Mushi's most pressing concerns was that if he allowed his men to be surrounded and killed by the Boxers, they would capture all his weapons and ammunition. In a letter to the Secretary of State, Hill, the American Consul McWade wrote from Guangzhou on 9 July of daily executions by decapitation:

> One of yesterday's victims was the Captain of a Chinese guardboat, caught smuggling 20,000 Mauser rifles, part of which he had already delivered to the Boxer leaders. He was led to his place of execution dressed in the robes of his Mandarin rank.[70]

Franz Michael has pointed out that:

> There was always a conflict between the government's inclination to prohibit the possession of all weapons by anyone except its own military forces and the necessity to tolerate private possession by the civilian population of some weapons for self defense against banditry and in times of unrest.[71]

Thus there was a tradition allowing "the people" to have weapons but this was not interpreted by Li Hongzhang in July 1900 in such a way that Boxers should be given Mauser rifles. While some contemporary writers noted that the Boxers used "old-fashioned and obsolete weapons" in their sniping activities,[72] the whole body of military literature stresses the deterrent nuisance value of Boxer snipers and the deaths of those who failed to take them seriously. To an enemy with a shattered arm, it would not seem relevant whether the bullet had come from an obsolete matchlock or a Winchester repeating rifle. On the question of efficiency of firepower, Dorothy Shineberg quotes H. L. Blackmore's *British Military Firearms* to the effect that in one of the Kaffir Wars it was estimated that it took 80,000 bullets to put twenty-five of the enemy hors de combat. In European conflicts the effective bullet ranged between 250/1 and 437/1.[73] When Western soldiers fought non-European enemies, the overwhelming evidence suggests that if their weaponry was more sophisticated, this was rarely if ever the decisive factor in Western success.[74]

With regard to Boxer fighting tactics, again these reflected the proportion of the men in the Boxer bands who were discharged soldiers still unemployed since the Sino-Japanese War as well as disaffected soldiers from various armies.[75] Boxer "drill" certainly incorporated supernatural ritual scorned by European and Chinese observers alike.[76] However, it also contained elements of Western military drill as well as hereditary military knowledge suitable for small militia units for use in minor engagements with banditry endemic in China towards the end of the Qing dynasty.[77] Thus when the Allied military noticed that the Boxers fought courageously and were orderly and tenacious both in attacking and withdrawing, they were observing what they understood as "orderly." That is, what they saw reflected some military training and knowledge on the part of some elements of Boxer forces.[78] The defeat of Admiral Seymour was due perhaps less to crazed fanatic patriotism armed with primitive weapons,[79] than to a semblance of tactical skill, military training and organisation, and some familiarity with modern weapons visible as such to the members of the Allied invading force describing their experience during the abortive Seymour expedition and the subsequent siege of Tianjin. Writing of Boxer action during the siege of Tianjin, Captain McCalla noted:

> About daylight, on the 11th July, the Boxers armed with rifles, came out in the open, and advanced on the station with great courage. The attack was well delivered and well sustained ...[80]

The Seymour Expedition and the Imperial Chinese Army

Before discussing the evidence concerning the military skill of the Chinese regular army with their modern weaponry and evaluating General Nie Shicheng's performance in forcing the Allied expedition to return to Tianjin, we must briefly acknowledge the nature of the military action undertaken by General Nie in and around Tianjin. He had been instructed to put down Boxer activities. General Nie was committed to obeying his instructions to protect the railway despite his realisation of the fact that by doing so, he risked disastrous professional consequences.

The problems facing General Nie were two-fold. Contradictory instructions from the Court as to the action he was to take concerning the Boxers and the fact that there had been successful Boxer action against his soldiers on several occasions, made his position extremely difficult. Fighting rebellious nationals for whatever reason had always been one of the major tasks of Imperial forces. General Nie had had experience of the Nian Rebellion and more recently, in the Sino-Japanese War he "was one of the generals who saved their [the Chinese] reputation by not being absolutely beaten."[81] This tantalising excerpt from a contemporary British dictionary of information on the Chinese armies and their leaders makes one wonder just how well General Nie did, in fact, perform. The British Captain Barnes took particular pride in the fact that he and his fellow officers had trained Chinese soldiers to fight against their own nationals.[82] Chinese officers also had no difficulty leading their men against Chinese insurgents. The Taiping Rebellion was an important and recent precedent in this context. In the Boxer War, General Nie's achievement in fighting two different enemies, at times simultaneously, while retaining the loyalty of the great majority of his army, is impressive. There must have been some soldiers of the Imperial Chinese Army who came from the same areas as the Boxers and they would certainly have come from the same social milieu. As well as the testimony of Yang Mushi, Liu Mengyang and Sawara Tokusake, Captain McCalla of the US Marines observed that:

> There was much bickering and ill-feeling and many fights, between the Boxers and the Imperial troops in Tianjin, the latter accusing the Boxers of having brought about the disastrous existing conditions.[83]

That is, rank and file Chinese soldiers had some concept of the broader consequences of the Boxer rising. Against this background, General Nie displayed qualities of professionalism and leadership of the highest order, giving his men a strong esprit de corps and holding them together to fight against combined Allied forces and a Chinese insurgency. Captain McCalla was among the foreign military observers who did observe this and he wrote of the Chinese soldiers with anything but condescension:

> These Chinese troops were composed of young men, admirable from a physical point of view, neatly uniformed in blue, with straw hats and were well armed with either new Mauser or Mannlicher rifles. I must confess that their appearance and arms surprised me, for it was not then generally known that the Agents of many companies in Europe and in the United States, had for several years flooding [sic] China with modern munitions of war. [On entering a train McCalla saw a Chinese general and several staff officers.] I saluted him courteously, saying "Good morning." Just after we were seated in our car, a young Chinese Officer came in, saluted me and said: "The General says 'Good morning!'," an evidence of national politeness.[84]

The Germans and the French were uncomfortable when faced with irregulars, however courageous, but were heartened when the soldiers of the Imperial Chinese Army joined the fray as now they saw fighting as they knew it. "This was suddenly a completely different picture, a different adversary who resisted with the same kind of weapons and fired back vigorously."[85] At an earlier date, Vice-Consul Carles described Li Hongzhang's Huai army troops who fought in 1900 as part of the Vanguard of the Wu Wei army as follows:

> The men that we saw were very favourable specimens of the Chinese lower classes. Few of them were over 35 (for this they accounted by the destruction

> wrought by the Taiping rebellion), and all were strong, healthy men, of courteous manners and intelligent countenance.[86]

Whatever the origins of the impressions that the Chinese soldier was a "neglected son of Mars" or that men were wasted in becoming soldiers in the same way good metal is wasted in making nails, they cannot be found in the writings of the officers and men who fought against the Imperial Chinese Army in 1900. The military literature abounds with examples of Chinese courage, particularly during the siege of Tianjin. The French naval captain Guillaumat wrote of the isolated Chinese snipers, "Several got themselves killed by Russian patrols very courageously after shooting their last cartridge rather than fleeing when it would have been easy for them to do so."[87] During the Boxer campaign the Russians were noted for not taking any prisoners. All agreed that the Chinese soldiers never failed to follow up a retirement. Those who took part in the retreat of the Seymour expedition unanimously observed how when the Chinese — both Boxers and regular soldiers — were driven back by the retreating Allied force, they would immediately regroup and counter attack.[88] Some attempt has been made to come to grips with the action during the retreat. However, the descriptions of the rout, like that of *The Times* and the text of Admiral Seymour's report itself, fail to relate the success of Chinese military action to the Allies' high casualty rate of nearly eighteen per cent. No English-language source notes these casualty figures correctly. Neither has it been observed that they are high in absolute terms and very high relative to the assertions that the Boxers were primitively armed disorganised peasants and the soldiers of the Imperial Chinese Army were poorly armed, badly lead and generally lacking in the skills required in the field. It comes as quite a shock having read scholarly accounts and contemporary accounts in *The Times*, for example, on the subject of the Seymour expedition, to see so many sketches of the helpless wounded in Captain Schlieper's book about his war experiences in China and to read his account of just how difficult their retreat was made by the fact of having to carry such a large number of wounded men. Knowing what forces General Nie had at his disposal, knowing that the Allied wounded were being towed along in sampans in a canal below a dyke, knowing that Admiral Seymour's force was exhausted, it is impossible to come to any other conclusion than that General Nie deliberately refrained from ordering his cavalry or artillery-supported infantry units to destroy the completely vulnerable sampans.

According to Sawara Tokusaki, Nie said on 8 June:

> The Boxers are weakening the country and will cause disaster in the long-term. Moreover Shiceng [himself] is the Commander-in-Chief [in Zhili] and when there are bandits in his jurisdiction, it is logical to put them down. After putting them down I will be punished severely but I will not attempt to evade punishment or even death.

On 10 June when Admiral Seymour's force marched by Yang village where a large part of Nie's force was stationed, Nie telegrammed Yulu for permission to stop the enemy force (one notes that Nie does not take action into his owns hands but defers to civil authority, the hallmark of the professional soldier trained on Western models and one which many an African military man trained at Sandhurst in the second half of the twentieth century had no difficulty ignoring once back home on his own ground). Yulu refused. "Nie was very angry and said to his subordinates, 'I am the Commander-in-Chief in Zhili. I cannot put down the Bandits and I also cannot stop the enemy. What is the use of this army?'" On 13 June, having received an Imperial decree to stop the expedition, General Nie went on to adopt the tactic of shepherding the enemy back to Tianjin. The Court gave the entire credit for this to the Boxers and gave them big rewards while the part played by General Nie and his men was totally ignored.[89]

Some of the troops of Generals Nie Shicheng and Dong Fuxiang joined the Boxers at Langfang to force the Seymour expedition back on Tianjin. Neither Admiral Seymour's official report nor the newspaper accounts give any idea of the number of skirmishes lost by the Allied force against Boxers or regular troops. The military accounts, by contrast, give full descriptions. Between 12 June and 25 June, apart from whole mornings or days spent fighting, there were seventeen separate engagements in which the Allied forces were attacked by Boxers or regular Imperial Army troops.

> Our progress was very slow. The enemy proved very persistent and difficult to dislodge. Once a village was cleared, it was certain that at the next village we would face even greater fire-power.[90]

In contrast to one scholar's assertion that "as the forces progressed, [the Allied troops] cleared the Boxers by rifle and bayonet from several villages along the way,"[91] Corporal Hicks described the retreat as the Boxers took up positions in the villages:

> [These] were easy to hold and the first lesson we learnt was that the attack must always be prepared to lose four or five times as much as the defence ... the Boxers had three and six pounders, pom pom and large native jingals and were frequently entrenched. We were also being continually harassed on our left flank by masses of Infantry and Cavalry accompanied by Horse Artillery (twelve and fifteen pounders) with which they regularly shelled us from the railway embankment as soon as we had again got into column.[92]

Contrary to the assertion by another scholar that "full use was not made of cavalry squadrons,"[93] it was the Chinese cavalry that bore the major part of the task of shepherding Admiral Seymour's force back to Tianjin. Moreover, the Chinese cavalry, "cette belle cavalerie bien en ordre, bien alignée"[94] on its first appearance, was universally recognised by the members of the retreating Seymour force as Cossack cavalry.[95] It would be difficult to think of a higher compliment to the Chinese cavalry of the Vanguard of the Wu Wei army in 1900 than to have been mistaken by foreign soldiers, including a detachment of Russian soldiers, for Cossacks.

McCalla's description of the overall effect of Chinese opposition as the expedition retreated to Tianjin is worth repeating:

> The character of the opposition can best be judged by the fact that, while we *advanced* nine miles on the 20th [June], the distance fell to four miles on the 21st, and to one mile on the 22nd, our casualties increasing with the resistance offered to our *progress*.[96] [emphasis added] [Note that McCalla is describing a retreat here.]

as is his implicit comment on Allied military intelligence and reconnaissance capacity. Most of the skirmishes resulting in the heavy casualties of the Seymour expedition arose either because the Allied forces made no attempt to reconnoitre or because such attempts were heavily punished by the Chinese before they gathered sufficient information. McCalla was writing of an exhausted body of men whose food, water and ammunition were now being heavily rationed. With numbers of wounded increasing daily, they "had practically fought [themselves] to a standstill":[97]

> The Column had unwittingly run into a cleverly prepared surprise, and we had then no knowledge that it was the Siku [sic] Arsenal in which the enemy was entrenched, nor indeed did anyone in Admiral Seymour's force know of the existence of such an arsenal ... I then found that the Chinese had stationed a heavy force of Infantry behind some graves ... and that there was also a force

> of Cavalry and Artillery posted a thousand yards on my left front. From this it will readily be seen that the Chinese had … skilfully prepared a trap for us to fall into.[98]

It is not a great tribute to the activities of the consuls and military attachés in Tianjin that the invading Allied forces knew nothing about an arsenal containing such valuable military equipment. In addition to this massive arsenal, there was also a report in the *North China Mail* on 28 July stating that General Nie's "artillery was posted at a fort in the native city of Tientsin which had been built unknown to the foreign attachés and commanded the foreign settlements." Colonel Pélacot commented bitterly on the inaccuracy of the information at the disposal of the Allies' guns and also noted that the Chinese forts hidden from the Allies had a commanding view of the foreign quarter. "Visiting these forts [after the battle] *which were not touched by our shells*, one would have been within one's right to ask if their very existence had been known [to the Allies]" (emphasis added).[99] Combined Western intelligence would appear to have failed lamentably.

McCalla attributed the Allied victory in the fight for the arsenal to the fact that the Chinese were not "well-officered."[100] General Yang's description of the fight shows complete agreement:

> Battalion Commanders Wang Chi-chung and Fang Te-chiang of the Rear Route and the companies led by Pien Ch'ang-sheng and T'ao Liang-ts'ai gazed on from a distance and did not advance with us. Although I urged them to advance, they stood their ground and ignored me.[101]

McCalla then went on to make a unique revelation. During the battle for the arsenal, he was fighting alongside the German Commander von Usedom. The Chinese cavalry suddenly moved off in the direction taken by Ensign Wurtsbaugh who was being commanded by von Usedom from an embankment above.

> Someone called attention to the body of Chinese infantry and to my surprise, the whole party turned and fled to their rear. In vain, I tried to call their attention to the fact that the enemy was in flight but it was impossible to make them understand, and von Usedom and I were left alone on the embankment. Thus *for the second time, within two days*, I witnessed a form of panic such as I had read of as being not infrequent in the stress of battle, among the bravest of troops.[102] [emphasis added]

Symptomatic of the way this campaign has been re-written, a biography of

McCalla, describes this incident but mentions only that the Chinese fled, omitting reference to the panic among the Allied troops.[103] With reference to the universally held belief that the Chinese were afraid to fight in the dark,[104] so decisively dispelled by this campaign, McCalla made this interesting observation:

> Seamen campaigning ashore, in an enemy's country are like all inexperienced troops: unusually susceptible to strange noises after dark. [On the first and second night of the Seymour expedition] all the pickets save those from the *Newark* [heard a sound and came] into the train on a run.[105]

Schlieper also mentioned the extreme fear of the Chinese among his men culminating in a number of soldiers fainting during the burial service for the Italians killed by Boxers in an attack on 14 June.[106]

In order to dispel finally the myth that the Chinese used weapons dating from the Middle Ages, the German naval Captain Schlieper's evidence is unequivocal. Schlieper wrote with relief that the poorly-equipped Allied Expeditionary Force which had run out of ammunition on its retreat to Tianjin, was able to replenish from the ammunition belts of dead Boxers and soldiers of the Imperial Chinese Army.[107] Moreover, Captain Schlieper had occasion to write that he "cursed the old powder and wished [he] had the new rifle which had only just been introduced."[108] As an officer of the Imperial German Navy, his weapon was inferior to those used by the men of Nie Shicheng's army and at least some of the "primitively" armed Boxers.

In the event, soldiers of all the Allied countries involved in this expedition were able to exchange their weapons for the more up-to-date hardware they found in the arsenal they captured at Xigu. The arsenal contained an estimated £1.5 to £3.5 million worth of modern weapons and ammunition.[109] As one of several arsenals in the vicinity of Tianjin alone, it is not possible to reconcile this with the assertion that "in the waning years of the century a few attempts were made by the dynasty [to reform the army] and a few modern weapons were purchased."[110] The Xigu arsenal also contained medical supplies which was fortuitous as Admiral Seymour's expedition of 2,044 had sixty-two killed and 312 wounded. Luckier still, the original instructions in German were found by the retreating Allied force still packed together with the medical supplies.[111] As an indication of the desirability of the weapons found by the retreating Allied expedition in the Xigu arsenal, several officers wrote that the soldiers were throwing away their own weapons and fighting to get superior weapons with the excitement of boys let loose in a toy shop. This was noted as constituting a real danger and as a serious discipline problem.[112]

As revealed by their writings, the mentality and professionalism of the soldiers of the invading forces does not leave any trace of incredulity at the ability of their non-white Western European foe. We may see such incredulity as indicative of an atypically irrational response. Implicit racism is irrational and therefore dominates over professionalism.[113] The comments of rank and file soldiers may have included bitterness or denigratory slang but they all acknowledged the fighting skill of the Chinese regular soldier. It was perhaps a deeply ingrained and unconscious racism that led some civilian contemporaries to refuse to acknowledge Chinese skill in warfare, despite obvious evidence to the contrary. Much earlier when superb gunnery was demonstrated during the First Opium War, a British lieutenant noted that he had heard the word "gunpowder" being shouted during the action, that is, that foreigners were manning the Chinese guns.[114] After the battle of Dagu, the *China Mail* and Captain Barnes advanced the hypothesis that the artillery fire was of such excellence that the guns must have been manned by Russians forcibly co-opted by the Chinese. Notably it was the soldier, Captain Barnes, who decided against the hypothesis but the public read the *China Mail* and not Captain Barnes.[115] Well into the twentieth century, John Dower recorded the fact that when Japanese aircraft wiped out General MacArthur's airforce on the ground in the Philippines nine hours after Pearl Harbour, "the General was caught by surprise and refused to believe that the pilots could have been Japanese. He [MacArthur] insisted that they must have been white mercenaries."[116] In the case of the battle of Dagu, it may have reflected better on the invading forces to say that the Chinese were good gunners but that the gunners of the seven Allies were better. The fact is that they were not. There is little evidence of such reasoning in the military accounts of the Boxer rising. General Frey's report, among many, singles out for praise the eyewitness account of Captain Frot of the *Lion*, of the tenacity with which the Chinese replaced wounded gunners and gunners' assistants during the battle of Dagu.[117] The tradition of Chinese artillerymen dying on their guns had begun in 1856.[118] Ruffi de Pontèves' account emphasises the precision of the gunners of the Tianjin forts firing on the retreating Seymour expedition.[119] The accuracy of Chinese artillery fire was taken as given by members of the

Allied forces. When members of the Seymour party, holed up in the Xigu arsenal three miles out of Tianjin, were debating whether or not an approaching force was a rescue force or a Chinese detachment, a French marine observed to de Pontèves

> Look! The shelling from the Tianjin forts is no longer directed at us. See how the shells are falling along the railway on what you take to be the Chinese army? How could this be an enemy force? The Chinese are stupid but not to the point where they would bombard their own forces.[120]

Not all compliments were as back-handed:

> June 25 … at about 8 am they commenced to shell us and knocked down our barricade as fast as we could build it up [the Italians tried to set up a field piece]. The first shot was a signal for them to open up on us with every little thing they had … [the Chinese wounded two Italian gunners] then Mitchell who had charge of the Colt gun tried his luck at it, but he would no sooner get the gun trained when the Chinks would open up with a three inch and all hands would lie down till the shell landed, they soon placed another gun in position and Captain Hall ordered us to take the guns below … those Chinks had us every way.[121]

> Great credit was given to [the Chinese] gunners [under General Nie] for their marvellous shooting. The men of the *Terrible* said that the shelling of Ladysmith, from which they had come, was mere child's play compared with the hot and well-directed fire of the Chinese artillery men.[122]

The Chinese were good gunners, they were using smokeless powder, and the supporting role of their engineers enabled them to plant and mask guns during the siege of Tianjin so that the Allies were unable to locate them.[123] As well, their fire-power was greater than that of the Allies both during the battle of Dagu and the siege of Tianjin. On the Seymour rout, the Allies accidentally and deliberately lost several pieces of artillery and some Maxim guns, putting the pieces in junks too light to hold them[124] or abandoning them in the fields.[125] The Chinese, by contrast, always held their artillery back and did not lose a gun in the initial four weeks of the campaign.

Furthermore, Chinese intelligence supplied quick and accurate information to the artillery so that positions were no sooner occupied by the Allied forces than they were being precision-shelled by the Chinese. Chinese intelligence was aided in this by superb mapping. See Figures 7.2a, b and c. When the Expeditionary Force was stopped by Chinese regular and irregular forces at the Xigu arsenal, it was located before it could make camp in the arsenal by guns from Tianjin firing in the dark.[126] Having found the range, the Chinese gunners turned their attention elsewhere. De Marolles noted that it was a dark night and that the Chinese signalled the movements of the retreating Allies by fires lit in the villages. The gunners at Tianjin had highly accurate maps.

The officers commanding the Seymour retreat were considerably confused as to whether or not they should occupy the Xigu arsenal.[127] Given the value of the ordnance and the military supplies in the arsenal, confusion as to the desirability of occupying and holding such a prize is indicative of the stress on those commanding this retreat forced by continuous Chinese pressure.[128] Only when the Expeditionary Force started bombarding neighbouring villages with Krupp guns from the arsenal or attempted to send a sortie for help from Tianjin, did it draw a riposte from Tianjin. As the Chinese gunners had already found the range, two shells exploded in the courtyard in front of the arsenal and another wrecked the roof of a dangerous powder magazine and started a fire in the tents housing the munitions depot established by the Allies. Captain de Marolles crowns his description of the precision of the Chinese artillery with a typically Gallic detail. Early on 25 June a shell clipped the pot in which the rice was being cooked, wounding a man and presumably delaying their breakfast.

A corollary to the excellence of Chinese intelligence and mapping and the accuracy of the artillery and rifle fire was their ability to catch the Allies unprepared throughout the abortive Seymour expedition, demonstrating that both Boxers and regulars were adept at scouting and reconnaissance.[129] The number of times this occurred opens to question the degree to which the Allies had really internalised the consequences of the military capacity they had noted. When the soldiers detrained to get water on 11 June, they did so unarmed and were immediately attacked by Boxers. On 14 June Schlieper's men were ordered to go to the village to do their washing, again unarmed, and once again they were attacked by Boxers. On 19 June Schlieper had just taken off his boots to wash his feet after dinner when an alarm heralded an attack by Chinese regular soldiers. While General Yang learned quickly that Boxer strategy relied on sudden, unexpected surprise attacks, it would seem that the officers on the Seymour retreat were slower to perceive a pattern in Boxer attacks. The Imperial Chinese Army was obviously capable of deploying men using their modern Western training or their traditional Chinese training as the circumstances required.

On the question of the state of weapons technology and training of the era, and assertions as to the primitive nature of Chinese weapons, particularly the gingal, Schlieper's reaction is notable "with my sabre in my right and my revolver in my left, leaving behind a sock ... I rushed out."[130] The cultural connotations of particular weapons can be immense. Moreover, differing combat conditions require different weapons. To have called a Prussian officer "primitive" because he prided himself on his duelling scars would have been unthinkable. After some experience losing battles with the Maori, there were fewer denigratory comments in British accounts about their "primitive" facial tattooing. American cadets of West Point were receiving instruction in fencing and broad sword in 1900[131] and British and French officers likewise took pride in their ability with the sabre up until the 1939–1945 War. German precision and organisation drew the admiration of military observers throughout the campaign. Captain Schlieper's strong preference for his sabre when taken by surprise is nothing more than what one would expect from a German officer of this era. In the specific circumstances of a surprise attack at night, preferences for weapons can thus also be seen to be a part of the cultural background and traditions, as much as the training of the military of any nation. Moreover, the contempt felt by some contemporary writers and echoed by some historians for particular kinds of Chinese weapons was not felt by the soldiers actually facing those weapons at the time. Wise wrote of the gingal which killed his friend Captain Davis:

> Those gingals were pure Chinese. Rifles with a seven-foot barrel and a modern breech-loading stock. They fired about a one-pounder projectile. It took three men to handle each gingal. The weapon was sighted over the shoulders of two and fired by the third. They could be sighted accurately to a very long range. They gave terrific wounds.[132]

The Chinese military philosophy with respect to the "weapons factor" and the "human factor" is epitomised by the gingal. The Chinese had the men trained to use the gingal, the industrial capacity to manufacture it and it was effective. The gingals were probably used by Lian troops most of whom had not yet been trained to use Mauser rifles.

The characterisation of war as "too complex a matter to be left to fighting men" is not borne out by the evidence regarding General Nie's actions. His stance on protecting the railway no matter what the cost would be to his career shows an awareness of the conflict between the elements of conservatism and modernisation in Imperial politics[133] and a determination to serve what he felt to be China's best interests. General Nie was the head of a modern foreign-drilled army. He had distinguished himself in the Sino-Japanese War and since then had implemented important changes in organisation and training.[134] Both the local civilian authorities and General Nie were aware of the commercial and logistic value of the railway line owned by the Chinese under bond to Britain, independent of its status as a hated foreign intrusion into many aspects of Chinese national, economic and spiritual life.[135] Furthermore, his experience in the Sino-Japanese War had made him fully cognizant of the political and military advisability of obeying his instructions concerning the Allied Expeditionary Force and acted to prevent it reaching its objective rather than to annihilate it. General Nie was under no military illusions about potential further foreign military action that would be consequent on the complete destruction of a force comprising soldiers from eight nations.[136] Chinese students had studied at Japanese, French, German and Russian military academies. General Nie had observed German, British and Russian military instructors working with his soldiers. Li Hongzhang, whose troops formed the backbone of General Nie's reconstructed army, had observed first hand the industrial and military strength of the West. The Chinese had had considerable experience of the French and British military in many contexts since the First Opium War in addition to the recent experience with the Japanese.

The military writers of the time marvelled at the fact that the defeated Allied column was allowed to march back into Tianjin right under the Chinese guns, McCalla incorrectly supposing this was because the Chinese troops had left the city.[137] Guillaumat drew a vivid picture of the return of the defeated force:

> I have never been able to understand how [the column] could have [got into Tianjin] without being welcomed by gun fire from the Chinese who shot incessantly from early morning to night from their ambuscades in the burnt houses on the right bank. Indeed [the column] crossed a completely exposed area marching very slowly because of the wounded they were carrying. It was highly imprudent ... The English who were at the head were marching in the greatest disorder.[138]

With such a wealth of evidence as to the military strength and skills of the Chinese regular forces and their ability to contain while depleting the Allied Expeditionary Force, the question as to why General Nie fought only to restrain rather than to annihilate the Seymour expedition must inevitably arise. The answers lie in the decrees which instructed him not to attack the Expeditionary Force but to prevent the foreigners from reaching Beijing; in the uneasy relationship between General Nie's forces and the Boxers; in General Nie's concepts of professionalism and loyalty to the long-term best interests of China; in Chinese military philosophy in which the value of future gains is considered more important than a short-term setback; and in his opposition to the anti-foreignism of elements of the Court.

Along with General Nie, General Ma Yukun, who was temporarily posted over his head[139] to command the siege of Tianjin, was also aware of the contents of decrees concerning the Allied expedition and the international repercussions which would certainly follow if the Seymour relief expedition was massacred as it limped back into Tianjin with two or even four men needed to carry each of the 312 wounded.[140] Like General Nie, General Ma had also seen service in the Sino-Japanese War and had been ordered by Li Hongzhang to protect Tianjin from disturbances.[141] There was considerable enmity between Boxers and the soldiers of the Imperial Chinese Army.[142] We have seen General Yang's evidence regarding the strength of the Boxers and the total support they commanded in the surrounding villages. However, Boxer allegiances changed and they had fought side by side at Langfang with regular soldiers to turn back the Seymour expedition. It is thus probable that the commanding officers of the Imperial Chinese Army were able to exert some influence over the Boxers. By this stage the Boxers certainly had the weapons and the capacity to have decimated the Allied force as it hobbled through Tianjin escorted by the 2000-strong rescue force. The "slanderous tissue of lies" regarding the performance of this Allied expedition began to be composed immediately.

There can be no doubt that at the battle of Dagu the Chinese fought to win and lost heroically. Under the circumstances, there is good reason to doubt that General Nie Shicheng instructed his officers to fight to win with respect to the Seymour foray. General Yang's correspondence shows him to have been technically very able in complying with his orders to withdraw from Boxer-dominated territory without using all the force at his disposal. Contemporaries theorised that there were elements of the Imperial Chinese

Army which had been ordered to "stay their hand"[143] during the siege of the Legations. It is possible that General Nie gave verbal orders to allow Admiral Seymour to regain Tianjin, that is, to impede but not to annihilate. If this were the case, it would argue the highest degree of professional discipline and competence on the part of officers and men of the Imperial Chinese Army. We know that soldiers under General Yang who had good reason to hate the Boxers, never once turned their guns full onto the Boxers despite the fact that they were hard-pressed and vastly outnumbered. How much greater was the hatred felt by Chinese regular and irregular forces for the foreigners. The distinctive Chinese hatred for foreigners developed from the massacre of the Roman Catholics and the burning of the cathedral in Tianjin in 1870 until by 1900, it was a unique and extremely powerful force. It will be remembered that many of General Nie's soldiers came from exactly the same provinces and even probably in some cases, the same counties as the Boxers. As remarked on in the journals of the men of the invading forces and other foreigners, Chinese hatred of foreigners had a palpable quality the like of which those who had fought in the Philippines, in South Africa, in the Sudan or in New Zealand had not encountered before. From the journals kept by men on the Seymour expedition, we know that the Chinese regular army had cavalry, superior gunnery and the advantageous position on top of the embankment above the helpless sampans weighed down by wounded foreign soldiers. We know that Chinese artillery work was brilliant. Given these elements, there is no other possible explanation for the Seymour expedition regaining its base than that General Nie Shicheng had complete control not only of his own troops, but also of the Boxers who were now fighting side-by-side with the regular army. We must argue for high-ranking Chinese military men's awareness of the longer and broader range of consequences for China of the use of maximum available armed force in and around Tianjin in June and July 1900. We know from his correspondence that General Yang had such capacities and perceptions and we know that Chinese military philosophy was replete with such concepts.

The Chinese Imperial Army and the Siege of Tianjin

In Chapter Six, we noted the detrimental results of Boxer attacks on the Imperial Chinese Army in respect of the army's ability to defend China against its enemies. There has been no serious evaluation of the military role played by the Boxers in the battle of Tianjin. To do this lies outside the purvue of the present study but it is a subject that calls for attention. During this four week long battle, in-fighting occurred between the Boxers and General Nie's army and between the Lian army (composed of local Zhili men) and General Nie. It was Sawara Tokusake's opinion that if there had not been such in-fighting and Nie's army had been able to focus on fighting the foreigners, Nie would not have died and his army would not have been defeated. Tokusake then goes on to make the astonishing claim that this writer has not seen written up in the literature anywhere, that in the best traditions of *The Three Kingdoms*, in a vicious coup, the Boxers kidnapped General Nie's wife, children and eighty-three year old mother who was ill and infirm. Whether they were held as hostages and eventually killed or whether they were eventually released has as yet to be established. This blow fell on General Nie just as enemy reinforcements reached Tianjin and Nie's army had withdrawn from the walled city to the suburbs. We must pause a little here and look more closely at this event. It is indeed entirely consistent with the possible range of military tactics as described in *The Three Kingdoms*. Not only in romantic fiction but in reality, it was common in China for the families of leading military men to be punished, exiled or even put to death. This was not something that any of the Commanding Officers of any of the Allied invading armies had to take into consideration when campaigning.

Hearing of the Boxers' dastardly move in taking his family hostage, General Nie led part of his army in pursuit. The Lian army and the Boxers opened fire on General Nie's force and the Allied army was behind him so he was thus caught between the rebels and the invading enemy. Tokusake wrote of General Nie's feelings saying that despite his experience and the scores of wounds he had received fighting for his country, he was still misunderstood by the Court and insulted and bullied by the Boxers. He was quite aware of the fact that "recently the Bandit faction at Court was trying to purge those who were not on their side" and had accused him of colluding with foreigners. The effect of this on General Nie was that he wanted to cleanse himself of this calumny by dying for his country. His death, after deliberately facing enemy artillery fire was "most gruesome" according to Tokusake. The Court refused to grant posthumous compensation but "castigated him for awkward deployment [something that never happened to Admiral Seymour], allowing himself to be wounded and causing harm to his country. However, the people grieved over this."[144]

Tokusake's account strengthens the evidence already discussed in Chapter Six that the reactionary forces at Court were powerful enough at this time to blight the performance of one of China's greatest modern-trained armies. It is not surprising that General Yuan Shikai who commanded an army also composed in part of the original Huai soldiers trained by Li Hongzhang and expert in the use of state-of-the-art weaponry, did not hurry to bring his army to Beijing or Tianjin in support of his country. By their attitude, the reactionaries utterly crushed one of China's greatest Generals. The tragedy of General Nie is not merely that he was insulted beyond all bearing by contemporaries but that posterity in China and the West seems to have been determined to write him out of the record. Whatever in-fighting there was between the Allies as to who should be the first to enter Tianjin or Beijing, it was child's play in comparison with the sorts of personal and political pressure under which General Nie Shiceng had to take on the task of defending Tianjin.

The siege of Tianjin showed the Imperial Chinese Army employing a range of effective tactics. Traditional Chinese tactics included the flooding of trenches and designated areas to stop enemy advance,[145] the cutting of river banks and the draining of the river to prevent the passage of large vessels,[146] rapid and methodical entrenching and fortification,[147] ingenious use of cover,[148] extensive use of the cover of darkness, and effective intelligence, mapping, signals and communications.[149] Powder mines and torpedoes were laid and night attacks were frequent.[150] The foreign military writers observed and experienced the consequences of the excellence of Chinese logistics. General Yang's correspondence makes it clear that ammunition and other supplies could be moved through enemy infested territory as quickly and efficiently as needed.[151] General Frey's report noted the operations of an ambulance corps.

Adapting modern weapons to these traditional tactics proved equally successful. The Chinese moved or constructed gun batteries throughout the siege without being observed by the Allies.[152] Their use of smokeless powder made it difficult if not impossible to locate the Chinese guns.[153] The precision of the Chinese snipers, riflemen and gunners would have become the stuff of legends had their weapons been manned by men of almost any other race.

Oscar J. Upham, taking part in the siege of the Legations, recorded that two more men were wounded at the loopholes, one in the eye, one in the elbow,

> those Chinks have got it down pat, they can put five shots out of six through a loophole three inches square and don't need a field glass to do it either. [154]

The French Commander Vidal had remarked on the high value placed on precision marksmanship as he observed it during peace time training in January 1899. Describing the marksmanship of the troops, Vidal noted that at every target practice a supplementary allowance was issued at a rate of approximately seven francs for five blacks (or bullseyes), five for four and two for three. This allowance was paid on the spot. In an era when all over the world, soldiers pay was constantly in arrears, an incentive of this dimension should not go unremarked as indicative of the importance attached to the training of Chinese soldiers on Western weaponry. "Marksmanship is excellent" observed Vidal tersely. The action as described by the military of the eight invading armies did not uphold his assessment that the troops he had seen would be useless as they had seen no active service.[155]

Thanks to accurate intelligence, the location of the Allied troops and their officers was known within hours to the Chinese gunners. They immediately began shelling the houses and warehouses concerned, destroying the buildings often before the Allies had completely settled in.[156] General Dorward and his staff chose the Temperance Hall for their quarters:

> Not more than six different sorts of shells struck the Temperance Hall … in about ten minutes, clearly proving that the Chinese spies had given us away. Two shells, fortunately both "blind," passed through the table where the Royal Artillery officers were at lunch, without hurting anyone. They ceased lunching. A shrapnel burst in the main entrance hall making a great mess, but hurting no one. The next was not so kind, for passing through in the same flight, it burst in the yard behind, and wounded Lieutenant Browne, R. E.… We all left the Temperance Hall for more retired quarters.… We had, that afternoon, an example of the excellence of the Chinese Intelligence Department … a shell burst on the verandah of the dining room [of the house to which the officers had moved]. Shortly after, another came into the bathroom of the room above the dining room … About the same time, Mr Cousens, into whose house General Dorward had moved, was hit in the leg by a sniper while he was in bed.[157]

An assessment of the quality of the Imperial Chinese Army was given in the US War Department's *Reports on Military Operations in South Africa and China*.

> The Chinese army, threatening the allies and opposing their advance to Pekin, was superior in fighting qualities to any previously known to Europeans. In addition to the modern weapons and the training received from their foes, the Chinese were inspired by hatred of foreigners and religious fanaticism to an intrepidity foreign to their ordinary habits, as shown by their repeated fierce attacks and stubborn resistance when themselves attacked. They had ample supplies of all kinds of modern warlike stores, the extent of their preparation being shown by [the Xigu and Western arsenal]. The heavy artillery at the disposal of the allies was markedly inadequate, and was much inferior to the Chinese, which seemed to increase daily in weight, and was worked with remarkable efficiency. It was believed by many that the positions of the allied troops from time to time were signalled … by spies inside the lines.[158]

In his journal of the siege of Tianjin, Captain Bayly of the British Royal Navy made frequent mention of the inadequacy of the guns at the disposal of the invading Allied forces:

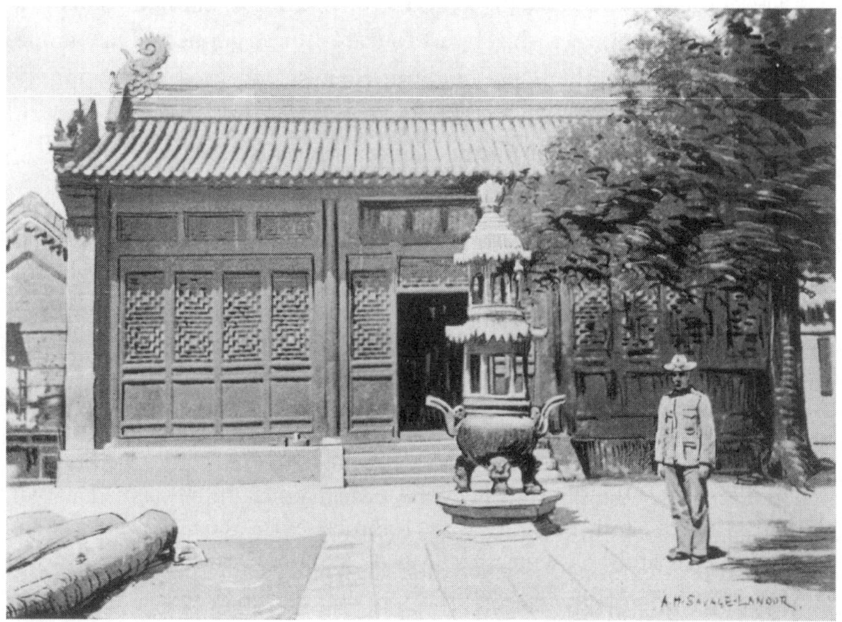

Figure 7.8(a) Although one of the armouries in Tianjin looked like this….

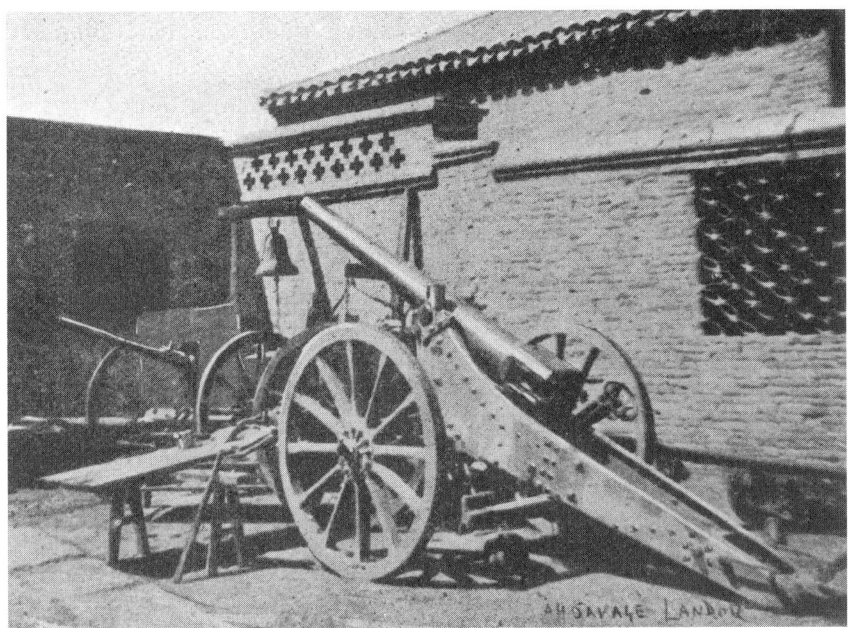

Figure 7.8(b) We can see from Savage-Landor's photographs that it contained the most modern guns in the world.[159]

> Having only the abominable 9-pounder ML field gun and 16-pounder QF available, can do little to annoy or silence guns in the Native City. The black smoke gives away the 9-pounder and its range is poor.[160]

Lieutenant Bernard Holbrooke of the British army when reviewing the whole campaign wrote:

> [the Chinese] fought well at Tientsin [sic] … at the best they are … the equal of the Boers … in artillery. They have hundreds of guns and their practice is wonderful; also their shells and fuses good — all our losses are nearly due to artillery fire.[161]

Above all, the siege of Tianjin which lasted for four weeks,[162] showed the Imperial Chinese Army inflicting heavy casualties on the Allies, defeating the Russian Cossacks in several engagements, severely punishing British and French sorties attempting to silence their guns, and decimating the American contingent in the final battle which resulted in the taking of Tianjin on 14 July. According to Sawara Tokusake, the Boxers had been severely punished by General Nie's troops and so they had taken "to pillaging here and there. waiting to see which way the action would turn."[163] The Amerian war correspondent Sydney Adamson gives a superb account of the way the Chinese gunners pinned down the US Ninth Infantry during the battle to take the walled city of Tianjin. His language allows us a rare glimpse of the effects of Chinese fire power on the enemy:

> Now the tide of men had stopped rushing through the gate and a bloody stream of wounded began to flow back. Twisted, dirty heaps that a few minutes before were bright, tidy Japanese soldiers were brought out and laid in rows. On their clothes were great Venetian-red patches, grayed with mud and covered with swarms of ravenous flies. A few writhed and groaned; others lay still. One seldom looks twice to tell the dead. There is a color, a something indescribable, that tells when life is gone, often the living were more awful to look at than the dead. I had seen men shot with bullets, but this was the first time that I had seen men mangled by shells.[164]

Brigadier General A. S. Daggett wrote of this battle, "no regiment in the service, regular or volunteer, was in so trying a situation during the recent wars as was the Ninth infantry on that dreadful day."[165] Frederick May Wise's accounts of some of the unsuccessful attacks by the Allies on Tianjin give evidence of Chinese fighting ability. Wise also offers the insight that the attack on 13 July showed the inadequate military deployment, weaponry and logistic support of the attacking Powers. In addition he wrote that:

> Somebody said the whole day's show had been the idea of the Japanese, who told the Allied Council that if we made a demonstration in force against the walls, the Chinese would lose their guts.[166]

The myth of the moribund Empire waiting to be divided by the vigorous Western nations was incompatible with an image of courageous soldiers fighting with fierce determination to hold off the combined forces of seven Western countries and the Japanese week after week. However this view of the moribund Empire was a commonly-held one.[167] It could not co-exist with the reality of a highly-trained army using modern weapons and ammunition to greater effect than their enemies who had to call for reinforcements to be able to take Beijing after four weeks of hard fighting in and around Tianjin. It is partly due to the strength of the pre-existing myth that the facts about the ability of the Imperial Chinese Army as recorded by the soldiers fighting against it, did not enter into the Western data base. The strength of this myth has prevented posterity from forming a detailed and accurate assessment of the degree of success in modernising selected armies in China. Most notably, it has prevented an evaluation of the fighting qualities of the soldiers and officers of the Imperial Chinese Army as demonstrated by the events of May, June and July 1900.

The literature does not detail the nature and extent of military resistance by the Chinese regular or irregular forces or the civilian population after the fall of Tianjin. It was three weeks before the Allied forces obtained sufficient reinforcements to march to the relief of the Legations. During this time Tianjin was shelled by Chinese regular forces and pinned down by sniper fire from Boxers. Chinese soldiers continued to harass the Allies. This also contributed to the thinking that caused the Allied command to estimate the strength of Chinese military opposition so highly. Although they were acutely aware that delay could and probably would[168] result in the massacre of the foreigners in the Legations in Beijing, they were unprepared to march on to Beijing without reinforcements.[169] A balanced assessment of the performance of the Chinese army would suggest a marked improvement since the Sino-Japanese War. History is full of "might-have-beens" but might the British have lost Trafalgar had Nelson been killed during the first hour of battle? With men like General Yang under his command, if General Nie had had the unconditional support of the Court instead of having to fight, knowing that his enemies had impeached him, might the battle of Tianjin have ended differently? One thing remains certain, in the judgment of the soldiers of the Allied armies the Chinese were a worthy foe.

Reflections

The making of erroneous assumptions and generalisations concerning the inevitable superiority in all situations of Western arms technology, in contrast with the primitive weapons of non-white opponents has been questioned by a number of historians in a number of contexts. Likewise, the relationship of arms technology to characterisation of fighting ability as (in the case of the Chinese) "uncivilised," "meek," "treacherous," "bloodthirsty and cruel," or "neglected sons of Mars" has been discussed in the literature.[170] Zhang Junbo and Yao Yunzhu explain that traditional Chinese military thinking "allots a weightier part to the human factor while the Westerners give a higher priority to the weapons factor."[171] There are still many Western writers who, knowing that one of the protagonists in a given war came out of a Western military culture and the other did not, assume that all victories were naturally the result of superior weapons technology without examining the details of the war or the battle in question. This assumption underlies the mind-set of a great many Western scholars in their evaluation of the degree of success of China's military modernisation in the nineteenth century.[172]

Recently John W. Garver, in a review of Zhang Shuguang's book *Mao's Military Romanticism: China and the Korea War, 1950–1953*, noted that Zhang's main contribution lies in his detailed military history of the Korean War from the Chinese side. "Zhang details exactly how Chinese forces adapted to and countered American technological and material supremacy in Korea to fight the war to what China's leaders viewed as a victorious conclusion."[173] What these military contexts have in common is that despite the actual performance of the enemy in battle, myths arose concerning these different enemies and their fighting ability. In the remarkable case of the Seymour rout, leading officers on the disastrous foray used the language of victory to describe their retreat. Officers on the Seymour expedition reported that Allied soldiers lost or threw away valuable artillery pieces, they were pinned down by accurate Chinese gunnery and were able to regain their base with high casualty rates only because they were rescued by a 2,000 man sortie from Tianjin. No journalist of the day could see beyond the mythical aura surrounding Admiral Seymour as the gallant leader of a glorious defeat. The public, certainly the British public, was quite prepared to accept the version of Admiral Seymour as hero. The working class American public were served a version showing Captain McCalla as hero. McCalla had brought extra supplies of food and water without which it is certain that very few men on that expedition would have survived. There were similarities between Western and Chinese illustrated newspapers in that both were able to present a pictorial image of the enemy without viciously caricaturing that enemy as "demon," or "yellow peril," or "foreign devil." There was no similarity in the Chinese press with regard to the glorification of the gallant leader who failed utterly. General Nie's performance was not written up for the Chinese in their press as heroic. He was not named "a matyr" for his country. We shall now so name him.

The case of China in 1900 takes the relationship between pre-existing stereotype, present action and resulting myth to an extreme. Chinese military capacity in the late Qing exists as a composite of myths regarding Chinese soldiery. There are many strands to this composite of myths. There is a refusal to acknowledge the extent to which the Chinese possessed and used modern weapons. There is a dearth of studies showing the re-assessment of Chinese military preparedness after defeats by foreigners and threats from internal revolts.[174] Any detailed and explicit reference to successful Chinese military action in 1900 has been omitted. There has been an unchallenged acceptance of the Allied invasion of Beijing as indicative of outright victory consequent on superior weapons, logistics, fighting power and military intelligence. The campaign, in fact, demonstrated startling weaknesses in all these aspects. In the same year when it was evident that the Boers, like the Chinese, possessed superior artillery, indignant letters were written to *The Times*. The Boers used field glasses and the British army had not been issued with them. This was regarded as reprehensible on the part of the War Office. The Americans noted during the siege of the Legations that the Chinese were such extraordinarily fine marksmen that they did not need field glasses.

No such letters were written about the Chinese whose ability and equipment, were regarded by soldiers who took part in both wars as superior to that of the Boers. Moreover, the notion of outright victory having been gained by the invading armies when they reached Beijing was questioned by Western observers of the day. It is of extreme military significance that a major consideration in the withdrawal of foreign troops was a common awareness by all senior officers that they lacked sufficient logistic support to remain in Beijing for another winter. With the benefit of hindsight, we may also reflect on the fact that because of the actions of the Generals commanding the five armies of the Wu Wei, these five armies were entirely or largely intact. The invading armies withdrew. The Boxer Protocol was imposed. Memories of near failure faded quickly. What emerged as part of a nation's and a culture's self-image was "a tradition of victory."[175] In the case of the British navy, this tradition was so strong that it could even turn defeat into victory, especially when it involved the dashing men and gallant leaders of the Senior Service.[176] In his memoirs, Admiral Seymour wrote of the British defeat by the Chinese at Dagu in August 1859:

> The boom proved too strong to be passed; our people behaved with great pluck and energy, but kept before the guns of the forts the fire was too hot and some of our vessals [sic] were sunk.... [The British tried to take the forts by land

> assault.] *It was probably a forlorn hope, and it failed; but we had incurred no dishonour.* The Admiral was wounded, and many officers and men killed and wounded.[177] [emphasis added]

Chinese forces when they failed automatically incurred dishonour and the taint of this "dishonour" even tarnished the distinguished performance of individual Chinese military leaders and their men to such an extent that little or nothing of their record appears in Western accounts of the Boxer rising. For different reasons, little or nothing of their record appears in Chinese accounts, not only of the Boxer War but of the Sino-Japanese War. The fact was that the "victors" were subsequently unable to consolidate their victory. The fact was that they had to leave or to sign treaties that did not give them the total power their victory at arms was expected to achieve. These facts indicate that what may be regarded as victory by one side may equally well have been built into a tradition of victory by the other side. The events of 1911 and 1949 prevented this happening in China in the case of the events of 1900 but it had happened before in Chinese military history and was to happen again.

Contemporaries saw that by removing her court, the Empress Dowager rendered the Allied victory meaningless.[178] Diplomatic correspondence fulminated against the skill of the Chinese officials in outmanoeuvring Western diplomats in the peace talks which were to formalise the terms of China's punishment for the throne's complicity in the Boxer troubles. Beijing was taken on 14 August 1900. The Boxer Protocol was signed over a year later on 7 September 1901. Political changes in twentieth century China have meant that the Imperial Chinese Army has been portrayed in Chinese history books in an extremely negative and simplistic light. However, it would be well within the Chinese tradition of looking at defeat and victory in warfare in terms of the longue durée, to revise the view of the events of 1900. A revised view would see the Chinese military response to them as indicative of a far more complex conception of what was entailed for China by the invasion of its sovereign territory by eight armies representing the most powerful countries in the world at that time.

The remarkable fact about the body of writing produced by professional military men is that when the victors took out their campaign-stained journals to compose their official reports or their memoirs, they wrote in a vein which eschewed the manufacture of data to support a simplistic view of right and wrong. They were all able to give many and precise examples of military excellence and courage on the part of their enemies. Yet by the time these memoirs were published, they reached a more esoteric audience and did not form part of mainstream culture either in newspaper reports or in histories of the Chinese army or the Boxer War. In the public and military mind there exists the concept of a "hierarchy of enemies" before battle is joined. Thus it may be that an enemy can be defeated and yet be regarded both in the contemporary public eye and by subsequent military writers as a skilful and heroic fighter. If this is the case, and the New Zealand Maori Wars afford examples of the phenomenon, then a pre-existing favourable image may predispose the popular mind to be receptive to new factual data about the success of alternative battle tactics, or the surprising effectiveness of non–Western-European weapons and fortifications, or even skill in the use of high technology weapons by non-white foes. The role of the press in sustaining or altering the image of the enemy is cardinal. After the relief of the besieged Legations, the missionary voice found strident expression in the pages of the popular press, particularly in America.[179] Sober accounts of the astounding accuracy of Chinese military intelligence and fire-power did not. Hence,

> the strange idea, which refuses to be eradicated, that the Chinese showed themselves in this Peking siege once and for all incompetent to carry to fruition any military plan, may be somewhat corrected by the plain and convincing terms in which the eyewitness describes the manner in which they stayed their hand whenever it could have slain, and the silent struggle which the Moderates of Chinese politics must have waged to avert the catastrophe by merely gaining time and allowing the Desperates to dash themselves to pieces when the inevitable swing of the pendulum took place.[180]

The notion of an effective military weapon exists as much in men's minds as in the capacity of the weapon itself.[181] Military history affords countless examples of rules placed upon the use of a weapon to limit its effectiveness either absolutely or under particular conditions or against a particular enemy. The history of the Western world from 1960 to 1980 was dogged by the consciousness of the existence of weapons, the capacity of which could only be limited by not using them at all. The effectiveness of a military weapon is thus not a finite given. The conservatism concerning changes in weapons technology illustrated by men in all cultures who have to use weapons to kill or be killed, is an inevitable concomitant of their mortal potential. However, attitudes towards weapons technology are not evenly evaluated by many scholars writing out of the Western cultural tradition. Thus Maori eagerness to seize Western firearms and use them effectively has been discussed in the literature for some time whereas Chinese drives not only to buy modern weapons but to manufacture them successfully in China, have not.[182]

Weapons technology can be seen to be not merely the capacity for death or destruction, but also a cultural construct which is a product of a particular historical environment. In Western Europe it was once allied to the notion of chivalry. Ideas about what constituted "chivalry" had had decisive implications for the ways weapons could be used until their demise in their then form at the battle of Agincourt. Such ideas retained currency in other forms and could be seen in the British Parliamentary debate on the use of explosive bullets against the Boers in 1900. Explosive bullets, it was argued, could be used against certain types of otherwise unstoppable natives but it was not deemed correct to use them against white Protestant Boers.[183]

In China, early technological advances in the use of weaponry and related tactical and strategic thinking developed sufficiently to answer the needs of the state until the nineteenth century. Where they did not so develop, the Chinese did not hesitate to borrow from Western knowledge and Western technology.[184] A reading of Sun Zi in almost any translation makes it clear that in Chinese military thinking, weapons technology was very low in priority. Charles Hucker's essay gives a lucid case-study of the Chinese preference for the defensive.[185] Basil Liddell Hart remarked in his introduction to General Samuel Griffith's translation that it was time Chinese officers returned to the study of Sun Zi "since in that one short book was embodied almost as much about the fundamentals of strategies and tactics as I had covered in more than twenty books."[186]

During the second half of the nineteenth century the similarities between China and the West in the factors forcing the development of arms manufacture, professional military training colleges and modern armies, are greater, on balance, than the differences. There was certainly a tremendous gap between the industrial base behind weapons development in China and that of the West. However, the degree of stimulation to and bifurcation of such development posed by internal revolts against the dynasty was a factor in China that did not exist to any comparable degree in the West. Likewise, the difficulties in the perennial struggle between the Court striving for central control and the regions striking out for autonomy became a factor in late nineteenth century China which had no parallel in any Western country at that time. Furthermore, the division inside the Court between the conservative faction and the modernising faction could literally mean life or death — or at the very least, exile and permanent disgrace — for the officials concerned. Such considerations were not a factor in the thinking of civilian or military leaders in Britain, Europe, Russia, America or Japan. In China, military modernisation was tied to the adoption of foreign thinking and foreign technologies; General Nie Shicheng was accused of having "Christian soldiers" in his army and impeached. He was one at the end of a very long line of men with a similar fate and for today's reader, there is more than a frisson as we think of what in-depth association with any form of Western culture or knowledge meant in China during the anti-Rightist movement and the Cultural Revolution. These kinds of internal factors had little or no parallel in the development of the military mind outside China. External stimulus such as defeat in war or fear of competition from a rival power, however, had the same sort of effect on leaders in China as it did in Britain and Western Europe.[187] There was certainly a difference of degree and also a crucial difference because stimulus to military expenditure and change in China did not effect one unified national army but was piecemeal in its application.

Conservatism in political and military circles regarding innovations in the organisation, training and equipment of the armed forces, was a major factor not only in China but also in some Western countries in the nineteenth century, as was reluctance to increase military budget expenditure. Nor should it be seen that China recognised the need to develop all aspects of its military capacity solely in order to defend herself against the West. Major influences in the thinking of powerful statesmen in China were the need to have independent means of suppressing internal rebellion and keeping the Empire united without having recourse to foreign military advice or assistance. There was also the imperative of being able to forestall changes in the regional power balance consequent on the expansionist ambitions of Japan and Russia.

As the rivalry between Western European states forced changes on the British military, particularly the navy, in the mid-nineteenth century, so did fear of Japan allow Li Hongzhang to secure funds to begin building up a navy. However, he and his generals read Sun Zi and not Clausewitz. Li was at all times well aware that the Chinese navy was inferior and so he rejected policies that would lead to "an eventual settlement of issues by force,"[188] "When he concentrates, prepare against him; where he is strong, avoid him." Furthermore, Li was well aware that "even if the foreigners were defeated, they could withdraw beyond reach only to return with additional strength when they chose."[189] Both Generals Ma Yukun and Nie Shicheng had served either under Li or, in the case of Nie Shicheng, had joined Li's Huai army under Liu Mingchuan in 1862.

What should the "correct" response have been? If Generals Nie Shiceng, Song Qing and Yuan Shikai had joined forces and wiped out the eight invading armies in the battle of Tianjin, what effect would this have had on subsequent Chinese history? We may ask this question for we may be reasonably sure that Generals Nie and Yuan at least asked themselves the question. They had fought against the Japanese. They had foreign-trained officers. Some of their men had been being foreign-drilled for thirty years. They read Sun Zi, not Clausewitz. This cannot be over-emphasised. In the short term, they could have wiped out the foreign invaders but each General had a view that included at least two factors. First, the foreigners would regroup and return in greater strength and with greater force of anger. Second, in Chinese military thought there is much emphasis on retaining the fighting strength of one's army. General Nie Shicheng's response in a hopeless position was the perfect response. Fight successfully and courageously, die in battle leading a strong resistance and leave an army almost intact. His response thus outlined, contains the best of Western and Chinese military thinking and tradition. General Nie died gloriously. He sacrificed himself but did not throw away his army. Not surprisingly, General Yang Mushi could look back on the performance of the army of the Vanguard and not have a crushing sense of defeat "I have been able to restore my former outlook and am more content than one could hope for."[190]

In terms of political and military awareness of the country's preparedness for war, there were many Chinese civilian and military leaders[191] towards the end of the Qing dynasty whose grasp of all the factors involved was as great as that of the British High Command in the Crimea or the Russian, French or German High Command in the 1914–1918 War. There were a select few whose understanding was greater. Chinese soldiers and statesmen had to include factors in their thinking that were of a high order of complexity, of immediate import and exclusive to Chinese political and military exigencies. At the same time, they had to be aware of the fact that exclusively Chinese exigencies might have to take priority over all. Lucien Bodard's *La Vallée des Roses* describes the parallel influence of these two factors on Chinese military performance in 1860.[192] The principal differences between Chinese and Western armies lay not in weapons technology, training, logistics and supply, methods of recruitment or even pay. The differences required an understanding that Court politics had far more decisive consequences for the leaders of modern-trained armies than was the case for Japan and the West and furthermore, that they concerned the fragmented nature of the military structure itself.[193] The nature of the command system in late Qing armies was based on a spirit of personal and often regional loyalty and was not highly integrated with easily replaceable and transferable officers. A crucial difference concerned cultural and political attitudes to the High Command, some of which undoubtedly arose from the effect of the study of Chinese military classics regarding the art of war. Other differences, however, came from fifty years experience of protracted internal warfare in major rebellions and insurgencies, as well as wars against the British, the French and the Japanese. Yet others came from a situation in which an alien dynasty wished to keep its power over China.

When Yuan Shikai refused to bring his army to the aid of the Court in 1900, he had many reasons for doing so. To have defeated the Allies would have brought further difficulties on China and possible difficulties for the victorious general;[194] to have lost would have been to lose his valuable army. The result of his action mirrored Sun Zi's writings on offensive strategy which to those inculcated at Saint Cyr, Sandhurst or West Point in the writings of Clausewitz would have appeared as incomprehensible nonsense.

> It is best to keep one's own army, battalion, company, or five-man squad intact; to rush the enemy's army … is only second best. So to win a hundred victories in a hundred battles is not the highest excellence; the highest excellence is to subdue the enemy's army without fighting at all.[195]

The least desirable alternatives in offence were to attack the enemy's army and to attack cities.[196] In writing of offensive strategy, Sun Zi's remarks on the ways in which a ruler can bring misfortune on his army[197] are also indicative of military thinking and its relationship to civilian authority that would have seemed like treason to late nineteenth century German, British or French officers and High Command. Yet the maxim, "He whose generals are able and not interfered with by the sovereign will be victorious"[198] bears reflection. The difficulties of Generals Nie and Yang were made insoluble by lack of clear consistent directives from the Court. Sun Zi had written "There are occasions when the commands of the sovereign need not be obeyed."[199] These remarks are necessarily simplified as this is not the place for an in-depth study of Chinese military initiatives in 1900 in the light of the overall context of Chinese strategic thinking. Nevertheless although the Chinese still had some way to go, they had come a very long way in a very short time in terms of their military preparedness for a wider range of strategic threat than that facing any Western country. This assessment of China's drive for military modernisation prepares a background to events in the twentieth century that has far greater historic logic than the hitherto unchallenged assumption that the events of 1900 demonstrated hopeless inferiority on the part of the Chinese both as fighting men and as the designers, producers and purchasers of modern military technology.

The first six weeks of the Boxer rising beginning with incidents involving Westerners in late May 1900, as discussed, seemed to many contemporary foreigners resident in China to have been decisively successful:

> The purpose of the rising has been so far successful that almost all foreigners in the interior apart from the treaty ports have been either murdered at their posts or forced to flee for their lives with the loss of all their property, whilst armed hordes of the "Boxers" and affiliated native troops have continuously bombarded and virtually destroyed the foreign settlements at Tientsin and Taku and the railways and other property throughout the region, and have forcibly prevented the rescue of the foreign Ministers and residents at Peking, who have been besieged in the Legations for over a month subject to incessant attack, and being, at the last advice, reduced to utter exhaustion and despair.[200]

"The highest excellence is to subdue the enemy's army without fighting at all." On the face of it after the eight invading armies occupied Beijing, this is actually what the Chinese did. A situation existed in which the armies of the eight invading Powers had to withdraw. While the governments of some of the eight Allied Powers clearly intended their armies to withdraw, no research has yet been done to demonstrate conclusively the intentions of all the governments involved. Only brief mention has been made of continued Chinese armed resistance. The effectiveness of this armed resistance needs further elucidating as do the questions as to precisely why the foreign armies withdrew; what exactly were the factors deliberated by the Commanders. After 1945, there was foreign armed presence in Germany and Japan for a lot longer than eighteen months. By 1898, the Powers were openly hungering to divide China. Although "victorious" in 1900, it was beyond the capacity of Western countries to ensure large permanent potentially deterrent military forces on Chinese soil. As to Russian and Japanese intentions, further research needs to be done. Most notably, their "victory" did not enable them to partition China at their hest. What, if anything, did Russia and Japan learn from their "victory"? We are reminded of the prophetic words of the French Captain d'Amade written in January 1888:

> In the event of a war, the military efforts made by China to increase its standing army and perfect its armaments will be beyond all rational forethought ... *this power will always adapt its pace to that of its adversary.*[201] [emphasis added]

The Japanese High Command did not digest thoughtfully the performance of Chinese regular and irregular forces in 1900.

Manuscript reports by American officers of the Sixth Cavalry describe successful Chinese resistance around Tianjin until 19 August although the city was taken and occupied by Allied forces on 14 July. This resistance, while not mentioned in the literature was of such a calibre that it "had been threatening our lines of communication and ... attack [on] the city."[202] While the sack of Beijing looms large in popular accounts and subsequent history books, there was an uneasy recognition by contemporaries that this victory of arms was hollow and meaningless. Centred on the flight of the Empress Dowager who continued to hold court, issue edicts and function effectively as shown by the compromises the Western diplomats were forced to make, the concept of "a tradition of victory" which had seemed so evident in the case of the British navy, now seemed less concrete, more elusive. Generals Ma and Nie were dead, Boxers were being shot and Princes were being hanged, but armed resistance to the Allies continued and was seen to continue. China was intact. Her most modern armies were intact. Let Bertram L. Simpson say the last word:

> We might have known that this loose jointed relief expedition could accomplish nothing, we would do everything wrong; and still we were acting as if everything was in our own hands.[203]

Notes*

1. James Belich, *The New Zealand Wars and the Victorian Interpretation of Racial Conflict*, Auckland University Press, New Zealand, 1986, pp. 12–13.
2. Jürgen Petschull, *Der Wahn vom Weltreich. Die Geschichte der Deutschen Kolonien*, Thomas Höpker, Würzburg, 1984, pp. 188–189. My thanks to Margaret Hosking for drawing this reference to my attention.
3. Joanna Waley-Cohen, "Religion, War, and Empire-Building in Eighteenth Century China," *The International History Review*, Vol. 20, No. 2. June 1998. During the 1770s in the Qianlong Emperor's wars in the Jinchuan area, the centre of the Tibetan Bon religion, the use of magic, hidden charms and loud chanting by Tibetan monks unnerved Qing troops and was responsible for undermining their morale as well as desertion.
4. Warned of a possible coup d'état against the Empress Dowager, Yuan Shikai put himself and his army at her disposal, effectively ending the coup and thus the Reform Movement led by the young Emperor.
5. By 1896 there was open discussion in the Shanghai press not merely of the possibility of the partitioning of China, but of its actual occurrence and what each power would get out of it. Captain Meillet referred to this in his report, Armée, Series 7N1674, p. 136. In Captain Meillet's opinion, such discussions were pointless as the country was too big and populous to be thus divided against the will of its peoples.
6. Nevertheless, popular tradition named General Dong as the man who fought the foreigners in Tianjin (see Chapter Three). We have seen how General Nie's actions with regard to the railway and the Boxers made him unpopular with the common people. However, it was Nie, not Dong who was initially responsible for the defence of Tianjin.
7. George Lynch, *The War of the Civilisations. Being a Record of a "Foreign Devil's" Experiences with the Allies in China*, Longmans, Green and Co., London, 1901. pp. 107–108.
8. US Department of State. Documents on the China Crisis (hereafter referred to as *China)*. Letters from Rear-Admiral Kempff to the Secretary of the Navy, 12 June and 17 June 1900.
9. There was an awareness that Chinese usages did not always respect the neutrality of bearers of diplomatic papers. A precedent that had shocked European minds was the imprisonment of the British diplomat Henry Parkes and members of his party in 1860 when they went ahead of the Anglo-French forces under a

* Many officers were promoted between the time of the Boxer War and the publication of their journals or memoirs. This accounts for the discrepancy in rank sometimes to be found when discussing the same officer.

flag of truce. It is not clear that the Chinese understood the conventions related to a flag of truce at that time.

10. Ruffi de Pontèves, *Souvenirs de la Colonne Seymour*, Librairie Plon, Paris, 1903, pp. 271–272.
11. "Photographies prises en Chine par le Commandant Corvisart, Attaché Militaire à la Légation de France au Japon, 1900." Manuscript Albums held at the Musée de l'Armée de Terre, Château de Vincennes, Paris, Album No. 1.
12. Frederick A. Sharf and Peter Harrington, *China, 1900. The Eyewitnesses Speak. The Boxer Rebellion as Described by Participants in Letters, Diaries and Photographs*, Greenhill Books, London, 2000, p. 93.
13. There is disagreement in the eye witness sources about the exact time the Dagu guns opened up; sources place the time between a little before 1 am and 0145h.
14. Chester C. Tan, *The Boxer Catastrophe*, Octagon Books Inc., New York, 1967. p. 70. See also Lin Huaguo, "Some Questions Concerning the High Tide of the Boxer Movement," pp. 142–145, in D. D. Buck (ed.), *Recent Studies of the Boxer Movement: Chinese Studies in History*, Vol. 20, No. 3–4, M. E. Sharpe Inc., New York, 1987.
15. Work needs to be done to clarify exactly when and where Boxers fought with or against units of the Imperial Chinese Army.
16. *Reports on Military Operations in South Africa and China*, War Department, Adjutant General's Office, No. XXXIII, Government Printing Office, Washington, 1901 (hereafter referred to as *Military Operations*), p. 533. The reason given by Purcell for the shelling of the Dagu forts cannot be found in any contemporary account (Victor W. Purcell, *The Boxer Uprising. A Background Study*, Cambridge University Press, Great Britain, 1963, p. 251). Esherick's description of the events at Dagu is also incorrect and misleading. He says, "the Powers felt compelled to issue an ultimatum for the surrender of the forts the next day — and then seized them an hour before the time was up," Joseph W. Esherick, *The Origins of the Boxer Uprising*, University of California Press, Berkeley, 1987, 302–303. That is, according to Esherick, no battle took place at all. Both Esherick's sources China — No. 3 (1900) "Correspondence Respecting the Insurrectionary Movement in China" (British Parliamentary Papers) p. 63 and *The Boxer Rising: A History of the Boxer Trouble in China*, reprinted from the "Shanghai Mercury," Paragon Book Reprint Corp., New York, 1967, p. 17 describe the battle accurately. Paul A. Cohen, *History in Three Keys. The Boxers as Event, Experience, and Myth*, Columbia University, New York, 1997, p. 50, describes the events at Dagu on 16–17 June as follows: the "foreign ships off the coast issued an ultimatum to the occupants of the Dagu forts on June 16 and seized them the following day." Again there is no mention of the battle. Roger R. Thompson, "Military Dimensions of the 'Boxer Uprising' in Shanxi, 1898–1901," in Hans van de Ven (ed.), *Warfare in Chinese History*, Sinica Leidensia,

Vol. 47, Brill, Leiden, 2000, p. 303 follows Cohen with the result that the reader has no idea that a savage artillery duel took place between the forces of the Imperial Chinese Army and the seven attacking Allied Powers. Bernard A. Weisberger, "Righteous Fists: The Boxer Rebellion Casts a Harsh and Vivid Light on America's Long Complex Relationship with China," *American Heritage*, Vol. 48, No. 3, May–June 1997, Part 14 (2) describes the events of Dagu, the Seymour rout and the siege of Tianjin as follows: "An International relief force of some nine thousand men … fought its way inland from the coast where it had easily landed under naval cover." My thanks to Dr Gerry Groot for drawing my attention to this reference. The battle of Dagu may have been short, but it was the first clash between the invading Powers and the Imperial Chinese Army, it was a key battle and it was a battle that had an extremely high profile at the time and even into 1901 with the making of a film of the battle. To omit reference to it or to deny that it took place is obviously unacceptable and is an example of a regrettable tendency in American scholarship which belittles or ignores Chinese military ability. The work of revisionist scholars Allen Fung and Joanna Waley-Cohen is important in this context as it indicates an awareness that there is a need for a reappraisal of all aspects of Chinese military preparedness. Allen Fung, "Testing the Self-Strengthening: The Chinese Army in the Sino-Japanese War of 1894–1895," *Modern Asian Studies*, Vol. 30, No. 4, 1996; Joanna Waley-Cohen, "China and Western Technology in the Late Eighteenth Century," *American Historical Review*, Vol. 98, No. 5, 1993 and *The Sextants of Beijing. Global Currents in Chinese History*, W. W. Norton, New York, 1999.

17. Rear-Admiral Bowman H. McCalla, "Memoirs of a Naval Career," typed manuscript held in the Marine Archives, Quantical, Virginia, USA undated.
18. *China*, op cit. Letter from Rear-Admiral Kempff to the Secretary of the Navy, 18 June 1900. See also *Military Operations*, op cit., p. 534.
19. McCalla, op cit., Ch. 28, p. 10.
20. *Military Operations*, op cit., p. 535.
21. Ibid., p. 533.
22. *The North China Herald and Supreme Court and Consular Gazette*, 26 June 1900.
23. Captain Paul Schlieper, *Meine Kriegs-Erlebnisse in China. Die Expedition Seymour*, Wilhelm Köhler, Westfalen, 1902. p. 8. For an interesting and detailed pictorial view of the state of the art of the Russian navy at the turn of the century, see Ron Blum, *The Siege at Port Arthur. The Russo-Japanese War Through the Stereoscope*, Adelaide, 1987.
24. *China*, op cit., Letter from Rear-Admiral Kempff to the Secretary of the Navy, 18 June 1900. See also *Military Operations*, op cit., p. 534.
25. Schlieper, op cit., p. 18 describes the extreme difficulty which confronted the German marines when they attempted to disembark. Schlieper attributes this to the particular conditions at Dagu.
26. McCalla, op cit., p. 10.

27. *Military Operations*, op cit., p. 535.
28. *China*, op cit., Letter from Admiral Kempff to the Secretary of the Navy, 18 June 1900.
29. Sharf and Harrington, *China, 1900. The Eyewitnesses Speak*, op cit., p. 96.
30. De Pontèves, op cit., p. 279 claimed that the shot had come from the *Lion*.
31. Frederick A. Sharf and Peter Harrington, *The Boxer Rebellion. China, 1900. The Artists' Perspective*, Greenhill Books, London, 2000, p. 45.
32. "Photographies prises en Chine par le Commandant Corvisart, Album No. 1, Photograph, No. 13.
33. *Twenty-first Century*, 15 February 2001.
34. Arnold H. Savage-Landor, *China and the Allies*, William Heinemann, London, 1901, 2 vols. Vol. 1, p. 178.; *Military-Operations*, op cit., p. 544; Sharf and Harrison, *China, 1900. The Eyewitnesses Speak*, op cit., pp. 203 and 237.
35. Neither Paul H. Clements, *The Boxer Rebellion: A Political and Diplomatic Review*, AMS Press, Inc., New York, 1967 (1915); Tan, op cit., George Nye Steiger, *China and the Occident. The Origins and Developments of the Boxer Movement*, Rusell and Rusell, New York, 1966; Esherick, op cit., nor Cohen, op cit., mention the military action at all. Purcell describes the battle of Dagu in one sentence (op cit., p. 251) and Duiker's brief discussion makes no mention of keen Chinese artillery action. See William J Duiker, *Cultures in Collision: The Boxer Rebellion*, Presidio Press, California, 1978.
36. *North China Herald*, 25 June 1900.
37. There are no scholarly English-language accounts of the Boxer rising which give accurate or detailed descriptions revealing the extent of preparedness and the military ability of the Chinese defending the Dagu forts.
38. A motion picture was made in 1901 of the battle of Dagu and may be seen in the Library of Congress. There is also a film of the taking of the walls of Beijing by the Ninth Cavalry. These films are very brief and very primitive. Nevertheless, at this stage of the development of the motion picture, their impact would have been extremely forceful. (Motion pictures were first shown in America in 1896). The films are also testimony to the fact that these high-profile battles stayed longer in the forefront of the consciousness of the public at the turn of the last century, than would be the case today.
39. "Photographies prises en Chine par le Commandant Corvisart," op cit., Album No. 1, Photograph No. 15.
40. Ibid., Album No. 7, Photograph No. 17.
41. Pierre Lorain, "Les Armes de la Guerre des Boxeurs 1900–1901," *Gazette des Armes*, No. 76, 1980, p. 27. "If the strength of the Allied Expeditionary Force was disproportionate to the regular and irregular Chinese forces, the technical superiority of their weapons was nonetheless crushing." Lorain was able to make this statement because of inadequate information concerning the weaponry of the Chinese army and Boxer irregulars. In the absence of such information, he

was able to conclude that the Allies had more and better weapons, a conclusion that the Allied military men fighting in and around Tianjin had frequent reason to dispute bitterly. See Schlieper, op cit., pp. 12–14, "If we had known beforehand that our small force would have to fight against the regular army, cavalry, infantry and artillery, equipped with all modern weaponry, it would have been greatly imprudent to start off as we did."

42. Captain Arthur A. S. Barnes, *On Active Service with the Chinese Regiment: A Record of the Operations of the First Chinese Regiment in North China from March to October 1900*, Grant Richards, London, 1902, p. 84 entertains the hypothesis but decides against it. See also *China Mail*, 26 June 1900.
43. An earlier version of this chapter was submitted to *Modern China* and rejected by a reader on the grounds that "the Chinese could not have had weapons more modern than those of the invading forces." When a letter was writtten to the Editor of *Modern China*, reminding him that readers are obliged to cite hard evidence in refuting hard evidence, no reply was forthcoming. See also Allen Fung, "China's Failure Reconsidered: An Analysis of the Defeat of the Chinese Army and the Chinese Military Culture During the Sino-Japanese War (1894–1895)," unpublished BA thesis, Oxford University, Oxford, 1990, p. 21. "The Lungmeontsuy forts outside Weihaiwei, equipped with a considerable number of 21 cm Krupp guns, were awesome by all standards." Fung gives his considered opinion that the defeat in 1894–1895 was not because of the "quality or quantity of Chinese weapons." Ibid., p. 22.
44. Commercial Stereograph of the Dagu Forts, 1900. From the collection of Mr Ron Blum.
45. Li Dezhang, Su Weizhi and Liu Tianlu, *Baguo lianjun qinhua shi* (A History of the Eight-Power Allied Forces Aggression Against China), Shandong University Press, Jinan, 1990, p. 81.
46. *North China Herald*, 25 June 1900.
47. See Hu Bin, "Contradictions and Conflicts among the Imperialist Powers in China at the Time of the Boxer Movement," in Buck, op cit, p. 157, who quotes von Bülow as representative of the school which attributed Seymour's failure to suspicion and difficulties among the Allies. The diaries and accounts of the military officers taking part do not permit the interpretation that this was a factor of any importance. This is yet another example of Seymour's failure being attributed to any factor other than skilful deliberate military initiatives taken by irregular and regular Chinese armed forces. Ralph Powell wrote, "The force … was delayed en route by Boxer attacks, but its greatest handicap was the destruction by the Chinese of sections of the railway," Ralph Powell, *The Rise of Chinese Military Power 1895–1912*, Princeton University Press, Princeton, 1955, p. 111. As this is all we learn about the Chinese military initiatives that were responsible for decimating and routing the Seymour expedition, it seems a little inadequate as a description of the initiatives of Chinese regular and irregular

forces. Powell did note that "the retreat of the Seymour expedition temporarily dispelled the popular myth that a small body of modern foreign troops could march from one end of China to the other without meeting effective resistance." Ibid., p. 116. However, the word "temporarily" carried such great weight in his thinking that his overall conclusion regarding the lessons to be learnt from the Boxer War failed to give the Chinese forces the credit they so richly deserved. Ibid., pp. 116–117.

48. Nathan Chaikin, *The Sino-Japanese War 1894–1895*, Imprimerie Pillet, Martigny, 1983, p. 38.
49. Fung, "Testing the Self-Strengthening," op cit., p. 1008.
50. Estimates of the length of railroad torn up by the Boxers only count their activity along the Tianjin–Beijing railway line. In the vicinity of Gaobeitian, they tore up about thirty kilometres of rail lines.
51. See Ding Mingnan, "Some Questions Concerning the Appraisal of the Boxer Movement," in Buck, op cit., pp. 34–35, Ding gives extensive evidence for Luddism as a motive for destroying the railway but he also says that "the Boxer's destruction of the railroads had military as well as economic grounds."
52. Schlieper, op cit., p. 35.
53. Liu Mengyang, "A Record of the Rebellion of the Boxer Bandits in Tientsin," manuscript translation by Professor Mark Elvin, p. 5; Cohen, op cit., p. 125.
54. Scott Dolby, "The Boxer Crisis as Seen Through the Eyes of Five Chinese Officials," unpublished PhD thesis, Columbia University, 1976, p. 268. Letter of 6 June, Yang Mushi to Nie Shicheng, "The Boxers do not have any skills, but each time they gather there are usually as many as several thousand to ten thousand of them and they are not afraid of dying."
55. Schlieper, op cit., p. 24.
56. The military accounts show a decided difference in national and cultural attitudes towards foraging for food, the French being observed to be the best. Although the troops in question were Annamites, they had successfully imbibed French culture in this respect. See Lynch, op cit., p. 32. See also Frank A. Kierman and John K. Fairbank, *Chinese Ways in Warfare*, Harvard University Press, Cambridge, Massachusetts, 1974, p. 20 for a description of Franke's study of siege warfare in the Song and Yuan dynasties. See further, *Sun Tzu. The Art of Warfare: The First English Translation Incorporating the Recently Discovered Yin-cheuh-shan Texts*, translated by Roger T. Ames, Ballantine Books, New York, 1993, p. 123.
57. Cohen, op cit., p. 52, notes that in another theatre of operations, Boxers joined with "Manchu" troops and "commenced destruction of the railway in part to hinder Russian military intervention." This railway had been built by the Russians.
58. Esherick, op cit., p. 289, notes simply that "much of the credit for stopping Seymour belonged to the Boxers, and their reputation increased enormously."

According to Sawara Tokusaki, it was the Court which gave credit to the Boxers and refused to give credit to the forces of the Imperial Chinese Army. See Jian Bozan et al. (eds), *Yihetuan* (The Boxers), Shenzhou guoguang she, Shanghai, 1953 (1951), 4 vols.

59. Esherick, op cit., p. 239 contains an interesting table showing the class background of Boxer leaders in Shandong province. It would be pertinent to have such information for Zhili province as well.
60. Liao Yuzhong, "Special Features of the Boxer Movement," in Buck, op cit., p. 176.
61. Li Jikui, "How to View the Boxers' Religious Superstitions," in Buck, op cit., p. 108. There is considerable disagreement as to the level of organisation among the Boxers, reflecting the widely disparate origins of the Boxers themselves. However, those accounts which show them to be capable of keeping good battle order may be taken to be representative of some groups of Boxers in some of the military action which took place. Observations concerning the Boxers' ability to act as an ordered military troop came from both Chinese and Western observers. See Zhong Fangshi, "Diaries of the Year 1900," p. 11, quoted in Li Jikui, ibid, p. 105, Schlieper, op cit., p. 38 and Yulu, Memorial K 26.5.24 cited in Tan, op cit., p. 101.
62. Esherick, op cit., p. 239.
63. Bertram L. Simpson, *Indiscreet Letters from Peking*, Arno Press, New York, 1970 (1907), pp. 422–423.
64. Barnes, op cit., pp. 6–8.
65. McCalla, op cit., Ch. 27, p. 21; Barnes, op cit., pp. 3 and 43; Lieutenant de Marolles in Colonel Pélacot, *Expédition de Chine de 1900 Jusqu'à L'arrivée du Général Voyron*, Henri Charles Lavauzelle, Paris, 1901, p. 33; *China*, op cit.
66. *Military Operations*, op cit., p. 528 and Colonel Cyril Field, *Britain's Sea Soldiers: A History of the Royal Marines and Their Predecessors*, Lyceum Press, Liverpool, 1924, Vol. 2, p. 256.
67. Arthur Cunningham, *The Chinese Soldier and Other Sketches with a Description of the Capture of Manila*, Hong Kong Daily Press, no date, possibly, 1901, p. 235.
68. Liu Tianlu et al., op cit., pp. 129–130.
69. Mark Elvin, "Mandarins and Millenarians," p. 219 in his *Another History. Essays on China from a European Perspective*, Wild Peony, Australia, 1996, op cit.
70. *China*, op cit., 9 July 1900, Consul McWade to Secretary of State.
71. Stanley Spector, *Li Hung Chang and the Huai Army. A Study in Nineteenth Century Chinese Regionalism*, University of Washington Press, 1974, footnote 1, p. xxiv. See also Mark Lewis, "The Han Abolition of Universal Military Service," in Hans van de Ven (ed.), op cit., as reviewed by Joanna Waley-Cohen in *China Review International*, Fall 2001.
72. *Military Operations*, op cit., p. 551.

73. Dorothy L. Shineberg, "Guns and Men in Melanesia," *Journal of Pacific History*, Vol. 6, 1971, p. 80.
74. The literature on the Maori Wars, the Zulu Wars, on Aboriginal resistance to white settlement in Australia, and on warfare between Pacific Islanders and Europeans makes this clear. See, for example, Bronwen Douglas, "Almost Constantly at War?", *Journal of Pacific History*, June 1990 and Belich, op cit.
75. Esherick, op cit., pp. 172 and 292; Purcell, op cit., pp. 176–177. See also Cunningham, op cit., pp. 58–68.
76. Powell, op cit., p. 112. Liu Mengyang, op cit., makes it clear that he is cynical to unbelieving about Boxer military prowess.
77. Anatol M. Kotenev, *The Chinese Soldier. Basic Principles, Spirit, Science of War and Heroes of the Chinese Armies*, Kelly and Walsh, Ltd., Shanghai, 1934, p. 75, "in compliance with the Imperial commands, [the Boxers] were drilled in accordance with the manual adopted by the modern troops of Peiyang. They diligently practised squad and company drill, the 'goose step,' and the 'setting up exercises'."
78. Barnes, op cit., p. 96 noted the discovery in former Boxer barracks of "receipts for money, lists of men, details of casualties, and of valiant deeds done by some of the members of this pleasant fraternity." Major E. W. Norrie, *History of the War in China, 1900–1901*, a one-off print edition, undated, p. 33, notes that when Boxers attacked they held formation "charging in line with great courage and enthusiasm." My thanks to Professor Mark Elvin for lending me this work.
79. Duiker, op cit., pp. 203–204. See also the language used in the editorial columns of *The Times*, June 1900.
80. McCalla, op cit., Ch. 28, p. 16.
81. *How to Read Chinese War News. A Vade-Mecum of Notes and Hints to Readers of Despatches and Intelligence from the Seat of War, with a Coloured War Map and a Glossary of Military Technical Terms, Local Titles, Places, Phrases*, etc., T. Fisher and Unwin, London, 1900, p. 41
82. Barnes, op cit., pp. 19–20.
83. McCalla, op cit., Ch. 28, p. 17.
84. Ibid., Ch. 26, pp. 12–13.
85. Schlieper, op cit., p. 61. The guerrilla tactics of the Boxers and their ability to take the invading forces by surprise at will had thoroughly disconcerted Schlieper. Unlike British and French officers of his era, he had had no experience in fighting irregular soldiers, using guerrilla tactics. The Americans were acquiring such experience in the Philippines and not finding it so easy.
86. Spector, op cit., pp. 211–212. See also pp. 119–121 for an account for the careful recruiting by Zeng Guofan and the short-term and long-term reasons for this.
87. "Rapport du Capitaine Guillaumat de la Légion Etrangère sur sa Mission en Chine du 30 Juin 1900 au 7 Janvier 1901," Hanoi, February 1901. Manuscript

held in the Archives Historiques de l'Armée de Terre, Château de Vincennes, Paris, p. 19. See also Schlieper, op cit., p. 84.

88. Midshipman G. Gipps, *The Fighting in North China Up to the Fall of Tientsin City*, Sampson, Low Marston and Co., London, 1901, p. 29.
89. Jian Bozan et al., op cit., Vol. 1, p. 256.
90. Schlieper, op cit., p. 77.
91. Duiker, op cit., p. 88.
92. Quoted in Field, op cit., Vol. 2, p. 256.
93. Powell, op cit., p. 116.
94. De Pontèves, op cit., p. 161, "This beautiful cavalry, well-ordered and well-aligned."
95. Ibid., pp. 161–162.
96. McCalla, op cit, Ch. 27, p. 21.
97. Ibid., p. 30.
98. Ibid., p. 29.
99. Pélacot, op cit., pp. 125–127.
100. McCalla, op cit., Ch. 27, p. 29.
101. Dolby, op cit., p. 287.
102. McCalla, p. 32.
103. Paolo E. Coletta, *Bowman Hendry McCalla, A Fighting Sailor*, University Press of America, Washington, DC, 1979, p. 118.
104. This belief when confronted with the reality that Chinese troops or insurgents fought equally well at night, was then twisted to put a pejorative gloss on the Chinese; "Mauser bullets are nightly fired at our sentries, and every night we have to turn out a number of times to repel the cowardly natives, whom we find sneaking down upon us, and who dare attack only under cover of darkness." Robert Coltman, *Beleaguered in Peking. The Boxers' War Against the Foreigner*, Philadelphia, 1901, p. 70. Coltman was a missionary and a medical doctor, not a soldier. Federick Brown, *From Tientsin to Peking with the Allied Forces*, Charles H. Kelly, London, 1902, p. 93. "The decision to march at night was a wise one, and in future wars with China it should be remembered that the Chinese have a strong dislike to being out at night." See also Schlieper, op cit., p. 30, cf. Simpson, op cit., p. 192, "by night they work as openly as they please." The hostilities were opened by the Chinese at Dagu after midnight and all the military accounts describe night attacks by Chinese regular and insurgent forces. See especially Pélacot, op cit., pp. 62, 84 and the accounts of General Nie's attack on the Seymour expedition holed up in the Xigu arsenal. See also de Pontèves, op cit., p. 174.
105. McCalla, op cit., Ch. 27, p. 42.
106. Schlieper, op cit., p. 41.
107. Ibid., op cit., p. 61.
108. Ibid., pp. 88–89.

109. Estimates of the monetary value of the contents of the Xigu arsenal vary from £1.5 million (McCalla, op cit., Ch. 27, p. 33) to £3.5 million (Norrie, p. 39) to $15 million (*Military Operations*, op cit., p. 531).
110. Duiker, op cit., p. 72.
111. Schlieper, op cit., p. 109.
112. See de Marolles, "Rapport du Capitaine de Vaisseau de Marolles," manuscript held in the Archives Historiques du Ministère des Armées.
113. Claude Lévi-Strauss, *Race et Histoire*, Denoël, France, 1995 (1952), p. 20.
114. Field, op cit., Vol. 1, p. 146.
115. *China Mail*, 26 June 1900 and Barnes op cit., p. 84.
116. John W. Dower, *War Without Mercy. Race and Power in the Pacific War*, Pantheon Books, New York, 1986.
117. General H. Frey, *Français et Alliés au Péi Tchi-Li. Campagne de Chine de 1900*, Hachette, Paris, 1904, p. 109. Although General Frey's account was one of the four military sources cited in Powell, op cit., and the General was not in China for the early weeks of the campaign, this positive statement about Chinese soldiery among many such also to be found in General Frey's own report, was not reflected in Powell's use of the French military accounts quoted in General Frey's work.
118. Field, op cit., Vol. 2, p. 126.
119. De Pontèves, op cit., pp. 234–235.
120. Ibid., p. 244.
121. Journal of Oscar J. Upham. Manuscript held in the Marine Archives, Quantical, Virginia, USA.
122. Savage-Landor, op cit., Vol. 1, p. 178.
123. *Military Operations*, op cit., p. 544.
124. Norrie, op cit., pp. 35–36.
125. Ibid., p. 30; Simpson, op cit., reported that the Russians accidentally left their guns behind at Tianjin railway station; de Marolles, op cit., reports that on 22 June 1900 the English dropped their guns into the river while trying to get them on to a junk and that the Russians sunk one and abandoned another in a field.
126. Norrie, op cit., p. 30.
127. De Marolles, op cit., 26 June 1900.
128. Schlieper, op cit., throughout gives a very clear picture of the morale of both officers and men of the Seymour expedition. See especially p. 57 for his account of Admiral Seymour's mien and his leadership qualities. See also de Marolles, op cit., 22 June 1900.
129. Schlieper, op cit., p. 84 comments on the "incredible fearlessness" of the Boxers who were able to lie still hidden in the long grass while the whole column passed by. One of the officers narrowly missed being killed by a Boxer who came after him with a long sword. "Probably the Boxers had lain in wait in order to do a reconnaissance at night or to attack our post."

130. Ibid., p. 79.
131. *Official Register, West Point*, 1900, p. 30, Schlieper, op cit., p. 20. See also McCalla, op cit., Ch. 27, p. 42.
132. Frederick May Wise, A *Marine Tells It to You*. As told by Frederick May Wise to M. O. Forst, Quantical, Virginia, Marine Corps Association, 1981, p. 34.
133. For further details concerning the effect of Court politics on various senior Chinese commanders, see Liu Tianlu et al., op cit., pp. 129–130.
134. *How to Read Chinese War News*, op cit., p. 41; Powell, op cit., p. 84; Spector, op cit., pp. 248–250; Fung, "China's Failure Reconsidered," op cit., pp. 24–25 considered that the Chinese paid insufficient attention to training and drilling. He mentioned the fact that "repeated drilling could often boost up the sense of solidarity among soldiers." This writer has argued in Chapter Six that among selected armies, such training and drilling had occurred as was observed by foreign defence attachés. It was certainly the case that after the Sino-Japanese War, Li Hongzhang and Nie Shiceng, among others, saw the need to intensify the drilling of the rank and file soldiers.
135. *North China Herald*, 13 June 1900, p. 1052, *Ostasiatische Lloyd-Extra*, Tientsin, 10 June 1900; cf. Ibid., p. 1065, "Report from our own correspondent, Shantung."
136. Dolby, op cit., p. 292. Letter 18 July, Yang Mushi to Li Hongzhang.
137. McCalla, op cit., Ch. 27, p. 41.
138. "Rapport du Capitaine Guillaumat," op cit., p. 35.
139. Dolby, op cit., p. 295; 18 July, letter from Yang Mushi to Li Hongzhang.
140. Many of the military accounts describe the anguish and extreme difficulty of withdrawing through hostile country with such a high proportion of wounded men. Captain Schlieper's book contains a lot of line drawings illustrating the makeshift stretchers used to carry the wounded and their defencelessness when placed in flat-bottomed sampans entirely at the mercy of the Chinese regular soldiers or the Boxers. Under the circumstances, such a small party encumbered with so many wounded men could only have regained their base if enemy High Command gave specific orders to impede but not annihilate it.
141. Spector, op cit., p. 269.
142. McCalla, op cit, Ch. 28, p. 16 describes two encounters between General Ma Yukun and the Boxers in which it is quite clear that General Ma had the upper hand in such a way as to ensure bad relations with the Boxers. This is also reflected in the Chinese accounts, see Dolby, op cit., Jiang Kai, p. 173 ff, pp. 190–191, pp. 193–194, p. 197; Zhu Zhaotang, pp. 220–22, p. 236. See also Liu Mengyang, op cit., pp. 8–10.
143. Simpson, op cit., p. 2.
144. Jian Bozan et al., Vol. 1, op cit., pp. 256–257.
145. Brown, op cit., pp. 40, 64, 69; Norrie, op cit., p. 67.
146. Brown, op cit., p. 75; Norrie, op cit., p. 62; Lynch, op cit., p. 33.
147. Norrie, op cit., pp. 62, 64; Brown, op cit., p. 82.

148. This was also evident in the siege of the Legations.
149. Barnes, op cit., pp. 51, 58, 85; Norrie, op cit., p. 46.
150. Brown, op cit., pp. 27, 49, 64; Schlieper, p. 119; *Military Operations*, op cit., p. 533.
151. Dolby op cit., p. 266, 6 June telegram from Zhang in the Military Secretariat to Governor General Yulu.
152. Frey, op cit., p. 108
153. Pélacot, op cit., p. 85; Schlieper, op cit., p. 88; *Military Operations*, op cit., p. 544.
154. Journal of Oscar J. Upham, op cit., 30 June 1900.
155. Armée, Series 7N1679, Letter from Commander Vidal to the Minister of War, Report No. 68 of 4 January 1899.
156. Guillaumat, op cit., p. 34.
157. Barnes, op cit., pp. 57–8. See also Brown, op cit, p. 98, "Ma was the man who had turned his guns so accurately on Tientsin settlement. Ten shells had entered the Temperance Hall in twenty minutes. British officers being quartered there, the Chinese had made a special target of it."
158. *Military Operations*, op cit., p. 548.
159. Savage-Landor, op cit., Vol. 1, facing p. 202 and facing p. 203. This type of gun was maufactured from 1896 onwards. Savage-Landor described the guns found at one of the arsensals inside Tianjin's city wall, "Forty beautiful Krupp and Nordenfeldt guns of the latest pattern were captured, with quantities of small arms and ammunition, including shells of all patterns and sizes." Ibid., pp. 203–204.
160. Sharf and Harrington, *China, 1900. The Eyewitnesses Speak*, op cit., p. 110. See also, p. 112.
161. Ibid., p. 237.
162. The siege of Tianjin is either written out of the English-language literature (see Clements, op cit. and Purcell, op cit.) or described in such a way as to minimise Chinese military prowess (see Tan, op cit. and Esherick, op cit.) or erroneously reported (see Steiger, op cit.).
163. Jian Bozan et al., Vol. 1, p. 257.
164. Sharf and Harrington, *China 1900. The Eyewitnesses Speak*, op cit., p. 127.
165. Brigadier A. S. Dagett, *America in the Chinese Relief Expedition*, Hudson-Kimberley Kansas City, 1903, p. 41.
166. Wise, op cit., p. 36.
167. Lévi-Strauss, op cit., pp. 42–47 gives a superb analysis of how the history of one culture is not composed of its intrinsic elements but derives from the situation in which the observer finds herself in relation to that culture or the number and diversity of the observer's interests which are engaged by the observed culture. He likens the opposition between "progressive" and "inert" cultures to the position of a traveller on a train who sees the speed and length of other trains

vary according to whether those trains are moving in the same direction or the opposite direction. His analysis of the relativity of history can profitably be applied to the ways China was perceived by various foreign countries in the eighteenth and nineteenth centuries as opposed to what was regarded as significant by the Chinese themselves at that time.

168. Norrie, op cit., pp. 61–62. Pélacot, op cit., pp. 127 and 131–132, make it clear that the Allies were totally unprepared to march on Beijing and that as well, knowledge and experience of Chinese military preparedness made it inadvisable to set out straight after the capture of Tianjin.
169. Powell, op cit., p. 114, "after the return of Admiral Seymour, official estimates of the forces needed to advance on Peking and maintain lines of communication were increased from 25,000 to from 40,000 to 100,000 men." It is notable that Powell did not draw any conclusions from this data. The journalist George Lynch mentioned the figure of 120,000. See Lynch, op cit., pp. 107–108.
170. B. Douglas, op cit.; H. Reynolds, "Aboriginal Resistance in Queensland," *Australian Journal of Politics and History*, Vol. 22, 1976; N. Shineberg, op cit.; A. P. Vayda, *Maori Warfare*, Wellington, 1960; M. Crowder (ed.), *West African Resistance. The Military Response to Colonial Occupation*, London, 1971.
171. Zhang Junbo and Yao Yunzhu, "Differences Between Traditional Chinese and Western Military Thinking and Their Philosophical Roots," *Journal of Contemporary China*, Vol. 5, No. 12, July 1966, p. 213.
172. The work and the approach of Joanna Waley-Cohen and Allen Fung constitute important exceptions to this generalisation.
173. John W Garver, "Feature Review," *Diplomatic History*, Vol. 22, No. 3, Summer 1998, pp. 492–493. My thanks to Dr Gerry Groot for drawing my attention to this reference.
174. One is reminded of the extreme interest and precision of the Qianlong Emperor's technical questions about warships and artillery. See Waley-Cohen, "China and Western Technology," op cit., p. 1534.
175. Oliver Warner, *The British Navy. A Concise History*, Thames and Hudson, 1975, p. 118.
176. Belich, op cit., p. 88.
177. Admiral Edward H. Seymour, My *Naval Career and Travels*, Smith, Elder and Co., London, 1911, p. 167.
178. Simpson, op cit., pp. 437 and 439.
179. The archives of the Hoover Institute of War and Peace hold collections of newspaper cuttings from regional newspapers such as *The Topeka Daily Capital*, *The St Louis Star*, *The Kansas Emporia Gazette* and *The Topeka State Journal* regarding the Boxer crisis. These reflect intense local interest in affairs in China corresponding to the numbers of missionaries and their families from those towns who were in China at this time. See also James Hevia, "Leaving a Brand

on China: Missionary Discourse in the Wake of the Boxer Movement," *Modern China*, Vol. 18, No. 3, July 1992.
180. Simpson, op cit., p. 2.
181. Zhang and Yao, op cit., pp. 213–217.
182. Waley-Cohen, *The Sextants of Beijing*, op. cit., is largely concerned with refuting the view that China has been a stubbornly isolationist civilisation. Her chapter "Shields and Swords, 1860–1914" is relevant in this context of industrialisation in China during the nineteenth century and its specific defence orientation.
183. See *Westminster Gazette*, letter to the editor, 11 June 1900 and *China Mail*, 23 July 1900.
184. Waley-Cohen, "China and Western Technology," op cit.
185. See Charles O. Hucker, "Hu Tsung-hsien's Campaign Against Hsü Hai, 1556," in Kierman and Fairbank, op cit., pp. 273–307. Fung, "China's Failure Reconsidered," op cit., p. 23 argued that overly defensive strategy and mentality were an important factor in China's defeat by Japan although there were generals, for example, Song Qing, who tried to press for a different approach.
186. *Sun Tzu, The Art of War*, translated by Samuel B. Griffith, Oxford University Press, UK, 1963, p.vii.
187. For Li Hongzhang's thinking on the development and use of the Chinese navy in the face of the Japanese threat, see Spector, op cit., pp. 184–185. See Thomas L. Kennedy, *The Arms of Kiangnan: Modernization in the Chinese Ordnance Industry, 1860–1895*, Westview Press, Colorado, 1978. See also Cunningham, op cit., pp. 72–73 for the impetus given to the Chinese military by the Sino-Japanese War. Similar crises forced European Powers to modernise equipment and organisation; see Lewis, op cit., p. 223. Spector, op cit., p. 184. Quite clearly different factions in Chinese power politics perceived the relationship of victory and defeat to the necessity for modernisation very differently from even the most widely differing factions in Western power politics.
188. *Sun Tzu*, Griffith, op cit., p. 67.
189. Spector, op cit., p. 176.
190. Dolby, op cit., p. 291, 18 July. Letter from Yang Mushi to Li Hongzhang.
191. The increase in the percentage of military governors relative to civilian governors has been documented by a number of writers. See Michael Franz, *Pacific Historical Review*, No. 18, 1949, pp. 479 and 484.
192. Lucien Bodard, *La Vallée des Roses*, Grasset, Paris, 1977.
193. Spector, op cit., p. 233.
194. Ibid., p. 39 for the influence of his awareness of past generals being put to death on Zeng Guofan's thinking in planning his moves against the Taiping Rebellion, and p. 104 for Zeng, the conqueror, having to ask to be retired. A comparison with an almost exact contemporary Ulysses Grant, shows that the relationship between the civilian and military arms of state cannot be conceptualised as emanating from a similar philosophy regarding the use of military force as an

extension of the power of the state. In his introduction to his translation of Sun Zi, Ames elaborates usefully on some of the Chinese philosophical concepts behind the art of warfare. *Sun Tzu*, Ames, op cit.

195. *Sun Tzu*, Ames, op cit., p. 111.
196. Ibid. See also *Sun Tzu*, Griffith, op cit., pp. 77–78.
197. *Sun Tzu*, Ames, op cit., pp. 112–113; *Sun Tsu*, Griffith, op cit, pp. 81–83. Thus when Zeng Guofan declined to accept the order to march and take the Taiping citadel, he was acting "according to traditional practice" (Spector, op cit., p. 45) in accordance with the precepts of Sun Zi which seem most pertinent when considered in relation to the military events in China in 1900.
198. Ibid, p. 83 and *Sun Tzu*, Ames, op cit., p. 113.
199. *Sun Tzu*, Griffith, op cit., p. 112 and *Sun Tzu*, Ames, op cit., p. 135.
200. *China*, op cit., Resolutions and Telegram adopted at the Public Meeting of Americans at Shanghai, 13 July 1900.
201. Armée, Series 7N1646, Captain d'Amade, "Chine, Armée du Pei-Tchi-Lì, Voyage, Rapport d'hiver, 1888," No. 5.
202. Reports of Battles, Manuscript, National Archives, Washington, Theo L. Wint, Lieut. Col. 6th Cavalry, Commanding Regiment Report of Reconnaissance and Engagement near Tientsin, *19 August 1900*. (emphasis added)
203. Simpson, op cit., p. 323.

Bibliography

Manuscripts

"Album de Photographies faites par le Commandant Laribe pendant les Manoeuvres de l'Armée Chinoise en 1908," Musée de l'Armée de Terre, Château de Vincennes, Paris.

Amade, Capitaine d', "Chine, Armée du Pei Tchi-Lì, Voyage d'hiver 1888." Five parts. Archives Militaires de l'Armée de Terre, Château de Vincennes, Paris. Series 7N1665.

Amade, Capitaine d', *Vues Diverses Provinces du Sse-Tchouen, Yunnan et Youang-si. Voyage du Capitaine d'Amade de Pékin aux Frontières du Tonkin* (1889), Tientsin, May 1890.

American Contingent to the China Relief Expedition. Reports of Battles, National Archives, Washington DC.

Archives Militaires de l'Armée de Terre, Château de Vincennes, Paris, Series 7N1665.

Archives Militaires de l'Armée de Terre, Château de Vincennes, Paris, Series 7N1666.

Archives Militaires de l'Armée de Terre, Château de Vincennes, Paris, Series 7N1668.

Archives Militaires de l'Armée de Terre, Château de Vincennes, Paris, Series 7N1674.

Archives Militaires de l'Armée de Terre, Château de Vincennes, Paris, Series 7N1679.

Archives Militaires de l'Armée de Terre, Château de Vincennes, Paris, Series 7N1680. (hereafter refer to as "Armée")

Bibliothèque Nationale de Paris, Bureau des Estampes, Series Oe 173, "Estampes populaires relatives à la guerre franco-chinoise de 1885."

Consular Records, Tientsin, January 1900–30 June 1903, Department of State held in National Archives, Washington M114.

Correspondance politique et commerciale-Nouvelle Série, sous-série: Chine.

Correspondence on the Subject of Looting. Letter from Mark Twain and letters in reply. Hoover Institute for War and Peace, Stanford University.

Reports of Battles, Manuscript, National Archives, Washington, Theo L. Wint, Lieut. Col. 6th Cavalry, Commanding Regiment. Report on Reconnaissance and Engagement near Tientsin, 19 August 1900.

Reverend Courtenay H. Fenn, "In the Matter of Loot," *The Presbyterian Banner*, 11 April 1901.

Liu Mengyang, "A Record of the Rebellion of the Boxer-Bandits in Tientsin," manuscript, translated by Mark Elvin.

McCalla, Rear-Admiral Bowman H., "Memoirs of a Naval Career," typed manuscript held in the Marine Archives, Quantical, Virginia, USA, undated.

"Photographies prises en Chine par le Commandant Corvisart, Attaché Militaire à la Légation de France au Japon, 1900." Manuscript albums held at the Musée de l'Armée de Terre, Château de Vincennes, Paris.

"Rapport du Capitaine Guillaumat de la Légion Etrangère sur sa Mission en Chine du 30 Juin 1900 au 7 Janvier 1901," dated Hanoi February 1901. Manuscript held in the Archives Historiques de l'Armée de Terre, Château de Vincennes, Paris.

"Rapport du Capitaine de Vaisseau de Marolles," manuscript held in the Archives Historiques de l'Armée de Terre, Château de Vincennes, Paris.

"Rapport du Capitaine Meillet adjoint à l'Atelier de Construction de Puteaux sur son Voyage en Chine, 1896," manuscript held at the Archives de l'Armée de Terre, Château de Vincennes, Paris, Series 7N1674.

Service Historique de la Marine, Château de Vincennes, Paris "Arsenal de Fou-tchéou [Fuzhou], 1866–1877, 1890". BB41555.

Service Historique de la Marine, Château de Vincennes, Paris, Prosper Giquel. CC71020.

State Department. Papers on the China Station, National Archives, Washington DC.

Upham, Oscar J., Manuscript held in the Marine Archives, Quantical, Virginia, USA.

US Consular Records, Department of State, National Archives, Washington DC.

US Department of State. Documents on the Chinese Crisis, National Archives, Washington.

Newspapers and Periodicals

Baihua huatu ribao
The Chicago Daily Tribune
The China Mail
Cilin huabao
The Daily Mail
Dianshizhai huabao
Emporia Gazette
Feiyingge huabao
Harper's Monthly Magazine
Harper's Weekly
The Hong Kong Daily Press
The Illustrated London News
L'Illustration
Die Illustrierte Zeitung
Kansas City Star

Manchoho
Marumaru Shimbun
Mingquan huabao
The Morning Oregonian
The Nation
The New York Times
The New York World
Nichiroko shinpo
North China Daily News
The North China Herald
The North China Herald and Supreme Court and Consular Gazette
Novoe Vremya
Der Oastasiatische–Lloyd Extra
The Peking and Tientsin Times
Le Point
The Presbyterian Banner
Punch
The Review of Reviews
La Revue des Troupes Coloniales
Le Rire
The Saint Louis Star
The San Francisco Examiner
The Shanghai Mercury
Shenbao
Shenbao tuhua
Shenjiang hengjintu
Shibao
Simplicissimus
The Spectator
Strekoza
The Times
Topeka Daily, Newspaper
Topeka State Journal
Twenty-First Century
The Westminster Gazette
The World
Xinshijie huabao
Xinwenbao
Zhongwai renwu huabao
Zhongwai renwu shanshui huabao
Zhongwaiguo renwu shanshui ribao tuhua
Zhongwai ribao

Contemporary Books and Publications

Allen, Roland, *The Siege of the Peking Legations*, Smith, Elder, London, 1902.

Barnes, Captain Arthur A. S., *On Active Service with the Chinese Regiment: A Record of the Operations of the First Chinese Regiment in North China from March to October 1900*, Grant Richards, London, 1902.

Bell, Mark, China: *Reconnaissance Journey Through the Central Western Provinces from Peking through Shansi, Shensi, Kansuh and Sin-Kiang to Ladakh and India* (Compiled from the various sources in the Intelligence Branch of the Quarter Master General's Department in India), Government Printer, Calcutta, 1888.

Beresford, Lord Charles, *The Break-up of China, with an Account of Its Present Commerce, Railways, Politics and Future Prospects*, Harper Brothers, New York, 1899.

Bernard, William D., *Narrative of the Voyages and the Services of the Nemesis from 1840 to 1843; and of the Combined Naval and Military Operations in China: Comprising a Complete Account of the Colony of Hong Kong and Remarks on the Character and Habits of the Chinese from Notes of Commander W. H. Hall R. N. with Personal Observations by W. D. Bernard*, Henry Colburn, London, 1844.

Bland, John O. P., *Houseboat Days in China*, William Heinemann, London, 1919 (1909).

Brown, Frederick, *From Tientsin to Peking with the Allied Forces*, Charles H. Kelly, London, 1902.

The Boxer Rising: A History of the Boxer Trouble in China. Reprinted from the "Shanghai Mercury", Paragon Book Reprint Corp., New York, 1967 (1901).

Bullard, Frederick L., *Famous War Correspondents*, Pitman and Sons, London, 1914.

Carl, Katharine A., *With the Empress Dowager of China*, Evelyn Nash, London, 1906.

Chamberlin, Wilbur, *Ordered to China*, Methuen, London, 1904.

Chou Han, (attributed) *The Cause of the Riots in the Yangtze Valley. A Complete Picture Gallery*, Hankow 1891.

China Yearbook 1903.

La Chine à Terre et en Ballon. Reproductions de Photographies des Officiers du Génie des Corps Expéditionnaires 1900–1901, Paris, 1902.

Chirol, Valentine, *The Middle Eastern Question or Some Problems in Indian Defence*, J. Murray, London, 1903.

———, *The Indian Unrest*, MacMillan, London, 1910.

———, *The Egyptian Problem*, MacMillan, London, 1920.

———, *India Old and New*, MacMillan, 1921.

———, *The Turkish Empire*, Unwin, London, 1923.

———, *The Occident and the Orient, Lectures on the Harris Foundation, 1924*, University of Chicago Press, Chicago, 1924.

———, *India*, Scribners, 1926.

Coltman, Robert, *Beleagured in Peking. The Boxers' War Against the Foreigner*, Philadelphia, 1901.

Conger, Sarah P., *Letters from China*, Hodder and Stoughton, London, 1909.

Cunningham, Arthur, *The Chinese Soldier and Other Sketches with a Description of the Capture of Manila*, Hong Kong Daily Press, Hong Kong, no date, possibly 1901.

Daggett, Brigadier-General A. S., *America in the China Relief Expedition*, Hudson-Kimberly, Kansas, 1903.

De Groot, J. J. M., *The Religious System of China: Its Ancient Forms, Evolution, History and Present Aspect, Manners, Customs and Social Institutions Connected Therewith* (1892–1910), 6 vols. Literature House, Taibei, 1964.

Frey, General H., *Français et Alliés au Péi Tchi-Li. Campagne de Chine de 1900*, Hachette, Paris, 1904.

Garnot, Captain, *L'Expédition Française de Formose 1884–1885*, Librairie Ch. Delagrave, Paris, 1894.

Giles, Lancelot, *The Siege of the Peking Legations. A Diary*, L. R. Marchant (ed.), University of Western Australia Press, Nedlands, 1970.

Gipps, Midshipman G., *The Fighting in North China Up to the Fall of Tientsin City*, Sampson Low, Marston and Co., London, 1901.

Giquel, Prosper, *The Foochow Arsenal and Its Results from the Commencement in 1867, to the End of the Foreign Directorate, on the 16th February, 1874*, translated from the French by H. Lang. Reprinted from the *Shanghai Evening Courier*, 1874.

Great Britain. British Parliamentary Papers. China, No. 3 (1900). "Correspondence Respecting the Insurrectionary Movement in China," Harrison and Sons, London, 1900.

Harper, Edith K., *Stead the Man: Personal Reminiscences*, W. Rider, London, 1918.

Hooker, Mary, *Behind the Scenes in Peking*, Oxford University Press, Hong Kong, 1987 (1910).

How to Read Chinese War News. A Vade-Mecum of Notes and Hints to Readers of Despatches and Intelligence from the Seat of War, with a Coloured War Map and a Glossary of Military Technical Terms, Local Titles, Places, Phrases etc, T. Fisher Unwin, London, 1900.

Jackson, Mason, *The Pictorial Press. Its Origin and Progress*, New York, 1969 (1885).

Lanning, George, *Old Forces in New China, An Effort to Exhibit Fundamental Relationships in China and the West in their True Light: Together with an Appendix dealing with the Story of the Chinese Revolution down to the End of June, 1912: And a New Map showing the Natural Resources of China*, Shanghai National Review Office, London, Probsthain, 1912.

Lynch, George, *The War of the Civilisations. Being a Record of a "Foreign Devil's" Experiences with the Allies in China*, Longmans, Green and Co., London, 1901.

Marchant, Leslie Ronald (ed.), *The Siege of the Peking Legations. A Diary* (by Lancelot Giles), Nedlands, University of Western Australia Press, 1970.

Mennie, Donald and Weale, Putnam (also wrote under the name of Simpson Betram L.) *The Pagent of Peking. Comprising Sixty-Six Vandyck Photogravures of Peking and Environs from Photographs*, Watson, Shanghai, 1920.

Norrie, Major E. W., *History of the War in China 1900–1901*, One-off Print Edition, Undated.

Official Register, West Point, 1900.

Palmer, Frederick, *With My Own Eyes. A Personal Story of Battle Years*, Jarrolds, London, 1934.

Pélacot, Colonel, *Expédition de Chine de 1900 Jusqu'à l'Arrivée du Général Voyron*, Henri-Charles Lavauzelle, Paris, 1901.

Pontèves, Ruffi, de, *Souvenirs de la Colonne Seymour*, Librairie Plon, Paris, 1903.

Rennie, David F. *The British Arms in China and Japan: Peking 1860; Kagosima 1862*, J, Murray, London, 1862.

Reports on Military Operations in South Africa and China, War Department, Adjutant General's Office, No. XXXIII, Government Printing Office, Washington, 1901.

Ricalton, James, see C. J. Lucas (ed.), *James Ricalton's Photographs of China During the Boxer Rebellion. His Illustrated Travelogue of 1900*, Edwin Mellen Press, New York, 1990.

Rogers, W. A., *Hits at Politics*, R. H. Russell, New York, 1899.

Savage-Landor, Arnold H., *China and the Allies*, William Heinemann, London, 1901.

Schlieper, Captain Paul, *Meine Kriegs-Erlebnisse in China. Die Expedition Seymour*, Wilhelm Köhler, Westfalen, 1902.

Seymour, Admiral Edward H., My *Naval Career and Travels*, Smith, Elder and Co., London, 1911.

Shanghai Mercury. The Boxer Rising: A History of the Boxer Trouble in China, Paragon Book Reprint Corp., New York, 1967 (1900).

Silbermann, Soldat, *Journal de Marche d'un Soldat Colonial en Chine*, Henri-Charles Lavauzelle, *Extrait de la Revue Coloniale*, Paris, 1902.

Simpson, Bertram L., *Indiscreet Letters from Peking*, Arno Press, New York, 1970 (1907).

Smith, Arthur H., *Everyday Village Life in China: A Study in Sociology*, 2 vols., Fleming H. Revell, New York, 1899.

———, *China in Convulsion*, Oliphant, Anderson and Ferrier, London, 1901.

Thirion, Commandant, *L'Expédition de Formose, Souvenirs d'un Soldat*, Paris, 1897.

Thomson, H. C., *China and the Powers: A Narrative of the Outbreak of 1900*, Longmans, Green, London, 1902.

Thomson, John, *Illustrations of China and Its People. A Series of Two Hundred Photographs with Letterpress Descriptive of the Places and People Represented*, Sampson Low, Marston, London, 1869–1874.

———, *Foochow and the River Min*, Autotype Fine Art Co., London, 1873.

———, *The Straits of Malacca, Indo-China and China or Ten Years' Travels, Adventures and Residence Abroad*, Samson Low, Marston, London, 1875.

———, *Through China with a Camera*, A. Constable, Westminster, 1898.

Thomson, John and Smith, Adolphe, *Street Life in London*, Sampson Low, London, 1878.

Wen Ching, *The Chinese Crisis from Within*, Grant Richards, London, 1901.

Later Books and Articles in Books

Ames, Roger T. (trans.), *Sun Tzu. The Art of Warfare: The First English Translation Incorporating the Recently Discovered Yin-Cheuh-Shan Texts*, Ballantine Books, New York, 1993.

Appel, John J., "Ethnicity in Cartoon Art," *Cartoons and Ethnicity*, The 1992 Festival of Cartoon Art, Ohio State University Libraries, 1992.

Appelbaum, S., *Simplicissimus, 180 Satirical Drawings from the Famous German Weekly*, Dover, New York, 1975.

Baker, Hugh and Feuchtwang, Stephen, *An Old State in New Settings*, J.A.S.O., Oxford, 1981.

Bales, W. C., *Tso Tsungt'ang, Soldier and Statesman of Old China*, Shanghai, 1937.

Banno, Masakata, *China and the West 1858–1861: The Origins of the Tsungli Yamen*, Harvard University Press, Cambridge, Massachusetts, 1964.

Belich, James, *The New Zealand Wars and the Victorian Interpretation of Racial Conflict*, Auckland University Press, New Zealand, 1986.

Berger, R. A., *Myth and Stereotype: Images of Japan in the German Press and in Japanese Self-Representation*, Verlag, Peter Lang, Frankfurt am Main, 1990.

Beurdeley, Cecile and Beurdeley, Michel, *Giuseppe Castiglione. A Jesuit Painter at the Court of the Chinese Emperors*, Lund Humphries, London, 1972.

Bi Keguan and Huang Yuanlin, *Zhongguo nianhua shi*, (A History of Chinese Year Pictures), Liaoning Fine Arts Publishers, Shenyang, 1986.

Bliss, Douglas Percy, *A History of Wood-Engraving*, Spring Books, London, 1928.

Blum, Ron, *The Siege at Port Arthur. The Russo-Japanese War Through the Stereoscope*, Adelaide, 1987.

Bodard, Lucien, *La Vallée des Roses*, Grasset, Paris, 1977.

Bo Songnian, *Zhongguo nianhua shi* (History of Chinese New Year Pictures), Liaoning meishu chubanshe, Liaoning, 1986.

Bo Songnian and Li Baoyi (eds), *Zhongguo minjian nianhua xuan* (Selection of Chinese Folk New Year Pictures), Jiangsu meishu chubanshe, Jiangsu, 1990.

———, *Zhongguo zaojun shenma* (Chinese Kitchen God Spirit Joss and Votive Prints), Bohaitang wenhua gongsi yinxing, Taibei, 1993.

Braive, Michael F., *The Era of the Photograph. A Social History*, Thomas and Hudson, London, 1966.

Bray, Francesca, *Technology and Power, Fabrics of Power in Late Imperial China*, University of California Press, Berkeley, 1997.

Britton, Roswell S., *The Chinese Periodical Press 1800–1912*, Kelly and Walsh, Shanghai, 1933.

Brown, Lucy, *Victorian News and Newspapers*, Oxford University Press, Oxford, 1985.

Buck, David D. (ed.), *Recent Studies of the Boxer Movement: Chinese Studies in History*, Vol. 20, Nos. 3–4, Spring–Summer 1987, M. E. Sharpe Inc., New York.

The Cambridge History of China, Vol. 2, Part 2, Chapters 4 and 10, Cambridge University Press, Cambridge, 1978 (1994).

Cahill, James, *The Painters Practice: How Artists Lived and Worked in Traditional China*, Columbia University Press, New York, 1994

Cameron, Nigel, *The Face of China. As Seen by Photographers and Travelers 1860–1912*, Aperture Inc., 1978.

Cartoons and Ethnicity, the 1992 Festival of Cartoon Art, Ohio State University Libraries, 1992.

Chaikin, Nathan, *The Sino-Japanese War 1894–1895*, Imprimerie Pillet, Martigny, 1983.

Chartier, Roger, *Introduction to Cultural History. The Making of a Racist Myth*, Trentham Books, Stroke-on-Trent, 1994.

——— (ed.), *The Culture of Print*, Princeton University Press, USA, 1989.

Ch'en, Jerome, "The Origin of the Boxers" in Ch'en Jerome and Tarling, Nicholas (eds), *Studies in the Social History of China and South East Asia: Essays in Memory of Victor Purcell*, Cambridge University Press, UK, 1970.

Chere, Louis, *The Diplomacy of the Sino-French War (1883-1885): Global Complications of an Undeclared War*, Cross Roads Books (publisher), Indiana, 1985.

Chiang Yee, *The Chinese Eye. An Interpretation of Chinese Painting*, Methuen, London, 1960 (1935).

Chipp, Herschel, *Picasso's Guernica. History, Transformations, Meanings*, Thames and Hudson, London, 1989.

Christ, R., *Simplicissimus 1896–1914*, Rütten and Loenig, Berlin, 1972.

Clegg, Jenny, *Fu Manchu and the "Yellow Peril": Between Practices and Representation*, Cambridge University Press, U.K., 1988.

——— (ed.), *The Culture of Print*, Princeton University Press, USA, 1989.

Clements, Paul H., *The Boxer Rebellion: A Political and Diplomatic Review*, AMS Press Inc., New York, 1967 (1915).

Clunas, Craig, *Pictures and Visuality in Early Modern China*, Reakton Books, London, 1977.

Coates, Austin, *City of Broken Promises*, Penguin, 1977.

Coe, Brian, *Cameras: From Daguerreotypes to Instant Pictures*, Nordbok, Gothenburg, 1978.

Coe, Brian and Haworth-Booth, Mark, *A Guide to Early Photographic Processes*, Victoria and Albert Museum, London, 1983.

Cohen, Paul A., *Discovering History in China: American Historical Writing on the Recent Chinese Past*, Columbia University Press, New York, 1984.

———, *History in Three Keys. The Boxers as Event, Experience, and Myth*, Columbia University Press, New York, 1997.

Cohen, Warren I., *East Asian Art and American Culture: A Study in International Relations*, Columbia Press, New York, 1992.

Coke, Van Deren (ed.), *One Hundred Years of Photographic History — Essays in Honor of Beaumont Newhall*, University of New Mexico Press, Albuquerque, 1975.

Coletta, Paolo E., *Bowman Hendry McCalla, A Fighting Sailor*, University Press of America, Washington, DC, 1979.

Collector's Show of Traditional Soochow Woodblock Prints in Taiwan, ROC, Taipei Fine Art Museum, Taibei, 1987.

Corfield, Justin, *The Australian Illustrated Encyclopaedia of the Boxer Uprising, 1899–1900*, Slouch Hat Publications, Australia, 2000.

Cosmo, Nicola di (ed.), *Warfare in Inner Asian History*, E. J. Brill, Leiden (forthcoming).

Coutes, Virginia, *The Kaiser*, Collins, London, 1963.

Crimée 1854–1856: Premiers Reportages de Guerre, Catalogue of the 1994–1995 Exhibition by the Musée de l'Armée.

Crossley, Pamela Kyle, *Orphan Warriors. Three Manchu Generations and the End of the Qing World*, Princeton University Press, Princeton, 1990.

———, *A Translucent Mirror: History and Identity in Qing Imperial Ideology*, University of California Press, Berkeley, 1999.

Crowder, Michael (ed.), *West African Resistance. The Military Response to Colonial Occupation*, Hutchinson, London, 1971.

Curtis, L. P., *Apes and Angels. The Irishman in Victorian Caricature*, David and Charles, Newton Abbott, 1971.

Darrah, W. C., *The World of Stereographs*, Darrah, Gettysburg, PA, 1977.

Davis, William C., *The Image of War, 1861–1865, The Embattled Confederacy*, Vol. 3, Doubleday and Co. Inc., New York, 1982.

Dège, Jean-Pierre, *La Commercial Presse de Shanghai 1897–1949*, Mémoires de l'Institut des Hautes Etudes Chinoises, Vol. VII, Presses Universitaires de France, 1998.

Deng Fuxing (ed.), *Zhongguo Minjian meishu quanji: Zhuangshi bian; Nianhua juan*, (Complete Collection of Chinese Folk Arts: Decoration Edition of New Year Pictures), Jiaoyu Publishers, Jinan, Shandong, 1995.

Desmond, R. W., *The Information Process: World News Reporting to the Twentieth Century*, University of Iowa Press, Iowa City, 1978.

Ding, Mingnan, "Some Questions Concerning the Appraisal of the Boxer Movement," in David D. Buck (ed.), *Recent Studies of the Boxer Movement: Chinese Studies in History*, Vol. 20, No. 3, Spring-Summer 1987.

Dittrich, Edith, *Glück Ohne Ende. Neujahrs Bilder aus China*, Catalogue of the Exhibition of the Cologne Museum for East Asian Art, 1984.

Dower, John W., *War Without Mercy. Race and Power in the Pacific War*, Pantheon Books, New York, 1986.

Duara, Prasenjit, *Culture, Power, and the State: Rural North China, 1900–1942*, Stanford University Press, Stanford, 1988.

———, *Rescuing History from the Nation: Questioning Narratives of Modern China*, University of Chicago Press, Chicago, 1995.

Duiker, William J., *Cultures in Collision: The Boxer Rebellion*, Presidio Press, California, 1978.

Eastman, Lloyd E., *Throne and Mandarins. China's Search for a Policy During the Sino-French Controversy, 1880–1885*, Harvard University Press, Cambridge, Massachusetts, 1967.

Edgren, Sören, *Chinese Rare Books in American Collections*, China House Gallery, 1985.

Elvin, Mark, *Another History. Essays on China from a European Perspective*, Wild Peony, Australia, 1996.

———, "Mandarins and Millenarians: Reflections on the Boxer Uprising of 1899–1900" in Baker, Hugh and Feuchtwang, Stephan, *An Old State in New Settings*, J.A.S.O, Oxford, 1991.

Encyclopaedia of American Journalism.

English Caricature 1620 to the Present: Caricaturists and Satirists, Their Art, Their Purpose and Influence, Victoria and Albert Museum, London, 1984.

Esherick, Joseph W., *Reform and Revolution in China: The 1911 Revolution in Hunan and Hubei*, University of California Press, Berkeley, 1976.

———, *The Origins of the Boxer Uprising*, University of California Press, Berkeley, 1987.

Feuerwerker, Albert, Rhodes Murphey and Mary C. Wright (eds), *Approaches to Modern Chinese History*, University of California Press, Berkeley, 1967.

Field, Colonel Cyril, *Britain's Sea Soldiers: A History of the Royal Marines and Their Predecessors*, Lyceum Press, Liverpool, 1924.

Finnane, Antonia and Anne McLaren (eds), *Dress, Sex and Text in Chinese Culture*, Monash Asia Institute, Australia, 1999.

Foot, Michael R. D., *Art and War. Twentieth Century Warfare as Depicted by War Artists*, Headline, London, 1990.

Foreigners in Chinese Art, The China Institute in America, New York, 1969.

Geertz, Clifford, *The Interpretation of Cultures*, Basic Books, New York, 1973.

Ghiglione, L., *The American Journalist. Paradox of the Press*, Library of Congress, Washington DC, 1990.

Gillard, Joseph, *The Struggle for Asia, 1824–1914*, London, Methuen, 1977.

Goldstein, J., J. Israel and Hilary Conroy (eds), *America Views China. American Images of China Then and Now*, Associated University Press, New Jersey, 1991.

Goldstein, R. J., *Censorship of Political Caricature in Nineteenth Century France*, Kent State University Press, Ohio, 1989.

Goldstein, Tom (ed.), *Killing the Messenger. 100 Years of Media Criticism*, Columbia University Press, New York, 1989.

Gombrich, Ernst, *Meditations on a Hobby Horse and Other Essays on the Theory of Art*, Phaidon Press, London, 1963.

———. "The Evidence of Images," in C. S. Singleton (ed.), *Interpretation Theory and Practice*, John Hopkins Press, Baltimore, 1969.

Gombrich, E. and E. Kris, *Caricature*, Penguin, London, 1940.

Goncharoff, Nicko and Robert, Storey, *Lonely Planet Guide to China*, Lonely Planet Publications, 5th Edition, Melbourne, 1996.

The Graphic Art of Chinese Folklore, National Museum of History, Republic of China, Taipei, 1977.

Griffith, Samuel B. (translator), *Sun Zi; The Art of War*, Oxford University Press, Oxford, 1963.

Hales, P. B., *William Henry Jackson and the Transformation of the American Landscape*, Temple University Press, Philadelphia, 1988.

Harrison, James, *The Communists and Chinese Peasant Rebellions: A Study in the Rewriting of Chinese History*, Atheneum, New York, 1971.

Harrist, Robert E., "A Letter from Wang Hsi-chih and the Culture of Chinese Calligraphy," in Robert E. Harrist and Wen C. Fong (eds), *The Embodied Image. Chinese Calligraphy from the John B. Elliott Collection*, The Art Museum, Princeton University Press, 1999.

Harrist, Robert E. and Wen C. Fong (eds), *The Embodied Image. Chinese Calligraphy from the John B. Elliott Collection*, The Art Museum, Princeton University Press, 1999.

Hegel, Robert E., "Distinguishing Levels of Audiences for Ming-Ching Vernacular Audiences: A Case Study," in E. Johnson, Andrew J. Nathan and Evelyn S. Rawski (eds), *Popular Culture in Late Imperial China*, University of California Press, Berkeley, 1985.

———, *Reading Chinese Illustrated Fiction in Late Imperial China*, Stanford University Press, Stanford, 1998.

Hevia, James L., *English Lessons: The Pedagogy of Imperialism in Nineteenth Century* (forthcoming).

The History of the Times: The Twentieth Century Test 1884–1912, Krause, London, 1971 (1947).

Hichberger, Joan W. M., *Images of the Army. The Military in British Art 1815–1914*, Manchester University Press, Manchester, 1988.

Hodgson, Pat, *The War Illustrators*, Osprey, London, 1977.

Hodnett, Edward, *English Woodcuts 1480–1535*, Oxford University Press, London, 1935.

Hoe, Susanne, *Women at the Siege, Peking, 1900*, The Women's History Press, Oxford, 2000.

Hsü, Immanuel C.Y., *The Rise of Modern China*, Oxford University Press, Oxford/New York, 1995.

Hu Bin, "Contradictions and Conflicts among the Imperialist Powers in China at the Time of the Boxer Movement," in David D. Buck (ed.), *Recent Studies of the Boxer Movement: Chinese Studies in History*, Vol. 20, No. 3–4, Spring–Summer 1987.

Hucker, Charles O., "Hu Tsung-hsien's Campaign Against Hsü Hai 1556," in Frank A. Kierman and John K. Fairbank, *Chinese Ways in Warfare*, Harvard University Press, Cambridge, Massachusetts, 1974.

Hunter, Jane, *The Gospel of Gentility: American Women Missionaries in Turn-of-the-Century China*, Yale University Press, New Haven, 1984.

Hu Zhaojing (ed.), *Yangliuqing nianhua* (Yanliuqing New Year Pictures), Wenwu chubanshe, Beijing, 1984.

Humbert, J., Dumarche, L. and Pierron, M., *Photographies Anciennes, 1848–1918, Regards sur le Soldat et la Societé*, Collections Historiques du Musée de l'Armée, Paris, 1985.

Hutchinson, Robert, *1800 Woodcuts by Thomas Bewick and His School*, Dover Publications, New York, 1962.

Isaacs, Harold, *Images of Asia. American Views of China and India* (originally *Scratches on Our Minds*), Harper and Rowe, New York, 1972.

Iwasaki, J. and Shimizu, K. (eds), *Yomeru Nenpyo-Bekkan. Meiji Taisho Fushi Mangato Seso-Fuzoku Nenpyo*, Dainippon Insatsu, Tokyo, 1982.

Jackson, Mason, *The Pictorial Press. Its Origin and Progress*, New York, 1969 (1885).

Jian Bozan et al. (eds), *Yihetuan* (The Boxers), 4 Vols., Shenzhou guoguang she, Shanghai, 1953 (1951).

Johnson, D., Nathan, A. J. and Rawski, E. (eds), *Popular Culture in Late Imperial China*, University of California Press, Berkeley, 1985.

Johnston, Alistair Iain, *Cultural Realism. Strategic Culture and Grand Strategy in Chinese History*, Princeton University Press, Princeton, 1995.

Jones, W. M., *The Cartoon History of Britain*, Tom Stacey, London, 1971.

Joseph, Philip, *Foreign Diplomacy in China, 1894–1900: A Study in Political and Economic Relations with China*, George Allen and Unwin, London, 1928.

Jussim, Elizabeth, *Visual Communication and the Graphic Arts: Photographic Technologies in the Nineteenth Century*, R. R. Bowker, New York, 1974.

Keegan, John, *The Face of Battle: A Study of Agincourt, Waterloo, and the Somme*, Viking, New York, 1976.

———, *A History of Warfare*, Hutchinson, London, 1993.

Keen, Sam, *Faces of the Enemy. Reflections of the Hostile Imagination*, Harper and Row, San Francisco, 1986.

Kelly, John S., *A Forgotten Conference: The Negotiations at Peking, 1900–1901*, Librairie E. Droz, Geneva, 1963.

Kennedy, Thomas L., *The Arms of Kiangnan: Modernization in the Chinese Ordnance Industry, 1860–1895*, Westview Press, Colorado, 1978.

Keown-Boyd, Henry, *Fists of Righteous Harmony: A History of the Boxer Uprising in China in the Year 1900*, Leo Cooper, London, 1991.

Kierman, Frank A. and John K. Fairbank, *Chinese Ways in Warfare*, Harvard University Press, Cambridge, Massachusetts, 1974.

Killy, Walter (ed.), *Literatur Lexicon. Autoren und Werke Deutsche Sprache*, Vol. 5, Bertelsmann Lexicon Verlag, Munich, 1990.

Knight, Ian, *Queen Victoria's Enemies (4): Asia, Australasia and the American's*, Osprey Publishing, London, 1990.

Kobre, Sidney, *Development of American Journalism*, William C. Brown, Iowa, 1969.

Kotenev, Anatol M., *The Chinese Soldier. Basic Principles, Spirit, Science of War and Heroes of the Chinese Armies*, Kelly and Walsh Ltd., Shanghai, 1937.

Kristeller, Paul, *Küpferstich und Holzschnitt in Vier Jahrhunderten*, Verlag von Bruno Cassirer, Berlin, 1922.

Kuhn, Philip A., *Rebellion and Its Enemies in Late Imperial China. Militarization and Social Structure 1796–1864*, Harvard University Press, Cambridge, Massachusetts, 1980.

———, *Soulstealers: The Chinese Sorcery Scare of 1768*, Harvard University Press, Cambridge, Massachusetts, 1990.

Kuo Li-ch'eng, *The Graphic Art of Chinese Folklore*, National Museum of History, Republic of China, 1977.

Lalumia, Matthew Paul, *Realism and Politics in Victorian Art of the Crimean War*, UMI Research Press, Michigan, 1984.

Landsberger, Stefan, *Chinese Propaganda Posters. From Revolution to Modernization*, The Pepin Press (Feiqing Shuju), Singapore, 1998 (1995).

Lee, Ou-Fan Lee and Andrew J. Nathan, "The Beginnings of Mass Culture: Journalism and Fiction in the Late Qing and Beyond," in D. Johnson, Andrew J. Nathan and Evelyn S. Rawski (eds), *Popular Culture in Late Imperial China*, University of California Press, Berkeley, 1985.

Leibo, Steven A., *Transferring Technology to China: Prosper Giquel and the Self-Strengthening Movement*, University of California Press, Berkeley, 1985.

Lévi-Strauss, Claude, *Race et Histoire*, Denoël, France, 1995 (1952).

Lewis, Hodous, *Folkways in China*, Probsthain, London, 1929.

Lewis, Michael, *The History of the British Navy*, Pelican, 1957.

Liaboeuf, Dominique and Jorge Svartzman (eds), *L'Oeuil du Consul. Auguste François en Chine (1896–1904)*, Musée Guimet, Paris, 1989.

Liang, Ellen J. *The Winking Owl: Art in the People's Republic of China*, University of California Press, Berkeley, 1988.

Liao Yizhong, Li Dezheng and Zhang Xuanru, *Yihetuan yundong shi* (A History of the Boxer Movement), Renmin chubanshe, Beijing, 1981.

Liao Yizhong, "Special Features of the Boxer Movement," in David D. Buck (ed.), *Recent Studies of the Boxer Movement: Chinese Studies in History*, Vol. 20, No. 3, Spring–Summer 1987.

Li Baoyi (ed.), *Zhongguo nianhua shi* (A History of Chinese New Year Prints), Liaoning Art Publisher, 1986.

Li Dezheng, Su Weizhi and Liu Tianlu, *Baguo lianjun qinhua shi* (A History of the Eight-Power Allied Forces Aggression Against China), Shandong University Press, Jinan, 1990.

Li Jikui, "How to View the Boxers' Religious Superstitions," in David D. Buck (ed.), *Recent Studies of the Boxer Movement: Chinese Studies in History*, Vol. 20, No. 3, Spring–Summer 1987.

Lin Yutang, *A History of the Press and Public Opinion in China*, Institute of Pacific Relations, Shanghai, 1936.

Liu Beisi and Xu Qixian (eds), *Gugong zhencang renwu zhaopian huicui* (Selection of

Photographs of People Kept at the Imperial Palace), Forbidden City Publishing House, Beijing, 1994.

Liu Kuili (ed.), *Zhongguo minjian wenhua congshu* (Selected Works of Chinese Folk Culture), Zhejiang Educational Publishers, 1989.

Liu Junyu, (illustrator), *Watermargin*, 1955.

Liu Zhicao and Guan Jian, *Zhengduo yu guonan. Jia cheng Ri-E zhanzheng* (Conflict and the Chinese Humiliation The Russo-Japanese War") Lionhai, Shenyang, 1999.

Loer, Max, *Chinese Landscape Woodcuts*, Belknap Press, Cambridge, Massachusetts, 1968.

Lo Hui-min (ed.), *The Correspondence of* G. E. *Morrison*, Cambridge University Press, New York, 1976.

Lu Shengzhong, *Zhongguo minjian muke banhua* (Chinese Folk Woodblock Prints), Hunan meishu chubanshe, Changsha, 1990.

Lu Yao et al. (eds), *Shandong yihetuan diaocha ziliao xuanbian* (Selections from Survey Materials on Fieldwork on the Shandong Boxers), Qilu shushe Jinan, 1980.

———, "The Origins of the Boxers," in David D. Buck (ed), *Recent Studies of the Boxer Movement: Chinese Studies in History*, Vol. 30, No. 3, Spring–Summer, 1987.

———, *Shandong daxue. Yihetuan diaocha ziliao huibian* (Shandong University. Documents Relating to the Oral History of the Boxers). Shandong University Press, Shandong, 2000.

Lucas, C. J. (ed.), *James Ricalton's Photographs of China During the Boxer Rebellion. His Illustrated Travelogue of 1900*, Edwin Mellen Press, New York, 1990.

Lust, John, *Chinese Popular Prints*, E. J. Brill, Leiden, 1996.

Mackerras, Colin, *The Chinese Theatre in Modern Times: From 1840 to the Present Day*. University of Massachusetts Press, 1975.

———, *Western Images of China*, Oxford University Press, Oxford, 1989.

MacDonald, G., *Camera, A Victorian Eyewitness*., B. T. Batsford, London, 1979.

Madaro, Adriano, *The Boxer Rebellion*, Europrint Edition, Milan, 2001.

Mak, Ricardo S and Danny S. L. Pau (eds), *Sino-German Relations since 1860: Multidisciplinary Explorations*, Peter Lang, Hamburg, 2000.

Marchant, L. R. (ed.), Lancelot Giles, *The Siege of the Peking Legations. A Diary*, University of Western Australia Press, Nedlands, 1970.

Marcus, Leonard S., *An Epinal Album, Popular Prints from Nineteenth Century France*, D. R. Godine, Boston, 1984.

Martin, Christopher, *The Boxer Rebellion*, Abelard-Schumann, London, 1968.

Masamichi, Asukai et al., *Meiji taisho zushi*, Vol. 16, Chikuma Shobo, Tokyo, 1979.

McAleary, Henry, *Black Flags in Vietnam: The Story of a Chinese Intervention*, George, Allen and Unwin, Great Britain, 1968.

McClellan, Robert, *The Heathen Chinee: A Study of American Attitudes Towards China 1890–1906*, Ohio State University Press, Columbus, 1971.

McIntyre, Tanya, "Images of Women in Popular Prots of the Early Modern Period," in Antonia Finnane and Anne McLaren (eds), *Dress, Sex and Text in Chinese Culture*, Monash Asia Institute, Australia, 1999.

Meyer, Maurits de, *Imagerie Populaire des Pays-bas. Belgique, Hollande*, Electra, Milan, 1970.

Miller, Stewart C., *The Unwelcome Immigrant. The American Image of the Chinese 1785–1882*, University of California Press, California, 1969.

Milton, Joyce, *The Yellow Kids: Foreign Correspondents in the Heyday of Yellow Journalism*, Harper and Rowe, New York, 1989.

Mo Anshi, *Yihetuan dikang lieqiang guafen shi* (The History of the Boxers' Struggle Against the Foreign Countries Who Wanted to Divide China), Jingji guanli, Beijing, 1997.

Moxy, Keith, *Peasants, Warriors and Wives. Popular Imagery in the Reformation*, University of Chicago Press, Chicago, 1989.

Moxy, Keith, *Peasants, Warriors and Wives. Popular Imagery in the Reformation*, University of Chicago Press, Chicago, 1989.

Mühlhanh, Klaus, "*Musterkolonie*", *Kiautschoui Interaktionen zwischen China und Deutschland, 1897–1914*, R. Oldenbourg, Munich, 2000.

Murrell, W., *A History of American Graphic Humor, 1865–1938*, Cooper Square Publishing, New York, 1976.

Nachbauer, A. and Wang Ngen Young, *Les Images Populaires Chinoises*, Na zhe bao, Peking, 1926.

Nathan, Joseph, *Uniforms and Non-Uniforms. Communication through Clothing*, Contributions in Sociology, No. 61, Greenwood Press, Westport, Connecticut, 1986.

Naquin, Susan, *Millenarian Rebellion in China: The Eight Trigrams Uprising of 1813*, Yale University Press, New Haven, 1976.

———, *Shantung Rebellion: The Wang Lun Uprising of 1774*, Yale University Press, New Haven, 1981.

Nicholls, Robert, *Bluejackets and Boxers, Australia's Naval Expedition to the Boxer Uprising*, Allen and Unwin, Sydney, 1986.

Ohle, Karl-Heinz, *Das Ich und das Andere. Grundzüge*, Metzler, Stuttgart, 1978.

Paret, Peter, *Imagined Battles. Reflections of War in European Art*, University of North Carolina Press, Chapel Hill, 1997.

Petschull, Jurgen, *Der Wahn vom Weltreich. Die Geschichte der Deutschen Kolonien*, Thomas Höpker, Würzburg, 1984.

Powell, Ralph L., *The Rise of Chinese Military Power, 1895–1912*, Princeton University Press, Princeton, 1955.

Preston, Diana, *The Boxer Rebellion: The Dramatic Story on Foreigners That Shook the World in the Summer of 1900*, Walker and Company, New York, 2000.

Price, Sally, *Primitive Art in Civilized Places*, University of Chicago Press, Chicago, 1989.

Purcell, Victor W., *The Boxer Uprising. A Background Study*, Cambridge University Press, Great Britain, 1963.

Rawlinson, John L., "China's Failure to Coordinate Her Modern Fleets in the Late Nineteenth Century," in A. Feuerwerker, R. Murphey and M. C. Wright (eds), *Approaches to Modern History*, University of California Press, Berkeley, 1967.

Rawski, Evelyn, "Economic and Social Foundations of Late Imperial Culture," in E. Johnson, A. J. Nathan and E. S. Rawski (eds), *Popular Culture in Late Imperial China*, University of California Press, Berkeley, 1985.

Régamey, F., *La Caricature Allemande pendant la Guerre*, Berger-Lerrault, Paris, 1921.

Reschef, O., *Guerre, Mythes et Caricature. Au Berceau d'une Mentalité Française*, Presses de la fondation nationale des sciences politiques, Paris, 1984.

Reynolds, Henry, *The Other Side of the Frontier: An Interpretation of Aboriginal Response to the Invasion and Settlement of Australia*, History Department, Townsville, Queensland, 1981.

Roberts, Moss (translator and editor), *The Three Kingdoms*, Pantheon Books, New York, 1976.

Rowley, George, *Principles of Chinese Painting*, Princeton University Press, Princeton, 1970 (1947).

Rudisill, R., *Mirror Image. The Lure of the Daguerreotype on American Society*, University of Mexico Press, Albuquerque, 1971.

Rudova, Maria, *Chinese Popular Prints*, Aurora Art Publishers, Leningrad, 1988.

Said, Edward W., *Orientalism*, Pantheon Books, New York, 1978.

Shi Yuceng, *Yihetuan yundong yibai zhounian jinian: Yihetuan yundong he baguo lianjun qinhua zhanzheng* (Commemoration of the Centennial of the Boxer Movement: The Boxer Movement and the Eight Allied Forces War of Agression), Chuzhong Huiguan, Tokyo, 2000.

Schodt, F. I., *Manga! Manga! The World of Japanese Comics*, Kodansha International, Japan, 1983.

Schrecker, John E., *Imperialism and Chinese Nationalism: Germany in Shantung*, Harvard University Press, Massachusetts, 1991.

Schultz, Raymond L., *Crusaders in Babylon. W.T. Stead and the Pall Mall Gazette*, University of Nebraska Press, 1972.

Seagrave, Sterling, *Dragon Lady: The Life and Legend of the Last Empress of China*, Alfred A. Knopf, New York, 1992.

Selby, John, *The Paper Dragon. An Account of the China Wars, 1840–1900*, Arthur Baker Ltd, London, 1969.

Sharf, Frederick A. and Peter Harrington, *The Boxer Rebellion. China, 1900. The Artists' Perspective*, Greenhill Books, London, 2000.

———, *China, 1900. The Eyewitnesses Speak. The Boxer Rebellion as Described by Participants in Letters, Diaries and Photographs*, Greenhill Books, London, 2000.

Singleton, Charles S. (ed.), *Interpretation, Theory and Practice*, Johns Hopkins Press, Baltimore, 1969.

Smith, Bernard, *European Vision and the South Pacific*, Harper and Rowe, Sydney, 1985.

Spector, Stanley, *Li Hung Chang and the Huai Army. A Study in Nineteenth Century Chinese Regionalism*, University of Washington Press, 1974.

Spence, Jonathan, *The Search for Modern China*, W.W. Norton, London, 1990.

Spufford, Margaret, *Small Books and Pleasant Histories. Popular Fiction and Its Readership in Seventeenth-Century England*, Cambridge University Press, Cambridge, 1981.

Ssu Yu Teng and John K. Fairbank (eds), *China's Response to the West*, Harvard University Press, Massachusetts, 1961.

Startt, James D., *Journalists for Empire: The Imperial Debate in the Edwardian Stately Press, 1903–1913*, Greenwood Press, New York, 1991.

Stavrianos, L. S., *Lifelines from Our Past. A New World History*, Pantheon Books, New York, 1989.

Steiger, George Nye, *China and the Occident. The Origins and Development of the Boxer Movement*, Russell and Russell, New York, 1966.

Steinberg, S.H., *Five Hundred Years of Printing*, Harmondsworth, Pelican, 1961.

Sullivan, Michael, *The Meeting of Eastern and Western Art from the Sixteenth Century to the Present Day*, Thames and Hudson, London, 1973.

Sun Qihai, *Tiexue bainianji: Baguo lianjun qinhua zhanzheng jishi* (Commemoration of the Centennial of the War Against the Eight Allied Forces Aggression) Huanghe, Jinan, 2000.

Sun Tzu, *The Art of War*, translated by Samuel B. Griffith, Oxford University Press, UK, 1963.

Sun-tzu, *The Art of Warfare: The First English Translation Incorporating the Recently Discovered Yin-chueh-shan Texts*, Translated by Roger T. Ames, Ballantine Books, New York, 1993.

Su Weizhi and Liu Tianlu (eds), *Yihetuan yundong yibai zhounian guoji xueshu taolun hui lunwen* (The Papers Collected at the International Meeting to Commemorate the Centennial Year of the Boxer Movement), Shandong daxue chubanshe, (forthcoming).

Suzhuo chuantong banhua Taiwan shoucang zhan (Collectors Show of Traditional Suzhuo Woodblock Prints in Taiwan), Xing Zhengyuan wenhua jianshe weiyuanhui, Taibei, 1987.

Sze Mai-mai (ed), *The Mustard Seed Garden Manual of Painting* (Jieziyuan huapu) Bollingren Series, Princeton University Press, Princeton, 1978.

Taboulet, Georges, *La Geste Française en Indochine. Histoire par les Textes de la France en Indochine des Origines à 1914*, Librairie Adrien-Maisonneuve, Paris, 1955.

Taft, Robert, *Photography and the American Scene. A Social History 1839–1889*, Dover Publications, New York, 1938.

Tagg, John, *The Burden of Representation. Essays on Photographies and Histories*, MacMillan Education, Minneapolis, USA, 1988.

Taiwan chuantong banhua yuanliu te zhan ("Special Exhibition of Traditional Woodblock Prints of Taiwan"), Taibei, 1985.

Tan, Chester C., *The Boxer Catastrophe*, Octagon Books Inc., New York, 1967.

Tanaka, Issei "The Social and Historical Content of Ming-Ch'ing Local Drama," in David Johnson, Andrew J. Nathan and Evelyn S. Rawski (eds), *Popular Culture in Late Imperial China*, University of California Press, Berkeley, 1985.

Thiriez, Régine, *Barbarian Lens: Western Photographers of the Qianlong European Emperor's Palaces*, Gordon and Breach Publishers, Amsterdam, 1998.

Thompson, E. P., *The Making of the English Working Class*, Victor Gollancz Ltd., London, 1956.

Thompson, Roger R., "Military Dimensions of the 'Boxer Uprising' in Shanxi, 1898–1901," in Hans van de Ven (ed.), *Warfare in Chinese History*, Sinica Leidensia, Brill, Leiden, 2000.

Tiedemann, Gary R., "Christian Civilization or Cultural Expansion? The German Missionary Enterprise in China," in Mak, Ricardo and Pau, Danny S. L. (eds), *Sino-German Relations since 1860: Multidisciplinary Explorations*, Peter Lang, Hamburg, 2000.

Toynbee, Arnold, *Half the World: The History and Culture of China and Japan*, Thames and Hudson, London, 1973.

Trachtenberg, Alan, *Reading American Photographs. Images as History. Mathew Brady to Walker Evans*, Hill and Wang, USA, 1989.

Trevor-Roper, Hugh, *Hermit of Peking: The Hidden Life of Sir Edmund Backhouse*, Alfred A. Knopf, New York, 1977.

Unterreider, Else, *Glück ein Ganzes Mondjahr Lang. Chinesische Neujahrsbilder*, Carinthia, Klagenfurt, 1984.

Vayda, Andrew P., *Maori Warfare*, Wellington, 1960.

Ven, Hans van de (ed.), *Warfare in Chinese History*, Vol. 47, Sinica Leidensia, Brill, Leiden, 2000.

Waley-Cohen, Joanna, *The Sextants of Beijing. Global Currents in Chinese History*, W. W. Norton, New York, 1999.

———. "Military Ritual and the Qing Empire" in Cosmo Nicola di (ed), *Warfare in Inner Asian History*, E. J. Brill, Leiden (forthcoming).

Wang Bomin, *Zhongguo banhua shi* (History of Chinese Prints), Peoples' Art Publishers, Shanghai, 1961.

Wang Shucun, *Ancient Woodblock New Year Prints*, Foreign Languages Press, Beijing, 1985.

———, *Zhongguo minjian nianhua baitu* (One Hundred Chinese Folk New Year Pictures), Renmin meishu chubanshe, Beijing, 1988.

———, *Sulian cang Zhongguo minjian nianhua zhenpin ji* (Compilation of Chinese Folk New Year Picture Treasures in Soviet Collections), Zhongguo renmin meishu chubanshe and Sulianafulia chubanshe, Beijing, 1989.

———, *Xiju Nianhua Zhongguo meishu shi tulu congshu* (Illustrative Record of the History of Chinese Folk New Year Pictures: Collection of Records of Chinese Fine Arts), Yingwen Hansheng Publishers, Taibei, 1991

———, *Zhongguo minjian nianhua shi lunji* (Collected Essays on the History of Chinese Folk New Year Pictures) , Yangliuqing hua chubanshe, Tianjin, 1991.

———, *Xiju Nianhua* (Theatrical New Year Prints), Hansheng Publishers, Taibei, Taiwan, 1991.

Wang Shucun (with Li Zhiqiang), *Zhongguo minjian nianhua shi tulu: Zhongguo meishu shi tulu congshu* (Illustrated Records of the History of Chinese Folk New Year Pictures: Collection of Records of Chinese Fine Arts), Shanghai renmin meishu chubanshe Publishers, Shanghai, 1991.

Wang Shucun (with Li Zhiqiang), *Zhongguo Yangliuqing muban nianhua ji* (Album of Paintings of Yangliuqing Woodblock New Year Pictures), Tianjin Yangliuqing huashe, Tianjin, 1992.

Warner, Marina, *The Dragon Empress: Life and Times of Tz'u-hsi (1835–1908, Empress Dowager of China*, London, Weidenfeld and Nicholson, 1972.

Warner, Oliver, *The British Navy. A Concise History*, Thames and Hudson, London, 1975.

Weaver, Paul H., *News and the Culture of Lying*, Free Press, New York, 1994.

Wechsler, Judith, *A Human Comedy: Physiognomy and Caricature in Nineteenth Century Paris*, Thames and Hudson, London, 1982.

Wiener, Joel H. (ed.), *Papers for the Millions: The New Journalism in Britain, 1850's to 1914*, Greenwood Press, New York, 1988.

Wise, Frederick May, *A Marine Tells It to You.* As told by Frederick May Wise to M. O. Forst, Quantical, Virginia, Marine Corps Association, 1981.

Wolff, Janet, *Social Production of Art*, MacMillan, London, 1981.

Wood, Walter, *Marvellous Escapes from Peril as told by Survivors*, Blackie and Son, London, no date.

Woodham-Smith, Cecil, *The Reason Why*, Penguin Books, 1958.

Worswick, Clark and Spence, Jonathan (eds), *Imperial China. Photographs 1850–1912*, ANU Press, Canberra, 1980.

Wright, Mary C., *The Last Stand of Chinese Conservatism. The T'ung Chih Restoration 1862–1874*, Stanford University Press, Stanford, 1957.

Wylie, R. F., "American Diplomacy in China, 1843–1857," in J. Goldstein, J. Israel and H. Controy (eds), *America Views China: American Images of China Then and Now*, Associated University Press, New Jersey, 1991.

Xiang, Lanxin, *The Origins of the Boxer War: A Multinational Study*, Curzon Press, London, 2001.

Yang Congsen, *Nafu yingxiang* (Enjoy Good Fortune, Welcome a Suspicious Things) Guoli zhongyang tushuguan tecangzu, Taibei, 1991.

Yao Qian (ed.), *Tuohuawu Nianhua* (Tuohuawu New Year Pictures), Wenwu chubanshe, Shanghai, 1985.

Yihetuan shiliao (Historical Materials on the Boxers), 2 Vols., Ed. Zhongguo shehui kexueyuan jindaishi yanjiusuo "jindaishi ziliao" bianjizu ("Modern Historical Materials" Editorial Group of the Modern History Institute of the Chinese

Academy of the Social Sciences), Zhongguo shehui kexue chubanshe, Beijing, 1982.

Yihetuan tongsu huashi, Cilian Publishers, Shanghai, 1954.

Zhang Daoyi (ed), *Minjian mubanhua* (Folk Woodblock Prints), Jiangsu Art Publishers, Jiangsu, 1990.

Zhang Dianying, *Yangjiabu muban Nianhua* (New Year Woodblock Prints from Yangjiabu), Wenwu chubanshe, Beijing, 1990.

Zhang Jinlan (ed.), *Weifang nianhua yanjiu* (Research on Weifang New Year Pictures), Xuelin chubanshe, Shanghai, 1991.

Zhao Jianli, *Yihetuan, baguo lianjun, xingchou tiaoyue. Gengzi zhi bian tuzhi* (The Boxers, the Eight Invading Powers, the Boxer Protocol. Illustrated Records of the Changes That Happened in the Year 1900), Shandong huabao, Jinan, 2000.

Zheng Zhenduo, *Zhongguo suwenxue shi* (The History of Chinese Popular Literature), Beijing, 1954.

Zhongfa zhanzheng xingshi tu (A Situation Map of the Sino-French War), Ditu chubanshe, Beijing, 1978.

Later Articles and Papers

Alba, Victor, "The Mexican Revolution and the Cartoon," *Comparative Studies in Society and History*, Vol. 9, No. 2, January 1967.

Ashton, Susanne "Compound Walls: Eva Jane Price's Letters From a Chinese Mission, 1890–1900," *Frontiers*, September 1996, Vol. 17, No. 3.

Bastid-Bruguière, Marianne, "Currents of Social Change," in Denis Twitchett and John K. Fairbank, *The Cambridge History of China*, Cambridge University Press, Cambridge, 1978 (1994), Vol II, Part 2, Chapter 10,

Bodde, Derk, and S. Galia "Chinese Folk Art and the Russian Sinologist, V. M. Alexeev," *Journal of Asian Studies*, Vol. 27, 1968.

Brinkman, D., "Do Educational Cartoons and Editorials Change Opinions?", *Journalism Quarterly*, Vol. 45, No. 4, 1968.

Brown, Aimée, "Official Artists and Not-so-official Art: Covert Caricaturists in Nineteenth Century France," *Art Journal*, 43, 1983.

Carl, L. M., "Educational Cartoons Fail to Catch Many Readers," *Journalism Quarterly*, Vol. 45, No. 4, 1968.

Ch'en, Jerome, "The Nature and Characteristics of the Boxer Movement: A Morphological Study," *Bulletin of the School of Oriental and African Studies*, Vol. 23, No. 2, 1960.

Cloud, Barbara., "News: Public Service or Profitable Property," *American Journalism*, Vol. 13, No. 2, 1996.

Congden, Kirsten G., "Finding the Tradition in Folk-Art: An Art Educator's Perspective," *Journal of Aesthetic Education*, Vol. 20, No. 3, 1986.

Corniot, Christine, "La Guerre des Boxeurs d'Après la Presse Française," *Etudes Chinoises*, Vol. VI, No. 2, 1987. *Annales du Musée Guimet et du Musée Cernuschi*, published by the Ecole Française d'Extrème Orient with the cooperation of the CNRS, 1978.

Coupe, W. A., "The German Cartoon and the Revolution of 1848," *Comparative Studies in Society and History*, Vol. 9, No. 2, January 1967.

———, "Observations on a Theory of Political Caricature," *Comparative Studies in Society and History*, Vol. 11, 1969.

Davis, Edward I., "Arms and the Tao: Hero, Cult and Empire in Traditional China," in Sodaishi Kenkyukai (ed) (Research Association for Song Dynasty History) *Sodai no Shakai to Shukyo* (Society and Religion in the Song Dynasty), Vol. 2, Tokyo, 1985.

Desnoyers, Charles, Review of Diana Preston, *The Boxer Rebellion: The Dramatic Story of China's War on Foreigners that Shook the World in the Summer of 1900*, in *Asian Affairs*, Vol. 3, Part 1, February 2000.

Doar, Bruce, "The Boxers in Chinese Drama: Questions of Interaction," *Papers in Far Eastern History*, Vol. 29, 1984.

Douglas, Bronwen, "Almost Constantly at War?" *Journal of Pacific History*, June 1990.

Duara, Prasenjit, "Superscribing Symbols: The Myth of Guandi, Chinese God of War," *Journal of Asian Studies*, Vol. 47, No. 4, November, 1988.

———, "Knowledge and Power in the Discourse of Modernity: The Campaigns Against Popular Religion in Early Twentieth-Century China," *Journal of Asian Studies*, Vol. 50, No. 1, February 1991.

Dubosc, Jean-Paul, "Images Popularies Chinoises," *Arts et Métiers Graphiques*, No. 37, 1933.

Dunsthemier, G. G. H., "Le Movement des Boxeurs: Documents et études publiés depuis le deuxième Guerre mondiale," *Revue Historique*, Vol. 232, No. 2, April–June 1964.

Durand, Maurice, "Imagerie Populaire Vietnamienne," *Ecole Française d'Extrème-Orient*, Vol. XLVII, Paris, 1960.

Eliasberg, Danielle, "Imagerie Populaire Chinoise du Nouvel An," *Arts Asiatiques. Annales du Musée Guimet et du Musée Cernuschi*, published by the Ecole Française d'Extrème Orient with the cooperation of the CNRS, 1978.

Elliott, Jane E., "Who Seeks the Truth Should Be of No Country. The British and American Press Report the Boxer Rebellion, June 1900," *American Journalism*, Vol. 13, No. 3, Summer 1996.

———, "American Photographs of the Boxer Rising," *History of Photography*, Vol. 21, No. 2, Summer 1997.

———, "The Choosers or the Dispossessed? Aspects of the Work of Some French Eighteenth Century Pacific Explorers," *Oceania*, Vol. 67, No. 3, March 1997.

———, "Shijiu shiji waiguoren paishe de Zhongguo shibing" (Nineteenth Century Foreign Photographs of Chinese Soldiers), *Lao Zhaopian*, Vol. 7, 1998.

Elvin, Mark E., Review of Jonathan Spence, *The Search for Modern China* in the *National Interest*, Fall, 1900.

Esherick, J. W., "Cherishing Sources from Afar," *Modern China*, Vol. 24, No. 2, April 1988.

———, "Tradutore, Traditore: A Reply to James Hevia," *Modern China*, Vol. 24, No. 3, July 1998.

———, Book review of Paul A. Cohen, *History in Three Keys. The Boxers as Event, Experience and Myth* in *Journal of Social History*, Vol. 32, 1988.

Franz, Michael, "The Military Organization and Power Structure of China During the Taiping Rebellion," *Pacific Historical Review*, No. 18, 1949.

Fung, Allen, "Testing the Self-strengthening: The Chinese Army in the Sino-Japanese War of 1894–1895," *Modern Asian Studies*, Vol. 30, No. 4, 1996.

Garver, John W., "Feature Review," *Diplomatic History*, Vol. 22, No. 3, Summer 1998.

Goodrich, Anne S., "Peking Paper Gods: A Look at Home Worship," *T'oung Pao*, Vol. LXXX, 1994.

Guttman, Jon, "Pride-Excessive, Wounded or Unrealistic — Influenced Events During the Boxer Rebellion and in Korea," *Military History*, Vol. 17, No. 2, June 2000.

Harr, Barend J. ter, Review of Po Song-nien and David Johnston, *Domesticated Deities and Auspicious Emblems: The Iconography of Everyday Life in Village China in T'oung Pao*, Vol. LXXX, 1994.

Harrison, Henrietta, "Justice on Behalf of Heaven," *History Today*, September 2000.

Henning, Stanley E., "Academia Encounters the Chinese Martial Arts," *National Physical Culture and Sports Commission Martial Arts Research Institute's Chinese Martial Arts History*, Vol. 6, No. 2, Fall 1999.

———, "Chinese Boxing: The Internal and External Schools in the Light of History and Theory," *Journal of Asian Martial Arts*, Vol. 6, No. 3, 1997.

———, "Observations on a Visit to Shaolin Monastery," *Journal of Asian Martial Arts*, Vol. 7, No. 1, 1988.

———, "Southern Fists and Northern Legs: The Geography of Chinese Boxing," *Journal of Asian Martial Arts*, Vol. 7, No, 3, 1988.

———, "The Chinese Martial Arts in Historical Perspective," *Journal of Military History*, December, 1981.

Hevia, James L., "Leaving a Brand on China: Misssionary Discourse in the Wake of the Boxer Movement," *Modern China*, Vol. 18, No. 3, July 1992.

———, "Loot's Fate. The Economy of Plunder and the Moral Life of Objects," *History and Anthropology*, Vol. 6, No. 4, 1994.

———, "The Archive State and the Fear of Pollution: From the Opium Wars to Fu Manchu," *Cultural Studies*, Vol. 12, No. 2, April 1998.

———, "Polemical Historiography: A Response to Joseph W. Esherick, *Modern China*, Vol. 24, No. 3, July 1998.

Hung, Chang-tai, "Two Images of Socialism: Woodcuts in Chinese Communist Politics," *Society for Comparative Study of Society and History*, Vol. 39, No. 1, January 1977.

———, *Going to the People: Chinese Intellectuals and Folk Literature, 1918–1937*, Council on East Asian Studies, Harvard University, Cambridge Massachusetts, 1985.

Jian Ai Lüe Te (Jane Elliott), "19 shiji waiguoren paishe de Zhongguo shibing" (Nineteenth Century Foreign Photographs of Chinese Soldiers), *Lao Zhaopian*, Vol. 7, 1998.

Johnston, R. F. "Cult of Military Heroes in China," *New China Review*, February 1921.

Kawano, Teruaki, "Allied Military Co-operation in the Boxer Rebellion and Japan's Policy," *Revue Internationale d'Histoire Militaire*, No. 70, 1988.

Kemnitz, Thomas M., "The Cartoon as a Historical Source," *The Journal of Interdisciplinary History*, Vol. 4, No. 1, Summer 1973.

Kunzle, David, "Between Broadsheet Caricature and 'Punch': Cheap Newspaper Cuts for the Lower Classes in the 1830's," *Art Journal*, 43, 1983.

Laing, Ellen J. "Reform, Revolutionary, Political and Resistance Themes in Chinese Popular Printers, 1900–1940," *Modern Chinese Literature and Culture*, Vol. 12, No. 2, Fall 2000.

Lo, Winston S., "The Self-image of the Chinese Military in Historical Perspective," *Journal of Asian History*, January 1997.

Lorain, Pierre, "Les Armes de la Guerre des Boxeurs, 1900–1901," *Gazette des Armes*, No. 76, 1980.

Luttwak, Edward N., "Towards Post-Heroic Warfare," *Foreign Affairs*, Vol. 74, No. 3, May/June 1995.

McCauley, A., "Caricature and Physiognomy in Second Empire Paris," *Art Journal*, No. 43, 1983.

McCord, Edward A., "Militia and Local Militarization in Late Qing and Early Republican China," *Modern China*, Vol. 14, No. 2, April 1988.

Medhurst, M. J. and Desousa, M. A., "Political Cartoons as Rhetorical Form: A Taxonomy of Graphic Discourse," *Communication Monographs*, Vol. 48, September 1981.

Peters, M. and Mergen , B., "'Doing the Rest': The Uses of Photographs in American Studies," *American Quarterly*, Vol. 29, No. 2, 1977.

Reynolds, Henry, "Aboriginal Resistance in Queensland," *Australian Journal of Politics and History*, Vol. 22, 1976.

Shepter, Joseph, "An American Missionary's Engineering Talents Made Him a Hero During the Boxer Rebellion," *Military History*, Vol. 17, No. 2, June 2000.

Shineberg, Dorothy L., "Guns and Men in Melanesia," *Journal of Pacific History*, Vol. 9, No. 4, July 1967.

Showalter, Dennis E., "Dien Bien Phu in Three Cultures," *War and Society*, Vol. 16, No. 2, October 1998.

Smith, Richard J., and Kwang-Ching Liu, "The Military Challenge: the North-West and the Coast," in Twitchett, Denis and Fairbank, John K. (eds), *The Cambridge History of China*, Cambridge University Press, Cambridge, 1978 (1994), Vol, 2, Part 2, Chapter 4.

Streicher, L. H., "On a Theory of Political Caricature," *Comparative Studies in Society and History*, Vol. 9, No. 4, July 1967.

Stuart, I. R., "Iconography of Group Personality Dynamics: Caricatures and Cartoons," *Journal of Social Psychology*, Vol. 46, 1964.

Tiedemann, R. Gary, "Baptism of Fire: China's Christians and the Boxer Uprising of 1900," *International Bulletin of Missionary Research*, Vol. 24, Part 1, January 2000.

Waley-Cohen, Joanna, "China and Western Technology in the Late Eighteenth Century," *American Historical Review*, Vol. 98, No. 5, December 1993.

———, "Commemorating War in Eighteenth Century China," *Modern Asian Studies*, Vol. 30, No. 4, 1996.

———, "Religion, War and Empire-Building in Eighteenth-Century China," *The International History Review*, Vol. 20, No. 2, June 1998.

———, Review of Hans van de Ven (ed.), *Chinese Ways in Warfare*, in *China Review International*, Fall 2000.

Ward, B. E., "Regional Operas and Their Audiences: Evidence from Hong Kong," in E. Johnson, A. J. Nathan and E. S. Rawski (eds), *Popular Culture in Late Imperial China*, University of California Press, Berkeley, 1985.

Weisberger, Bernard A., "Righteous Fists: The Boxer Rebellion Casts a Harsh and Vivid Light on America's Long Complex Relationship with China," *American Heritage*, Vol. 48, No. 3, May–June 1997.

White, Stephen, "Felix Beato and the First Korean War, 1871," *The Photographic Collector*, 1982, Vol. I.

Wiest, Jean-Paul, "Catholic Images of the Boxers," *The American Asian Review*, Vol. 9, No. 3, Fall 1991.

Wou, Odoric Y. K., "Financing the New Army: Yuan Shi-k'ai and the Peiyang Army, 1895–1907," *Asian Profile*, Vol. 2, No. 4, August 1983.

Wright, David, "Careers in Western Science in Nineteenth Century China: Xu Shou and Xu Jianyin," *Journal of the Royal Asiatic Society*, Third Series, Vol. 5, No. 1, April 1995.

Wyman, Judith, "The Ambiguities of Anti-foreignism: Chongqing, 1870–1900," *Late Imperial China*, Vol. 18, No. 2, December 1997.

Xu Youwei and Billingsley Philip, "When Worlds Collide. Chinese Bandits and Their 'Foreign Tickets'," *Modern China*, Vol. 26, No. 1, January 2000.

Yang Zhouhan and Yue Daiyun (eds.), *Literature, Histories, and Literary Histories: The Proceedings of the Second Sino-US Comparative Literature Symposium*, Liaoning Press, 1989.

Zhang Longxi, "The Myth of the Other: China in the Eyes of the West," *Critical Inquiry*, Vol. 15, No. 7, Autumn 1988.

Zhang Junbo and Yao Yunzhu, "Differences Between Traditional Chinese and Western Military Thinking and Their Philosophical Roots," *Journal of Contemporary China*, Vol. 5, No. 12, July 1966.

Zheng Zhenduo, "Zhongguo banhua shi" (History of the Chinese Woodblock Print), in *Suzhou Taohuawu muban nianhua*, (Suzhou Taohuawu Woodblock New Year Pictures), Jiangsu Art Publishers, Jiangsu, 1991.

PhD Theses and Unpublished Papers

Barmé, Geremie, "Feng Zikai: A Biographical and Critical Study, 1898–1975," unpublished PhD Thesis, Australian National University, 1989.

Chen Xiao, "Shequ jiangying qun de lianhe he xingdong" (The Coalition and Movement of Elite Groups in the Community), unpublished paper given at the centennial conference of Boxer Studies, Jinan, October 2000.

Cohen, Paul A., "Humanizing the Boxers," unpublished paper given at the conference "1900. The Boxers, China and the World," SOAS, London, June 2001.

Dolby, Scott, "The Boxer Crisis as Seen Through the Eyes of Five Chinese Officials," unpublished PhD thesis, Columbia University, 1976.

Eberspächer, Cord, "'Germans to the Front'. The German Navy and the Boxer Rising," unpublished paper given at the conference "1900. The Boxers, China and the World," SOAS, London, June 2001.

Elliott, J. E., "Why Western Cultural Inhibitions Prevented the Exploitation of a Technology for Over Half a Century. An Analysis of Photographic Portraits of the Chinese and American Photographs of the Boxer Rising," unpublished paper, Centre for Asian Studies, University of Adelaide, 1995.

———, "Cartoons of the Boxer War; China the Conscience of the 'Civilised' World," unpublished paper given at the centennial conference of Boxer Studies, Jinan, October 2000.

———, "The Greatest Unsung Heroes of All Time: Soldiers of the Imperial Chinese Army, Summer 1900," unpublished paper prepared for the conference "1900. The Boxers, China and the World," SOAS, London, June 2001.

Elliott, Mark E. "Manchu (Re) Definitions of the nation in the Early Qing," Indiana East Coast Working Paper Series on Language and Politics in Modern China, Paper 7, January 1996.

Flath, James A., "Printing Culture in Rural North China," unpublished PhD thesis, University of British Columbia, 1996.

Flath, James A., "Liu Mingjie — A Modern Peasant? Viewing the Boxer Uprising Through Nianhua Print," unpublished paper given at the conference "1900. The Boxers, China, and the World," SOAS, London, June 2001.

Fung, Allen, "China's Failure Reconsidered: An Analysis of the Defeat of the Chinese Army and the Chinese Military Culture During the Sino-Japanese War (1894–1895)," unpublished B.A. thesis, Oxford University, Oxford, 1990.

Harrist, Robert E. Jnr, "Qianlong Triumphant: Art and War at the Manchu Court of China," unpublished paper, Columbia University, 1998.

———, "Clothes Make the Man: Dress, Modernity and Masculinity in Early Modern China," unpublished paper, Columbia University, 1998.

Hevia, James L., "Plundering Beijing 1900–1901," unpublished paper given at the conference "1900. The Boxers, China and the World," SOAS, London, June 2001.

Kuss, Susanne, "Elements of a War of Extermination During the Boxer Uprising:

German and British Soldiers in China," unpublished paper given at the conference "1900. The Boxers, China and the World," SOAS, London, June 2001.

Lili, "Koushu shiliao yu yihetuan yanjiu" (Oral Historical Materials and Boxer Studies), unpublished discussion paper given at the centennial conference of Boxer Studies, Jinan, October 2000.

Liu Tianlu, "Boxer Studies in China in the Last Fifty Years," presentation given at the conference "1900. The Boxers, China and the World," SOAS, London, June 2001.

Lu Yao, "Minjian mimi jiaopai" (The Boxer Movement and the Secret Sects), presentation given at the conference "1900. The Boxers, China and the World," SOAS, London, 2001.

McIntyre, Tanya, "Chinese New Year Pictures: The Process of Modernisation, 1842–1942," unpublished PhD thesis, Melbourne University, 1997.

Middleton, Ben, "Scandals of Imperialism: Kotoku Shusui, the Yorozu choho and Japanese Critiques of Empire at the Time of the Boxer War," unpublished paper given at the conference "1900. The Boxers, China and the World," SOAS, London, June 2001.

Mühlhahn, Klaus, "Religious Exclusion: Interactions Between German Missionaries and Local Chinese Society in Shandong, 1880–1900," paper prepared for the conference "1900. The Boxers, China and the World," SOAS, London, June 2001.

Narramore, Terry, "Making the News in Shanghai — *Shen Bao* and the Politics of Newspaper Journalism, 1912–1939," unpublished PhD Thesis, Australian National University, 1989.

Otte, Thomas G., "The Boxer Uprising and British Foreign Policy: The End of Splendid Isolation," unpublished paper given at the conference "1900. The Boxers, China and the World," SOAS, London, June 2001.

Tiedemann, R. Garry, "The Big Sword Society and Its Relations with the Boxer Movement, 1894–1900," unpublished paper given at the centennial conference of Boxer Studies, Jinan, October 2000.

———, "The Church Militant: Armed Conflicts Between Boxers and Christians in North China," unpublished paper given at the conference "1900. The Boxers, China and the World," SOAS, London, June 2001.

Wachs, Iris, "The Politics of Style: Chinese Woodblock Prints, 1945–1980," unpublished paper given at the China Seminar, University of Leiden, 2001.

Wagner, Rudolf G, "The Making of Shanghai Into the Chinese Media Capital: The Role of the Shenbaoguan Publishing House 1872–1895," unpublished paper presented at the New York University workshop on Shanghai Urban Culture, April 2001. Centre of Chinese Studies, Heidelberg University.

Yang, Anand, "Suburltern's Boxers: An Indain Soldier's Account of China and the World in 1900," unpublished paper given at the conference "1900. The Boxers, China and the World," SOAS, London, June 2001.

Ye Xiaoqing, "Popular Culture in Shanghai, 1884–1898," unpublished PhD Thesis, Australian National University, 1991.

Yeh, Catherine V., "A Public Love-Affair: the Tabloid Newspaper and the Rise of the Opera Singer as Star," unpublished paper presented at the New York University workshop on Shanghai Urban Culture, April 2001.

Yoshizawa, Seiichiro, "Tianjin yihetuan yundong yu difang shehui de jiyi" (The Tianjin Boxer Movement and the Memory of Local Society), unpublished working paper given at the centennial conference of Boxer Studies, Jinan, October 2000.

Zhang Ming, "Yihetuan de xiangzheng yinyu yishi wenhua yuzheng zhi" (The Cultural Symbols and Political Metaphors of the Boxer's Rituals), unpublished paper given at the centennial conference of Boxer Studies, Jinan, October 2000.

Others

Tape-recording: "Memories of Wai H. Tan (1891–1990) concerning the Boxer Rising," Hoover Institute, Stanford University.

Films: "The Battle of Dagu" (1902) Library of Congress.
"The Ninth Cavalry Charge the Walls of Peking" (1902) Library of Congress.
"Li Hong Chang Being Presented with a Mutoscope" (1902) Library of Congress.
"The American Soldier in Love and War" (1903) Library of congress.

Index

Related Titles from The Chinese University Press

New Year Celebrations in Central China in Late Imperial Times
Göran Aijmer (Forthcoming)

Building in China: Henry K. Murphy's "Adaptive Architecture" 1914–1935
Jeffrey W. Cody (2001)

The Yale-China Association: A Centennial History
Nancy E. Chapman with Jessica C. Plumb (2001)

Changing Chinese Foodways in Asia
Edited by David Y. H. Wu and Tan Chee-beng (2001)

Soul of Chaos: Critical Perspectives on Gao Xingjian
Edited by Kwok-kan Tam (2001)

Cantonese Society in a Time of Change
Göran Aijmer and Virgil K. Y. Ho (2000)

The Other Shore: Plays by Gao Xingjian
Translated by Gilbert C. F. Fong (1999)

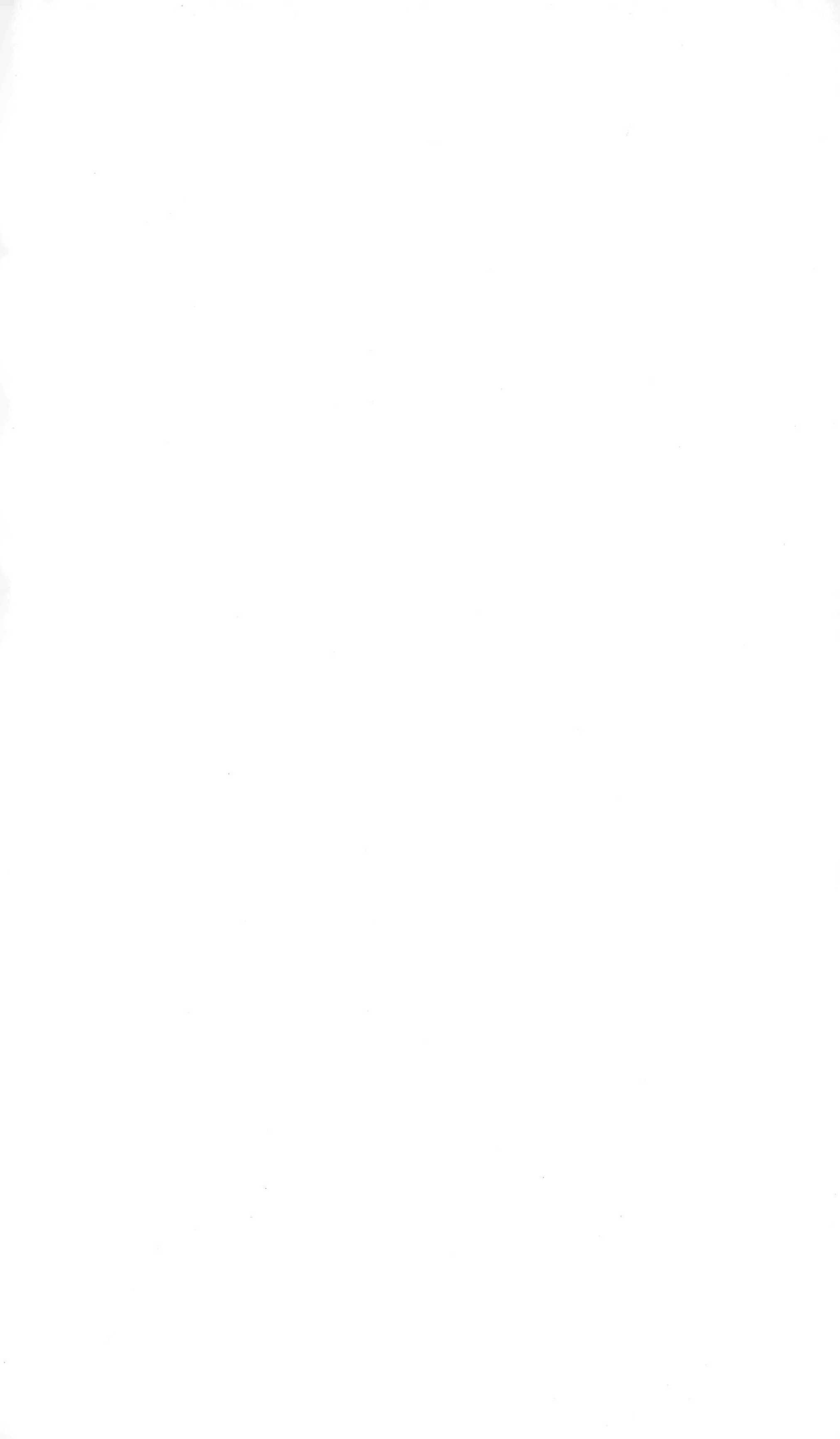

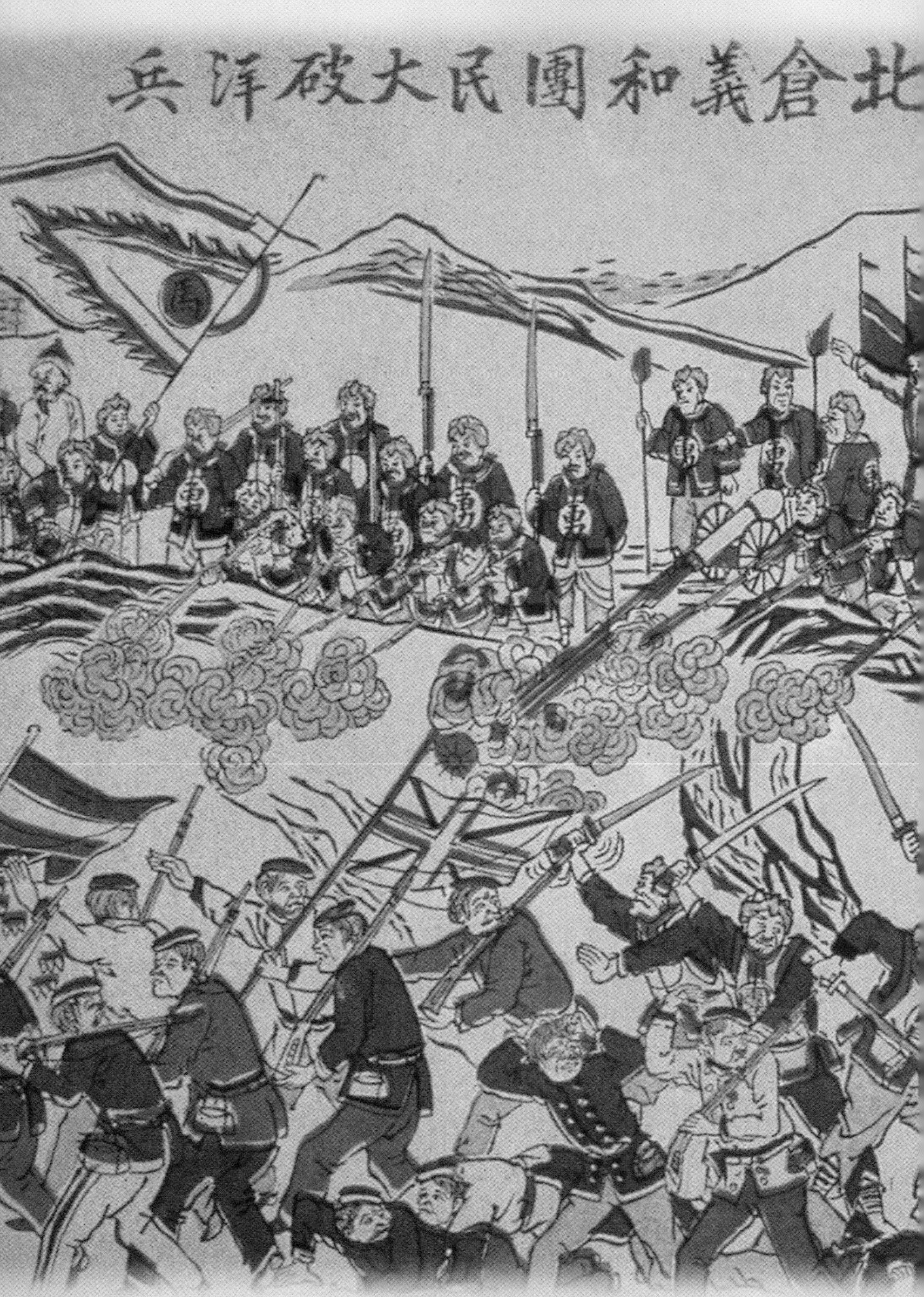

The Boxers of Beicang at Tianjin Defeat Foreign Allied Armies. (By courtesy of the trustees of the British Lib

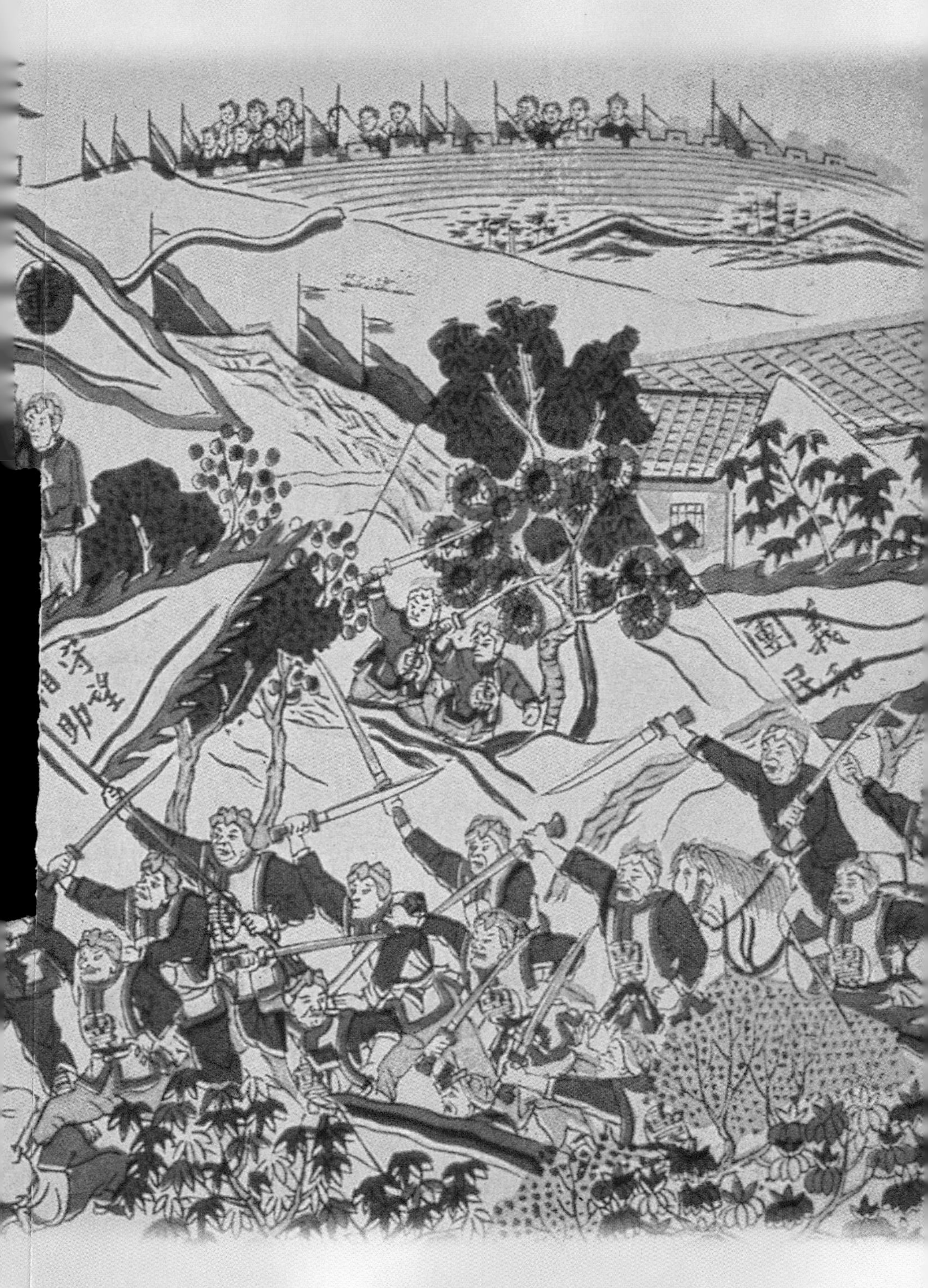
守望相助
義和民團